BEGINNING SHAREPOINT® 2013: BUILDING BUSINESS SOLUTIONS

D0608263

BEGINNING

SharePoint® 2013

BEGINNING

SharePoint® 2013

BUILDING BUSINESS SOLUTIONS

Amanda Perran
Shane Perran
Jennifer Mason
Laura Rogers

WILEY

John Wiley & Sons, Inc.

Beginning SharePoint® 2013: Building Business Solutions

Published by
John Wiley & Sons, Inc.
10475 Crosspoint Boulevard
Indianapolis, IN 46256
www.wiley.com

Copyright © 2013 by John Wiley & Sons, Inc., Indianapolis, Indiana

Published simultaneously in Canada

ISBN: 978-1-118-49589-6
ISBN: 978--1118-49587-2 (ebk)
ISBN: 978-1-118-65491-0 (ebk)
ISBN: 978-1-118-65502-3 (ebk)

Manufactured in the United States of America

10 9 8 7 6 5 4

For general information on our other products and services please contact our Customer Care Department within the United States at (877) 762-2974, outside the United States at (317) 572-3993 or fax (317) 572-4002.

Wiley publishes in a variety of print and electronic formats and by print-on-demand. Some material included with standard print versions of this book may not be included in e-books or in print-on-demand. If this book refers to media such as a CD or DVD that is not included in the version you purchased, you may download this material at http://booksupport.wiley.com. For more information about Wiley products, visit www.wiley.com.

Library of Congress Control Number: 2012954767

ABOUT THE AUTHORS

AMANDA PERRAN is a seven-time recipient of the Microsoft Most Valuable Professional for Microsoft SharePoint Server, located in St. John's, Newfoundland and Labrador. She has been working as a consultant and trainer with SharePoint for more than 10 years. Amanda is a regular speaker and presenter at user group meetings, webcasts, and conferences, on topics such as Information Architecture, Enterprise Content Management and Governance. She is the co-founder of SharePoint Nation (www.sharepointnation.org), a virtual user group for SharePoint. You can follow her on Twitter as @amandaperran or visit her weblog at www.sharepointmentors.com.

SHANE PERRAN is a five-time recipient of the Microsoft Most Valuable Professional for Microsoft SharePoint Server, located in St. John's, Newfoundland and Labrador. He has been designing online user experiences for more than 15 years. His strong passion for visual presentation, web standards, and usability has paved the way for a successful transition into the SharePoint Products and Technologies space, where, over the past 10 years, Shane has become highly involved and focused in the SharePoint customization space. He is the co-founder of SharePoint Nation (www.sharepointnation.org), a virtual user group for SharePoint. Shane's SharePoint Customization Blog (www.graphicalwonder.com) is a popular stop for customization enthusiasts across the globe. You can follow Shane on Twitter as @shaneperran.

JENNIFER MASON, as a SharePoint Server MVP, has spent the last several years consulting others on best practices for implementing business solutions using SharePoint technologies. She is passionate about SharePoint and loves using out-of-the-box features to bring immediate ROI to her clients. She has worked with a range of companies, leading teams responsible for the design, implantation, and maintenance of SharePoint environments. When she isn't riding the slide at her new company, Rackspace Hosting, Jennifer focuses on strategy, planning, governance, and sharing her knowledge with the SharePoint community. After a recent move to the Lone Star State from Ohio, where she was a founding member of the Columbus, Ohio SharePoint Users Group, Jennifer is learning how to be a true Texan, cowboy boots and all.

You can learn more about Jennifer by viewing her blog at http://sharepoint911 .com/blogs/jennifer. You can follow Jennifer on Twitter as @jennifermason.

LAURA DERBES ROGERS is a Senior SharePoint Consultant at Rackspace Hosting, and a Microsoft MVP. Her background is in server administration. She has been working with SharePoint implementations, training, customization, and administration since 2004. Her focus is on making the most of SharePoint's out-of-the-box capabilities without writing code. She works extensively with automating business processes with SharePoint Designer workflows and forms. Laura is a regular speaker at several different SharePoint conferences and loves sharing ideas on her blog at www.wonderlaura.com. A graduate of Louisiana State University, Laura currently resides in Birmingham, Alabama with her husband and two daughters. You can follow Laura on Twitter as @WonderLaura.

ABOUT THE TECHNICAL EDITORS

JAVIER BARRERA is a SharePoint Engineer at Rackspace (USA), a premier service leader focusing on a business class audience. He is the Senior Lead Engineer who serves as an architect and administrator to hundreds of enterprise-level SharePoint farms. Javier has delivered more than 30 presentations at SharePoint-focused events, and authored numerous blogs and articles. He is a contributing author to the forthcoming *Professional SharePoint 2013 Administration*. Javier, his beautiful wife, Roxanne, and three children live in San Antonio, Texas. His speaking engagement information and writing references are available at `http://JavierBarrera.com`.

COREY BURKE is a SharePoint Architect at Rackspace (UK). Corey has designed and built farms of more than 100,000 users and uses his experience to give back to the community. He is also a contributing author for *Professional SharePoint 2013 Administration*.

CREDITS

Acquisitions Editor
Mary James

Project Editor
John Sleeva

Technical Editors
Javier Barrera
Corey Burke

Production Editor
Christine Mugnolo

Copy Editor
Kim Cofer

Editorial Manager
Mary Beth Wakefield

Freelancer Editorial Manager
Rosemarie Graham

Associate Director of Marketing
David Mayhew

Marketing Manager
Ashley Zurcher

Business Manager
Amy Knies

Production Manager
Tim Tate

**Vice President and Executive
Group Publisher**
Richard Swadley

Vice President and Executive Publisher
Neil Edde

Associate Publisher
Jim Minatel

Project Coordinator, Cover
Katie Crocker

Proofreader
Nancy Carrasco

Indexer
Robert Swanson

Cover Designer
Elizabeth Brooks

Cover Image
© Anthia Cumming / iStockphoto

ACKNOWLEDGMENTS

IT IS COMMON FOR AUTHORS to thank their spouses or partners for their understanding and support during the book-writing process. In our case, this was a project by a husband-and-wife team, which meant that the late nights, deadlines, and missed holidays were spent together, side by side, for better or worse. Of course, we would have it no other way.

We would like to thank our families for their love, support, and encouragement throughout this book and all the other challenges and surprises that life can bring.

It is an honor and a pleasure to share a title with talented professionals such as Laura and Jennifer. Thank you again for your excellent work on this book.

As always, we would like to thank Jim Minatel for introducing us to the Wrox team so many years ago. Thank you to Mary E. James for leading this project and for helping us get focused very early in the game. Thank you to John Sleeva for your excellent professionalism and support. It was an extreme pleasure to work with you on this project and we hope our paths cross again. Thank you Javier Barrera, Corey Burke, and Kim Cofer for your diligence and attention to detail throughout the editing process. Each of your talents contributed significantly to this project and we are so very grateful to each of you.

Finally, to Dylan. We would especially like to thank you for providing an excellent source of motivation and perspective during the entire process. Everything we do and experience in life is made so much better because of you. You are a light like no other.

—AMANDA AND SHANE

WRITING TECHNICAL BOOKS is one of the things that I consider a huge blessing to be able to do. So many people along the way have helped get me to a point where this is possible. It would be impossible to thank them all by name, but it is important to call out some that have specifically helped me with this project.

Cathy, Diane, and Jane, who would have thought that hiring an intern would be such an adventure? I think back very often on the crazy times we had and am thankful that I was able to get my start with such a wonderful team. The time I spent with you was rich in learning and more fun than anyone should have at work! I think of you ladies often and credit many of my successes today on the investments you made in me. I am truly thankful and blessed for the time I was able to work with you!

When Amanda and Shane asked Laura and me to join this project a few years ago, little did I realize the changes it would have on my career. This is one of my proudest accomplishments, and I am so happy to be able to work on such a great team of people! Shane, Amanda, and Laura, I appreciate the long hours and the sacrifices you have put into this project. I couldn't ask for a better team to work with!

To the team at Wrox, especially Mary James and John Sleeva, thank you for all the hard work and effort you put into polishing this work and making it ready for print. I know you have quite a task when you have to deal with authors, and I appreciate all that you do.

Javier Barrera and Corey Burke, thanks so much for all the technical editing you did for this book. Your dedication and hard work has made for a better book. I am lucky to have you two as coworkers and thankful for the fanatical investment you have made for this book.

Jeff DeVerter, this year has been full of changes, and I am thankful for all you have done for me as I have transitioned into my new role at Rackspace. I consider myself lucky to have you as a manager, and this project definitely wouldn't have been possible without you helping me clear my schedule and make time for me to dedicate to the project.

Finally, I want to thank the SharePoint community, without whom none of this would be possible. I appreciate the time we get to spend together, and I consider so many of you close friends. I look forward to a future of learning more things together!

—JENNIFER

WORKING ON THIS BOOK has been quite an experience, and there are several people who I would like to thank. The major influencers in my life exist on both the personal and the professional sides.

First, my husband, Chris, has been wonderful and supportive. His sarcasm and wit have always kept me laughing despite any book-deadline stresses. Speaking of family, I thank my daughters, who are growing up to be so intelligent, lovely, and poised. Also, thanks to my parents and my brother for being such a supportive family.

Thanks to Jennifer Mason and to Shane and Amanda Perran for being so inspiring to work with. I really have enjoyed being a part of this endeavor with all of you. You are outstanding and inspiring, and I look forward to working with you in many future endeavors.

Of course, I would also like to extend my thanks to the Wrox team, especially Mary James and John Sleeva. It has been more than a pleasure working with you on this book. You have been wonderful, professional, and patient, and I sincerely hope that we cross paths again soon.

Lastly, I would like to thank those of you who have been a major part of my path as a SharePoint professional: Shane Young, Todd Klindt, Bill English, Brett Lonsdale, Mark Miller, and Lori Gowin. Thanks to all my colleagues at Rackspace. You are like family to me, and I truly enjoy working with you every day.

—LAURA

CONTENTS

INTRODUCTION

MICROSOFT SHAREPOINT SERVER 2013 has improved and changed dramatically over previous versions of the product, including significant enhancements to the web content management, social media, business connectivity, and search features of the platform. However, the value of this tool to an enterprise depends primarily on the ability of individuals in the organization to understand the features and capabilities of the platform and effectively map those to specific business requirements.

This book is designed to mentor and coach an organization's business and technical thought leaders on the use and configuration of SharePoint to address critical information-management problems. It gives detailed descriptions and illustrations of the product's functionality and includes realistic usage scenarios to provide contextual relevance and a personalized learning experience.

WHO THIS BOOK IS FOR

The mission of this book is to provide extensive knowledge to information workers and site managers that will empower them to become SharePoint application champions in their organizations. This book should be the premier handbook of any active or aspiring SharePoint expert.

To complete the exercises (known as *Try It Outs*) in this book, you should have a basic comfort level using Microsoft Office client applications to create content and a general understanding of how to interact with a website through the browser. This book is intended as a starting point for any SharePoint 2013 user, whether that user has never used SharePoint before or has some familiarity with a previous version and just wants to understand the differences with the new release.

WHAT THIS BOOK COVERS

SharePoint 2013 represents the latest release of Microsoft's portal and collaborative technology platform. This book covers in detail many of the features of Microsoft SharePoint Server 2013 that will assist you in creating an effective collaboration, content management, business intelligence, business process, or social media solution for your organization. It addresses core functionality that has existed in SharePoint within previous versions as well as new concepts that have been introduced in this latest release.

HOW THIS BOOK IS STRUCTURED

This book covers the essential elements of using and configuring SharePoint 2013 as an effective tool for business. Each chapter focuses on a dedicated topic and provides hands-on exercises to assist with your learning experience. The following is a short summary of each chapter of this book.

➤ **Chapter 1, "Understanding SharePoint":** This chapter serves as an introduction to SharePoint and lays the foundation for important terminology and concepts explored in the following chapters.

➤ **Chapter 2, "Working with List Apps":** This chapter introduces one of the core mechanisms for sharing and organizing content in a SharePoint site. You will review what list apps are and how they are used, and then explore the various types that exist in SharePoint 2013.

➤ **Chapter 3, "Working with Library Apps":** After reviewing some of the fundamental concepts relating to lists, this chapter introduces the other major storage mechanism in SharePoint, known as libraries. This chapter discusses some of the various apps that exist for libraries.

➤ **Chapter 4, "Managing and Customizing Lists and Libraries":** SharePoint apps for lists and libraries provide a great starting point for collaboration and information sharing. This chapter shows how you can extend these base templates to address an organization's specific requirements for a collaborative site or information management tool.

➤ **Chapter 5, "Working with Workflows":** This chapter discusses the templates that SharePoint provides for workflows and demonstrates how to create custom workflow solutions using the SharePoint Designer application.

➤ **Chapter 6, "Working with Content Types":** Most organizations have documents that use consistent templates, processes, and policies each time they are created. Therefore, SharePoint has content types, which allow an organization to package templates and information to ensure that reusable components are rolled out in the organization to enforce consistency and ease of use. This chapter demonstrates what content types are and explores how they can be used through some hands-on examples.

➤ **Chapter 7, "Working with Web Parts":** Web parts are an important element in SharePoint because they enable teams to present information on their sites to users in many different ways. This chapter explores the various groups of Web Parts that exist in SharePoint 2013, and gives examples on how specific types of Web Parts can be configured and used to present information in a desired manner.

➤ **Chapter 8, "Working with Sites":** The fundamental components of any SharePoint environment are its sites and workspaces. These collaborative work areas contain all the components discussed in previous chapters and represent how each of those items comes together to provide an effective environment for collaboration, communication, and document management. In this chapter, topics such as site templates and features are covered.

➤ **Chapter 9, "Managing Permissions":** Effective management of users is of ultimate importance to any information system. The two primary tiers of effective user management are securing content and personalizing information on the portal. This chapter explains in simple terms how to effectively secure a SharePoint environment at the site level, the list or library level, and down to the unique content items stored on a SharePoint site. In addition, the chapter introduces personalization to ensure that readers understand how to effectively target information to users in a portal.

➤ **Chapter 10, "Working with Business Intelligence":** This chapter demonstrates how to improve the overall decision making of an organization, including providing access to important information, using browser-based worksheets and visual indicators of performance information, and building personalized, interactive dashboards.

➤ **Chapter 11, "Working with Social Features":** Social networking has been an area of major enhancement in SharePoint 2013. In this chapter, you will learn how to make the most of SharePoint's social networking, such as My Sites, tags, blogs, wikis, and ratings.

➤ **Chapter 12, "Managing Forms":** Microsoft InfoPath is the ideal companion to SharePoint for many business solutions. This chapter introduces readers to creating simple business applications using Microsoft InfoPath, including creating template parts, creating flexible form interfaces, and connecting to business data.

➤ **Chapter 13, "Working with Access Services":** This chapter provides an overview of the new and simplified Access application model in SharePoint 2013, which empowers users to create Access applications that leverage SharePoint 2013 as the front end.

➤ **Chapter 14, "Branding and the User Experience":** SharePoint 2013 offers a significantly improved experience for changing the look and feel of your site. In this chapter we will take a look at some of these enhancements, including the Design Manager and an improved mobile experience through channels.

➤ **Chapter 15, "Getting Started with Web Content Management":** This chapter provides an overview of the web content management capabilities of the system, including the use of publishing sites and features, the automatic provisioning of multilingual content through variations, and the creation of custom page templates known as *page layouts*.

➤ **Chapter 16, "Managing Records":** This chapter provides an overview of and introduction to the establishment of a records management practice in your organization using SharePoint 2013. The chapter covers topics including term sets, archive-based records management features, as well as in-place records management features.

➤ **Chapter 17, "Working with Search":** An information system is useful to an organization only if stakeholders can easily access and locate the information it contains. This chapter discusses the search engine capabilities of the SharePoint platform, including methods that improve the search experience through the use of effective queries, configurations, and analytics.

➤ **Chapter 18, "Building Solutions in SharePoint":** This chapter explores the practical usage of SharePoint 2013, exploring realistic scenarios that leverage SharePoint features to perform critical business functions.

WHAT YOU NEED TO USE THIS BOOK

To complete the examples in this book effectively, you should have access to a Microsoft SharePoint Server 2013 environment or site collection, and have administrative rights to the server. If you do not have administrative rights, your server administrator may have to assist you with some exercises in this book.

You should also have a client computer running either Windows 7 or Windows 8 along with Microsoft Office 2013 Professional or Professional Plus, and SharePoint Designer 2013. Although many exercises can be completed with earlier versions of Office, certain exercises may function better with Office 2013.

The resource files for the samples is available for download from the Wrox website at:

```
www.wrox.com/remtitle.cgi?isbn=1118495896
```

CONVENTIONS

To help you get the most from the text and keep track of what's happening, we've used a number of conventions throughout the book.

TRY IT OUT

The *Try It Out* is an exercise you should work through, following the text in the book.

1. They usually consist of a set of steps.
2. Each step has a number.
3. Follow the steps through with your copy of the database.

How It Works

After each *Try It Out*, the code you've typed will be explained in detail.

> **WARNING** *Warnings hold important, not-to-be-forgotten information that is directly relevant to the surrounding text.*

> **NOTE** *Notes indicate notes, tips, hints, tricks, and asides to the current discussion.*

As for styles in the text:

➤ We *highlight* new terms and important words when we introduce them.

➤ We show keyboard strokes like this: Ctrl+A.

➤ We show file names, URLs, and code within the text like so: `persistence.properties`.

➤ We present code in two different ways:

```
We use a monofont type with no highlighting for most code examples.
```

```
We use bold to emphasize code that is particularly important in the present context
or to show changes from a previous code snippet.
```

SOURCE CODE

As you work through the examples in this book, you may choose either to type in all the code manually or to use the source code files that accompany the book. All the source code used in this book is available for download at `www.wrox.com`. Once at the site, simply locate the book's title (either by using the Search box or by using one of the title lists) and click on the "Download Code" link on the book's detail page to obtain all the source code for the book.

> **NOTE** *Because many books have similar titles, you may find it easiest to search by ISBN; this book's ISBN is 978-1-118-49589-6.*

Once you download the code, just decompress it with your favorite compression tool. Alternately, you can go to the main Wrox code download page at `www.wrox.com/dynamic/books/download.aspx` to see the code available for this book and all other Wrox books.

ERRATA

We make every effort to ensure that there are no errors in the text or in the code. However, no one is perfect, and mistakes do occur. If you find an error in one of our books, like a spelling mistake or faulty piece of code, we would be very grateful for your feedback. By sending in errata, you may save another reader hours of frustration, and at the same time, you will be helping us provide even higher quality information.

A complete book list including links to errata is also available at

`www.wrox.com/misc-pages/booklist.shtml`.

If you don't spot "your" error on the Book Errata page, go to www.wrox.com/contact/ techsupport.shtml and complete the form there to send us the error you have found. We'll check the information and, if appropriate, post a message to the book's errata page and fix the problem in subsequent editions of the book.

P2P.WROX.COM

For author and peer discussion, join the P2P forums at http://p2p.wrox.com. The forums are a Web-based system for you to post messages relating to Wrox books and related technologies and interact with other readers and technology users. The forums offer a subscription feature to e-mail you topics of interest of your choosing when new posts are made to the forums. Wrox authors, editors, other industry experts, and your fellow readers are present on these forums.

At http://p2p.wrox.com, you will find a number of different forums that will help you, not only as you read this book, but also as you develop your own applications. To join the forums, just follow these steps:

1. Go to http://p2p.wrox.com and click the Register link.

2. Read the terms of use and click Agree.

3. Complete the required information to join, as well as any optional information you wish to provide, and click Submit.

4. You will receive an e-mail with information describing how to verify your account and complete the joining process.

> **NOTE** *You can read messages in the forums without joining P2P, but in order to post your own messages, you must join.*

Once you join, you can post new messages and respond to messages other users post. You can read messages at any time on the Web. If you would like to have new messages from a particular forum e-mailed to you, click the Subscribe to this Forum icon by the forum name in the forum listing.

For more information about how to use the Wrox P2P, be sure to read the P2P FAQs for answers to questions about how the forum software works, as well as many common questions specific to P2P and Wrox books. To read the FAQs, click the FAQ link on any P2P page.

1

Understanding SharePoint

WHAT YOU WILL LEARN IN THIS CHAPTER:

➤ The differences between SharePoint product versions

➤ Common usage scenarios for SharePoint

➤ An overview of important SharePoint concepts and features

The goal of this book is to provide you with experience using the tools and features of SharePoint in a way that enables you to craft and develop powerful, no-code business solutions within SharePoint. An important part of understanding how best to manage and use SharePoint from either an end user, information worker, developer, or IT pro perspective is first to understand the core capabilities of the product and how they can be extended to meet your organization's unique and specific business needs. Along those lines, this chapter introduces you to the exciting features and capabilities of Microsoft SharePoint Technologies. With it, you will learn how to put the platform to work for your organization to create scalable business solutions. In this chapter, you get an overview of how SharePoint is used and gain an understanding of the different combinations of licensing and configuration available within your environment.

UNDERSTANDING PORTALS

Before getting started on the technical tasks associated with managing and working with SharePoint content, it is important to understand the purpose of common usage scenarios for the technology. The power associated with SharePoint solutions is directly related to the ability for organizations to customize solutions to fit their needs. SharePoint offers many things, in many different formats. Although Microsoft provides a high level of direction, it is really up to the internal organization to build a solution structure that matches its specific requirements.

At a high level, SharePoint is a solution that provides features and capabilities to help organizations perform the following key business tasks:

➤ Share

➤ Organize

➤ Discover

➤ Build

➤ Manage

SharePoint enables organizations to build specific solutions that guide their users to desired behaviors. By creating solutions to provide alternate options for sharing and collaborating on data, organizations can enhance user satisfaction and increase productivity. In this age of the consumerization of IT, users expect to quickly, easily, and efficiently use technology in a self-serve fashion to solve needs as they arise. When deployed within an organization, SharePoint provides a platform that satisfies this need. But, like all good technology, without an understanding of what it can do and how to best use the features, things often are not used to their full potential. By reading this book, you will gain an understanding of the basic features available and will be prepared with many tools to get started building powerful, efficient business solutions.

Because SharePoint is one of the industry's leading portal technologies, we start with a review of portal technologies, followed by some common reasons that organizations are driven to these types of solutions. With the framework laid, we continue with a discussion of the different versions of SharePoint and how they differ from each other. Then, we provide a high-level overview of some of the primary components of SharePoint. This overview will give you a sampling of what is to come in the remainder of this book.

What Is Portal Technology?

A corporate portal is a gateway through which members can access business information and, if set up properly, should be the first place an employee goes to access anything of importance. Portals differ from regular websites in that they are customized specifically for each organization. In many cases, a portal may actually consist of numerous websites, with information stored either directly on those sites or in other systems, such as file shares, business applications, or a regular Internet website. This allows the portal to be the central location users can visit to find information regardless of its actual storage location. Because making informed business decisions is key to becoming and remaining successful, it's important that the information placed on a portal be secure, up to date, and easily accessible. Because a business's marketplace may span the globe, an organization also needs to have the information that reflects the needs of employees from multiple specific regions.

As an example, consider a new employee who has just joined an organization. In addition to learning her new job responsibilities, this employee must quickly get up to speed on the various company processes and policies. A good portal should provide all the company reference and policy information that the employee needs to review, as well as links to all the information systems and websites that employee needs to do her job. Information should be stored in easy-to-browse locations, based on subject or topic. In situations where the location of a document or information is not obvious, the employee should be able to type words into a search box and receive suggestions. The employee should also be able to share information with others. In many ways, a good portal should act as a table of contents for all the information and websites related to an organization or topic.

In summary, portal technology provides ways for users to share and consume information from a central location. Though this may mean that all data lives within a single portal application, it is also very likely that the data is spread across many systems and solutions; the portal technologies are just a way to simplify access to the data.

Why Do Organizations Invest in Portal Technologies?

The following list provides just a few of the reasons why many enterprise organizations opt to invest in portal technologies:

➤ Users have become used to working with technology and, in many cases, expect to have access to simple, easy-to-access and easy-to-use tools to find and do their jobs. Because their personal lives include many of these technologies, the expectation that their work will use the same technologies is very high.

➤ The adoption of the web and web-related technologies makes portal technologies an obvious choice. Because portal technologies are web-based, decision makers can access important information via the Internet regardless of where they are located.

➤ Portal technologies enable information workers to handle day-to-day tasks from a single starting point, whereas previously things were spread out across multiple places and applications.

➤ With important regulatory initiatives, such as the Sarbanes-Oxley Act, organizations are using portal technologies to ensure that an accurate audit trail is kept on important documents and that business processes remain compliant.

➤ The file-share–based approach previously used to store most information was highly dependent on the habits and practices of the person creating it. Portal technologies store and share information based on the organizational structure, making them intuitive to use for everyone in the organization. This structure translates into productivity boosts because workers can more easily locate and retrieve information.

➤ Portal technologies are designed to scale with an organization, offering a model that will grow as the company grows.

➤ Although a company may be tempted by the latest and greatest information management system, most organizations still have legacy systems and data sources such as file shares, databases, or business applications. You can massage portal technologies so that they integrate with these systems, allowing easier data mining or migration.

WHAT IS SHAREPOINT?

SharePoint is one of the leading portal technologies. Many organizations implement SharePoint to satisfy the needs that were stated in the preceding section. Part of the Microsoft Office family, SharePoint provides a scalable, extensible, and customizable portal solution for organizations of any size. SharePoint consists of tools and technologies that support the collaboration and sharing of information within teams, throughout the enterprise, and on the web. The total package is a platform on which you can build business applications to help you better store, share, and manage digital information within your organization. Because you can build with or without code, the package empowers the average business user to create, deploy, and manage team websites, without depending on skilled resources, such as systems administrators or developers. Using lists, libraries, and Web Parts, you can transform team websites into business applications built specifically around making your organization's business processes more efficient.

SharePoint is available to organizations in two primary ways:

➤ **On-Premise SharePoint Deployment:** With an on-premise deployment your organization builds, configures, and manages its own SharePoint environment. You can do this using many different approaches, which include maintaining your own data center or dedicated hosting in an offsite data center, partnered with a hosting provider. The main component of this type of environment is that you have full control of the environment and can deploy custom solutions without restraint.

➤ **Office 365 SharePoint Subscription:** Office 365 is a shared multi-tenant hosting experience where you subscribe to SharePoint services that are hosted and maintained by Microsoft in its data centers. You are given a set of guidelines around storage space and development options and must follow those within your environment. The benefits of this arrangement enable you to quickly and easily take advantage of SharePoint features without having to take on the extra overhead of managing and supporting a fully dedicated environment.

Many different organizational needs drive the choice between the two preceding options. To best determine which option is best for your organization, you need to determine the current as well as future planned needs of your organization. With those needs in mind, you will then be able to determine what type of environment you need to support and maintain. Once you know what you need, you can focus on how best to do it. Some questions to consider at this stage include the following:

➤ What level of control and segregation is required for the data within my environment?

➤ What types of service-level agreements (SLAs) are in place for the data within my organization?

➤ Do we have the internal resources needed to support our environment?

➤ What types of customizations and custom code will need to be supported within our environment?

These, along with other factors, will help you determine which approach is best for your organization. In many cases it is a clear distinction as to which path to take. In other cases, a hybrid approach is often a desirable option, allowing users to have the best of both configurations.

Once you determine the deployment type that is best for you, you have to determine what level of licensing you will need to have. Each of the different deployment options have different licensing options available, giving you a choice with the different features you will need to acquire for your organization. Although this book assumes you are using SharePoint Enterprise features within an on-premise deployment, the following section provides descriptions and details on the different options available to you.

COMPARING DIFFERENT SHAREPOINT VERSIONS

For SharePoint on-premise, you have two options for installation:

➤ SharePoint Foundation 2013

➤ SharePoint Server 2013

For Office 365, you also have several options, as discussed at the end of this section.

SharePoint Foundation

SharePoint Foundation provides you with the basic collaboration features that are included within SharePoint. These features are the foundation required to build standard collaboration and communication solutions within your organization. The primary features of SharePoint Foundation revolve around document management and collaboration. The following list outlines the major features of the platform that have been responsible for its wide adoption in businesses:

➤ **Effective document and task collaboration:** Team websites offer access to information in a central location as well as the following capabilities:

  ➤ Sites for teams to share documents and information, coordinate schedules and tasks, and participate in forum-like discussions. Team members can use these sites to share information regardless of their physical proximity or boundaries. Because SharePoint uses many of the same features users are accustomed to in Office, such as the ribbon, it is easy for users to navigate through the sites.

  ➤ Libraries provide a better document creation and management environment than standard file shares solutions. You can configure libraries to ensure that a document is checked out before editing, track a document's revision history, or allow users to collaborate on its review and approval.

  ➤ Role-based security settings ensure that sensitive information is secure and available only to select individuals.

  ➤ Advanced task-tracking lists and alert systems keep users updated on current and upcoming tasks.

  ➤ Templates for creating wikis and blogs enable you to share information across your organization quickly and easily.

➤ **Reduced implementation and deployment resources:** Because SharePoint Foundation is available to Windows Server customers as a free download, implementation time and cost are greatly reduced, resulting in the following benefits:

  ➤ Deploying team collaboration sites is easy, so organizations can free up skilled resources and focus on more important and complex tasks.

  ➤ Users can immediately create and apply professional-looking site themes directly from within their browser.

  ➤ Because SharePoint Foundation offers seamless integration with the Microsoft Office system, employees can use common applications, such as Microsoft Word, to create and manage documents, without the need for expensive training or process changes.

➤ **Better control of your organization's important business data:** SharePoint Foundation offers the following features for data and information management and security:

> ➤ Enhanced browser and command-line–based administrative controls enable you to perform site provisioning, content management, support, and backup. Subsequently, a business can become more efficient and reduce costs.
>
> ➤ Using advanced administrative features, IT can set the parameters under which business units can provision sites and allow access, ensuring that all units fall within an acceptable security policy.
>
> ➤ The Recycle Bin item retrieval and document versioning capabilities provide a safe storage environment.

➤ **Embrace the web for collaboration:** By extending and customizing SharePoint Foundation, you can:

> ➤ Create collaborative websites complete with document libraries that act as central repositories for creating, managing, and sharing documents with your team.
>
> ➤ Create, connect, and customize a set of business applications specific to scaling your organizational needs.

In short, SharePoint Foundation represents the core content storage and collaboration features of SharePoint. It is the ideal edition for teams and small organizations looking to improve on their ability to work with one another in a secure, easy-to-use, collaborative workspace.

SHAREPOINT FOUNDATION USAGE EXAMPLE

The fictional organization Rossco Tech Consulting offers professional services and technology mentoring to startup companies. The following scenario outlines Rossco's experience with SharePoint, beginning with SharePoint Foundation and later expanding to SharePoint Server.

Because so much of Rossco's business revolves around process documentation, having a central repository with which to manage information surrounding projects is imperative. Because Rossco was using Windows Server, SharePoint Foundation became the obvious and most cost-efficient foundation on which to build solutions to manage its projects.

Planning

To identify what improvements it needed to make to enhance efficiency, the company asked team leads about the problems they were encountering when collaborating within their respective teams. From these results, the company identified the common issues each team shared and created a site hierarchy that best represented the organization's corporate culture and business processes. Because the organization consisted of only three divisions (Finance, Marketing, and Operations), it opted for a single collection of sites: a main site for the organization as a whole and three subsites, one for each division.

Because each division followed similar processes for most projects, the company could use SharePoint's template system to create a single "project" site template that all teams could use to create a collaborative project location. The sites created from this template would then have the following features:

➤ A document library to create, store, and organize any documents related to the project

➤ A contact list to store and organize important contacts involved with the project

➤ A task list to coordinate important tasks for team members involved with the project

➤ An issue-tracking list to highlight any potential project concerns

The template was created and then saved in a central site template gallery, where each division could use it to generate a new site for each project.

Moving from Plan to Practice

After defining the organizational structure via team sites on the intranet, it was time for Rossco Tech Consulting to put its hard work and planning into real-world practice. As teams began to understand the tools that they now had available, the following practices started to drive more efficient operations within the organization:

➤ Projects were quickly defined via sites created using the project site template. This enabled teams to set up a central environment in which to create, store, and share information about a particular project with the entire organization in just seconds.

➤ Appointments and important deadlines were created and tracked from a single shared calendar on the project site that everyone on a team could easily view.

➤ Contact information was added to a central location so that team members could easily contact one another and other key partners or stakeholders for the project.

➤ Important project documents were moved to the document repository of their respective project sites where changes became easier to track and security became more manageable.

➤ Users began to create e-mail alerts on the task and issues lists, ensuring that tasks and issues were dealt with in a timely manner.

➤ As each division began defining its role in important projects, executives realized that they now had a bird's-eye view of operations within the organization, which was met with great enthusiasm.

SharePoint Server

SharePoint Server extends upon what is available in Foundation by including additional feature sets that provide a richer, more advanced collection of features that you can utilize in your organization's solutions. Some of these additional features are described in the following list:

➤ **Advanced Search:** Although it is true that search is included in the Foundation installation of SharePoint, the search features and functionality features available within the Server versions offer a great deal more flexibility. They allow for customized Search Results pages that you can configure with customized search Web Parts. You can also use these search Web Parts on other pages within the organization, enabling you to create customized search experiences for your users based on their business needs. These features are explored in more detail in Chapter 17, "Working with Search."

➤ **Web Content Management:** SharePoint Server supports web content creation and publishing for the Internet. Publishing features range from a content approval workflow to page layouts and content types, which allow you to create and publish branded web content without writing any complex code. These features are often used very extensively for public-facing websites created in SharePoint or for internal intranet environments created within SharePoint. These features enable you to create a solution that utilizes some of the following features (which are explored in more detail in Chapter 15, "Getting Started with Web Content Management"):

  ➤ Easy Content Authoring

  ➤ Multi-Lingual Site Support

  ➤ Cross-Site Publishing

  ➤ Catalog-Enabled Lists & Libraries

  ➤ Managed Navigation

  ➤ Friendly URLs

➤ **Enterprise Services:** These services provide ways for you to quickly and easily build custom solutions using tools that are available to you within the Office product family, and include the following:

  ➤ InfoPath Forms Services (see Chapter 12, "Managing Forms")

  ➤ Excel Services, Visio Services, and PerformancePoint Services (see Chapter 10, "Working with Business Intelligence")

  ➤ Access Services (see Chapter 13, "Working with Access Services")

➤ **Business Connectivity Services:** Although SharePoint may be your central application, your organization may have legacy business applications. Business Connectivity Services (BCS) enables you to connect to these external data sources and display business data via Web Parts, user profiles, or SharePoint lists. Although BCS does not contain the information from these systems, it acts as the virtual bridge between the alternate system and the user. Working with BCS usually requires some custom code and because of that, this particular topic is not explored in detail within this book.

➤ **Social networking and computing:** Social networking is everywhere and has become an expected feature set of many solutions. Features such as ratings and tagging provide a less structured approach to classification of content, but truly help drive user adoption and relevance of content within the system. Many business users have become accustomed to these features in many of the online portals they use outside of the business world. For example, you may have purchased this book by visiting an online book retailer. From this retailer's site, you may have reviewed ratings that other readers left to describe the content of the book. Subsequently, you may also choose to rate your own personal experience in an effort to provide feedback for other potential buyers. This concept also works extremely well in the business world. As users rate content and provide comments or notes related to specific topics, it helps other users understand the content's relevance and subsequently reduces much of the time required to find the right content. You can learn more about these specific features in Chapter 11, "Working with Social Features."

➤ **Records management:** SharePoint Server provides excellent support for the management of content throughout its entire life cycle. This includes features such as auditing of content access, review and disposal of expired content, and the creation of multistage retention policies and file plans. Depending on the type of organization you work within, records management may be something that has existed for years or it may be a new concept. Whatever your situation, Chapter 16, "Managing Records," takes you through the effective usage and configuration of SharePoint Server as a records management system.

SharePoint Server typically comes with several different licensing options, each one allowing different features to be used in different ways. Because licensing and feature sets can be updated often, it is important to review the current options available to you by accessing the Microsoft product website. SharePoint has an additive client access license (CAL) structure that enables you to continually and easily add additional features as needed to your environment.

ANOTHER SHAREPOINT SERVER USAGE EXAMPLE

This section again presents the fictional company, Rossco Tech Consulting, to show how Microsoft SharePoint Server can be used effectively by an organization that has outgrown the capabilities of SharePoint Foundation and requires more advanced features and functionality. Rossco Tech Consulting has expanded operations to support a major software manufacturer.

This means providing English-, French-, and German-speaking customers with an Internet support portal where they can access up-to-the-minute information on the manufacturer's various software offerings.

continues

continued

Planning

While performing a needs analysis, the following factors were major contributors in Rossco's decision to use Microsoft SharePoint Server as the platform on which to build its customer support portal:

➤ The portal must accommodate multiple products from a central Internet-facing location. Each product has its own unique support materials.

➤ The portal must serve up content in multiple languages, although the original content will be created in English and then translated.

➤ For legal reasons, support documentation must be published via a strict approval process, involving several individuals in the organization.

➤ The portal must accommodate speedy publishing of up-to-date information on emerging products.

➤ Additional documentation exists beyond what is stored in the SharePoint sites. This content must be indexed and accessible via the SharePoint search interface.

➤ Specific reporting requirements exist for dashboard scorecards on progress related to specific requirements, as well as the aggregation of information from multiple sources on a single page.

Moving from Plan to Practice

With the planning needs in mind, Rossco set out to plan and implement a Microsoft SharePoint Server solution. The following list outlines the company's experience.

➤ **Internet-facing sites in SharePoint Server:** Because users will access a major part of the portal via the Internet, Rossco created the initial site collection with a special publishing feature available only in SharePoint Server. This makes it possible to publish content through an automated and scheduled process from an internal and secured location to an external anonymous Internet-facing site. No technical skills are required for publishing this content, so Rossco can empower business users directly with the creation and publishing of web content, which cuts down considerably on the duration of updates to the website.

➤ **Multilingual design:** Because the portal needed to service three languages, the company used variations, a feature that helps create a site hierarchy for each language. This feature simplifies the management of content in multiple languages by creating a source site and a site for each language.

➤ **Content creation:** After creating the main subsites, the product teams created intuitively named lists and libraries (introduced later in this chapter) and added important documents and information. Making use of built-in features such as content types, site columns, and views, they created and presented the data more efficiently. To ensure that the portal was in line with the corporate brand, the portal was customized. Using the master pages feature, they created custom style sheets, page layouts, and content types to remodel the look and feel of the portal. This transformed the original site with its generic SharePoint look into an easy-to-use support interface. Using page layouts, they were able to empower key business users with no programming knowledge to create and publish branded web content such as newsletters and product updates.

➤ **Automating operations:** Taking advantage of SharePoint's workflow features, Rossco created a strict content approval process that routed documents from approver to approver before finally publishing them to the Internet-facing portal.

➤ **Content aggregation:** Using built-in Web Parts, such as the Content Query web part, Rossco could gather the most sought-after and important information in its subsites and funnel this information to the Internet-facing portal where users had quick and easy access to support information for multiple products at a glance.

Choosing between Foundation and Server

Many organizations struggle with understanding which of the SharePoint products is most appropriate for their needs. The following sections identify some differences between the editions and usage scenarios for each. Although this book has been written specifically to review features and functionality from the perspective of SharePoint Server, the following list shows some comparisons between SharePoint Foundation and SharePoint Server:

➤ **SharePoint Foundation contains the core document management and collaboration platform features.** With Foundation, the average information user can build web-based business applications without the need for technical resources or code. Because Foundation is available free with the Windows Server system, it has become a very popular collaborative tool for teams. This is largely because of the templates and existing site modules, which enable users to add documents, images, and information via a simple form rather than by using code. Users can create a new site based on an existing template in just a few seconds. SharePoint Foundation is tightly integrated with Microsoft Office applications, such as Word, Excel, PowerPoint, Access, and Outlook, so users can create and share content using a familiar, comfortable environment.

➤ **SharePoint Server includes the more advanced features that can be implemented within the environment.** It can accelerate the adoption of business process management, content management, and business intelligence across the intranet, extranet, and Internet. SharePoint Server delivers the tools to create, publish, and manage web-based content from a cohesive environment. SharePoint Server also offers the tools to automatically aggregate content from the SharePoint team sites, rolling up content from multiple sources to a central location, making information management even easier.

It is common for many organizations to have both a short-term and long-term plan for their SharePoint environment. In many cases, it is beneficial to start with a SharePoint Foundation environment and focus mostly on the collaboration effort. Once your needs have matured, you can upgrade to one of the SharePoint Server options. The main thing you want to try to avoid, though, is trying to fit a square peg in a round hole by attempting to build solutions that require Server features on the Foundation environment.

Options for Office 365

The options for licensing SharePoint Online through Office 365 are based on factors such as the number of users you want to add, the amount of data you need to store, and the features you need to be available. In addition to the features described previously for SharePoint Foundation and SharePoint Server, Office 365 includes options for hosting your e-mail in Exchange and for making Office Professional available to your users.

Different pricing options are available for desk-less kiosk workers, education organizations, and government agencies.

> **NOTE** *The best advice we can give about the licensing available is to refer you to the Office 365 website (*`www.microsoft.com/en-us/office365/`
> `compare-plans.aspx`*) to compare plans. Plans are designed to be flexible and are known to change over time. The main premise, though, is that you can supply a SharePoint solution for a small or large organization at varying costs, depending on required needs.*

SHAREPOINT COMPONENTS OVERVIEW

Regardless of an on-premise SharePoint Server environment, on-premise SharePoint Foundation environment, or an Office 365 implementation, several components serve as a foundation for all things within SharePoint and are key to the effective use of the system. These will be very important concepts to master as you progress through this book. Although each of these items is addressed in detail in later chapters, the following sections offer a brief overview. This overview serves as a way for you to become familiar with several key concepts before you begin to work through the remaining chapters.

The Ribbon

The *ribbon* is a tool within SharePoint aimed at making management and navigation activities much easier than the traditional menu-based system that was available in previous versions of the tool. The goal of the ribbon is to provide a simpler user experience when interacting with the site. Small icons are used rather than text to give a quicker visual indication of the setting you may be seeking. In addition, as you select various objects on a page, the ribbon adjusts itself to display tabs that may be of interest to you based on your selection. Figure 1-1 shows an example of the ribbon. In the image, because a Media web part is selected on the page, the ribbon is displaying options that relate to managing the Media web part.

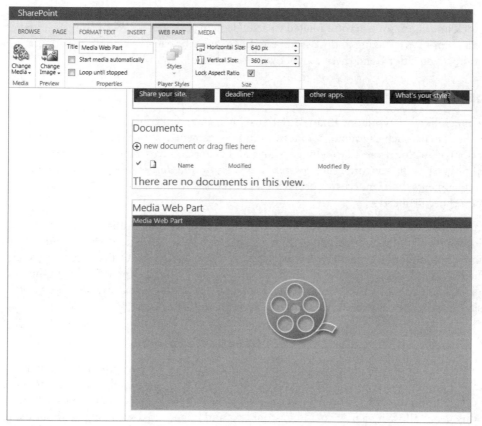

FIGURE 1-1

List Applications

The *list* is a fundamental application used in SharePoint Products and Technologies. A list is a storage location for a group of items. Items can be defined as any object that you are tracking information about. To create an item, you must fill out a form that describes the item, and the data from this form is then stored in a list. For example, you may have a list in SharePoint to track customer orders. Each customer order would be added to the list through the completion of the form. The form provides a controlled environment in which to collect information in a structured manner to ensure that all information tracked about customers is the same. Each customer order is considered an item. A list can have many items; however, an item can belong only to a single list.

Although advanced and dynamic, SharePoint lists are easy to create, requiring absolutely no code, special development skills, or tools. In the past, such lists took time to create and required using an application and hiring a developer or having a user with technical skills. By using SharePoint, users most familiar with the information-tracking and -sharing needs of the organization can create the tools they need.

You can use lists to store virtually any type of information. The most commonly used list types are contacts, tasks, announcements, and calendars. You can create other lists for just about any usage scenario to track and share information related to a single item. Chapter 2, "Working with List Apps," and Chapter 4, "Managing and Customizing Lists and Libraries," examine the common list templates and how you can extend them to meet your team's goals and objectives.

Library Applications

Libraries are much like lists with one major difference: their intended content. Whereas lists store information about items such as events, contacts, or announcements, libraries store documents. You can think of libraries as locations that help users find files faster and easier than ever through the use of special properties or keywords such as *status*, *owner*, or *due date*. Once you add a number of properties to documents, you can create special views or reports to filter, sort, and organize documents based on those properties.

Through SharePoint-specific technologies, such as content types, document libraries can now manage multiple types of files and templates from a single library, making it possible to quickly create and manage common document types such as those from Microsoft Office Word or Excel right from the browser. Chapter 3, "Working with Library Apps," and Chapter 4, "Managing and Customizing Lists and Libraries," explain how you can use document libraries within your SharePoint sites and further customize them to meet your team's needs.

Web Parts

When you create a list or library, SharePoint automatically generates a corresponding web part that you can later add to a web part page. You can think of *Web Parts* as mini-applications or modules that display information on a page or perform a special function. Web Parts can perform any number of functions, from allowing a user to add custom text and images to a web page without using Hypertext Markup Language (HTML) code, to displaying a financial report based on information stored in a completely separate application.

Although many common business Web Parts come with SharePoint, the model is extensible, and you can create custom Web Parts to accommodate the specific needs of your organization. You store Web Parts in a *web part gallery*, and you place them on a web page by dragging and dropping them into an appropriately marked *web part zone* or *content area*. Users can reuse, move, and customize Web Parts on multiple pages. For example, you can place a small module on the page to display the weather and have each division in your organization decide whether and where to display it on their site. Chapter 7, "Working with Web Parts," examines the various types of Web Parts that are available in SharePoint and discusses common usage scenarios for each primary category.

With the newest release of SharePoint, the SharePoint Marketplace will become a common location for you to purchase custom Web Parts that can be used within your environment. You can think of this as a process similar to going to the marketplace on your mobile device and downloading applications. The applications available in the Marketplace will come from many different sources, including Microsoft and Microsoft Partners, and will be available in a range of costs.

Workflows

A *workflow* automates a business process by breaking it into a set of steps that users must take to complete a specific business activity, such as approving content or routing a document from one location to another. Automation eliminates manual tasks and reduces the chance of data entry errors or documents getting lost in the system.

Workflows can be as simple or complex as your organization's needs. They can be very rigid and clearly defined or offer a greater level of flexibility and decision making. You learn more about the various alternatives for participating in and creating workflows in Chapter 5, "Working with Workflows."

Content Types

A *content type* represents a group of informational items in your organization that share common settings. They enable you to manage multiple types of information from a single location. You can associate content types with a document library, for example, to manage multiple file types, such as Word, PowerPoint, and Excel documents. Content types can also manage multiple templates of the same document type such as a Sales Presentation or Customer Order. As you associate a content type with a document library or list, it appears in the library's or list's New Document drop-down menu, as shown in the Figure 1-2.

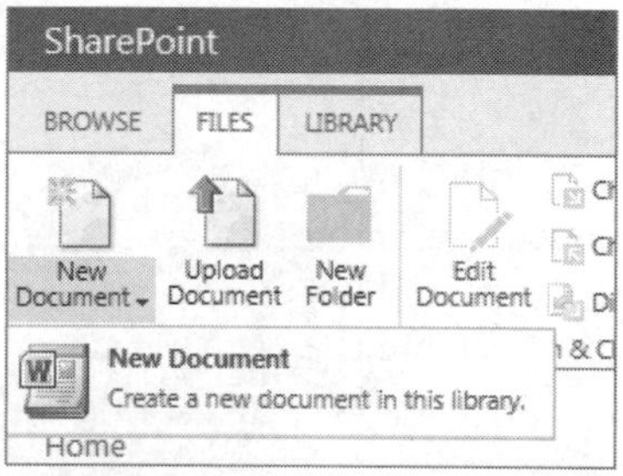

FIGURE 1-2

Content types make extensive use of global properties known as *site columns*, which means you can associate *metadata* (descriptive information) with your item to more easily find it. *Columns* are properties that help define an item; you use them similarly to the way you can use a field in a form. For example, for a task list, the field value for describing when an item is due is a column, used much like a field is for identifying who is responsible for completing a task. Content types make use of site columns because they, too, can be associated with multiple lists or libraries across a number of sites.

A more advanced use of content types involves templates known as *page layouts*, which you use to publish only certain types of content on your site. For example, you can create a newsletter article content type so that the web pages reflect your content—in this instance, a column for the title, another for the date, and a third for main text body. You can create page layouts via the browser or using SharePoint Designer; after creation, they become available in the Site Actions menu under the Create Pages option as page templates. Content types are introduced and explored in Chapter 6, "Working with Content Types."

Sites, Workspaces, and Site Collections

Both the terms sites and site *collections* refer to SharePoint sites. These websites, which you can create using available SharePoint templates, are also called *team collaboration* sites, and they store and share information using Web Parts, lists, and libraries as their various components. The following list explains how they differ:

➤ **Sites:** These share information in the form of list items and documents within a team or organization. Sites come in a variety of templates, and each template contains a unique set of lists, libraries, and pages. The template you select depends highly on which template most closely matches your needs.

➤ **Site collections:** These are a group of sites that form a hierarchy with a single top-level website with a collection of subsites, and another level of subsites below it. Figure 1-3 shows a graphical representation of a site collection.

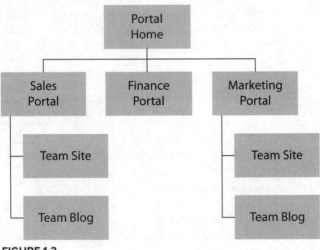

FIGURE 1-3

In the first exercise for this book, you create a new site collection based on the Collaboration Portal template, which will be known in all future exercises as the Corporate Intranet site. If you do not have the ability to create a new site collection within your SharePoint environment, you can ask your system administrator to complete this task for you and specify that your account is a site collection administrator account. Ideally, you should have a unique site collection to complete the exercises in this book; this will give you the most flexibility and a complete learning experience. If, for some reason, you are unable to get your own site collection, you will still be able to complete the exercises, but you may need to complete some additional steps in certain cases.

TRY IT OUT Creating a Site Collection

When learning an application such as SharePoint, it is a good idea to create an area where you can perform exercises without impacting existing environments or users. You select the Publishing Portal template because it closely matches the requirements of most organizations for an intranet site. From this site, you can create many of the content elements such as lists, libraries, and workflows that are required for the next four chapters.

To create a new site collection, you must visit the Central Administration site of your SharePoint environment. If you are unsure what the address for this site is, you should contact your system administrator or the person who installed SharePoint. You can also access the Central Administration site by logging directly into the server and selecting SharePoint 2013 Central Administration from the Microsoft SharePoint 2013 Products option on the Programs menu.

1. Log in to the SharePoint Central Administration site for your server farm.

2. Select Create Site Collections from the Application Management group of links.

3. The first item in your list of things to identify is the web application on which you will create the site. Make sure that the web application you select is the correct application. If it is not, you can click the down arrow to the right of the selected web application and click Change Web Application.

> **NOTE** *Typically, you create most SharePoint sites under the web application that is hosted on port 80 so that end users do not have to see a port number in the address of their sites. For example, a web address of* `http://servername` *is much nicer than* `http://servername:32124`*. If you are unsure which application to select, ask your system administrator or the person who installed SharePoint.*

4. To create a site collection, you must provide a title, description, and URL for the site. Name the site **Corporate Intranet**, and enter the following description:

   Collaborative portal for practicing exercises within the Beginning SharePoint 2013 book.

5. For URL options, select the "/sites/" managed path from the drop-down menu and then enter **intranet** in the blank field to the right of the drop-down.

> **NOTE** *If no other sites exist in your web application, you can also create your intranet portal site at the root of the website (for example,* `http://servername`*). Only one site collection can exist at the root of a website.*

6. You have a variety of choices for the site template. As described earlier, each template has a unique blend of lists, libraries, and pages. The optimal template for a corporate intranet is the Publishing Portal template, and you should use that template for this site.

7. Enter your own name as the primary site collection administrator.

> **NOTE** *If you are having another user create this site collection on your behalf, you should request that your name be entered in the Secondary Site Collection Administrator field.*

8. Click OK. The process for creating your site takes a few minutes. After it is completed, you are redirected to a page advising you that the process has completed successfully, and a URL is displayed for you to select to visit your site. Beginning in the next chapter, you use this site collection to start exploring the different features available within SharePoint.

How It Works

In this Try It Out, you access Central Administration to create a new site collection. When selecting the template, you chose what the default layout of the site would be and which libraries would be included. Since the first example was a Corporate Intranet site, you used the Publishing Portal template.

SUMMARY

This chapter provided basic knowledge about the features available in Microsoft Office SharePoint Technologies and how you can use them to provide various services to enterprise-level organizations, drive more efficient business processes, and connect people with the information required to make informed business decisions. After reading this chapter, you should also better understand how SharePoint Foundation differs from SharePoint Server and how they both differ from SharePoint Online, which is part of Office 365. You should also better understand the core components of SharePoint, including lists, libraries, content types, sites and workspaces, and workflow.

EXERCISES

1. What is the difference between a site and a site collection?

2. Your manager informs you that the organization is currently reviewing the need for a corporate portal. List two reasons that justify why organizations invest in portal technologies.

3. True or false: You must deploy SharePoint Server to have access to the collaboration features within SharePoint.

▶ **WHAT YOU LEARNED IN THIS CHAPTER**

TOPIC	KEY CONCEPTS
What SharePoint is	SharePoint is an extensible and scalable web-based platform consisting of tools and technologies that support the collaboration and sharing of information within teams, throughout the enterprise, and on the web.
The difference between an on-premise installation and an Office 365 implementation	With an on-premise installation of SharePoint, you have full control and responsibility of the entire environment, whereas with Office 365, you are relying on services provided by Microsoft. While using Office 365 and customizations, you must follow the provided guidelines and restrictions for applications or development. If your solutions need more access or control than allowed within Office 365, you will need to deploy an on-premise solution. You can install on-premise environments locally, or you can partner with a hosting provider to help you manage the environment.

2

Working with List Apps

WHAT YOU WILL LEARN IN THIS CHAPTER:

➤ What a SharePoint list is

➤ How to use lists

➤ The type of information that you can store in lists

➤ The primary activities available for interacting with lists

➤ The various default list templates

➤ How to work with lists to create and view information

This chapter reviews lists, a very important concept that you use throughout SharePoint to store and display information. By gaining a solid understanding of how they work early in this book, you can construct highly effective business applications and solutions in later chapters by combining multiple lists with other important SharePoint components.

This chapter focuses mainly on working with the basic features and functionality of lists. In Chapter 4, you learn how to customize and manage lists to create working environments that suit your specific business requirements and needs.

UNDERSTANDING LIST ELEMENTS

Lists have items, columns, and views. Items and columns correspond to the rows and columns that you see on a grid layout in a spreadsheet. Views present list data in a friendlier format that acts very similarly to a report.

➤ **Items:** An item is a row in a list. For example, for a list that stores information on customers, each customer may have a unique item in the list, which is also called the customer row or customer record.

➤ **Columns:** A column is a field in a list. You may also see columns referred to as *metadata*, which is a descriptive piece of information related to the item. In the case of a customer item in a list, the phone number, physical address, mailing address, and e-mail address would be columns that describe the customer.

➤ **Views:** A single list can have multiple views. You create a view to address a user's informational needs relating to list data. A view displays a subset of information from the list — for example, customers who have been added during a specific time period. You may also create a view to show all information on a list but have items displayed in a predefined order.

DISCOVERING SHAREPOINT LIST COLUMN TYPES

SharePoint lists can store information in the following types of columns:

➤ **Single line of text:** Possibly the most commonly used column type, it can store a variety of formats, such as names, phone numbers, e-mail addresses, the item's title, and virtually anything else that you can enter into a single-line textbox.

➤ **Multiple lines of text:** Occasionally, this type of column is useful because it can store larger amounts of information, such as a customer's background information or billing address. For this column type, you can select whether the information should contain plain, rich, or enhanced text elements, such as bold, italic, pictures, or tables. You can expand this column as you add text to it or you can select how many lines in the box to display initially. When you use this field to collect information from users, it is a good idea to determine the number of lines to display so that users will know how much content is expected from them.

➤ **Choice:** When gathering information on an item, you can offer users a selection of values or answers from which to choose. Using the example of a customers list, you may want to find out what types of services the customer purchases from you. If your organization provides only a fixed number of key services, it makes sense to present the user with this set of choices to ensure that the field always contains valid information. When creating a Choice column, you can choose whether to have the choices appear in a drop-down list, as radio buttons, or as checkboxes. For checkboxes, the user can select more than one item. Alternatively, you can have users fill in their own choices if their item does not appear in the list. This is known as allowing "fill-in choices."

➤ **Number:** You commonly need to associate numerical information with an item so that you can later perform calculations on the information stored in it. You can configure Number columns to store numbers that fall within a specific range or percentage value.

➤ **Currency:** This is similar to the Number column but specifically displays financial or monetary values. You can select what type of currency to display and the appropriate format based on region, such as $123,000.00 for the United States or £123,000.00 for the United Kingdom.

➤ **Date and Time:** You typically have a list containing dates or times. This might include when an organization first became a customer or the last time it purchased a product. Date columns allow users to enter the date information directly into a textbox or select the date from an easy-to-use calendar tool. When configuring a Date column, you can control whether to allow only dates or dates with times. You can also select a default value for the date, including a special setting that detects "Today's Date" as the user is filling out the item.

➤ **Lookup:** As your SharePoint environment expands, you may have many lists containing important information about things such as projects, products, and employees. In some cases, you need to take information from one list and associate it with information from another. In the example of the customers list, you may have a listing of projects that display the name of the customer for which the project is being completed. Because your customers list will contain that information, it makes sense to have a column in the projects list that displays the names of all the customers. Lookup columns encourage users to store information in a single location rather than duplicate items throughout the organization. New in SharePoint 2013 is the ability to select an item in a Lookup column and have additional fields related to that item displayed in the list. For example, when selecting a customer within your projects list, the name of the key contact for that customer and an associated phone number will also be associated with the list item.

➤ **Yes/No:** This checkbox column indicates whether an item matches a specific criterion. In the case of the customers list, you may create a Yes/No column named Active. If the customer is active, you select the checkbox. In the customer in not active, the checkbox remains blank.

➤ **Person or Group:** Users can select people or groups from the site's membership source (for example, Active Directory) and associate them with items in a list. In the customers list example, you may use this column type to associate an account manager with a customer. Optionally, you can include a display picture along with the account manager's name.

➤ **Hyperlink or Picture:** You can use this column type to allow users to enter a web address into a list item to create a hyperlink or display an image located at the source location. In the customers list example, you can use this type of column to display the company's website address or the company's logo.

➤ **Calculated:** Rather than have users enter information manually, you may want to calculate values based on other columns within the list. For this type of column, you can select the names of other columns from the list and identify relationships and formulas. For example, you may have a calculated value that displays how many years the customer has been a client of the organization based on other information in the customer record. You can then select a format for the column.

➤ **Task Outcome:** You can use this column type when defining workflow solutions. It is very similar to the Choice column in its properties, but is often leveraged related to the tracking on tasks for workflow.

➤ **External Data:** In some cases, you may want to associate business data from an external business application with your list items. For example, you may have a listing of all products in a sales database and instead of re-creating it in SharePoint, you can connect to it and reuse that information. Using an External Data column, you can associate a products list with your list so that, as you define customers, you can also select which products the customer typically purchases.

➤ **Managed Metadata:** In some cases within your organization, another administrative user may have already defined a set of metadata to describe important aspects of your organization. Therefore, there is no requirement for you to redefine this information yourself. In such cases, it would be more appropriate for you to create a column that connects to the managed metadata service to select the values that have been predefined by your system administrator or another user who has been empowered to configure this shared feature. Managed metadata is described in detail in Chapter 16, "Managing Records."

➤ **Audiences:** If a list has audience targeting enabled, this column type is added to it automatically. Audiences are groups of users that you define based on a set of criteria. When you use audiences on list items, the items appear only to members of the audiences associated with the item. Chapter 11 provides in-depth information on audiences.

UNDERSTANDING THE STANDARD LIST APPS

With the basic components of a list explained, you can now look at some of the list templates that are available in SharePoint as apps. Apps are special tools you can create and use on your site to better track, store, and access information. A variety of apps exist; this chapter reviews the apps that are related to lists. Many of these apps address common collaborative scenarios that exist within organizations, such as tracking tasks and sharing contact and meeting information. You should think of these apps as a starting point because you can further customize them to suit the needs of any organization. More advanced techniques for customizing and managing lists are discussed in Chapter 4.

To demonstrate common collaborative scenarios that might exist in relation to the usage of lists within teams, the remainder of this chapter considers the example of using SharePoint lists for tracking information related to a project. Within a project, there is often a large amount of information to be tracked and many of the built-in templates can assist in providing an excellent starting point for sharing such information.

| TRY IT OUT | Creating a Project Team Site |

To get started, you create a site that acts as a collaborative location for sharing information about a new project that is about to start, called Project Gros Morne. This is a project that evaluates the feasibility of expanding a travel company's operations into a popular tourist location in eastern Canada. You create this site using the Team Site template. If you already have a site available for your use that is based on this template, you can skip this exercise.

1. From the main page of your training site collection, select Site Contents from the Settings menu.

2. Select the New Subsite link. The New SharePoint Site dialog box appears, as shown in Figure 2-1.

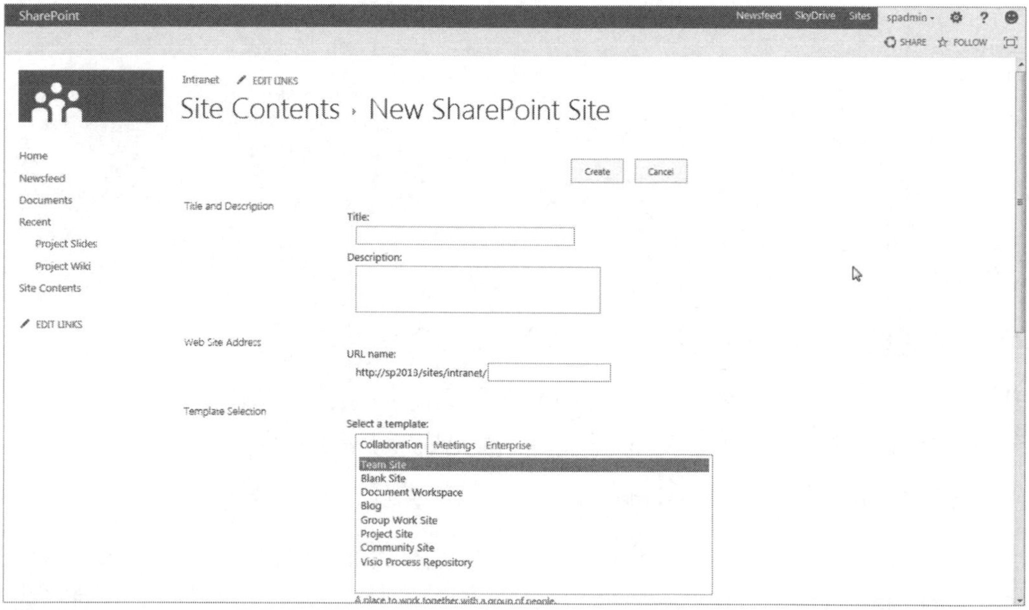

FIGURE 2-1

3. Select the Team Site template from the template list under the Collaboration tab.

> **NOTE** *Sites created based on the Publishing Portal template may require the ability to enable the creation of subsites based on any site template to complete this exercise. You do this by going to the main page of your intranet site collection, selecting Site Settings from the Settings menu, and selecting "Page layouts and site templates" from the Look and Feel Group of links. You must then enable the subsites so that you can use any site template option within the Subsite Templates section of the page. Then you must click OK to save your changes. Now you can create a subsite using any template from your intranet site.*

4. Complete the fields shown in Figure 2-2 using the information in the following table.

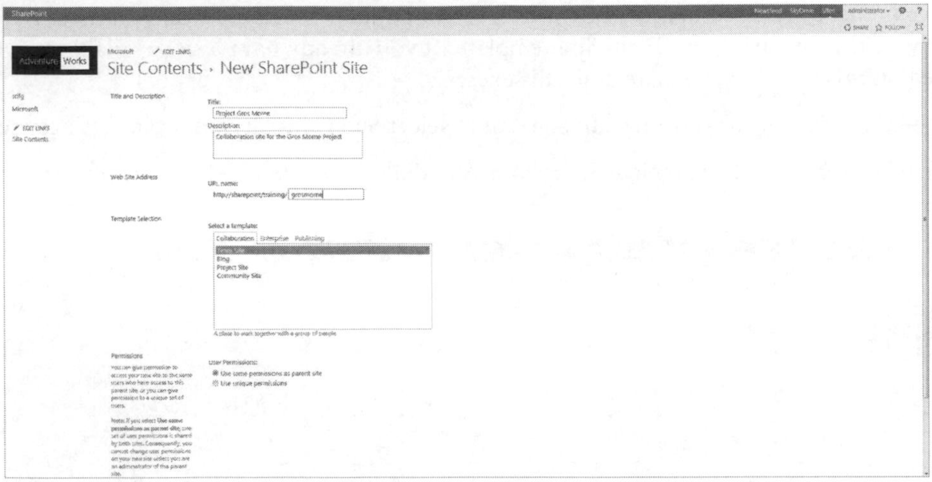

FIGURE 2-2

FIELD	VALUE
Title	Project Gros Morne
Description	Collaboration site for the Gros Morne Project
Web Site Address	grosmorne
Permissions	Use same permissions as parent site
Navigation Inheritance	Yes

5. Click Create. The site creation process starts, and upon its completion you are redirected to the main page of your new site.

How It Works

Users with the appropriate privileges can create sites for projects, initiatives, or any other collaborative scenarios simply by completing a form to specify a template, site title, description, and URL. In this exercise, you selected the Team Site template because it contains many of the lists that you would like to use for tracking your project. If you have Project Server installed, a template is available called Project Site that is useful for such scenarios, as well.

When creating the site, you selected the option to use the top link bar from the parent site. This ensures that as users visit your site, they will see the same top-level navigation links that they saw when on the previous site. This can sometimes be considered a best practice, because users typically find it easier to navigate across multiple sites if the primary navigation stays consistent. You can change this setting after the site has been created by visiting the Settings page for the site and changing the navigational settings. This activity is covered in Chapter 8.

The Contacts List App

Within a project team, you commonly need to share contact information. This may be the contact information of team members, but may also include contact information of other key stakeholders such as customers, vendors, partners, or industry experts. SharePoint provides a very easy-to-use interface just for this purpose that you can create via an app. It's known as a *Contacts list*. Rather than storing contact information of key stakeholders within individual address books, team members add contacts to a list on a SharePoint site so that the information becomes available to everyone.

A Contacts list has the columns shown in the following table. However, as is the case with any list, you can create or delete columns at any time. The Last Name column is considered to be the title column, and you cannot remove it from the list. You can rename it if you like, however.

COLUMN NAME	COLUMN TYPE
Last Name (required)	Single Line of Text
First Name	Single Line of Text
Full Name	Single Line of Text
E-mail Address	Single Line of Text
Company	Single Line of Text
Job Title	Single Line of Text
Business Phone	Single Line of Text
Home Phone	Single Line of Text
Mobile Phone	Single Line of Text
Fax Number	Single Line of Text
Address	Multiple Lines of Text
City	Single Line of Text
State/Province	Single Line of Text
ZIP/Postal Code	Single Line of Text
Country/Region	Single Line of Text
Web Page	Hyperlink or Picture
Notes	Multiple Lines of Text

Adding an item to a Contacts list is quite easy, and you can do it using one of the following methods:

➤ **Click the "new item" link:** You can click this link, as shown in Figure 2-3, and then enter all the details for the list manually using a form.

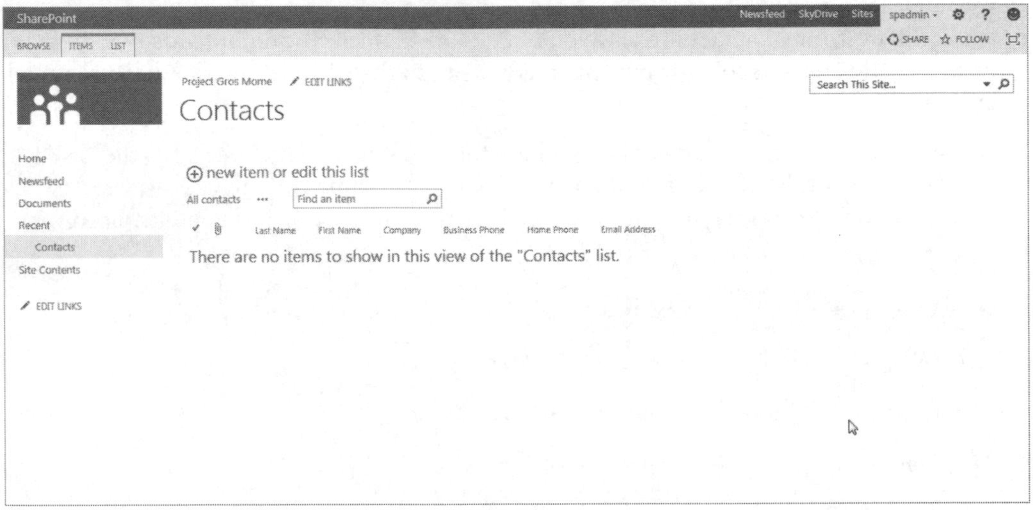

FIGURE 2-3

➤ **Synchronize data using an offline client application:** You can update Contacts lists using Microsoft Outlook, SharePoint Workspace, or Microsoft Access. The methods for each are described later in this chapter within the Try It Out exercises.

The Contacts list features only one view upon creation:

➤ **All Contacts:** This standard list view displays all items (in groups of 30) in the list sorted by Last Name. Site visitors can access it either from the list itself or a web part related to the list.

The Announcements List App

Virtually every team needs to track news related to important events and activities. Instead of sending distracting direct e-mail messages to team members, you can use the Announcements list app to drive members to your site to look for the latest information on key activities and events. Using the Announcements list app, site managers can alert team members to key events and milestones related to their business activities, without having to adopt a more formalized news-publishing feature.

When you create an Announcements list, it contains the columns shown in the following table. However, you can add more columns or remove unwanted ones. Because the Title column is considered to be a required column, you cannot remove it from the list.

COLUMN NAME	COLUMN TYPE	COLUMN DESCRIPTION
Title (required)	Single Line of Text	Generally, this column is used to store the headline of the announcement you are creating.
Body	Multiple Lines of Text	This column is typically used to feature the details of the announcement you are creating. It supports enhanced text with formatting, pictures, and tables by default.
Expires	Date and Time	This column is used in cases where an announcement should not appear within certain views after a specific date. You can then configure views to show only items where the expiry date is blank or occurs in the future.
Created By	Person or Group	This is a system-generated value that displays the name of the user who originally created the announcement.
Modified By	Person or Group	This is a system-generated value that displays the name of the user who last modified the announcement.

The Announcements list app features two standard views upon creation:

➤ **All Items:** This standard list view displays all items (in groups of 30) in the list sorted by their creation date. Site visitors can access it either from the list itself or a web part related to the list.

➤ **Summary:** The Announcements list web part uses this view to display the item title followed by a segment of the story and the author's name. This view displays the latest stories for which the expiry date has not been specified or has not passed. There is no way to edit the properties or behavior of this view.

The Tasks List App

An important requirement when running a project is having the ability to effectively monitor and track task progress. SharePoint includes an app designed specifically around the management of tasks. Using this app, you can create a list of tasks for team members and e-mail notifications are automatically sent to the assigned parties containing details of the assignment. A Tasks list app features the ability to be connected to Microsoft Outlook, which allows users to view, create, and update tasks within SharePoint directly from within Microsoft Outlook. In addition, you can export information from a Tasks list directly into a Microsoft project plan or Excel spreadsheet. This allows team leaders or project managers to create a Tasks list for the initial activities related to a project within their SharePoint team site, which can later be promoted into a more formal project plan when the project becomes more defined or complex. Similarly, team leaders or project managers can synchronize existing Microsoft Project plans with a SharePoint Tasks list. This is an activity you review later in this chapter in a Try It Out exercise.

When you create a Tasks list app, it has the columns listed in the following table; however, you can add more columns at any time. Because the Task Name column is required, you cannot remove it from the app.

COLUMN NAME	COLUMN TYPE	COLUMN DESCRIPTION
Task Name (required)	Single Line of Text	This column is typically used to provide a name for the task. This name is displayed in web parts to allow users to easily identify it from others.
Priority	Choice	This column is used to associate a priority level with tasks to allow users to easily identify which tasks they should resolve first. Like all other columns, you can customize this column to reflect priority values that would be relevant to your organization.
Task Status	Choice	This column is used to track the status of the task. Applying a status value enables your team to stay informed about how the task is progressing by visiting the list.
% Complete	Number	This column is used to track the progress of the task. Applying a % complete enables your team to stay informed about how the task is progressing by visiting the list.
Assigned To	Person or Group	This column is used to select a team member who has been assigned to complete the task. By default, only a single team member can be assigned to a task. However, you can modify the settings for this column to allow multiple users to be assigned to a single task. This customization is covered in Chapter 4.
Description	Multiple Lines of Text	This column contains details of the task, such as the original request as well as any notes on how the task is progressing.
Start Date	Date and Time	This column is used to identify when the task is scheduled to start.
Due Date	Date and Time	This column is used to identify when the task is scheduled to be completed.
Predecessors	Lookup	This column helps team members easily identify which tasks must be completed before the task in question can be worked on or resolved.

The Tasks list features the following standard views upon creation:

➤ **All Tasks:** This view displays all items (in groups of 30) in the list sorted by their creation date.

➤ **My Tasks:** This personalized view of items is a good default view for team members because it displays the tasks that have been assigned to the current user.

➤ **Upcoming:** This view displays summary information related to tasks that are incomplete and due either today or in the future.

➤ **Late Tasks:** This view displays summary information related to tasks that are incomplete and due in the past.

➤ **Completed:** This view displays summary information related to tasks that are complete.

➤ **Calendar:** This view displays the listing of tasks in a calendar format that defaults to a month view. Users can change it to either weekly or daily view.

➤ **Gantt Chart:** This view displays the listing of tasks in a Gantt chart format that demonstrates the progression of tasks over time. Users can zoom in and out using the timescale. Tasks show schedule information that is useful for planning in project or team scenarios.

The Issues Tracking List App

Unfortunately, it's not uncommon for unexpected issues to arise when you conduct business or run a project. An *issue* is an event that requires resolution. In a software environment, this may be a bug that someone discovered in the software. In a shipping company, this may be a transportation delay because of a snowstorm. Because issues can have a huge impact on business operations and the success of an initiative, it is important to effectively track and resolve them. The SharePoint Issues Tracking app provides an easy-to-use method for doing so.

As with the Tasks list app, you can export information from an Issues list to Microsoft Access, Excel, and SharePoint Workspace. Although the Issues list app does support the offline synchronization features of certain Microsoft client applications, there is no default support for Microsoft Outlook integration.

By default, an Issues list contains the columns shown in the following table, but you can add columns to meet your needs. Because the Title column is considered to be the required column, you cannot remove it from the list.

COLUMN NAME	COLUMN TYPE	COLUMN DESCRIPTION
Title (required)	Single Line of Text	This column is typically used to provide a name for the issue. This name is displayed in web parts to allow users to easily identify it and differentiate it from others.
Assigned To	Person or Group	This column is used to select a team member who has been assigned to complete the issue. By default, only a single team member can be assigned to an issue. However, you can modify the settings for this column to allow multiple users to be assigned to a single issue. This customization is covered in Chapter 4.
Issue Status	Choice	This column is used to track the status of the issue. Applying a status value enables your team to stay informed about how the resolution of the issue is progressing by visiting the list.
Priority	Choice	This column is used to associate a priority level with issues to allow users to easily identify which issues they should resolve first. Like all other columns, you can customize this column to reflect priority values that are relevant to your organization.

continues

(continued)

COLUMN NAME	COLUMN TYPE	COLUMN DESCRIPTION
Description	Multiples Lines of Text	This column contains details of the issue. Clearly documenting the details on an issue enables team members to better identify an approach for resolution.
Category	Choice	This column is an optional column that is meant to be customized to include relevant categories for issues. Assigning an appropriate category to each issue enables team members to more easily identify which items are related, and the list remains easy to manage as it expands.
Due Date	Date and Time	This column is used to identify when the issue is scheduled to be completed.
Related Issues	Lookup	Because sometimes you cannot resolve one issue until you find a resolution for another issue, the Issues list has built-in functionality for tracking related items.
Comments	Multiple Lines of Text	The Comments column of an Issues list timestamps and labels each entry that team members make over the duration of the issue. This provides excellent insight into the progress of a specific item.

The Calendar List App

Having a shared calendar that all team members can access improves the communication of important information, such as availability, deadlines, and progress. The Calendar list app offers a variety of views and features that make tracking and viewing date-based information easy within team-based environments.

When you create a Calendar list, it contains the columns shown in the following table. You can add or remove columns at any time, but you cannot remove the default columns: Title, Start Time, and End Time.

COLUMN NAME	COLUMN TYPE	COLUMN DESCRIPTION
Title (required)	Single Line of Text	This column is typically used to provide a name for an event. This name is displayed in web parts to allow users to easily identify it and differentiate it from others.
Location	Single Line of Text	This column is used to identify the location of the event.
Start Time (required)	Date and Time	This column is used to identify the starting time of the event. The values selected here will determine where the event is displayed within the calendar-based views of the list.

End Time (required)	Date and Time	This column is used to identify the end time of the event. The values selected here will determine where the event is displayed within the calendar-based views of the list.
Description	Multiple Lines of Text	This column is used to provide details of the event.
Category	Choice	This column is used to help provide classification of the different events. This list contains many common event types but can be configured to suit your organization's specific requirements.
All Day Event	Checkbox	Similar to an event created in Microsoft Outlook, an event in SharePoint can be specified as an All Day Event. When an event is designated as All Day, the ability to select hourly time values for Start and End Time are disabled.
Recurrence	Checkbox (Special)	This special setting enables you to set a recurring schedule on an event. For example, if your team has a weekly status meeting, you can set up recurrence on a single event rather than creating a new event for each week.

Calendar lists can be connected to Microsoft Outlook or Access. When you connect with either of these two applications, information is synchronized between the SharePoint list and a local copy within the application. In addition, information from a SharePoint Calendar list can be exported to Microsoft Excel.

The Calendar list features three standard views upon creation:

➤ **Calendar:** This view displays all list information in a month, week, and day calendar format, as shown in Figure 2-4. Users can switch between month, week, and day views of the list items or select a specific date to view all items for the selected day.

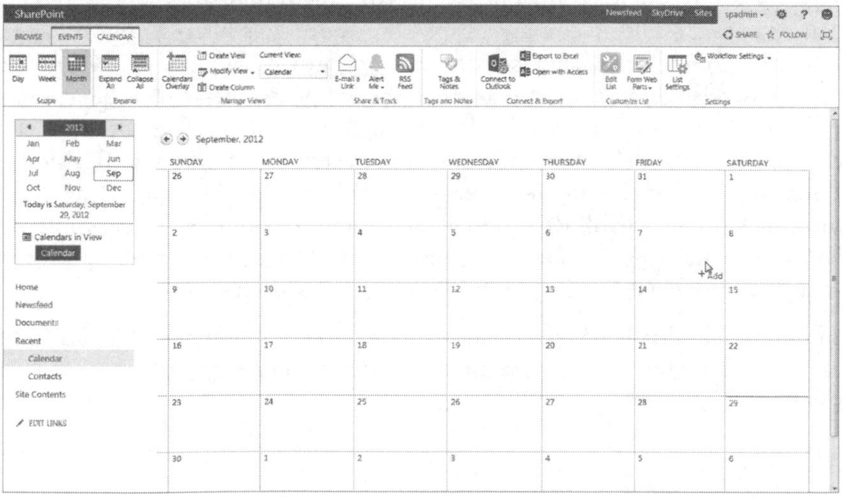

FIGURE 2-4

➤ **All Items:** This standard list view displays all items (in groups of 30) of the list sorted by their creation date.

➤ **Current Events:** This list view filters out items that have taken place in the past and displays upcoming items in the order that they will take place.

The Links List App

Commonly, working on a project or initiative requires a team to set up website links to share with one another — for example, links to third-party information sources. SharePoint provides an app that makes it easy to share links with team members. Upon creation, the links list app has the columns listed in the following table; however, you can add more columns later. The URL column is considered to be a required column and, therefore, you cannot remove it from the list.

COLUMN NAME	COLUMN TYPE	COLUMN DESCRIPTION
URL (Required)	Hyperlink or Picture	When adding a new link item to a list, you must specify a URL along with a description. The description gives your URL a title so that the full web address does not display in the list views. When you specify the URL, you can click a link that tests the address to confirm that it is a valid location. You should test your address before you publish it to all your team members.
Notes	Multiple Lines of Text	You may choose to include notes on why you feel this link is useful to other team members.

The Discussion Board List App

Because team members may be collaborating on projects from different geographic locations and have different working schedules, having an effective mode of electronic communication is critical. Although e-mail has traditionally played this role, the proliferation of e-mail messages within organizations often results in employees spending more time filtering and sorting through their inboxes than they can afford. As a result, SharePoint provides a more passive electronic communication. A threaded discussion enables an author to post a message or question, and allows others to reply to that message or question through the web interface. Because all the communication occurs on the website, team members can stay informed about decision-making processes without directly participating in a specific thread. In addition, as you learn in Chapter 17, Working with Search, all this content can be indexed and made accessible via the built-in search engine. This helps provide a long-term knowledge center for users to search for answers to commonly asked questions prior to initiating a new discussion.

The Discussion Board list initially has the columns shown in the following table; however, you can add more columns. Because the Subject column is considered to be required, you cannot remove it from the list.

COLUMN NAME	COLUMN TYPE	COLUMN DESCRIPTION
Subject (required)	Single Line of Text	Similar to an e-mail subject, this column provides high-level information that describes the topic of the discussion.
Body	Multiple Lines of Text	This column contains the message that is being shared between team members and is similar to the body of an e-mail message.
Question	Checkbox	This column is intended to allow users to flag certain discussion topics as questions.

In addition to these columns, multiple views are associated with a discussion list that allow users to view discussions they have created themselves as well as discussions that might be unanswered questions. These views make a discussion list app a valuable tool for sharing information and frequently asked questions on a SharePoint site. Figure 2-5 demonstrates an example of a discussion that was marked as a question and has received multiple replies, including a single reply that has been flagged as the best reply.

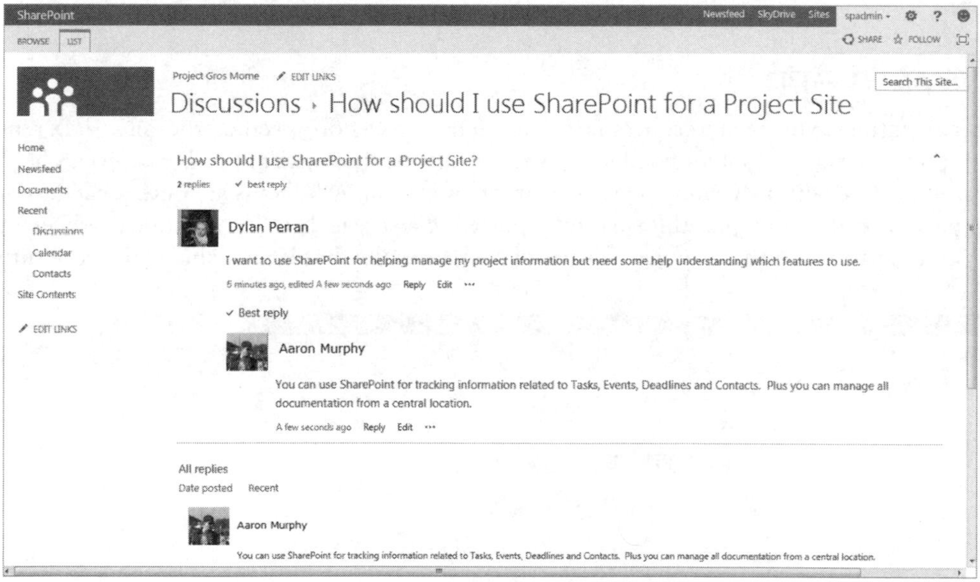

FIGURE 2-5

For team members who prefer to control their communications from an e-mail client, you can connect to Outlook in this list app. Clicking Connect to Outlook from the ribbon menu of a discussion list enables team members to view a new folder specifically for discussion in their Outlook SharePoint lists. Users can make new posts and send replies from Outlook in the very same way that they create a new e-mail message. However, instead of sending a message directly to someone's inbox, the message is posted to a central location where everybody can share the information. Figure 2-6 shows an example of a Discussion Board list item in Flat view. This view is available by clicking a discussion subject.

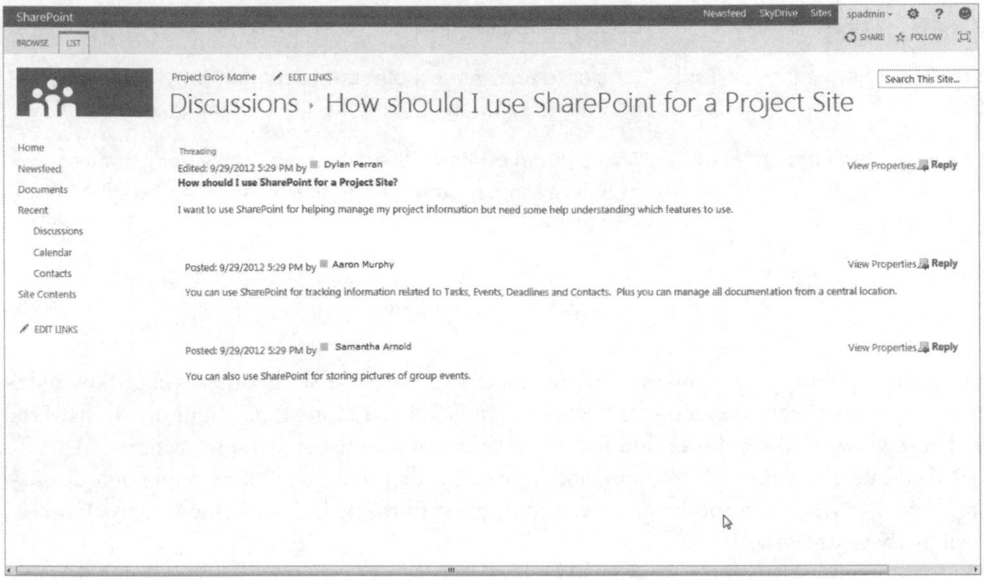

FIGURE 2-6

The Survey List App

In most organizations, you need to collect information from users on specific programs and events. SharePoint provides a great tool for conducting surveys via the Survey list app. This app can be highly customized to deliver dynamic surveys to an organization. All data is submitted back to the list and can be viewed in a graphical format or exported to a spreadsheet for additional processing. Figure 2-7 is an example of the graphical format of survey results that is available with every survey.

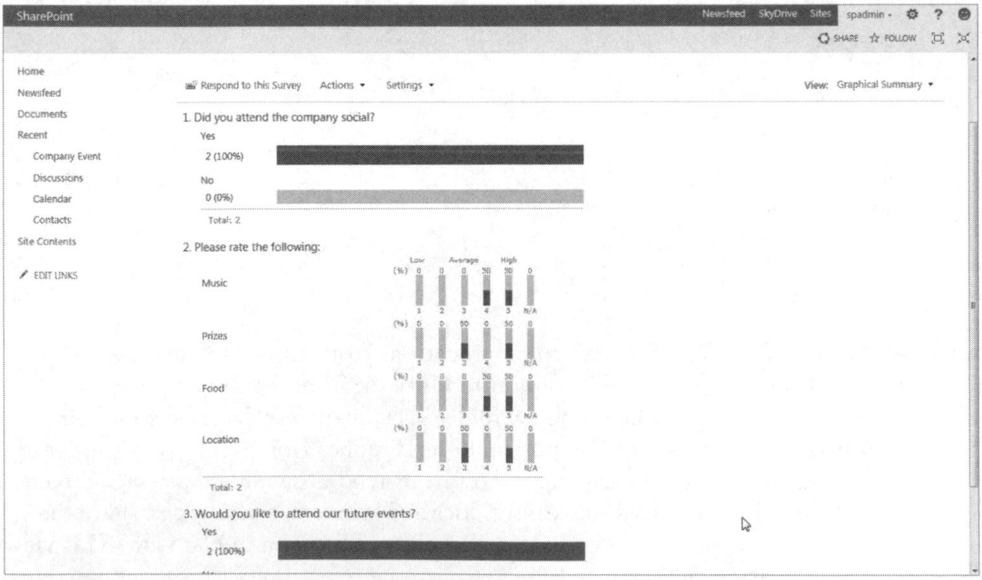

FIGURE 2-7

Creating questions in a SharePoint survey is similar to creating columns, with the exception that no default (required) columns exist. Instead, the author must complete a wizard type interface to create the questions required for the survey.

In a SharePoint Survey list, you can create the question types shown in the following list:

- Single line of text

- Multiple lines of text

- Choice (menu to choose from)

- Rating Scale (a matrix of choices or a Likert scale)

- Number (1, 1.0, 100)

- Currency ($, ¥, €)

- Date and Time

- Lookup (information already on this site)

- Yes/No (checkbox)

- Person or Group

- Page Separator (inserts a page break into your survey)

- External Data

- Managed Metadata

The Survey list app has a unique feature that enables you to create page separators and rating scales to improve a survey form's usability and design. Once you create questions, you can add branching logic to improve the flow of questions and ensure that you're only asking users to answer questions relevant to them. For example, if a question asks if the user has attended the company social, you can insert branching logic to ensure that, if the user selects no, she can skip questions that focus on the company social and redirect her to the next relevant question.

The Status List App

The Status list app is a specialized list template for tracking progress toward organizational goals and objectives. Because this feature is related to the business intelligence features of SharePoint Server 2013, it is explored in detail in Chapter 10.

The External List App

An External list is a feature within SharePoint 2013 that supports the viewing and interaction of external business data from within a SharePoint list. To use this list app, you must create what is known as an *External content type*, which is a special mechanism for accessing data that is located in external systems. This list is dependent on the Business Connectivity Services feature of SharePoint, which is not explored in this book. For more information, see `http://technet`
`.microsoft.com/en-us/library/fp161238(v=office.15)`.

WORKING WITH LISTS

Now that you know the various lists that are available in SharePoint, you need to understand how you can interact and work with lists to gain the insight you require from a SharePoint site and the information it contains.

Working with List Content

In the next three examples, you learn how to create a list app, add content to the list, and make updates to existing content within the list. Because SharePoint lists are useful only if they contain information, it is very important that you understand how to update them effectively.

In SharePoint, a variety of list apps can store just about any type of information or data. In the following examples, you walk through the steps of creating a new list and item using the Announcements app. However, the same steps apply regardless of the list app you use. Therefore, we recommend that you repeat these exercises using the different list apps within the Project Team Site you created earlier in this chapter.

TRY IT OUT Creating a New List

When you created your Project Team Site earlier in the chapter, the site contained certain lists and libraries by default. In some situations, you may need to add additional lists to your site that use other apps or meet your specific requirements. In this example, you create a new list based on the Announcements template. This list is used for sharing progress information throughout the project.

1. From the main page of your Project Gros Morne site, expand the Settings menu and select the "Add an app" menu item, as shown in Figure 2-8.

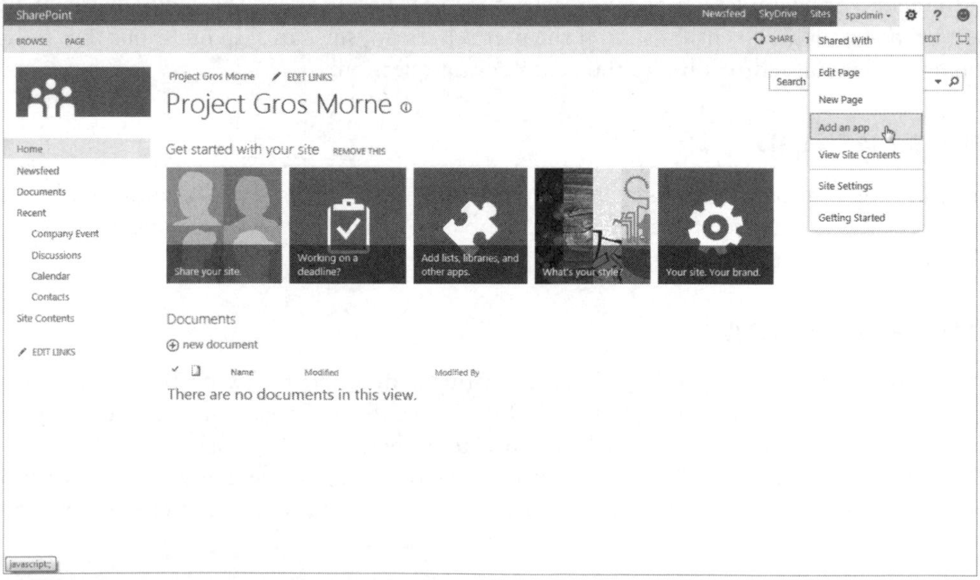

FIGURE 2-8

2. Select the Announcements app.

3. Enter **Announcements** as the name of your list.

4. Click the Create button.

5. The new list is created, click its name to be redirected to it (See Figure 2-19).

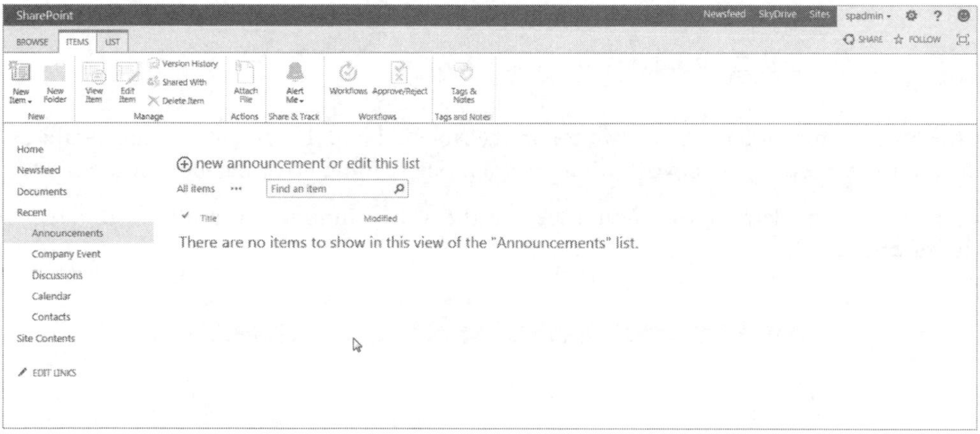

FIGURE 2-9

How It Works

In this example, you created a new list on your site using the Announcements app. You can use this same process to create any list on your site.

TRY IT OUT   **Adding a New Item to a List**

Your boss has requested that you create a news story announcing the launch of the new project. Rather than creating this story as an e-mail message and potentially distracting your team members from more important and time-sensitive activities, you choose to create an announcement on your newly created team site.

1. From the main page of your Project Gros Morne site, select the Site Contents link from the side navigation. You are redirected to a page listing all lists and libraries that exist within the current site.

2. Click the Announcements link. This brings you to the Announcements list.

3. At the top of the page, click the Items tab within the List Tools menu. This displays the List Items ribbon menu associated with the Announcements list (refer to Figure 2-9). From this menu, you can create new announcements or interact with existing announcements, as well as access more advanced features that are covered later in this book.

4. Click the New Item menu option. This launches a form for you to complete to specify the details of your announcement.

5. Complete the form using the following details:

COLUMN	VALUE
Title	New Project Launched
Body	We are excited to annonce the launch of our new project. This project will last approximately 12 months and will focus on the exploration of a National Park located in Newfoundland and Labrador for a suitable location for a company office.
Expires	Enter a date 12 months in the future.

6. Click the Spelling menu item of the Edit tab in the ribbon menu. If you entered the details as specified in the preceding table, you will notice that one spelling error has been found.

7. Click OK to view the details. You should see that the word "annonce" is underlined in red, as shown in Figure 2-10.

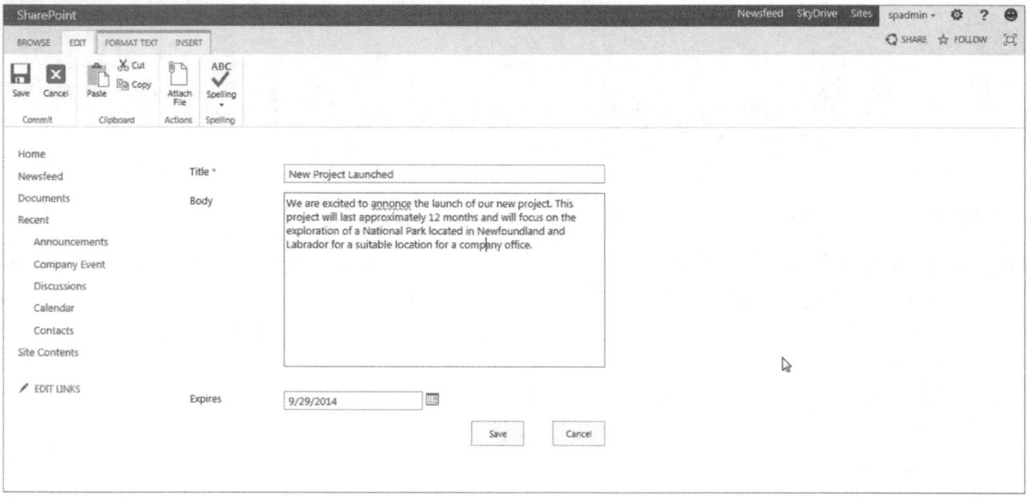

FIGURE 2-10

8. Click the word using your right mouse button. A listing of suggested words appears.

9. Select the first choice: announce. The text of your announcement body is updated to feature the correct spelling.

10. Click Save to complete the creation of your new announcement. You are returned to the list, and your new announcement appears on the screen with a new icon.

How It Works

In the preceding example, you navigated to the Announcements list of your project site to create a new entry related to the launch of a new project. The Announcements list is an excellent location for content such as this, which does not require an immediate response or action from readers. Quite often in organizations, messages such as this are sent via e-mail. Using an Announcements list, team members can receive their updates on topics at times that are more convenient for them. When you specify an expiration date for your entry, it is only displayed in the Summary view until that date. You can configure other views for filtering based on the Expires column as well. The creation of custom views is covered in Chapter 4.

When navigating to the Announcements list, you selected Site Content from the side navigation. This option enables you to access all lists and libraries on the site. In some cases, a list may have been created but not have been added to the side navigation. Therefore, you must access it using the Site Contents option.

TRY IT OUT   Editing an Existing Item in a List

Upon reading the new Announcement that you created on your Project Team Site, you realize it would have been useful to also include details related to how others can become involved. Therefore, you must update the announcement to include additional details.

1. From the main page of your project site, select the View Site Contents link from the Settings menu. This is an alternative method to access the page containing links to all lists and libraries on the site.

2. Select your Announcements list.

3. Select the checkmark to the left of your New Project Launched announcement.

4. Select the Edit Item option from the Items tab of the ribbon, as shown in Figure 2-11.

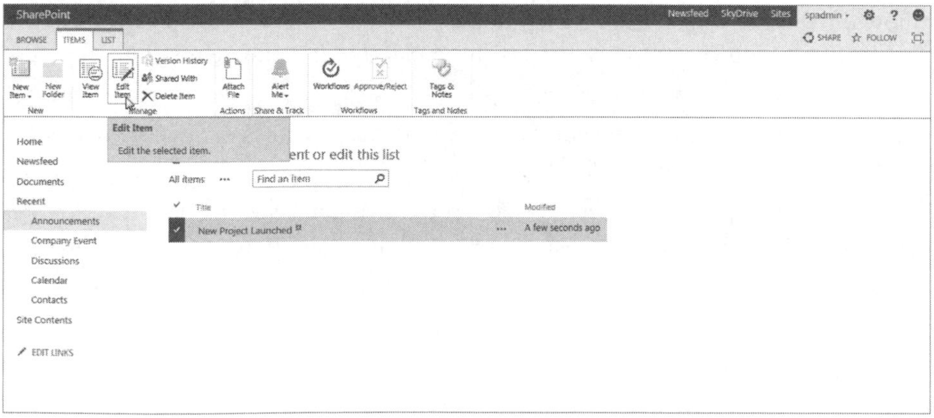

FIGURE 2-11

5. Within the Body column, add the following text:

To become involved in this project, please contact Dylan Perran, the Project Manager at `dylan.perran@discovern1.com`.

6. Click Save.

Now when team members view your announcement, they will see your latest changes.

How It Works

In the preceding example, you added a new announcement to an Announcements list. Users with the appropriate privileges can modify these items by editing the properties and making the appropriate changes to the corresponding form.

When you select to edit properties of a list item, you are presented with a form allowing you to modify the metadata columns associated with the list. By modifying these fields, you modify what the users will see when viewing the contents of the list—in this case, the announcements.

> **NOTE** *The previous examples focused on creating and editing items in an Announcements list. However, you can use the steps to create new items on all lists. It is highly recommended that you take some time to enter items in the other list templates that exist on your Project Team Site before completing additional exercises.*

TRY IT OUT　　Changing the View of a List

In this Try It Out, you create a list and change its view. In a collaborative environment, it is common for multiple people to store information in shared lists. As these individuals go about their day-to-day activities, it is also common that they will need to interact with subsets of the information stored in those lists. Views allow you to filter a group of list items based on preset criteria, such as "Show only my items" or "Show only items where sales are not final." As you create views, they become available from the ribbon, where you can select them and subsequently filter the items from all items to a subset.

1. Following the steps described in the previous example for creating an Announcements list, create a new list on the project site using the Tasks app.

2. Once the list is created, expand the Current View drop-down and select the Gantt Chart view, as shown in Figure 2-12. The page refreshes, and you will notice that a new view of the list appears.

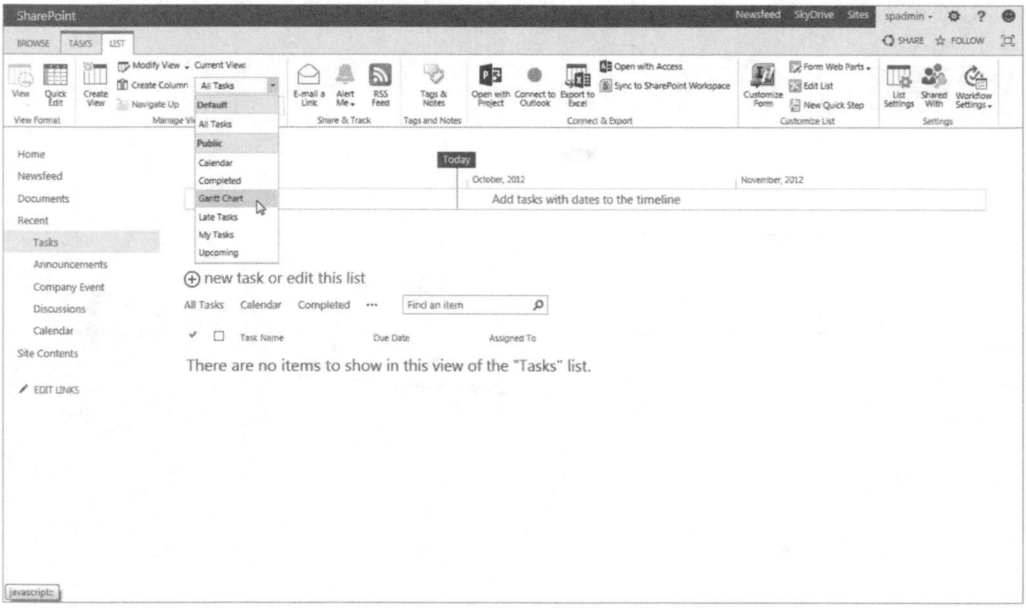

FIGURE 2-12

How It Works

As you add more and more data to SharePoint lists, it is important that you have methods to organize and access the information in a timely and effective manner. In the previous example, you created a Tasks list and changed the view of the list to a Gantt view. The Gantt view is designed to display tasks in a graphical format so that you can compare the progress and timeline of each visually. Other views exist on the Tasks list as well, including My Tasks, which displays a listing of tasks assigned to the current user.

In the example shown, you selected the My Tasks view. This view has a filter that only displays items assigned to the current user. The view uses a special property, called [me], which identifies the current user and displays only items that have that user's name in the Assigned To column.

TRY IT OUT Editing Items in a Gantt View

The Gantt View is a special view for Tasks lists, giving you a visual presentation of tasks over time. In this Try It Out, you will track tasks across a date range using the Gantt View and get hands-on experience adding and modifying a series of tasks in a SharePoint Tasks list.

1. You may notice that the presentation of the Gantt view selected in the previous exercise is slightly different from that of the lists previously explored in the chapter. In the middle of your screen, you will notice a view divider bar. Hover near the middle of the bar, as shown in Figure 2-13, to highlight the area on the bar that you can click and drag to the right.

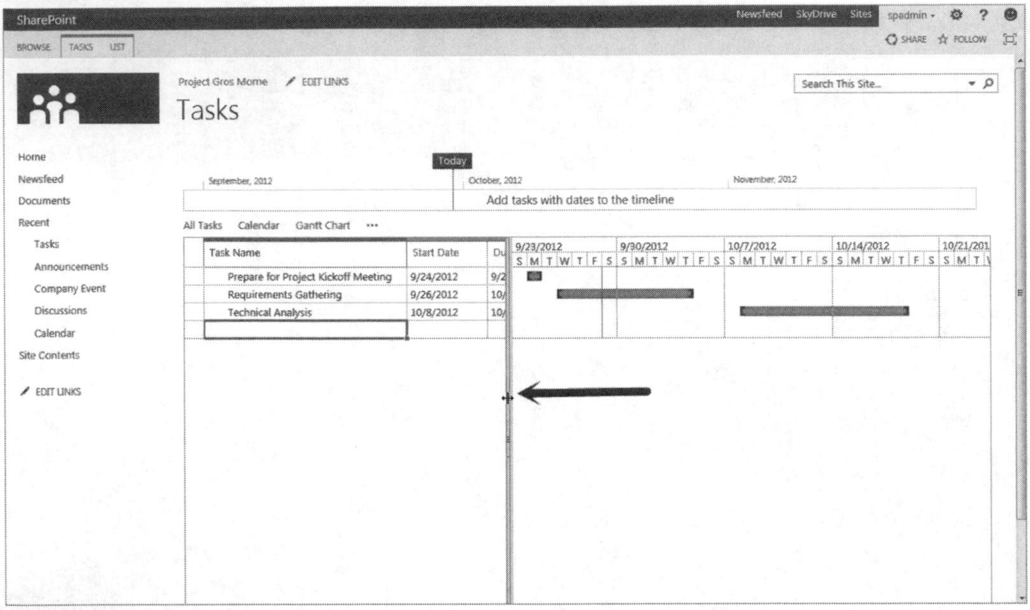

FIGURE 2-13

2. Drag the bar to the right so that all columns are displayed in the left-hand panel of the view, as shown in Figure 2-14.

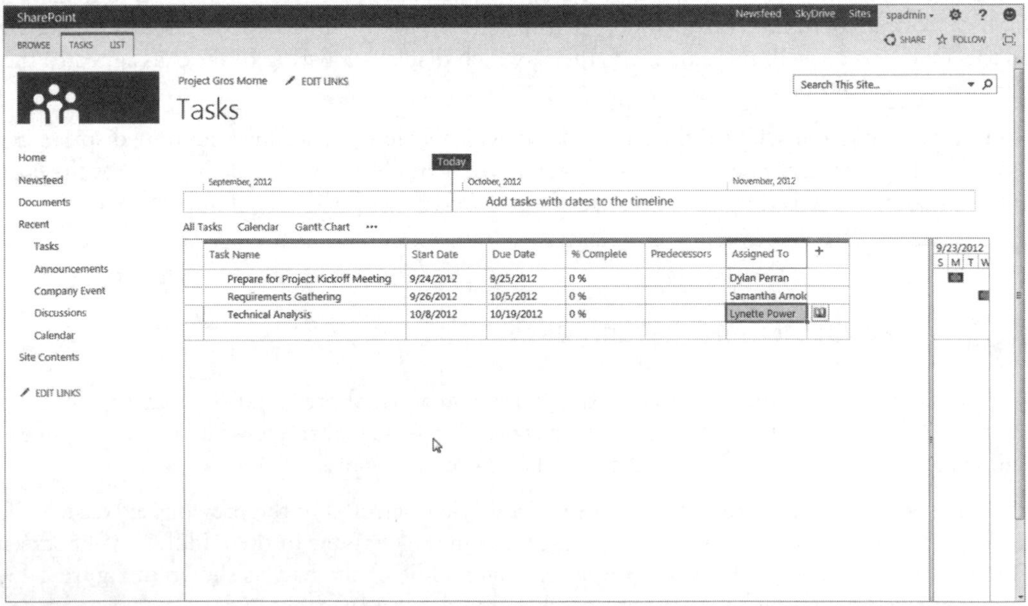

FIGURE 2-14

3. Update the list by clicking within the table cells of each column on the left side to create the following tasks:

TITLE	START DATE	DUE DATE	% COMPLETE	PREDECESSORS
Project Kickoff Meeting	January 3, 2011	January 3, 2011	100	
Complete Stakeholder Interviews	January 4, 2011	January 11, 2011	50	Project Kickoff Meeting
Create Requirements Document	January 12, 2011	January 26, 2011	0	Complete Stakeholder Interviews

4. Enter your own name in the Assigned To column for the Complete Stakeholder Interviews task. Leave the Assigned To column blank for the other two tasks.

5. Drag the view divider bar back to the left, and select Scroll to Task from the List tab within the ribbon menu bar, as shown in Figure 2-15. You may be required to also zoom out or zoom in using the buttons on the ribbon menu.

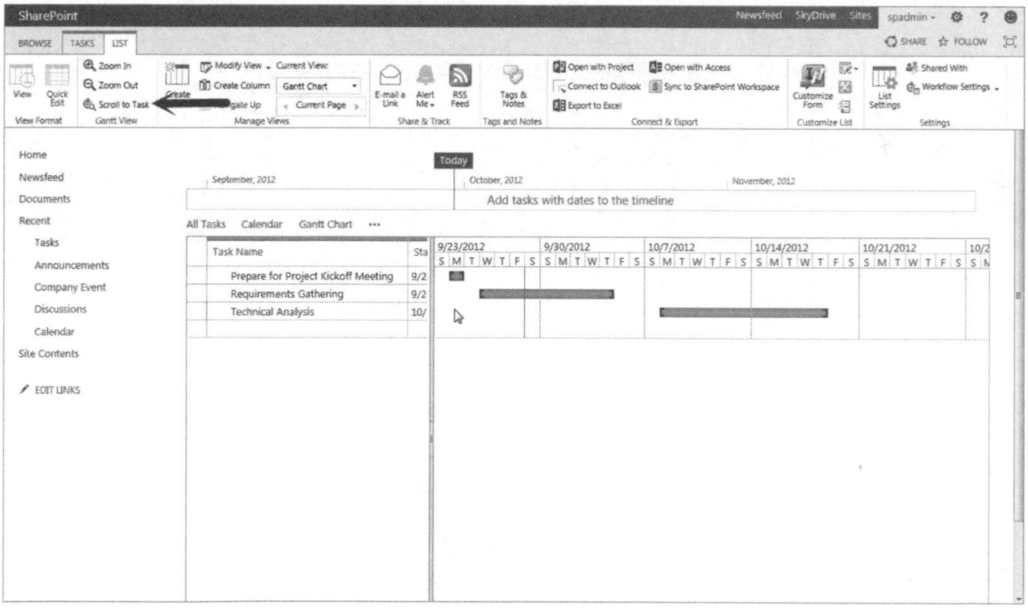

FIGURE 2-15

You will now see a graphical representation of your task schedule displayed in the right-hand portion of your view.

How It Works

In this exercise, you explored using the Gantt view of a Tasks list. This specialized view is helpful for viewing date-based information in a format that clearly indicates the schedule and dependencies of tasks. You will notice that lines are drawn between tasks to indicate relationships where one task has been defined as a predecessor of another. In addition, you will notice that the Complete Stakeholder Interviews task is partially filled with a black line to indicate that it is 50% complete. This helps ensure that team members can easily identify the status of the various tasks that are assigned to them.

TRY IT OUT   Exporting List Items to Excel

Although SharePoint 2013 offers a rich experience right from the browser, you may require advanced calculations and activities that are available only through Microsoft Excel. In this Try It Out, you will leverage the Export to Excel feature from the ribbon to export your list data to an Excel spreadsheet, where you will be able to run even more in-depth analyses.

1. From your Tasks list, select the List tab on the ribbon.

2. Expand the Current View drop-down and select All Tasks. The view refreshes, and all three tasks are visible in the listing.

3. Select the List tab on the ribbon menu once again.

4. Select the Export to Excel option, as shown in Figure 2-16.

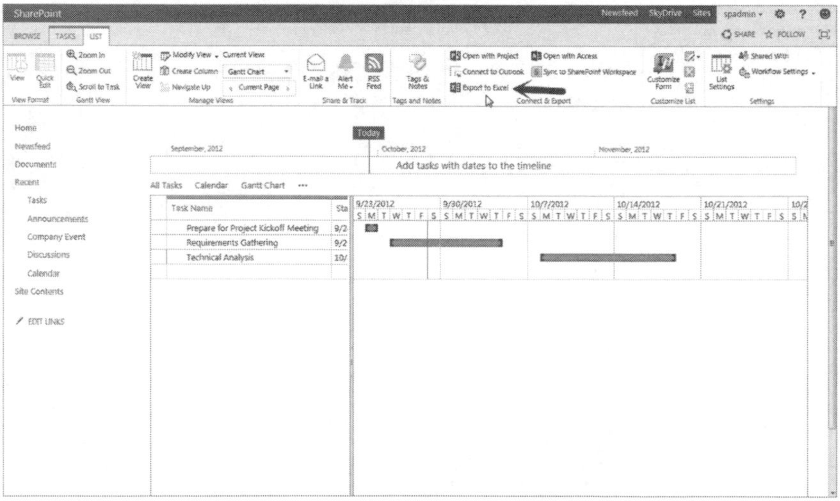

FIGURE 2-16

5. A prompt appears asking you to Open, Save, or Cancel. Select the Open option.

6. Microsoft Excel opens on your desktop, and you will likely receive a security warning. Click the Enable button.

7. A spreadsheet opens, containing the information from your SharePoint list.

How It Works

SharePoint is a fantastic collaborative environment for storing up-to-date information in a centralized store. Editing lists is very similar to editing information in Excel, especially if you are using a Datasheet view, but in Excel you can do certain things that are impossible on the browser, such as advanced calculations, data analysis, what-if analysis, and complex rich formatting. However, you can have the best of both the SharePoint and the Excel worlds; you can create custom views on large amounts of data to filter and display only relevant information. Then, through the Export to Spreadsheet functionality views of list data, you can move data into Excel worksheets to share information or run further analysis.

TRY IT OUT   Subscribing to an Alert

When you work with SharePoint lists, you may want to be notified of changed or added content because receiving this information via an e-mail is less time-consuming than physically visiting every SharePoint site to manually check for new content. SharePoint offers a special Alerts feature, to which you can subscribe and from which you can create lists to keep aware of changes.

Creating alerts enables team members to stay up to date on the changes to a SharePoint list or library in a manner that is appropriate to their unique work preferences, or to receive immediate notifications on items that are of high relevance to them. For example, if you are responsible for responding to trouble tickets submitted to a list, you'll likely want notification as soon as an item is created or edited. However, you may choose to select only a weekly summary report for another list that tracks menu choices for the cafeteria.

1. From the main page of your Project Gros Morne site, select the Tasks link from the side navigation.

2. Select the List tab on the ribbon menu.

3. Select the Alert Me item from the menu. A small menu appears.

4. Select the "Set alert on this list" option from the menu, as shown in Figure 2-17.

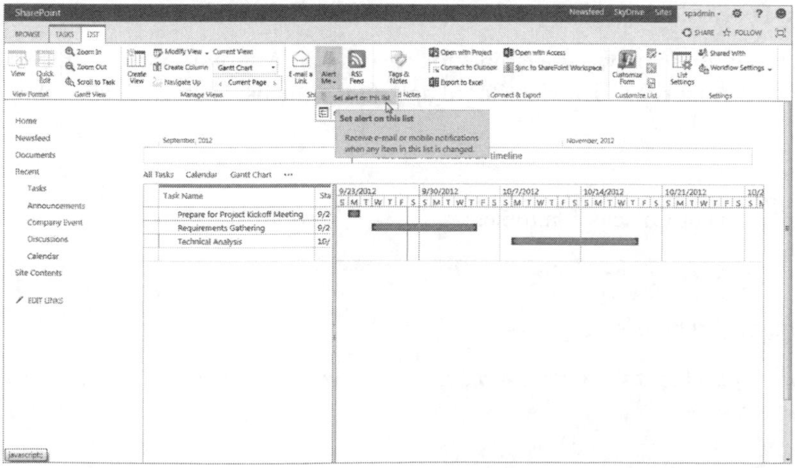

FIGURE 2-17

5. A New Alert window appears. Enter the following settings for your new alert:

SETTING	VALUE
Alert Title	Workplan task updated by team member
Send Alerts To	Your name
Delivery Method	E-mail
Change Type	Existing items are modified
Send Alerts for These Changes	Someone else changes an item
When to Send Alerts	Send a daily summary

6. Click OK.

How It Works

In the preceding example, you created an alert on the Tasks list so that you would be notified whenever a team member other than yourself makes a change to an existing task. You chose to receive your alert via e-mail. Changing the Alert Title to an informative value enables you to easily distinguish the type of update you are receiving as it appears in your inbox, because the Alert Title will be the subject of the e-mail message that is sent. By selecting a daily summary, you can choose which hour of the day you want to receive the alert. As a project manager, you may want to receive a single report at the end of each business day outlining what progress has been made on your team's tasks for the current business day. This may be more effective and efficient than receiving a single e-mail message every time a task is updated.

TRY IT OUT   **Creating a Threaded Discussion**

Discussion boards allow you to quickly set up topic-based, threaded conversations in SharePoint 2013. In this Try It Out, you create a Discussion Board app and configure it with a simple starter topic.

1. Following the steps described in the previous example for creating an Announcements list, create a new list on the project site using the Discussion Board app. Once the list is created, click the Discussions list.

2. Click the "new discussion" link.

3. Enter the following details for your discussion topic:

COLUMN	VALUE
Subject	How can SharePoint be used for projects?
Body	Now that we have a team site for our project, how do you feel we might best use it to manage our project?
Question	Selected

4. Click Save.

5. Your new discussion topic appears, as shown in Figure 2-18.

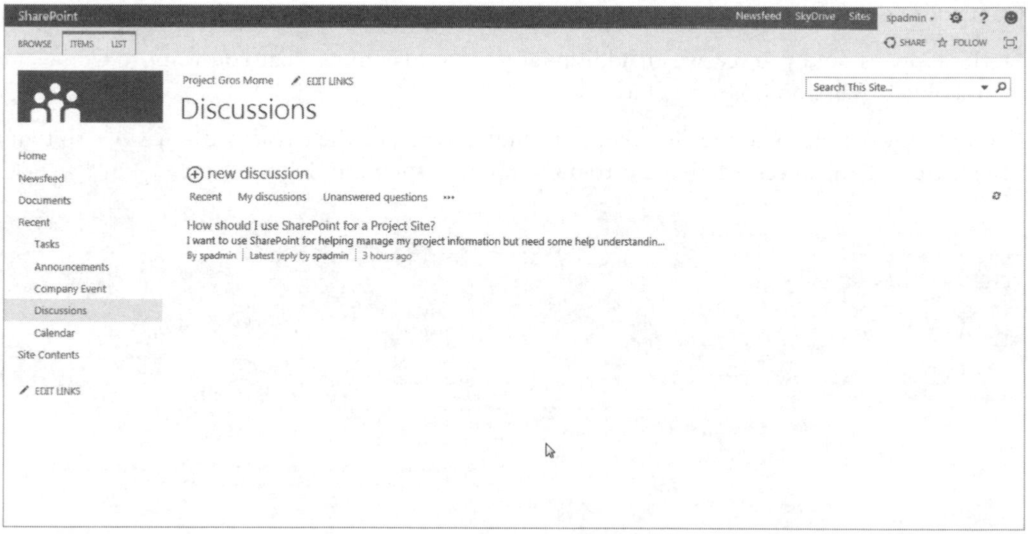

FIGURE 2-18

Now that your new discussion topic has been added to the site, other team members can come to the site and reply to your post.

How It Works

In this example, you created a new list on your site using the Discussion Board app. Discussion boards give you a great way to quickly create threaded discussions, allowing you and your colleagues to collaborate on a topic of choice.

The process for creating this list is repeatable for any other type of list you choose to create in your site.

TRY IT OUT   **Connecting a List to Outlook**

For many team members, Microsoft Outlook is an application that is open on their computer continuously throughout the day. It is an application that many people are familiar with and, therefore, it can be a great tool for updating information on your SharePoint site. If you use Outlook as your mail client, you can connect specific lists to your profile so that information stored within the list is available as a folder in Outlook. This means that you can work directly on list items through Outlook and the application automatically synchronizes your changes with the list when you reconnect. This keeps the SharePoint list information up to date, even when you are away from the office or disconnected from the network. If a conflict exists, you receive a notification and you have a choice on how you want to resolve the conflict.

1. From the discussion list you created in the previous example, select the List tab from the ribbon.

2. Select the Connect to Outlook option from the Connect & Export group.

3. You receive a security prompt to ensure that you want to allow the website to open the application from your computer. Click Allow.

4. Outlook opens, and you receive an additional prompt to confirm that you want to Connect that SharePoint Discussion Board to Outlook. Click Yes.

5. Outlook now connects to the SharePoint list and downloads the existing discussions so that they can be viewed and accessed directly from Outlook, as shown in Figure 2-19.

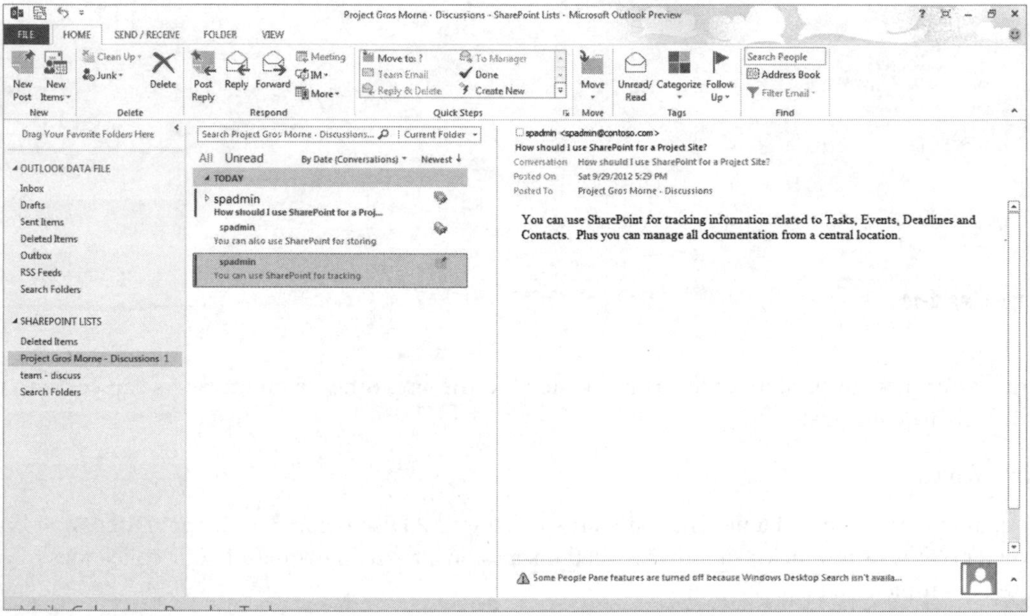

FIGURE 2-19

How It Works

SharePoint is a fantastic tool for storing up-to-date information in a centralized store. Although editing lists from within SharePoint offers a familiar experience across other applications, many users spend a large portion of their day in Outlook and prefer to manage lists from there, rather than visiting the SharePoint site.

As reviewed in the preceding example, this need has been accommodated. To manage a list through Outlook, simply choose Connect to Outlook from the ribbon. A connection with the list is made and, from that point forward, you are able to add or edit items from Outlook just as you would from your SharePoint site.

TRY IT OUT   **Replying to an Existing Discussion from Outlook**

Outlook supports a two-way synchronization of content. This means that, in addition to receiving updates within Outlook from the SharePoint list, team members can submit updates to the SharePoint list from Outlook. In this example, you reply to your previously created discussion topic from within Outlook.

1. Open Microsoft Outlook.

2. Select your Team Discussion list from the SharePoint Lists on the left (refer to Figure 2-19).

3. Select the "How can SharePoint be used for projects?" message.

4. Click the Post Reply button from the Home tab on the ribbon.

5. Enter the following for your reply:

> **SharePoint could be very useful for tracking customer complaints. I hear there is an Issue Tracking list that we could use to log complaints that we receive from our customers.**

6. Click Post.

When you return to your team site, you will notice that, in just a few moments, your new reply appears with the Team Discussion list.

How It Works

Because Outlook supports two-way synchronization of SharePoint lists, once a list is connected to Outlook, you are free to add or edit list items from Outlook, and your SharePoint list will be updated.

Connecting lists to Outlook and interacting with them is mostly a universal process; it works the same across all lists that can be connected to Outlook.

SUMMARY

In this chapter, you learned about the basic content storage mechanism in SharePoint, called lists. A list is a type of app in SharePoint that enables you to collect information and share it with other team members in a manner that is easy to update and maintain. You learned the following:

➤ Lists contain columns of data that describe an item. Columns can contain information in a variety of formats, such as a single line of text, multiple lines of text, date, or numerical data.

➤ You can link some lists, such as Tasks, Discussion Boards, Contacts, and Calendar, to Microsoft Outlook to allow users to update and create new content on the SharePoint site directly from their e-mail client. This is convenient for those users who are less familiar and comfortable in a web environment, but very much at ease when they work with their e-mail program.

➤ By linking lists to Outlook, you can create an offline store that you can synchronize with later when the SharePoint site is available.

➤ You can link some list apps with an Access database. This also creates an offline store and provides a rich reporting environment for users on data that is stored on the SharePoint site.

➤ SharePoint has a variety of list apps that you can use to create task assignments, and perform event management and issue tracking. You can use these templates exactly as they are created, or you can customize them by creating custom views or columns.

➤ You can subscribe to information that is stored within lists via alerts, which are customizable e-mail notifications that you can define directly from the List toolbar menu.

➤ When you need to share information stored on a SharePoint site with stakeholders who do not have access to the physical environment, you can export certain SharePoint list views into Excel spreadsheets or Visio diagrams and save the data offline for further analysis or sharing.

This chapter focused mainly on lists basics, describing the various functionality and features. In Chapter 4, you learn how to customize and manage lists to create working environments that suit your specific business requirements and needs.

EXERCISES

1. If you wanted to receive an e-mail notification every time a new item was added to a list, how would you do that?

2. Describe the difference between a Lookup column and a Choice column.

3. Describe how you would send a report of information stored in a list to a partner outside your organization who did not have access to your SharePoint list.

4. True or false: You can allow users to skip specific questions based on their responses to specific survey questions.

▶ **WHAT YOU LEARNED IN THIS CHAPTER**

TOPIC	KEY CONCEPTS
The core elements of a list	Lists have items, columns, and views. Items and columns correspond to the rows and columns that you see on a grid layout in a spreadsheet. Views present list data in a friendlier format that acts very similarly to a report.
Alerts	An alert is a subscription you can create on a list to be notified via e-mail or text message based on activities that occur within the list, such as new items added and existing items edited or deleted.
Standard list types	In this chapter you learned about the different types of lists that you can create in SharePoint including Tasks, Threaded Discussions, Calendar, Status, Contacts, Issues, Announcements, Survey, and External lists.

3

Working with Library Apps

WHAT YOU WILL LEARN IN THIS CHAPTER:

➤ The key activities related to a document library such as the creation, uploading, and updating of files

➤ The core functionality available related to tracking unique versions of files

➤ Features available within the various library templates in SharePoint 2010

WROX.COM CODE DOWNLOADS FOR THIS CHAPTER

The wrox.com code downloads for this chapter are found at www.wrox.com/remtitle
.cgi?isbn=1118495896 on the Download Code tab. The code is in the Chapter 3 download
and individually named according to the names throughout the chapter.

In this chapter, you discover the magic behind document collaboration: the document library.
Document libraries are a type of SharePoint app that enables you to create, store, manage,
and collaborate on documents. SharePoint has a variety of library apps, each designed to
allow maximum efficiency when you work with particular types of documents. This chapter
discusses the major elements of a document library and walks you through some of the different library templates and how you can use them to manage the documents crucial to business
operations.

In Chapter 4, "Managing and Customizing Lists and Libraries," you learn how to configure the properties and features of a document library to fit your business needs. This
chapter focuses on interacting with document libraries that have been previously created or
configured.

UNDERSTANDING LIBRARIES AND DOCUMENTS

You can think of a document library as a Windows file folder, but better. Like folders, libraries act as document storage, but they also store the document's metadata or version history (more about these a little later), which folders do not. Also, Windows file folders lend themselves to user personalization in that they may stay on a user's drive or be labeled differently from another user's folder, which leads to inefficiency. Libraries are intended to act as central stores, shared across an organization or team. SharePoint also offers collaboration features that go well beyond the traditional file-sharing techniques that you may have used in the past. Also, because SharePoint stores lists and libraries in a database rather than the filesystem, it is arguably more secure, more efficient, and enables more sophisticated document workflow and content management scenarios. Users are only able to see files that they have been granted access to, which exposes only relevant files to their role and improves the ease by which information can be found.

While we often refer to the storage of documents in SharePoint libraries, it is important to know that you can store a variety of file types, including presentations, images, forms, and spreadsheets. You can store virtually any file type in a SharePoint library as long as the file type has not been added to the Blocked File Types listing.

BLOCKED FILE TYPES

You can view the listing of blocked file types for your SharePoint environment by visiting the SharePoint Central Administration site for your server farm. Once there, you can find a link to view blocked file types, under the Security group of links.

You can remove items from this list to allow users to upload files of that type to SharePoint libraries within a web application; however, you should be very careful not to allow certain executables or file types that may cause security risks or performance issues. It is recommended that you speak with someone familiar with managing security within your network before removing a file type from this list. As a general rule, this list should not be modified unless a well-justified business case exists.

Administrators may allow users more or less flexibility for managing certain file types within their personal sites versus their collaborative sites. This may include blocking certain media file formats in the MySites application that may typically be used within the various departmental and team sites for training or reference.

The core components of a SharePoint document library include:

> **Metadata information:** Document libraries have metadata columns for attaching information to the document, such as document owner or status, and, thus, tailoring it to your corporate practices. Metadata is useful for running searches on documents, which you learn more about in Chapter 17, "Working with Search." Users with appropriate permissions can quickly and easily create extra metadata columns to describe the contents of a library. In fact, SharePoint document libraries offer many of the same features of lists that you explored in Chapter 2, "Working with List Apps," such as rows, columns, and views.

➤ **Document protection:** Documents in libraries are protected by a check-in and check-out feature, which ensures that only one user at a time can edit a document. Later in this chapter, you learn about the various methods available for working with documents in this manner.

➤ **Document history:** Libraries keep a document audit trail, known as *version history*. This feature enables you to easily and quickly revert to a previously saved version of the document, directly from the browser. The version history feature tracks changes that are made to the document's content as well as its metadata. Depending on which site template you are using, you may need to enable this feature prior to its availability for use. The process for doing so is described later in this chapter.

➤ **Major and minor versions:** Although both lists and libraries support versioning of information, document libraries support minor and major versions. Major versions are published files that are accessible to all site users, whereas the minor versions are files in a draft state that typically only a document's author or members of an approver's group can access.

On the surface, a document library view page (shown in Figure 3-1) looks similar to a list, with a few additions, including:

➤ **Upload Document button:** Located on the Files tab of the ribbon, this button supports the uploading of single or multiple files to the library.

➤ **Open with Explorer button:** Located on the Library tab of the ribbon, this button opens the library in a Windows Explorer-type folder. Using this option, you can drag and drop files into folders, delete multiple files at once, and create new folders the same way you would when interacting with a standard Windows file folder. This feature requires the use of Internet Explorer 7.0 or later.

➤ **Copies:** Unique to the document library, this section of buttons located on the Files tab of the ribbon enables you to interact with the document by downloading a copy of it, sending it to another location, creating a document workspace, or managing copies of the file within the system. These actions are covered later in this chapter.

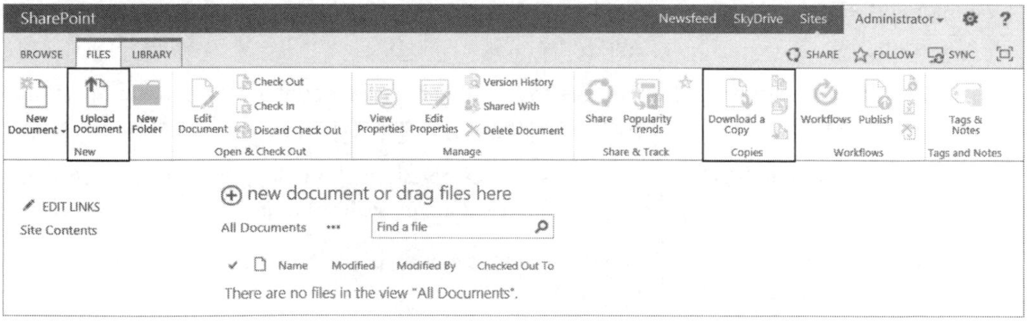

FIGURE 3-1

Creating and Managing Documents in a Library

Both employees and organizations benefit from SharePoint libraries. Organizations commonly roll out SharePoint to help ensure that documents are stored in a secure system where access, versioning, templates, columns, and content are controlled. From a user's perspective, creating and managing documents in a library is a simple process. You start by creating a document that is based on the latest version of a template. You can also easily upload single or multiple files to a location that is shared by other members of your team.

This section has a series of Try It Outs that walk you through many of the actions available within document libraries. Before you start, however, you need to understand the various document templates (shown in the following table) that you can create by clicking the New button within a document library. The obvious purpose of these templates is to start with blank documents or files; however, you can also create custom templates that help your company to maintain a consistent look and feel for common document types. For example, you can have a sales proposal presentation template that contains important elements, such as your company's name, logo, and website information, on every slide. Associating this template with the sales team document library allows an account manager to launch a presentation containing these elements with a single click.

TEMPLATE	PURPOSE
None	This option disables the New Document button within the ribbon of your library. Users will only be able to upload documents to the library.
Microsoft Word 97-2003 Document	Creates a blank Word document compatible with versions of Microsoft Office prior to the 2007 release.
Microsoft Excel 97-2003 Spreadsheet	Creates a blank Excel spreadsheet compatible with versions of Microsoft Office prior to the 2007 release.
Microsoft PowerPoint 97-2003 Presentation	Creates a blank PowerPoint presentation compatible with versions of Microsoft Office prior to the 2007 release.
Microsoft Word Document	Creates a new Word document using the new file formats. Supported only by Microsoft Office 2007 or later.
Microsoft Excel Spreadsheet	Creates a new Excel spreadsheet using the new file formats. Supported only by Microsoft Office 2007 or later.
Microsoft PowerPoint Presentation	Creates a new PowerPoint presentation using the new file formats. Supported only by Microsoft Office 2007 or later.
Microsoft OneNote 2010 Notebook	Creates a new OneNote section using the new file formats. Supported only by Microsoft Office 2010 or later.
Microsoft SharePoint Designer Web page	Creates a standard web page that you can edit using SharePoint Designer.
Basic Page	Creates a blank SharePoint web page containing a Content Editor Web Part to allow authorized users to add text and basic HTML to the page.
Web Part Page	Creates a blank SharePoint web page with a series of Web Part zones to support the addition and configuration of multiple Web Parts in a desired layout.

TRY IT OUT Creating a New Document from a Document Library

You can create new documents while working in applications, such as Microsoft Office Word, and then save them to a SharePoint site, or you can create them within SharePoint by selecting the New button from within a document library. By default, each document library has a single blank Word document template associated with it. You are presented with this template as a starting point to create your document. This is the case for any standard document library that you create in a SharePoint site, unless the site manager specifies otherwise or uploads a custom template.

1. From the main page of the Project Team Site you created in Chapter 2, select the Documents link from the side navigation bar. This will bring you to the Documents library on the site.

> **NOTE** *If you did not complete the exercises in Chapter 2, you can complete the exercises by creating a site based upon the Team Site template. If you require the steps to create a site, please review the first exercise in Chapter 2.*

2. Click the Files tab from the ribbon to display the available options for creating or interacting with documents in this document library.

3. Expand the New Document menu item, as shown previously in Figure 3-1, and select the option to "Create a new document in this library." A new blank document opens within Microsoft Word.

> **NOTE** *Though it is possible to just click the New Document menu item, it is recommended that you always expand the menu to see what options are available. Chapter 6, "Working with Content Types," explores a way to allow the creation of multiple document types from a single library.*

4. Enter the following text in the new document:

> **This is a new document for my project. Even though I am using SharePoint to store and manage my files, I can still create and update the content from Microsoft applications such as Word the same way I have in the past.**

5. From the File menu, select Save.

6. You are prompted to enter a filename for the document. Notice that the save location is automatically recognized as the library that you initiated the document from. Enter **My Project Document** as the filename and click the Save button.

7. Close the Microsoft Word application.

How It Works

In this Try It Out you created a new document in a document library on your SharePoint site. When you saved the file, Word allowed you to save it directly within the document library you launched it from. When you return to the document library after completing the exercise, you can refresh your browser window or click the F5 button, and you will see that your file is now there. This file can be shared with team members for collaboration purposes.

 TRY IT OUT   **Uploading a New Document**

With SharePoint, uploading previously created documents happens as frequently as creating new ones. The following example guides you through the process of uploading a document from your personal computer or network share to a SharePoint document library.

Imagine that you are the project manager for the Gros Morne project, and you want to upload a recently created project plan to the team library. In the previous Try It Out, you created a new document from a library. However, you may want to share or manage documents created outside of the SharePoint environment. To accommodate this common situation, SharePoint document libraries support the uploading of content to the library from another location.

In this exercise, you browse to the location of a project plan called `GrosMorneProject.mpp`, which is available as part of this chapter's resources, and upload it to the Shared Documents library.

1. Return to the Documents library of your team site, as shown in the last Try It Out.

2. Click the Files tab on the ribbon.

3. Click the Upload Document menu item. An Upload Document prompt appears, as shown in Figure 3-2.

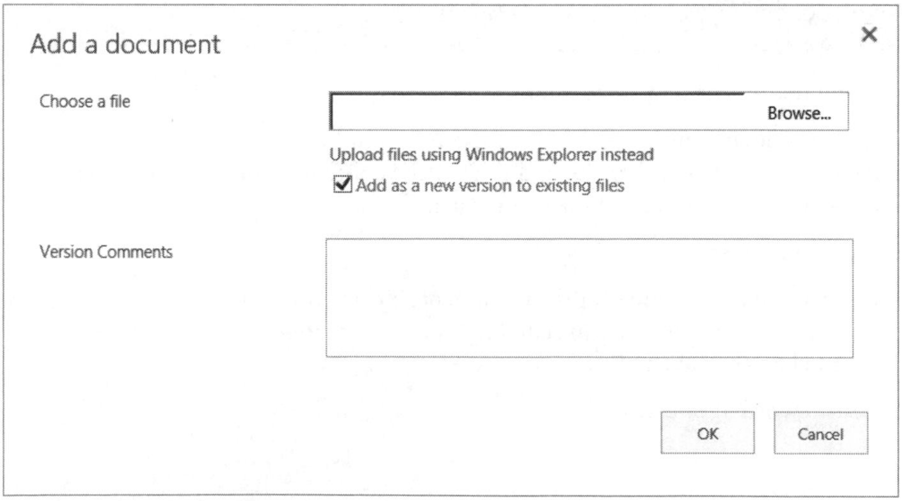

Add a document   ✕

Choose a file

                                              Browse...

Upload files using Windows Explorer instead

☑ Add as a new version to existing files

Version Comments

                                                             OK   Cancel

FIGURE 3-2

4. From the Upload Document prompt, select the Browse button. The Choose File dialog box appears.

5. Browse to the location of the `GrosMorneProject.mpp` file from this chapter's resources, and select Open, as shown in Figure 3-3.

6. You will be returned to the upload prompt. Click the OK button. You are returned to the document library where you will see the project plan within it.

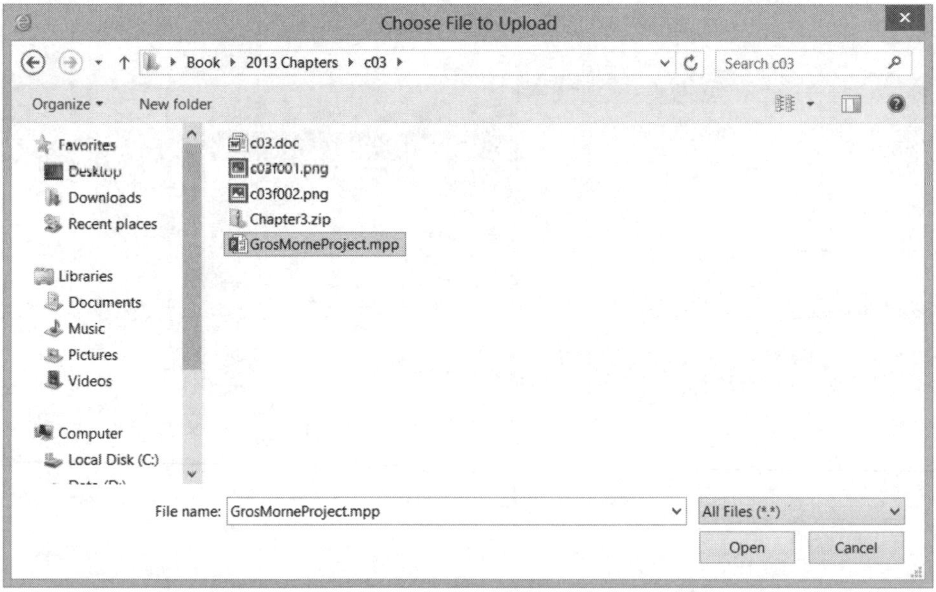

FIGURE 3-3

How It Works

When you upload in step 4, you are presented with a standard file-open dialog box from which you can navigate to and select the file. After selecting your file and clicking OK, your document is transferred to the document library and, if applicable, you are prompted to enter any metadata that your document library requires. When uploading the file, you may have noticed the checkbox in Figure 3-2 to add the file as a new version to existing files. By selecting this box, any files that exist in the library that contain the same filename are overwritten by the newly uploaded file. If version history is enabled in the library, the previous version of the file will be accessible through the version history.

Uploading Multiple Documents to a Document Library

The previous Try It Out works great if you need to upload only a single document to the document library. This example reviews the process for uploading multiple files at once.

1. From the main page of your Project Team Site, select the Documents link from the side navigation bar.

2. Open File Explorer on your computer and select the files you want to upload. You can select one or more files.

3. Drag the selected files from your File Explorer window into the main area of the document library, as shown in Figure 3-4.

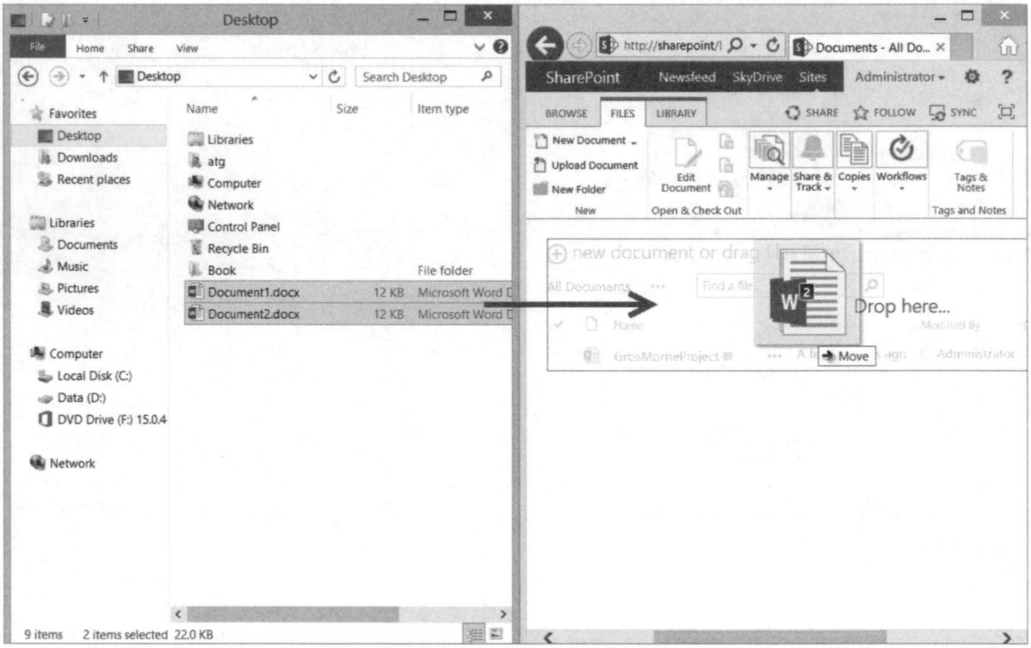

FIGURE 3-4

4. Your progress is displayed as the files are uploaded.

In addition to the preceding method, you can also upload files using Windows Explorer. Select the Upload Document option from the ribbon menu, and then select "Upload files using Windows Explorer instead," as shown in Figure 3-5.

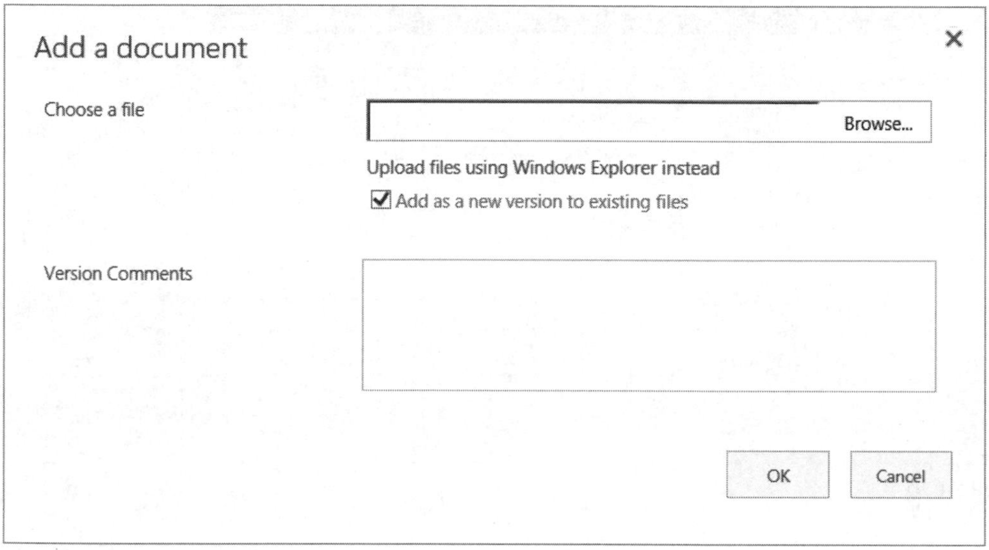

Add a document   ✕

Choose a file   [   ] Browse...

Upload files using Windows Explorer instead

☑ Add as a new version to existing files

Version Comments   [   ]

                                                    [OK]   [Cancel]

FIGURE 3-5

How It Works

In this Try It Out you uploaded multiple files to the document library by simply dragging them from a folder on your computer into the library. This can be a convenient method of uploading files and reduces the number of clicks or steps you have to perform.

TRY IT OUT   **Editing a Document Library Using Quick Edit**

One important thing to remember when uploading files in bulk is that you are not prompted to complete the metadata for each item. Incomplete metadata can negatively impact searches that users perform to locate your documents. If you have to meet a deadline and can't fill in metadata information during the upload, remember to return to the library afterward and do so. The most efficient way to update multiple items at once is to use the Quick Edit option. This command, which is shown in the following steps, enables you to update document metadata in a manner similar to updating a spreadsheet in Excel.

1. From the main page of your Project Team Site, select the Documents link from the side navigation bar.

2. Select the Library tab from the ribbon.

3. Select the Quick Edit option.

4. Update columns, as necessary. Figure 3-6 shows an example of how this could look in a customized library with metadata.

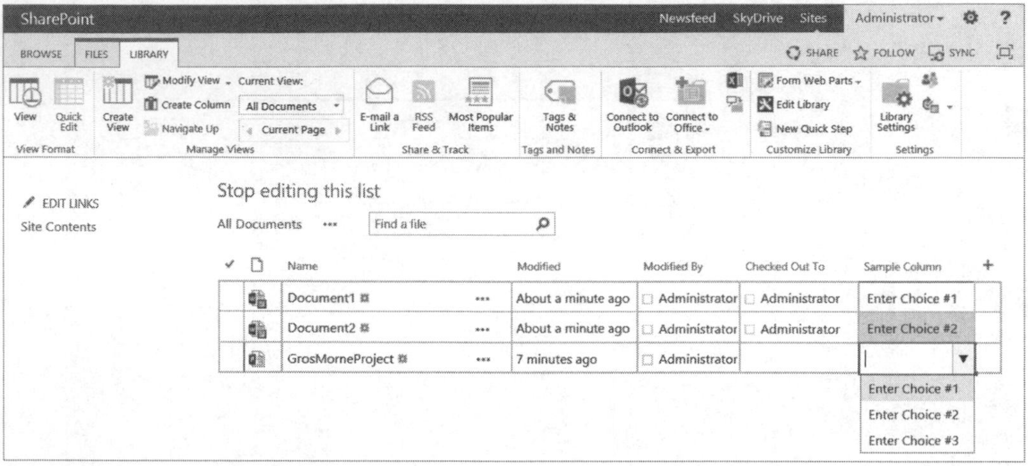

FIGURE 3-6

> **NOTE** *Chapter 4 reviews adding metadata to lists and libraries. On your current team site, you may not have any metadata available yet to update.*

5. When changes are complete, you can click View option from the Library tab of the ribbon to return to the original view.

How It Works

In this example, you temporarily changed a standard document library view to the Quick Edit view. This allows updates to be made to the metadata associated with all documents within your document library. Using Quick Edit is very similar to completing information within a spreadsheet application and is, therefore, ideal for occasions where a team member must update metadata in bulk. Although you can create views that are always in datasheet mode, you can edit any standard list view in datasheet mode as shown here.

You now know how to create documents within your libraries as well as how to upload documents and update the metadata associated with them. Next is to understand how to update documents that are already in a library.

Updating and Sharing Documents

Your document's life cycle will probably require you to perform updates and edits over time. You can quickly open and edit any document inside its document library via either of the following methods:

➤ Select the Open Menu button, which is accessible by clicking on the ellipses located to the right of every document and exposes a variety of actions related to a single document. Select

Edit, Share, or Follow from the list of menu options, as shown in Figure 3-7. You have several other options, such as Edit Properties, which edits the metadata, or View Properties, where you can view additional information associated with the document. These are available by selecting secondary ellipses that appear to the right of the word Follow.

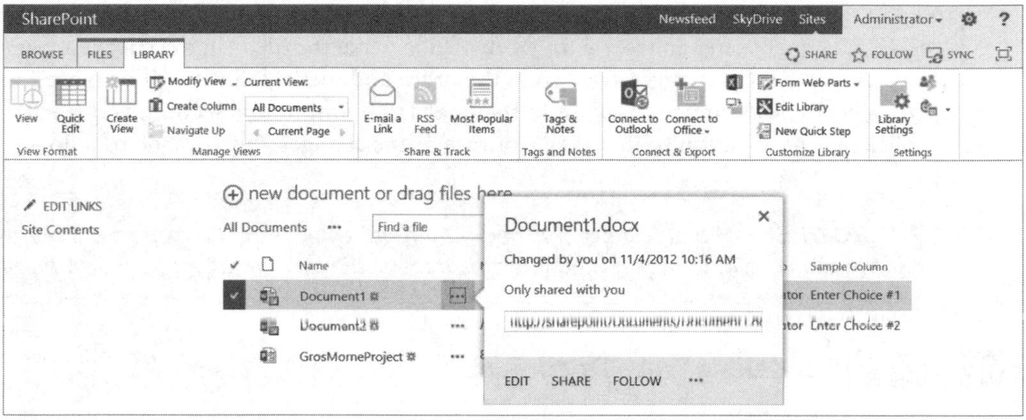

FIGURE 3-7

➤ Select an item in a document library and click the Edit Document item from the ribbon, as shown in Figure 3-8. The associated application opens so that you can begin editing.

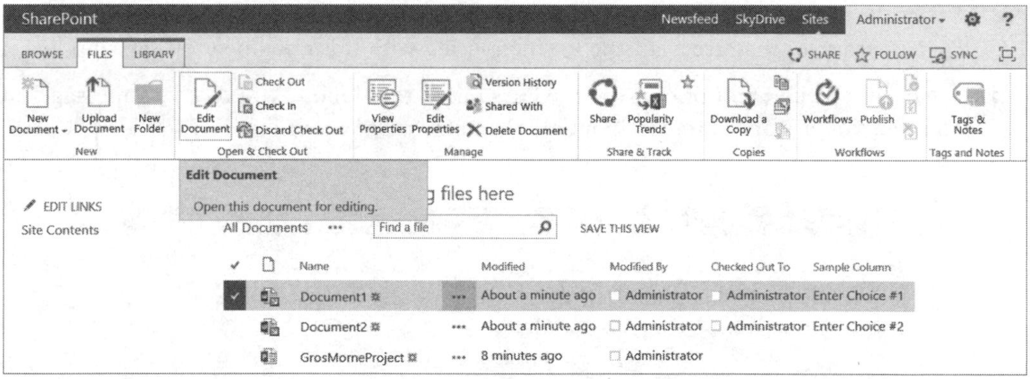

FIGURE 3-8

Obviously, collaborating often requires that people work on the same document; however, this can lead to version conflict. For example, if you work on a document but leave the office for an extended period of time, another user can make changes to your document that conflict with your version or upload an older version of the document that could lead to confusion or lost work. When you resume your work, you definitely will notice changes, but not necessarily know why or how the document was changed.

To minimize frustration, instead of directly editing the document via the contextual menu or from the document library, you can select the Check In/Check Out options beforehand. Checking out a document locks it so that others can view the last published version but cannot edit it or upload a version of the document until you check the document back in.

The next three Try It Outs cover how to check out and check in a document, either from the SharePoint library or from an Office application, such as Word. The Check In/Check Out feature has the added benefit of enabling you to work offline while the file is in the checked-out stage. This means you can perform changes away from the office and these changes will be placed in the library when you check the document back in. In the final Try It Out in this section, you learn how to send your colleagues notification so that they're aware of the changes you've made to a document.

> **NOTE** *SharePoint's Check In/Check Out feature is controlled as part of library versioning. To configure and customize the settings for this feature, see Chapter 4.*

TRY IT OUT Checking Out a Document

Checking out a document greatly reduces the chances of version conflicts because only one person can make changes to the document at a time. When a document is checked out, only the user who checked it out can edit the document. The following example shows you how to check out an item from a document library.

1. From the main page of your Project Team Site, select the Documents link from the side navigation bar.

2. Select the checkmark to the left of the document you want to edit. This selects the file and enables specific features that are available for interacting with this document on the ribbon.

3. Select the Check Out option from the Files tab of the ribbon. You receive a message informing you that you are about to check out a document, as shown in Figure 3-9.

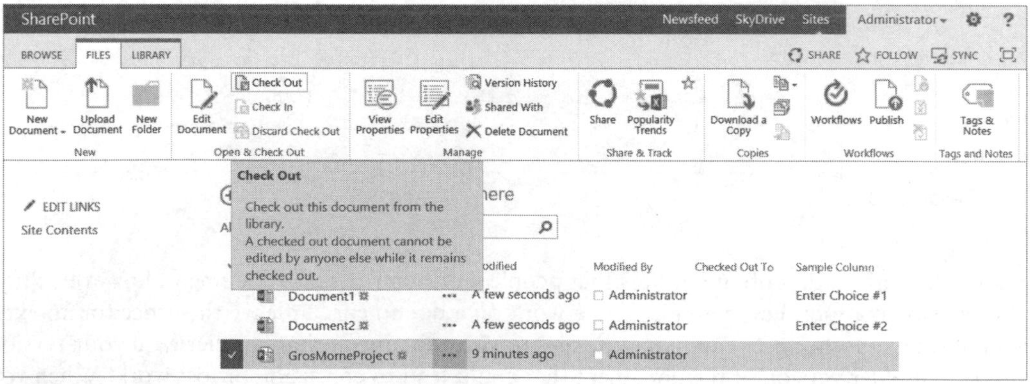

FIGURE 3-9

4. Do not select the "Use my local drafts folder" checkbox, as it is not needed in this exercise. Selecting this option will download the file for storage on your local system in case you want to access it offline. This file would be stored in a folder called SharePoint Drafts in your Documents folder on your workstation associated with your profile. The SharePoint Drafts folder is created automatically the first time you check a file out from a library and select the checkbox to Use my local drafts folder.

5. Click OK to check the document out. The document icon to the left of the document name changes to a document with a green arrow next to it, as shown in Figure 3-10.

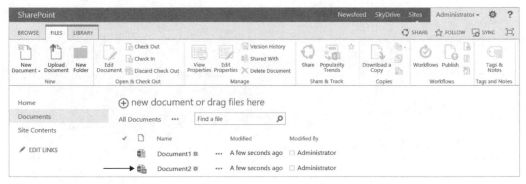

FIGURE 3-10

How It Works

When you check a document out from a library, it becomes locked and reserved to you for editing. Other members of your team can still open the file; however, they will be unable to make changes to it. When other team members view the document, they will not see the changes you are making until the document has been checked into the library again.

TRY IT OUT Checking In a Document

After you make changes to your checked-out document, you need to check it back in. This creates a new version, complete with your changes, and makes the document available for others to check out. The check-in process is very similar to the check-out process, but you have the additional option of checking in changes while keeping the document checked out. This means that others can see changes you've made so far but that you can continue working on the document. It is best practice to include comments when checking a document in so that others understand what changes you made. Comments are visible in the version history, which makes tracking down problems easier in the future. The following steps show this process:

1. From the Documents library, select the checkmark to the left of the document you want to check in.

2. Select the Check In option from the Files tab of the ribbon. You receive a message informing you that you are about to check in a document, as shown in Figure 3-11.

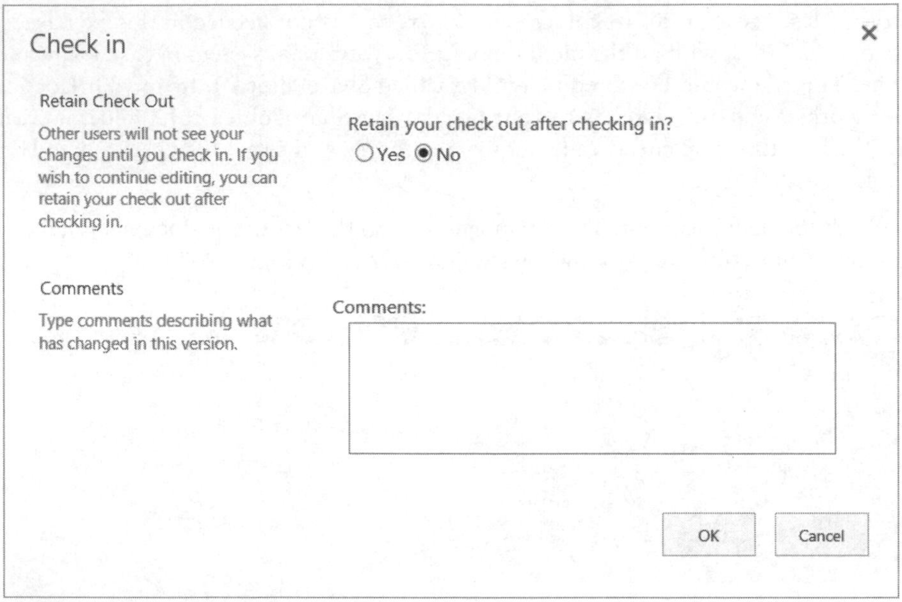

FIGURE 3-11

3. Select No for the "Retain your check out after checking in" option. This is the default selection.

4. Enter notes into the Comments field to describe the changes you made to the document.

5. Click OK to complete the check-in process.

How It Works

In this Try It Out you checked in a file that you had performed edits to. Once a file is checked in, other users can view the changes that have been made and, optionally, check out the file to make edits. You had the option in step 3 to keep the file checked out after you save your changes. By selecting this option, you can make interim versions of the file available to other users in read-only mode, but you still retain control over the file for editing until you check it back into the library.

TRY IT OUT **Checking In a Document from a Microsoft Office Application**

If you are editing a document with Microsoft Office Word, instead of saving your changes, closing the document, going back to the browser, and checking in your document, you can check the document back in straight from the application to cut out some steps. This functionality is available only in Microsoft Office 2007 client applications or later. All other applications and previous versions of Microsoft Office require you to check in the document using the SharePoint interface via the browser.

The following steps show you how to check in a document using Word, but they are similar to how you would check in a document in Excel or PowerPoint. Before you perform these steps, you should check out the My Project Document from your Documents library following the steps described in the "Checking Out a Document" Try it Out earlier in this chapter. Checking a document in using the Microsoft Office Word client application has the same effect as checking it in via the browser (shown in the "Checking in a Document" Try It Out above).

1. From the Documents library, select the checkmark to the left of My Project Document.

2. Select the Edit Document option from the Documents tab of the ribbon.

3. You receive a prompt to confirm that you want to open the document. Click OK to continue.

4. Make the desired changes to your document. You may need to click the Edit button that appears at the top of your document to enable edit mode. When it is complete, switch to the File tab of the ribbon, as shown in Figure 3-12.

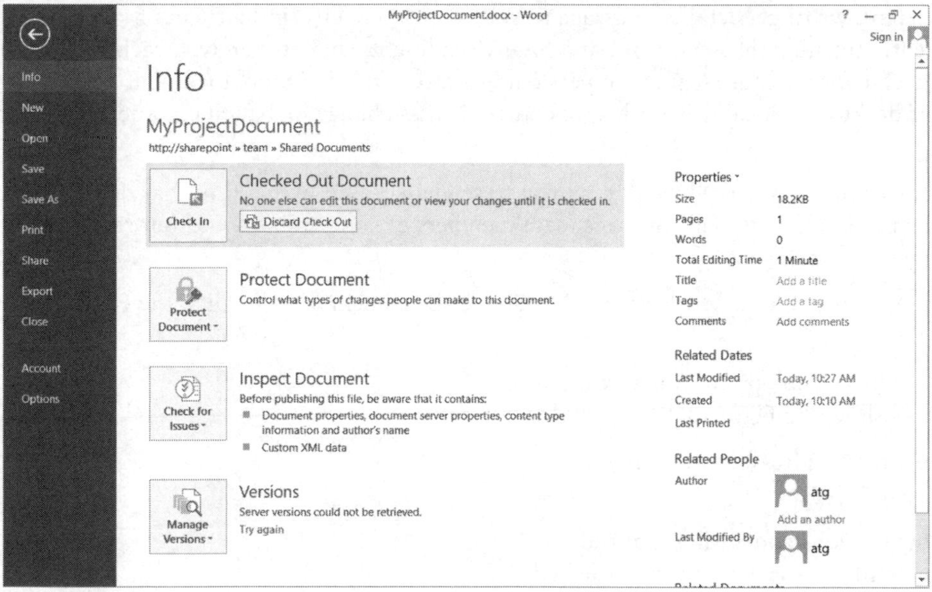

FIGURE 3-12

5. Click the Check In option from the Info menu of the File tab.

6. Enter comments describing the changes made to the document, and click OK.

7. Close the document. Your file is now checked back into the library, and your latest changes are available to members of your team.

How It Works

In this Try It Out you checked in the file directly from within Microsoft Office. This is very convenient in that you can complete the check out/check in process without having to return to the library, as you had done in the "Checking in a Document" Try it Out.

To this point, the Try It Outs in this section have dealt with checking a document in or out and working with it on a computer that is connected to a network. As mentioned previously, you have the option of checking out a document and working offline by saving it to your local drafts folder, which is automatically created the first time you check out and save a document. SharePoint creates a physical copy that you can edit away from the office. When you check a document back in via the browser or through Microsoft Word using the steps shown in the previous Try It Outs, the offline copy of the document is synchronized with and uploaded to the document library so that your changes become available to team members.

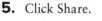 **TRY IT OUT**   Sending an E-mail Link of a Document to Others

After uploading or updating a document, you commonly want to share your changes with other team members so that they can review, collaborate, or make their own changes. In the past, this involved opening your e-mail, writing a detailed message to your coworkers informing them of your intention to share a document, attaching the document, and finally sending it. Unfortunately, attaching a document can lead to duplicate files because team members tend to save versions of the document from the e-mail message to their desktop or local drive. This, of course, makes change management and document control very difficult.

SharePoint bypasses this confusion by enabling you to send an e-mail with a link that directs colleagues to your document in the library. This informs team members of your updates without removing the file from the document management system.

1. From the Documents library, select your My Project Document file and click the Files tab of the ribbon.

2. Select the Share menu option. A new window launches, as shown in Figure 3-13.

3. Fill in the e-mail addresses to which you want to send the link.

4. Click Show Options and ensure that the "Send an email invitation" option is selected.

5. Click Share.

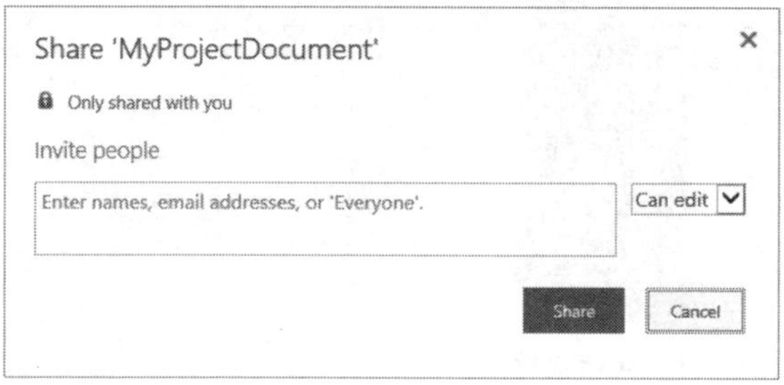

Share 'MyProjectDocument'   ✕

🔒 Only shared with you

Invite people

Enter names, email addresses, or 'Everyone'.   Can edit ▾

Share   Cancel

FIGURE 3-13

How It Works

In this Try It Out you selected a file and shared it with other team members via e-mail. When the team members receive an e-mail message, they will be able to click a link to open the file. This is different from scenarios you may have followed in the past that included attaching a file. When you attach a file, you make copies that become uncontrolled. In this example, however, the file still resides in SharePoint, and the users can access it directly from there.

Review Document Version History

Imagine working all night on a document and saving your changes to your team's collaborative location, only to have a team member overwrite your document with an older version of the document. For a collaborative team, multiple versions of a single document or overwritten files can translate into lost work and frustration. That's why most organizations implement a document audit trail, which helps users understand when changes were made and why. SharePoint's Version History option enables you to view this trail as well as restore previous versions if you catch errors or omissions in the active version. If versions after a certain date are in doubt, you can restore the document to the point where you know the information is accurate and relevant. In addition, having a version history can help organizations identify what a document looked like at an exact point in time.

In the upcoming exercises, you learn how to enable version history tracking on a library and how to view the version history related to a document, and optionally restore a previous version of a document as the active version.

> **NOTE** *In Chapter 4, you learn how you can customize version history settings of a document library.*

TRY IT OUT **Enabling Version History Tracking on a Document Library**

Some libraries may not have version history tracking enabled upon creation. Therefore, a user with permissions to manage the list will be required to enable this setting. In the case of the Gros Morne Project site, because it was created based on the Team Site template, the Shared Documents library must be configured to track version history.

1. From the Documents library, click the Library tab on the ribbon.

2. Select the Library Settings menu option. You are redirected to a page where all the settings related to the Documents library are managed.

> **NOTE** *You explore the settings displayed on this page in greater detail in Chapter 4.*

3. Select the Versioning settings link. The Version Settings page appears.

4. Select the option to "Create major versions," as shown in Figure 3-14.

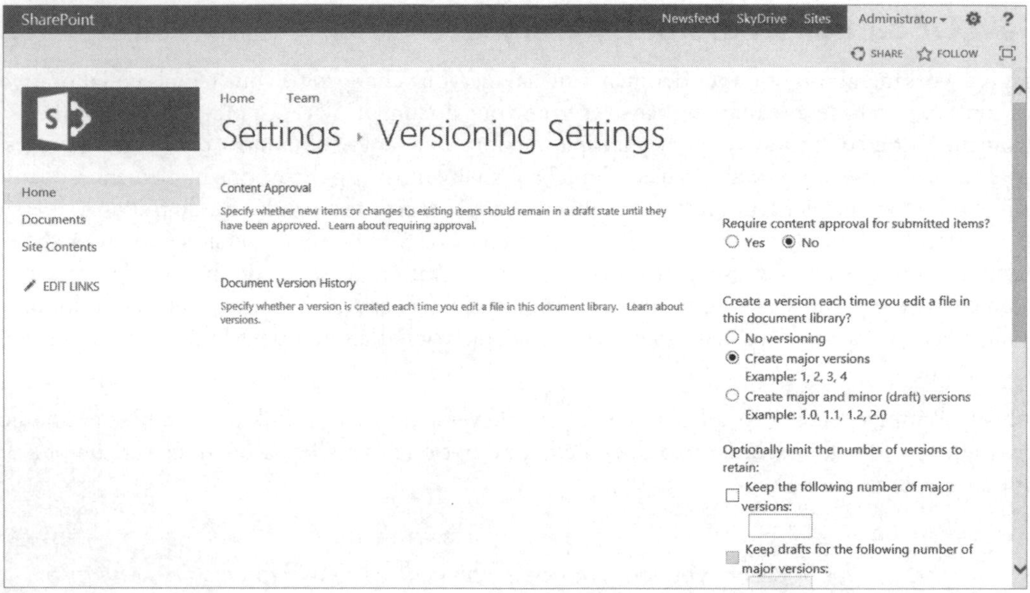

FIGURE 3-14

5. Click the OK button located at the bottom of the page. You are returned to the Documents library settings page. Click Documents from the side navigation to return to the library.

How It Works

In this Try It Out you configured your library to track version history. As a result, users are no longer required to track manual versions of files; instead, all file version history will be stored as part of the document's properties. You selected the Major Version option, which will track file versions in a sequence such as 1.0, 2.0, 3.0, etc.

Now that your library has been configured to track version history, it is recommended that you make multiple edits to your My Project Document file and add comments upon check-in prior to completing the next exercise.

TRY IT OUT   **Reviewing a Document's Version History**

SharePoint updates a document's version history each time a user changes or saves the document. Imagine that while you were away from the office someone made changes to your document that you either were not satisfied with or wanted clarification on. You can visit the version history of the document and review the various versions and associated comments to determine what changes were made. In addition, you may find it useful to review versions of a document to find out what information was published and is available to users of the SharePoint site or via the File tab of the ribbon menu of your document.

1. From the Documents library, click the Files tab of the ribbon.

2. Select your My Project Document file.

3. Select the Version History option from the Files tab of the ribbon. The Version History window appears, as shown in Figure 3-15.

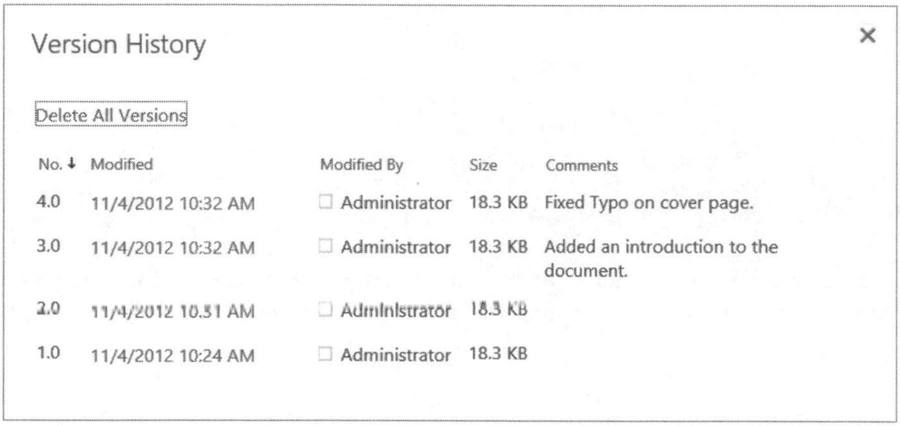

	Version History				✕

Delete All Versions

No. ↓	Modified	Modified By	Size	Comments
4.0	11/4/2012 10:32 AM	☐ Administrator	18.3 KB	Fixed Typo on cover page.
3.0	11/4/2012 10:32 AM	☐ Administrator	18.3 KB	Added an introduction to the document.
2.0	11/4/2012 10:31 AM	☐ Administrator	18.3 KB	
1.0	11/4/2012 10:24 AM	☐ Administrator	18.3 KB	

FIGURE 3-15

4. Click the date and time of a version to preview it. The version of the document opens for you to review in the associated application.

How It Works

In this Try It Out you reviewed the version history of a single file. When you opened the version history, you were able to view the date and time associated with each version, along with any comments that were entered by the author when the file was checked in. As you can likely see, it is a good practice to enter brief but descriptive comments so that other users can easily identify what has changed from version to version.

TRY IT OUT **Restoring a Previous Version of a Document**

When multiple team members work on a document, on occasion they may need to revert to a previous version of the document. This may be necessary because unwanted changes were made or just to perform a what-if analysis to see how changes impact a report. With SharePoint, you can easily follow a document's entire version history and, if need be, restore a previous version of the document by following these steps:

1. From your My Project Document's Version History window, hover over a previous version to expose the actions menu, as shown in Figure 3-16.

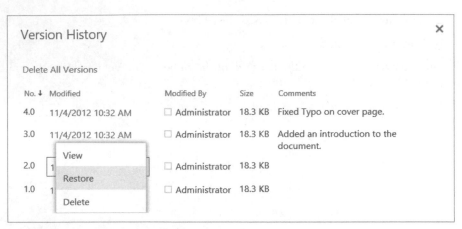

FIGURE 3-16

2. Select the Restore option from the menu. You are prompted with a message informing you that you are about to replace the current version of the document with the one you have selected.

3. Click OK.

How It Works

When you restore a previous version of a document, the document reverts to reflect that state of the document, and it becomes the new current version of the document. The restoration of a document does not overwrite or delete previous versions. Instead, it creates a completely new version within the library. For example, if you view a listing of a document's versions, you may see that there are five versions of the document. If you were to restore version 2.0, then a new version would be created called 6.0. All previous versions would remain unaffected.

UNDERSTANDING SHAREPOINT LIBRARY TEMPLATES

So far this chapter has generically referred to libraries as document libraries. However, SharePoint actually has various library apps, just as it has multiple varieties of list apps. Libraries are generally defined by what you place in them. Once you create your library from the appropriate app, you can have others access the library and add content to it. Chapter 4 shows how to create and customize new lists and libraries; however, in this section, you learn about the features and functions of each so that you select the proper library for your team. The SharePoint library templates are described in the following list:

➤ **Document libraries:** This library stores the majority of documents and files in a SharePoint site and is the most common type of document library created.

➤ **Form libraries:** You use this template to create libraries that store InfoPath form data and templates. You can use this to store submitted forms, such as purchase requests or status reports created using the Microsoft InfoPath client application or Forms Services.

Chapter 12, "Managing Forms," reviews this library and InfoPath in greater detail.

➤ **Wiki page libraries:** You use this kind of library for wiki pages, which are collaborative web pages that teams use to share information in a highly interactive and less structured environment. This is perfect for storing a knowledge base or FAQ section.

➤ **Picture libraries:** This library is for sharing photos and images in a collaborative environment. This library uses columns and properties to define images, and has special thumbnail views of the stored files. It's ideal for storing team member photos or your company's logos.

➤ **Asset libraries:** This library is for sharing rich media assets such as images, audio, and video. When an asset library is created, it is preconfigured with metadata and settings required for sharing rich media files.

➤ **Slide libraries:** You use this library to share PowerPoint presentation slides. Users can upload slides to the library so that other users can browse for slides and use them in new presentations. This template works well for teams that are responsible for creating presentations and want a central gallery from which to select the latest slides and information.

➤ **Data connection libraries:** These libraries store trusted data connection information that link SharePoint with documents created using InfoPath or Excel. Chapters 12 and 13 explore this library type further.

➤ **Report library:** This specialized template creates libraries that store spreadsheets and dashboards as part of the business intelligence capabilities of SharePoint Server 2013. You would use this template to create a location for reporting that would allow business managers to publish spreadsheets to others that could be viewed via the browser and that would hide any protected information from users. This type of library is discussed in Chapter 10, "Working with Business Intelligence," because this template type is specific to that feature of SharePoint.

Document Libraries

Document libraries can store just about any kind of file and are at the center of SharePoint's file-sharing and collaboration features. The anatomy of a document library is very similar to a list and includes the following elements:

➤ **File items:** From Chapter 2, you know that the primary element of a list is an item. Likewise, the primary element of a document library is a file. Most organizations collaborate using Microsoft Office documents (Word, Excel, and PowerPoint) or other common formats, such as PDF, HTML, or JPEG. Document libraries support just about any file type, assuming that an administrator has not explicitly blocked it.

➤ **Columns:** The column types available for lists are also available for document libraries. Depending on which template you select, certain columns may already be created for you. Most libraries share a common set of columns; however, special templates, such as the picture and asset libraries, contain additional columns such as image size and copyright. You can create additional columns at any time if you have the appropriate rights to the site.

> **NOTE** *You can find out how to add new columns to a library in Chapter 4.*

➤ **Views:** Similar to lists, document libraries display their items in views. The default view for a document library is the All Documents view, which shows all documents stored within the library in groups of 30 in the following columns:

➤ **Document Type:** Displays an icon representing the document's file type

➤ **Name:** The file name of the document

➤ **Modified:** The date and time the document was last modified

➤ **Modified By:** The name of the user who last modified the document linked directly to his or her user profile or MySite

> **NOTE** *Users with the appropriate rights can create custom views at any time. This activity is explored in Chapter 4.*

TRY IT OUT Opening a Document Library in Windows Explorer

In addition to the All Documents view, you can open a document library in Windows Explorer via the ribbon. This enables you to interact with your library with the usual Windows behaviors, including dragging and dropping content. In this example, you open a Documents library in Windows Explorer and create a new folder within it called Project Documentation.

1. From the main page of your team site, click the Documents link on the side navigation bar.

2. Click the Library tab on the ribbon.

3. Select the Open with Explorer menu option.

4. A new window opens listing the entire contents of your Documents library in a Windows Explorer view, as shown in Figure 3-17. Right-click the window and create a new folder called Project Documentation.

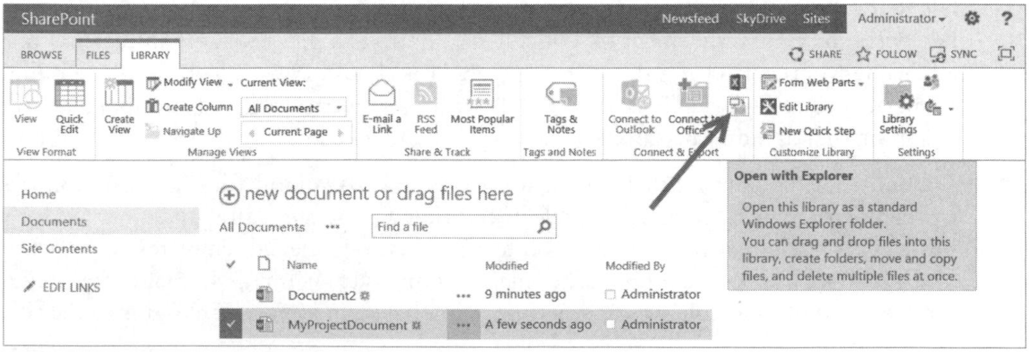

FIGURE 3-17

5. Select the files you have created in the Documents library and drag them into the Project Documentation folder.

How it Works

In this Try It Out, instead of creating a new folder and uploading the documents via the SharePoint browser interface, you opened the document library in a Windows Explorer view and created a new folder. You then moved the existing files into the folder in the same manner you would if you were working in a folder on your computer. This method of updating can be very easy and helpful when performing bulk operations, such as creating folders or moving files within a set of folders.

Form Libraries

Form libraries are special types of libraries that store InfoPath forms. *Microsoft InfoPath* is an application that enables you to collect and share data via highly customizable electronic forms. You can use this application to create form templates that reflect their data collection needs without requiring code or special development skills. The application makes it very easy for business users to craft an electronic form that suits their needs by dragging and dropping form elements onto a page. Users can complete InfoPath forms using either the InfoPath application or via the browser using the Enterprise Edition of SharePoint Server.

You can promote data stored in InfoPath forms to the library so that you display the data in views. This gives you more advanced reporting options on the data contained in multiple forms. You might find it advantageous, for example, to create an InfoPath form to collect data from your portal users instead of using standard list functionality because with InfoPath, you can do the following:

➤ Connect to external data sources such as databases, SharePoint lists, or web services to either retrieve or submit data.

➤ Customize the interface in ways not possible using standard lists via the browser.

➤ Use code to extend forms to provide additional functionality and enhancements related to more complex data calculations or routing.

Chapter 12 explores InfoPath forms and the libraries in which they are stored.

Wiki Page Libraries

With wikis, a very popular collaborative tool for group sharing and editing content, you can add, edit, or remove web page content in an open and informal manner without following a restrictive editing or approval process. Users can edit wikis using SharePoint's built-in content editor without knowing a special language. Because of the informality and lack of restriction, wiki pages are a more inviting way for team members to record their experiences and goals.

WHAT'S A WIKI?

A wiki article or website is a site where users can freely expand or change the published content, often without registration requirements. Wiki, named for a Hawaiian term meaning "fast," is a popular method for sharing information in a quick and easy-to-use format.

A good example of a wiki is the Wikipedia project (see www.wikipedia.org), which formerly began in January 2001. Wikipedia delivers a free content encyclopedia to which anyone can contribute. The website has grown to become one of the largest content libraries in existence, serving up millions articles, if you're just counting the English ones.

SharePoint has an option for creating either an entire site to act as a wiki or just a wiki document library within a site:

- ➤ **A wiki site:** Useful for a technical support team's knowledge base or a training department's tips and tricks documentation. Any collaborative site in SharePoint can be transitioned into a wiki site using a special feature that transforms the main page of the site into a wiki page. Chapter 8, "Working with Sites," reviews wiki sites further.

- ➤ **A wiki document library:** Provides a collaboration tool for planning and sharing ideas around specific operational events. This is illustrated in the next Try It Out.

The next two Try It Outs show how to create a wiki document library as well as how to create a new wiki page.

TRY IT OUT   Creating a Wiki Library

In this example, you create a wiki document library in your site to brainstorm for ideas for your project. The wiki page library has special features that enable you to share and publish wiki content pages within a single location. Team members can create these pages around a specific topic or set of topics.

1. From the main page of your project or team site, select the Add an App option from the settings menu.

2. Select the Wiki Page Library template list of apps, as shown in Figure 3-18.

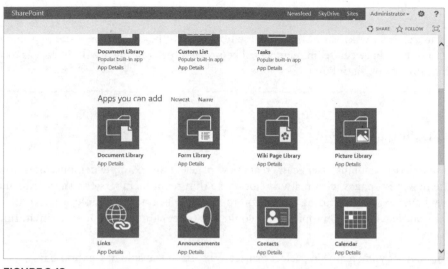

FIGURE 3-18

3. Click the Advanced Options button.

4. Enter a name and description for the library. For this example, enter **Project Wiki** for the name and the following for the description:

> **This wiki will be used to track information related to initial planning around scope, milestones, and timelines related to the Gros Morne project.**

5. Click Create. The wiki library is created and you are redirected to the wiki homepage, as shown in Figure 3-19.

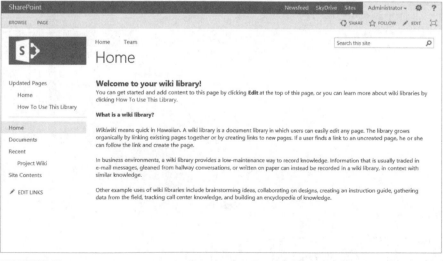

FIGURE 3-19

How It Works

In this Try It Out you created a wiki page library. These libraries can be created on a site to allow for quick and easy collaboration between team members. The process for creating a wiki library is exactly the same as any other library in SharePoint.

TRY IT OUT | **Creating a Wiki Page**

In addition to editing existing content, users can create new pages. This example demonstrates how easily you can create new wiki pages within a wiki library so that team members can share information about what they have learned regarding a common topic, such as a new technology (SharePoint). In addition, members can leave notes on topics they would like to learn more about as an invitation for others to provide content.

1. From the main page of your team site, select Project Wiki from the side navigation bar.

2. Select the Page tab of the ribbon.

3. Click the Edit menu option.

4. Remove the existing content from the page and add a Welcome to Your Project Wiki heading.

5. Below the welcome message, type [[**Project Ideas**]], as shown in Figure 3-20.

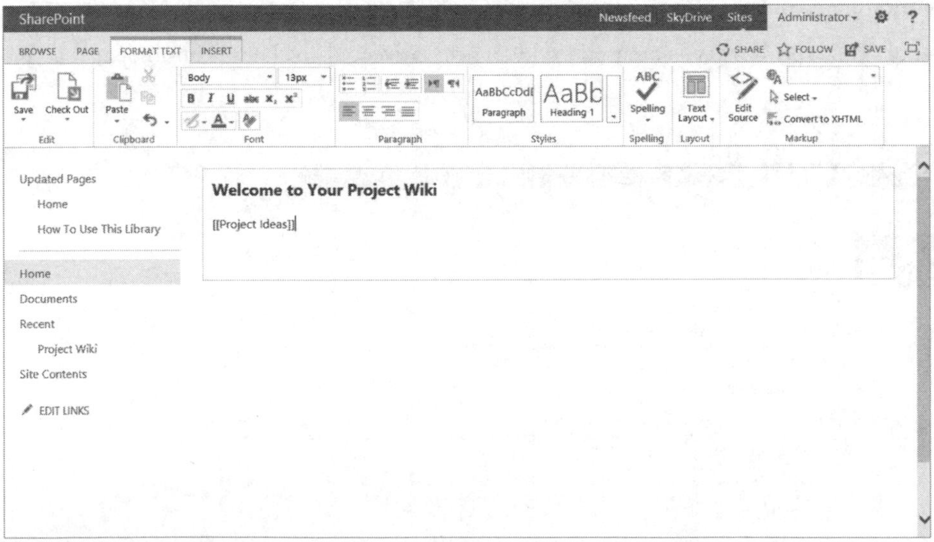

FIGURE 3-20

6. Click the Save menu option.

7. The page refreshes and the Project Ideas phrase is displayed as a link with a dashed line underneath, as shown in Figure 3-21. Click the link.

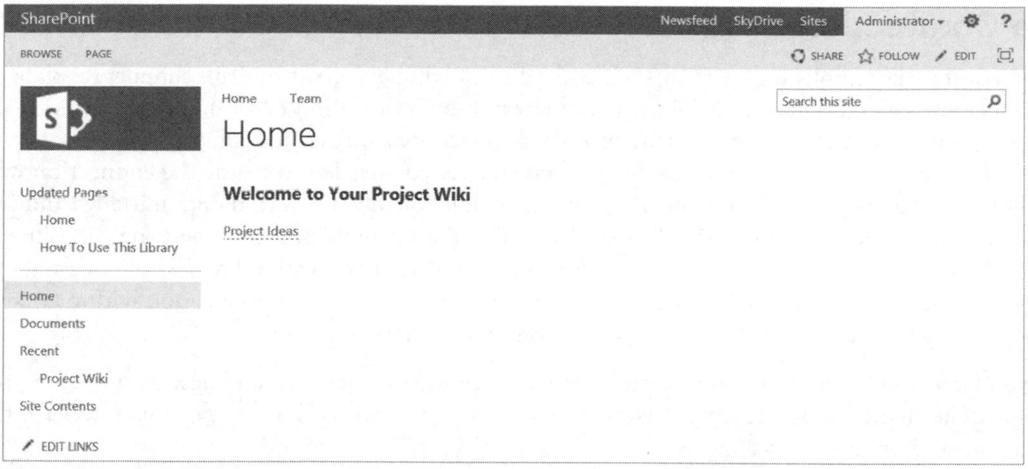

SharePoint | Newsfeed SkyDrive Sites | Administrator ▾ ⚙ ?

BROWSE PAGE | ◯ SHARE ☆ FOLLOW ✎ EDIT ⧉

S

Home   Team

Home

Updated Pages

   Home

   How To Use This Library

Home

Documents

Recent

   Project Wiki

Site Contents

✎ EDIT LINKS

Search this site 🔎

Welcome to Your Project Wiki

Project Ideas

FIGURE 3-21

8. A dialog box appears stating that the page does not exist. Click Create to create the new page in the wiki page library.

9. You are redirected to your new page. Add content as necessary, and when you have finished, add the word **home** in between the double brackets shown at the bottom of the page.

10. Click the Save and Close menu option.

11. When the page refreshes, you will see that the word "home" now appears as a link and by clicking it, you can return to the home page of your wiki library.

How It Works

Wiki pages are both easy to edit and simple to create. You can create new pages on-the-fly by putting the name of the page in between double square brackets, as follows:

[[**page name**]]

To link to an existing page, you can use the same technique by placing the name of the existing page between the square brackets.

Picture Libraries

Although document libraries can store just about any file type, in some cases it's better to have a library that caters to a specific file format. Such is the case with the Picture Library template, which efficiently displays pictures and images because it includes a thumbnail preview feature. This is an invaluable feature for locating the correct image in a large collection of images.

Data Connection Libraries

Microsoft Office applications, such as Excel and InfoPath, have great built-in support for data connectivity to external sources such as databases, web services, and even SharePoint sites. Traditionally, this meant that you managed data connections on an individual usage basis. Therefore, every time you connected to the data source, you needed to define the connection within the file or settings. This often made it very cumbersome to embed external data into files and subsequently make changes to the data source or file. For example, it might seem logical to use a SharePoint customer list in your InfoPath forms any time that you wanted to display a listing of customer names. To do this, however, you would need to create a data connection within your form template each time you wanted to include customer information.

If you later decided to move your SharePoint list to another location or add new columns, in order to have the changes updated within your InfoPath form, you would have to go back into each form template and update the settings.

Data connection libraries solve the cumbersome connection dilemma of how to deal with past versions by enabling you to create data connection files. These Universal Data Connection (UDC) files contain all the connection settings applicable to the data source and usage scenario. Therefore, instead of specifying the connection settings in each of your form templates, you save the connection settings as a file and have your form templates point directly to this file, as shown in Figure 3-22. When you do this, making changes to a single file updates multiple templates.

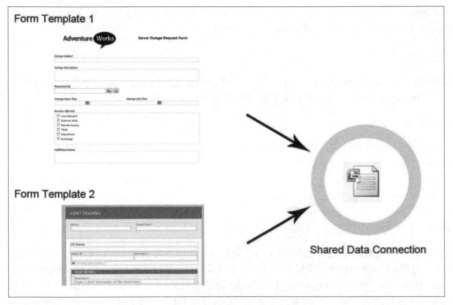

FIGURE 3-22

> **NOTE** *You work in greater detail with data connections in Chapters 10 and 12. These chapters have specific examples of how beneficial data connection files can be and how you can store them centrally in a data connection library.*

SUMMARY

This chapter discussed document collaboration in a team environment and then detailed the benefits and pitfalls arising from managing a single document with multiple editors. Things to remember about this chapter are:

➤ SharePoint's library feature enables you to create, store, and manage your documents from a central location.

➤ Document libraries let you track a variety of different types of information. It is the most common type of SharePoint library.

➤ SharePoint also offers you libraries that are for a specific type of file or information and has templates to create these libraries, including InfoPath form data, images and pictures, Excel spreadsheets for browser-based reporting and dashboards, data connection files, and media and presentation slides.

➤ Throughout this chapter, you looked at the ways that a user can interact with document libraries and the content within them. In Chapter 4, you take a deeper look at customizing libraries along with lists to suit specific needs your organization might have.

EXERCISES

1. Your project manager informs you that the version of the document you submitted for approval was not correct and that the version that was sent earlier in the week is more appropriate. How do you remedy the situation?

2. You've been given the task of archiving an old document. Currently, these documents are stored in a common file share. What is the best method of mass-copying these documents to a document library?

3. You need to change the metadata information for multiple documents. What is the fastest way to change the metadata of a particular column for multiple documents?

▶ **WHAT YOU LEARNED IN THIS CHAPTER**

TOPIC	KEY CONCEPTS
Document libraries	A document library is a location for storing files in SharePoint. You can store a number of file types including Microsoft Office files, PDFs, images, or data connection files.
Library templates	A number of templates are available for libraries in SharePoint, including form libraries, picture libraries, and asset libraries.
The benefits of version history	Version history is a feature in SharePoint that enables you to store all previous copies of a document within a single location in an organized fashion. This enables you to easily retrieve and restore previous versions of a file at any time.

4

Managing and Customizing Lists and Libraries

WHAT YOU WILL LEARN IN THIS CHAPTER:

➤ Specific reasons for customizing a SharePoint list or library

➤ Best practices for customizing lists

➤ Working with lists and libraries

➤ Working with list and library templates

The previous two chapters discussed how to use lists and libraries in their most basic format. SharePoint includes many great default templates that you can use as a jumping point as you are building your specific solutions. The previous chapters also looked at some of the default functionality that you can configure on these templates, but within this chapter you look at the different features available for managing and customizing these lists. By looking at the various configuration options you will start to see that the possibilities for unique configurations are almost limitless. As a user who is responsible for managing a SharePoint solution, it is your responsibility to understand the different configuration options available and then combine them to build a solution for your organization. Because each organization is unique, almost every SharePoint solution will be unique as well.

After reading this chapter, you should feel comfortable taking a specific list or library template and customizing it to suit your specific needs. You should also understand the steps and value associated with adding your custom list to the central list of templates so that teams and users can benefit from your customization efforts.

CREATING AN ENVIRONMENT THAT REFLECTS YOUR BUSINESS

Information is not very useful if it is disorganized and hard to find. Traditionally, electronic documents are stored in a filesystem consisting of folders and subfolders, often many levels deep. In computer lingo, this is often called a *tree structure*. You create the document tree according to your needs or whims, and then you share it with your associates. However, they may not understand your organizational approach and so may have difficulty finding documents in your folder structure. For example, you may have a folder for each city in your territory, and within each city folder you may have folders for your customers in that city. In each customer folder, you store project specifications, statements of work, proposals, project status reports, and other documents related to that customer. However, what if an associate simply wants a list of the current project status reports for all of your customers? This is pretty hard to get because status reports are scattered throughout your folder structure.

This example shows the major limitation of using the filesystem to share documents: Because you have only one way to organize and categorize information, you must develop a system in advance that is useful for everyone, and that usually results in a compromise that no one wants. Further, once you choose a folder structure, it may become both difficult to change and difficult to teach to others.

By depending on files to store and organize your data in your file server, you are limiting the amount of information that you can associate with each file. If you wanted to find all of the client documents that had been generated over the past month, you would need to search through each of the file structures and look at the dates. If you wanted to classify each type of document based on its type and sorted by contract number, you could potentially end up with the same folder structure repeated multiple times for each contract. The truth is that you need this level of information to help you find and classify the data, because without it you wouldn't fully understand the context of the stored files. But the issue is that when the additional data is required, the file server quickly becomes limited in how it can accurately meet the demands of the business. This is one area in which SharePoint provides a much-needed solution to the limitations within a file-share solution. Because of the structure of lists and libraries, you are able to build a solution that is unique and customized for your organization. Once the list structure is built, you can use views to access the information quickly and easily.

Because of the flexibility in creating the attributes of a list or library, you can customize the solution to meet your organization's specific needs. SharePoint enables you to create a solution that not only lets you store your data, but also provides tools to classify and filter your data based on your common needs. Throughout the remainder of this chapter you see the various techniques and tools that you can use to achieve this level of customization. With standard file shares, it's impossible to store this information and have it easily associated with a specific document. However, with SharePoint, you simply add columns to the document library. By capturing the appropriate information, your associates can search and view the document library in the ways they prefer. For example, one colleague might search for projects by client, whereas another might search by author. Through the use of metadata and views, you can create reusable reports to allow your colleagues to find information more efficiently.

BEST PRACTICES FOR BUILDING A DYNAMIC SYSTEM FOR MANAGING CONTENT

In this section, you learn the best practices to ensure that your SharePoint site offers the maximum value to your organization based on the customizations that you implement. This is an important consideration because the right customizations can make your site user-friendly and efficient, whereas the wrong ones can make data entry burdensome and can cause user confusion.

Start with the Users

The first thing that you should always consider is the users who will be accessing the content. How will they need to view the content? What will they need to do next? The more that your solution can guide them through the process they are taking, the higher the level of satisfaction they will have when they use the solution. Any configuration you add to a list or library should make the system easier to use and the information intuitive to find and work with. The fancy bells and whistles you can add to a solution pale in comparison to the basic level of functionality that is required for the users to work efficiently in the solution. If the solution isn't simple, intuitive, and easy to use, it simply won't matter what extra features you are using.

The best approach to take when looking at what lists and libraries you should create and how you should configure them is to first take some time to get to know your audience. One way to do this is to take some time to familiarize yourself with their day-to-day tasks and activities. This enables you to see how they are working and find ways that you can improve their processes. Here is a list of common approaches you can take as you are learning about your users:

➤   Hold meetings or send questionnaires to gather information on users' frustration points.

➤   From these discussions, create a list of problems that you need to address.

➤   Rank and prioritize the list based on the number of people who are affected and the productivity impact they experience because of the issues.

➤   Look at how SharePoint lists and libraries can improve the situation. For example, if people have a difficult time finding documents created during a specific timeframe, you can create views that filter and sort documents based on when they were completed.

Select the Best Tool

Once you have spent the time understanding your users, it is up to you to determine the best tool for the solution. In terms of using lists and libraries, this typically means you need to determine the following items:

➤   The number of lists or libraries you need within the solution

➤   The templates that you should use to create each list and library

➤   The customizations that you should make to each list or library to create the best overall experience for the end users

In addition to these items, it is important to look at some of the required conditions on the library in terms of size and security. As a general rule, SharePoint lists and libraries can contain many items.

But in terms of performance, you need to be careful about how many items you want to show to your users at one time. The typical guideline is 5,000 items returned at one time. If you need to return a larger number of items in one view, it is recommended that you work with your SharePoint governance team to determine if a SharePoint list is the best tool to use in that particular scenario. Security is another issue that you should consider prior to the creation of lists. Within SharePoint you can secure content as low as the items level; however, in many cases this adds an extra burden to the person who has to maintain and manage the list. As an alternative to having one highly secured list, you could consider creating several lists with items grouped into the list based on their security requirements. For more information on permissions and how to best incorporate them into your solutions, refer to Chapter 9, "Managing Permissions."

Plan for the Future

Finally, once you have looked at the business case for the solution and selected the best tools for it, you then need to spend some time planning for the future. You want to look at how the lists will be used today and then how you think they will be used over time. You also want to think about the different things you have created in the past to ensure that you are using similar methods and approaches. Here are some examples of how this type of planning could look within your organization:

➤ A column that describes the status of a list item or document should offer the user consistent choices. If you use a certain set of status values for one list or library, use the same for all other lists and libraries. Do not use values such as "Not Started," "In Progress," and "In Review" in one location and then use completely different values to represent the same type of information elsewhere.

➤ If you start creating custom views, offer some level of standardization, such as consistent ordering and sorting of columns based on the type of information you're presenting.

WORKING WITH COLUMNS

A list or library in SharePoint is a way to store various items. These items can be anything from a document to a task associated with a project to a list of contacts. For each of the items stored within a list, columns enable you to further classify or describe that item. Defining information effectively is a key reason you use SharePoint and, by default, many of the list templates within SharePoint contain default columns to help you get started. After reviewing the default list templates, you may find that you need to add additional columns to your lists. For example, you can add a column to track document status to a document library so that users can easily identify a document's current state strictly by looking at its properties, rather than making an assumption or asking the author directly.

You may hear people describe columns as metadata, or properties of an item. As described in Chapter 2, "Working with List Apps," metadata is essentially information about information. In the case of a document, metadata is information that describes the document, such as its status, owner, or due date. A single document might have multiple metadata values because, quite often, many things describe a document.

You can create and associate columns with a single list or library, or you can create them at a higher level and reuse them throughout the site or site collection. For the first Try It Out, you add a column to a single library. The "Choosing a Column's Scope" section discusses in greater detail how each column type differs and how to select the correct one for your solution.

TRY IT OUT   Creating a Column

In this example, you create a column for the Documents library so that business users can track the status of project-related documents, such as user manuals, planning documents, and training presentations. Because you do not want users to enter just any value for the status, you provide a list of common choices. This example assumes that you require a choice column that enables you to specify the release status of documents in a document library as Alpha, Beta, or Final Release. A choice column, one of several column types, gives users a list of values from which to select and presents them in a drop-down menu. The remaining column types are discussed in the next section.

For this example you work within the default Team Site template. To get started, create a new site collection or site using the Team Site template from the Collaboration templates.

1. From the main page of your team site, select Documents from the side navigation bar.

2. Select the Library tab from the ribbon.

3. From the Manage Views section of the Library tab, select Create Column. The Create Column window appears, as shown in Figure 4-1.

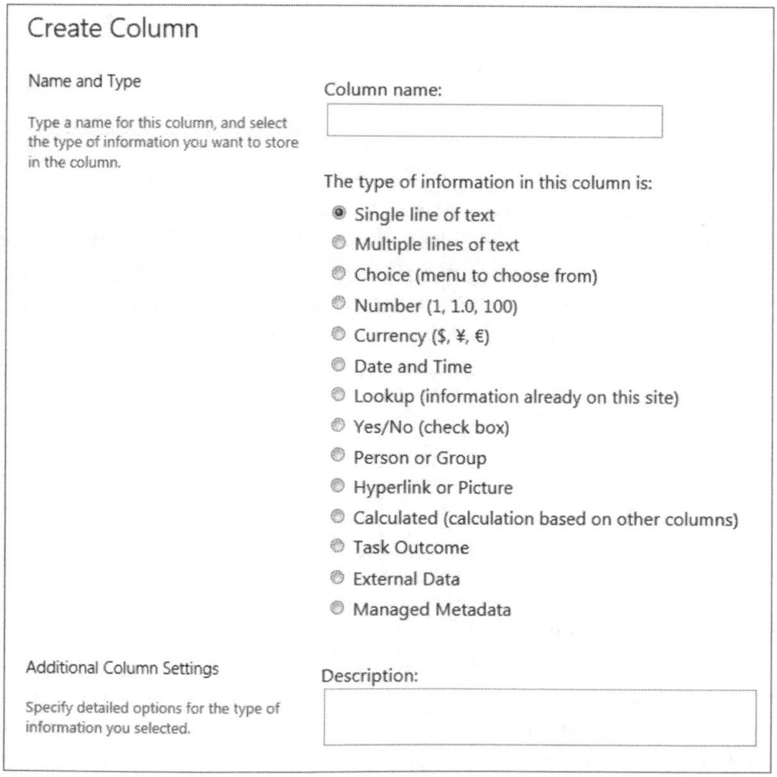

Create Column

Name and Type

Type a name for this column, and select the type of information you want to store in the column.

Column name:

The type of information in this column is:

- Single line of text
- Multiple lines of text
- Choice (menu to choose from)
- Number (1, 1.0, 100)
- Currency ($, ¥, €)
- Date and Time
- Lookup (information already on this site)
- Yes/No (check box)
- Person or Group
- Hyperlink or Picture
- Calculated (calculation based on other columns)
- Task Outcome
- External Data
- Managed Metadata

Additional Column Settings

Specify detailed options for the type of information you selected.

Description:

FIGURE 4-1

4. Enter the following properties for your column:

PROPERTY	VALUE
Column name	Release Status
The type of information in this column is	Choice (menu to choose from)
Description	This column contains the current release stage of the document.
Require that this column contains information	Yes
Enforce unique values	No
Type each choice on a separate line	Alpha Beta Final
Display choices using	Radio Buttons
Allow "Fill-in" Choices	No
Default value	Alpha

5. Click OK to complete the creation of your new column.

How It Works

In the preceding example, you created a new column that will appear whenever users are uploading or editing documents within your Documents library. Because you selected the Choice column type, the users will have a predefined list of values from which to select. You specified that the column required information; this means that a user cannot check a document into the library unless this value is specified. By making certain important columns required, you can help ensure that all documents have this value specified, which will make it easier for users to locate the files within the library.

You specified that the choices be displayed as radio buttons. This ensures that, as users complete the metadata form when uploading or editing a file, they see what the available values to select are directly within the form. This is a suitable choice when you have just a few values. If you have a large number of items in your selection list, a drop-down menu may be more suitable.

Types of Columns

In the preceding Try It Out you added a column to the Documents library. You may have noticed that once you selected the type of data you wanted to use for your column you could configure additional attributes for it. These attributes, or column properties, describe how the column will behave. Several attributes are based on the specific data type you select for your column, but several common properties also can apply to any data type. The following table describes these common attributes and provides an example of how you can use them within a list or library.

PROPERTY	CONFIGURATION VALUE	EXAMPLE
Description	Multi-Lines of Text	Use this to give your users guidance on what values should be entered for the column.
Require that this column contains information:	Yes / No	If this property is set to Yes, users must first enter in a value before they can save the list item. For document libraries where this is selected, items can be updated but must have this column completed before they can be checked in.
Enforce Unique Values:	Yes / No	When this is set to Yes. only one item in the list can have the value selected for the item. In the example from the preceding Try It Out, it would mean that only one document in the list could have the value of Beta.
Column Validation	Formula that varies based on column data type and a User Message for when the value equates to False.	This enables you to validate an entry before it is saved to the list. An example could be a help desk ticketing system. Within the system all tickets must be given a due date greater than the current date. Using this option you could require that the [Due Date] > [Today]. If the date entered didn't meet the criteria, the user would see the message you entered when you configured the column.

You can configure these properties for each of the different types of columns that you can create within a list. By configuring them to match your specific business requirements, you are helping to ensure that your users have the best user experience possible when working with the list data. By configuring items such as validation and required fields, you are helping to ensure that your site contains relevant and meaningful data.

Chapter 2 discussed at a high level the different types of data that you can store in a column. This section looks even more deeply at the types of columns you can have in SharePoint, and discusses some of the various customization options that exist with them. In the "Creating a Column" Try It Out you just completed, you selected a Choice column type to collect information from a radio button control, but you have other options at your disposal. The method used to create additional columns is exactly the same as described previously, but each type of column has different attributes that you can configure. You can even have multiple columns of the same data type, each with different attributes. Your options are pretty limitless, which enables you to easily configure a solution that can meet your specific business needs.

Single Line of Text

Virtually every list starts with the Single Line of Text column type, possibly the most commonly used within SharePoint lists, as its primary or title column. When creating a Single Line of Text column, you have very few options for customization, as you can see from Figure 4-2. However, you can select whether the column is required or optional. You can also limit the number of characters that a user can enter to prevent users from entering unnecessary data in a column. You also have the option to specify a default value, which users can enter manually or which you can allow SharePoint to calculate.

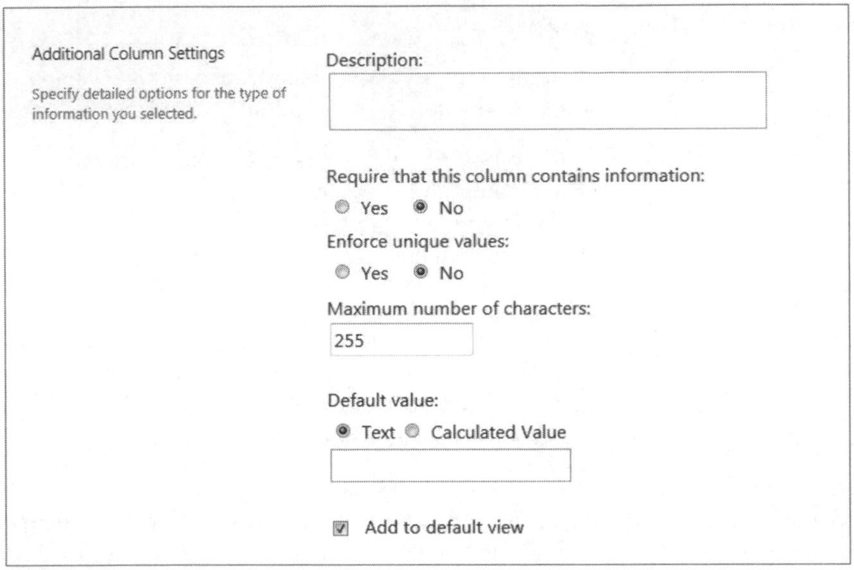

Additional Column Settings

Specify detailed options for the type of information you selected.

Description:

Require that this column contains information:

⚪ Yes ⚫ No

Enforce unique values:

⚪ Yes ⚫ No

Maximum number of characters:

255

Default value:

⚫ Text ⚪ Calculated Value

☑ Add to default view

FIGURE 4-2

Multiple Lines of Text

A Multiple Lines of Text column allows for a variable amount of text to be entered by the users. You can specify how many lines the field should display when users complete the information. You should give users plenty of space for situations where you expect them to enter a great deal of data; the size gives users a visual cue of how much information you want them to enter.

The Multiple Lines of Text column type has more advanced formatting options, including the following:

➤ **Plain Text:** Most appropriate for scenarios where no special formatting is required, such as in the example of a mailing address.

➤ **Rich Text:** Users can format the text using the Rich Text Editor, which is ideal when users input a larger amount of text that doesn't have specially formatted elements, such as tables or pictures, but may require some formatting and text alignment. You select this for notes and comments related to an item.

➤ **Enhanced Text:** Allows your users to add images, tables, and hyperlink elements to the column via the Advanced List Text Editor. This format is ideal for article body columns in an announcements list or employee biography content columns.

➤ **Append Changes to Existing Text:** This feature enables you to create a running list of all changes to this field. Whenever the column value changes, the new value is stored but the previous value is retained and can be viewed in a running history list. For you to use this attribute, the list must have versioning enabled.

It is important to note that not all list or library templates can support the advanced configuration settings. As an example, you do not have the ability to configure these advanced settings within a document library. This has to do with the type of template that you have selected for your list. For any list template that doesn't support the features, you will not see them as an option for configuration. Figure 4-3 shows a multi-line text column that is associated with a document library. Notice that the additional features described in the preceding list are not available for configuration.

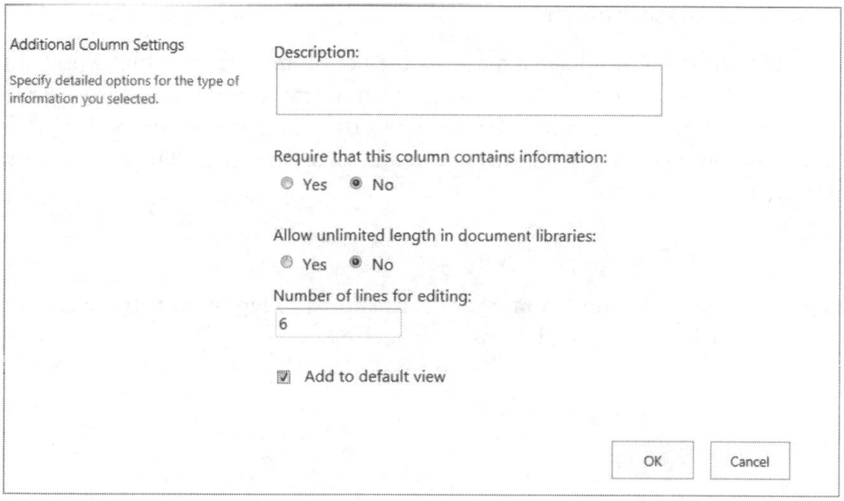

Additional Column Settings

Specify detailed options for the type of information you selected.

Description:

Require that this column contains information:

○ Yes ● No

Allow unlimited length in document libraries:

○ Yes ● No

Number of lines for editing:

6

☑ Add to default view

OK   Cancel

FIGURE 4-3

Choice

The Choice column enables you to define a list of values from which a user can select, as shown in Figure 4-4.

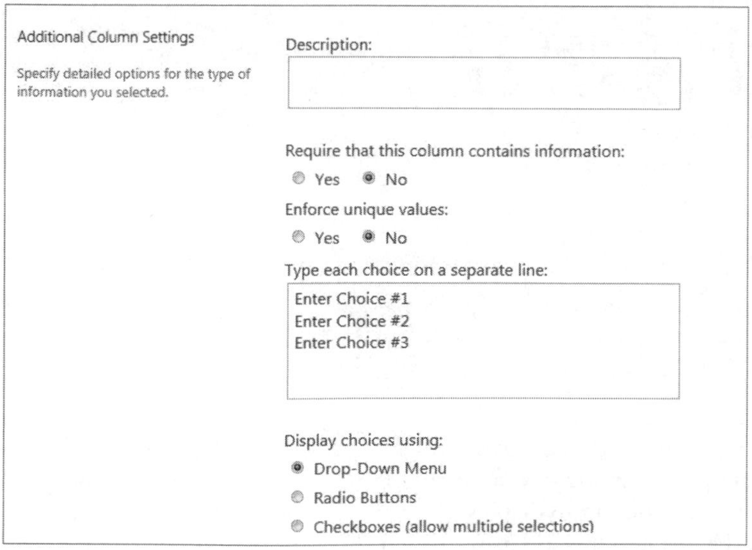

Additional Column Settings

Specify detailed options for the type of information you selected.

Description:

Require that this column contains information:

○ Yes ● No

Enforce unique values:

○ Yes ● No

Type each choice on a separate line:

Enter Choice #1
Enter Choice #2
Enter Choice #3

Display choices using:

● Drop-Down Menu

○ Radio Buttons

○ Checkboxes (allow multiple selections)

FIGURE 4-4

You enter all values by placing each value on a separate line. Users see this as a drop-down list, a set of radio buttons, or a series of checkboxes. A drop-down list or set of radio buttons means users can select only one option, whereas checkboxes allow them to select more than one item from the list of values. You can also specify whether users can fill in their own item if an appropriate value does not appear in the list. The value that they enter will be associated with the current list item, but will not be added to the list of choices for the column.

The choice data type is a great option if you have a manageable list of items from which you want users to select a value. As your list of options grows longer, it is important to review the scenario and make sure that you are not creating a scenario that becomes difficult for your users. If you find that your choice selection is becoming difficult to use or to manage, an alternate data type to consider is the Managed Metadata column type.

Number

A Number column has pretty simple customization options, as shown in Figure 4-5, but is extremely useful in many lists because it's helpful for calculations or reporting.

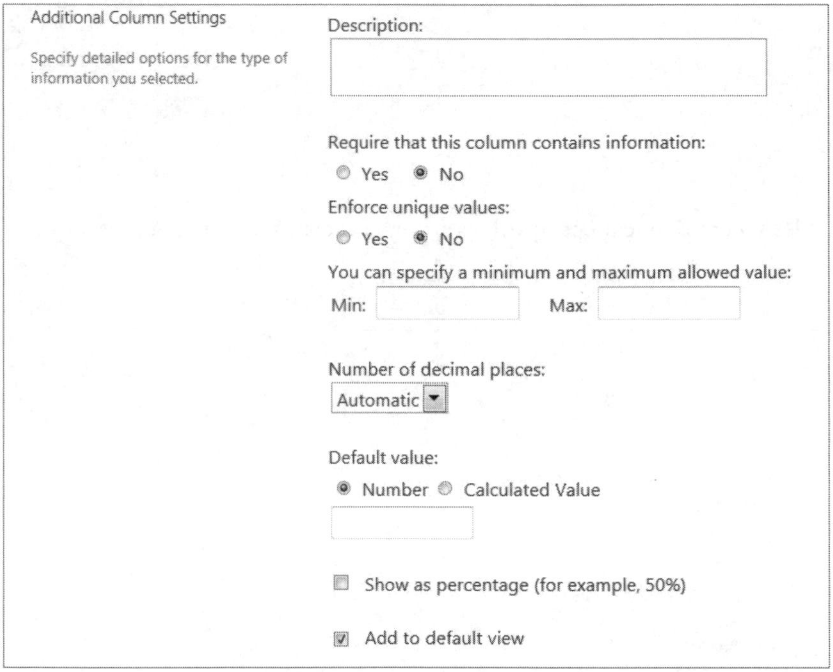

FIGURE 4-5

You can specify an allowed range of numbers that users can enter. For example, if you have a column to represent a user's rating of an item, you can have a minimum value of 1 and a maximum value of 10. You can also configure a column to display a specific number of decimal places or percentage value regardless of the format a person uses to enter the information.

Currency

A Currency column has the same customization options as the Number column type with one addition, as shown in Figure 4-6.

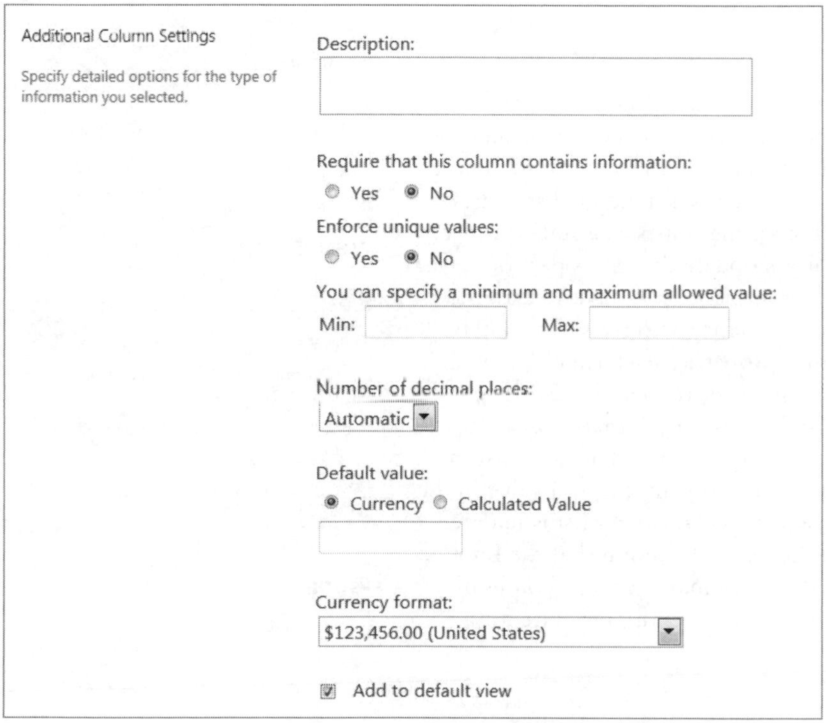

Additional Column Settings

Specify detailed options for the type of information you selected.

Description:

Require that this column contains information:
◯ Yes ◉ No

Enforce unique values:
◯ Yes ◉ No

You can specify a minimum and maximum allowed value:
Min: [   ]   Max: [   ]

Number of decimal places:
[Automatic ▼]

Default value:
◉ Currency ◯ Calculated Value
[   ]

Currency format:
[$123,456.00 (United States) ▼]

☑ Add to default view

FIGURE 4-6

The Currency column enables a user to specify the regional format in which the data displays, such as $123,456.00 for the United States or £123,456.00 for the United Kingdom. There is no direct link between the regional setting and currency exchange rates.

Date and Time

Every list, by default, has Date and Time columns for tracking when an item was created or last modified. For your solution, you may need to add columns containing date and time information because many of the items you track in a list have some level of time relevance, such as an expiration date, review date, or completion date.

Beyond the options that determine whether this column is required and that add a description, you can have the column display only a date or a time value. Time values are particularly useful if you intend to display your list information in a daily calendar view or if you define details on events, such as meetings or appointments. You can also select that your date value will be displayed in a Standard format (8/12/12) or a Friendly format (Next Tuesday). Figure 4-7 shows the results of selecting a Friendly display format.

You also have the option to use a calculation for the default value, as shown in Figure 4-8. This is useful if you are setting a value such as the default due date for an item. In that case, you can select the default value as [today] + 180, which sets the value to 6 months past the current date.

Lookup

A Lookup column is very similar to a Choice column because it supplies users with a set of predefined values for a column. The advantage is that you can point it to another list on the site and, thus, create more dynamic list values. This is better than storing all the values as a static property of the column because users update the list as part of normal business operations. For example, if you have a customer list, it's unrealistic for a site manager to constantly log in and change a list column's properties each time a company acquires a new customer. Instead, you can have this column point to a centralized customer list that those closest to the business operations can maintain. The new customer's name would then automatically appear as a value in the column as soon as the centralized customer list is updated. In addition to selecting the list and column that the Lookup column uses to display data, site managers can configure the column so that users can select multiple values for a list, as shown in Figure 4-9.

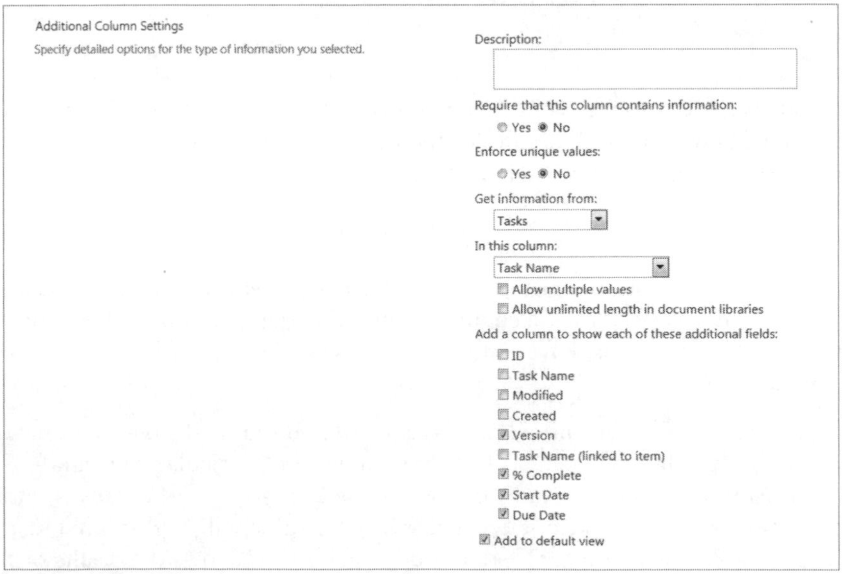

Review Date	Owner
December 15	SP_Admin
Today	SP_Admin
February 09, 2013	SP_Admin
Wednesday	SP_Admin

FIGURE 4-7

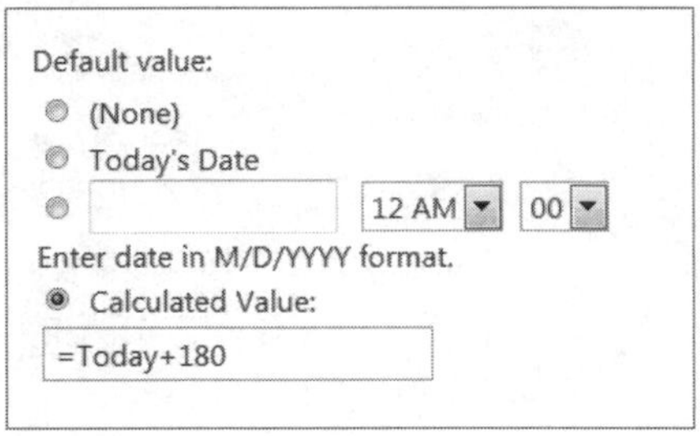

Default value:
- ○ (None)
- ○ Today's Date
- ○ [ ] [12 AM ▾] [00 ▾]
  Enter date in M/D/YYYY format.
- ● Calculated Value:
  [=Today+180]

FIGURE 4-8

Additional Column Settings
Specify detailed options for the type of information you selected.

Description:
[   ]

Require that this column contains information:
○ Yes ● No

Enforce unique values:
○ Yes ● No

Get information from:
[Tasks ▾]

In this column:
[Task Name ▾]
☐ Allow multiple values
☐ Allow unlimited length in document libraries

Add a column to show each of these additional fields:
☐ ID
☐ Task Name
☐ Modified
☐ Created
☑ Version
☐ Task Name (linked to item)
☑ % Complete
☑ Start Date
☑ Due Date

☑ Add to default view

FIGURE 4-9

Another powerful feature of the Lookup list is that site managers can configure the list to display additional properties of the item that was selected within the list. As an example, if a user selects Customer XYZ, the customer's address and phone number may also be displayed within the list item along with the customer's name.

Lookup columns also can enforce a relationship behavior. This is a powerful feature that enables you to ensure that data between the two lists remains in sync. If you select the option to Restrict delete within the relationship behavior, you are saying that no items from the source list can be deleted if they have an item in this list that references it. This means that if I have a document that is associated with a customer, that customer cannot be deleted from the customers list as long as the document is referencing the customer. The other relationship behavior is to delete all associated content when the source item is deleted. This means that if the customer is deleted, all of the documents associated with that customer are also deleted.

Yes/No

A Yes/No column type is essentially a checkbox column that defines whether an item meets a specific criterion. The primary configuration option when defining a Yes/No column is determining whether the default value should be selected or unselected.

Person or Group

The Person or Group column is ideal for assigning ownership of an item or personalizing the display of data to users of a list. You have the option of selecting multiple items, which enables you to assign a single task to multiple people. In fact, for a default tasks list, the Assigned To column is based on the Person or Group column type. You can also allow the selection of groups of people rather than individuals. For example, you can create a task and assign it to the Technical Support group. Then any member of the Technical Support group can complete the request rather than rely on users to specify which technician should complete the task.

You have the added option of defining whether a person from this column is drawn from the list of all users or from a single SharePoint group, which is useful if you want to have an Assigned To column to represent who should review the document next. Because only those with approval rights should be reviewing items, it may make sense to specify that only members of the Approvers SharePoint site group be assigned to the column. This will help ensure that your users are able to select the desired values for the column. The more you can help restrict the values to meaningful choices, the more user-friendly your solutions will be.

Your final customization option involves how the information is displayed. You can have the person identified by a variety of personal profile properties, including display name, e-mail address, and job title or picture. An example of the configuration options for the Person or Group column type is shown in Figure 4-10.

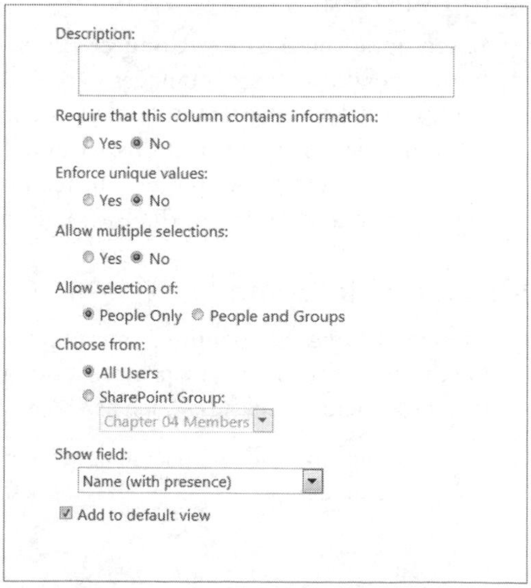

FIGURE 4-10

Hyperlink or Picture

This column offers very little from a customization perspective beyond specifying whether the item is required, but it does offer one significant attribute. You can format the URL of the item as either a web address that users can click to open or as a picture that is displayed as a thumbnail.

Calculated (Calculation Based on other Columns)

This special column type allows a site manager to define a formula that will automatically determine the value of a column without requiring a user's input. This formula can be based upon other columns within the list. An example of such a formula is [Items Sold] × [Price], which would calculate the total revenue associated with a list item that represents a customer sale. As shown in Figure 4-11, the available columns to reference in your formula are displayed for your ease of use.

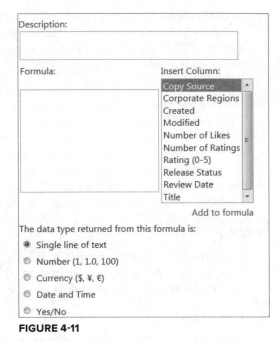

FIGURE 4-11

Task Outcome

This column type is used specifically for lists that have an associated workflow. This column is intended to be used within the workflow to show the outcome of the workflow. This column type is discussed more in Chapter 5, "Working with Workflows."

External Data

Based upon the Business Connectivity Services feature of SharePoint Server, the External Data column type allows a site manager to reference an external business system as the lookup location for a column's values. For example, if your company has a customer relationship management system, all customer data may exist in this system. Therefore, it would not make sense to export and replicate that information in SharePoint. Instead, you could create a column that looks up that external business system and points to the Customer database for its values.

Managed Metadata

Managed Metadata columns can support hierarchical information as well as large volumes of choices. Columns of this data type provide a rich interface for users as they enter data into the column. The interface includes features such as:

➤ **Type Ahead:** As users begin to enter text they are presented with existing values from which they can select.

➤ **Synonyms:** For each term loaded into the term store, additional synonyms or labels can be configured for it. This means that a user may enter the value of "RFP" and the actual value stored in the list could be "Request for Proposal." In this example, the commonly used abbreviation was loaded in place of the term. Using features like this enables users to experience a more natural term set.

➤ **Open term sets:** Open term sets allow users to add data values that become part of the selection tree. This means that users can add values that are then available for selection by other users.

Managed Metadata is a large concept within SharePoint, and it is explored further in Chapter 16, "Managing Records."

TRY IT OUT | **Creating Additional Columns**

In this example, you add two additional columns to the Documents list that you used in the previous Try It Out.

1. From the main page of your team site, select Documents from the side navigation bar.

2. Select the Library tab from the ribbon.

3. From the Manage Views section of the Library tab, select Create Column.

4. Enter the following properties for your column:

PROPERTY	VALUE
Column Name	Review Date
The type of information that is in this column	Date and Time
Description	This column contains the date that the admin will need to review the document.
Require that this column contains information	Yes
Enforce unique values	No
Date and Time Format	Date Only
Display Format	Friendly
Default value	Calculated Value
Calculated Value	[Today] + 180
Add to default view	Selected

5. Click OK to complete the creation of your new column.

6. Repeat steps 1–5, using the following table for step 4:

PROPERTY	VALUE
Column Name	Owner
The type of information that is in this column	Person or Group
Description	This column contains the name of the person who is responsible for this document.
Require that this column contains information	Yes
Enforce Unique Values	No
Allow multiple selections	No
Allow selection of	People Only
Choose from	All Users
Show field	Name (with picture and details)
Add to default view	Selected

Figure 4-12 shows the default view of the list once your columns have been created.

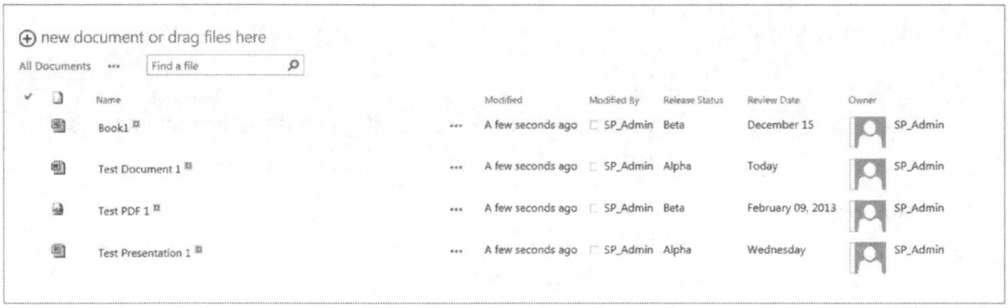

FIGURE 4-12

How It Works

In the preceding example, you added additional columns to the documents list. You used the data and people data types. These additional customizations to the list allow users to quickly see additional information about the documents.

Configuring Column Ordering

As you create new columns they will be associated with the list items in the order they were created. This is something that you can update easily, and it is recommended that you update the order of the columns to match the most intuitive order for the users that will be required to work with the data.

TRY IT OUT   Changing the Order of Columns on a List

Once you have defined a list or library with the columns you want to track, you may at times realize that you would prefer to have the columns appear in a form in a slightly different order. Building on the preceding example, you have decided that it is important to show the owner before the status and the status before the review date.

1. From the main page of your team site, select Documents from the side navigation bar.

2. Select the Library tab from the ribbon.

3. Select the Library Settings menu option. You are redirected to the Library Settings page.

4. Scroll to the Columns section of the page.

5. Select the Column Order link. You are redirected to the Change Column Ordering page, as shown in Figure 4-13.

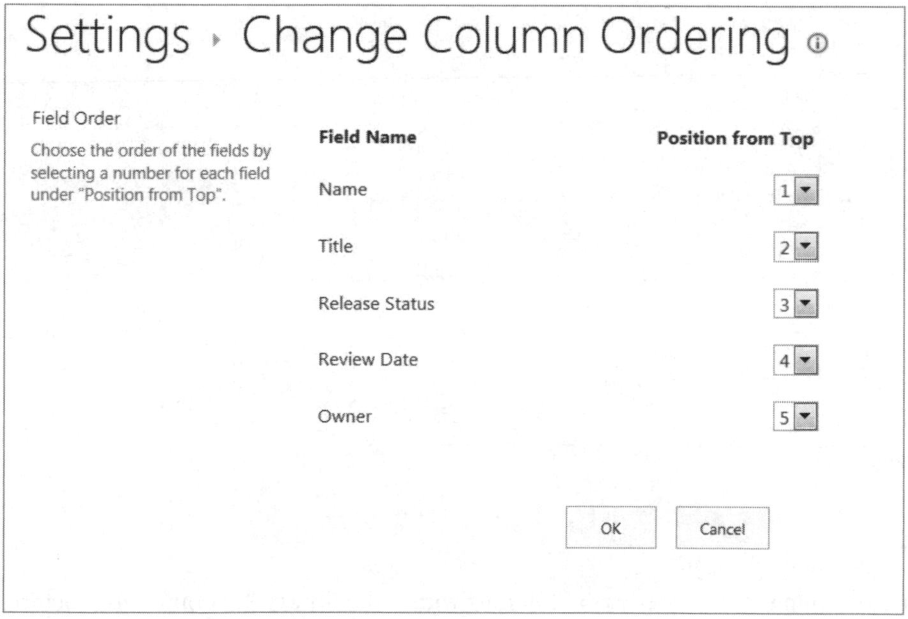

FIGURE 4-13

6. Update the fields based on the following table:

FIELD NAME	POSITION FROM TOP
Name	1
Title	2
Owner	3
Release Status	4
Review Date	5

7. Click OK.

By changing the Column Order, users will now see the order as displayed in Figure 4-14 when editing the properties of a document stored in the Documents library.

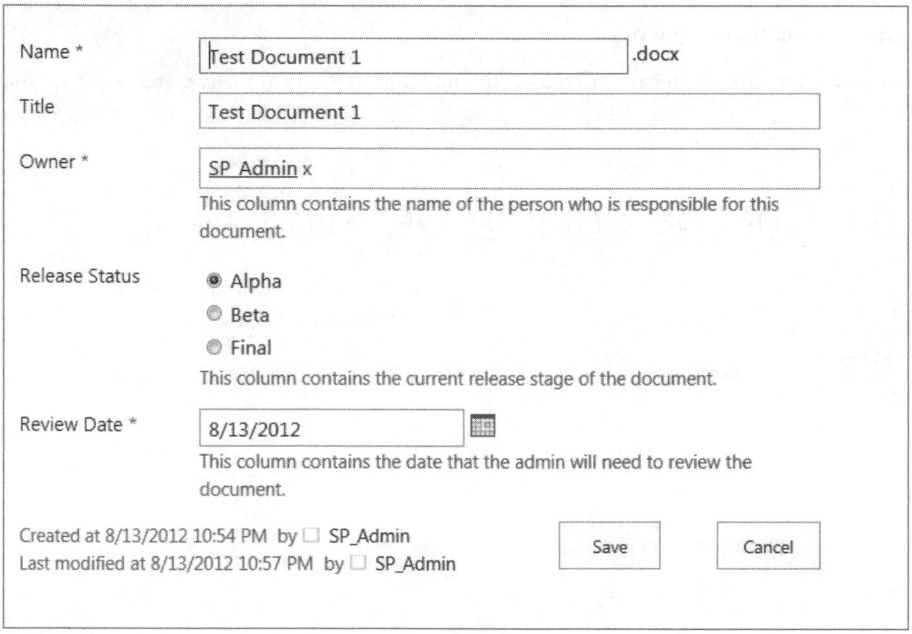

FIGURE 4-14

How It Works

In this Try It Out, you changed the order of the columns within the library. By doing this, you are controlling the order that users see the columns on the View, Edit, and Display forms for the list item.

Choosing a Column's Scope

So far, all examples in this chapter have been limited to creating a column for a list or library, but you can associate the information for a single list with multiple lists. For example, for a column that defines customers, you commonly associate a customer's name with items from multiple lists and libraries. Because the steps for creating a suitable customer list are somewhat time-consuming, it's inefficient to reproduce the column in each list where you want to associate client information. Instead, you can create what is known as a *site column*, which makes a column available to all sites and subsites. Generally speaking, if many lists will use your column at all levels of a corporate intranet or collaboration site, you should create it at the top-level site of a site collection. This makes the site column available on all sites throughout the site collection.

A site column may only be relevant to a specific division or team. In that case, you may want to create the column only on the divisional site itself. It will still be available to all lists within that site and all sites below it; however, it will not be listed under the Available Site columns for the other subsites within the site collection.

If you have a column that will need to be used across multiple site collections, you can associate the column with a specific content type and then publish that content type to all the site collections consuming the service application. This concept is covered in detail in Chapter 6, "Working with Content Types."

Earlier in the chapter it was mentioned that planning is one of the key elements to successfully configuring lists and libraries. This is an example of how planning ahead can save you time. If you look at all of the components your solution will need, you should be able to identify what columns could be shared across different lists or libraries. By sharing these columns you will reduce the amount of configuration and management required to maintain your solution over time. Although it's tempting to create a site column for everything and thus make it accessible to everyone, remember the following:

- ➤ **List-centric columns:** Some column types are relevant only for a specific list and only clutter the site column gallery for all other users and usage scenarios. For example, a software development team's issue list may have a column that tracks whether a client called about an application bug or feature request, and that column isn't appropriate for any other list or site. Or, a column may contain important data that should not be shared with the entire organization, such as manually entered items or data from an external business system. In either of these cases, it's more appropriate to create a column that is attached to a single list.

- ➤ **Site columns:** These are more appropriate when you have a column of data that needs to be associated with multiple lists and libraries. You would use a site column to ensure that there is consistency in how a column is configured. Because you create the column once and it's placed in a central gallery for others to reuse, you save time and effort.

The next two Try It Outs show you how to create a site column as well as how to add a site column to a list.

TRY IT OUT   Creating a Site Column

In the "Creating a Column" Try It Out, you learned how to create a list-centric column. This Try It Out walks you through creating a site column within the central gallery of columns so that it can later be used by multiple lists with a site and its subsites. For this example, you create the site column that holds all the regions in which an organization has a presence. Because you want to ensure that your column is available to the maximum number of sites in your environment, you create it at the very top level of your site collection.

1. From the top-level site of your site collection, select Site Settings from the Site Actions menu (the gear icon in the top right of the page). You are redirected to the Site Settings page for the site collection, as shown in Figure 4-15.

FIGURE 4-15

2. Select the Site columns option from the Web Designer Galleries section.

> Note that SharePoint has a wide range of preexisting site columns, which are good starting points. It is always a good practice to search this listing to ensure that a similar column does not already exist.

3. Click Create. The Create Column window appears, as shown in Figure 4-16. You may notice some differences in this window compared to Figure 4-1. These differences are discussed in the How It Works following this exercise.

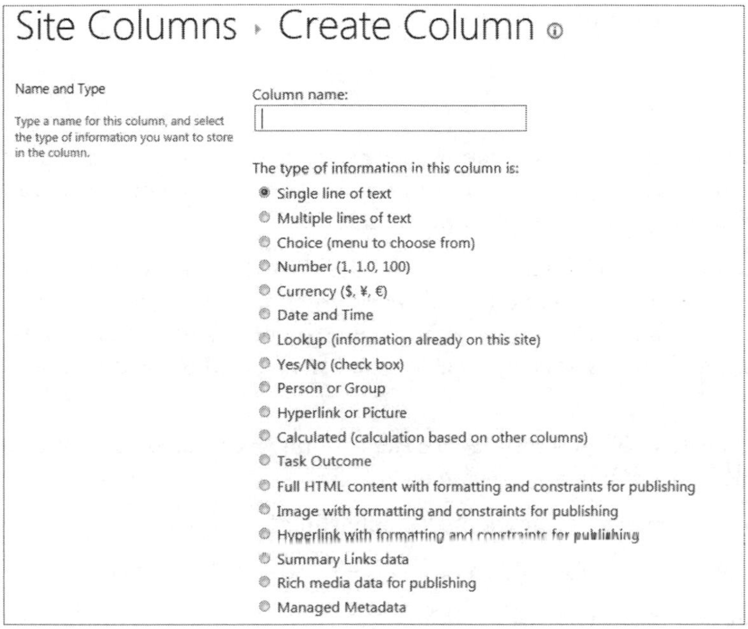

Site Columns ▸ Create Column ⓘ

Name and Type

Type a name for this column, and select the type of information you want to store in the column.

Column name:

[   ]

The type of information in this column is:

- ⦿ Single line of text
- ○ Multiple lines of text
- ○ Choice (menu to choose from)
- ○ Number (1, 1.0, 100)
- ○ Currency ($, ¥, €)
- ○ Date and Time
- ○ Lookup (information already on this site)
- ○ Yes/No (check box)
- ○ Person or Group
- ○ Hyperlink or Picture
- ○ Calculated (calculation based on other columns)
- ○ Task Outcome
- ○ Full HTML content with formatting and constraints for publishing
- ○ Image with formatting and constraints for publishing
- ○ Hyperlink with formatting and constraints for publishing
- ○ Summary Links data
- ○ Rich media data for publishing
- ○ Managed Metadata

FIGURE 4-16

4. Give the site column a name. This example uses the name Corporate Regions.

5. Select the "Choice (menu to choose from)" option as the type of information in this column.

6. To better organize your site columns, you can choose a group for your site column. You can create a custom group for your custom site columns. To do this, select New Group, and type **Corporate Columns** in the field provided.

7. In the Additional Column Settings section, enter the following properties:

PROPERTY	VALUE
Description	This is a list of regions in which your organization has offices.
Require that this column contains information	Yes
Enforce unique values	No
Type each choice on a separate line	Canada United States Europe Asia Africa
Display choices using	Drop-Down Menu
Allow "Fill-in" Choices	No
Default value	Leave this field blank

8. Click OK. Your site column is now available to share and use across all lists and libraries throughout your site collection.

How It Works

When users add a list item that is utilizing this site column, they are required to select a region from this list of choices. If you want to update the region choices available in your site column, you can return to the site column web designer gallery to edit your column.

In addition to the previous selection options, you also see a new checkbox that enables you to update all lists and libraries using this site column, so that they include your changes. Thus, you can update a large number of lists to accommodate a change in your organization from one single location. As you accumulate more and more lists and libraries, this valuable feature becomes more powerful and offers great time savings.

You may have noticed that the Create Column screen for the site column you created in the previous example offered additional choices for column type. These included:

➤ Full HTML content with formatting and constraints for publishing

➤ Image with formatting and constraints for publishing

➤ Hyperlink with formatting and constraints for publishing

➤ Summary Links data

➤ Rich media data for publishing

These columns are for the publishing capabilities of SharePoint Server, which is explored in Chapter 15, "Getting Started with Web Content Management." In addition, you will notice that you cannot create site columns based on external data. This option is available only on list-centric columns.

TRY IT OUT   **Adding a Site Column to a List**

The previous example guided you through creating a new site column. You can now use this site column on any list or library in your site collection. This saves you the time and energy required to re-create list-centric columns. The following example guides you through the process of attaching a site column to a list or library. Instead of creating a column on the list from scratch, you add an existing site column to the list. The steps for doing so are considerably easier, and future updates to the column properties can be streamlined and rolled out to all lists from a single location.

As you add site columns to a list, they become fields that users are required to fill out as they add list items. Most organizations like to enforce a standard set of required items that users must complete on lists and libraries, such as Owner or Status. Based on this methodology, an organization can create a site column for each type of information it wants to enforce and then reuse this column on all lists and libraries throughout the site collection. This greatly reduces the amount of maintenance.

1. From the main page of your team site, select the Documents library from the side navigation.

2. Click the Library tab on the ribbon.

3. Select the Library Settings menu option. You are redirected to the Library Settings page.

4. Scroll to the Columns section of the page.

5. Select the option to Add from existing site columns. You are redirected to the Add Columns from Site Columns page, as shown in Figure 4-17.

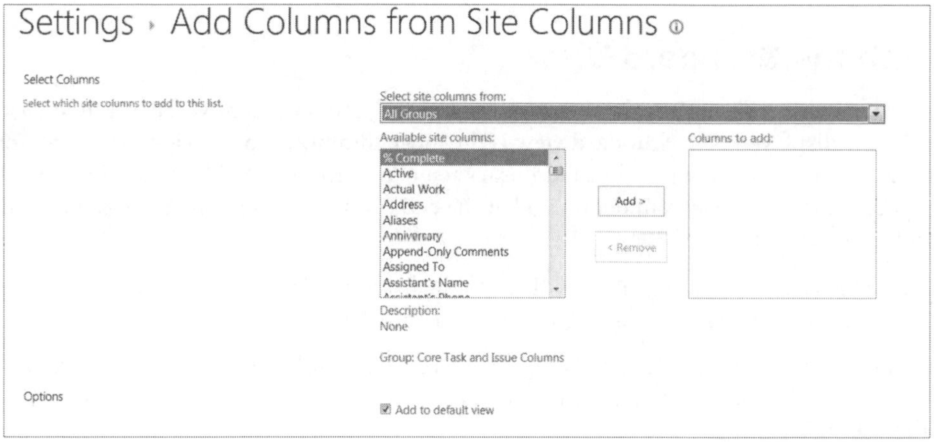

Settings ▸ Add Columns from Site Columns ⓘ

Select Columns
Select which site columns to add to this list.

Select site columns from:
All Groups

Available site columns:
% Complete
Active
Actual Work
Address
Aliases
Anniversary
Append-Only Comments
Assigned To
Assistant's Name
Assistant's Phone

Add >

< Remove

Columns to add:

Description:
None

Group: Core Task and Issue Columns

Options

☑ Add to default view

FIGURE 4-17

6. Select the Corporate Columns group from the "Select site columns from" drop-down.

7. Select the Corporate Regions field and click the Add button.

8. Click OK.

Now when you edit the properties of an existing file within the Documents library, you will see the Region column appear as a required value.

How It Works

In this Try It Out, you added a site column to a list. Using this feature will allow you to create a column once and then use it in multiple locations.

CREATING AND CUSTOMIZING VIEWS

So far in this chapter you have looked at the various columns you can add to list or libraries. In this section you look at how you can customize the various views associated with a list or library. A *view* basically displays the information about a list in different ways. By creating different views you are able to help users access the data in a format and style that is appropriate for the way they are interacting with the data. Some views display all the items in the list, whereas others show specific items based on their properties or metadata values. Every list has at least one view, and many of them come preconfigured with additional views.

You can customize views, allowing users to quickly find relevant information. In addition to customizing existing views, you can also create new views. Views are based off of several view templates, including the Standard view, the Gantt view, Datasheet view, and the Calendar view. Imagine opening the telephone book and having it display only the numbers that are relevant to you. That's the type of flexibility you have with a custom view.

Working with the Standard View

The Standard view within SharePoint has a standard set of components that you can use to customize the way the data is displayed. The Standard view is the most common type of view within SharePoint and is often the default view on which list and library templates are based. The following list describes each of the view elements in detail, and at the end of this section you get an opportunity to create a Standard view in a Try It Out.

➤ **Name:** This is the name that users will see in the list view drop-down. This is also where you can select if this view is the default view for the library.

➤ **Audience:** This is where you can choose to create a personal view that is accessible only to you or where you can create a public view that is accessible to everyone who has access to the list or library.

> **NOTE** *It is important to remember that Audiences are a way to restrict who can see the views, but they are not a way to secure list content. Whenever you see the term "audience" you should note that this is just about hiding or displaying data, but that it does not secure the data. For more information on securing data, refer to Chapter 9.*

➤ **Columns:** In this section you configure the specific columns that should be included in your view as well as the order in which they should be displayed.

➤ **Sort Order:** You can select up to two columns by which items in the list are sorted. Sort order can either be ascending (A to Z) or descending (Z to A).

➤ **Filter:** You can customize a view by defining the items that are displayed, based on specific column values or properties. You first select a column from the drop-down list and specify a rule so that only items that meet your criteria are displayed in the view. You can add up to 10 filter rules for a single view.

➤ **Tabular view:** You can specify whether checkboxes should be enabled on the view. When you allow checkboxes on a view, users can select multiple items to perform bulk actions such as Delete or Check Out. An example of this is shown in Figure 4-18.

Documents

⊕ new document or drag files here

All Documents   •••   [Find a file   🔍]

✓	🗋	Name		Modified	Modified By	Release Status
✓	📄	Book1	•••	10 minutes ago	☐ SP_Admin	Beta
	📄	Test Document 1	•••	3 minutes ago	☐ SP_Admin	Alpha
✓	📄	Test PDF 1	•••	10 minutes ago	☐ SP_Admin	Beta
	📄	Test Presentation 1	•••	10 minutes ago	☐ SP_Admin	Alpha

FIGURE 4-18

➤ **Group By:** Because views can quite often contain a large amount of information, SharePoint enables you to group up to two columns of similar items together. The first column acts as a parent item and the second acts as a child of the parent. For example, you can group a task list by "Project" and then by "Assigned To." This allows users to see a report of all tasks grouped first by the project name and then by each person to whom the tasks are assigned.

➤ **Totals:** For numerical columns, it's beneficial to display total values for all your items. These might be the sum, average, or standard deviation of all items in a view or group. For other columns, the total value is useful to display the number of items in a view or group by selecting Count.

➤ **Style:** Depending on your presentation requirements, you can select a style for your view. For example, you can select "Newsletter, No Lines" for a plain view of items in a list, or "Boxed" to display items in a series of rectangular boxes. Take a few minutes to try out each view style so that you can familiarize yourself with the options that are the most appropriate choice for your views.

> **NOTE** Styles are one of the most unused features when configuring lists and libraries. You can do many different things when you are working with the styles. It is valuable to become familiar with these different styles so that you can configure views that provide the most benefit to the organization. A good way to get started is to create a test list with various data types for columns and then to create various views using the different styles. This will help you get the most benefit from the different view styles.

➤ **Folders:** In a list or library, folders organize items or documents. However, you may not want to show folders for a particular view. Instead, you can show items that meet specific criteria, regardless of their folder location. For example, if you have 10 layers of folders in your document library and you want to view all documents associated with a specific project, rather than manually clicking through the various levels of folders, you can create a custom view that displays items with no folders that gives a complete listing of all documents that meet your criteria in a single level. No additional clicks are required.

➤ **Item Limit:** For performance reasons, you commonly may only want to display a specific number of items; for example, it's not very efficient to display 10,000 documents in a single view, but groups of 30 may be more beneficial. In fact, the All Items view for most lists displays items in groups of 30 by default. In other cases, you may want to limit the number of items to a goal number and display them to meet a criterion. For example, you may want to show the last 25 documents that have been added to a library. You first sort the view by either the created or modified date in descending order. You then specify the limit for the view to be 25 items.

➤ **Mobile:** When creating or editing a view, you can select whether it is enabled for mobile access. A mobile view is one that is suitable for access from a device such as a cell phone or PDA. Many of the user interface elements, such as tables and images that would typically be seen via a standard browser, are left out of these views. Only views that are public views can be created as mobile views. When creating a mobile view, you are given an option to limit the number of items that are displayed. Because mobile devices typically have smaller screens, it is recommended that you use a smaller value. By default, this value is 3.

Because you can create multiple views, it is possible for you to create a wide combination of the views that help users navigate to the right content at the right time. For each list or library you create, it is important to spend time understanding how users will be working with the data so that you can create views that help them be efficient and effective as they complete their tasks.

TRY IT OUT **Creating a Standard View**

By sorting, filtering, and grouping the columns of metadata, SharePoint can display the contents of a list in a personalized way, one that is directly relevant to the information you want to see. This is particularly useful when you have lists shared across an organization, or when you have large lists. For this Try It Out, you sort items in the Documents list by their Review Date so that items appear in the order in which they need to be responded to. In addition, you create the view with a special filter that will only display items Owned by the current user.

1. From the main page of your team site, select the Documents list from the side navigation.

2. Click the Library tab on the ribbon.

3. Select the Create View menu option. You are redirected to the Create View page, where a choice of view types is displayed, as shown in Figure 4-19.

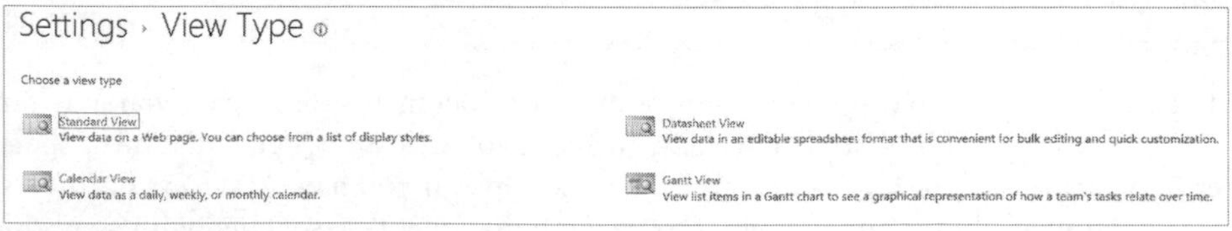

FIGURE 4-19

4. Select Standard View. The page refreshes to display options relevant to a standard view.

5. Define the view as follows:

VIEW PROPERTY	VALUE
View Name	My Upcoming Reviews
Make this the default view	No
View Audience	Create a Public View
Columns	Type (icon linked to document)
	Name (linked to document with edit menu)
	Release Status
	Review Date
	Owner
	Corporate Regions
Sort	Review Date (Show items in ascending order)
Filter (Show Items only when the following values are true)	Owner is equal to[me]

6. Click the OK button. You are redirected to a page displaying your new view, as shown in Figure 4-20.

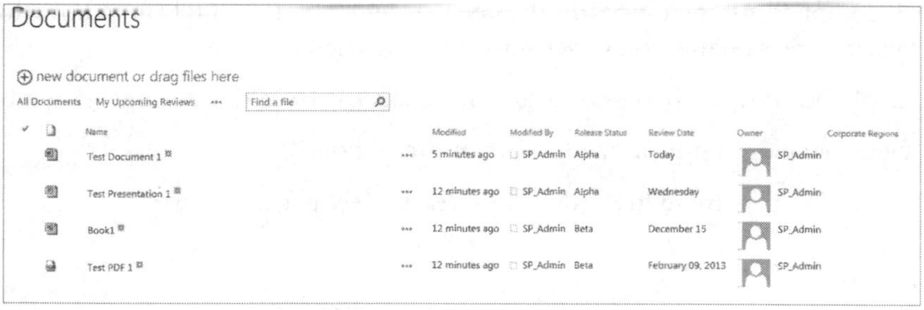

FIGURE 4-20

How It Works

In the preceding example, you created a custom view that displayed only items assigned to the current user. You did this by using a special property on the filter, known as [me] on the Assigned to column. Whenever a column is of the Person or Group type, you can personalize the view by using the [me] property and only the items in the list where the current user's name is selected within the Person or Group field will be displayed. In addition to filtering the view, you specified a sort order that displays items according to their due date. This is practical because users will see the items that are due the soonest at the very top of their list. This results in a sense of priority for the items that must be completed first.

Setting Up a Gantt, Calendar, or Datasheet View

In addition to the Standard view, SharePoint has several other view types:

➤ **Gantt view:** This view displays a graphical representation of tasks and how they are progressing over time. It gives you a clear picture of how a project or task is evolving at a glance, and helps you easily identity bottlenecks in the process. You can use this view type on any list or library type as long as there is date-based information to reference. For many small teams, the Gantt chart view is the ideal solution for managing and reporting a project. This particular view is a big hit with project and resource managers who need to track how tasks are evolving and give updated status reports to an executive team.

➤ **Calendar view:** This view enables you to create a daily, weekly, or monthly view of your data. You can create a Calendar view on any list or library as long as there is a date range that can be referenced for the start and end data points on the calendar.

➤ **Datasheet view:** This view gives you a spreadsheet-like view of your data, very similar to an Excel spreadsheet. This view is particularly useful when you want to customize multiple columns of data.

In addition to showing you how to set up these views, this section also has a Try It Out that shows you how to create a view based on an existing view. This is particularly useful when you have columns that are similar but with slightly different requirements.

TRY IT OUT   Creating a Gantt View

When configuring a Gantt view, you must select a start and end date. Based on this elapsed time and the percentage of the task complete, SharePoint can calculate a graphical representation of how things are progressing. The following steps enable you to get starting using the Gantt view.

1. From the main page of your Project Team site, select the Tasks list from the side navigation bar.

2. Select the Create View menu option from the List tab of the ribbon.

3. Select the Gantt View type. You are redirected to the Create View page.

4. Define the view as follows:

VIEW PROPERTY	VALUE
View Name	Task Tracking
Make this the default view	No
View Audience	Create a Public View
Columns	Attachments Title (linked to item with edit menu) Start Date Due Date % Complete

5. For the Gantt Columns section, enter the values as follows:

GANTT COLUMN	VALUE
Title	Title
Start Date	Start Date
Due Date	Due Date
Percent Complete	% Complete
Predecessors	Predecessors

6. Click the OK button to complete the view. You are directed to a page displaying the new view (see Figure 4-21).

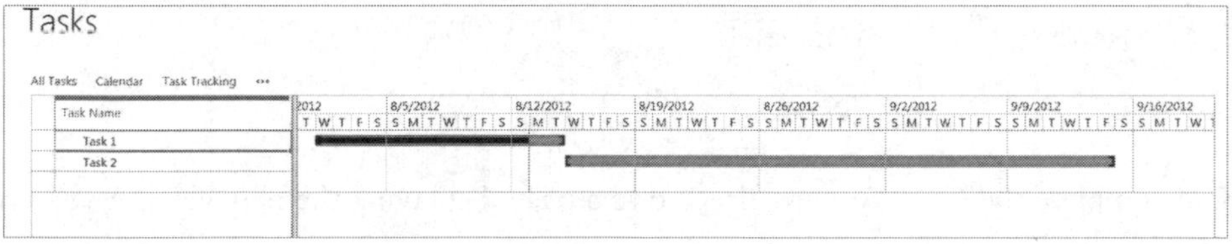

FIGURE 4-21

How It Works

After creating and selecting your Gantt view, you can see a timeline view of the data. With this view, you can easily track project dates over periods of time.

TRY IT OUT   Creating a Calendar View

This view enables you to move back and forth between months, add tasks to your calendar, and even connect your calendar to Outlook, a familiar interface for managing calendars. The following steps walk you through setting up the Calendar view on your Tasks list.

1. From your Tasks list, select the Create View option from the ribbon.

2. Select the Calendar View type.

3. Define the view as follows:

VIEW PROPERTY	VALUE
View Name	Task Calendar
Make this the default view	No
View Audience	Create a Public View
Time Interval (Begin)	Start Date
Time Interval (End)	Due Date
Month View Title	Title
Week View Title	Title
Week View Sub Heading	% Complete
Day View Title	Title
Day View Sub Heading	% Complete
Default Scope	Week

4. Click OK to complete the view. You are directed to a page displaying the new view. An example is shown in Figure 4-22.

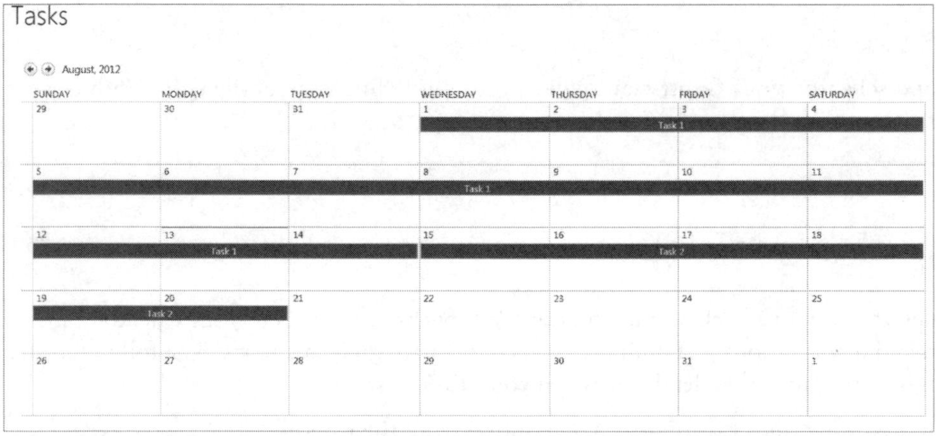

Tasks

August, 2012

SUNDAY	MONDAY	TUESDAY	WEDNESDAY	THURSDAY	FRIDAY	SATURDAY
29	30	31	1	2	3	4
5	6	7	8	9	10	11
12	13	14	15	16	17	18
19	20	21	22	23	24	25
26	27	28	29	30	31	1

FIGURE 4-22

How It Works

After creating and selecting your Calendar view, you can easily see the tasks spread out over a period of time. Using this view gives you an easy way to understand the events occurring within your list for any date.

TRY IT OUT   Creating a Datasheet View

The Datasheet view gives you a spreadsheet view much like Excel but allows for much easier and faster mass updates and data customization.

1. From your Tasks list, select the Create View option from the ribbon.

2. Select the Datasheet View type.

3. Define the view as follows:

VIEW PROPERTY	VALUE
View Name	Task Datasheet
Make this the default view	No
View Audience	Create a Public View
Columns	Attachments
	Type
	Title
	Assigned To
	Status
	Priority
	Due Date
	% Complete

4. Click the OK button to complete the view. You are directed to a page displaying the new view. An example is shown in Figure 4-23.

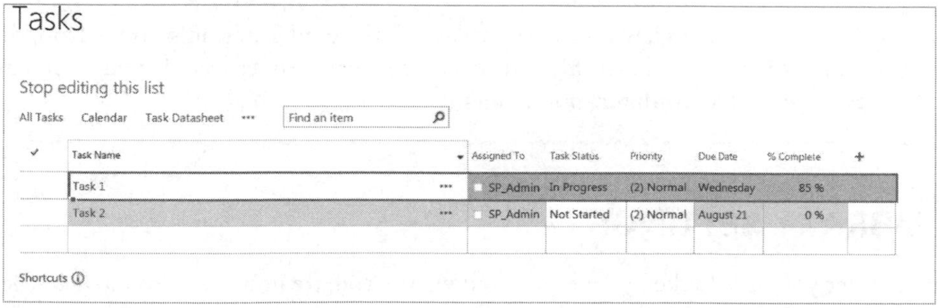

FIGURE 4-23

How It Works

After creating and selecting your datasheet view, you are presented with a spreadsheet-like view of your list's data. With this view, you can update multiple columns at the same time. This is a big timesaver, particularly if you have a large number of updates to perform.

TRY IT OUT   Creating a View Based on an Existing View

In some situations, a single list or library may contain multiple views that are similar but have slight differences to meet specific information requirements. Instead of creating each new view from scratch, you can use a particular view as a starting point and alter it slightly to meet your needs.

Each time you add a new view to a list, it appears in the Start from Existing View section in the Create View window. Selecting one of these views generates a view based on the filtering, sorting, and meta-data columns of the existing view. This saves you time and helps you efficiently customize views to meet your needs. By creating a starting point, you can reuse this view to minimize your efforts for all remaining views for the list. You can also think of customization using an existing view as a way to create structure because it acts as a template for displaying common components.

1. From your Tasks list, select the Create View option from the ribbon.

2. Below the listed view types is the Start from Existing View heading with any views currently available for your list. Select an existing view from which to start building your custom view. For this example, select the Tasks Tracking view.

3. Specify a view name and define any unique properties of the view that did not exist in the previous view. For example, select the option to "Filter based on tasks that are assigned to the current user" using the method described in "Creating a Standard View."

4. Click OK to complete the view.

How It Works

Creating a new view from an existing view allows you to use all the configuration settings from the starting view as a baseline for the new view. This feature can be a great timesaver, as you often have many views that differ on just a few configuration points.

LIST AND LIBRARY SETTINGS

So far in this chapter you have looked at columns and views. You are now ready to move to the last set of configuration options for lists. Some of the options are discussed in detail and others simply reference future chapters. In addition to what we have already covered in terms of configuring lists, these additional settings will enable you to customize your lists in very specific configurations, which provides a unique and specific experience for your users. Figure 4-24 shows a view of the list settings page, highlighting the specific configuration options that are discussed.

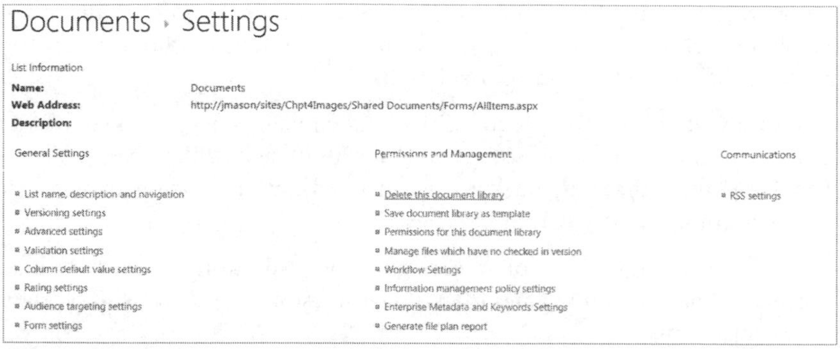

Documents ▸ Settings

List Information

Name: Documents
Web Address: http://jmason/sites/Chpt4Images/Shared Documents/Forms/AllItems.aspx
Description:

General Settings   Permissions and Management   Communications

▪ List name, description and navigation   ▪ Delete this document library   ▪ RSS settings
▪ Versioning settings   ▪ Save document library as template
▪ Advanced settings   ▪ Permissions for this document library
▪ Validation settings   ▪ Manage files which have no checked in version
▪ Column default value settings   ▪ Workflow Settings
▪ Rating settings   ▪ Information management policy settings
▪ Audience targeting settings   ▪ Enterprise Metadata and Keywords Settings
▪ Form settings   ▪ Generate file plan report

FIGURE 4-24

General Settings

The General Settings for the list or library enable you to configure a set of default configurations for the location. Although different templates will have a few additional options, for the most part all lists and libraries have the same configuration options.

➤ **List name, description and navigation:** This option enables you to update the list title and description that were created when the list was created. You can also select if you would like to display the list on the Quick Launch menu.

➤ **Versioning settings:** These settings enable you to customize how item versions will be managed within the list. These settings can be configured only at the list level and therefore apply to all content within the list:

➤ **Content Approval:** This feature determines if content must first be approved by someone who has approval rights on the list before it becomes available within the list. When this option is selected, all content is uploaded and remains in the draft stage until it is approved as a major version.

➤ **Major version:** This is considered the same as a published version of a document. Over the life of a key organizational document, a site admin is more concerned with a previous major version of a document rather than the minor versions that show specific iterations of the document's creation or modification. You can limit the number of major versions that are retained. This is useful, particularly for libraries, where documents are fairly large in size and change very seldom.

➤ **Minor version:** This is an iteration of the document while in draft mode. This is helpful for scenarios where many people must do work on a document before it is published to the entire organization. Each time a user works on the document and saves it, SharePoint creates a new minor version. However, for long-term editing purposes, the minor versions are not as relevant.

➤ **Draft Item Security:** This setting determines who can read items that are in the draft stage. You can configure this so only the creator and approvers can see it, only the people who can edit content can see it, or so that anyone who can read the content can see the draft versions. You could use different configurations depending on your business requirements. It is important that your users understand how the draft documents are being used within your solution.

➤ **Require Check Out:** This setting requires that a document is first checked out to a user before he or she can edit the document and save it back to the library. This is a great tool to enforce that only one person can be editing the document at a time. This feature is available only within libraries.

➤ **Advanced settings:** These settings allow you to configure some additional items within a library. These settings all have default values that allow the list or library to work without any additional customizations.

➤ **Content Types:** This is where you can configure what specific content types will be associated with your list or library. This topic is covered in detail in Chapter 6.

➤ **Document Template:** When you create a document library, you are asked to select the document template that will be associated with the library by default. An example of this is shown in Figure 4-25. This association does not affect what type of documents you can store in a library, but instead determines the type of file that is created when a user clicks the New button on the Document Library toolbar.

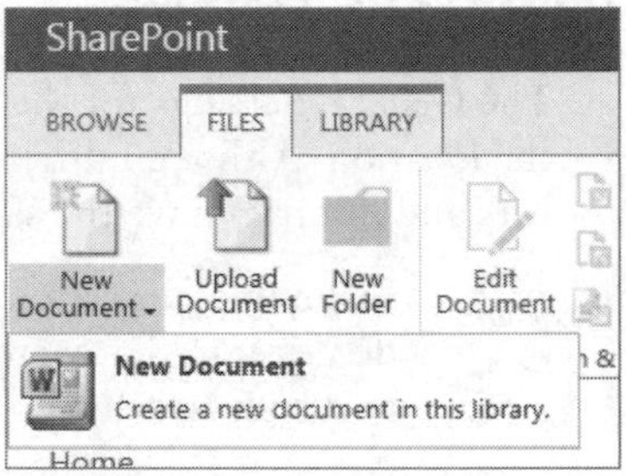

FIGURE 4-25

➤ **Opening Documents in the Browser:** This setting enables you to configure how browser-enabled documents will be opened by default. You can configure them to always open in the browser or always open in the client. Whenever the client application isn't available, they will open in the browser.

➤ **Custom Send to Destination:** This enables you to create a location that is available on the item menu drop-down that can be used to send a copy of an existing document to a new location. It is recommended that you use this feature with caution because it creates additional copies of the same document within the environment.

➤ **Folders:** You can use this setting to disable the ability to create folders within the list or library. This is especially good to do if you are concerned with users creating a deep folder structure.

➤ **Search:** If you do not want the contents of your list or library to be included in the search results, you can restrict them from being added to the index. Oftentimes this isn't necessary, because search results are security trimmed by default.

➤ **Reindex the Document Library:** Clicking this button causes the entire contents of your library to be reindexed during the next scheduled crawl.

> ➤ **Offline Client Availability:** This feature enables you to restrict users from syncing the content with offline clients.

> ➤ **Datasheet:** You would select No for this option if you want to restrict users from editing the list in Datasheet view. This is especially helpful for lists where check out/check in are required or where specific fields (such as enhanced rich text) are not able to be edited in datasheet.

> ➤ **Dialogs:** This feature enables you to configure that all pages open in the full page mode instead of the module dialog (where applicable).

➤ **Validation settings:** The validation settings at the list level (versus the column level discussed previously) enable you to do a comparison of two columns together. An example of this type of validation could include you configuring that the Due Date of the Task in a task list must occur later than the Start Date. If a user enters a value that causes the validation to fail, he or she would see the error message that you configure on this screen.

➤ **Column default value settings:** You can use this page to see all of the columns within the list that have a default value set. This is a shortcut that enables you to see all columns at once instead of having to open each column individually.

➤ **Rating settings:** This is a document library-only feature that allows you to enable ratings for the content within the library. When this has been enabled, users will be able to provide a ranking for the content stored within the library. Figure 4-26 shows a document library that has had the ratings configured.

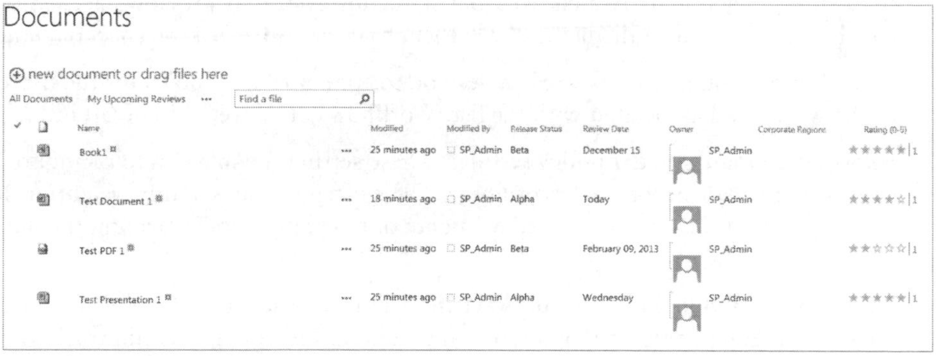

FIGURE 4-26

➤ **Audience targeting settings:** This setting allows you to enable audience targeting for the list, which would allow you to specify a particular audience for each item in the list. Audience settings are part of the User Profile Services and are covered in more detail in Chapter 11, "Working with Social Features."

➤ **Form settings:** For libraries or lists that are compatible with InfoPath forms customization, this setting allows you to enable the form customizations and then to also revert back to the default list views as needed.

Permissions and Management

The Permissions and Management settings for the list or library give you access to some of the list associations such as Workflows and Information Management Policies as well as some of the management tools that can be referenced.

➤ **Delete:** You use this option whenever you need to delete a list. Once the list is deleted you are returned to the homepage.

➤ **Save as a Template:** This option enables you to create a template based on the current list. When created, the template is stored within the site collection gallery and can be used to create new lists within the site collection. This is a great feature that allows you to save time by reusing common list configurations. The following Try It Out walks you through the process of creating a list template.

➤ **Permissions:** This is where you can configure unique permissions for the list or library. For more information on this topic, refer to Chapter 9.

➤ **Manage Files which have no checked in version:** For document libraries you can use this feature to take control of any documents that have been checked out to another user. This is where you can go to access all the files that Raymond has checked out and forgot to check back in before heading out on his weeklong fishing vacation. When you take ownership of the files, they remain in a checked-out state; however, they are now checked out to you, enabling you to update them and check them back in or discard the checkout status.

➤ **Workflow Settings:** This feature enables you to configure workflows for the list and see all of the workflows associated with the list. Workflows are covered in detail in Chapter 5.

➤ **Information management policy settings:** These settings enable you to configure in-place records management for the list or library. This often includes adding retention stages that enable you to start a process based on a date or to create a policy around the management of barcodes or labels.

➤ **Enterprise Metadata and Keywords Settings:** This feature enables you to activate some of the social tagging features that allow you to add tags to content within the library. This feature is covered in greater detail in Chapter 11.

➤ **Generate file plan report:** You can use this link to generate a report that provides a summary view into the configuration of the library. This report gives you details on the number of items in the list, the policies associated with the items, and details around how security is managed for the list. Figure 4-27 shows an example of a File Plan Report for a document library. This is a great tool for troubleshooting configuration issues within a document library.

	A	B	C
1	**Documents: File Plan Report**		
2		Site:	Chapter 04 Screenshots
3		URL:	http://jmason/sites/Chpt4Images/Shared Documents/Forms/AllItems.aspx
4		Description:	
5		Report Generated	2012-08-13T23:22:54
6		Created By:	SP_Admin
7			
8		FolderCount:	1
9		Item Count:	4
10		Versioning:	No versioning
11		Require Content Approval:	No
12		Draft Item Security:	Any user who can read items can see drafts
13		Source of retention schedules:	Content types
14			
15		Has Records:	No
16		Has Items on Hold:	No
17			
18	Content Type	Policy Name	Policy Description
19	Document		
20	Folder		
21			
22			

FIGURE 4-27

Communications

The final area of configuration for a list or library is the communication group. Within this group you can manage the RSS settings for the specific list. Configuring these settings enables you to streamline the data that is available within the default RSS feed for the library.

TRY IT OUT Creating a Custom List

Now that you have covered the basic configuration settings for lists and libraries, in this Try It Out you work through an example that allows you to practice using some of the items that have been discussed. In this example, you create a custom list to represent all the projects for an organization. Based on your meetings with Project Management Office (PMO), you determine that you must implement a project list containing the columns for the project status, due date, project manager, project summary, and client. To effectively track project information, the PMO must have this information on active projects. Clicking the project name should make more detailed information on the summary available.

To meet these requirements, you create a list based on the Custom List template, which has just a single column, called Title. To this, you must add five list-centric columns. In real life, you might want to make some of these site columns so that other lists and sites could use them. However, for simplicity's sake, the example uses the list column model.

Next, you create a custom view on your list based on the information requirements of your stake holders. Because the PMO requested a listing of all active projects, you create a filtered view to show projects with a project status value of In Progress. You then include information that is concise enough for the user to consume easily to gain a high-level understanding of the project, which in this case is the Project Manager, Client, and Due Date. Because the information in the Project Summary tends to be lengthy, you omit it from the initial view.

1. From the main page of your team Site, select the Site Contents item from the navigation menu.
2. Click the "Add an app" option on the Site Contents page.

3. Enter the term **Custom** in the "Find an app" search box.

4. Select the Custom List App.

5. Enter **Projects** for the list name and click OK.

6. Click the new application to open the custom list you just created.

7. From the List tab of the ribbon, select List Settings.

8. From the Columns section, select the Create Column link. The Create Column window appears, similar to what is shown in Figure 4-1.

9. Enter the following details for your column:

PROPERTY	DETAILS
Name	Project Status
Column Type	Choice
Description	Please specify the current status of your project.
Require That This Column Contains Information	Yes
Choice Values	Not Started In Progress Complete Halted
Display Choices Using	Radio buttons
Default Value	Leave blank

10. Click OK to create your column.

11. Create another column using the same steps described previously based on the settings in the following table:

PROPERTY	DETAILS
Name	Project Due Date
Column Type	Date and time
Description	Please enter the date your project is scheduled to be complete.
Require That This Column Contains Information	Yes
Date and Time Format	Date only
Default Value	(none)

12. Click OK to create your column.

13. Create another column based on the following settings:

PROPERTY	DETAILS
Name	Project Manager
Column Type	Person or group
Description	Please specify the project manager for this project.
Require That This Column Contains Information	Yes
Allow Multiple Sections	No
Allow Selection of	People only
Choose From	All users
Show Field	Name (with presence)

14. Click OK to create your column.

15. Create a column based on the following settings:

PROPERTY	DETAILS
Name	Project Summary
Column Type	Multiple Lines of Text
Description	Describe the project by providing some background information and outlining the deliverables.
Require That This Column Contains Information	Yes
Number of lines for editing	25
Type of text to allow	Enhanced Rich Text
Append Changes to Existing Text	No

16. Click OK to create your column.

17. Create another column based on the following settings:

PROPERTY	DETAILS
Name	Client
Column Type	Choice
Description	Specify the client's name
Require That This Column Contains Information	Yes
Choice Values	Customer A Customer B Customer C
Display Choices Using	Drop-down menu
Default Value	Leave blank

18. Click OK to create your column.

19. From the Views section, click the link to Create a new view.

20. Select Standard View.

21. Specify the following details for your view:

PROPERTY	DETAILS
View Name	Active Projects
Audience	Create a Public View
Display Columns and Order	Select to display the columns in the following order: Attachments Title (linked to item with Edit menu) Project Manager Project Due Date Client
Sort	Project Due Date
Filter	Show items when Project Status is equal to In Progress
Group By	None

22. Click OK to create your view.

How It Works

When you create a custom list, you are selecting and choosing all the columns you want to have associated with the list, rather than starting with one of the default list templates. This flexibility allows you to create a list that meets your specific needs.

TRY IT OUT Saving a List as a Template

Once your list is complete, members of your organization can use it. You may even want to save the list as a template so that other teams can use it as a starting point in the future rather than repeating all the steps you took to create this list in the previous Try It Out. Follow these steps to save a list or library as a template:

1. From the Projects list you created in the previous Try It Out, select List Settings from the Lists tab of the ribbon. You are redirected to the Lists Settings page.

2. From the Permissions and Management group of links, select the option to Save list as template. The Save as Template page appears, as shown in Figure 4-28.

FIGURE 4-28

3. Complete the template's properties as follows:

PROPERTY	VALUE
File name	Projects
Template name	Project Listing
Template description	Centralized list template for tracking project status. Includes Active Projects view.
Include Content	Do not select

4. Click OK to create your template. You will receive a message confirming that the operation has completed successfully and your template will be saved in the central list gallery for your site collection. The list will now appear to users when creating new lists on the list creation page, as shown in Figure 4-29.

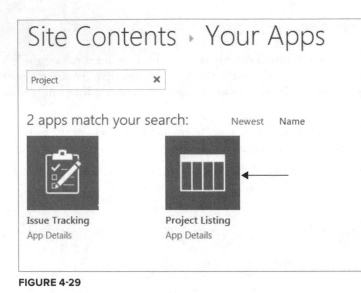

FIGURE 4-29

How It Works

When you save a list template, you are able to create future lists based on the settings and configurations of the current list. The template is added to the Solution Gallery in the site collection and is visible on the new application's page whenever you create a new application for the site collection.

SUMMARY

This chapter discussed how to customize column types and views that are associated with lists and libraries. From it, you learned the following:

➤ The advantages of creating a work environment that closely reflects the users' actual business activities. By customizing SharePoint to operate in accordance with common business processes, users can focus more on their specific work duties rather than on technology. However, it is always important to remember not to over-customize. You should only implement changes that offer value to the business and operational environment.

➤ The types of columns that you can create in SharePoint and their specific configuration alternatives. Understanding what is possible from a configuration perspective is a key element in recognizing the appropriate customization approach.

➤ The difference between the different types of columns in SharePoint.

➤ The various view types in SharePoint and the process for creating each.

➤ The configuration options that you can customize for each list or library that you create. Being able to customize these lists and libraries enables you to easily create a very specific and focused business solution for your users.

EXERCISES

You've just been assigned the task of customizing the SharePoint site for your company's sales team. The team has struggled with having a central location in which to store all information related to its various opportunities, contacts, meetings, and tasks. It has had a SharePoint site for a few months; however, the team has expressed some concerns that information is too difficult to find. The following exercises focus on ways in which you need to develop the site to become a more useful tool for the sales team.

1. After conducting a planning workshop with some members of the sales team, you determine that while the sales manager wants to see all information stored in a single location, the actual sales team members struggle with seeing too much information. As a result, it takes sales team members longer than necessary to look up contact phone numbers. The sales team prefers to see contacts only from their own region. What can you do to make both groups happy?

2. Whenever a salesperson views the central list of contacts, he/she wants to see specific contacts that he/she has added. How would you accomplish that?

3. The sales manager wants to see a list of all opportunities that are in the pipeline for his staff. Because he has some concerns about the length of time certain sales staff members are taking to close their leads, he wants to visually identify leads that have the longest duration from initial point of contact to the expected date of sale. What can you suggest to help address this situation?

▶ **WHAT YOU LEARNED IN THIS CHAPTER**

TOPIC	KEY CONCEPTS
Site columns	A site column is a column that is defined within a central gallery and may be used within multiple lists or libraries.
Major versions versus minor versions	A major version is considered to be a published release of a document, whereas minor versions typically represent a draft.
Configuration options for lists and libraries	Many different configurations are available for lists and libraries. Each list or library can be configured in a very granular approach, enabling you to easily configure a custom solution that maps directly to user requirements.

5

Working with Workflows

WHAT YOU WILL LEARN IN THIS CHAPTER:

➤ The definition of workflows and basic workflow concepts

➤ How to create powerful custom workflows using SharePoint Designer 2013

➤ How to use tasks and workflow history in workflows

➤ Troubleshooting steps and basic workflow administration processes

Business processes exist within all companies. These processes not only consist of computer interactions, but more importantly, they are between individuals. SharePoint brings processes together with tasks and the people who are part of these day-to-day interactions.

Workflows are used to automate business processes, promoting a more efficient work experience. When defined and created in SharePoint, automated workflows lessen confusion and save time and money.

This chapter covers SharePoint 2013 workflows and their features and capabilities. The new SharePoint 2013 workflow engine, which your server administrator can install on your server, is a prerequisite. This chapter does not cover the old SharePoint 2010 workflows, which means that if the 2013 workflow engine is not there, this chapter will not be applicable to your environment.

> **NOTE** *Your server administrator can follow the instructions in the following links:*
>
> ➤ *Installing and configuring workflow for SharePoint Server 2013*: `http://technet.microsoft.com/en-us/library/jj658588`
>
> ➤ *Installing Workflow Manager 1.0*: `http://technet.microsoft.com/en-us/library/jj193448`

Some steps in this chapter also use the new workflow Visual Designer. The prerequisite for this is to have Visio 2013 Professional installed on the same computer as SharePoint Designer 2013.

UNDERSTANDING WORKFLOWS

Before delving into the details of how to use workflows in SharePoint 2013, it is important to have a basic understanding of some of the terminology and the components that you use to create workflows. This section introduces you to the basic building blocks of workflows. Business users can use logic to create their own applications and processes, without having to know a single line of code.

Initiating Workflows

You can use four different methods to start a workflow, which is referred to as *initiation*. The first three are available options within the user interface during workflow creation, and the fourth is available from within Information Management Policy settings. You can set up each workflow to use one or multiple methods of initiation:

➤ **On Creation:** The workflow is started only once, when a new item is created.

➤ **On Change:** The workflow is started each time an item is edited.

➤ **Manual Initiation:** The workflow is started manually. This entails a user clicking a Start button. The out-of-the-box workflows specify that the user who manually starts the workflow must have Edit Item permissions, and you have an option to increase the security by opting to Require Manage Lists Permissions to start the workflow.

➤ **Information Management Policies:** When workflows are associated with content types, you can set up information management policies at the site or library content type level. When you define a retention policy, you can set it to initiate a workflow relative to a date column. To set up a workflow to only be initiated based on a policy, none of the other initiation types needs to be selected. You can even configure retention policies as repeating — for example, if there is a need to start a workflow every 30 days. The Information Management Policies link is in the list or library settings page.

Initiation Forms

When a workflow is set up to be started manually, it uses an initiation form. The person who makes the workflow can create predefined fields to be filled out by the person who manually starts the workflow (the initiator). When workflows are automatically initiated on creation or on change, there is no prompt to fill out a form.

Steps

Steps in a workflow define the order in which processes are supposed to happen. Each step can contain conditions and actions. Arrange the steps in the order in which the process should take place.

Stages

Stages are placed in a workflow to make use of the new "Go to a stage" action that you can use in the Transition stage at the end of each stage. This means that instead of the workflow running once from top to bottom, you can set it to go to another specific stage of the workflow. The action called "Go to a stage" enables you to jump from one spot (stage) in the workflow to another, either forward or backward.

Conditions and Actions

Conditions can be thought of as rules. According to conditions that are set up, specified actions take place. Conditions are not a required component in a workflow. Actions *without* conditions in front of them will take place every time the workflow is initiated.

If the first condition is not met, the next condition is checked. This type of logic requires an else-if branch. When a condition is reached, and that condition is true, then its actions take place. If you've ever created rules in Microsoft Outlook, the basic concept is similar.

Loops

Loops allow the workflow to run a certain set of conditions and/or actions over and over again. You can add a loop and set it to run a specific number of times, or you can set a loop to run repeatedly while a certain condition exists. For example, you can set a condition so that the loop runs repeatedly when one value or field is equal to another value or field.

Workflow Associations

Each time a workflow is created, it is associated with *something* in SharePoint. To associate a workflow is to attach it to something. Lists, libraries, content types, and even sites are all things that workflows can be associated with.

➤ **Content workflows:** Content workflows are associated with specific content in SharePoint, such as a specific list or library. These are also referred to as *list workflows*.

➤ **Site workflows:** Site workflows are not connected to any particular list or library, and these types of workflows are usually initiated manually. On a SharePoint site, click View All Site Content on the left side of the screen. The Site Workflows button is next to the Create button.

➤ **Reusable workflows:** Similar to site workflows, these types of workflows are not bound to any specific list when they are initially created. Reusable workflows are created to be used multiple times and can be reused on different sites. These workflows can be connected to different lists and libraries. When you create a reusable workflow in SharePoint Designer, you have an option to pick a base content type to limit the workflow to. You can select all content types or one particular one, such as Announcement.

CREATING CUSTOM WORKFLOW SOLUTIONS

In SharePoint Designer 2013, the easy user interface lets you create your own rules-based workflows.

You can also create custom workflows with Visual Studio, and these are even more flexible and scalable than the ones in SharePoint Designer. These types of workflows are created by developers, and are tested and then installed in the production environment.

In this section, you get an in-depth understanding of how to get around in the SharePoint Designer interface and create custom workflows. SharePoint Designer 2013 is a free application that you can obtain from Microsoft's download site.

> **WARNING** *When the top-level site (root of the site collection) is opened in SharePoint Designer, be careful with the out-of-the-box workflow templates. Changes made at this level do propagate down to every subsite. If it is necessary to change an out-of-the-box workflow, the best practice is to click Copy & Modify. Make changes to the copy instead of the original and then publish it.*

Getting around the List of Workflows

The first thing to get familiar with is the workflow design interface. Open a SharePoint site in SharePoint Designer 2013 and click Workflows in the left navigation's Site Objects section. The contextual ribbon contains options for creating new workflows, editing workflow properties, and managing workflows (see Figure 5-1). The main content section of the page displays a list of the existing workflows on the site.

FIGURE 5-1

New

Use these buttons to create new workflows. These options were discussed in the "Workflow Associations" section earlier in this chapter.

Edit

Select an existing workflow's row in the list of workflows, and use these buttons to access that workflow's settings, edit the workflow itself, or delete it.

Manage

This section enables you to manage workflows and their associations. These buttons are related to how each workflow is associated with lists and content types, and the options in this section all enable you to take action on the workflow as a whole.

➤ **Save as Template:** Save the selected workflow to the Site Assets of the current site. Go to the site's Site Assets library to find the saved template as a WSP solution file.

➤ **Copy & Modify:** This option is available only for reusable workflows. It enables you to create a duplicate copy of the workflow, which you can then modify.

➤ **Import from Visio:** Create a SharePoint workflow flowchart in Microsoft Visio 2013, and import the diagram into SharePoint to create a workflow based from it.

➤ **Export to Visio:** You can export all types of workflows, except for site workflows, to become Visio Workflow Interchange (VWI) files.

➤ **Associate to List:** Available only to reusable workflows, this button shows a drop-down list of the lists on the site that can be associated with the workflow. Clicking a list name creates the association. If a workflow has been created to be associated with a certain content type, only the lists of that same content type will be displayed as options to choose from.

➤ **Associate to Content Type:** This button is also available only when a reusable workflow is selected. Pick a site content type to associate the workflow with. Every list on the site that contains that content type will then have that workflow associated with it.

Getting around the Workflow Settings

For existing workflows, you have several configuration options within that workflow's settings page. Figure 5-2 shows the contextual ribbon options.

FIGURE 5-2

Save

You can save workflows before publishing them, which means that if a workflow isn't ready to go into production and needs to be completed later, you save it without having to publish it and go live. Making a workflow available on the site or library is now a two-step process: Save the workflow and then publish it.

Edit

Edit the workflow itself by setting up the order of the steps, conditions, and actions. You can also delete or rename the workflow from here.

Manage

Use the Save as Template button to make the workflow portable and usable on another site. This template file gets saved as a `.WSP` file in your Site Assets library.

For reusable workflows, use the Associate to List button to attach that workflow to one or more lists. Once the workflow has been associated with a list or library, it can be initiated from that location using the start options that you specify.

Variables

Variables are values that exist in a workflow only during the time that the workflow is running. For example, if a new list item is created via a workflow, the ID of that item is automatically returned to the workflow as a variable. This ID can be utilized later in the workflow, in cases where data needs to be obtained *from* or sent *to* the other list. Once the workflow is finished, this variable does not exist anymore.

➤ **Initiation form parameters:** When a workflow is manually initiated, the initiation form parameters are the fields that users fill out when they start the workflow. The association parameters are collected when a reusable workflow is attached to a list. For each parameter that you add on this screen, choose the field type and whether it is to be collected during initiation, association, or both. Read more about this subject later in this chapter in the section called "Variables and Parameters."

➤ **Local variables:** This is a list of all the variables that exist in the workflow. Each variable has a type, such as string, number, or date.

The Content Section

The options on the main content section of the page differ depending on the type of workflow.

Workflow Information

The workflow information is basic data such as the name and description of the workflow. Some of these basics will vary according to the type of workflow. Simply click the name or description to edit them. Figure 5-3 shows an example of the Workflow Information section for a list workflow. This screen shows when you open an existing workflow or when you click the Workflow Settings button in an already opened workflow.

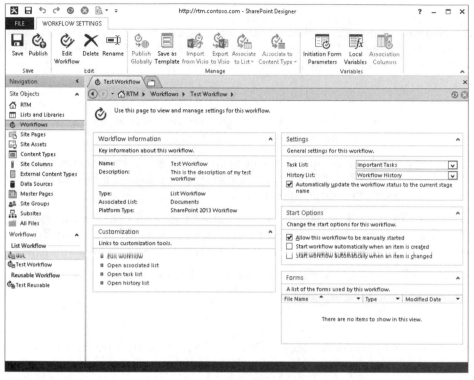

FIGURE 5-3

➤ **Name:** Descriptive naming of workflows is important not only for you as the workflow's creator, but also for the workflow initiator as well. The name should give you a quick indication of what the workflow does and what it is associated with. For workflows that automatically run when items are created or changed, the end users won't see the names. As the administrator, you will see the list of workflow names when administrating the workflows. For example, the workflow could be named "Create Announcements," if it were set up to run each time a new announcement is created.

➤ **Description:** When workflows are manually initiated, this description is displayed to end users along with the workflow name. Describe to the users why they would run this workflow.

➤ **Type:** This is the workflow type, such as List Workflow, Site Workflow, or Reusable Workflow.

➤ **Associated List:** List workflows display the name of the associated list.

➤ **Platform Type:** This indicates whether the workflow runs on the SharePoint 2010 or 2013 workflow engine.

➤ **Content Types:** Only reusable workflows display the name of the content type that they are associated with.

Customization

This section contains quick links to open the associated list, associated task or history lists, or to edit the current workflow. If the workflow is reusable, you will see only an Edit Workflow link here. All workflows have an Edit Workflow link here and in the ribbon.

Settings

You can select a task list and history list here. If you assign tasks anywhere within the workflow, this is where you create them. Reusable workflows do not give these options.

There is also a checkbox called "Automatically update the workflow status to the current stage name." The first time that a workflow is run in a list or library, a new column is created automatically in that list with the same name as the workflow.

With this box checked, this column displays the current status of the workflow. If a workflow only has a stage called "Stage 1," then after that workflow has run on an item, the value in this column will be a hyperlink that says "Stage 1," which you can click to get to the workflow status page.

If this box is *not* checked, the workflow column will be empty. In this case, you can get to the workflow status page by using the Workflows button on the Items tab in the ribbon.

Start Options

Determine when the workflow will be initiated by checking the appropriate boxes here in the Start Options. You can select all or any one of the options. Choose for the workflow to run manually, on item creation, or when an item is changed. By default, when a workflow is created, it is only set to be manually started. For a list workflow, when the workflow can be manually started, there is an additional checkbox, Require Manage List permissions, which means that only users with that permission level or higher on the list will be able to initiate the workflow. Reusable workflows use the opposite syntax than list workflows. With these, all start options are available by default, and you can check each box to *disable* that option.

Forms

This section contains the list of InfoPath forms that are used in the current workflow, only if you are currently using an old SharePoint 2010 workflow. In SharePoint 2013, InfoPath is no longer used for these forms. If your workflow has any initiation parameters, a file called `WFInitForm.aspx` will be generated automatically when the workflow is published.

Editing Workflows

The Workflow Editor is the meat and potatoes of the workflow. This is where you do most of your work. Figure 5-4 shows the ribbon commands available.

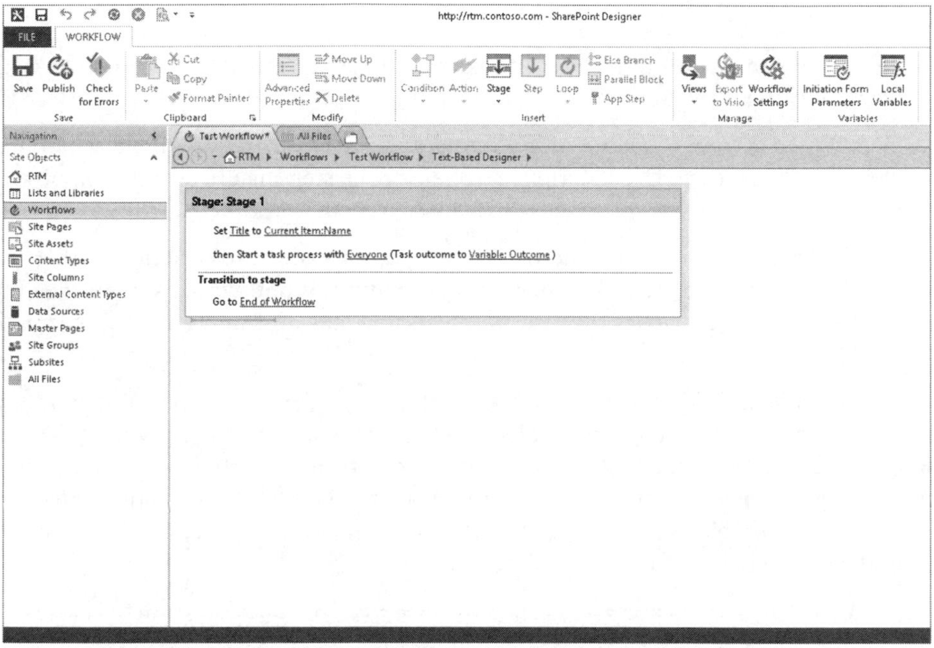

FIGURE 5-4

➤ Save:

  ➤ **Save:** Save your changes without putting them in production yet.

  ➤ **Publish:** Put your workflow into production.

  ➤ **Check for Errors:** Check the logic in the workflow to make sure that it makes sense and will run correctly.

➤ Clipboard:

  ➤ **Paste, Cut, Copy:** New in SharePoint Designer 2013 is the ability to cut, copy, and paste components of the workflow in different places within the workflow. These options are also available by right-clicking any object in the workflow.

➤ Modify:

  ➤ **Advanced Properties:** Each condition and action in the workflow has advanced properties for further configuration. Select the name of the condition or action, and click this button to modify the properties. They are different depending on what kind of item is selected.

  ➤ **Move Up and Move Down:** Rearrange the pieces of the workflow by selecting one and clicking the Move Up or Move Down buttons.

  ➤ **Delete:** Delete the selected action from the workflow.

➤ **Insert:**

>   ➤ **Stage:** Put your cursor outside of any existing stage in order to create another stage before or after it.

>   ➤ **Step:** A step is the next group of conditions and actions that is to take place in the workflow's sequence. Use descriptive names for the steps as documentation of your process.

>   ➤ **Else-If Branch:** If a certain condition is met, you can add several actions under that condition, but what needs to happen if the condition is not met? Insert an else-if branch to define processes this way. If a workflow has no conditions, this button is disabled.

>   ➤ **Parallel Block:** When several actions need to take place at the exact same time, and not in sequence, insert a parallel block and place the actions inside of it. Do not use a parallel block if any its actions rely on something that took place in a previous action in the block. A new advanced property of a parallel block enables you to add a Boolean variable as a completion condition. If the value is true, only the first item in the parallel block will be completed.

> **NOTE** *You can also insert conditions and actions, as covered in the next two sections, respectively.*

➤ **Manage:**

>   ➤ **Views:** Switch back and forth between the text-based designer, and the Visual Designer. When you are on the Visual Designer, there is a button in the ribbon called Generate Stage Outline, next to the Views button. When dealing with a large and complex workflow, it's nice to be able to see the big picture view, where you can jump to a specific stage of the workflow.

>   ➤ **Workflow Settings:** Go to the Workflow Settings screen (refer to Figure 5-3).

Conditions

Several conditions are available, depending on which type of workflow you create. You can select multiple conditions, and you can set up the workflow to look at *all* or *any* of them. As shown in Figure 5-5 (in the highlighted part of the workflow), when conditions are set, the "and" link can be toggled to "or."

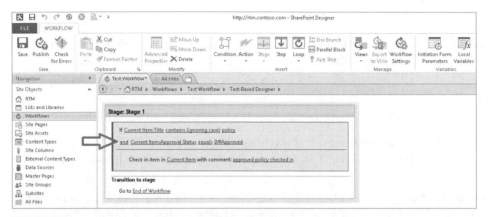

FIGURE 5-5

The following table contains a list of conditions with their descriptions, along with the types of workflows in which they are available.

CONDITION NAME	TYPE OF WORKFLOW	DESCRIPTION
If any value equals value	All Workflows	Compare any two fields to each other, from any list or library on the site. When fields from other lists are selected, a matching field must be selected in the "Find the List Item" section.
Created by a specific person	List and Reusable Workflows	Pick a person from groups on the site, from within the list (Workflow Lookup), or simply "User who created current item."
Created in a specific date span	List and Reusable Workflows	Pick two dates as the beginning and end of the span, from date fields in the list or by typing specific dates.
Modified by a specific person	List and Reusable Workflows	Pick a person from groups on the site, from within the list (Workflow Lookup), or simply "User who created current item."
Modified in a specific date span	List and Reusable Workflows	Pick two dates as the beginning and end of the span, from date fields in the list or by typing specific dates.
Person is a valid SharePoint user	All Workflows	This condition ensures that the person selected is not anonymous. This condition is commonly used to look at the "User who created current item."
Title field contains keywords	List and Reusable Workflows	Look at the title field of the current list. This condition is case sensitive.

Actions

Whether or not any conditions exist in a workflow, actions are the activities that happen when a workflow is triggered. This section describes each action and includes some examples.

Core Actions

The core actions are the most commonly used actions in SharePoint Designer workflows:

➤ **Add a Comment:** Add a comment that stays here in the workflow designer and does not have any effect on the site data. This is simply for documentation purposes for the workflow creator.

➤ **Add Time to Date:** Do a calculation that adds time to a date field. Pick from minutes, hours, days, months, or years, and obtain a variable that contains this new calculation.

➤ **Build Dictionary:** In programming terms, this could be likened to an array. Build a list of items that will be used or referenced from within the workflow. Give each item in the dictionary a name, type, and a value.

➤ **Count Items in a Dictionary:** After you use the Build Dictionary action, use this action to count the items in that specific dictionary's variable output.

➤ **Get an Item from a Dictionary:** Once you build a dictionary, retrieve a specific item and output that value to a variable.

➤ **Call HTTP Web Service:** Enter the URL to a web service, and pick GET, PUT, POST, or DELETE. Pick a variable as a request to send, and decide in which variables to store the response and response headers. Not only can you tap into SharePoint's built-in web services, but you can also use custom ones that a programmer has written, or from third-party applications.

➤ **Do Calculation:** Perform calculations between two different number columns, or manually typed numbers. The available calculations are addition, subtraction, division, multiplication, or mod. The answer is set as a variable in the workflow.

➤ **Log to History List:** This is an important action, and should be used often. This action logs information to the workflow history regarding what is going on during the workflow. It is a best practice, especially when troubleshooting, to create these actions after each step and action that happens in the workflow. When you view the workflow status, this logged information lets you see what has taken place so far. Without any "Log to History List" actions in a workflow, it will often run and show as "Completed" without any further detailed information.

➤ **Pause for Duration:** Put the workflow on hold for a certain number of days, hours, or minutes. You can type each of the number fields in this step manually, or you can select them from existing number fields.

➤ **Pause until Date:** Put the workflow on hold until a specific date, or until the value of a date column.

➤ **Send an Email:** Send a custom e-mail to recipients. Pick recipients from members of the site or from values within fields. The subject and body of the e-mail can contain manually typed text in combination with fields inserted from a list. You can also insert hyperlinks into the body of the e-mail, with fully customizable links and text.

➤ **Set Time Portion of Date/Time Field:** Pick a date field and select the exact time that should exist as the time portion of that field, and the new date/time becomes a variable in the workflow.

➤ **Set Workflow Status:** Choose to set the workflow status to any value.

➤ **Set Workflow Variable:** Create a new workflow variable, and set it to a certain value. Select from a list of existing variables or create a new one. You can set the value of the variable as the exact value from a field, or you can use the String Builder to create a custom one.

Coordination Actions

These actions involve interactions with another workflow on the site.

➤ **Start a List Workflow:** Initiate a SharePoint 2010 workflow that runs on the same site, and pass a parameter to it.

➤ **Start a Site Workflow:** Initiate a specific SharePoint 2010 site workflow on the site, and pass a parameter to it.

List Actions

The title of this section of actions is a bit misleading. You can perform a lot of the list actions on both lists and libraries.

➤ **Check-In Item:** Because list items do not have the check-in/out capability, checking items in and out through a workflow applies only to items in libraries. The item will be set as checked in by the user who is currently running the workflow.

➤ **Check-Out Item:** The item will be set as checked out by the user who is currently running the workflow.

➤ **Copy Document:** When copying a document from one list to another, it helps if the lists contain the same content type. Only the common site columns will be copied when a document is copied from one library to another. This action can only be performed from library to library, and lists are not available to choose from.

➤ **Create List Item:** In contrast to the Copy List Item action, this action allows for more granular creation of an item in another list or library. Select a destination list or library in the current List drop-down box, and then pick each field in the list one at a time to set what the value needs to be. Figure 5-6 shows the creation of a new list item in a calendar. By default, because the Title, Start Time, and End Time are required fields in

FIGURE 5-6

the list, they each have asterisks next to them. The values in the Field column are in the calendar, and the values in the Value column can be either manually typed in or selected from list values or workflow variables.

➤ **Delete Item:** Delete an item in a list or library.

➤ **Discard Check Out Item:** When a checked-out item is discarded, this means that the changes made during the current check out are lost.

➤ **Set Field in Current Item:** Set the value of any field in the current list to a certain value. This value can be taken from any other field in any list in the current site, or workflow variables, or context. This action is not available in site workflows.

➤ **Update List Item:** Compared to the Create List Item action, which creates a new item, this action finds an already existing item and modifies it. The interface is similar to that of the Create List Item action, but an additional section is required, called Find the List Item. To find the correct list item to update, a field in the target list must match up with a workflow variable or other list value, so that a join is defined between the updated list and the current list.

➤ **Wait for Event in List Item:** This action lets you wait for an item to be created or changed in another list or library in the same site, or in the current list or library.

➤ **Wait for Field Change in Current Item:** Pick a field, and then pick a value that you would like to wait for it to be changed to. The workflow will stay in a pending state until the field has been changed.

Task Actions

The assignment of tasks plays a huge role in many workflows; therefore, you can use two different methods to assign tasks from within the workflow designer. Each task that is created will contain a Complete Task button for the assignee to click. Not only are there options to select the participant(s) for approval, with a task title and description and due date, but some enhancements are worth pointing out:

➤ **Assignee Options:** The "Wait for task completion" checkbox enables you to determine whether or not the workflow itself should keep moving to the next action after the task is assigned, or if it should wait in a pending state for the task to be completed. Previous versions of SharePoint did not give this option, and workflows always waited for task completion before moving on. The Associated Item box has a grayed-out appearance, but this does not mean it is not functional. Click the little ellipsis button to the right to select other lists in your site, so that the workflow action can be run on an item other than the current item in the current list or library.

➤ **Email Options:** When you check the Send Emails box, you have options to edit the task creation e-mail and the overdue task e-mail, along with the frequency of overdue notifications.

➤ **Outcome Options:** At first glance, it appears that you don't have many options to choose from here, besides determining the default outcome. On the Site Settings screen, you can create new workflow task content types and new Task Outcome site columns.

The following table compares the differences between the two task actions.

ACTION	RETURNS TASK ID AS VARIABLE	ASSIGN TO MULTIPLE GROUPS AND USERS	ASSIGNEE OPTIONS
Assign a Task	Yes	No	Pick one participant.
Start a Task Process	No	Yes	Pick more than one participant, select serial or parallel, and select completion criteria.

> **NOTE** To create new task columns that are not already included in the task, you must create a new content type based on the Task content type and add new columns to that content type. In the workflow task's Outcome Options, pick your new content type in the Task Content Type drop-down.

Utility Actions

The utility actions allow granular control over how strings are structured. If you are familiar with Excel functions such as LEFT, RIGHT, and MID, these utilities will be easy to understand. For each of these actions, the data that is extracted becomes a workflow variable.

➤ **Extract Substring from End of String:** Define the number of characters needed from the end (right) of a specified field.

➤ **Extract Substring from Start of String:** Define the number of characters needed from the beginning (left) of a specified field.

➤ **Extract Substring from Index of String:** Set the number of characters at which to start copying the data from a field. Starting at that number, the value of the rest of the field will be obtained.

➤ **Extract Substring of String from Index with Length:** This one is similar to the previous action, except that instead of grabbing the rest of the field's value starting with a character number, this action lets you start at a certain character number, and obtain only a defined number of characters from that point.

➤ **Find Interval Between Dates:** Find out the number of minutes, hours, or days between one date and another.

➤ **Find Substring in String:** Define the string that needs to be found, and then pick the field in which to search. The output will be an integer.

➤ **Replace Substring in String:** Define the string that needs to be replaced, then define what you want to replace it with, followed by the field where this string exists. The output variable will be the new string value with the string replaced.

➤ **Trim String:** This action removes all the blanks from the beginning and end of the field that is selected, and outputs the new trimmed value to a string variable.

Custom Ribbon Buttons

A commonly asked question about starting workflows is: "Why does it take so many clicks to initiate a workflow? Can't I just click a button there on the item?" This issue has been addressed with the ability to create custom actions in SharePoint Designer. You do this not from within the workflows, but from within the Lists and Libraries.

In SharePoint Designer, click Lists & Libraries on the left, and click the name of a list. Click inside of the Custom Actions section at the bottom right. A new Custom Actions section of the ribbon appears. The Custom Actions button is a drop-down box (see Figure 5-7).

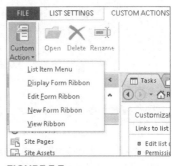

Click the name of the location where you would like this new button to appear. After you type the name and description, choose the Initiate Workflow option and pick the name of a workflow from the drop-down box. Only workflows that are associated with the list will be displayed here.

FIGURE 5-7

Variables and Parameters

Variables and parameters are values that are used within a workflow. Parameters are values that are filled in on an initiation form by a user when the workflow is being manually started. Variables are values that exist within the workflow only while it is running, and were defined earlier in the chapter in the section called "Variables." As you work through the next example, the meaning of a variable will become clearer within the context of the workflow.

TRY IT OUT Creating a SharePoint Designer Workflow

In this Try It Out, you learn how to create your own custom SharePoint Designer workflow from beginning to end. The scenario is a very simple company store, where employees can have items delivered to their office. The store site consists of a library of items and an order list. You use the workflow to calculate the total cost of an item when it is ordered. This workflow consists of two actions, as follows:

➤ Multiply item quantity by the price.

➤ Use the result of the calculation to set the total cost.

1. On your SharePoint site, create a custom list called Store Items.

2. Create a new currency column in the list called Price.

3. Create several sample items in this list, each with a title and price.

4. Create a new custom list on the site called Store Orders.

5. In the Store Orders list, create new columns as defined in the following table.

COLUMN NAME	COLUMN TYPE	DETAILS
Store Item	Lookup	Get information from the Store Items list, in the Title column
Quantity	Number	Zero decimal places
Total Cost	Currency	Two decimal places

6. The goal is that when people fill out the Store Orders list, the workflow will run when an item is created, which will automatically fill in the total cost. Therefore, you can hide the title and total cost from the user filling out the form. In the Store Orders List Settings, click Advanced Settings link in the General Settings area of the page.

7. In the Content Types section, change "Allow management of content types" to Yes. Click OK.

8. Now that the management of content types is turned on, you can set form fields as hidden. In the Content Types section in the middle of the list settings page, click the "Item" content type.

9. Change Title and Total Cost to Hidden, as shown in Figure 5-8. Note that even though certain fields have been hidden from the forms that users fill out, these columns are still shown in the default view of the list.

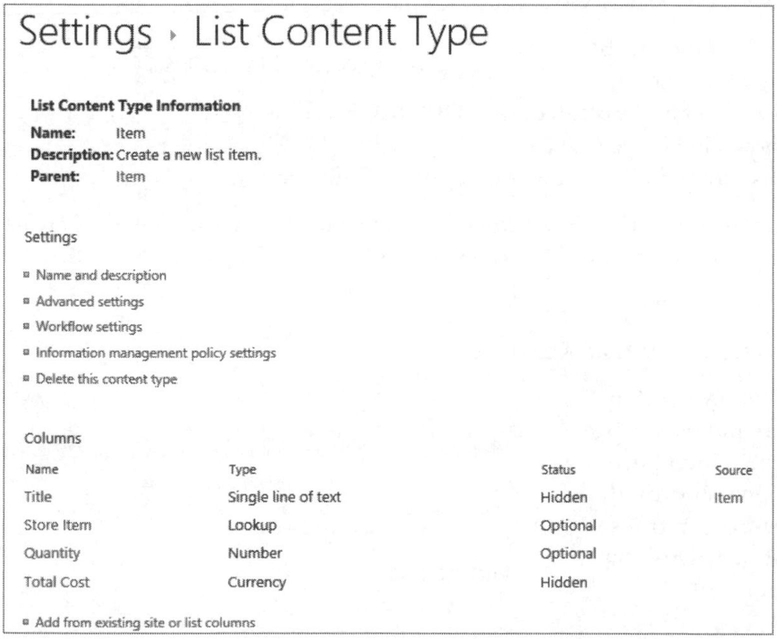

Settings › List Content Type

List Content Type Information
Name: Item
Description: Create a new list item.
Parent: Item

Settings

▫ Name and description
▫ Advanced settings
▫ Workflow settings
▫ Information management policy settings
▫ Delete this content type

Columns

Name	Type	Status	Source
Title	Single line of text	Hidden	Item
Store Item	Lookup	Optional	
Quantity	Number	Optional	
Total Cost	Currency	Hidden	

▫ Add from existing site or list columns

FIGURE 5-8

10. Back on the Store Orders list, click the ellipsis next to the name of the All Items view at the top of the list. Choose Modify this view.

11. Uncheck the box next to the Title column. Make sure that the boxes *are* checked next to Quantity, Store Item, Total Cost, and Created By. Click OK.

12. Now it's time to create the workflow. Still on the Store Orders list, click the List tab in the ribbon.

13. Click the Workflow drop-down box at the top right. Choose Create a Workflow in SharePoint Designer.

> **NOTE** *You can also access SharePoint Designer 2013 workflows by clicking Start and choosing All Programs ⇨ SharePoint ⇨ Microsoft SharePoint Designer 2013. Click to Open Site, and use the full URL to your site. Once the site is opened in SharePoint Designer, click Workflows on the left.*

14. The SharePoint Designer 2013 application runs, and a Create List Workflow screen pops up. Name the workflow **Create Store Order**, and type the description as **This workflow is used to process new orders in the company store.** Click OK.

> **WARNING** *On step 14, if the platform type is not SharePoint 2013 Workflow, this exercise will not work. These steps are only for creating SharePoint 2013 workflows, and do not apply to SharePoint 2010 workflows.*

15. The Workflow Editor is now shown. Before adding any actions, you need to set up the workflow to run each time an item is created. In the breadcrumb trail shown in Figure 5-9, click Create Store Order. This shows the workflow's main information screen.

◀ ▶ ▾ 🏠 Home ▶ Workflows ▶ Create Store Order ▶ Text-Based Designer ▶

FIGURE 5-9

16. In the Start Options section, select the "Start workflow automatically when an item is created" checkbox. Uncheck the "Allow this workflow to be manually started" option.

17. Click Save at the top left.

18. In the Customization section, click Edit Workflow.

19. The text-based editor is shown with a blank "Stage 1," with a blinking orange line inside of it. Click the Action button in the ribbon, which shows a list of all the available actions. In the Core Actions section, choose Do Calculation. This empty action is shown in Figure 5-10.

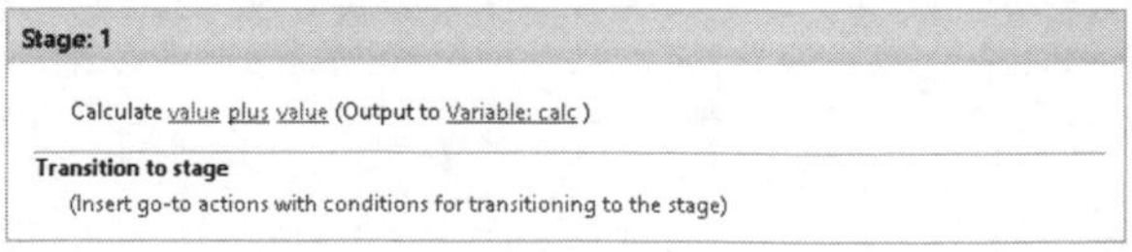

Stage: 1

    Calculate <u>value</u> <u>plus</u> <u>value</u> (Output to <u>Variable: calc</u>)

Transition to stage
(Insert go-to actions with conditions for transitioning to the stage)

FIGURE 5-10

20. Each of the underlined text items is configurable. Click on the first word "value," and click the function button (fx). Select the Quantity field from the data source called Current Item, as shown in Figure 5-11. Click OK.

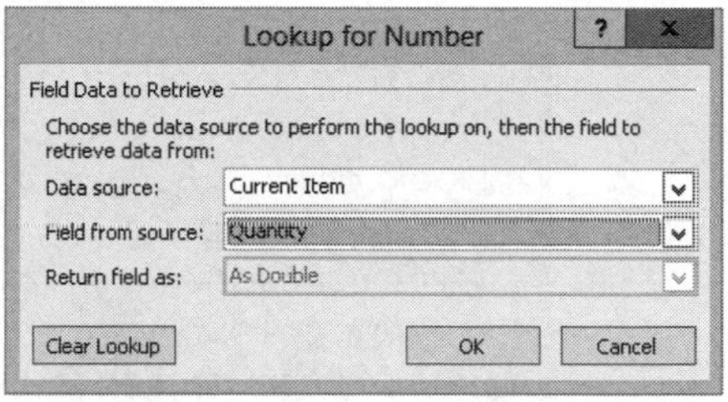

21. Click the word "plus," and change it to "multiply by." Click the second underlined word "value."

This is where the workflow gets fancy, because the cost of the item will be looked up from another list.

FIGURE 5-11

22. Change the Data source to the Store Items list. In Field from source, select Price.

23. Because the source was changed to another list, a new section appears in the bottom of the dialog box, called Find the List Item. In the Field drop-down, select ID.

24. For the Value, click the function button (fx) and choose the Store Item field from the Current Item data source drop-down menu.

25. In the "Return field as" box, select "Lookup ID (as Integer)." Click OK. These dialog boxes are shown in Figure 5-12.

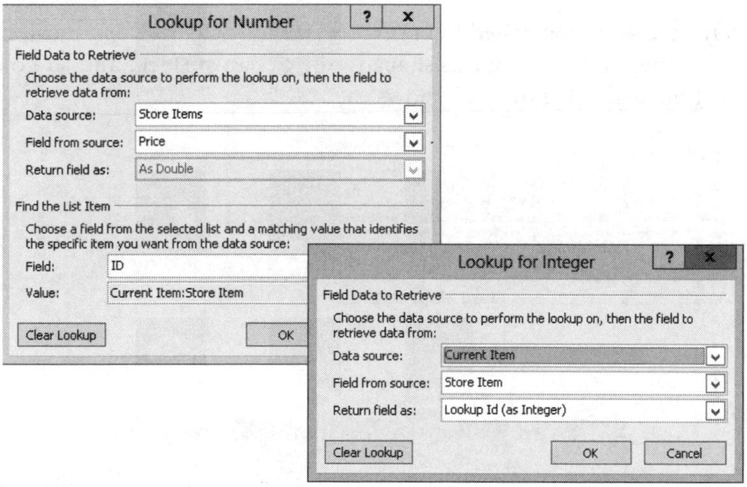

FIGURE 5-12

26. After you have clicked OK on both dialog boxes, back on the workflow edit screen, click the name of the Variable: calc. It's a good practice to give good descriptive names to workflow variables, instead of using the generic default ones. Click "Create a new variable."

> **NOTE** It is important to understand at this point that when looking up the price for the item that is being ordered, the "Store Item" that the user selects in the lookup field is being matched with the ID of the item in the Store Items list. Every SharePoint list and library has a built-in field called ID that is always unique. When one list contains a Lookup column to another list, the selected item's ID is what is actually stored in the lookup field. In workflows, when using the Find the List Item section to match one list to another, it is not required that ID fields are used, but these are simply preferable because they are guaranteed to be unique.

27. Name the new variable **Total Cost Calculation,** with a type of Number. Click OK.

28. The next step is to add a second action to occur after the first Do Calculation action. So far, you have used the text-based editor, so it's time to try out the new visual editor as you continue editing the workflow. In the ribbon at the top of SharePoint Designer, click Views, and choose Visual Designer.

> **WARNING** If Visio 2013 is not installed on your computer, the Visual Designer will not be available.

29. In the Shapes area on the left, in the section called "Actions - SharePoint 2013 Workflow", find the shape called "Set field in current item." Drag this shape to the design surface, and let go of it to the right of the Do calculation shape. Figure 5-13 shows the result.

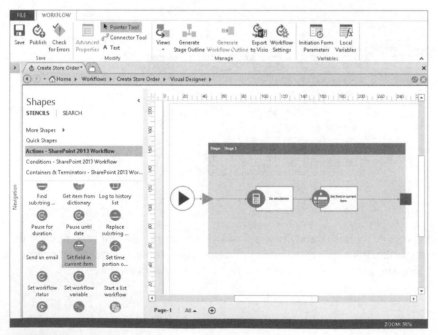

FIGURE 5-13

30. Hover over the "Set field in current item" shape, and click the drop-down box shown in Figure 5-14. Click the word "Field," and choose the Total Cost field from the drop-down box.

31. Click the word "value," and click the function (fx) button. Change the Data source to Workflow Variables and Parameters.

FIGURE 5-14

32. In the "Field from source" box, choose the name of the variable that you just defined: Total Cost Calculation. Click OK and then OK again.

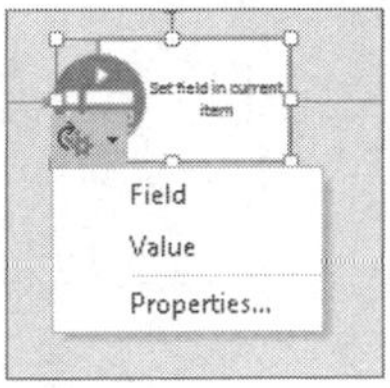

33. Click the Save button at the top left, and then click the Publish button (leave the workflow screen open after publishing).

34. On the Store Orders list in the browser, click New Item. Add a new item in the list. Pick an item and quantity, and click Save. This new item form is shown in Figure 5-15

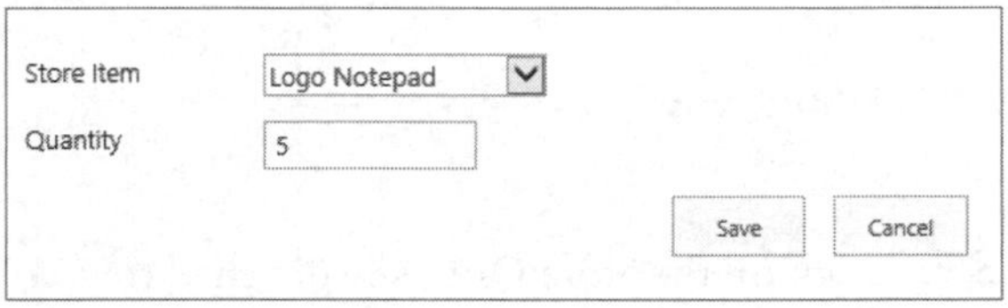

FIGURE 5-15

Notice that after the workflow has run for the first time and after the page has been refreshed, the Total Cost column has been filled out and there is a new column in the list with the same name as the workflow. Because the workflow completed" successfully, you can click the word Stage 1 to see the workflow status page, which contains the workflow history for that item (which is empty). You have just two more things to do, so go back over to the workflow in SharePoint Designer.

35. Because there was no information on the workflow status page that you viewed when you clicked Stage 1, it's time to add some log information. In SharePoint Designer (still on the Visual Designer view), drag the action called "Log to history list," letting go of it to the right of "Do calculation." Drag another "Log to history list" action to the right of the "Set field in current item" shape.

In the Visual Designer, if you see shapes that do not have connecting lines between them, this can be easily fixed. In the ribbon, click on the Connector Tool button, and use your cursor to draw a line from one shape to the next. There should be lines between each shape, and a line from the last shape to the red stop square. If all shapes are not connected, an error will occur when you try to publish the workflow When you are done drawing the connections, click the Pointer Tool button in the ribbon, to toggle back to it.

36. Hover over the first Log to history list shape, click the drop-down box, and click Message. For the message, type the information to log, as follows: **Total cost has been calculated**. Click OK.

37. On the second Log to history list shape, type **The total cost field has been filled in**. Click OK.

38. The goal here is to insert log history information after every step in the workflow for informational and documentation purposes. The workflow should now look like Figure 5-16. Publish the workflow.

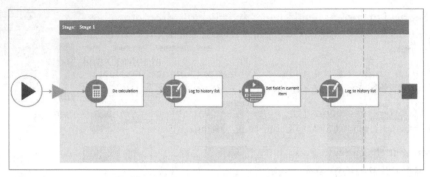

FIGURE 5-16

39. Back on the Store Orders list in the browser, click New Item to add a new item in the list. Pick an item and quantity, and click Save.

> **NOTE** Publishing the workflow also automatically saves it, so it is not necessary to click the Save button each time you publish. Alternately, if a workflow is not ready to go to production, you can use the Save button to simply save your latest changes and work more on the workflow later.

How It Works

You have finished creating your first SharePoint Designer 2013 workflow. When a new store order item is first saved, the Create Store Order column will be empty. When you refresh the web page, the workflow is shown as Stage 1. Click Stage 1 to look at the Workflow Status page. Notice that the Workflow History section contains the text that you created in the Log to History List actions.

> **WARNING** When you are logged in to SharePoint as the System Account (the SharePoint administrator), workflows may not run as they should. If you have a problem where a workflow will not run automatically when a new item is created or changed, it could be because of the account that you are logged in as. Look at the top-right corner of the SharePoint page in the browser where it says the name of the current logged-in user. If this says "System Account," try logging in as a regular user account instead, and run the workflow again. To log in as another user, right-click the Internet Explorer icon on the desktop or Start menu, and hold down the Shift key at the same time. Choose "Run as a different user."

Sending E-mails

E-mails are one of the most common actions in workflows, and are also heavily customizable. There is already an easy alternative, which is to create alerts on all SharePoint lists and libraries; however, sometimes these canned alerts are not enough. Create workflow e-mails when they need to be more specific and customized.

TRY IT OUT Creating a Workflow E-mail

In the previous Try It Out, you created a workflow to calculate a total and set information in a field. In this Try It Out, you add on to the Create Store Order workflow by adding an e-mail action to let the recipient know the details of his or her order, and that it was received.

1. In SharePoint Designer 2013, open the workflow that you created in the previous Try It Out section. Click Edit Workflow.

2. In the Visual Designer, Inside of Stage 1, drag the shape for the "Send an email" action and drop it to the right of the last action, and before the red square (which represents the end of the workflow).

> **NOTE** When working in the Visual Designer, you can expand the big rectangular shape that represents the stage to make room for more actions. Hover over any edge of the shape to find the little white handles that allow the resizing of the shape, and drag the edges out.

3. Hover your mouse over the "Send an email" action, and in the shape's drop-down box, choose Email.

4. Click the address book icon next to the To box, choose "User who created current item," click the Add button, and click OK.

5. Click the ellipsis button next to the Subject box. This lets you create a string that combines free-form text with values from the form.

6. Fill in the String Builder as shown in Figure 5-17. The Add or Change Lookup button at the bottom of the String Builder is used to insert the Store Item text into the string. Click OK on both dialog boxes.

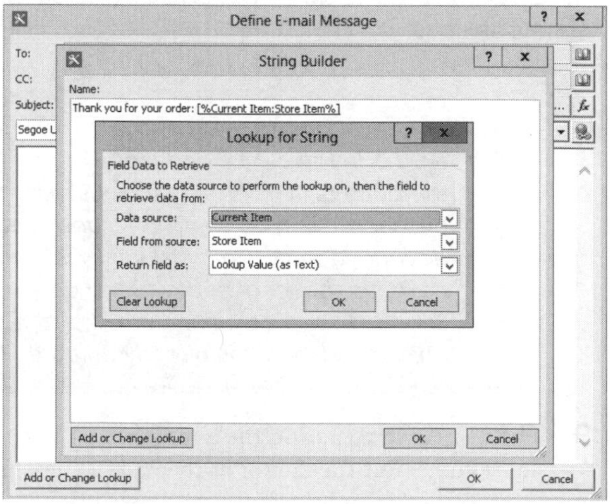

FIGURE 5-17

7. The body of the e-mail can contain some "Thank You" text, and optionally details about the order, such as the item, price, quantity, and total. Use the Add or Change Lookup button to add each field's value.

8. The Price is the tricky field, because that value is a lookup to an item in another list. Figure 5-18 shows an example of the e-mail message, with the Price lookup interface displayed. See the earlier note that explains the concept of creating lookups to other lists.

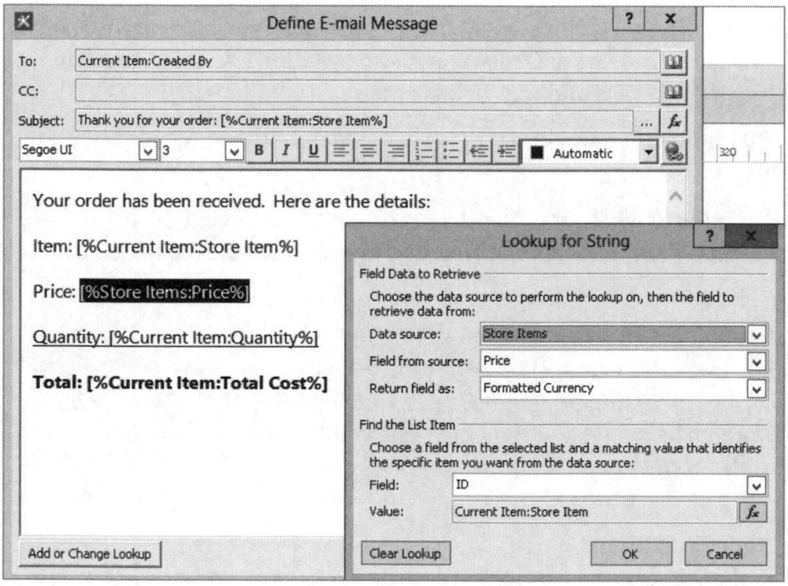

FIGURE 5-18

> **NOTE** *In the e-mail body for workflow e-mails, you can do some formatting of the body text. There are icons similar to what you see in other Microsoft Office products, such as bold, italic, and font sizes. There is a way to do even more advanced e-mail formatting, if you know how to write HTML code. In the workflow designer, hover over the "Send an email" action, click the drop-down box and choose Properties, and then click the ellipsis button next to the Body text box. This screen lets you directly edit the HTML of the message.*

9. The last thing to add to the e-mail is a link for the e-mail recipient to open the order in SharePoint. Put the cursor at the end of the e-mail, and click the hyperlink icon (under the Subject box, to the far right) to insert a hyperlink.

10. For the Text to display, type **Click to view order.**

11. Click the function (fx) button next to the Address box. The address must be an absolute URL, not a relative one. Choose Workflow Context as the Data source and then choose Current Item URL in the "Field from source" box, as shown in Figure 5-19. Click OK, OK, and then OK again to save the e-mail.

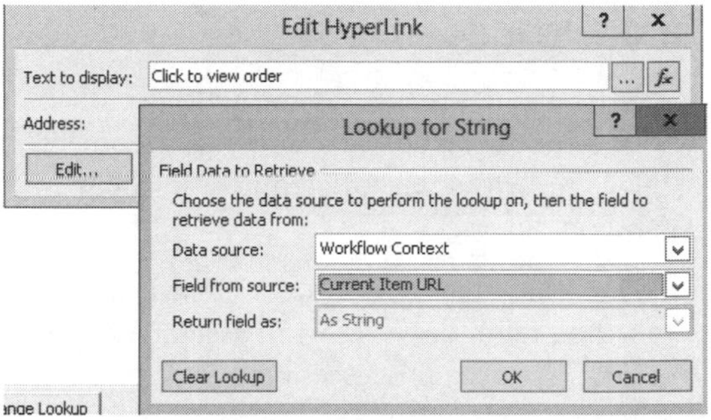

12. Back on the visual design surface, click to select the "Send an email" action's drop-down box, and click Properties. In the BCC box, add your own name. This enables you to receive a blind copy of each e-mail. Notice that on this properties screen, you can click the ellipsis button next to Body if you would like to directly edit the HTML code behind the e-mail. Click OK.

13. In the workflow, after the "Send an email" action, add another "Log to history list" shape, with the message "Confirmation email has been sent."

14. Publish the workflow.

FIGURE 5-19

How It Works

In this Try It Out, you test the workflow by creating a new order in the Store Orders list. You will receive the e-mail about the item you ordered, with a link that takes you back to that list item.

WORKFLOW TASKS AND HISTORY

When workflows are created on lists and libraries, the task and workflow history lists are two secondary lists that the workflow utilizes. Every workflow doesn't necessarily make use of a task list, but every workflow does write to a workflow history list.

On the Workflow Settings screen of any workflow in SharePoint Designer 2013, the Settings section on the right has drop-down boxes to pick the task list and workflow history list that you would like your workflow to be associated with.

Tasks

So far in this chapter, you may have noticed that the use of tasks in SharePoint workflows is substantial. Assigning tasks to workflow participants enables you to allocate accountability to individuals. Knowing that you can rely on workflows not only to assign tasks as part of defined business processes but also to automatically follow up with individuals, allows you to become more efficient in your day-to-day work.

When tasks are assigned using workflow actions, they look a bit different from tasks that are normally created in a SharePoint task list. This is because workflows automatically add new content types to task lists, and they also make use of InfoPath as a custom form interface.

Task Process Designer

"Start a task process" is the action that uses the Task Process Designer to assign tasks to more than one person, such as to approve a document. It not only contains conditions and actions that take place regarding task assignment in the workflow, but it also has easy interfaces to customize e-mails and outcomes.

When these task processes are used, the associated tasks perform follow-up actions by automatically sending reminder e-mails to assignees when due dates arrive. This is one of many functionalities built into these processes.

TRY IT OUT   Creating Task Processes

In the previous Try It Out, you created a workflow and set it up to run when new items are ordered in a store. The last action you added was an e-mail notification to the person who ordered the item. Next, you must assign tasks so that the order gets shipped out. In this example, the Processor Group is a SharePoint group containing those in charge of processing the order, and the Shipper Group contains those in charge of shipping it out.

In this Try It Out, you learn how to use the new Task Process Designer to assign tasks. This is not an approval process. Each assignee simply needs to mark his or her task as completed, as opposed to approving or rejecting it.

1. Create two new SharePoint groups on the site, called Processor Group and Shipper Group. If the workflow is still open from the previous exercise, you need to close and reopen SharePoint Designer so that the new groups will be visible in the workflow.

2. Open the previously created workflow called "Create Store Order" in SharePoint Designer.

3. Click Edit Workflow.

4. In the Visual Designer view, after the last Log to history list shape, drag another action called "Start a task process."

5. Click the drop-down box on the shape, and click Process Settings, which takes you to the Task Process Designer.

6. For the participants, select the Processor Group and then the Shipper Group. Use the Add button to move each group to the right. These are SharePoint groups on the site. *For testing purposes, it is okay to insert two individuals' names instead of groups here.* Leave the order as "Serial (one at a time)."

7. Click the ellipsis icon next to the Task Title box to elicit the String Builder.

8. Type **New Store Order,** and then use the Add or Change Lookup button to insert the ID field from the current item. This ID field is unique to each order that is placed.

9. In the Description box, type **Please perform your role in the new order process**. Expand all the sections on the Task Process dialog box to see all the available options. This screen is shown in Figure 5-20.

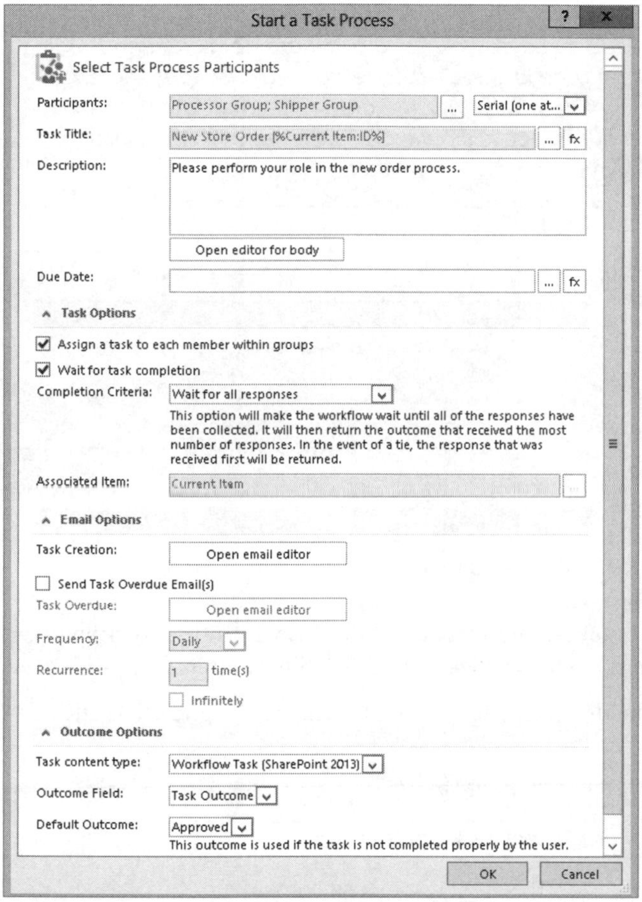

FIGURE 5-20

10. For the due date, the goal is to set each of these tasks as due three days after they are assigned, *not* to simply pick a specific date. To achieve this goal, you need to set a variable ahead of time. Click OK to close the Task Process Designer.

11. To get a different perspective on the structure of this workflow so far, click Views and switch back to the text-based designer view. Put the cursor above the "Start a task process" action so that you see an orange blinking line between the last Log action and the "Start a task process" action. Using the Action button in the ribbon, add the action called Add Time to Date.

12. Set up this action to say Add 0 Months, 3 days, 0 hours, 0 minutes. Click the blue word Date, click the function (fx) button, and select the Modified field from the current item.

> **NOTE** At step 12 when you add three days to today, you are not selecting the current date. When the current date is selected, it defaults to midnight. Instead, the Modified date of the current item will store the date and time right now, and will add three days to it. The difference is significant, especially when adding hours or minutes instead of days.

13. In the Output to Variable drop-down box, click Create a new variable. Name the variable **Task Due Date,** as a Date/Time. Click OK. Figure 5-21 shows what the workflow looks like so far in the text-based designer. Save the workflow.

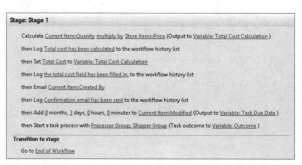

FIGURE 5-21

14. Before going back into the Task Process Designer, you still need to do a couple of things in preparation. The goal of this workflow is not to get approvals (Accepted and Rejected are the default outcomes), so you need to create some different outcomes, and you do *not* do this within the workflow. On your SharePoint site in the browser, go to the Site Settings page. Click Site Content Types.

15. Click the Create button. Fill in the fields according to the following table, and click OK.

FIELD NAME	FIELD VALUE
Name	Test Task Content Type
Description	This is a custom task content type
Select parent content type from	List Content Types
Parent content type	Workflow Task (SharePoint 2013)

16. Now that the new content type has been created, scroll down to the bottom of the page, under the columns, and click "Add from new site column."

17. Name the new column **Workflow Task Completion,** and for the type of column, select Task Outcome. Scroll down to the box called "Type each choice on a separate line." Type one choice called **Completed,** and on the next line, type **Not Completed.** Click OK.

18. Now that the content type has been created, you need to apply it to the task list. In the browser, click the name of the task list in the left navigation. In the List tab in the ribbon, click the List Settings button.

19. In the Content Types section, click "Add from existing site content types." On the left, find Test Task Content Type, and use the Add button to add it to the right side. Click OK.

20. Go back to the workflow in SharePoint Designer, and click the small green Refresh button at the top-left corner.

21. On the Start a Task Process action, click the text that says Processor Group; Shipper Group. Click the function (fx) button next to the Due Date box. For the Data source, choose Workflow Variables and Parameters. For Field from source, choose the Task Due Date variable. Click OK.

22. Expand the section called Task Options. Uncheck the box next to the "Assign a task to each member within groups" box. The goal is that each group will be assigned one task, and anyone in the group can complete it.

23. Expand the Email Options section. Check the box to "Send Task Overdue Email(s)." Click each of the Open editor buttons, and see that the task notification e-mail and the overdue notification e-mail can both be customized. Change the frequency of overdue e-mails to Weekly.

24. Remember that custom content type you created at step 15? Expand the Outcome Options section. Change the Task content type drop-down box to your Test Task Content Type. Change the Outcome field to Workflow Task Completion. Notice that your custom outcomes of Completed and Not Completed are choices in the Default Outcome drop-down box. Click OK. These outcome options are shown in Figure 5-22.

25. Publish the workflow.

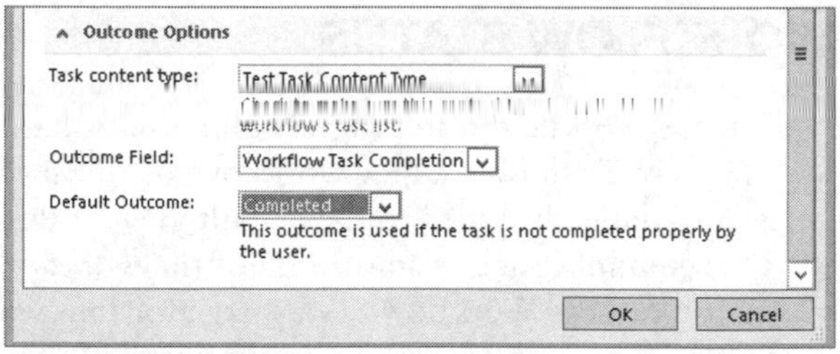

How It Works

FIGURE 5-22

Try out the workflow now by adding a new item to the Store Orders list. A few seconds after you create the new item, a task, called *Tasks*, will be created in the list. In the Store Orders list, click the Stage 1 link in the Create Store Order column. In the Tasks section of the Workflow Status page, click the title of the task that was created.

Notice that the button at the bottom of the task is called *Completed*, which you modified in the Outcomes section of the Task Process Designer. Each person or group in the workflow will be assigned a task in order, since we created a serial task process.

> **NOTE** *When assigning tasks, sending e-mails, or performing any other action in a workflow that involves people, it is recommended that SharePoint groups or variables be used instead of individuals. For example, if a file needs to be approved by the company's CEO, even though there is only one, create a SharePoint group called CEO. Put that one person in the group. In the workflow, send an e-mail to the group. When groups are used, people can easily be added and removed from them, so that the workflow itself does not need to be modified.*
>
> *In the Task Options section of the task process, there is an option called "Assign a task to each member within groups". If this box is checked, it means that each individual in the group will be assigned his or her own task. If the box is unchecked, only one task will be assigned for the whole group, and anyone in the group can complete that task.*

History

On every SharePoint site, there is a built-in list called *workflow history*. All workflows that run on the site are logged in this list, which also includes all errors. Knowing that there is a history log and where it lives gives you a good basis of understanding when it comes to workflow status pages and troubleshooting. The location of the workflow history list is:

```
http://your_site_url/lists/workflow%20history
```

This list is automatically sorted in ascending by Date Occurred order, but just as with any list, you can create your own views for sorting and filtering purposes. The data in the workflow history does seem a bit cryptic, because it makes use of unique IDs for lists and workflows, but it is a good reference sometimes.

WORKFLOW STATUS

When a workflow is in progress and after it has completed, there is a workflow status page that you can view. Each time a new workflow is published for the first time on a list or library, a new column is automatically added to the default view of the list. The column name is the name of the workflow. This column contains status text of the workflow, such as In Progress or Completed. This status text is a link to the Workflow Status page for that workflow, specific to that list item. The following are the sections of the workflow status page.

Workflow Information

This section shows basic facts about who started the workflow, when, and what the status is.

There is a link here called "Terminate this workflow," which is very useful when it comes to errors. When a workflow gets stuck, terminate the workflow so that it can be modified, published, and tried again.

Tasks

This is a list of all the tasks that have taken place so far or are currently in progress. Information about each task and assignee is listed, along with the outcome, such as Approved. Click any task's name to open it.

Workflow History

This section contains a list of everything that happens in the workflow on that item, including any errors. When you use out-of-the-box workflows, they output some pretty detailed information; however, when you create workflows from scratch, it is up to you to use the Log to Workflow History action to create this data.

SUMMARY

SharePoint workflows are fundamental in the creation of automated business processes, and in making jobs and tasks more efficient. This chapter has supplied you with introductory information about out-of-the-box and custom workflows, so that you can effortlessly create and configure your own. You also learned how to get around in SharePoint Designer, and practiced creating workflows from scratch.

EXERCISES

1. The marketing department has a custom approval workflow for pictures in a picture library. You would like to see a visual representation of the workflow. Which view in SharePoint Designer shows this?

2. Each document in the company policies library needs to go through a strenuous collaboration and approval process. When the workflow is kicked off, it needs to be sent to each individual in the taxation department for review and feedback, all at the same time. Which action should you use for this approval process?

3. The personnel department has an approval workflow in which a document needs to be set with an outcome of approved if at least 50% of the participants approve it. In the Task Process Designer, which completion criteria should you select?

4. Sue Ellen would like to customize the colors in a workflow e-mail. Where can she click to get to the HTML code of the e-mail in order to modify it?

5. Bob is attempting to manually start his workflow called "Policy Approval," but he does not see it in the "Start a New Workflow" section of the workflows page for that item. He has verified that the workflow is allowed to be manually started, and it has been published. Where can you look to troubleshoot his problem?

▶ **WHAT YOU LEARNED IN THIS CHAPTER**

TOPIC	KEY CONCEPTS
Workflows	Business processes are everywhere, and workflows are how you automate them.
Actions and conditions	Workflow actions and conditions are the main principles behind the way workflows can be structured. Conditions are the "if" statements, and actions are what happens if the conditions exist.
SharePoint Designer 2013 workflows	The workflow engine in SharePoint 2013 has been rebuilt and is a separate installation on the server. SharePoint Designer 2013 workflows have many new functionalities, one of them being the Visual Designer, which uses Visio 2013 behind the scenes.
Task and history lists	The task list is used for assigning tasks to people from within the workflow. The workflow history list, which exists on every site, is where all the workflow status information is recorded.

6

Working with Content Types

WHAT YOU WILL LEARN IN THIS CHAPTER:

➤   What a content type is and why it is such an important part of SharePoint

➤   The various content types you can create

➤   How to create the major content types

➤   What a content type hub is and why you might use it

➤   Best practices for creating and managing content types for your organization

WROX.COM CODE DOWNLOADS FOR THIS CHAPTER

The wrox.com code downloads for this chapter are found at www.wrox.com/remtitle .cgi?isbn=1118495896 on the Download Code tab. The code is in the Chapter 6 download and individually named according to the names throughout the chapter.

Thus far, this book has discussed components that can help you organize information in a SharePoint site. You should now know how to create list and library apps, and assign metadata values to content items. You should also know how to associate business processes with lists and libraries so that you can track, review, and approve items in a consistent and automatic manner. Using this functionality in your work environment means that you spend more time doing actual work, rather than trying to locate information in disorganized filing systems.

This chapter takes the concepts discussed thus far and brings them together to create an information management package that ties to your content. After reading this chapter, you should feel comfortable creating content types suitable for efficiently managing the information that is vital to your organization.

CONTENT TYPES OVERVIEW

A *content type* represents a group of informational items in your organization that share common properties such as meeting minutes. You can define these properties, which include name, description, and a grouping category, to meet your business needs. In addition, you can adjust the properties associated with templates, workflow, site columns, and information policies as well as the settings for the document information panel. You can change these properties at any time and optionally apply those changes to your entire environment.

> **NOTE** *For more on the various content type properties and what they do, see the section "The Anatomy of a Content Type."*

SharePoint offers several content types that provide solid foundations for all future content types. You can select one of these content types, and use it to create your content type in the central gallery, where you can then apply it to multiple lists and libraries throughout a site collection. By creating new content types, you can apply rules and properties to customize information and tie it to your business activities. Once you define your content type, you can create a new item by selecting the appropriate template from a drop-down menu presented by the New Document command on your list or library's ribbon (see Figure 6-1). This chapter discusses the various elements of a content type as well as some of the configuration and customization alternatives of the most common content types.

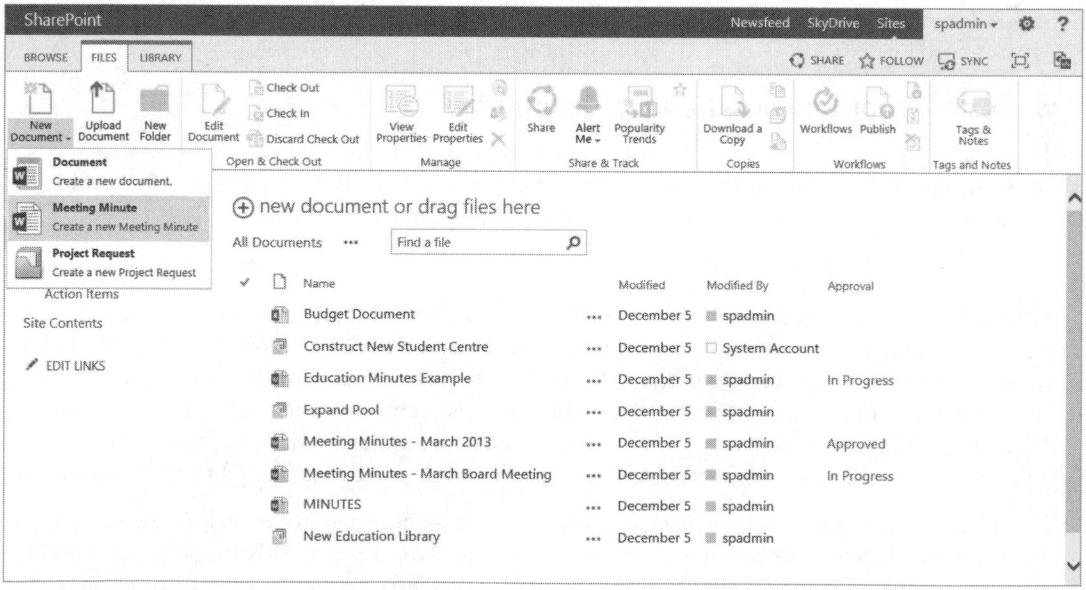

FIGURE 6-1

KNOWING WHERE TO CREATE CUSTOM CONTENT TYPES

It's important where you create a custom content type in the site hierarchy. If you plan to use it throughout your organization in many sites, you should store it in the content type gallery of the top-level site. For more specialized content, you might create content types that apply to a specific site and its subsites. Figure 6-2 displays a site hierarchy. In this example, a content type created at the top-level site (Portal Home) would be available for use within every site in the site collection. However, a content type that was created on the Marketing site would only be available for use on the Marketing site and the team sites below it. It is important to create your content types at the appropriate location in the site collection, because they cannot be moved once they have been created.

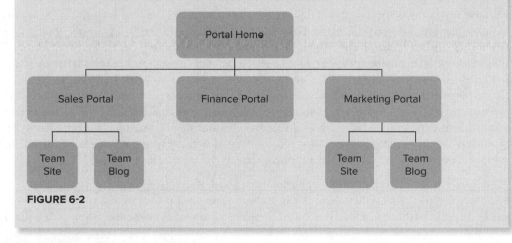

FIGURE 6-2

When you create a content type, you must select a parent from which it automatically inherits any existing settings for a template, workflow, or metadata columns. You should consider the content types you need for your organization and then identify any relations they may have with each other or inheritances that they share so that you can place similar content types into groups. Using the same parent for each of these content types means you can filter based on the parent and include information from all child content types. For example, to manage your workflow, you may need a general purchase request form that manages the approval process for new purchases within each division. You can create a standard purchase request content type and then create each divisional content type using it as the template. All metadata and the form template become associated with each divisional content type automatically; however, you can define a unique workflow process for each child content type to allow different departmental managers to approve requests. You can easily update the form; because each divisional content type is based on the same parent, edits to the parent are copied down into each child.

THE ANATOMY OF A CONTENT TYPE

The magic of SharePoint is making its various pieces fit your business situation, and nowhere is that more evident than in content types. Content types all have properties, the basic ones being the name, description, and grouping category. In addition, you have properties associated with templates, workflow, site columns, and policy management as well as settings for the document information panel. You can define and redefine these properties to fit your business situations, but to do that, you need an understanding of how to work with them. For example, you can change a content type's name to reflect a change in process, but it's important for you to make the name consistent and intuitive when you redefine it. In this section, you learn about the various content type properties and how to work with them.

Name and Description

Because the name is displayed on all the buttons and labels associated with the content, you should assign a clear and descriptive name. For example, users should intuitively know what name to select when they click the button for creating a new item in a document library. You should consider who will work with this content type and make sure that they understand exactly what they are creating when they select a name. This is especially critical when you work with the automated workflows, templates, and policies. For example, if your company sells multiple product lines related to aerospace and transportation, and you create a content type that contains the proposal template, approval process, and metadata related to a specific marine product line, consider using a name that clearly defines which product line it is associated with. Naming it "sales document" or "marine product documents" would not be as appropriate as "marine sales proposal."

As with all other SharePoint content elements, a good description helps communicate the purpose and intended use of a content type. If you state concisely what the content type is, users can more easily fill in information, modify settings, or select a content type for inclusion with a list or library.

Parent Content Type

You must define hierarchical relationships between two content types. In SharePoint, the *parent content type* defines the properties for a child content type, which, in turn, inherits all the parent's properties. For example, going back to the marine sales proposals scenario, you can create a new content type called "Marine Documents," which has specific site columns and metadata that you want to apply to all marine-related documents. By basing all Marine Sales Proposals on the Marine Document content type, they will inherit the existing properties of the parent — in this case, Marine Sales Proposals. Likewise, if you later need to add a new site column to all marine content types, you simply add columns to the Marine Documents parent content type to have them added to the children of the content type automatically. Once you create a content type, you cannot change its parent. Therefore, it is strongly recommended that you plan your content types carefully and work out the logistics of the hierarchy on paper before starting to define your content types in SharePoint.

Group

You can organize your various customized content types by grouping them. As you create or edit a content type, you must specify a group name either by selecting an existing group name or by creating a custom group. Instituting some standards for groups provides a solid base for expanding and organizing content types as you create them. For example, using the Marine Sales Proposals as an example, it may be appropriate to associate the content type with a custom group called "Marine Sales Documents" that can store all content types related to the marine product line.

Template

In many organizations, standard templates are used for business documents. Content types can be associated with these templates to improve the functionality and information flow within SharePoint and to make document libraries, for example, more useful to you. When you associate document templates with a content type, you can better control the quality of the data that you collect. You can base the template on a variety of file formats, including Word documents, Excel spreadsheets, InfoPath forms, and custom web pages. You can either upload a custom template to the content type, or you can point to a template stored at another location. If you want to point to an existing template, be sure that all members using the content type can access the location of the template. For example, if you create a sales proposal content type and a document template for sales proposals already exists on the sales team site, make sure that the people who will create content based on your newly created content type have access to that sales team site.

For Microsoft Office files, such as Word and Excel, updating or changing the document template associated with a content type has no effect on items that users have already created and that are stored in the document library. This is because of the way these files relate to a template. In Word, a document template is primarily relevant only for the initial creation of the document. However, for content types based on InfoPath or publishing templates such as page layouts, changing the template associated with the content type updates the existing documents to display the information as detailed in the template. This will become clearer when you explore those content types in greater detail later in this book.

When a document library is created, users are given the ability to create new documents. If desired, a site owner may change the association of the New Document link to a custom template. This association means that users can automatically generate documents based on that template by clicking the New Item button for a document library. With content types, you can have more than one item in the New Item menu, which gives you a single document repository in which to store several different types of information and simplify how people access materials.

To show you how to create and specify some of the reviewed properties of content types, this section presents two Try It Outs. In the first, you see how to create a new content type, and in the second, you see how to edit one of the content types that SharePoint has to offer to suit your needs by specifying a template.

TRY IT OUT   Creating a New Content Type

You need to manage your company's sales proposals in a more organized fashion as well as provide more automated support to the sales team during the proposal-creation stage. This includes giving them access to a standard proposal template as well as an automated review and approval workflow process. To reach your goal, you must first create the initial shell of the content type, which you can later modify to include elements such as templates, standard metadata, and workflow processes. In this Try It Out, you create a company document content type based on the document parent content type and place it in a group. Then, you create a second content type that inherits from that content type.

1. From the top level of your site collection, select Site Settings from the Settings menu. The Site Settings page appears.

2. Under the Web Designer Galleries group, select Site Content Types. The Site Content Types page appears listing all content types available within the site collection.

3. Click Create. The New Site Content Type screen appears, as shown in Figure 6-3.

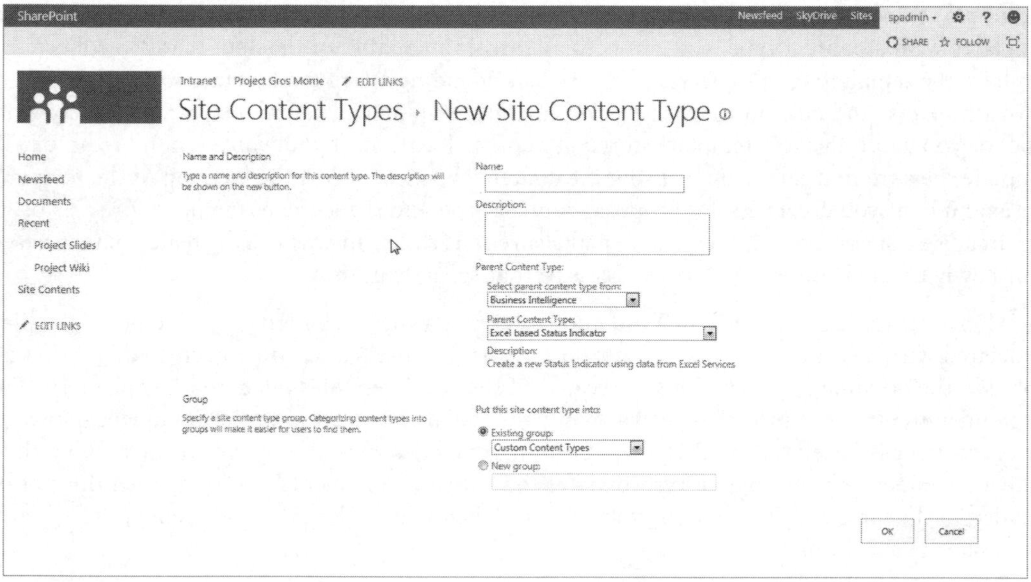

FIGURE 6-3

4. Define your new content type as follows:

PROPERTY	VALUE
Name	AW Document
Description	AdventureWorks Standard Document
Select Parent Content Type From	Document Content Types
Parent Content Type	Document
Put this Content Type into (New Group)	Company Documents

5. Click OK. You are redirected to the administration page for the new content type, as shown in Figure 6-4. From this page, you can manage the properties of the content type, such as metadata, workflow settings, and template.

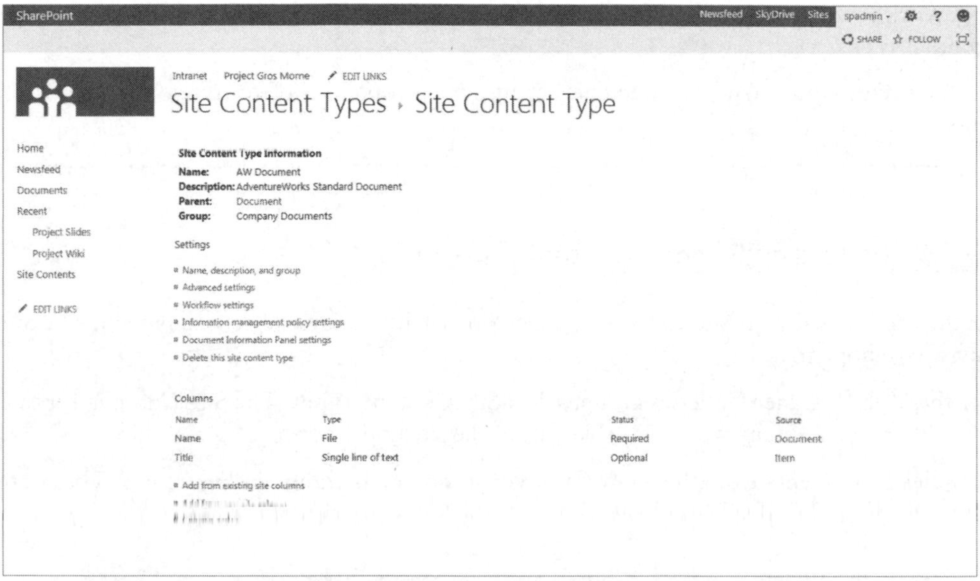

FIGURE 6-4

6. From the breadcrumb navigational menu, select Site Content Types to return to the Site Content Types page.

7. Click Create.

8. Define your new content type as follows:

PROPERTY	VALUE
Name	Sales Proposal
Description	AdventureWorks Sales Proposal
Select Parent Content Type From	Company Documents
Parent Content Type	AW Document
Put this Content Type into (New Group)	Sales Documents

9. Click OK.

How It Works

In this Try It Out, you created two custom content types. The AW Document content type is the base document content type for your organization. You created it from the default system content type of Document. It is good practice to always create at least one custom content type that will act as the parent for all other custom content types in your organization. This enables you to apply settings to the AW Document content type that will cascade down through all its children without impacting or changing the default Document content type. You then created a Sales Proposal content type that is based upon the AW Document content type. Therefore, any custom settings related to template, metadata, or workflow applied to the AW Document content type can be pushed down to the Sales Proposal content type.

In the next Try It Out, you learn how to update settings for a content type to suit your business requirements.

TRY IT OUT Editing an Existing Content Type

1. From the top level of your site collection, select Site Settings from the Settings menu. The Site Settings page appears.

2. Under the Web Designer Galleries group, select Site Content Types. The Site Content Types page appears listing all content types available within the site collection.

3. Select Sales Documents from the Show Group drop-down, as shown in Figure 6-5. The content type will be filtered to display only items within the Sales Documents group.

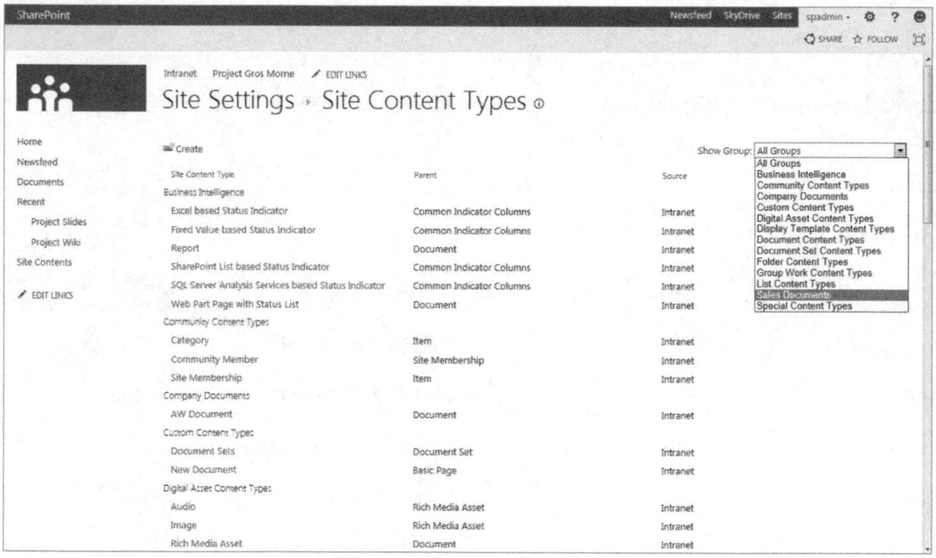

FIGURE 6-5

4. Select the Sales Proposal content type created from the previous exercise.

5. Select the Advanced Settings link.

6. Select the option to Upload a new document template.

7. Click the Browse button.

8. Locate the Proposal Template.docx file from this chapter's resource files and click Open.

9. Click OK. The page refreshes, and you are returned to the Sales Proposal content type administration page.

How It Works

In steps 4–9, you specified a custom document template for your Sales Proposal content type. This means that whenever users create a New document based on the Sales Proposal content type, the document you specified will open based on the associated document template. This helps address a common challenge in many organizations, whereby users have difficulty locating the latest version of a template when creating new documents.

Workflow

Creating important documents often requires the creator to follow an equally important business process. This process ensures that everyone involved in the collaboration activity is doing their part and communicating properly. When people follow processes without the aid of automated tools, they often encounter or create roadblocks because of distractions and other duties. For example, if a sales manager completes an important sales proposal and sends it to a colleague or supervisor for feedback with an e-mail notification, that colleague may not immediately respond because of another task or emergency and, as a result, the request gets buried in an inbox or lost in the shuffle. This is a common situation because many people struggle to keep up with e-mail and daily responsibilities. Unfortunately, this means missed deadlines, frustration between team members, and missed opportunities, and it may ultimately impact the overall operations of the company.

By assigning a workflow template with a content type, you can define a realistic series of tasks with built-in reminders for a specific business activity so that workers can focus on their duties. For example, in the previous scenario, whenever a salesperson creates a sales proposal, he or she can send it to the sales team or a supervisor for feedback with tasks and deadlines automatically created so that the request for feedback is less likely to be lost. Even if the sales team supervisor does forget the task, the system will send reminder messages to the supervisor until the task is complete. This means that the salesperson doesn't have to follow up on the task.

Depending on the parent content type you select when you define your custom content type, you may already have workflows enabled. If these workflow processes do not apply, you can remove them, but be careful not to remove a workflow that is important to the operations of a specific content type. By updating the workflow settings of a parent, you can optionally update any content types that are inheriting from that content type.

Adding a custom workflow to a content type is a fairly simple process and similar to adding a workflow to a document library or list as described in Chapter 5, "Working with Workflows." The advantage here, however, is that you typically have to define the process only once, and it is then applied to multiple document libraries that utilize that content type. If you add multiple content types to a single library, each content type can have its own unique workflow or set of processes that are independent of the others.

TRY IT OUT Defining a Workflow for a Content Type

To better track approvals related to sales proposals, you have decided to configure a workflow on the Sales Proposal content type that tracks the approval process of each proposal that is added to the library.

1. From the Sales Proposal content type administration page, select Workflow settings. You are redirected to the Workflow Settings page.

2. Select the Add a Workflow link. You are redirected to the Add a Workflow page.

3. Select the Approval - SharePoint 2010 template, as shown in Figure 6-6.

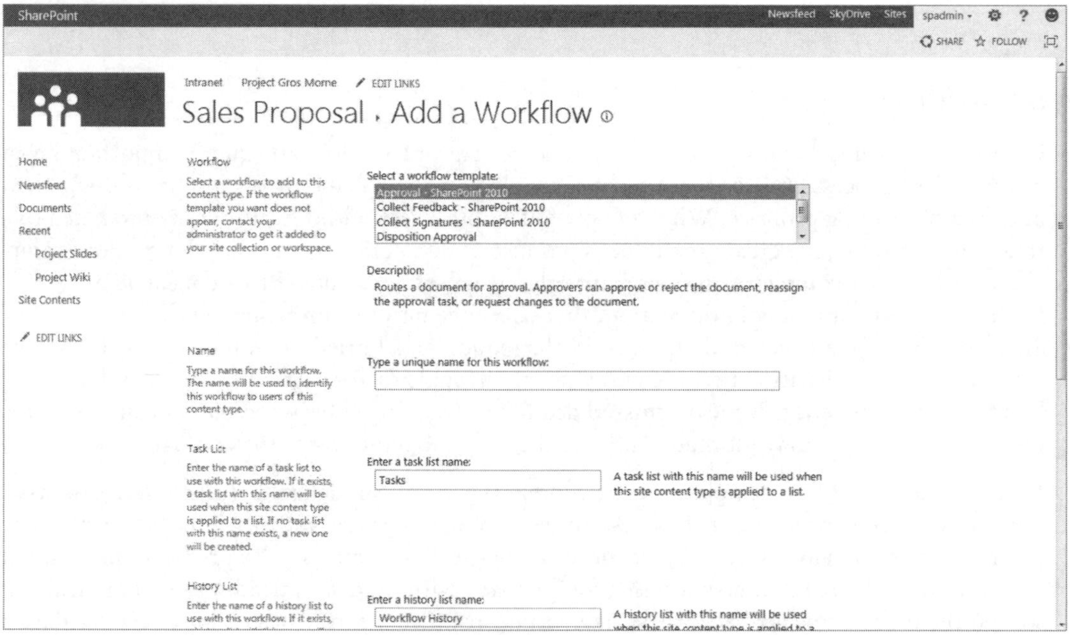

FIGURE 6-6

4. Specify the details as follows for the new workflow:

PROPERTY	VALUE
Name	Sales Proposal Approval
Task List	Tasks
History List	Workflow History
Start Options	Start this workflow when a new item is created.
Update List and Site Content Types	Yes

5. Click the Next button to enter the remaining workflow details.

6. Enter the following details for the remaining properties:

PROPERTY	VALUE
Approvers	Assign To: Enter your own name Order: One at a time (serial)
Expand Groups	Deselect
Request	The following sales proposal has been added to the library. Please review it and provide an approval decision.
Duration Per Task	2
Duration Units	Day(s)
End on First Rejection	Select
End on Document Change	Select

7. Click Save. You are returned to the Workflow Settings page, as shown in Figure 6-7.

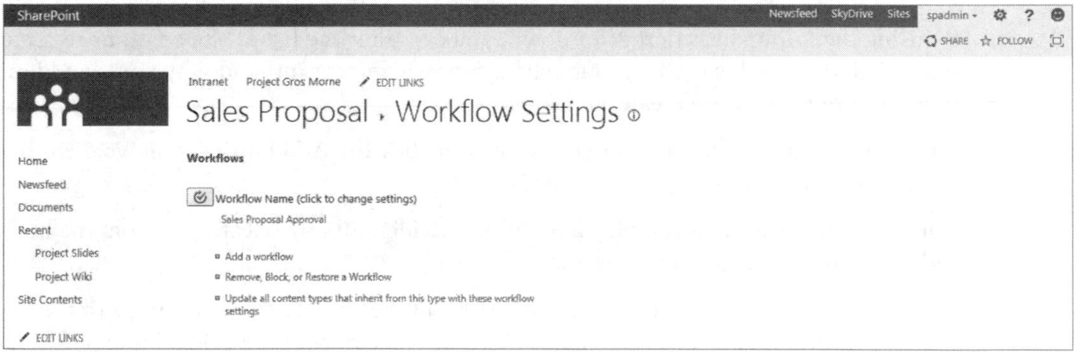

FIGURE 6-7

How It Works

The workflow activity you created launches whenever a new item is created based on that content type, and a task is created for you because you selected your own name as an approver for the serial work-flow. The due date for the task is two days from the point the document is created. If you do not complete the task by the assigned date, you will receive a reminder. Because you selected the option to end on first rejection, the workflow ends if you reject the item. Similarly, if the document is changed after the workflow has launched, the workflow is canceled.

Site Columns

In Chapter 4, "Managing and Customizing Lists and Libraries," you learned about the importance of site columns when creating standard metadata properties for lists and libraries. To recap, site columns are stored in a central gallery on each site, and any list or library can use them on the same site or any site below it. Site columns provide standardization and ease of use when you want to share important information across multiple lists, libraries, or sites.

Site columns are also very important in content types. Because content types are created and stored in a central gallery, all associated components must be centralized as well. Therefore, you can only associate site columns with a content type. When you add a content type to a library, the required site columns are automatically associated with that library for use by the content type. You can create custom views on the columns and Web Parts, such as the Content Query Web Part, and you can apply advanced filtering.

> **NOTE** Web Parts are explained in Chapter 7, "Working with Web Parts."

Remember the following when working with site columns:

➤ When defining metadata for a content type, you can use existing site columns or create new site columns directly from the Content Type Settings page. When you use existing site columns, you are redirected to a site column selection page.

➤ By using the Group Selection drop-down, you can filter the list of site columns to a more manageable size. This is why group names are very important, and why you should make them intuitive when you create site columns.

➤ Once you select the site columns you want, you click the Add button to move them from the left-hand list box to the right-hand list box.

➤ You can remove an item you may have added accidentally by selecting it from the box on the right and clicking the Remove button.

➤ You can update all content types that inherit from the current content type with the new columns you selected. For example, imagine you have a content type called Human Resources Document and another content type called Policy that is a child of Human Resources document. You can make changes to the site column settings of Human Resources document and have those applied to Policy automatically.

You can also create a new site column as you create a content type. Even though you're creating the site column from the administration interface of the specific content type, SharePoint still adds it to the central gallery of the site, making it available to other content types, lists, and libraries on the current site and sites below it.

Adding a Site Column to a Content Type

To better track the owner of each sales proposal, you decide it would be a good idea to add a column to the Sales Proposal content type to track the account manager who is assigned to the specific opportunity.

1. From the Columns section of the Sales Proposal content type administration page, select "Add from new site column."

2. Enter the details for your new column as follows:

PROPERTY	VALUE
Column Name	Account Manager
The type of information in this column is	Person or Group
Group	Sales Related
Description	Enter the account manager for this opportunity.
Allow Multiple Sections	No
Allow Selection of	People Only
Show Field	Name (with picture)

3. Click OK to save your column. You are returned to the content type administration page, and your new column appears in the column listing.

How It Works

In this Try It Out, you created a new site column for your content type. Now whenever a document is created based on the Sales Proposal content type, the Account Manager column will appear in the document information panel or the edit properties page associated with the file.

Adding a Site Column to a Parent Content Type

You have decided that, for every document that is created within your organization, you want to track its confidentiality rating. It would not be realistic to manually update every single library with this column, nor would it be practical to manually add the column to each content type. Therefore, you decide instead to create a column called Confidentiality Rating to the content type AW Document, because all other document-based content types in your organization will inherit from that content type. Therefore, all existing and new content types will be created with that column.

1. From the Columns section of the AW Document content type administration page, select "Add from new site column."

2. Enter the details for your new column as follows:

PROPERTY	VALUE
Column Name	Confidentiality Rating
The type of information in this column is	Choice
Group	Corporate Classification
Description	Please select the appropriate confidentiality rating for this document.
Type each choice on a separate line	Private - InternalPrivate - TeamPublic
Display Choices Using	Radio Buttons
Allow "Fill-in" Choices	No
Default Value	Blank

3. Click OK to save your column. You are returned to the content type administration page, and your new column appears in the column listing. Also notice that when you visit the Sales Proposal content type, the new column appears in the listing, as shown in Figure 6-8.

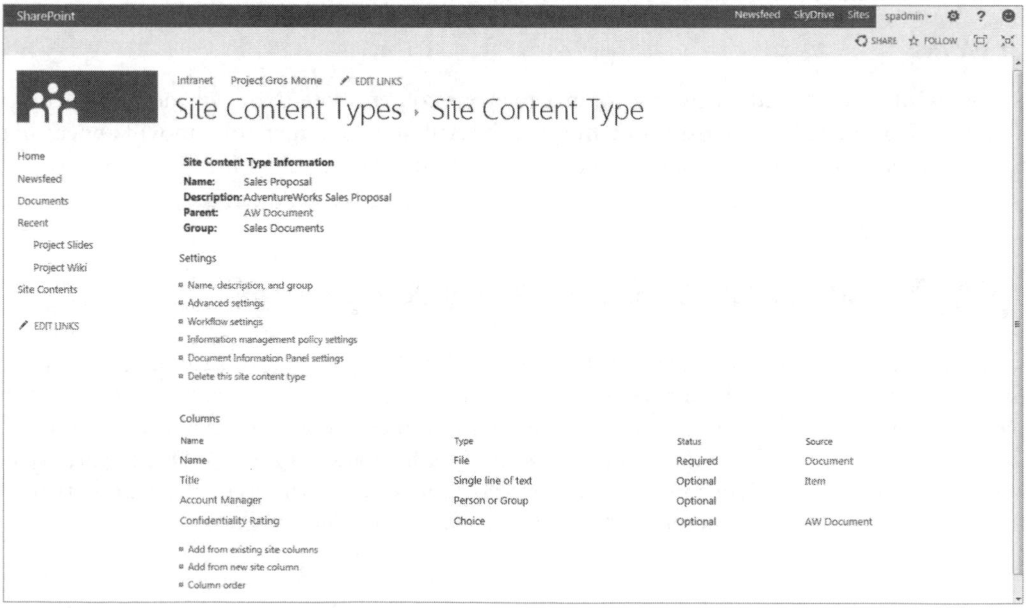

FIGURE 6-8

How It Works

In this Try It Out, you created a new site column for your content type. Because AW Document is a parent content type for the Sales Proposal content type, the column will appear in both. This is because when you made the change, you kept the default setting of Yes to the question "Update all content types inheriting from this type?" By selecting this setting, the changes made to AW Document are also applied to its children.

Document Information Panel Settings

Whenever you are saving a file in a Microsoft application such as Word or Excel, you will notice a form appear at the top of the application containing all the columns that are associated with the content type or library you are saving to. This is the *document information panel*, which asks you to complete metadata as shown in Figure 6-9, and which is the subject of the next Try It Out.

FIGURE 6-9

If you desire, you can modify the document information panel for a content type. You review the process for doing this in the following Try It Out.

 TRY IT OUT Editing the Document Information Panel of a Content Type

1. From the Sales Proposal content type administration page, select the Document Information Panel settings link.

2. Select the Create a New Custom Template link. Microsoft InfoPath Designer 2013 opens and a dialog box message appears, as shown in Figure 6-10. Click the Finish button to open the document information panel.

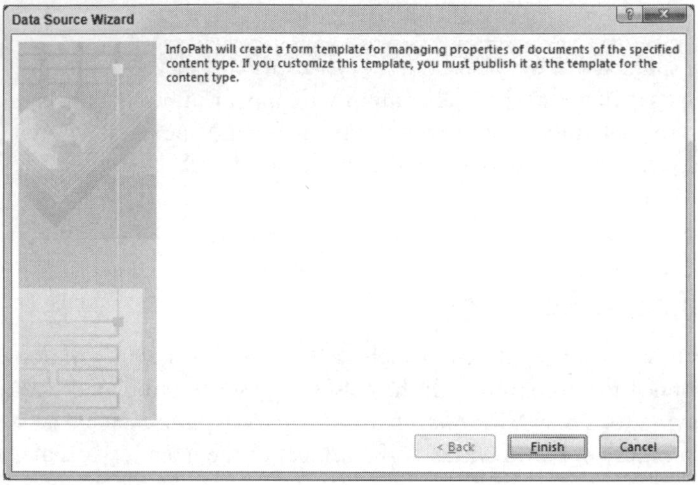

FIGURE 6-10

3. Select to the left of the Title field and click the Return button on your keyboard to insert a space above the three fields.

4. Select the blank row above the fields and select the Insert tab from the ribbon menu.

5. Select the Picture button and browse to the location of this chapter's resources to locate the `awlogo.png` file.

6. Click the Insert button. Your logo should now appear above the three fields, as shown in Figure 6-11.

FIGURE 6-11

7. Click the Publish button on the File tab of the ribbon menu.

8. Select the Document Information Panel publish option.

9. You are prompted to save the form template. Click OK.

10. Save the file to your chapter resources using the same proposal form.

11. The Publishing Wizard displays a final verification page listing details for the form. Click the Publish button to complete the process.

12. Click the Close button.

13. You are returned to a page with a link to return to the Document Information Panel settings page. Click the link.

14. Select the checkbox to Always show Document Information Panel on document open and initial save for this content type.

15. Click OK.

How It Works

In this Try It Out, you created a custom information panel for your content type that displays a custom logo. Though it may not be considered best practice to add logos to this user interface, this example demonstrated how easy it is to use InfoPath to customize your organization's document information panels. Once you create a single custom panel, you can reuse it for other content types by pointing to it from the Document Information Panel settings of your other content types. You would do this by selecting Use Existing Custom Template (URL, UNC, or URN) from the Document Information Panel settings instead of creating a new template as you did previously.

You enabled a checkbox in step 14 on your content type so that the document information panel always appears whenever your content type is opened within a Microsoft Office application such as Word or Excel. Because you display the panel whenever the document is opened, users treat the panel as a form that they must update before closing the document. If an item is required, it will have to be completed or added before the document is closed. However, if a required column is already specified but outdated, having the values front and center while someone is working on the document should help reduce the probability that they will close the document without updating the latest information. There is no way to force someone to update a column if a value already exists, so communicating the importance of keeping information up to date to your team is still important. Figure 6-12 is an example of how the document information panel for the sales proposal document will look to users when creating a new document based on that template.

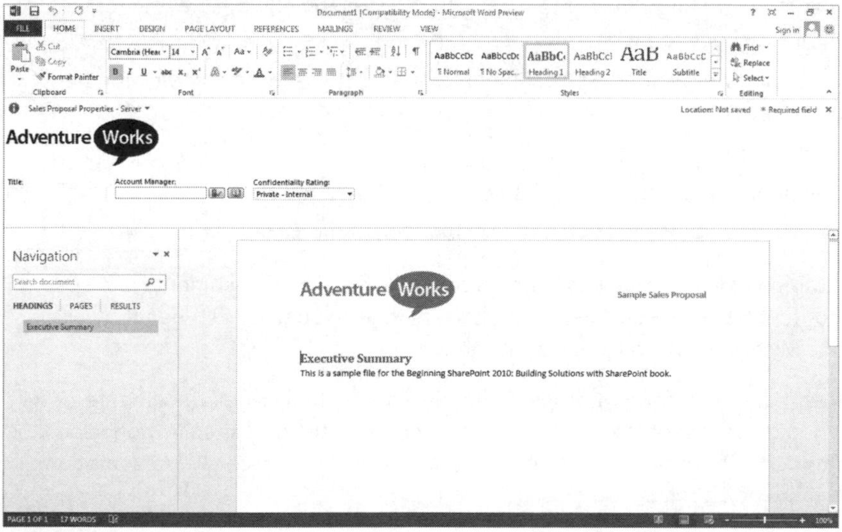

FIGURE 6-12

Information Management Policies

Another great feature of content types is how you can define certain policies and behaviors around how they are managed. Because content of a specific type quite often has the same requirements for retention and management, it is beneficial to define a set of policies around a content type and have those inherited by all documents that are created from it. Although it is possible to define information management policies on a library, it is often a better practice to define the policy based on the content type so that you can have specific rules for each type of content that can be reused throughout your organization in a consistent manner.

You can configure the items in relation to a content type's information policies as listed in the following table:

POLICY SETTING	DESCRIPTION
Administrative Description	Provide some background information to users who are responsible for managing the policies related to the content type.
Policy Statement	A customizable message that appears when users open documents associated with the content type. A message bar appears at the top of the document in an Information Management Policy box. Users can click a Details button to view all the details related to the policy message. By using a policy statement, content type owners can ensure that users have all the information they need concerning the important policies related to specific content.
Retention	Enables you to control the life span of specific types of content. You can configure content types to be deleted automatically after a certain time based on a document property. Alternatively, you can launch a workflow that gives the user a final chance to review the document before it is archived or deleted.
Auditing	If you enable auditing on a content type, the following activities related to documents associated with the content type are tracked: ➤ Opening or downloading documents, viewing items in lists, or viewing item properties ➤ Editing items ➤ Checking out or checking in items ➤ Moving or copying items to another location in the site
Barcodes	This automatically inserts an auto-generated barcode into documents of a specific content type. You can also prompt users to insert barcodes when they use specific Microsoft Office client applications.
Labels	Ensures that important properties or messages are printed with documents related to a specific content type, such as a confidential or a specific noncalculated document property. Content type owners can customize the presentation of the label by choosing font formatting and size.

We review information management policies in detail in Chapter 16, "Managing Records."

Document Conversion

If the document conversion feature is enabled on your web server, you can configure rules for each content type that support the files being automatically converted to an alternate file type, such as a web page or image file. This feature is reviewed as part of Chapter 15, "Getting Started with Web Content Management."

BASE CONTENT TYPES

SharePoint offers a repertoire of content types that address basic business needs. These are organized into groups according to their purpose. This section details some of the more common built-in content groups and types. Additional content types exist out-of-the-box that are used by the system for the operations of built-in lists and features, but they are not explored in this book.

Business Intelligence Content Types

SharePoint offers powerful features that organize, track, and display data from a variety of sources so that you can monitor the status of your business. This section discusses the business intelligence content types, and Chapter 10, "Working with Business Intelligence," describes the useful set of business reporting tools included in SharePoint. The content types in the following table are available as part of the Business Intelligence group. The indicator types contain columns that collect business intelligence information from a data source so that it can be presented as a key performance indicator (KPI) or in a report. By creating a new content type based on one of these base content types, you can augment the information that is gathered by default. You can also customize the dashboard and report types to meet your needs.

CONTENT TYPE	PARENT	DESCRIPTION
Excel-Based Status Indicator	Common Indicator Columns	A key performance indicator based on information stored within an Excel workbook. You can create this type of indicator from the Status list template.
Fixed-Value-Based Status Indicator	Common Indicator Columns	A key performance indicator based on information entered manually into a list item. You can create this type of indicator from the Status list template.
Report	Document	An Excel document page for the browser-based display of spreadsheet information.
SharePoint List-Based Status Indicator	Common Indicator Columns	A key performance indicator based on information stored within a SharePoint list. You can create this type of indicator from the Status list template.
SQL Server Analysis Services-Based Status Indicator	Common Indicator Columns	A key performance indicator based on information stored within SQL Server Analysis Services. You can create this type of indicator from the Status list template.
Web Part Page with Status List	Document	A preconfigured Web Part page with an associated Status List. You can further configure this page to provide an informative dashboard page to business stakeholders.

Community Content Types

SharePoint has a number of features that focus on the creation and enabling of communities. The following content types are used by these features and are available for further expansion.

CONTENT TYPE	PARENT	DESCRIPTION
Category	Item	This content type is used in the Community site template for tracking categories related to community discussions.
Community Member	Site Membership	This content type is used for the built-in Community Members list that is part of the Community site template.
Site Membership	Item	This content type is leveraged by the Community Member content type.

Digital Asset Content Types

In addition to being an excellent storage location for files such as spreadsheets, documents, and presentations, SharePoint can also be a location for storing digital assets, such as videos, audio clips, and images. An asset library is a document library in SharePoint that is designed for the storage of images, videos and audio files. These libraries support a number of content types related to this area and are described in the following table.

CONTENT TYPE	PARENT	DESCRIPTION
Audio	Rich Media Asset	Content type used in Asset libraries for the storage of audio clips.
Image	Rich Media Asset	Content type used in Asset libraries for the storage of images.
Rich Media Asset	Document	Base media content type that contains the majority of core properties relevant to rich media, such as Thumbnails, Preview, and Keywords.
Video	System Media Collection	Content type associated with Asset libraries for the upload and storage of videos. Users can select options such as whether the video can be downloaded or embedded, and tag people as appearing in a video.
Video Rendition	Rich Media Asset	SharePoint 2013 offers support for creating renditions of video files so that you can have videos of different qualities and sizes. This is useful in scenarios where some of your users may be in low bandwidth locations and you want to provide a lower quality file that will stream better due to smaller size.

Document Content Types

You will probably use the document types frequently in your SharePoint sites because the typical site functions as a document repository and viewing system for your team. The following document types are built into SharePoint, many of which are explored throughout this book.

CONTENT TYPE	PARENT	DESCRIPTION
Basic Page	Document	Standard web page containing location for sharing text-based information.
Document	Item	Standard base content type for the storage of documents in SharePoint.
Dublin Core Columns	Document	Based on the Document content type but contains many standard columns to conform to the requirements for the popular classification system known as Dublin Core.
Form	Document	Based on the Document content type and is specifically designed to support the use of InfoPath. See Chapter 12, "Managing Forms," for more information on this content type.
Link to a Document	Document	In some cases, a document may be stored in one location and linked from another library. This content type helps support such scenarios by creating a record or row in a document library that references the document located in the other location.
List View Style	Document	System content type for the definition of list view styles.
Master Page	Document	Content type for the definition of master pages. See Chapter 14, "Branding and the User Experience," for more information on this content type.
Master Page Preview	Document	Based on the Document content type and is used for providing a preview of master pages.
Picture	Document	Based on the Document content type and is the primary content type associated with a picture library.
Web Part Page	Basic Page	A web page with a number of Web Part zones for the use of Web Parts. These web pages can come in a variety of layouts and templates.
Wiki Page	Document	A web page for use within a wiki library.

Document Set Content Types

Only one content type exists within the Document Set group. The Document Set content type is a specialized content type that supports the management of a group of documents.

CONTENT TYPE	PARENT	DESCRIPTION
Document Set	Document Collection Folder	Specialized content type for the grouping and management of related files as a single entity.

When defining a Document Set, you associate one or more content types that can be created within the set as well as define specific templates or content that can exist within the document set folder when it is created. In the next two Try It Outs, you enable the use of Document Set content types on your site collection and then define a Document Set for managing the sign-up process for new customers.

TRY IT OUT **Enabling Document Sets on a Site Collection**

1. From the top level of your site collection, select Site Settings from the Settings menu. The Site Settings page appears.

2. Select the Site Collection Features link from the Site Collection Administration group of links. You are redirected to a page listing all features available within the site collection.

> **NOTE** *If you do not see that group, you are not listed as a Site Collection Administrator of the site and you will need to work with your system administrator to be added to this group or to complete this exercise.*

3. Select the Activate button associated with the Document Sets feature. The page refreshes and the feature now appears as Active, as shown in Figure 6-13.

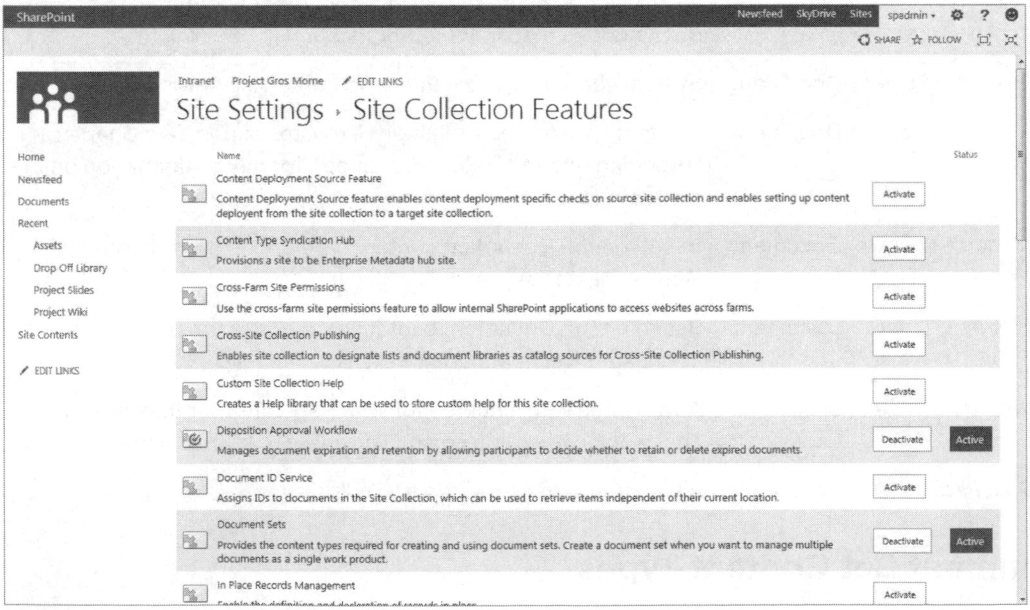

FIGURE 6-13

How It Works

SharePoint supports a wide range of functionality. Each site template is configured with certain features enabled while others are inactive until a user with appropriate privileges activates the feature for use. Once the feature is activated, the functionality it represents becomes enabled within the site or site collection. In the preceding example, the Document Sets' functionality was not available until you selected the Activate button. Now when you visit the Site Content Types gallery, you will be able to create Document Set content types.

TRY IT OUT Creating a Document Set

1. From the top level of your site collection, select Site Settings from the Site Actions menu. The Site Settings page appears.

2. Under the Galleries group, select Site Content Types. The Site Content Types page appears listing all content types available within the site collection.

3. Click the Create button.

4. Create the content type using the following settings:

PROPERTY	VALUE
Name	New Customer
Description	Package for Creating a New Customer
Select Parent Content Type From	Document Set Content Types
Parent Content Type	Document Set
Put this Content Type into (New Group)	Sales Documents

5. Click OK. You are redirected to the New Customer Content Type administration page.

6. Select the Document Set settings link. You are directed to a specialized administration page for Document Set content types, as shown in Figure 6-14.

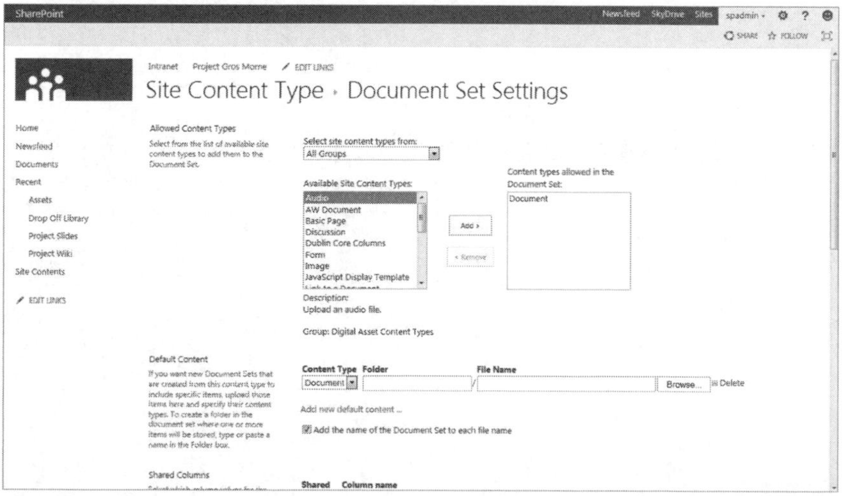

FIGURE 6-14

7. Select the content types that you want to allow users to utilize when creating a new customer. In this example, select AW Document and Sales Proposal.

8. In the Default Content section, click the Delete button next to the Browse button. This removes the Document content type from this library.

9. Select Add new default content link.

10. Select Sales Proposal as the content type, and upload the Proposal Template from this chapter's resource files.

11. Return to the Allowed Content Types section, and remove Document from the allowed listing.

12. Scroll to the bottom of the page, and click OK.

How It Works

In this example, you created a new Document Set content type for new customers. Whenever a user selects this content type from the new document option of the ribbon menu, a window appears, as shown in Figure 6-15. Users define the details of the new customer and then are redirected to a details page list for the document set. From this details page, users can create new documents based upon the allowed content types, as well as fill in documents such as the Proposal Template that exists already upon creation, as shown in Figure 6-16.

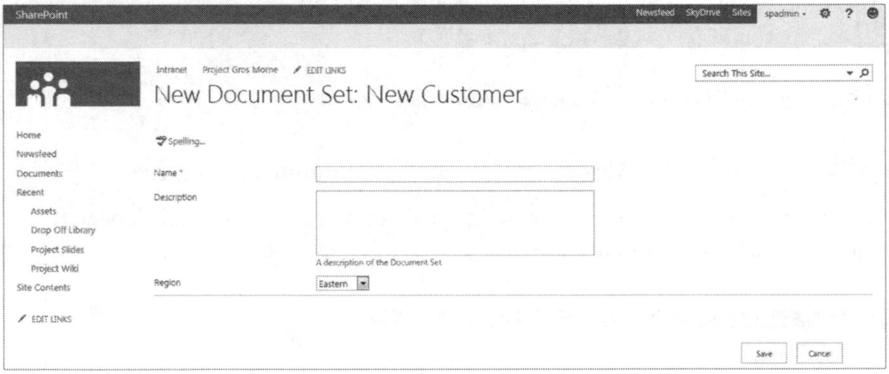

FIGURE 6-15

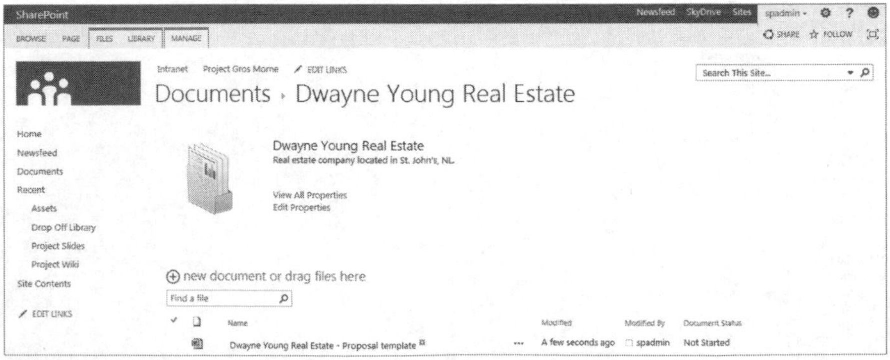

FIGURE 6-16

There is also a specific ribbon menu tab for Documents Sets, as shown in Figure 6-17. From this menu, users can edit properties, manage permissions, or capture version history of the entire set of documents. In addition, workflows can be launched based upon the available workflows that have been assigned to the content type. For example, account managers may run an approval workflow once all documentation related to the new customer is complete so that the sales manager can approve the new customer.

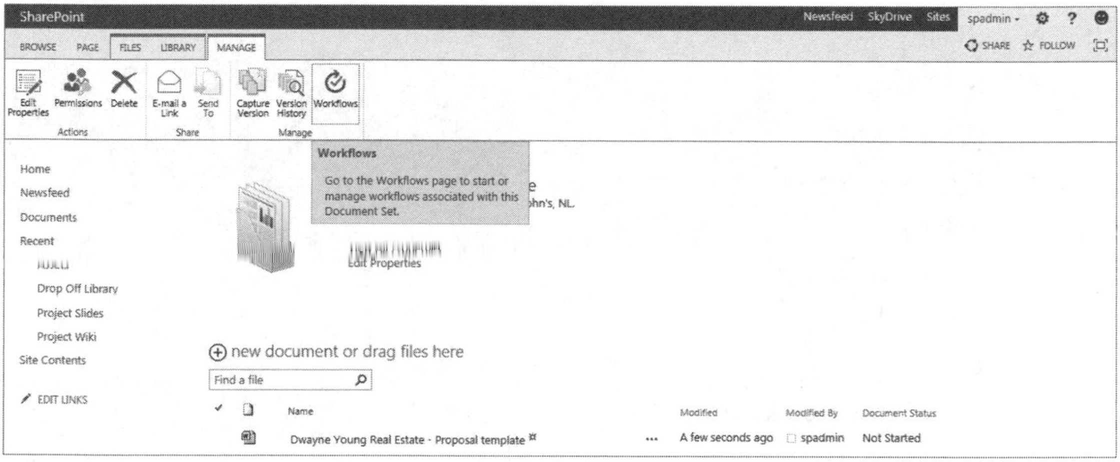

FIGURE 6-17

Folder Content Types

You use this type of content type for folders and discussion boards in SharePoint. Because individual discussions in SharePoint are stored within folders, it is appropriate that the base content type be affiliated with the Folder Content Types group. The following base content types are what SharePoint has to offer as part of the Folder Content Types group.

CONTENT TYPE	PARENT	DESCRIPTION
Folder	Item	Specialized folder that supports columns and metadata like any other element stored within a list or library.
Discussion	Folder	This content type is associated with a Discussion list, which was discussed in Chapter 2.
Summary Task	Folder	This content type is associated with the Tasks lists, which were discussed in Chapter 2, "Working with List Apps."

Group Work Content Types

The Group Work content types are a set of specialized content types associated with lists available within the Group Work Site template. This site template is designed to be a collaborative location for sharing data between team members of subjects such as whereabouts, phone calls, assignments, and schedules. The content types associated with this group all inherit from the Item content type and are as follows:

➤ Circulation

➤ Holiday

➤ New Word

➤ Official Notice

➤ Phone Call Memo

➤ Resource

➤ Resource Groups

➤ Timecard

➤ Users

➤ What's New Notification

List Content Types

An important SharePoint feature is the capability to easily create and store information in lists. Lists can hold any type of information, from a simple To-Do list, to a more complex resource-tracking list. The following base content types are what SharePoint has to offer as part of the List Content Types group.

CONTENT TYPE	PARENT	DESCRIPTION
Announcement	Item	Based on the Item content type and used for tracking simple news updates for a team. This content type is associated with an Announcements list, which was covered in Chapter 2.
Comment	Item	Based on an Item content type and contains the columns required to post responses to blog articles. Blogs are covered in Chapter 11, "Working with Social Features."
Contact	Item	Based on an Item content type and contains the columns required to share contact information. This content type is associated with the Contacts list, which was covered in Chapter 2.
East Asia Contact	Item	Very similar to the Contact content type but contains special columns related to phonetic information. We do not cover this content type in this book.

Event	Item	Based on the Item content type and used for tracking date-based information such as appointments, meetings, and events. This content type is associated with a Calendar list, which was covered in Chapter 2.
Issue	Item	Contains columns for tracking problems that may arise within a collaborative or work environment. This content type is associated with the Issues list, which was covered in Chapter 2.
Item	System	A parent content type of the Document content type and many list items. It is created by default with a single column for Title.
Link	Item	Based on the Item content type and used for hyperlink references to sites or documents. This content type is associated with a Links list, which was covered in Chapter 2.
Message	Item	Based on the Item content type and is used for storing replies associated with discussion topics. This content type is associated with a Discussion Board list, which was covered in Chapter 2.
Post	Item	Based on an Item content type and contains the columns required to post articles within a blog. Blogs are covered in Chapter 8.
Reservations	Event	This content type contains information related to the Group Calendar list.
Schedule	Event	This content type contains information related to the Group Calendar list.
Schedule and Reservations	Event	This content type contains information related to the Group Calendar list.
Task	Item	Based on an Item content type and contains the columns required to share task information. This content type is associated with the Tasks list, which was covered in Chapter 2.

Page Layout Content Types

One of the most significant advancements of SharePoint over the past few versions has been its advancement as a web content management system. This great functionality allows users to create content for a site directly from the browser without having any special web development knowledge or skills.

Most sites have unique types of pages. For example, you might have a main page, a generic sub-page, and a newsletter page. Each of these page types, in turn, has specific content elements that make it unique to the site. For example, the Newsletter page likely has a Title, Newsletter Body, and Published Date. A Page Layout content type defines these unique content elements by attaching site columns to your content type. You can later use this content type to create a Page Layout, which is a special type of template page that users can use to create new pages in a site. The following base content types are what SharePoint has to offer as part of the Page Layout Content Types group.

CONTENT TYPE	PARENT	DESCRIPTION
Article Page	Page	Contains many of the common properties that a page should have, including elements used for publishing, such as scheduling date, and others that are used for content display, such as page content.
Catalog Item Reuse Page	Page	The Catalog Item Reuse content type is best if you want to create article pages that can be easily reused or republished across your site collections.
Enterprise Wiki Page	Page	Enterprise Wiki Page is the default content type for the Enterprise Wiki site template. It provides a basic content area as well as ratings and categories.
Error Page	Page	The Error page is used to create system and custom error pages in sites that have the publishing feature enabled.
Project Page	Enterprise Wiki Page	Project Page is a content type included with the Enterprise Wiki site template. It provides some basic information to describe a project, including a project status and a contact name.
Redirect Page	Page	Redirect Page is a content type associated with a specialized page template that supports the definition of a URL that will redirect visitors automatically to the described location.
Welcome Page	Page	Contains a number of columns for the displaying and publishing of content.

PerformancePoint Content Types

The PerformancePoint content types are used by the business intelligence features of SharePoint. They are discussed in detail in Chapter 10. These content types are used for the display of reporting information such as dashboards, key performance indicators, and reports. The PerformancePoint content types include the following:

- ➤ PerformancePoint Dashboard
- ➤ PerformancePoint Data Source
- ➤ PerformancePoint Filter
- ➤ PerformancePoint Indicator
- ➤ PerformancePoint KPI
- ➤ PerformancePoint Report
- ➤ PerformancePoint Scorecard

Publishing Content Types

Another web content management-related content type group in SharePoint Server is Publishing content types. The base Publishing content types provide the structure for all major web publishing components. The following base content types are available as part of the Publishing Content Types group.

CONTENT TYPE	PARENT	DESCRIPTION
ASP.NET Master Page	System Master Page	Master Page is a system content type template created by the Publishing Resources feature. All master pages will have the column templates from Master Page added.
HTML Master Page	ASP.NET Master Page	HTML Master Page enables users to build custom master pages that contain a header, footer, and navigation using only HTML.
HTML Page Layout	Page Layout	HTML Page Layout is used as a template for authored page data within a master page using only HTML.
Page	System Page	Page is a system content type template created by the Publishing Resources feature. The column templates from Page will be added to all Pages libraries created by the Publishing feature.
Page Layout	System Page Layout	Page Layout is a system content type template created by the Publishing Resources feature. All page layouts will have the column templates from Page Layout added.

Special Content Types

The Special content type group allows users to upload documents to a library regardless of content type. It offers no special customization characteristics and is intended for use in situations where the content type is unknown or not important.

MANAGING CONTENT TYPES

An important aspect of managing a SharePoint site or environment is to understand how to combine and manage the information that a team or group shares. In this section, you discover some of the common management tasks that ensure that users in your organization can easily share and use your content types.

Enabling Content Type Management on a Library

For content types to be used within a SharePoint document library, the library must first be configured to utilize content types. You review this process in the next Try It Out. The steps for enabling content types on a document library apply to configuring a list to utilize content types as well.

TRY IT OUT Enabling Content Types on a Library

1. From the document library you want to configure, select Library Settings from the Library tab of the ribbon menu.

2. Select the Advanced Settings link. You are redirected to the Advanced Settings page, as shown in Figure 6-18.

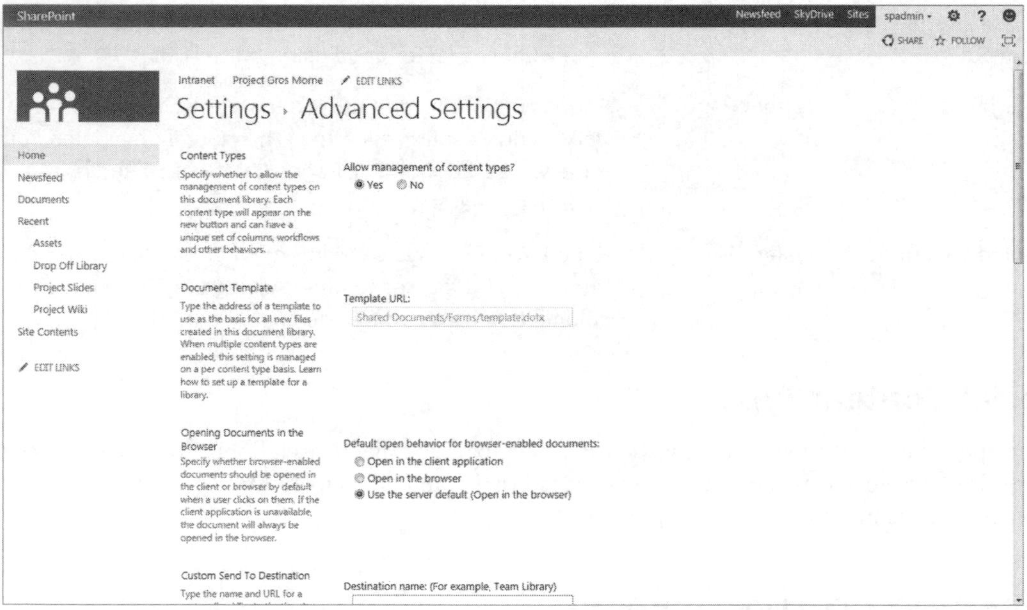

FIGURE 6-18

3. Select Yes for the Allow management of content types option.

4. Scroll to the bottom of the page, and click OK.

How It Works

Once you enable the management of content types from a list or library, you will notice that a Content Types section appears on the administration page for that list or library, as shown in Figure 6-19. From this section, users can add or remove content types for use within the library.

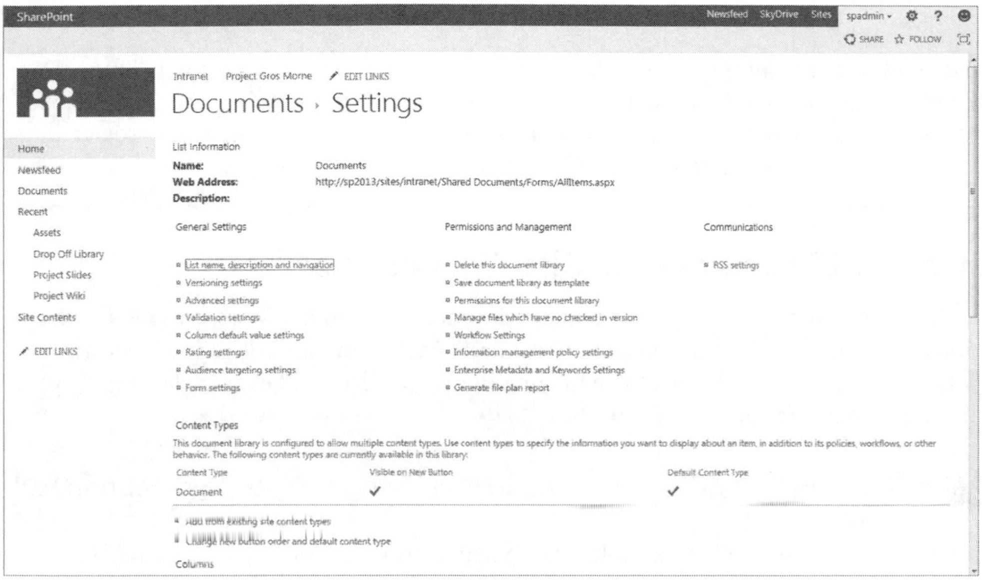

FIGURE 6-19

Managing Multiple Content Types in a Library

Today's business world often requires working with various types of content, which means managing many document templates, business processes, and information policies. Using the standard configuration of a document library, you can associate only a single document template with a document library, so you would require a large number of document libraries just to accommodate unique document templates and classification requirements. By associating multiple content types with a document library (shown in the next Try It Out), however, you can freely manage all the important information from a single location. These can be different types of templates using the same format, or completely different applications such as Microsoft Office Excel, InfoPath, PowerPoint, or Word. This means that you can save a tremendous amount of time because you can edit and share multiple types of documents from the same location.

TRY IT OUT Associating Multiple Content Types with a Library

1. From the document library on which you enabled the management of content types in the previous example, select Library Settings from the Library tab of the ribbon menu.

2. From the Content Types section of the page, select the "Add from existing site content types" link. You are redirected to the Add Content Types page.

3. Select the Sales Documents group from the drop-down menu. The content types associated with that group appear. Add the Sales Proposal and New Customer content types.

4. Click OK. You are returned to the Library Settings page.

How It Works

When you associate multiple content types with a document library, they become available in the drop-down menu of the New item on your document library toolbar, where you can select the type of document you want to create. For example, you might have a content type for Sales Proposals associated with a Microsoft Office Word template and a New Customer Document Set content type.

Managing Content Types across Site Collections

Once you have defined your content types for a single site collection, you may want to make them available to other site collections. To do this, you must first enable your site collection to be an Enterprise Metadata hub site. You do this by managing the Site Collection Features settings of your site. You review this process in the next Try It Out.

TRY IT OUT Configuring Your Site Collection to Be a Content Type Syndication Hub

1. From the top level of your site collection, select Site Settings from the Site Actions menu. The Site Settings page appears.

2. Click the Site Collection Features link from the Site Collection Administration group of links. You are redirected to a page listing all features available within the site collection.

> **NOTE** If you do not see that group, you are not listed as a Site Collection Administrator of the site and you will need to work with your system administrator to be added to this group or to complete this exercise.

3. Select the Activate button associated with the Content Type Syndication Hub feature. The page refreshes and the feature now appears as Active, as shown in Figure 6-20.

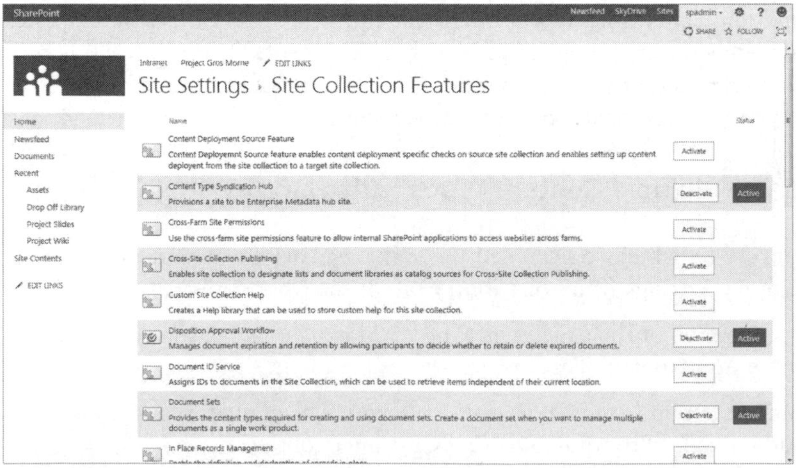

FIGURE 6-20

How It Works

Once your site collection is configured to be a content type syndication hub, the administration page of each content type now displays a new option to support the publishing of that content type to other web applications or site collections, as shown in Figure 6-21.

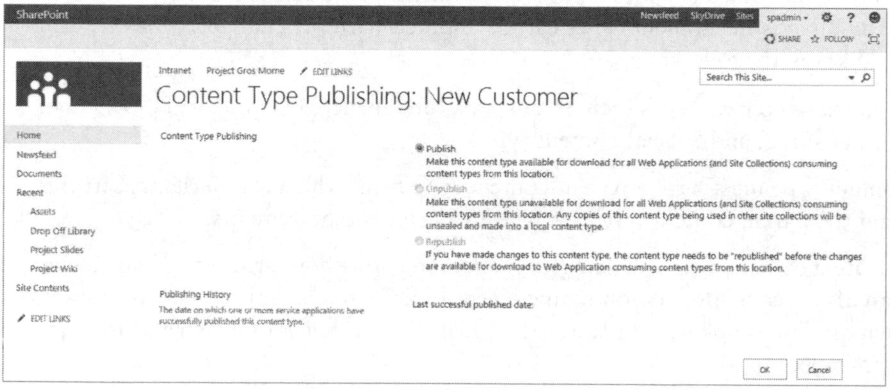

FIGURE 6-21

To complete the configuration of the content type syndication hub, you must also indicate the site collection that is the content type hub within the Managed Metadata Service application. This is done by navigating to the Central Administration site and selecting Manage Service Applications. Once on the service application listing page, select the Managed Metadata Service application and click the Properties button from the ribbon. Scroll to the bottom of the page and specify your site collection as the Content Type hub, as shown in Figure 6-22.

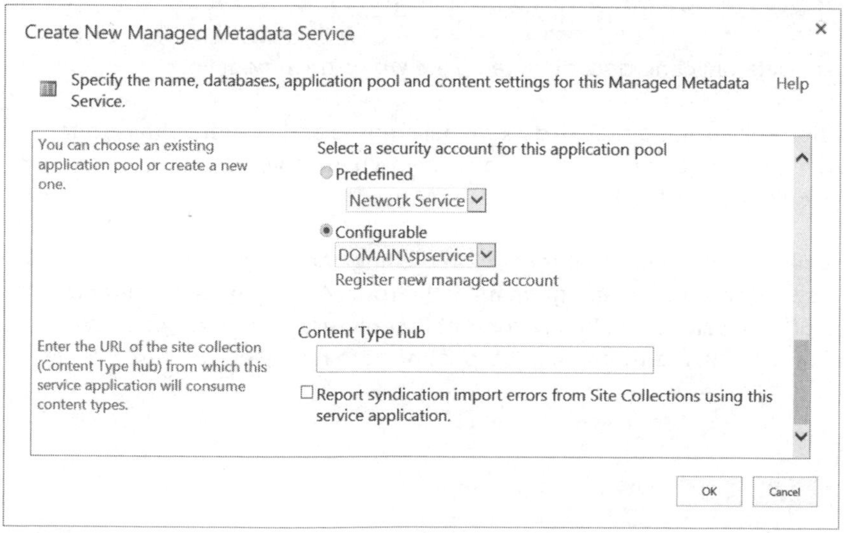

FIGURE 6-22

SUMMARY

This chapter discussed the very important SharePoint feature known as *content types*. Content types enable you to package and manage elements such as templates, workflow processes, policies, and metadata columns as a single reusable component. You can then associate these components with lists and libraries throughout a site collection. Users can then make edits centrally to the site content type gallery, and all existing content types can be updated with the changes. After reading this chapter, you should know the following:

➤ The default groups of content types include Business Intelligence, Document, Folder, List, Page Layout, Publishing, and Special content types.

➤ Every new content type must have a parent content type from which it inherits its settings. You can extend the parent content type to suit your business requirements.

➤ You can associate a content type with a custom template, workflow processes, and site columns. You can also create information management policies to control what information is displayed when an item is opened or printed. In addition, you can configure rules to determine when it must expire.

➤ Some content types are very basic in nature and do not require configuration; however, other content types may be more heavily regulated and controlled.

➤ A single document library or list can host multiple content types. This allows users to work from a single repository for related content. However, when managing multiple content types and large amounts of data within a single library, consider using custom views to maintain an acceptable level of usability for users. Information should always be well organized and easy to find.

EXERCISES

1. True or false: You can associate only one document template with a document library.

2. Imagine you are responsible for ensuring that all documents created and printed within your organization have the words Private and Confidential on them. What are your options for making this happen, and which would provide the best results?

3. People in your company have complained that recent job postings are being published on the corporate intranet website with typos and grammatical errors. Your management team demands a certain level of professionalism in any content that division members post. What are some steps you can take to ensure that future job postings are reviewed prior to publishing them?

▶ **WHAT YOU LEARNED IN THIS CHAPTER**

TOPIC	KEY CONCEPTS
Content types	A content type represents a type of information in your organization that shares common properties such as a template, workflow, site columns, and information policies.
Parent content types	Content types are organized in a hierarchy and each new content type must have a parent from which it inherits the basic properties.
Base content types	The base content types in SharePoint include Business Intelligence, Content Organizer, Document, Document Sets, Folders, Group Work, List, PerformancePoint, Page Layout, Publishing, and Special content types.

7

Working with Web Parts

WHAT YOU WILL LEARN IN THIS CHAPTER:

➤ How to add and configure Web Parts

➤ How to remove Web Parts

➤ How to import and export Web Parts

➤ How to connect Web Parts

➤ How to use out-of-the-box Web Parts

You can think of Web Parts as visual information blocks that you use to build a team or portal site. Essentially, they are modules or applications that you retrieve from a site's gallery and add to a web page. Every time you create a list or library app, SharePoint creates a corresponding Web Part that you can drag onto a Web Part page to view the contents of that list or library. Web parts can be as simple as an application allowing you to view a list of members of your site, to something more complex that displays data from an external business system.

Although SharePoint 2013 has Web Parts ready for your use, you can also create your own Web Parts using Visual Studio. For example, if you need a special module on your site that allows users to submit, update, and review support incidents from an external helpdesk application, you can develop a Web Part for that purpose. However, before you create anything custom, it is always important to understand what is available out-of-the-box. This chapter focuses on the core Web Parts that are available as part of a SharePoint Server installation and discusses the most common methods for interacting with them.

USING WEB PARTS

To get started, this section explores the more common techniques for interacting with Web Parts, including adding a Web Part to a page, editing its properties, and removing it from a page.

Adding Web Parts to a Page

It is important to know that two types of pages in SharePoint relate to Web Parts: a Web Part page and a wiki page. Both support the use of Web Parts, but are different in how you edit and manage them.

A Web Part page, as you can imagine, is designed specifically for the use of Web Parts. It contains a series of predefined areas known as *Web Part zones*. Users with the appropriate privileges can add or move Web Parts between zones. Figure 7-1 shows a typical Web Part page that is associated with a site created with the Document Center template.

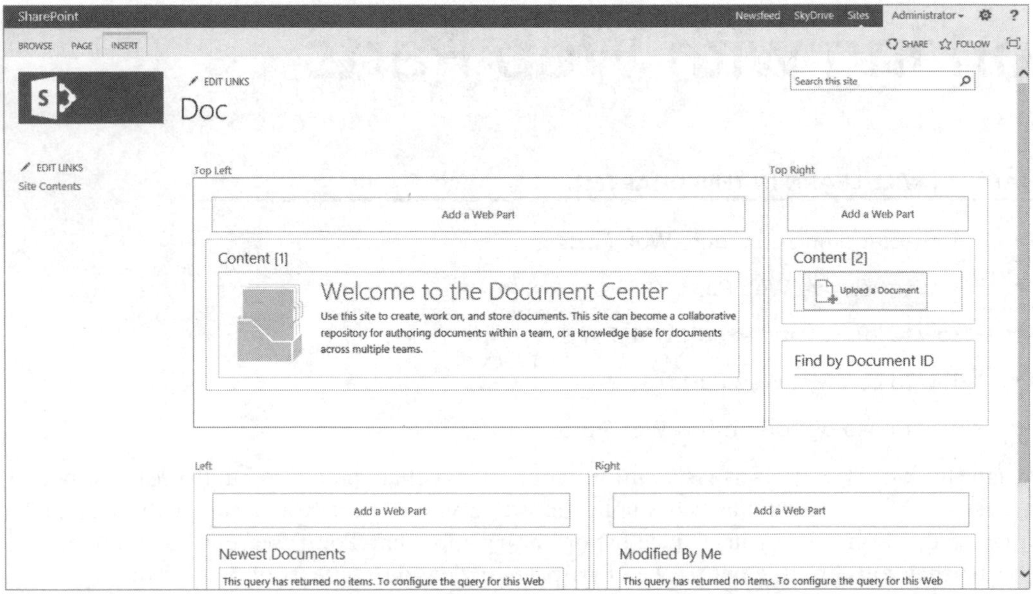

FIGURE 7-1

> **WARNING** *You cannot modify the layout of standard Web Part pages that you create with a site template.*

Wiki pages are pages that allow users to type freeform rich text directly on the page and format it as desired in addition to adding Web Parts to it. When a new site is created based on the Team Site template, the homepage for that site is a wiki page. Figure 7-2 shows a wiki page from a team site. Authorized users can edit this page by typing directly into the content area or they can choose to insert items such as Web Parts, video players, or images. If desired, users can change the layout of a wiki page as well.

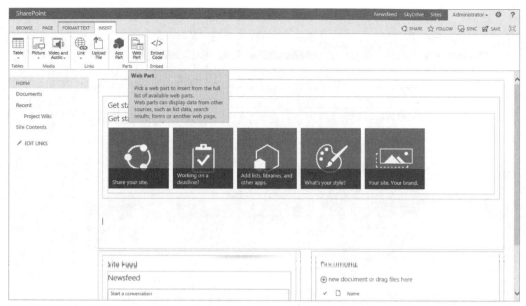

FIGURE 7-2

Chapter 15 reviews the web content management features of SharePoint Server, which include an additional type of page, the *publishing page*, that supports the use of Web Part zones, but also allows for the insertion of additional types of content and layout changes.

The following examples cover the process for adding a Web Part to a Web Part page, followed by an example of doing so on a wiki page.

CHANGING A HOMEPAGE FROM A WEB PART PAGE TO A WIKI PAGE

A Document Center site is one type of site template that has a Web Part page as a homepage. To change any site's homepage to a wiki page, click Site Actions and choose Site Settings. Click Manage Site Features and activate the Wiki Page Home Page feature, as shown in Figure 7-3.

continues

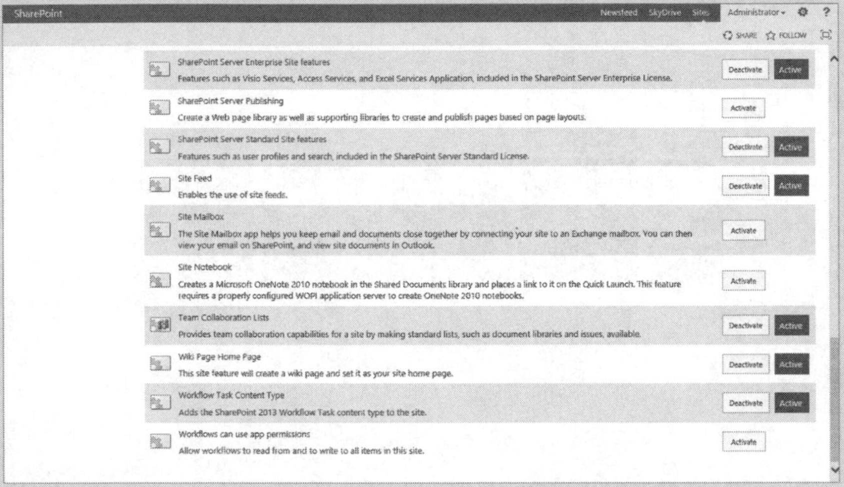

FIGURE 7-3

TRY IT OUT Adding a Web Part to a Page

In this Try It Out, you go through the steps of adding a Web Part to a page. In many of the remaining activities in this chapter, you add different Web Parts to pages, so it's important to understand this procedure.

1. On your homepage, click Settings ⇨ Edit Page.

2. Depending on the type of page you are editing, your process may be slightly different for the next step:

   ➤ If the page is a Web Part page, you will see blocks on the page that have Add a Web Part links. Click the Add a Web Part link for the desired area of the page to which you want to add a Web Part.

   ➤ If the page is a wiki page, put your mouse cursor in the area of the page to which you want to add a Web Part, click the Insert tab of the ribbon menu at the top of the page, and click the Web Part button.

3. A new pane is now displayed at the top of the page. Select the category of the Web Part you want to add. You will want to become familiar with the different types of Web Parts and which categories they belong to by reading the "Configuring a Web Parts" section later in this chapter.

4. Once you select a category, all Web Parts associated with that category are listed in the Parts area of the screen. Select the Web Part you want to add. Once you select a Web Parts, you can view details regarding that Web Part in the "About the part" section of the screen, as shown in Figure 7-4.

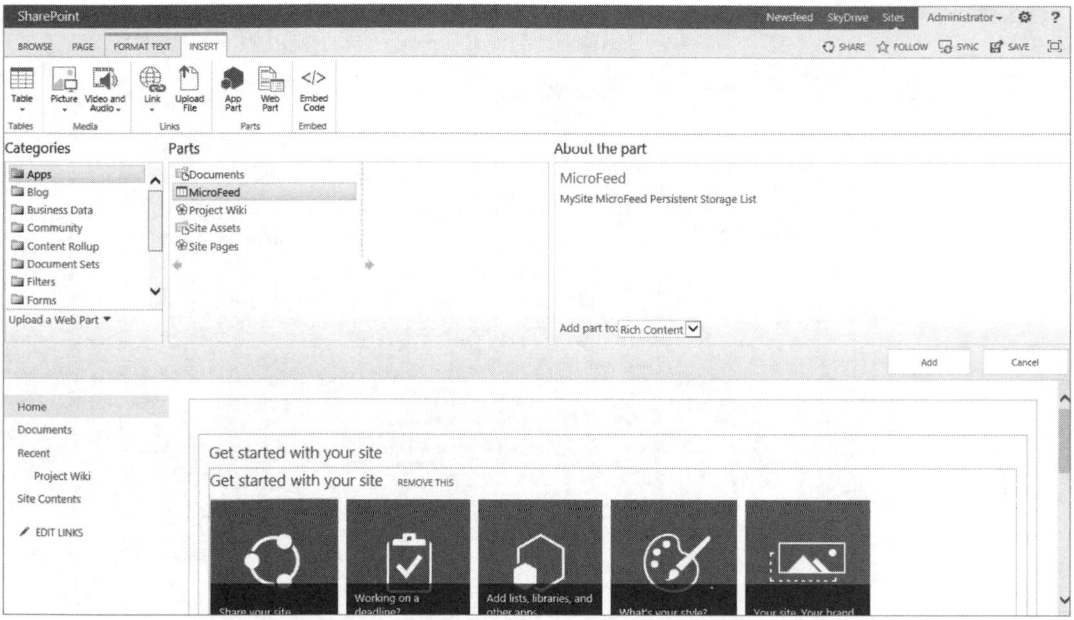

FIGURE 7-4

5. Once you select your Web Part, you can click the Add button to complete the process of adding the Web Part to the page.

If you added the Web Part to a Web Part page, you can move it from zone to zone by clicking the title part of the Web Part and dragging it around the page.

How It Works

In this Try it Out, you added a Web Part to a page. The Web Part will now be available on the page to be configured and viewed by other users. You can add multiple Web Parts to a page using the same process defined in this exercise.

Configuring Web Parts

Whenever you add a Web Part to a page, it contains default settings and may likely require additional configuration to display content exactly how you want. To further configure a Web Part, you can use the Web Part properties pane, which is accessible via every Web Part's Edit Web Part menu, as shown in Figure 7-5.

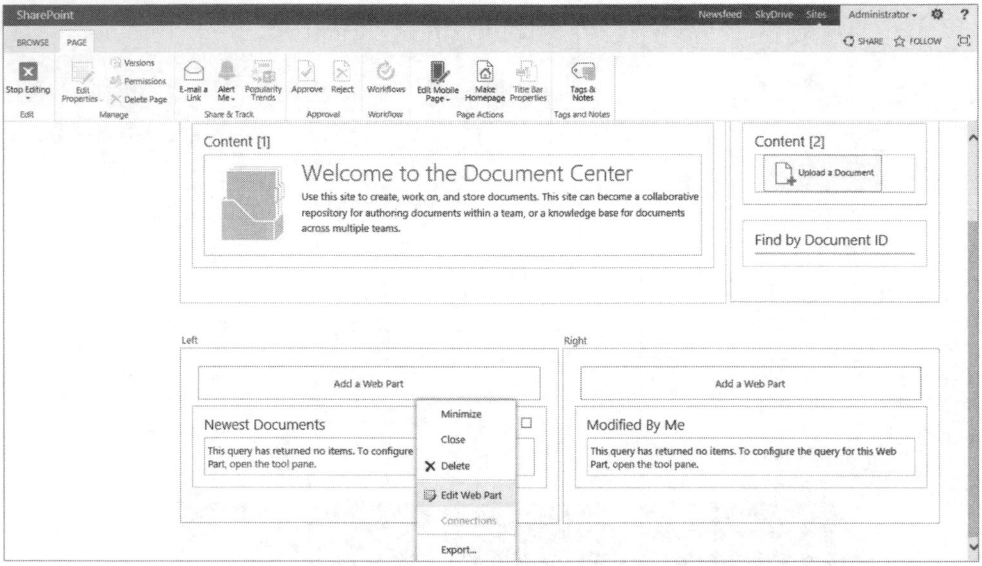

FIGURE 7-5

The Web Part properties that are available vary between different types of Web Parts, but a standard set of options exists across all Web Parts. This section describes each of the standard Web Part settings.

Appearance

The Appearance setting of a Web Part refers to the various properties that you can define related to how the Web Part appears on the page. These might include details such as the title that appears above the Web Part, the size of the Web Part on the page, or whether a title or frame appears around the Web Part's content.

NAME	DESCRIPTION
Title	This is the title that displays in the top of the frame of the Web Part. For list (and library) app Web Parts, by default the title is the name of the list. Note that changing the Web Part title does not change the actual name of the list. Changing the name of a list can be done in the list settings, in the Title, Description, and Navigation section.
Height	The height of the Web Part, in a selectable measurement, such as pixels or inches.
Width	The width of a Web Part, in a selectable measurement.
Chrome State	The options are Minimized and Normal, with Normal being the default.
Chrome Type	These options consist of various combinations of the title and border of the Web Part. This setting can be very useful when you want to have the title of a Web Part displayed or hidden based on your preferences for the look of a page.

Layout

The layout options reflect how the Web Part is positioned on the page. You can use these options to move the Web Part from one zone to another or to hide it on the page.

NAME	DESCRIPTION
Hidden	Hide the Web Part. This Web Part can be seen only by the page designer while the page is in edit mode. This option is sometimes useful for testing purposes, or in cases where the Web Part contains code or script and does not need to be displayed. This is not configurable in a wiki page.
Direction	Right to left or left to right.
Zone	Pick which Web Part zone to put the Web Part in. This is not configurable in wiki pages.
Zone Index	Type the number of the zone index. This is the order in which the Web Parts are displayed within the Web Part zone. Typing a "1" here brings the Web Part to the top of the page. You can optionally use this instead of dragging Web Parts with the mouse. This is also not configurable in wiki pages.

Advanced

These settings relate to some of the options that are available for users of the site to interact with the Web Part. In addition, you can use the Advanced settings for Audience Targeting to specify which groups are able to view the Web Part when it is on the page. This can be useful for creating personalized experiences on pages for each of the main roles of the site.

NAME	DESCRIPTION
Allow Minimize	Uncheck this box to disallow the option to minimize the Web Part.
Allow Close	Uncheck this box to disallow the option to close the Web Part. Not available on wiki pages.
Allow Hide	Uncheck this box to disallow other page designers from checking the box in the layout options that changes the Web Part to hidden. Not available on wiki pages.
Allow Zone Change	Site members will not be able to put the page in edit mode and rearrange Web Parts using their mouse, but they will be able to click Edit My Web Part to open the Web Part tool pane. When Allow Zone Change is unchecked, the site members will not have the ability to change zone information for a Web Part. This option is not available on wiki pages.

continues

(continued)

NAME	DESCRIPTION
Allow Connections	Uncheck this to disallow creating connections from this Web Part to other Web Parts on the page.
Allow Editing in Personal View	Uncheck this to disable the Edit My Web Part button for site members.
Title URL	If this value is set, end users of the site will be able to click the title of the Web Part. The page that they will be directed to will be the URL specified in this property.
Description	If the Title URL property is specified, the information specified in the Description property can be displayed as a tooltip to users that hover their mouse over the link.
Help URL	If you have created a specific page for users to obtain help regarding this Web Part, enter the URL to that page here. When a URL exists here, there will be a new option called Help, available to users when they click the Web Part's drop-down box.
Help Mode	Choose from modal, modeless, or navigate. When users click the Help button on the Web Part's drop-down menu, they will view the help page that was specified in the Help URL. Based on the Help Mode, either the page will appear in a new window or the user will be redirected to the specified page.
Catalog Icon Image URL	This is the image that represents this Web Part.
Title Icon Image URL	This icon is displayed next to the title of the Web Part. By default, there is no icon in this location.
Import Error Message	Type the error message that you would like to be displayed if there is ever an error importing the Web Part.
Target Audiences	Pick the target audience of people who you would like to see this Web Part. By default, this setting is blank, and the Web Part is shown to everyone who visits the page. Pick from global audiences, distribution/security groups, or SharePoint groups. Audience targeting is not a substitute for security, but is used to personalize the way that the page is viewed, according to the viewer. Show the most relevant information to any audience.
Export Mode	This appears only in the properties for Web Parts that are exportable. Choose from Do Not Allow, Non-sensitive data only, or Export all data.

Removing Web Parts

At times you may have a Web Part on your page that you no longer require or that you want to remove. If your page is a Web Part page, you can either close or delete it. Wiki web pages only allow for deletion of Web Parts. When you close the Web Part, it is added to a gallery called *Closed Web Parts*, which you can access later. All settings you have applied to that instance of the Web Part are retained. When you delete a Web Part, it is deleted from the page completely. Any configurations or content that you have added directly to the Web Part (such as text in a content editor Web Part) are deleted as well. However, it is important to understand that if your Web Part points to content displayed on the site, such as a list or library Web Part, the content within the list or library is unaffected by the Web Part being deleted.

Importing and Exporting Web Parts

You can import and export certain Web Parts, which is a way of saving a Web Part and its settings and adding it to another page or site. List app (list and library apps) Web Parts cannot be exported, but most other types can. When in edit mode, click the drop-down box at the top right of a Web Part to see if Export is listed as an option, as shown in Figure 7-6. When you click the Export button, you are prompted to save the Web Part to your computer. Pick a location on your computer to save the Web Part to.

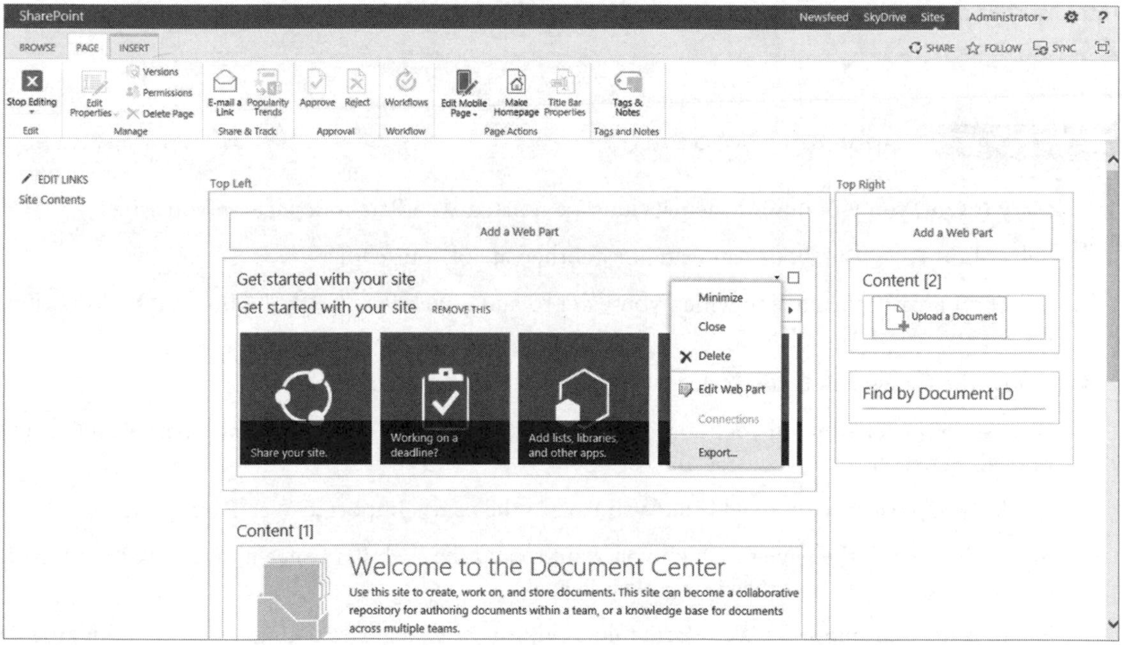

FIGURE 7-6

TRY IT OUT   Exporting a Web Part

In this Try It Out, you will export a Web Part from a page. This will allow you to save it for reuse on another page.

1. From your team site, add the "Getting started with your site" Web Part, which is part of the Media and Content category of Web Parts, to the homepage using the method described earlier in the chapter.

2. Hover on the right side of the Web Part till a small black arrow appears.

3. Click the arrow to expand the Web Part menu, as shown in Figure 7-6, and select Edit Web Part. The Web Part properties pane appears.

4. Enter **Important Tasks** as the title of your Web Part and click the Apply and OK buttons to save the changes.

5. Expand the Web Part menu again, as in step 2, and select the Export option.

6. Save the Web Part to a location on your computer to be used in the next example.

How It Works

In this Try It Out, you configured your Web Part by changing the title to a preferred value. You then exported the Web Part from the page and saved it to your computer. This will allow you to import it into another page, which we will explore in the next Try It Out.

TRY IT OUT   Importing a Web Part

In this Try It Out, you will import the previously exported Web Part to a page on your site.

1. Select Edit Page from your team site (or another site of your choice).

2. Select an area of the page to which you want to add a Web Part, click the Insert tab of the ribbon menu, and select Web Part.

3. Below the Categories listing, select the Update a Web Part link.

4. Browse to the location on your computer to which you saved the Important Tasks Web Part in the preceding exercise.

5. Click the Upload button to add the Web Part to the page's Imported Web Parts gallery.

6. Select the area of the page to which you want to add the Web Part once more, click the Insert tab of the ribbon menu, and then select Web Part.

7. There is now an Imported Web Parts folder within the Categories listing, as shown in Figure 7-7. Select the Important Tasks Web Part from this gallery and click Add.

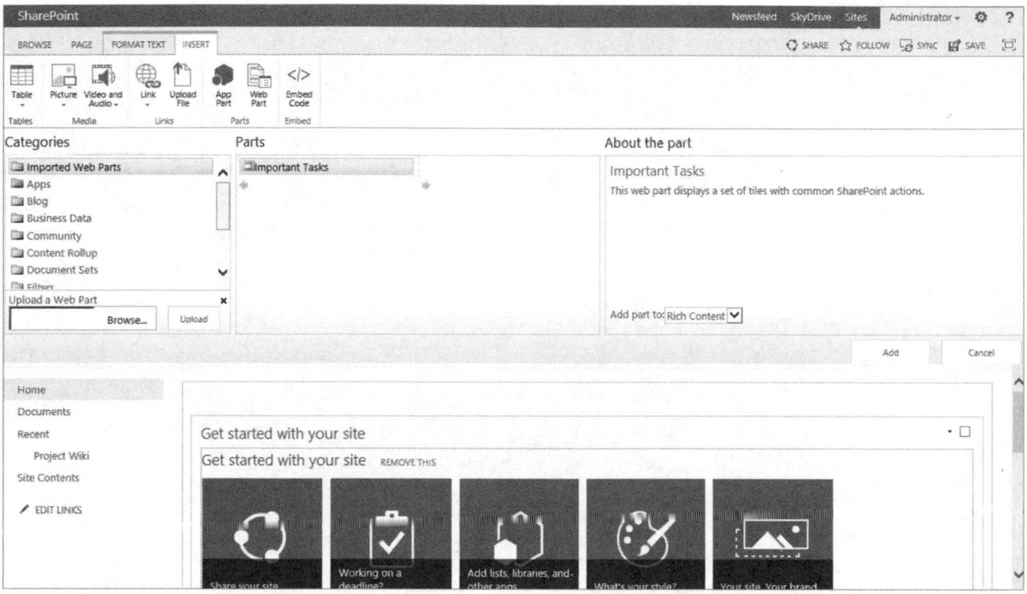

FIGURE 7-7

How It Works

In this Try It Out, you imported the Important Tasks Web Part to a new page. This Web Part is now available to be added to the page.

This approach requires you to import a Web Part to each page that you want to add it to. You can also upload the Web Part to the Web Parts gallery, which is accessible by clicking the Web Parts link from the Site Settings page of the top-level site of the site collection. When an exported Web Part is uploaded to this location, it will be accessible to all pages within the site collection.

Connecting Web Parts

You can add Web Parts to the page as independent pieces of information, or you can connect them to one another to share common information so that the selection of an item in one Web Part automatically filters the items displayed in the other. For example, two Web Parts can exist on a page displaying a column called *customer*. You can connect these two Web Parts so that selecting a customer in one Web Part (such as customer name) filters the second Web Part to display only orders that include the selected customer name. This helps to provide a more interactive experience to users of your site, as they can select items and have the contents of the page change to suit their selection. The Web Part that sends the filter information is called the *provider*, and the Web Part that gets filtered is referred to as the *consumer*. When a page is in edit mode, click the drop-down box in the top-right corner of a Web Part to see the Connections option, as shown in Figure 7-8.

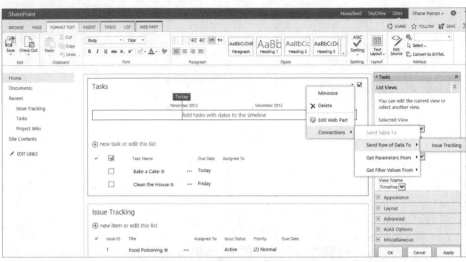

FIGURE 7-8

TRY IT OUT | **Connecting Web Parts**

In this Try It Out, you connect two Web Parts to each other. This example explores a scenario where a Tasks list is being used for tracking activities related to a project. However, in some cases issues may arise from these tasks. Therefore, an Issues list is also being used on the site to track issues that may relate to a specific task. To make this scenario work, you must have two lists with the following configurations:

➤ **Tasks list** — Standard list based on the Tasks app. Add two to three sample tasks as data to the list.

➤ **Issues list** — Standard list based on the Issues Tracking app with an additional column called Related Task that is a lookup to the Task Name column of the Tasks list. Include five to six sample issues related to the tasks created within the Tasks list.

If you do not create these lists, you will not be able to complete this exercise exactly as written. If you are unsure how to create the lists, see Chapter 4, "Managing and Customizing Lists and Libraries."

1. Add the Tasks App Web Part to the homepage of your site using the method described in the "Adding a Web Parts to a Page" section earlier in this chapter.

2. Add the Issues Tracking App Web Part to the homepage of your site.

3. With the page in edit mode, expand the Web Part menu of the Tasks App Web Part and select Edit Web Part. This puts the Web Part in edit mode and enables you to create connections.

This step is required only for Web Parts on a wiki page. If the Web Parts were on a Web Part page, this step would not be required.

4. Expand the Web Part menu of the Tasks App Web Part and select Connections ⇨ Send Row of Data To ⇨ Issue Tracking (refer to Figure 7-8). The page refreshes and a pop-up window appears requesting details related to the connection between the two Web Parts.

5. In the pop-up window, select the option to Get Filter Values From for Connection Type and click the Configure button. The pop-up window refreshes and two drop-down fields appear.

The Provider Field Name refers to the field within the Tasks list that will be passed to the Issues Tracking list. The Consumer Field Name refers to the field within the Issues Tracking list that will be a match for the field being sent from the Tasks list.

6. Select Task Name for the Provider Field Name value.

7. Select Related Task for the Consumer Field Name.

8. Click the Finish button.

The screen refreshes and the two Web Parts will now be connected. If you select a task in the Tasks Web Part, the Issues Tracking Web Part refreshes and displays on those that are associated with the selected task, as shown in Figure 7-9.

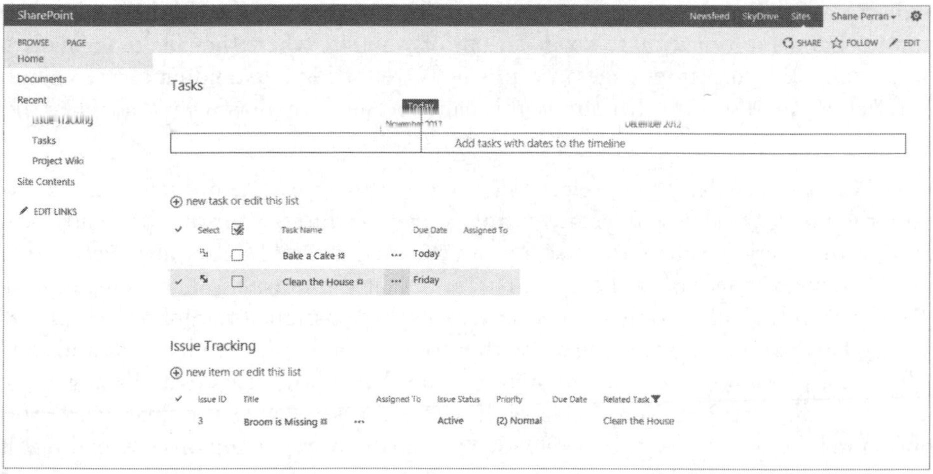

FIGURE 7-9

To remove a Web Part connection, follow steps 3-5, and then click the Remove Connection button on the Configure Connection screen. Sometimes it is necessary to temporarily remove connections in order to make changes to the filter Web Part configurations.

How It Works

In this Try It Out, you created a connection between a Tasks App Web Part and an Issues Tracking App Web Part. By creating this connection, you have configured the page so that if a user selects a task from the Tasks list, it will filter the Issues list to show only items that are related to that task.

THE OUT-OF-THE-BOX WEB PARTS

Now that you know the basics of working with Web Parts, it's time to find out what Web Parts SharePoint has to offer. Each SharePoint Web Part is designed to aid in the display of content or information on your website. Some Web Parts display information based on the SharePoint site or environment, such as the Table of Contents Web Part, which is a navigational tool to display links to sites, lists, and libraries. Other Web Parts, such as the Media Viewer Web Part, can be configured to include content that site owners may want to share with others. Finally, some Web Parts work in combination with other Web Parts to control how a page displays information, such as the Filter Web Parts.

The previous section discussed operations that are common to most Web Parts. This section introduces the different Web Parts as well as some of the unique characteristics of each.

List and Library

One of SharePoint's best collaborative features is the lists and libraries where teams can store and organize documents. Each time you create a list or library, SharePoint creates a corresponding Web Part in the gallery so you can place a view of the list or library on any page within the site. This empowers you to channel information to key locations of your site where they make the most sense. For example, you may have a custom page on your site for reporting outstanding tasks. Therefore, you can add a Web Part of the Tasks list app to this page so users can view what tasks they should focus on next.

List and library Web Parts enable you to select views in order to access the information that you need. In Chapter 4, you learned how to create custom views to address your requirements for information display. In this section, you learn how you can use the List and Library app Web Parts to display these views on any page you want. The first Try It Out shows you how to change the view of a List Web Part so the user can see only the tasks that have been assigned to him or her. In addition, each list app Web Part has a toolbar associated with it to help you work with list data and settings. The toolbar has multiple states. The Full and Summary toolbars allow users to add a new item to the list directly from the Web Part. You also have the option of not having a toolbar at all. You can select that option in cases where the page is intended primarily for reporting or viewing information and no interaction is expected or desired from viewers. Regardless of which option you select for the toolbar, the users of your site will see the option to add new content only if they are allowed to do so.

For more on lists and libraries and how to manage them, see Chapters 2 through 4.

TRY IT OUT   Changing the View of a List App Web Part

In this example, you add a Tasks App Web Part to the homepage of your team site. The views associated with the Tasks App will be available for selection within the Web Part. You want to have users see all tasks assigned to them within the Web Part, so you select the My Tasks view to be displayed within the Web Part.

1. Add the Tasks list Web Part to the homepage of your site using the method described earlier in this chapter.

2. Select the checkbox in the top right of the Web Part. The ribbon menu now displays a new tab called Web Part.

3. Select Web Part Properties from the Web Part tab of the ribbon menu. This displays the Web Part properties pane that was previously viewed by selecting Edit Web Part.

4. Select the My Tasks view from the Selected View drop-down menu, as shown in Figure 7-10.

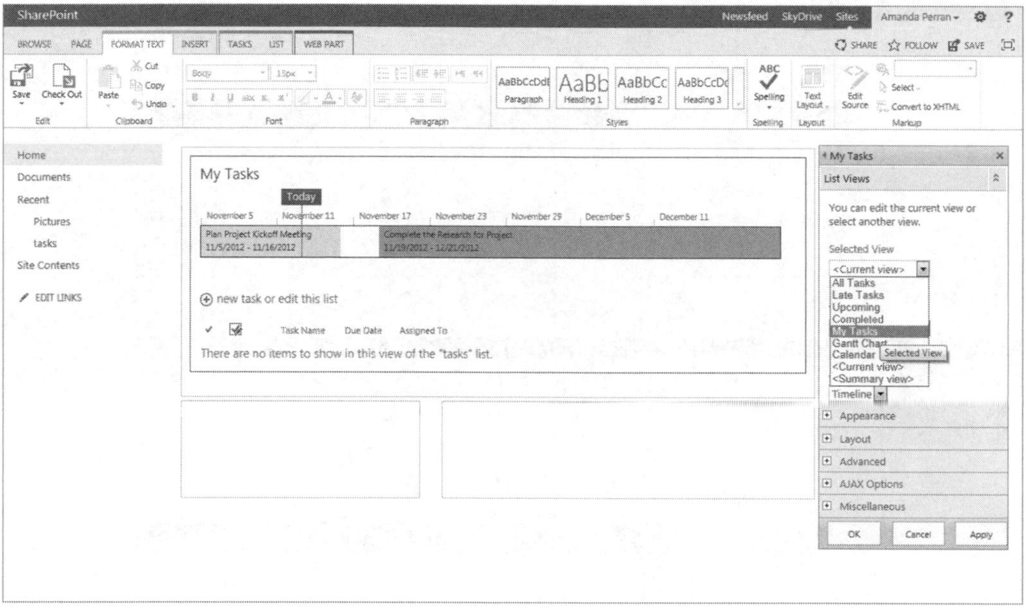

FIGURE 7-10

5. For the Toolbar Type drop-down, select the option for No Toolbar.

6. Expand the Appearance section of the Web Part properties pane.

7. Enter **My Tasks** as the title of the Web Part.

8. Click the Apply button and then save your changes.

9. Click the OK button to close the Web Part properties pane.

How It Works

In this Try It Out, you selected the My Tasks view and then changed the title of the Web Part to describe the view to be displayed. This informs users that they are viewing a subset of the data available in the list and not the default view of All Items. You can use this same process for custom views you create on any list or library. In addition, you selected that No Toolbar should appear on the Web Part. This setting removed the link for users to add a new task or edit this list from the Web Part. It is useful to use this setting in scenarios where you may have a page that is only for displaying content but you do not want to clutter up the display with additional menu options or links. Changing the Web Part properties for the toolbar does not impact any security permissions related to the list. It just disables the ability for any user to add items via the Web Part. Figure 7-11 is an example of a Tasks Web Part with the Summary toolbar enabled. This is typically viewable whenever the Web Part is added to the page. Figure 7-12 is an example of how the Web Part looked once you changed the toolbar type to No Toolbar.

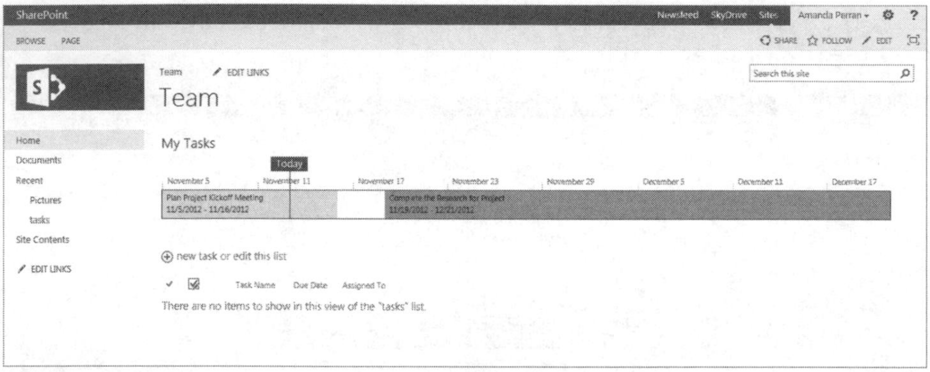

FIGURE 7-11

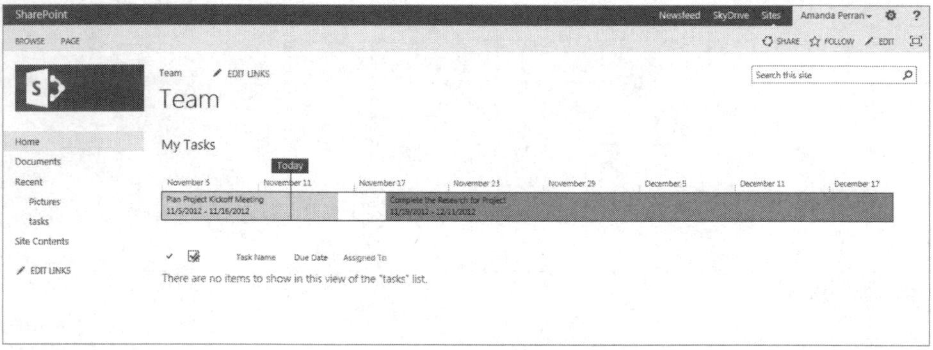

FIGURE 7-12

In addition to these settings, you could have also selected Show Toolbar, which would display a menu bar at the top of the Web Part to allow users to add new items, perform actions on the Web Part, or modify settings associated with the list. An example of this toolbar is shown in Figure 7-13.

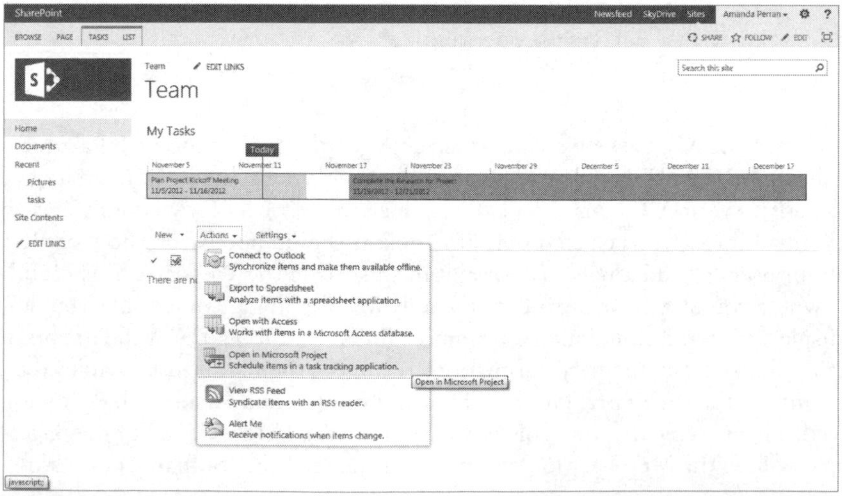

FIGURE 7-13

Blog

The blog Web Parts enable site administrators on sites using the Blog template to provide additional links to a monthly archive listing, provide links for end users to subscribe to notifications, or insert a set of links that allow blog owners to publish or manage new content. These Web Parts are built specifically for blog sites and not intended for use on other site templates.

Business Data

Although SharePoint is an excellent data repository, many organizations keep a great deal of operational and historical data in other systems — usually called *back-end systems* — such as custom or commercial line-of-business (LOB) applications. Back-end systems often run on infrastructure that has been in place for many years. Because it may be impractical for organizations to manage such information in SharePoint but they still need to extract data for reports, key performance indicators (KPIs), and other SharePoint collaboration features, SharePoint offers *Business Connectivity Services* (BCS). BCS enables organizations to access data from these other data sources via specialized Web Parts, external lists, and content types.

As shown in the following table, the business data Web Parts are a group of powerful Web Parts that enable you to connect to and interact with important business data from various sources:

WEB PART	DESCRIPTION
Business Data Actions	Displays a list of actions from the Business Connectivity Services (BCS) data connection that enable you to view or interact with business data. For example, you may be able to e-mail a customer by selecting an action from this Web Part on a page that displays information about the customer.
Business Data Connectivity Filter	Filters the contents of Web Parts on the page based on filters that have been associated with the content source with the business data connection.
Business Data Item	Displays information related to a single item from a data source in the BCS. For example, you may be able to view contact details of a customer that is being pulled from an external customer database in this Web Part.
Business Data Item Builder	Used on business data profile pages, this Web Part creates a business data item from parameters on the query string and then provides it to other Web Parts.
Business Data List	Displays a list of items from a data source in the BDC. An example of this might be a listing of customers.
Business Data Related List	Displays a list of items as they pertain to child-parent relationships from a data source in the BCS. An example of this is a listing of orders made by a single customer who had been selected in a connected Business Data List Web Part.

continues

(continued)

WEB PART	DESCRIPTION
Excel Web Access	Enables you to interact with an Excel workbook as a web page. This is helpful for displaying financial or numerical reports based on information stored in a spreadsheet by displaying it directly in a Web Part. Using this Web Part provides great flexibility in reporting due to Excel's rich features.
Indicator Details	Displays the details of a single KPI Status Indicator.
Status List	Shows a list of Status Indicators from a SharePoint Status list.
Visio Web Access	Enables the viewing and refreshing of a Visio drawing in a Web Part. Visio is an Office Suite application that allows for the creation of advanced visuals such as charts, diagrams, flowcharts, and even network diagrams and floor plans. When you are working in Visio, you can save files as Web Drawing (VDW) files. In the properties of the Visio Web Access Web Part, an existing VDW file is selected for display. Additional settings can be configured, such as the toolbar and drawing interactivity.

Community

Community Web Parts display information relevant to a community and its members, such as top contributors, discussion listings, and member details. These Web Parts are intended for use on a site created based on the Community Site template or that has been turned into a community site through the activation of a feature called Community Features. Figure 7-14 is an example of a Community Site page with the community Web Parts added.

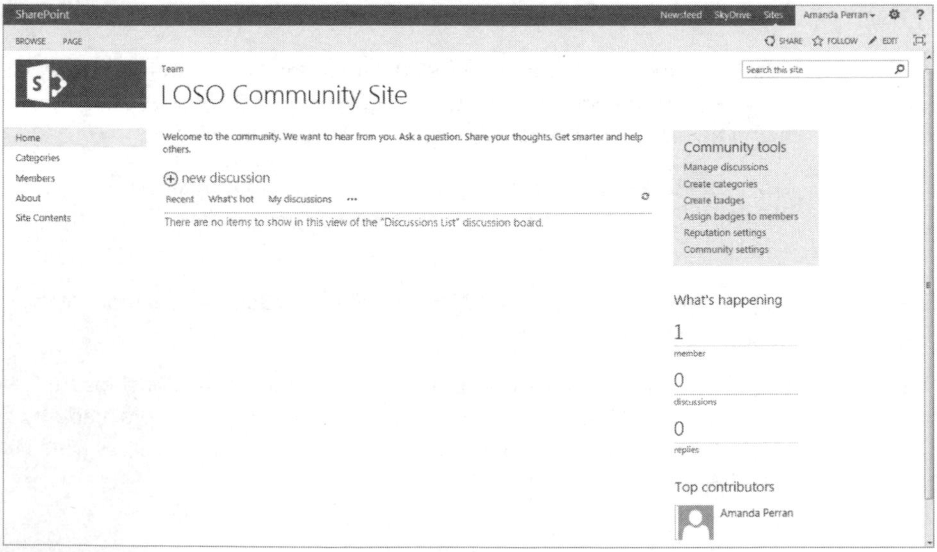

FIGURE 7-14

Content Rollup

Content rollup Web Parts enable you to gather information from multiple content locations, such as subsites within a site collection. These Web Parts create an aggregated view of that information in a single location. This section defines the most commonly used content rollup web parts, but note that others may exist based on specific usage scenarios or backward compatibility with previous versions of SharePoint.

Content Query

Content Query Web Parts are useful for displaying information that exists within the current site collection based on a set of predefined parameters and filters. Content Query Web Parts are also particularly helpful when you have multiple divisions or teams represented in a single site collection. You can use this Web Part to allow each division to display content such as policies or templates on a single page, even though the content is stored in a number of libraries spread throughout the site collection.

The Content Query Web Part contains two primary groups of properties that are unique to this Web Part: Query and Presentation.

Query

The Query group of settings refers to specific details of where the content you want to display resides. You can filter the query based on the location of the information so that only items from a specific site or subsites are included, or you can narrow results down to a single list. If you want to have a broader scope of items displayed, you can elect to display all items in the site collection that meet the criteria you define. This may be useful in situations where you want to display all forms and templates from every departmental or team site in the site collection.

Within the Query group of settings, you can also create filters based on list type or content type. An example of this may be that you want to show all updated wiki pages, so you would filter the Web Part to display only items from a Wiki Page library. Or if you have a custom content type created for Policies and Procedures, you would filter the Web Part to display only items related to that content type if you were building a page dedicated to Policies and Procedures–based content.

In the event you want to get very specific about which content is displayed to users, you would create a custom filter. You can create custom filters based on site columns values that are associated with the content. For example, if you were querying for a listing of incomplete tasks in a Web Part, you might use the filter to narrow results to items where Task Status is not equal to Completed.

You can also enable Audience Targeting on a Content Query Web Part. This feature leverages the built-in audience feature of lists that, if enabled, causes the content query to only display individual content items in the Web Part to users to which the content has been targeted. An example of this may be if you were using the Web Part to display Procedure documents. If the Audience Targeting feature is enabled on the document library, then as documents are added to the library, content owners could define which group or audience in the organization the procedure is relevant to. Then when individuals view the Content Query Web Part listing all Procedure documents in the library, they would see links only to the documents that are targeted at their group.

Presentation

From the Presentation group of settings, authorized users can select how the Web Part will be displayed on the page. This includes specifying from a list of available styles for the content links and any headings. In addition, you can select what information is displayed in the Web Part, including which columns are displayed for Title, Description, Link, and Image. Figure 7-15 is an example of the Presentation settings for a Content Query Web Part.

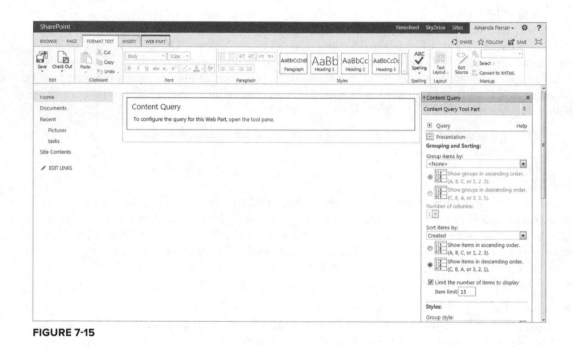

FIGURE 7-15

TRY IT OUT **Configuring a Content Query Web Part to Display All Tasks in a Site Collection**

In this example, you add a Content Query Web Part that displays all tasks within your site collection that are incomplete and assigned to the user that is looking at the page. This is a common requirement for many organizations that have many project or team sites with Task apps deployed to track assignments. Rather than users having to visit each Task app individually to see what has been assigned to them, they would prefer to go to a single page where all active tasks are listed.

> **NOTE** *You must complete the following example on a site collection that has the Publishing feature enabled. If the Publishing feature is not enabled, you will not see the Content Query Web Part listed under Content Rollup Category in the Web Part Gallery when you try to add it to the page. If this is the case, you must activate the SharePoint Server Publishing Infrastructure feature by visiting the Site Collection Features within the Site Settings of the top site within your site collection. This will enable you to utilize the Content Query Web Part on your site. Once that is completed, you can also activate the SharePoint Server Publishing feature located within Manage Site Features under the Site Settings option to make all other publishing features available on your site.*

1. Select Add a Page from your site's Settings menu.

2. Enter **My Active Tasks** for the page name and click Create.

3. Click inside the Page Content area of the Web Part and select the Insert tab of the ribbon menu.

4. Select Web Part. The Web Part Gallery appears.

5. Select the Content Rollup Category. The Gallery refreshes and the available Web Parts appear. If you do not see the Content Query Web Part, please review the note preceding step 1 of this exercise.

6. Select the Content Query Web Part and click the Add button. The Content Query Web Part appears on the page.

7. Select the checkbox in the top right of the Web Part. You might need to hover over the Web Part with your mouse for the checkbox to appear. The ribbon menu now displays a new tab called Web Part.

8. Select Web Part Properties from the Web Part tab of the ribbon menu. The Web Part panel appears.

9. Expand the Query section of the Web Part and specify the following values:

SETTING	VALUE
Source	Show items from all sites in this site collection.
List Type	Tasks
Content Type	All Content Types

continues

(continued)

SETTING	VALUE
Filters	Show items when:
	Task Status
	is not equal to
	Completed
	and
	Assigned to
	Is equal to
	[me]

10. Expand the Presentation section of the Web Part. Specify the following values within the Presentation section:

SETTING	VALUE
Group items by	<Site>
Number of columns	1
Sort items by	Due Date (Core Task and Issue Columns)
Limit the number of items to display	25
Fields to display (Link)	Leave this field Blank
Fields to display (Image)	Leave this field Blank
Fields to display (Title)	Title
Fields to display (Description)	Task Status

11. Expand the Appearance section of the Web Part and set Title to **My Active Tasks.**

12. Click the Apply button at the bottom of the Web Part.

13. Click the OK button at the bottom of the Web Part.

How It Works

In this Try It Out, you added a Web Part that was configured to display all tasks within the site collection that have been assigned to the user that is viewing the page. You did this by creating a query that listed all sites in the site collection as the source and by filtering the Web Part to show items that were set to Completed and that were assigned to [me]. The [me] value is a specialized function that identifies items for which the current user has been specified as the value for the Assigned to column. When the preceding steps are performed on a site collection containing multiple subsites, the end result will be similar to what is displayed in Figure 7-16.

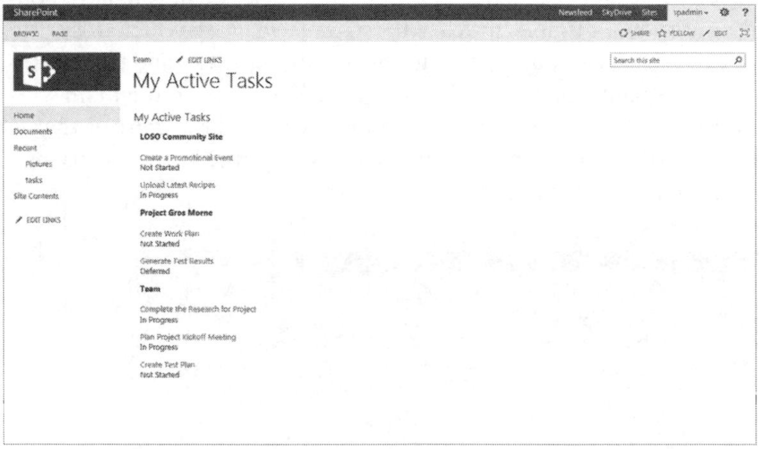

FIGURE 7-16

Content Search

The Content Search Web Part allows content that appears in the search engine related to a specific search query to be displayed on a Web Part on the site. By default, when added to the page, it displays recently modified items on the site. This can be useful for easily displaying the most recent content to site visitors. However, you can add custom search queries to build relevant results related to a specific topic. For example, if you had a site related to Employee Safety Awareness, you might use this Web Part to display anything related to the topic of Employee Safety Programs. An example of the query options when defining this Web Part is shown in Figure 7-17.

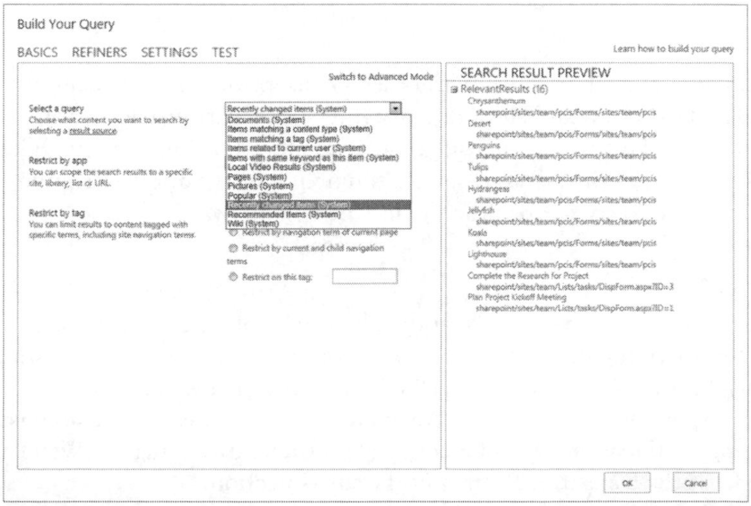

FIGURE 7-17

Relevant Documents

On certain sites you may have multiple document libraries that contain content. This is often seen in sites created from the Document or Record Center templates because these types of sites tend to contain large volumes of documents. You may want to make it easy for users to identify which documents they have created, updated, or have checked out on the site across all libraries. The Relevant Documents Web Part is designed for that specific purpose. By placing the Web Part on the main page of the site, you can keep users from having to navigate to each library to find the content that is most likely of relevance to them. Figure 7-18 displays the options that are available when specifying what content will appear to users in a Relevant Documents Web Part.

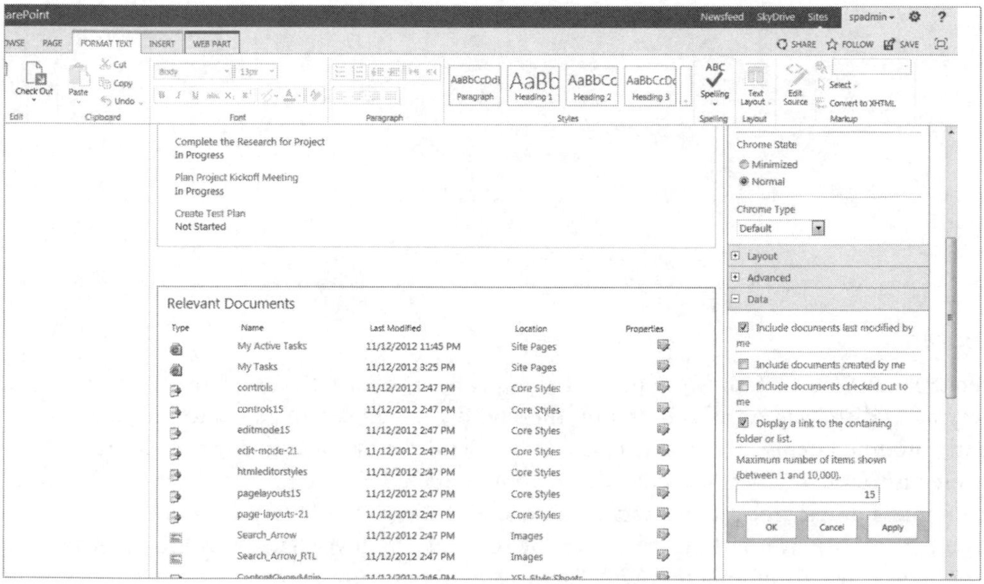

FIGURE 7-18

Summary Links

A common requirement on many sites is to share links with other site users and present them in a manner that is well organized and easy to read. The Summary Links Web Part provides more options for how links are organized and displayed on a site than a standard links list app provides. When adding a link to the Web Part, you can elect to display a thumbnail image and description with the link, or have users select a checkbox to open the site in a new window.

Table of Contents

The Table of Contents Web Part is used to embed a navigational hierarchy of a site or section of a site on a page. It can be useful for providing drill-down navigation on sites to augment the existing site navigational tools. You can add this Web Part to a page and select any area within the site collection from which you want to display site or page links. An example of how this may be used is to have a Departmental site listing on the main page of a corporate intranet by having the Web Part configured to display site links from the Departments area of the site collection.

Timeline

You can add the Timeline Web Part to any page of your site to display information from a Task app on that site or another site. This may be useful in situations where you may want to clearly identify important milestones or deadlines that are in focus and share them with others on your site without displaying the entire Task list. Figure 7-19 shows an example of a Department site that is displaying a Timeline Web Part for an important initiative.

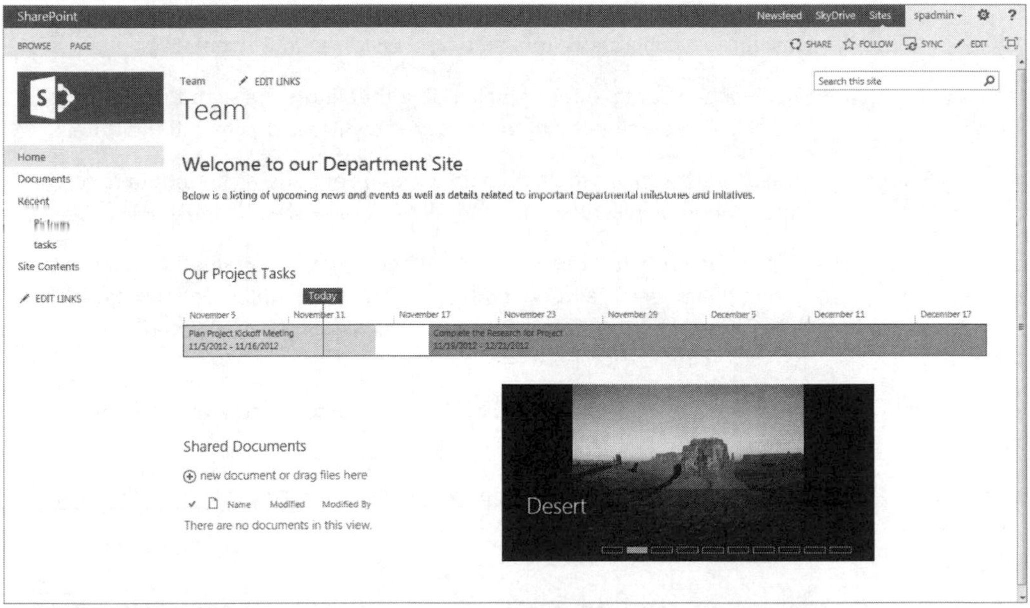

FIGURE 7-19

Document Sets

Document sets are groups of files that can be managed as an individual entity to share metadata, workflows, and version history. The document set Web Parts are built-in Web Parts that are used to either display the contents of a document set, which are the files that have been added to a document set folder, or the properties of a document set, which is the metadata that has been applied to it.

Filters

As explored previously in this chapter, Web Parts can be connected to one another so that one Web Part provides values to filter the display of information on the other Web Part. For example, one Web Part may contain a listing of customers, which is connected to another Web Part that displays a listing of orders. When a user selects a customer from the first Web Part, the orders list refreshes to display only orders that contain the customer's name. Filter Web Parts provide you with more options on how you can filter data between connected Web Parts.

WEB PART	DESCRIPTION
Apply Filters Button	A Web Part that adds a button to a page so that users can decide when to apply their filter choices.
Choice Filter	Allows page viewers to filter the contents of the connected Web Parts via a choice listing that has been specified by the page author.
Current User Filter	Filters the contents of connected Web Parts to items that contain the current user in a predetermined column. An example may be a Tasks Web Part that is filtered to only show items that are assigned to Current User.
Date Filter	Allows the user to enter or pick a date that filters the Web Parts that have been connected on the page to only show items that match the date.
Page Field Filter	Uses information associated with the current page as metadata to filter information displayed within connected Web Parts.
Query String (URL) Filter	Filters the Web Part based on information that is contained within the query string of a page. The query string is information that appears in the URL after a ? symbol and is defined by certain parameter names, which must be specified in the Web Part.
SharePoint List Filter	Uses a list of values from a SharePoint list to filter the Web Parts on the page.
SQL Server Analysis Services Filter	Filters information in connected Web Parts by using values from a SQL Server Analysis Services cube.
Text Filter	Allows the user to enter text values to filter the information that is displayed on the page in connected Web Parts.

Forms

Two form Web Parts are available in SharePoint Server. The HTML Form Web Part enables a page author to write HTML source code to define a simple form that can be connected to other Web Parts on the page. The InfoPath Form Web Part supports the display of browser-enabled forms within a page. When this Web Part is added to the page, you can point to a library where a form template has been published to and select the view of the form that should be displayed within the Web Part. You can then determine whether the form ribbon is displayed or how the form will behave once it is submitted. You can find more information on InfoPath and browser-based forms in Chapter 12, "Managing Forms."

Media and Content

The media and content Web Parts are a variety of Web Parts that can be used to share and embed content within a web page. This may include an image using the Image Viewer Web Part or a video clip using the Media Web Part. Depending on the desired content to be shared, a variety of options are available:

WEB PART	DESCRIPTION
Content Editor	Used for rich text or HTML-based content
Image Viewer	Used for sharing images
Media Web Part	Used for media clips such as video files
Page Viewer	Used for embedding content from other live websites
Picture Library Slideshow	Used for displaying a slideshow of images from a picture library on the current site
Script Editor	Used for inserting HTML based snippets or scripts onto a page
Silverlight Web Part	Used for displaying Silverlight applications on a page

Search

The search Web Parts represent the core search elements of a search interface and include Search Box, Search Results, Search Navigation, and Taxonomy Refinement Panel Web Parts. Using these Web Parts, authorized users can create a completely custom search interface to suit their specific business requirements. These Web Parts are covered in greater detail in Chapter 17, "Working with Search."

Search-Driven Content

The search Web Parts described in the preceding section are primarily focused on the creation of search interfaces so that users can visit and execute searches based on their information requirements. The search-driven content category of Web Parts refers to search Web Parts that can be added to a page as content that relates to a topic in order to display relevant information to visitors. For example, the Pictures Web Part displays images that have appeared in the site that have been associated with the Picture or Images content type. Figure 7-20 displays an example of the Pictures Web Part. Each small rectangle is an interactive tile that users can click to view an associated image. Otherwise, the Web Part rotates between images.

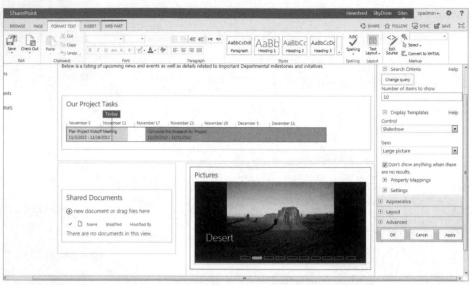

FIGURE 7-20

Using these Web Parts, site authors can create interactive and intuitive interfaces that will guide users to content of interest without having to rely solely on the user's ability to navigate or search for the content. These Web Parts are discussed further in Chapter 17.

Social Collaboration

The social collaboration Web Parts are designed to be added to pages for social interaction purposes so that users can learn more about or communicate with one another. The following table lists the Web Parts available in this category.

WEB PART	DESCRIPTION
Contact Details	Used to point to a single user that can be identified as the contact for the site. Users can click the contact's name to be redirected to the personal site and/or contact information for that user.
Note Board	Adding this Web Part to a page allows users to leave messages that are viewable by others. This can help to generate conversations related to relevant topics.
Organization Browser	Used to display an interactive org chart of site users.
Site Feed	Used to display microblogging conversations on a group site.
Site Users	Used to display a member of a site or group. Clicking the name of a user displays contact information for that user.

Tag Cloud	Used to display a listing of tags that are relevant to the current site. Clicking a tag redirects a user to a profile page for the tag.
User Tasks	Displays a listing of tasks assigned to the current user from the current site. This Web Part can be used to aggregate task information on a site with multiple Tasks lists.

SUMMARY

Web parts are an integral part of SharePoint and are used, to some degree, in every chapter in this book. This chapter discussed the various Web Parts that can help your team with any business problem. In this chapter, you learned the following

➤ Web parts are applications that you can only add to a Web Part page that allow users to interact with the site. SharePoint has various Web Parts, which were discussed in detail, and you can create your own using custom code.

➤ Web part pages have a Web Part properties pane where you can select and modify Web Part properties. You add Web Parts to zones by dragging and dropping them to different positions within a zone, or dragging them to completely separate zones on the page. Wiki pages do not have Web Part zones, but instead have content areas to which Web Parts can be added. You learned the basics of adding Web Parts, customizing the title and border, and importing or exporting them from one page or site to another.

You then learned the various types of Web Parts that you can add to pages within SharePoint 2013 along with realistic examples of how you can leverage them in business solutions.

EXERCISES

1. You get an e-mail from marketing informing you that the executive team would like to add a list of key contacts to the main page of the corporate intranet. What do you do?

2. It's requested that you move the main news Web Part from the small right column to a more prominent section of the homepage of the human resources team's collaboration site. How can you make this happen?

3. Sales makes a change in its division so that all current tasks displayed on the homepage of the team site via a Web Part must also display which of the two team leaders is responsible for the task. How can you modify the Web Part to display who the team leader is?

4. During a meeting, an executive asks if you can display a listing of all upcoming events for the organization. What is your answer?

5. You have been asked to add a Web Part to the main page of the social committee site that rotates through the images from the last social event. What are your options?

▶ **WHAT YOU LEARNED IN THIS CHAPTER**

TOPIC	KEY CONCEPTS
Description of Web Parts	Web parts are modular and can be added to pages on SharePoint sites in order to display pertinent content to site users.
Adding Web Parts	To learn how to work effectively with Web Parts, it is important to understand first how to add them to a page. There are multiple methods for adding Web Parts to a page, depending partially on whether you are adding them to a Web Part page or wiki page.
Configuring Web Parts	When configuring Web Parts, some settings are standard across all of them. Some other settings are unique, depending on the type of Web Part.
Importing and exporting Web Parts	Some types of Web Parts can be exported from one page and imported to be displayed on another page, usually to save time in configuring another Web Part.
Connecting Web Parts	Web parts can be connected to each other to allow for the passing of filter information or parameters.
List app Web Parts	List and library app Web Parts automatically exist for every list and library on the site.
Blog Web Parts	Web parts used by the system to display key navigational and action details related to blog sites.
Business data Web Parts	These give you different ways of viewing and analyzing business data stored in other systems or within SharePoint.
Content rollup Web Parts	These display data from multiple locations, or from another location besides the current site.
Document set Web Parts	These are used by the system to display information and details related to document sets.
Media and content Web Parts	In general, these can display media on a page, such as pictures or video.
Form Web Parts	These allow site users to fill out and submit forms directly on the page, which saves them time and clicks.
Social collaboration Web Parts	Web Parts that allow for social interaction and contact information to be shared on a site.
Filter Web Parts	These are extremely powerful, and enable you to highly customize the interactivity of a SharePoint page. All of these require connections to other Web Parts.
Search Web Parts	Used to build search interfaces so that users can perform searches on pages.
Search-driven content Web Parts	Used to aggregate content on a site based on search properties, metadata, and usage information.

8

Working with Sites

WHAT YOU WILL LEARN IN THIS CHAPTER:

➤ The difference between sites and site collections

➤ How to manage the structure of a site

➤ Out-of-the-box templates and when to use them

➤ How to create a custom template based on an existing site

So far this book has covered many of the different components that can be included within a SharePoint site. This chapter is dedicated to understanding the container that you are building the objects within, and you look at several key concepts that should help you pull all the pieces together. This chapter also looks at the creation process for new site collections and sites, and provides you with the information on when to create each one.

UNDERSTANDING SITES AND SITE COLLECTIONS

When an organization stores information in a disorganized or haphazard manner, systems become difficult to navigate and information difficult to find. An increase in storage locations results, such as personal drives, network file shares, or removable media. Different people catalog information using different methods, which leads to co-workers relying on each other to find information, which leads to a serious loss in productivity. SharePoint introduces great potential at addressing challenges that businesses face with respect to how content is organized and subsequently located. However, it is still important to apply good design principles when configuring your SharePoint environment. A key aspect of doing so is to understand the various containers and building blocks within a SharePoint environment: site collections and sites.

The terms *sites* and *site collections* both refer to SharePoint websites. They use Web Parts, lists, and libraries to store and share information. The following list explains how they differ:

➤ **Sites:** These share information in the form of list items and documents within a team or organization. Sites come in a variety of templates. Each template contains a unique set of lists, libraries, and pages. The template you select depends highly on which template most closely matches your needs.

➤ **Site collections:** These are a group of sites and/or workspaces that form a hierarchy, with a single top-level website and a collection of subsites, and then another level of subsites below it (see Figure 8-1).

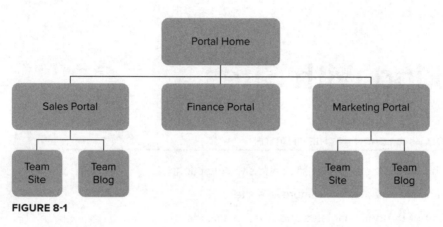

FIGURE 8-1

Sites

SharePoint organizes pages, lists, libraries, and other components into containers known as *sites*. Each site typically contains information related to a common subject or topic, such as an intranet site for a project team or an extranet site for collaboration with business partners.

By gathering related information in SharePoint sites, organizations can adopt consistent procedures and practices concerning content management. Users no longer have to wait for others to supply them with details related to the location of important information. Instead, content access and processes become more self-service-oriented, resulting in more efficient work patterns.

Sites can be created based on a template. The templates contain the elements such as lists, libraries, Web Parts, and workflows that are best suited for a specific usage scenario. For example, a community site template contains discussion and configuration lists that are best suited for building dynamic user communities, whereas a team site contains elements that would most likely be required for team members who need to collaborate with one another.

Site Collections

A *site collection* is a group of sites that share common elements, organized into a tree structure. A site can be either a subsite within the site collection or the top-level site that stores the common templates and components for the entire group of sites below it. A subsite has a parent and may also have additional sites below it.

An individual site, whether it is a top-level site or a sub site, can have its own security and access profile. Similarly, a subsite can be configured to inherit the access rules of its parent site. In an organization's SharePoint structure, every site in an intranet can be in a single site collection, or multiple site collections may exist to distinguish between groups or provide greater flexibility related to storage of content. Today's workplaces often use site collections to represent their various divisions and projects. Typically, each division has its own top-level site, with subsites representing projects assigned to a division. The subsites have lists and libraries where teams can share information and collaborate on the project.

In the first Try It Out in this section, you create the site collection's top level using the Publishing Portal. Then, in the second Try It Out, you see how to add subsites to this top-level site using the Team Site template.

TRY IT OUT   Creating a Site Collection

In this first Try It Out, you create a site collection. To create a site collection, you need to have access to the Central Administration site. If you do not have access, talk with your SharePoint administrator.

1. Open the Central Administration site.

2. Select the "Create site collections" link within the Application Management group, as shown in Figure 8-2.

FIGURE 8-2

3. Enter the following properties for the new site collection and then click OK. An example is shown in Figure 8-3.

PROPERTY	VALUE
Web Application	Accept the default option, unless directed otherwise by your server administrator.
Title	Projects
Description	Location to create and store all internal project information
URL	/sites/projects

continues

(continued)

PROPERTY	VALUE
Experience Version	2013
Template Selection	Publishing Portal
Primary Site Collection Administrator	Your username
Secondary Site Collection Administrator	Enter the username of the primary SharePoint Administrator for the farm.
Quota Template	No Quota

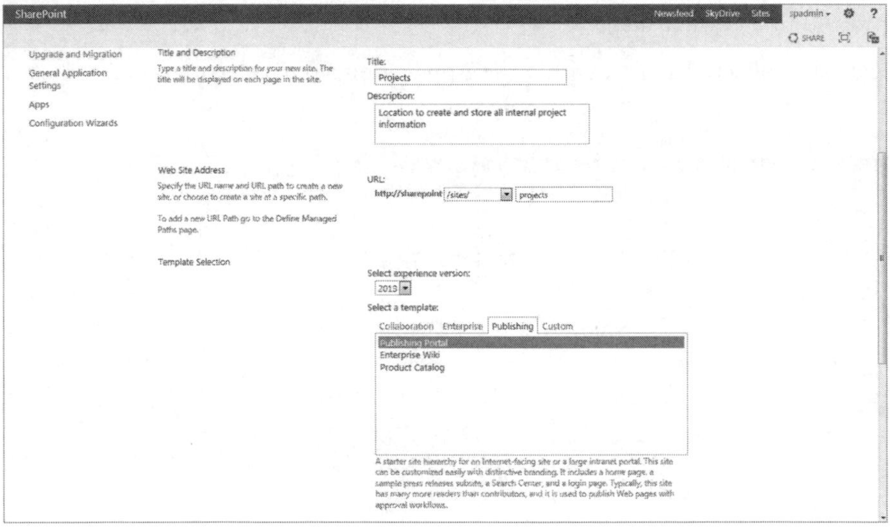

FIGURE 8-3

> **NOTE** *The user that you enter as the primary site collection administrator will be the user that is notified by the system when something needs attention. This can include site access requests and quote notifications. This user will have full control to the site collection. It is good practice to specify a farm administration or management account as the secondary site collection administrator so that account has access as required.*

4. Click the OK button.

On the Top-Level Site Successfully Created page, click the link to open the new site collection. Your site should look similar to the site in Figure 8-4.

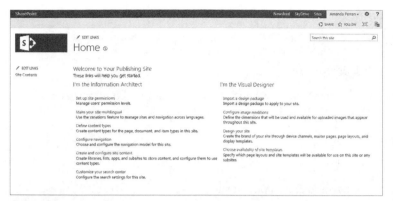

FIGURE 8-4

How It Works

When you create a site collection in Central Administration, you provide all of the details for your site collection, and then the site is provisioned for you and a link is returned. You can then visit the site to perform additional configurations or invite other users, as required.

TRY IT OUT Creating a Web (Subsite)

In this Try It Out, you create a site within your Projects site collection. This allows you to start to build a site hierarchy that can be used for the remaining chapter examples.

1. Open the Projects site collection that you created in the previous Try It Out.

2. Select Site Contents from the Settings menu. You will be redirected to a page listing all the content elements of the current site. From here, you can see links to the apps that are created automatically as part of the Publishing Portal template.

3. From the bottom of the page, select the "new subsite" link, as shown in Figure 8-5.

FIGURE 8-5

4. Enter the following properties for the site. An example is shown in Figure 8-6.

PROPERTY	VALUE
Title	Signal Hill Restoration
Description	Project site to manage news and content related to the restoration of historic monuments at Signal Hill in St. John's, NL.
URL Name	signalhill
Template Selection	Publishing Site
User Permissions	Use same permissions as parent site
Use the top link bar from the parent site?	Yes

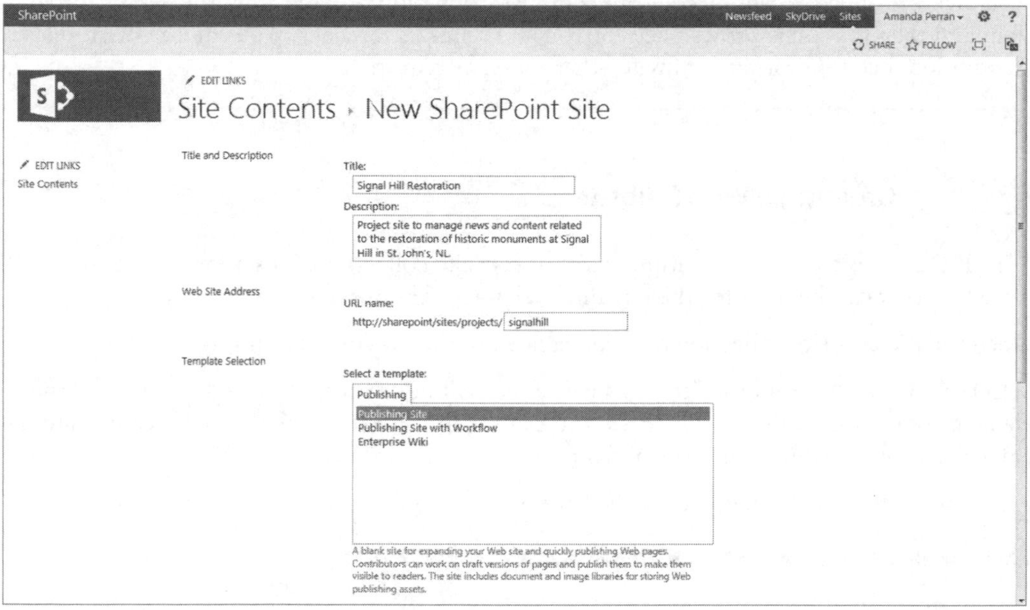

FIGURE 8-6

5. Once the site has been created, you will be redirected to the new blank site. Your screen should look similar to the one shown in Figure 8-7.

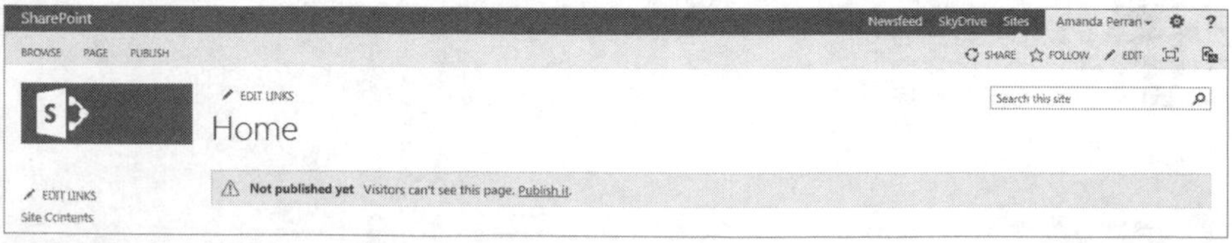

FIGURE 8-7

How It Works

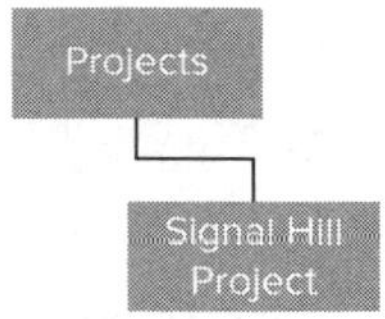

Now that you have created a new site, the site collection that you created in the first example has a hierarchy similar to that outlined in Figure 8-8.

The Projects site was the top-level site created in the first Try It Out. This represents the first site in your site collection and contains the locations where most templates and roles related to the site collection will be stored. Then you added the Signal

FIGURE 8-8

Hill Project site. You may have noticed that when you created the Signal Hill site in this example, there were only a few options for the template selection. This is because by default, only a select number of sites are available for selection as a subsite of a publishing portal. However, in the next Try It Out, you will configure the top-level Projects site to allow for any site template to be used.

TRY IT OUT   Changing the Available Site Templates for a Site

In this Try It Out, you configure the Projects site collection so that sites can be created using any of the available site templates that exist within SharePoint 2013.

1. Open the Projects site collection that you created in the first Try It Out of this chapter.

2. From the Settings menu, select the Site Settings link.

3. From the Look and Feel group of links, select "Page layouts and site templates." You will be redirected to a page where you can select which site templates and page layouts can be used from this location (see Figure 8-9).

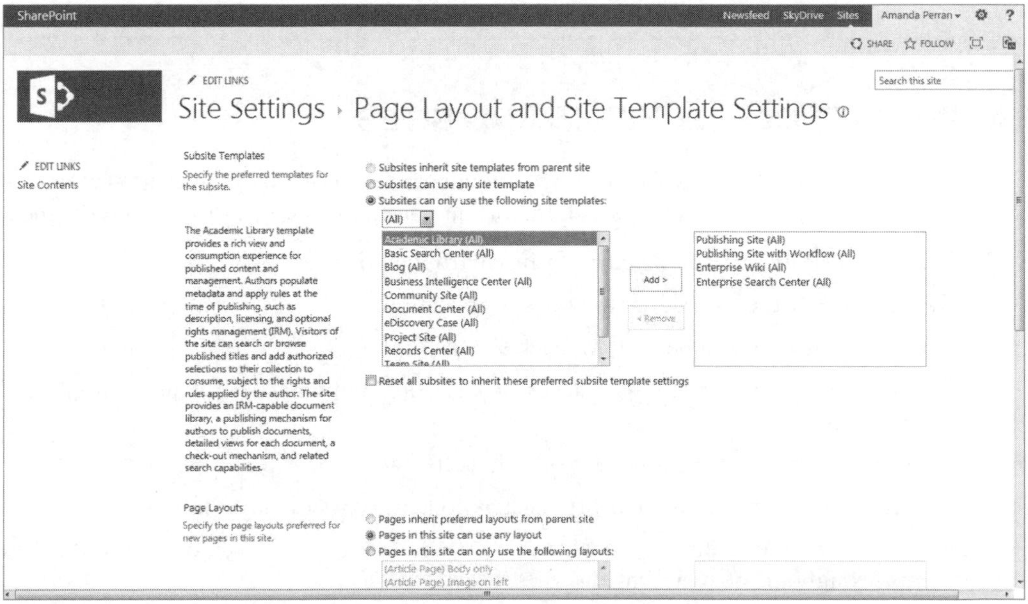

FIGURE 8-9

4. Select the "Subsites can use any site template" option.

5. Select the checkbox to "Reset all subsites to inherit these preferred subsite template settings."

6. Click the OK button.

How It Works

Now that you have changed the settings for which site templates can be created from the Projects site, the site template selection panel that you will see when you create a new site will have additional options available (see Figure 8-10).

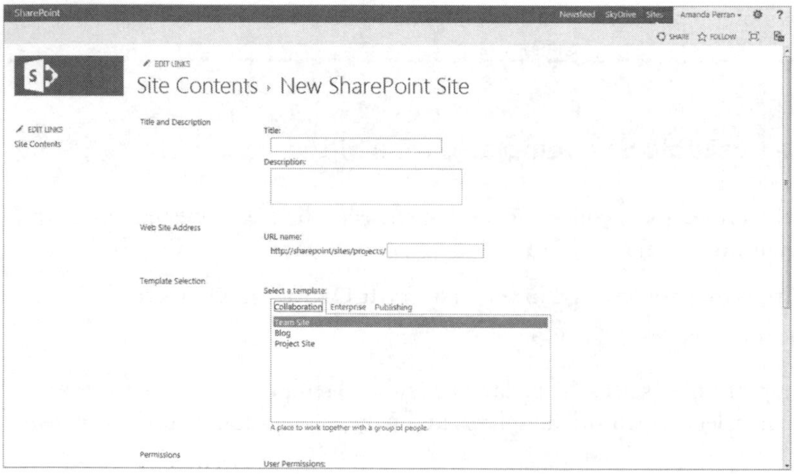

FIGURE 8-10

MANAGING SITE COLLECTIONS AND SITES

As you create a new SharePoint environment, you should consider how to organize its sites and content so that users can easily access what they need. Important questions that you should consider include:

➤ What primary sites should be part of this environment?

➤ What content will be stored within the site collection?

➤ What site templates will be used for each site?

➤ What users or groups should have access to each site, and what are the users' needs and requirements?

➤ Should site permissions be inherited or unique for each site?

➤ Will any sites share any components, such as content types or site columns?

➤ Should the users see a different navigation interface at each site level, or should this be consistent throughout the hierarchy?

➤ Should all sites in the hierarchy have the same look and feel, or should sites have their own color schemes and branding?

The answers to these questions may vary, depending on the situation, so there's not really a set of rules on how to create a SharePoint site hierarchy. However, by taking the answers to the questions under consideration, you can determine the best approach and build around whatever situation you encounter.

When designing a SharePoint environment, draw out the site hierarchy's primary structure. You can use drawing tools, such as Microsoft Visio or something as simple as a sketchpad, to help you through the planning stage. From there, you can add information such as what templates to use, where to define permissions, or where to create content elements such as content types. Figure 8-11 shows an example. Planned sites are laid out in a logical hierarchy, and the preferred template for each is defined. Sites that will not inherit the permissions of their parent have been flagged so that it is easily identifiable that those sites will have unique permissions. You can take additional steps to highlight which users and groups should have access at each site, as well as any preferences around branding or templates.

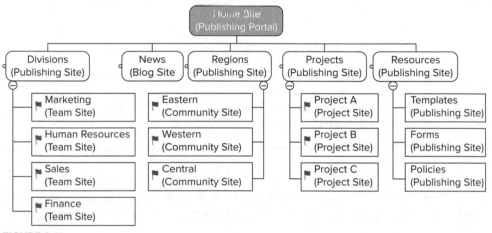

FIGURE 8-11

Although SharePoint is very flexible when you want to change something, identifying the core structure of a SharePoint environment early in the game has a positive effect on the environment's growth and prevents costly reworks and downtime later on.

Navigation

Navigation is one of the most important parts of any site. Users expect a clear and easy path to the information they require. As a site designer, you need to supply your users with a consistent navigation experience that becomes familiar to them. As a general rule, you should answer the following key questions concerning your site's navigation menu:

➤ Where am I?

➤ Where can I go?

➤ Where have I been?

SharePoint offers several built-in navigation menus and items, and allows you to tailor things to your environment so that users are never lost when they look for information.

Global Navigation

The *global navigation* (also known as the *top link bar*) is the primary navigation for a site collection. It is the navigation menu that appears at the top of each page. This navigation menu can be either unique for each site in the site collection or shared. In many cases, site collection administrators will elect to make this navigational menu consistent throughout the site collection so that users can easily move between sites in the hierarchy. Figure 8-12 shows an example of a global navigation.

FIGURE 8-12

When defining your global navigation, you can either have the navigation based on the structure of the site collection or based on custom properties such as managed metadata. For the purposes of this chapter, we will be reviewing how to manage the navigation based on the site's structure. Metadata-based navigation is covered in Chapter 15, "Getting Started with Web Content Management."

Current Navigation

The *current navigation* is the navigation that is displayed on the left side of the page. It is typically known as a contextual navigation that will display the relevant items of the particular site that you are visiting. When configuring the current navigation, you have multiple options, as described in the following table:

SETTING	DESCRIPTION
Display the same navigation items as the parent site	This setting will display the exact same links that are displayed on the parent within the current navigation. You may use this in a scenario where you have a hierarchy of sites defined but you don't want the user to be aware of the fact that they are navigating between multiple sites for content. You may also use this in a situation where you have a managed navigation and you want to keep the links consistent between all sites within the hierarchy.
Managed Navigation	Sites using this type of navigation will display links to pages that are generated based on values of a managed metadata term set. This might be useful if you have a products list that you want to manage centrally and may contain a hierarchy of product categories and subcategories. Attempting to manually maintain a navigation structure to match this type of hierarchy might be unrealistic and prone to error.

Structural Navigation	Sites using this type of navigation will display links based on the actual content structure that exists on the site such as lists, libraries and subsites. When selecting this option, site admins have the option to either display the site's siblings in the side navigation or not.

Site admins can also choose to use a navigation feature known as tree view for the side navigation. The standard side navigation, known as *Quick Launch*, allows site managers to be selective over which links are available in the side navigation and how they are ordered. Figure 8-13 shows an example of a typical Quick Launch navigation.

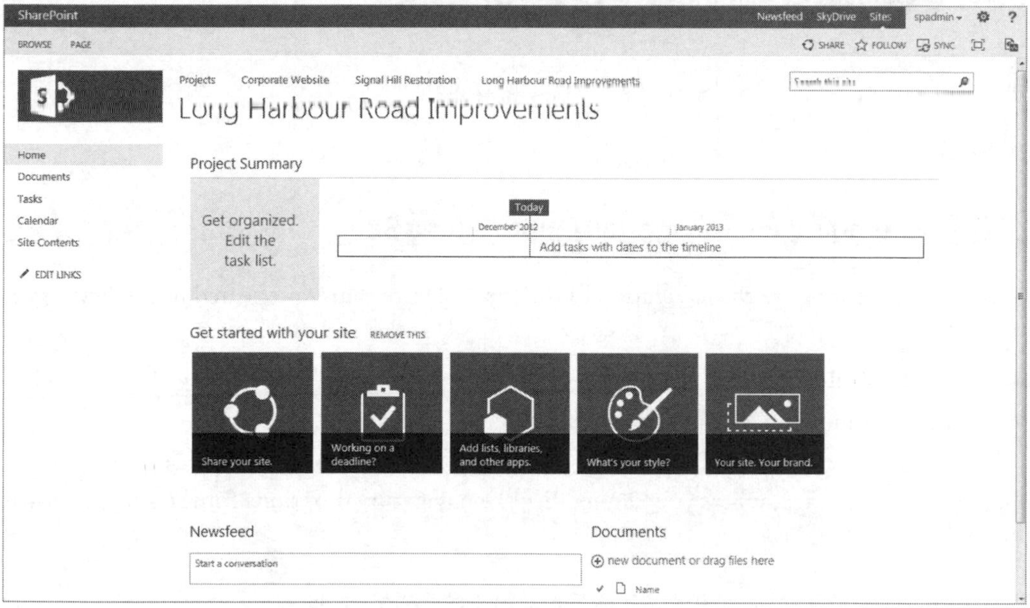

FIGURE 8-13

Optionally, site admins can change the type of navigation to tree view to enable users to drill down into the entire site structure, including folders within the lists and libraries. This type of navigation is most suitable for sites that contain a large number of folders within apps and for which users have a requirement to easily drill down to navigate between folders. Figure 8-14 shows an example of a typical tree view navigation.

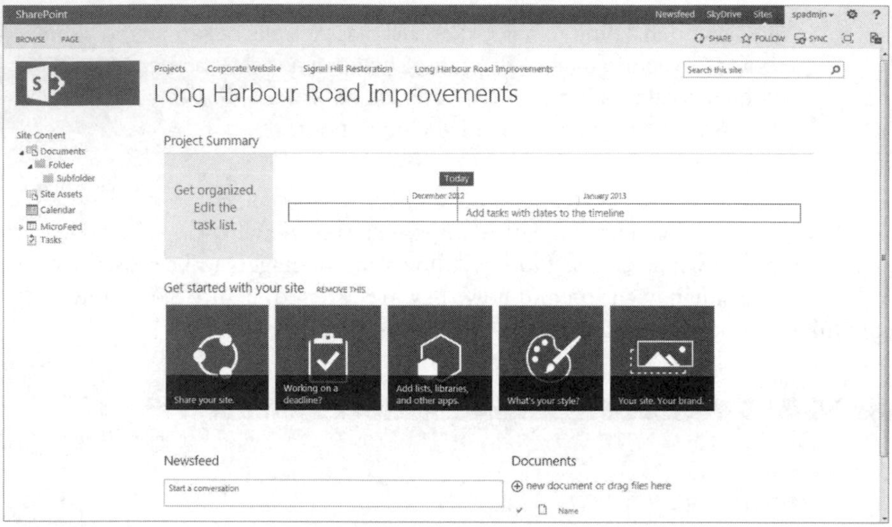

FIGURE 8-14

TRY IT OUT   **Changing the Navigation Options for a Site**

In this Try It Out, you configure the navigation of the top-level site that you created in the first Try It Out of this chapter.

1. Open the Projects site collection that you created in the first Try It Out of this chapter.

2. From the Settings menu, select the Site Settings link.

3. From the Look and Feel group of links, select Navigation. You will be redirected to the Navigation Settings page, where you can modify the navigational options for the site, as shown in Figure 8-15.

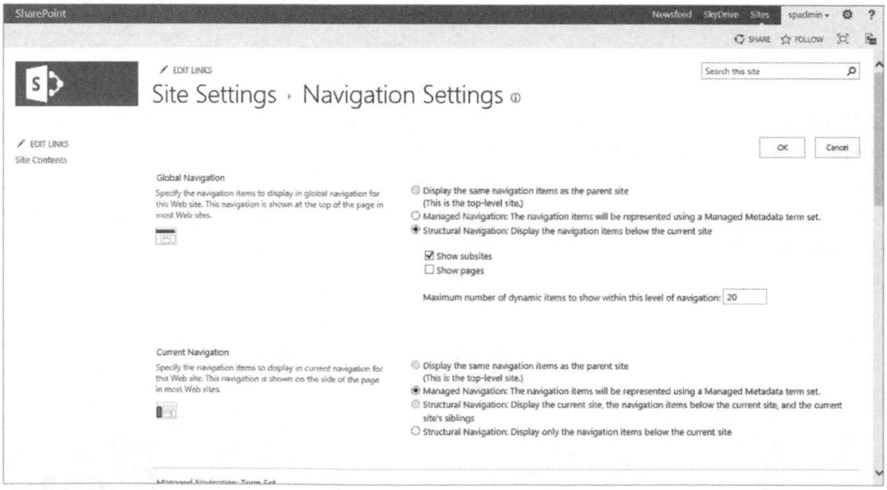

FIGURE 8-15

4. From the Global Navigation section, select the "Structural Navigation: Display the navigation items below the current site" option.

5. Click the OK button.

How It Works

Now that you have changed the settings for the top-level site, you likely have noticed that the subsite that you previously created is now showing in the navigation as shown in Figure 8-16. This is because you changed the navigation to be structure-based and to display subsites. By doing so, you exposed a direct link to the Signal Hill site, which is a subsite of the Projects site. This will enable users of the site to find it more easily when accessing it through the Projects site. Also, because you selected to use the top link bar of the parent site when you created the Signal Hill site, when users navigate to the Signal Hill site, they will see the same links in the global navigation.

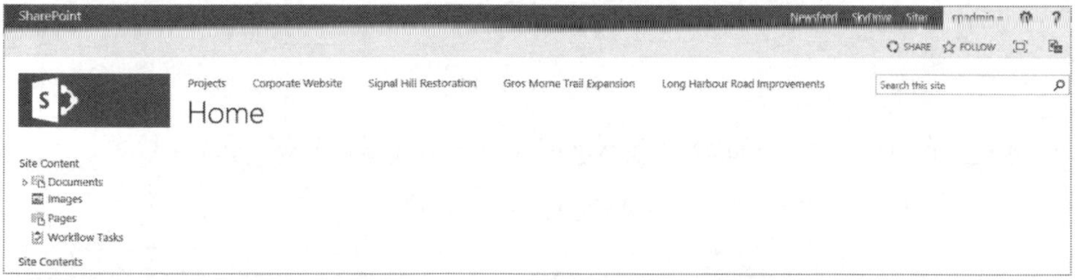

FIGURE 8-16

The next Try It Out looks at how you can modify the navigation one more time to add a custom link to the global navigation that points to the company's corporate website.

TRY IT OUT Adding a Custom Link to a Navigation

In this Try It Out, you configure the navigation of the top-level site that you created in the first Try It Out of this chapter.

1. Open the Projects site collection that you created in the first Try It Out of this chapter.

2. From the Settings menu, select the Site Settings link.

3. From the Look and Feel group of links, select Navigation.

4. Scroll down the page to the Structural Navigation: Editing and Sorting section of the page.

5. Select the Global Navigation heading, as shown in Figure 8-17.

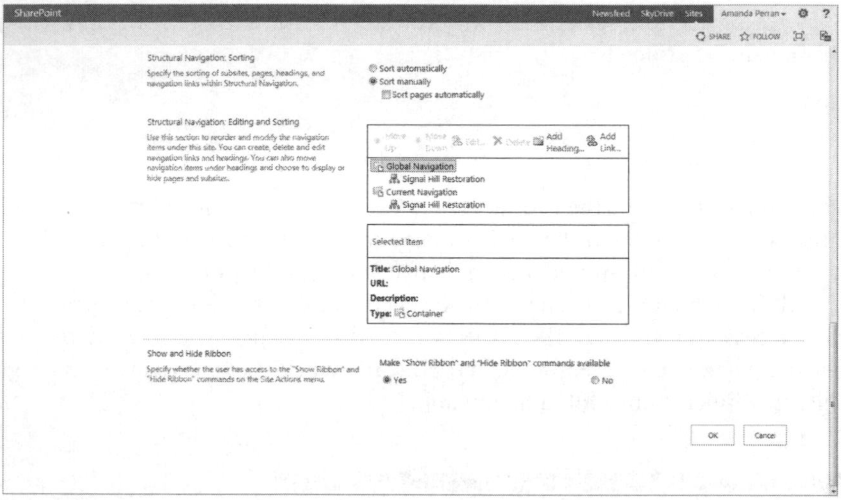

FIGURE 8-17

6. Click the Add Heading link from the toolbar. A Navigation Heading window appears.

7. Enter the following details for the heading, as shown in Figure 8-18.

PROPERTY	VALUE
Title	Corporate Website
URL	Enter the URL of your organization's public website
Open link in new window	Yes (Select)
Description	Click this link to view our public corporate website.
Audience	Leave blank

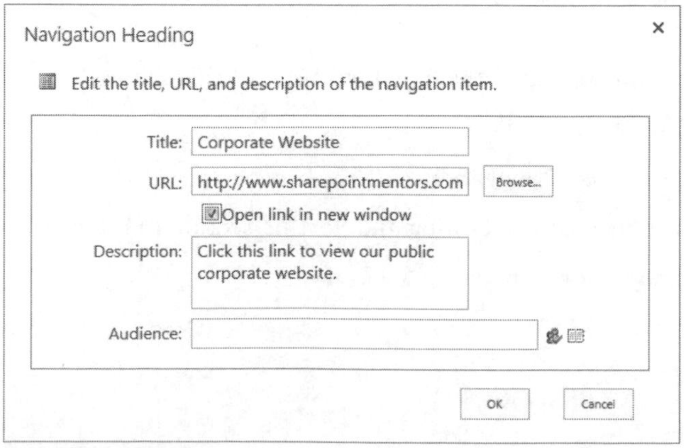

FIGURE 8-18

8. Click the OK button.

How It Works

After completing this Try It Out, you will see the Corporate Website link appear in the top link bar. If you click the link, it will open in a new window. This is a great technique for adding custom links and pages to your SharePoint sites. In step 7, you could have also specified an audience that the link could be targeted at. By doing this you could point to an Active Directory group or role within your SharePoint site that would be able to see the link. All other users would not see the link in their navigation bar. This can be useful in situations in which you want to provide users with a very personalized navigation experience where links that are most relevant to them are displayed throughout the portal.

TRY IT OUT   Changing the Order of Navigation Links

In this Try It Out, you reorder the links that are displayed in the global navigation.

1. Open the Projects site collection that you created in the first Try It Out of this chapter.

2. From the Settings menu, select the Site Settings link.

3. From the Look and Feel group of links, select Navigation.

4. Scroll down the page to the Structural Navigation: Editing and Sorting section of the page.

5. Select the Corporate Website link, as shown in Figure 8-19.

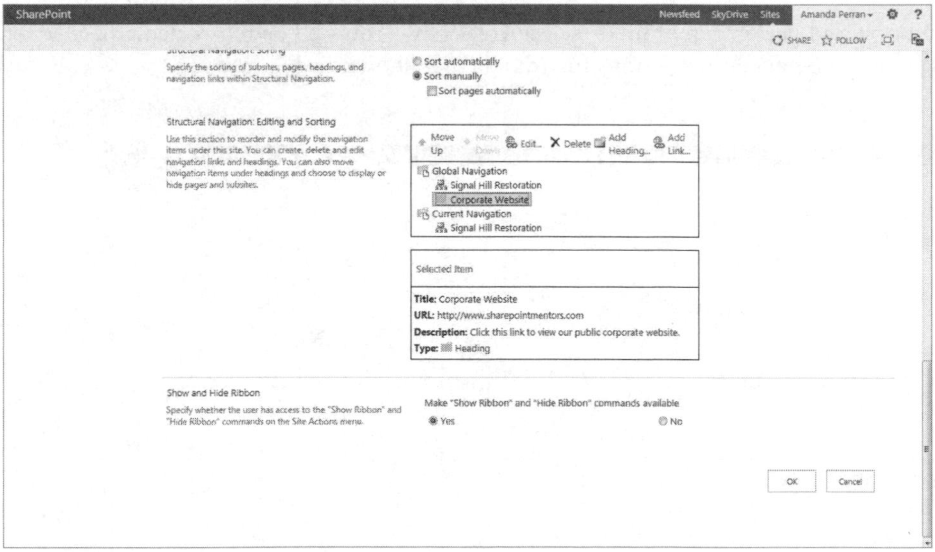

FIGURE 8-19

6. Click the Move Up link on the toolbar.

7. Click the OK button.

How It Works

After making the preceding change, you will see that the Corporate Website link appears to the left of the Signal Hill site, as shown in Figure 8-20. Because the navigation of the Signal Hill site inherits from the Projects site, the links will appear in the same order on that site as well.

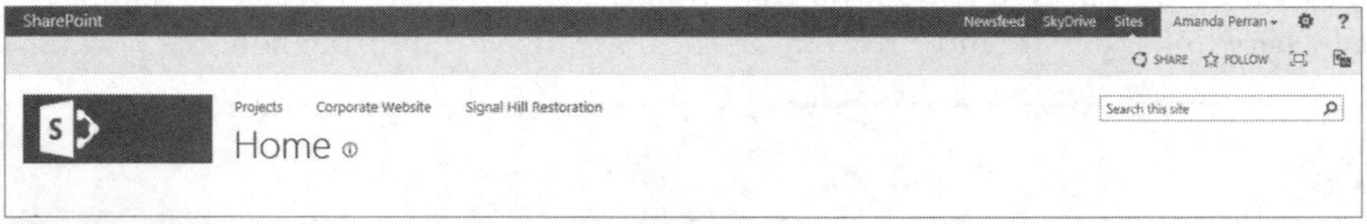

FIGURE 8-20

TRY IT OUT   **Enabling the Tree View Menu**

Earlier in the chapter we mentioned that the side navigation for a site has two options. In this Try It Out, you will change the side navigation from the Quick Launch type to the tree view.

1. Open the Signal Hill Restoration site created in a previous Try It Out.

2. From the Settings menu, select the Site Settings link.

3. From the Look and Feel group of links, select Tree View. You will be redirected a page where you can change the side navigation options for your site, as shown in Figure 8-21.

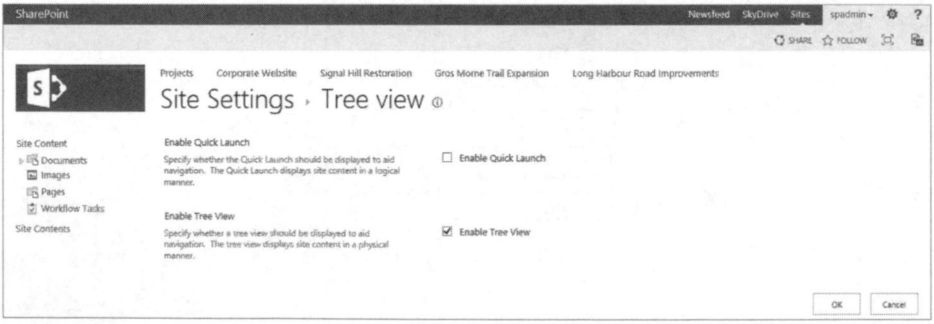

FIGURE 8-21

4. Deselect the Enable Quick Launch checkbox.

5. Select the Enable Tree View checkbox.

6. Click OK.

How It Works

Once you make the preceding change, the Signal Hill Restoration site will no longer show the Quick Launch, as was available previously (refer to Figure 8-13), but will instead show the tree view menu (refer to Figure 8-14).

Features

SharePoint has a wide variety of functions and capabilities. Not every site template uses every capability, so certain functions are packaged into elements known as *features*. Features are modular packages of functionality that can be activated within a site. For example, the Team Collaboration Lists feature, which is activated by default when you create a team site, enables you to create list apps such as Tasks, Discussions, and Issues. However, you may have noticed that in the first example, when you created the Projects site based on the Publishing Portal, those list apps are not available for use or creation. In other words, when you go to the Add an App page from the settings menu, you see only the options displayed in Figure 8-22. To make more apps available for selection from the Add an App page, you must activate the Team Collaboration Lists feature.

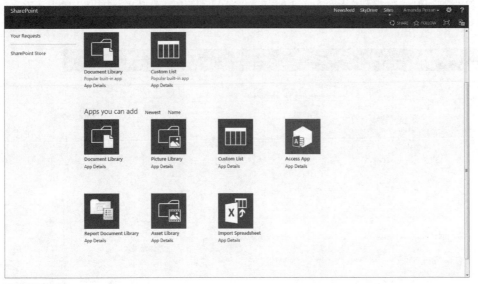

FIGURE 8-22

Features can be activated at the site collection level and the site level. When you activate features at the site collection level, the functionality affects the entire site collection, whereas when you activate them at the site level, the functionality will be available only for that site. In the next example, you will activate the Team Collaboration Lists feature on the top-level site of your site collection so that you can create additional list apps from that location for your Projects Collaboration area.

NOTE *The publishing features are pre-activated on the Publishing sites and Enterprise sites and will have an impact on how pages are created and stored, including the home page. You can still activate the publishing features on other site collections, but this will not move the home page to the pages folder. You would need to create a new home page in the pages folder and then set that page to be the home page for the site.*

TRY IT OUT Activating a Feature

When you activate a feature, you enable that functionality on the site or site collection (depending on the type of feature you activated) for which you activated it. In this Try It Out, you will enable the ability to create collaboration lists from the top-level site of your site collection by activating the Team Collaboration Lists feature.

1. Open the Projects site collection that you created in the first Try It Out of this chapter.

2. From the Settings menu, select the Site Settings link.

3. From the Site Actions group of links, select Manage Site Features. You will be redirected to a page listing all features that can be activated within the Projects site, as shown in Figure 8-23.

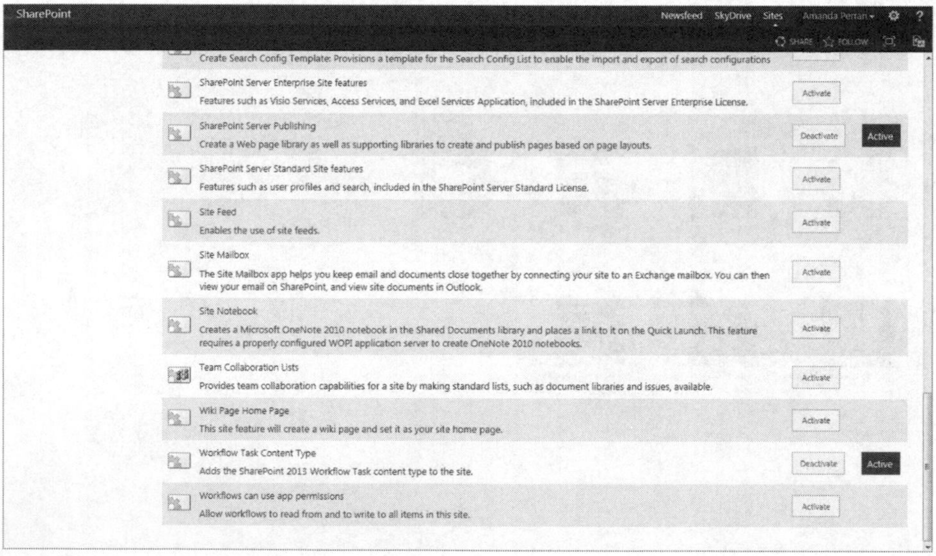

FIGURE 8-23

4. Scroll to the bottom of the page and click the Activate button associated with the Team Collaboration Lists feature.

5. From the Settings menu, select the Add an App option. You will see that more collaboration apps are available, as shown in Figure 8-24.

FIGURE 8-24

How It Works

In this Try It Out, you activated the Team Collaboration Lists feature on the Projects site collection, which was created based on the Publishing Portal template. This template does not have that feature enabled by default. By activating it, you enabled the ability to create collaboration apps, such as Calendar, Links, and Tasks list apps. Some sites such as the Team Site template, have this feature enabled by default.

Managing Content and Structure

Once a site is created, typically the first thing you need to do is to customize it to match your requirements. Although the out-of-the-box templates provide a great set of features to start with, it is very likely you will want to do additional configurations to make a site completely suit your business needs. We covered how to create lists and libraries in earlier chapters, but it is likely that you are wondering if there is an easy way to view all of the different types of content within your site. There are several different ways to view the content within a site collection, including those discussed in the following sections.

Site Contents

As shown in Figure 8-25 and accessed from the Settings menu, this page displays all the list and library apps within your site. You can also see all the subsites that exist for a particular site. This option is available as part of the Quick Launch menu as well as via the Settings menu.

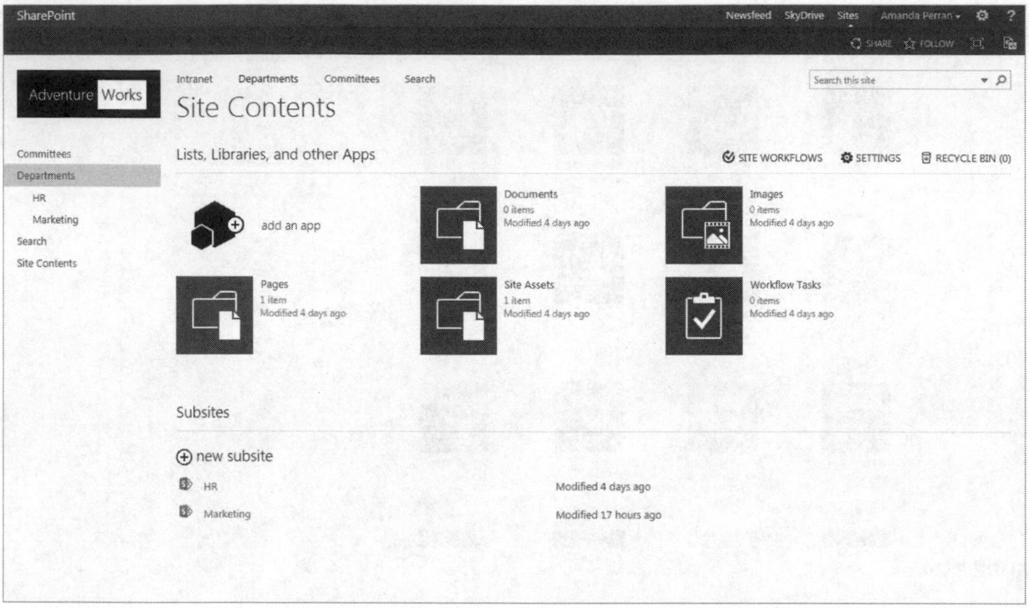

FIGURE 8-25

Site Hierarchy

If you want to see a listing of all sites and subsites associated with a site collection, you can access the Site Hierarchy page. This page is accessible via the Site Settings page for the top-level site within your site collection within the Site Collection Administration set of links. It displays a listing of all sites within a site collection, along with the URL of the site and a link directly to the Site Settings page for that site (see Figure 8-26).

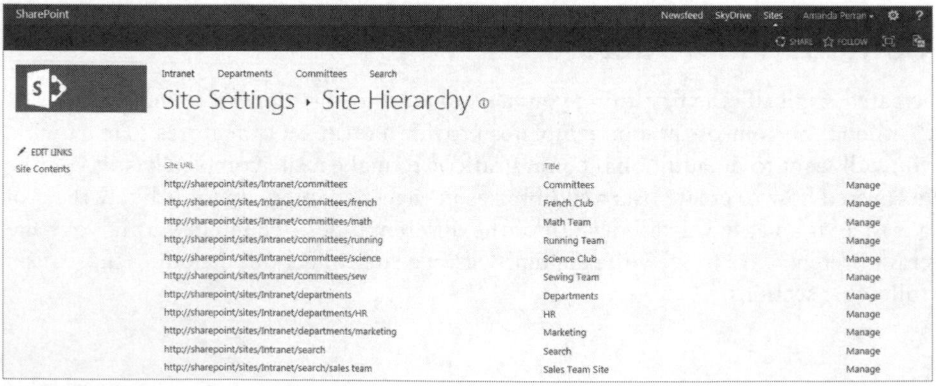

FIGURE 8-26

Site Content and Structure

If you require the ability to perform multiple updates to a group of sites or have more administrative options for a site, such as to move or copy it to another location in the site collection, the Site

Content and Structure section enables you to see a tree view of the content within the site collection (see Figure 8-27). From this view, you can easily create content, move content, and configure the content's behavior (general settings, advanced settings, and permissions). This provides a quick way to work with content within the site collection. The Site Content and Structure section can be a great asset for any site collection administrator, because it provides additional administrative options that are not accessible from the standard Site Settings page.

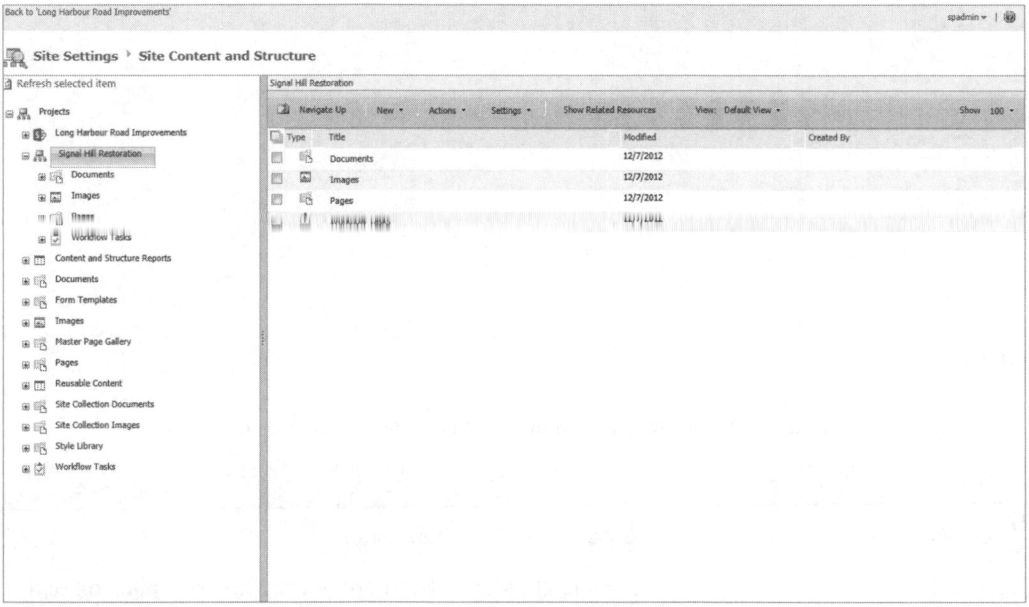

FIGURE 8-27

TRY IT OUT   Creating and Moving a Site from the Site Content and Structure Page

In this Try It Out, you use the Site Content and Structure page to create a new project site. You create the site as a project site under Signal Hill and then move the site so that it is a sibling to the Signal Hill project instead of a child. Although creating a site and moving it immediately afterwards may not always be a common scenario, there may be times where you create a site in the wrong location and need to move it. In addition, you may elect to move sites from one location in a site collection to another based on changes to your organizational structure or archival requirements.

1. Open the Projects site collection that you created in the first Try It Out of this chapter.

2. From the Settings menu, select the Site Settings link.

3. From the Site Administration group, select the Content and structure link.

4. Select the drop-down menu next to the Signal Hill Project site. Select the arrow next to the word "New" and then select Site, as shown in Figure 8-28.

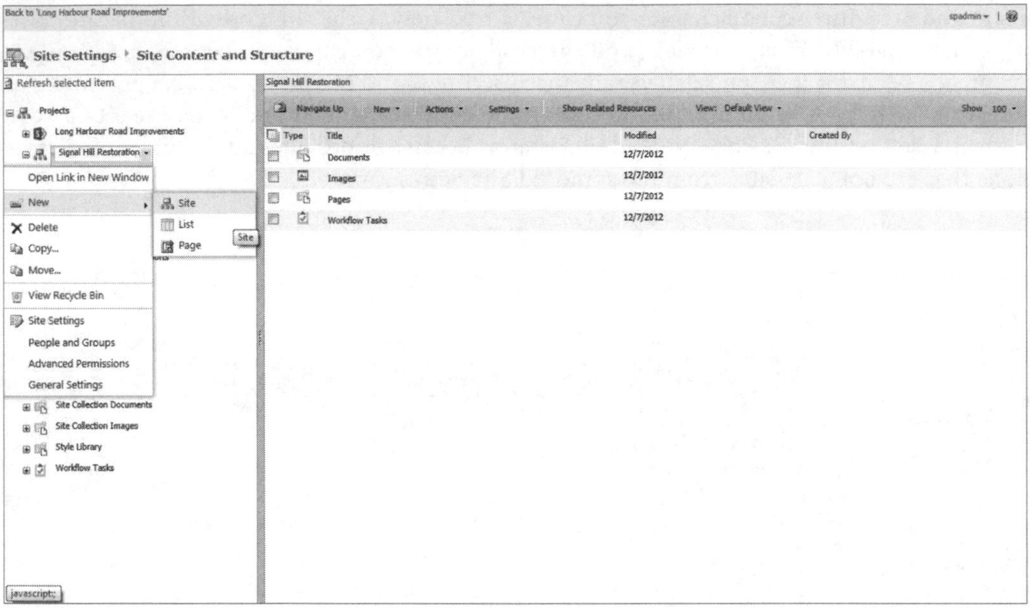

FIGURE 8-28

5. When the page loads, enter the following properties for the site and then click Create:

PROPERTY	VALUE
Title	Gros Morne Trail Expansion
Description	Location to store all content related to the expansion of a hiking trail in Gros Morne National Park.
URL	gmtrail
Template Selection	Team Site
Permissions	Use same permissions as parent site
Use the top link bar from the parent site?	Yes

6. Click OK. You will be redirected to the Site Content and Structure page. You should now see the Gros Morne Trail Expansion site listed under the Signal Hill site.

7. Now that you have the site created, you realize that you created it in the wrong location and want to move the site so that it is directly under the projects site. Remember that you could have created the site directly under projects; we are just using this as an example so that you understand the process for moving sites.

8. Select the drop-down next to the Gros Morne Trail Expansion and select the Move option, as shown in Figure 8-29.

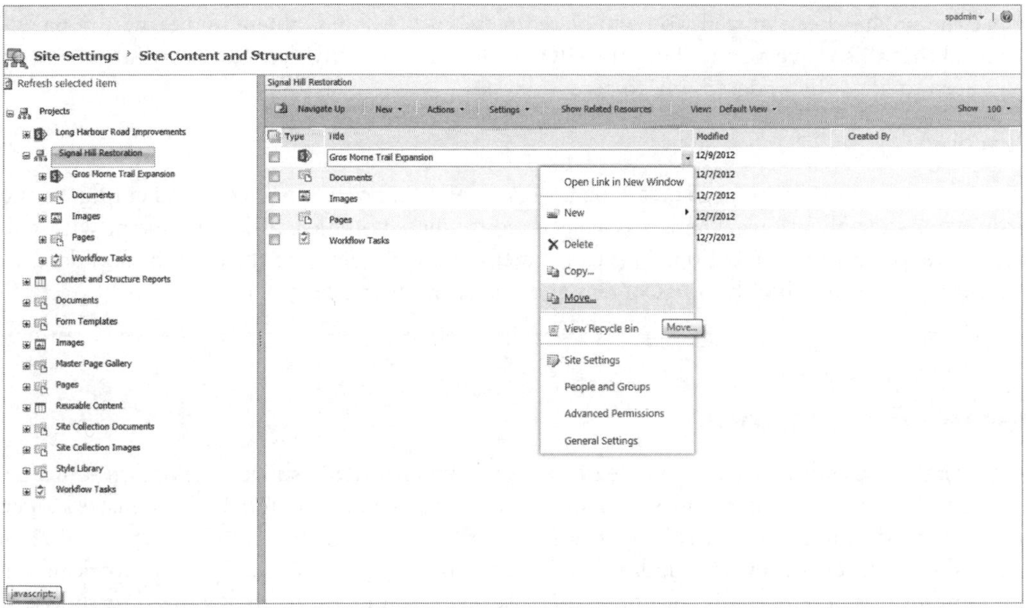

FIGURE 8-29

9. Select Projects within the move dialog box, as shown in Figure 8-30, and then click OK.

FIGURE 8-30

10. Once the site has been moved, you will be redirected to the Site Content and Structure page. Keep in mind that this move also updates the URL of the site, so if any users had the link saved, they will need to have the updated link to access the site.

How It Works

The Content and Site Structure page gives you an easy way to quickly work with and configure the content within your site collections. There may be occasions where you have a site or content within a site that must move to a different location. This can sometimes be challenging through the standard web interface but works well using the Site Content and Structure interface.

Managing Permissions

You may have noticed that when you create new sites, you are always given the option to inherit permissions or to create unique permissions. So far, you have been inheriting permissions. As a general rule, it is a good practice to inherit permissions for ease of management and to ensure that changes made at the top level site are also updated across its child sites. However, if you are working with a site that needs restricted permissions or contains sensitive data, you likely will need to choose the option that allows for unique permissions. Regardless of what you choose when creating the site, you can always modify it later if circumstances change. Simply go to the Site Settings page of a site and select Site Permissions.

> **NOTE** Chapter 9, "Managing Permissions," describes in detail how to manage permissions for a site and its contents.

SharePoint Designer Settings

The typical progression of SharePoint development is to start with what you can do within the browser, then what you can do within SharePoint Designer, and finally what you can do with custom code solutions. SharePoint Designer is a powerful design tool that can be used to do many great things, including customizing and configuring SharePoint sites and workflows. However, like any good tool, you must monitor its usage to ensure that it doesn't negatively impact the experience of your environment's users.

> **NOTE** Chapter 5, "Working with Workflows," and Chapter 14, "Branding and the User Experience" include examples of using SharePoint Designer.

If you want to restrict how SharePoint Designer is used within a particular site collection, you can use the SharePoint Designer Settings associated with the site collection. To access this configuration, go to the Site Settings page and select the SharePoint Designer Settings under the Site Collection

Administration Group. From this screen, you can enable/disable particular feature sets within SharePoint Designer (see Figure 8-31). In the event that your system administrator has configured settings at the farm level, the settings displayed within the site collection will inherit these settings.

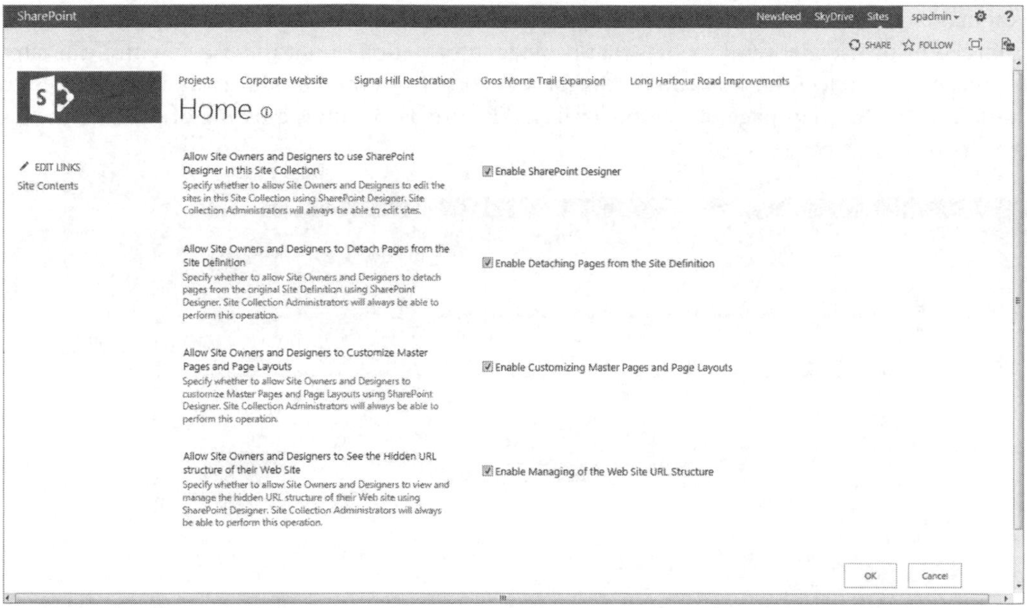

FIGURE 8-31

Help Settings

To address the variety of user types that could be using the system, SharePoint has a variety of Help collections, which are tailored to suit the needs of specific types of users. By clicking the Help Settings link from the Site Settings page of every top-level site, a site collection administrator can select which Help collections are available within a specific site collection. Figure 8-32 shows an example.

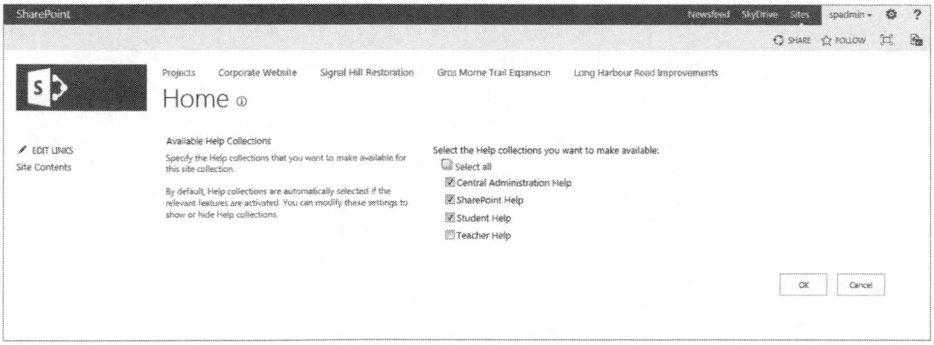

FIGURE 8-32

Popularity and Search Reports

One thing that will be important to you as you manage your sites is the ability to understand how the site is being used. Are users accessing the site consistently? When they access the site, what pages are they viewing? What are they searching for? Having all this information easily accessible will help you make modifications to your site that improve its usability and functionality. Out-of-the-box, SharePoint provides several reports that provide information about the usage within the site and within the site collection. You can access these reports from the Popularity and Search Reports link under the Site Settings page of the top level site. Figure 8-33 shows a listing of some of the available reports from this page.

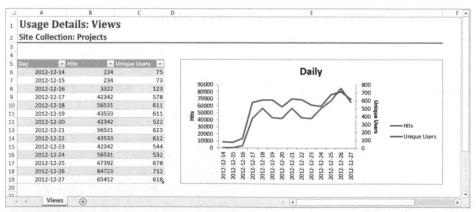

FIGURE 8-33

To open a report, click on its link. You will be required to choose a location to save the report. The report is available in a convenient Excel format, which makes it ideal for sharing or performing additional analysis. An example is shown in Figure 8-34.

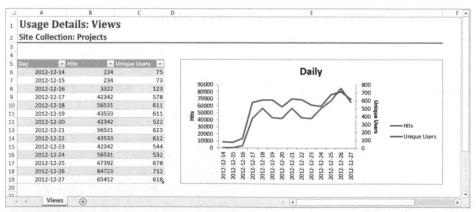

FIGURE 8-34

Working with Content across Sites

As you start working with site collections and sites, you may start to wonder how you can start to "roll-up" (aggregate) certain content so that it can be displayed on different sites from where it is stored. This is possible using Web Parts such as the Content Query Web Part or Content Search Web Part. For more information, see Chapter 7, "Working with Web Parts."

UNDERSTANDING SHAREPOINT'S OUT-OF-THE-BOX TEMPLATES

In SharePoint, whenever you create a new site, you start with a template, which has preconfigured components, including a Home page, list and libraries, Web Parts, features, and content types. Based on the type of activities you want to perform within a site, you will likely choose different templates. For example, if you were creating a site that is to be a collaboration area for members of a team working toward a common goal, you might select the team site or project site. If you want your site to be more suited toward discussions and collaboration related to a club or committee, you might choose the community site. Once you create a site based a template, you have a starting point that you can further extend by performing additional configurations to suit your specific business requirements. For example, you might start with a Team Site template but then create additional apps, such as Issues, Tasks, Calendar, and Links. Within each app, you might then create custom views and enable metadata navigation or other settings, similar to what we reviewed in Chapter 4. After finishing these configurations, you can save the modified site as a template and use it as the starting point for all other sites of that type.

In the following sections, we briefly review the templates that are available for sites out-of-the-box with SharePoint, and then look at how to save a configured site as a template.

Collaboration Templates

The templates in the collaboration category are designed to help you create an environment where users can easily share, build, and collaborate on content. The following table describes the specific templates that are available:

TEMPLATE	DESCRIPTION	WHEN TO USE
Team Site	A site for groups of people working together on a common topic. This site utilizes wiki-type functionality to ensure that site pages can be easily created and organized by team members.	This template is useful for a team that needs to share general content. By default, several list and library apps are preconfigured for you. A team could take this template and quickly develop it further to suit their specific needs.

continues

(continued)

TEMPLATE	DESCRIPTION	WHEN TO USE
Blog	A web log where authors can create news stories and posts related to a specific topic or variety of topics. This site includes built-in capabilities for collecting user comments so that a dialog can occur between the post's author and members of the community or organization.	This template is useful when you want to empower a user or group of users to publish information related to a topic on an intranet or employee portal. Due to its ability to accept feedback and comments directly from stakeholders, this template can also be useful as a corporate news site for internal postings and announcements.
Project Site	A site that has been preconfigured with the basic elements that most project teams would require, including a document library, Tasks list app and Calendar list app.	This site, as its name implies, is an ideal starting point for a project team that requires a common location for the storage of project documentation, milestones, and assignments.
Community Site	A group discussion forum with statistics, replies, and badges for its participants.	This site is useful for teams, clubs, or communities that can benefit from discussions and Q&A exchanges. This site can also be used as an enterprise knowledge base that enables staff to search for frequently asked questions.

Enterprise Templates

The enterprise templates are used to implement the Enterprise Features within SharePoint. Typically, system administrators use these site collection templates when they are configuring the farm. In some cases, your environment may have multiple sites collections that use these templates; however, it is likely that they will still be configured by one of the administrators. The following table describes each of the available templates:

TEMPLATE	DESCRIPTION	WHEN TO USE
Document Center	A site designed for the storage and sharing of documents. The Document Center template is one of two templates within SharePoint that is preconfigured for large volumes of data.	This site can be used as a documents repository on an intranet or shared location.

Records Center	SharePoint enables users to assign rules and policies to certain types of content in order to consistently manage and control the access, expiry, and deletion of important corporate records. This is an area of major concern for many large organizations that store customers' personal information or manage information that has specific access and retention rights. The Records Center template has several lists and libraries that help control and store records and managed content. It can be used as a repository for records-based content and is the other site template designed to be capable of storing large volumes of documents.	This site template is used for creating a records repository or formal archive location for files.
Business Intelligence Center	This site is designed for use with the reporting features of SharePoint. To use this template, you should have the Site Collection feature for PerformancePoint Reporting enabled.	A site created with this template will have many of the elements required to create a reporting center, such as a data connection library and PerformancePoint content list for the creation of reports, scorecards, and key performance indicators (KPIs).
Enterprise Search Center	A site for delivering the search experience. This template, used in the examples in Chapter 17, provides pages preconfigured for enterprise search and displays results pages for common result types, such as people, videos, and conversations.	This site is used within any site collection where more control and flexibility around search interfaces is required.
Basic Search Center	A site for delivering the core search experience. The site includes pages for search results and advanced searches.	This site is used within any site collection where more control and flexibility around search interfaces is required.
Visio Process Repository	A site for groups or teams that are dedicated to the purpose of defining processes and procedures that are based on Visio flow diagrams.	This site comes with a library preconfigured for the storage of flow charts and diagrams.

Publishing Templates

As described in the following table, the publishing templates are preconfigured to take advantage of the rich content management features across the development of site pages:

TEMPLATE	DESCRIPTION	WHEN TO USE
Publishing Portal	Available only for the creation of site collections, the Publishing Portal template contains many preconfigurations that make it useful as a starting point for a corporate intranet, web portal, or Internet-based site. This template was used in the first Try It Out of this chapter.	This site is used for Internet-facing sites, corporate Intranets, and any other sites that want to leverage the publishing functionality provided by this template.
Publishing Site	A site that can be used as a subsite within any site collection, this template relies on the publishing features of SharePoint, which must be enabled for this site to be created. Within this site, authors can create new pages from a variety of templates and use web content management features, such as page controls and rich media, within the publishing of their pages. These pages are covered extensively in Chapter 15.	This site template is used as a subsite to any site in a Publishing Portal (described above) that requires the ability to easily create and publish pages. This template would be used in scenarios where the site owners want flexibility in how content approval and workflows are defined.
Publishing Site (with Workflow)	The same as the Publishing Site template but preconfigured with approval workflows for site libraries so that published content must go through an approval process.	This site template is used as a subsite to any site in a Publishing Portal (described above) that requires the ability to easily create and publish pages. This template would be chosen in scenarios where approval is required for all published content.
Enterprise Wiki	A site that is suitable for creating a library of wiki-based content to be used as a knowledge management or sharing portal within your organization, empowering users to publish, edit, and share content related to specific topics.	This site would be used for creating a corporate wiki or knowledge base.

These templates are configured with all the publishing features activated and ready for use. Out-of-the-box, they allow you to create pages from preconfigured page layouts and to publish these pages through an approval workflow.

CREATING CUSTOM TEMPLATES

As mentioned previously, the templates discussed in this chapter so far may give you only some of the elements you need for an effective collaboration or information management site. To create a site for your specific business requirements, you can use an existing template that provides some of the elements you require, and then create the additional components you need after the site has been created. Once you have a site that works for you, you can then save your site as a template for future use. Companies commonly do this to create uniform sites and to save time and effort when creating new sites.

When creating templates, you have the option to include content of the site when saving. This may include documents that are stored within library apps, content within the list apps, or content stored within specific Web Parts. You can select this option if you want to include certain placeholders or starting points for users that they can reference after the site is created.

If you are responsible for a SharePoint environment, remember the following timesaving tips when creating customized templates for your site:

➤ **Identify the key templates your organization will need.** Anticipating your users' needs prevents site owners from creating their own templates.

➤ **Don't create too many templates.** Too many templates are difficult to manage, and site owners may not intuitively know which template to use.

➤ **Make sure that your template is an adequate starting point.** Having too few or too many elements will frustrate site owners and cause them to either create their own template or spend too much time fixing your template.

➤ **Create sites from a consistent set of templates with common interface elements and component names.** This helps drive user adoption and overall acceptance of the environment.

Saving a Site as a Template

The option to save a site as a template is located in the Site Settings page in the Site Actions grouping. It is important to note that you will only see the "Save site as template" link when the site you are working within can be saved as a template. Some sites, including those that enable publishing within the site, do not support the "Save as template" option.

TRY IT OUT Saving a Site as a Template

In this Try It Out, you create a new site based on the Project Site template and make some minor additions to it that reflect your organization's requirements for project tracking and collaboration. Then you save the site as a template so that it can be used for other sites in the future.

1. Open the Projects site collection that you created in the first Try It Out of this chapter.
2. From the Settings menu, select the Site Contents link.
3. Select the option to create a New Subsite.

4. Enter the following details for your subsite:

PROPERTY	VALUE
Title	Long Harbour Road Improvements
Description	Project site to manage Long Harbour Road Improvements
Web Site Address	roadimp
Permissions	Use same permissions as parent site.
Top Navigation Bar	Use top link bar from the parent site.

5. Click the Create button to create the site.

6. Once the site is created, create the following list and library apps (refer to Chapters 2 and 3, respectively):

➤ Links list app named `Links`

➤ Issues Tracking list app named `Issues`

➤ Announcements app named `News`

7. Create an Announcement within the News app stating that the project has started and welcoming users to the site.

8. Add the News App Web Part to the home page and display the Summary View, as described in Chapter 7.

9. Using the method described earlier in this chapter, enable the tree view navigation for the current navigation. When you have finished, your site will be similar to Figure 8-35.

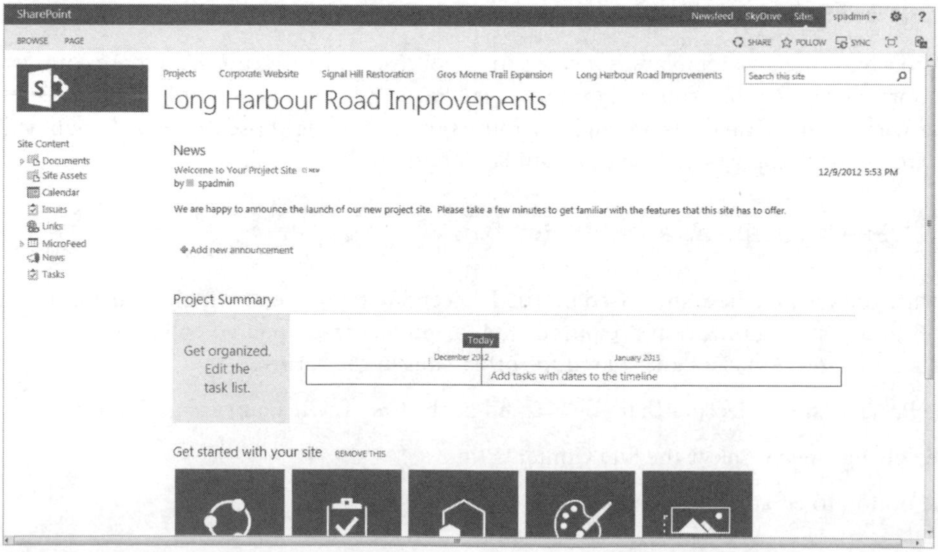

FIGURE 8-35

10. Once the apps and content have been created, select Site Settings from the Settings menu. You will be redirected to the Settings page for the site.

11. Select the "Save site as template" link from the Site Actions group. The "Save as template" page will appear.

12. Enter the following details for your template:

PROPERTY	VALUE
File Name	Official Project Site
Template Name	Official Project Site
Description	Official site for corporate projects.
Include Content	Yes

13. Click OK to save the template.

How It Works

When you saved your site as a template, the configurations and content were saved to the site's Solutions Gallery and made available for use within the site collection. When you create a new site, the template will appear in the site's Solutions Gallery, as shown in Figure 8-36. Selecting that template creates a new site with all the same configurations and content as your site.

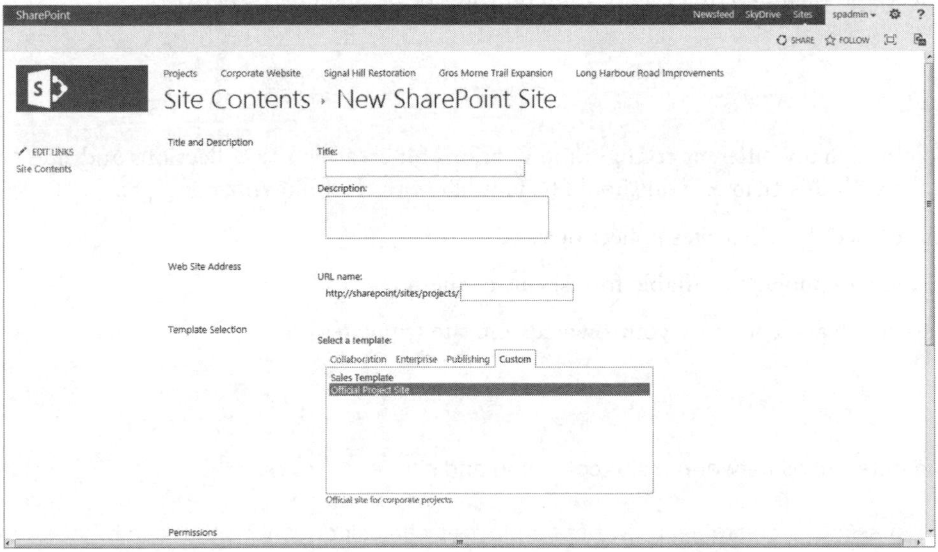

FIGURE 8-36

Moving the Template to a New Location

When you create a template, it is stored as a `.wsp` file in the Solutions gallery (see Figure 8-37). You can access this gallery through the Solutions Gallery link in the Galleries section of the Site Settings page.

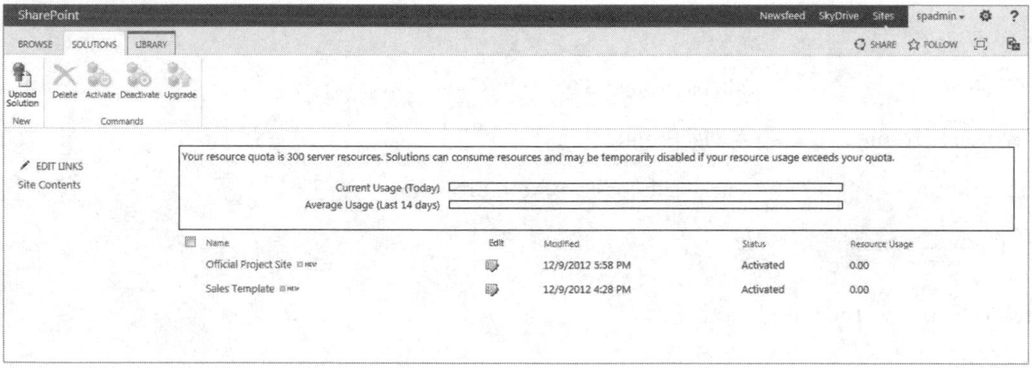

FIGURE 8-37

Basically, the Solutions gallery is a list of the solutions that are used within the site collection. Because it is a library, you can upload additional solutions. This means that you can move templates between different site collections simply by saving them locally and then uploading them to a different site collection's Solutions gallery. You can save a solution locally by clicking its name from within the gallery and then selecting the location on your local computer or network.

SUMMARY

This chapter covered many different configuration options for creating site collections and sites. After reading through this chapter, you should be familiar with the following concepts:

➤ The differences between sites collections and sites

➤ The different templates available for use out-of-the-box

➤ How to create and configure your own custom site templates

EXERCISES

1. Describe the differences between a site collection and site.

2. You have been asked to create a site where employees can ask questions that can be answered by other employees and rated. What template would be appropriate for managing this content?

3. You have spent a considerable amount of time configuring a project site that you manage. You want to make that site available to other users for future sites. What should you do?

▶ **WHAT YOU LEARNED IN THIS CHAPTER**

TOPIC	KEY CONCEPTS
Sites vs. site collections	You can create a variety of sites in SharePoint that can be used for storing content. These sites are organized as groups and stored within site collections. Each site collection shares certain elements, such as templates, content types, and security groups.
Site templates	SharePoint provides many out-of-the-box site templates that are preconfigured for use within your environment. Sites can be created based on the templates and then customized further to meet project needs.
Custom site templates	If no template exists for your needs, you can create a custom template, with the lists and libraries configured as you require.

Managing Permissions

The goal of this book is to provide you with experience using the tools and features of SharePoint in a way that enables you to craft and develop powerful, no-code business solutions, and no solution that is highly related to the business can be completed without an in-depth understanding of managing permissions. Permissions are one of the central elements to any organization and should be managed with care and attention to detail. This chapter reviews the most common methods for managing permissions and discusses some of the tools and techniques that you can use in the ongoing process of managing users.

UNDERSTANDING USER ACCESS AND AUDIENCE TARGETING

Within SharePoint you can take two different approaches to managing access. One is through the management of permissions. Using this approach, you assign an access level to different users that determines what content they have access to and what they can do with the content once they access it. The other approach is what is referred to as *audience targeting*. Audience targeting does not deal with the permissions of content, but instead is a way to push relevant information to users. An example of this is if you have a list of events for the entire corporation. All the events are stored in one central location, but the various offices don't really need to see the onsite events for other locations. Using the concept of audience targeting, you can push the relevant content (that is, events relevant to a particular location) to the users and not bombard them with content that doesn't apply to them. There is no reason that they can't see all the events, but there is value in just showing users what applies directly to them. This chapter discusses both approaches, but it is important to remember that there is a large difference between the two. If you need to secure data and ensure that only a select set of users can access the data, you need to use permissions. Audiences should never be considered a security feature.

The Login Process

When users click a link or enter the web address of a SharePoint site, they are either logged in to the site automatically because they are already authenticated on the site due to the configuration of their network, or they are prompted for a username and password via a dialog box or form. In some cases, there may be no need for authentication because the site is configured for anonymous access. In this chapter, you primarily review scenarios where the user is connecting in an authenticated environment.

If users try to enter a site for which they do not have access, they are directed to one of two different pages. The first thing they might see is a page that informs them that they do not have access to the site, but they can submit a request to the site owner asking for permission to access it. An example of this is shown in Figure 9-1.

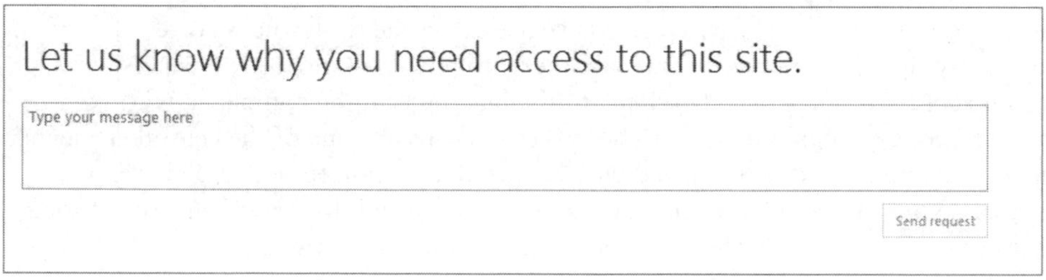

Let us know why you need access to this site.

Type your message here

Send request

FIGURE 9-1

This is the experience they will have if the site has been configured to allow Site Access Requests. If this feature has been enabled, users can enter their request for access and an e-mail will be sent to one of the site owners who can then approve or reject the request. While the request is being processed (or pending approval), users can return to the site URL to supply any updates and see the history of the request. An example of this feature is shown in Figure 9-2.

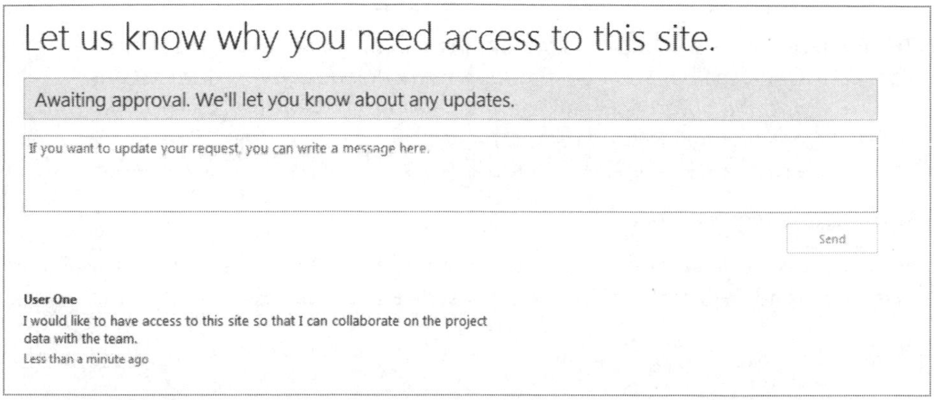

Let us know why you need access to this site.

Awaiting approval. We'll let you know about any updates.

If you want to update your request, you can write a message here.

Send

User One
I would like to have access to this site so that I can collaborate on the project
data with the team.
Less than a minute ago

FIGURE 9-2

If a site owner does not want users to be able to request access, users will simply see a message that informs them that the site has not been shared with them. An example of this message is shown in Figure 9-3.

Sorry, this site hasn't been shared with you.

FIGURE 9-3

TRY IT OUT | **Enabling Site Access Requests**

To configure the experience that users will have when they try to access a site for which they do not have permission, you need to configure the Manage Access Requests properties.

1. From the top-level site of your site collection, select Site Settings from the Site Actions menu (the gear icon in the top right of the page).

2. Select Site Permissions from the Users and Permissions group.

3. Select the Access Requests Settings option from the ribbon. A window appears, as shown in Figure 9-4.

Access Requests Settings   ✕

Access Requests Settings
Allow users to request access to this   ☑ Allow access requests
Web site.
                                           Send all access requests to the following e-mail address:
                                           siteadmin@demo.com

                                                          OK   Cancel

FIGURE 9-4

> **NOTE** *If you do not see this item in the Settings menu, your server may not be configured to send e-mail. You can change this by having your system administrator configure the outgoing e-mail settings from the Operations tab of the SharePoint Central Administration site.*

4. Select the "Allow access requests" checkbox.

5. Enter the e-mail address to which all access requests should be sent. It is good practice to use a distribution list for this address rather than a single user's e-mail address.

6. Click OK.

How It Works

When users who do not have access to the site attempt to visit the address, they are presented with a dialog box that allows them to enter a request for site access. This request is then sent to the site administrator for processing.

> **NOTE** *For more information on the process that a site administrator follows when a new site access request has been made, refer to the "Understanding the Share Option" section later in this chapter.*

Once users are logged in to a site where they have been given access, they will only see content and user interface elements that they have been given permission to view. The content that users view and edit is determined by their SharePoint site group membership and permission levels. *Site groups* are specific roles in SharePoint that determine what a user can do within a site. Permission levels define the activities that a user or group is allowed to perform in a specified location.

Active Directory Integration

Most organizations using SharePoint in a corporate or enterprise setting, such as an intranet, use Active Directory to manage user profiles and determine how users log in to the network, which is also known as the *authentication process*. If your organization uses Active Directory, SharePoint becomes a great browser-based tool in which to work because a user who logs in to the domain does not typically need to enter credentials again to access a SharePoint site. This is because when the system administrator configured the SharePoint Server, it was added as a member of your Active Directory domain. Therefore, when you enter your username and password to connect to the network, the SharePoint environment will recognize you as a member and, therefore, not require you to specify your username and password again. In addition, SharePoint will allow you to connect to sites based on your site group membership and will retain your permissions as you access various other Windows-based systems such as file shares or printers. Most users prefer this type of experience because it can be tedious and confusing to manage both multiple usernames and passwords.

OTHER AUTHENTICATION METHODS

In SharePoint, you can connect your membership database to stores aside from Active Directory or Windows. In fact, because SharePoint is built on the .NET Framework, any membership provider that you can use in ASP.NET can control access to the SharePoint environment using forms-based authentication.

Configuring alternate authentication providers is beyond the scope of this book. Within this book all examples are based on an environment that has been configured using Active Directory.

MANAGING ACCESS IN SHAREPOINT

As your SharePoint environment starts to become populated with important business documents, it's important to manage access properly. Users who require information to do their jobs should be able to locate and then access information easily. In cases where you have sensitive information, it's crucial that only users who have a business requirement to access it have the rights to do so. Finally, because SharePoint will become a central storage location for important business information, it is critical that this information be protected. This means locking out those who could cause harm to the system or should not have access to information.

SharePoint Permissions

A *permission level* represents a set of rights that can be assigned to a user or group on a specific SharePoint object such as site, list, or document. Out-of-the-box, several permission levels exist to reflect the most common usage scenarios of the system. The following table outlines the default out-of-the-box permission levels in a SharePoint 2013 Team Site template:

PERMISSION LEVEL	HIGH-LEVEL SUMMARY
Full Control	Has full control
Design	Can view, add, update, delete, approve, and customize
Edit	Can add, edit, and delete lists; can view, add, update, and delete list items and documents
Contribute	Can view, add, update, and delete list items and documents
Read	Can view pages and list items and download documents
Limited Access	Can view specific lists, document libraries, list items, folders, or documents when given permissions
View Only	Can view pages, list items, and documents; document types with server-side file handlers can be viewed in the browser but not downloaded

ACTIVATING FEATURES CAN ADD ADDITIONAL ROLES

When you activate additional features, additional permission levels might be added automatically. For example, when you activate the publishing features, publishing permissions are added by default because they are needed when the features are used.

If the permission levels that come with the site by default do not meet your needs, you can create your own custom permission levels. However, you should do this with caution. You need to ensure when you create new permission levels that you do not modify the ones that are included by default. This is a best practice that helps to ensure that your customizations are not lost or overwritten when a new system patch, hotfix, or version is released.

TRY IT OUT **Creating a Custom Permission Level**

In certain cases, you may want to assign a set of rights that isn't completely covered by the out-of-the-box permission levels in SharePoint. For example, you may want to allow users to read and write, but you may not want to allow them to delete items. Therefore, the Contribute permission level will not be suitable for your requirements. In this Try It Out, you create a new permission level by copying the Contribute permission level and making modifications to the copy to suit your requirements.

1. From the top-level site of your site collection, select Site Settings from the Site Actions menu.

2. Select Site Permissions from the Users and Permissions group of links. You are redirected to the Site Permissions page, as shown in Figure 9-5.

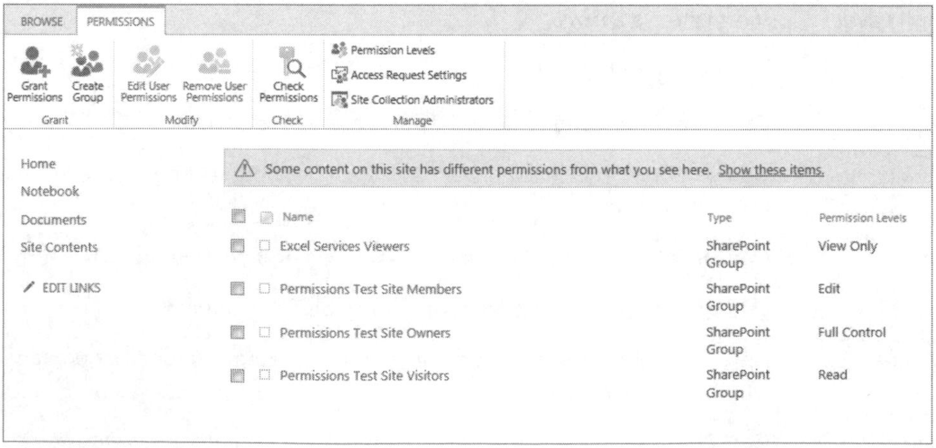

FIGURE 9-5

3. Select Permission Levels from the ribbon.

4. Select the Contribute permission level. You are redirected to a page containing the various rights and activities allowed within the Contribute permission level.

5. Scroll to the bottom of the page and click the Copy Permission Level button. A new blank permission level is created containing the same settings as the Contribute permission level.

6. Enter **Contribute No-Delete** as the name for the new permission level.

7. Enter the following for the description: **Can read and write but cannot delete.**

8. Deselect the options to Delete Items and Delete Versions.

9. Scroll to the bottom of the page and click Create. Your new permission level is now displayed within the permission level listing, as shown in Figure 9-6.

☐	Contribute No Delete	Can read and write but cannot delete.

FIGURE 9-6

How It Works

The Contribute permission level contained rights similar to those you wanted to provide to the end users of your site, except for the fact that it allowed users to delete items. Because you do not want to allow users to delete documents or list items, you created a custom permission level called Contribute No-Delete. Rather than create everything from scratch, you created the Contribute No-Delete permission level from a copy of the Contribute permission level and removed the rights for deleting items and versions. Your new permission level is now available for use within your site and its subsites.

SharePoint Groups

SharePoint permission levels enable you to determine what level of access is available within a SharePoint site. SharePoint Groups enable you to take a collection of users and assign them to a permission level. Out-of-the-box, each new site you create also contains several default groups that have been assigned a default permission level. The three most common groups are:

➤ Site Visitors

➤ Site Members

➤ Site Owners

Depending on what features and what template you use for your site, additional default groups can exist. These default groups exist so that you can have a starting point for giving users access to your content.

TRY IT OUT   Adding a User to a Site Group

In this example, you add users to the default Members group. This gives the users access to contribute to the lists and libraries within the site.

1. From the top-level site of your site collection, select Site Settings from the Site Actions menu.

2. Select People and Groups from the Users and Permissions group of links. You are redirected to the Group Management area of the site. By default, you will be viewing the membership of the Site Members group, as shown in Figure 9-7.

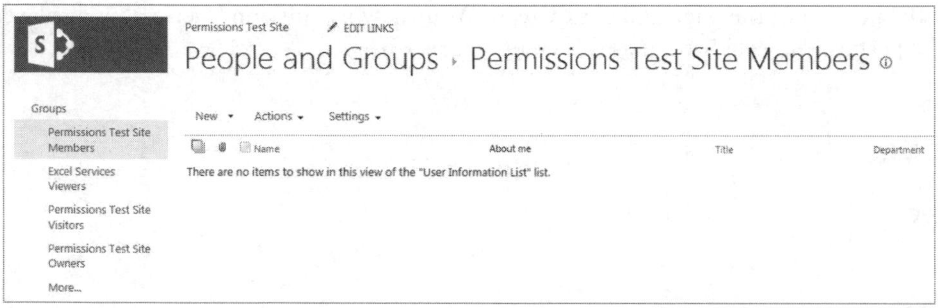

FIGURE 9-7

3. On the New menu of the toolbar, select Add Users. The grant permissions window appears, as shown in Figure 9-8.

4. Enter the name of the user that you want to add to the group. For this example, add **User One** to the site.

5. Enter a message to include in the e-mail invitation that will be sent to the user. An example of this is shown in Figure 9-9.

6. Click Share.

FIGURE 9-8

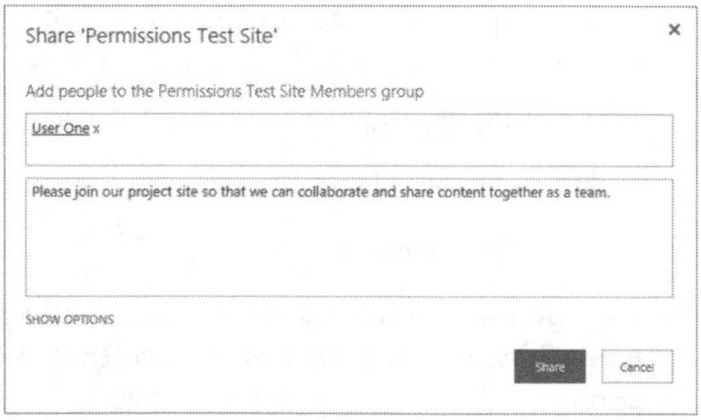

FIGURE 9-9

E-MAIL INVITATIONS

If you do not want to send an e-mail invitation to users you are adding to a group, you can select the Show Option link on the page and deselect the Send an e-mail invitation option. By default the system is configured to send notification e-mails whenever you assign new permissions.

How It Works

Adding users to the default SharePoint Group provides a way for them to be given access to the site. In this example, you gave User One contribute permissions through the Site Members group.

In real-world scenarios you will often create custom groups that reflect your organization's structure and then add users to those custom groups. An example of this scenario can include having a group of managers that needs to have approval rights. You could create a custom group called Managers and assign that group to have approval rights within the site. Then as managers come and go within the organization, you can simply add and remove them from the group.

TRY IT OUT   Creating a New Site Group

In this Try It Out, you creat a new group within your site. This will allow you to more easily manage the permissions within your solution.

1. From the top-level site of your site collection, select Site Settings from the Site Actions menu.

2. Select People and Groups from the Users and Permissions group of links. You are redirected to the Group Management area of the site. By default, you will be viewing the membership of the Site Members group.

3. Select the Groups link from the left-hand navigation menu. You are redirected to the Groups listing page.

4. On the New menu of the toolbar, select Create New Group. You are redirected to the Create Group page, as shown in Figure 9-10.

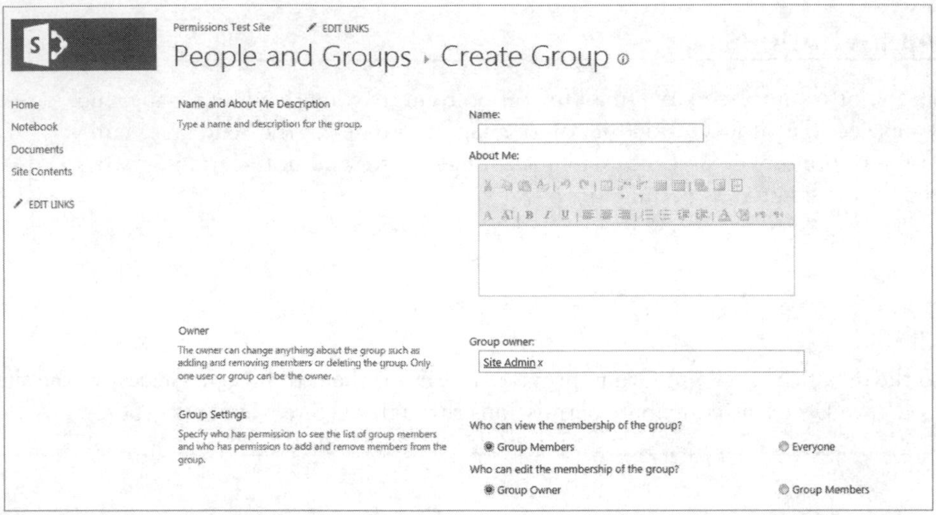

FIGURE 9-10

5. Enter **Team Contributors** for the name of the group.

6. Enter the following description into the About Me field for the group: **These are the team members who need to contribute content but can't delete any content from the site.**

7. For this example, you should enter your name for the Group owner value. However, it is a best practice to create a SharePoint Administration group and specify that group as the owner for all other SharePoint Groups.

8. Retain the default configurations for Group Settings and Access Requests.

9. For the Give Group Permission to this Site section, select the Contribute No-Delete permission level. This gives all members of the Team Contributors group Contribute No-Delete access to the site.

10. Click Create. Your new group is now displayed on the Quick Launch bar of the People and Groups page, as shown in Figure 9-11. As you need to add people to the group, you simply return to the People and Groups page and follow the instructions from the previous Try It Out to add new users.

FIGURE 9-11

How It Works

When you create your group, you automatically become a member because you are the creator. You add new users to a custom group by following the same process described earlier for adding users to one of the default SharePoint Groups.

In addition to creating new permissions and groups and adding users, it is important to also know how to modify the existing settings. The remaining Try It Out exercises in this chapter deal with some of the common scenarios you will face as a site administrator.

TRY IT OUT Modifying the Permissions of an Existing User or Group

In some scenarios, it's necessary to change the specific rights that a single user or site group has on a site. This may be related to a direct request from a business manager, a change in requirements, or perhaps because you need to grant a certain user rights to a workspace beyond what he or she currently has. This may be because the user has demonstrated exceptional skills and would make a good candidate to assume more responsibility for managing the SharePoint site. In the next example, you modify the permissions of one of the existing SharePoint Groups.

1. From the top-level site of your site collection, select Site Settings from the Site Actions menu.

2. Select Site Permissions from the Users and Permissions group of links.

3. Select the checkbox associated with the Team Contributors group, as shown in Figure 9-12.

| ☑ ☐ Team Contributors | SharePoint Group | Contribute No-Delete |

FIGURE 9-12

4. Select the Edit User Permissions option from the ribbon.

5. Deselect the Contribute No-Delete option and select the Contribute permission level.

6. Click the OK button. You are returned to the Site Permissions page, where you will see that the Team Contributors group now has Contribute access to the site.

How It Works

In this example, you changed the permissions associated with the Team Contributors group from Collaborate No-Delete to Collaborate. This may be because of a recent requirements change that would allow for more flexibility in storing content, thus removing the need to restrict who had the ability to delete site content.

> **TRY IT OUT**   Removing a User from a Group

In a previous Try It Out you added User One to the Team Contributors group. As of now he is no longer working on your team due to a transfer to another unit. Because he is no longer on the team, you should remove him from the SharePoint Group.

1. From the top-level site of your site collection, select Site Settings from the Site Actions menu.

2. Select People and Groups. You are redirected to the Group Management area of the site. By default, you will see the membership of the Site Members group.

3. Select the Team Contributors link from the left-hand navigation menu.

4. Select the checkbox to the left of User One from the membership listing.

5. Select the Remove Users from Group option from the Actions menu. You receive a warning message, as shown in Figure 9-13.

6. Click OK to confirm your action and complete the operation.

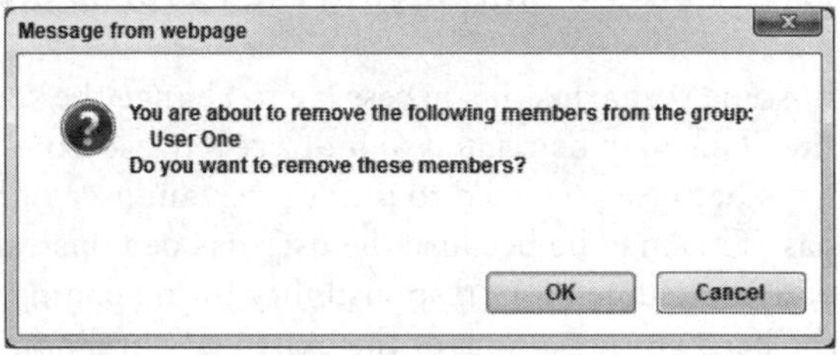

FIGURE 9-13

How It Works

In this Try It Out, you located the single user within the site and modified the permissions he had been assigned. Selecting a single user and modifying his permissions modifies the access he has to the site.

SharePoint Groups vs. Active Directory Domain Services Groups

In addition to being able to create SharePoint Groups to manage collections of users, you can use existing Active Directory Domain Services (AD DS) groups and assign permissions to those groups. When groups from AD DS are used you manage the group membership within AD DS. Whenever AD DS is updated, those updates are available within SharePoint. The choice to use AD DS or SharePoint Groups is up to the organization and typically depends on many internal factors. In most cases, the best practice is to use an existing AD DS group and then to use a SharePoint Group if one doesn't exist within AD DS. There is typically a balance to be achieved through governance policies that dictate how to best manage permissions. This balance should be considered unique within each organization and discussed with both the site administrators and the system administrators. Working together to find the best solution, given your environment, will ensure that you are managing permissions in a way that can be maintained over the long term.

NESTED GROUPS IN AD DS

It is possible that you could have various AD DS groups that do not work within SharePoint. In many cases this has to do with the groups having references that cross multiple AD DS structures. It is a best practice for you to work with your organization to determine which approach will be best for you within SharePoint. Understanding how your organization manages AD DS will help determine if you should be using AD DS groups or SharePoint Groups.

Navigating the User Permissions Pages

Managing permissions can often be a difficult task, especially if you are a new site administrator. As you completed the preceding Try It Outs, you probably noticed that you were navigating between several different pages. So far, all the examples have been focused on specific scenarios. This section switches the focus to each of these pages that exists for managing Users and Permissions. By reviewing these pages, you should gain a high-level understanding of how to navigate as you complete additional scenarios for managing permissions. The pages that you review in this section are in the Users and Permissions section of the Site Settings page, as shown in Figure 9-14.

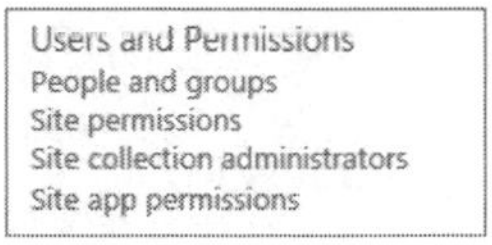

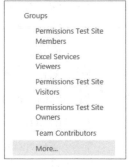

FIGURE 9-14

People and Groups

The People and Groups pages provide a way to view all of the groups that exist within the site. By selecting one of the groups in the Quick Launch bar, you can view all of the members of the group. From this screen you can also add and remove members from the group. By default, the most common groups are listed in the Quick Launch bar and the top group listed is selected when the page loads. To see a group that is not displayed on the Quick Launch bar, select the More option below the groups (see Figure 9-15).

FIGURE 9-15

Selecting this option takes you to the People and Groups listing. From this page you can create new groups using the New menu, and modify what groups are displayed by default on the Quick Launch bar by using the Settings menu. Figure 9-16 shows an example of the Settings menu with the option to display groups that are displayed on the Quick Launch bar.

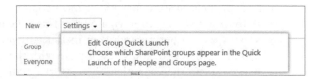

FIGURE 9-16

Site Permissions

The Site Permissions link on the Site Settings page takes you to the central hub for managing permissions within your site collection. If you are new to managing permissions within SharePoint, it is recommended that you start with this page first. In most cases, as you select items from the menus on this page, other pages discussed in this chapter are opened for you. By having separate links, you have the option to quickly go right to the location you know you need. However, if you are new to managing a site collection it will likely be easier for you to work with this page and let it help you navigate to the other pages. An example of this page is shown in Figure 9-17.

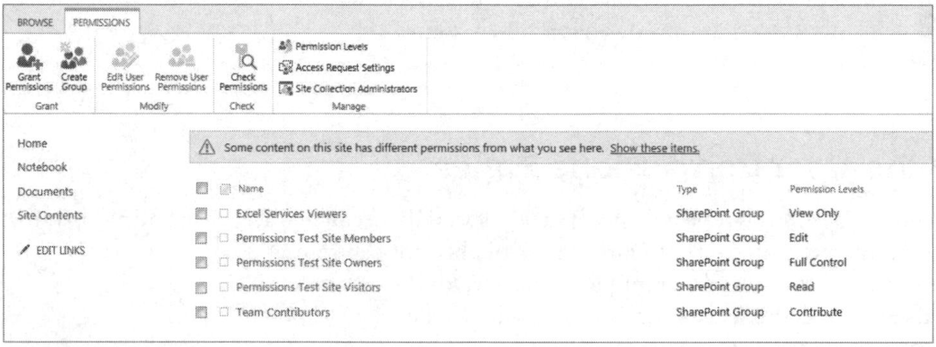

FIGURE 9-17

From this page you can complete the following administrative tasks:

➤ Grant permissions

➤ Create new groups

➤ Edit user permissions

➤ Remove user permissions

➤ Check permissions

➤ Manage permission levels

➤ Manage access request settings

➤ Manage site collection administrators

You have completed many of these tasks in the Try It Out exercises within this chapter. Although this page provides a summary of the most common actions for managing permissions, you will realize that as you start to navigate from this page it is just directing you to the other management pages that exist for permissions. For instance, if you select one of the groups listed on this page, you will open the Users and Groups page with the group you selected as the default group. From that page you can then complete the required management tasks. This is just one of many examples within SharePoint of how navigating through two different options can still lead you to the same settings page. At the end of the day, it doesn't matter how you navigate to the page; it only matters what you do once you are on the page.

Site Collection Administrators

From this page you can manage all of the users who are Site Collection Administrators. These users have full control of all content within the site collection. You can give multiple users this level of access; however, it is important that you understand the implications of granting this access level. If you give many users full control, it will quickly become difficult to manage and maintain any structure within the site. If everyone has full control, they have the ability to use the site as they please without limitations.

Site App Permissions

This page exists so that you can set the permissions for the various apps that you install from the SharePoint Marketplace. When you install an app, specific permissions are granted to that app, based on how it is designed. If you need to remove those permissions at a later date, you would do so from this page.

ITEMS THAT CAN HAVE PERMISSIONS APPLIED

Everything you have done so far has applied to the entire site collection. By default, this is how permissions work for each site collection. Items are managed at the site-collection level (the parent), and then all the contents below (the children) inherit the permissions. SharePoint supports a unique permissions configuration in which the child item stops inheriting from the parent and takes on its own permissions. This means that you can have a site collection (parent) with multiple document library apps (children), each of which has its own unique permissions. Although a user may contribute to his team's collaboration site, he may have read-only rights for a particular document library or even a single document in a library. This section discusses the different levels of access that you can have on a SharePoint site.

Site Permissions

Site permissions apply to the subsites that you create within your site collection. With the creation of each new subsite, you will need to choose if you would like the subsite to inherit the permissions of the parent site or if you would like to configure unique permissions. Your decision generally depends on your requirements:

➤ **Inheriting permissions:** When you allow a subsite to inherit permissions from a parent site, you create a scenario in which any user who has permission to the parent site will have the same permissions and rights on the child site. This cuts down on the tasks and effort associated with managing permissions and creates a consistent access experience for all users.

➤ **Creating unique permissions:** Creating a site with unique permissions enables you to manage permissions and access to your child site, independent of the settings specified for the parent site. Therefore, a user who can add content on the parent site may not necessarily have access to the child site. Users perform different roles from site to site. This means that you'll have to spend more time setting up and managing the site, but you will have greater flexibility in meeting the access requirements of each individual team. Sometimes it's beneficial to give users greater access rights on a subsite than they have on a parent site. For example, in a sales proposal workspace, members of the sales team may be able to create lists and libraries to aid in their production of the proposal, whereas on the sales team site they may only have permissions to add content to existing lists.

TRY IT OUT   **Stop Inheriting Permissions from a Parent Site**

You may have created a site and selected the option to inherit permissions from the parent, but at a later time, realized you needed to manage the site's permissions independently of the parent site. The following example uses the project site that you created in Chapter 2, "Working with List Apps," and assumes that the site has different usage requirements than your main intranet site. You change the permissions settings on the existing site, which copies all permissions settings from the parent into the project site so that you can manage them separately.

Remember that if users have permissions on the parent site and you do not want them to have access to the project site, you must remove them after breaking the inheritance because SharePoint copies the permissions, groups, and users from the parent into the child. You wouldn't have to do this if you had opted to create unique permissions when you first created the site. In that case, once the site is created, it has a blank set of permissions, and no users of the parent have access to the site unless explicitly given access. The exception, of course, is a site collection administrator or site owner on the parent site.

> **NOTE** *If you did not complete the exercises from Chapter 2, you can create any subsite on your site collection that inherits the permissions of the parent. The same steps apply regardless of what site template you use.*

1. From the main page of the subsite site, select Site Settings from the Site Actions menu.

2. Select Site Permissions.

3. Click the Stop Inheriting Permissions option on the ribbon, as shown in Figure 9-18.

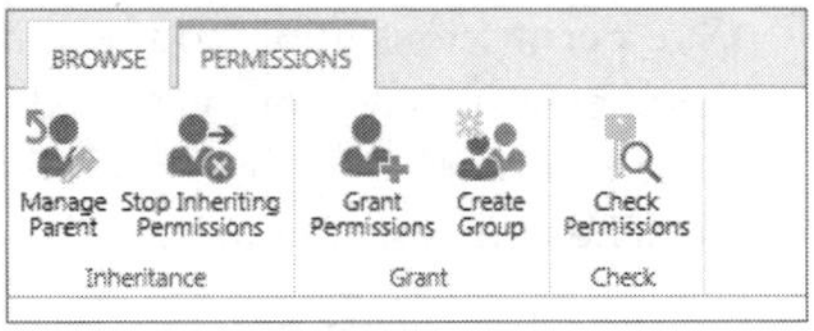

FIGURE 9-18

4. You receive a warning message. Click OK to confirm your action.

5. A page is displayed prompting you to set up the groups for the site. You can choose to use existing groups from the site collection or create new groups. In this example, choose to create three new groups, as shown in Figure 9-19. Click OK.

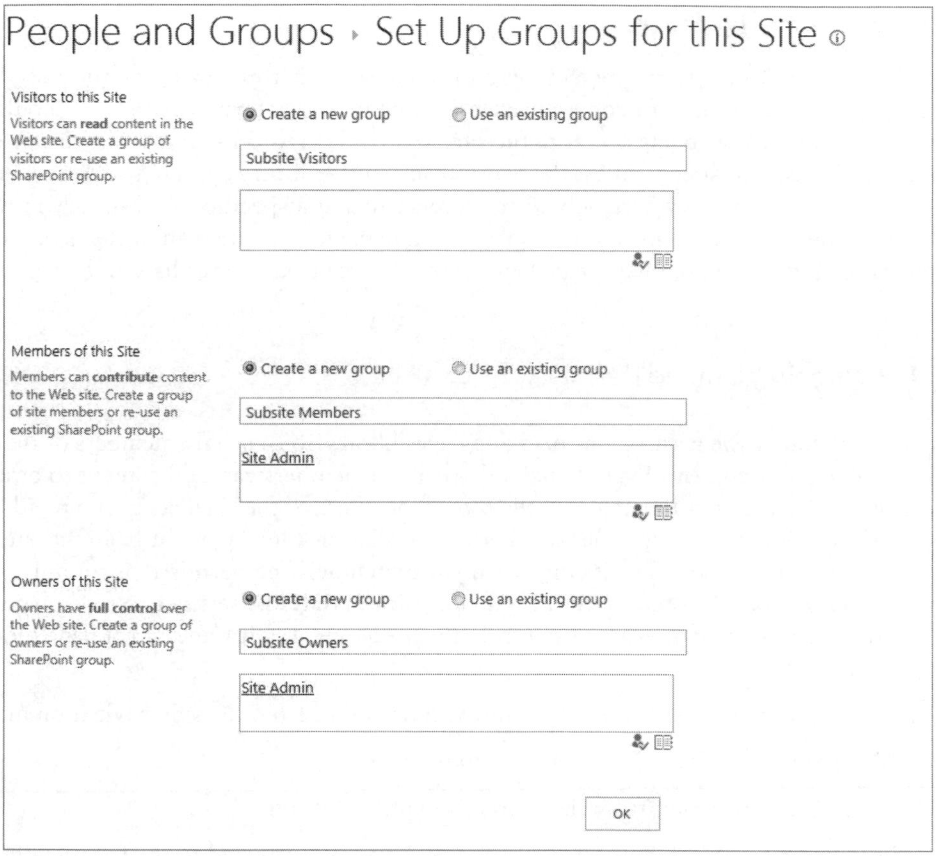

People and Groups › Set Up Groups for this Site ⓘ

Visitors to this Site

Visitors can **read** content in the Web site. Create a group of visitors or re-use an existing SharePoint group.

○ Create a new group   ○ Use an existing group

Subsite Visitors

Members of this Site

Members can **contribute** content to the Web site. Create a group of site members or re-use an existing SharePoint group.

○ Create a new group   ○ Use an existing group

Subsite Members

Site Admin

Owners of this Site

Owners have **full control** over the Web site. Create a group of owners or re-use an existing SharePoint group.

○ Create a new group   ○ Use an existing group

Subsite Owners

Site Admin

OK

FIGURE 9-19

6. Using the Site Actions menu, navigate to the Site Settings page.

7. Notice that the site now contains the new groups that you created in step 5, along with all the permissions from the parent site. You can now delete the permissions that came from the parent site without impacting the parent site.

How It Works

Once you selected the option to stop inheriting permissions, the users, groups, and permissions from the main intranet site were copied down into the project site. You can now make additional changes such as removing groups or adding users. Any changes you make to the project site will not have any impact on the main intranet site.

List or Library Permissions

Sometimes a list or library on a team site requires a different set of permissions than the rest of the site. For example, a document library containing sensitive financial performance reports should not be shared with everyone who has access to the site. You could create a separate site to store this information, but it's easier to simply adjust the permissions on the library so that a subset of users can access it. Another example is where only certain users can edit a specific list or library in which team members can only view content. For example, only a manager can create new items on an Announcements list for a team, but team members can contribute to the other lists and libraries in the site.

TRY IT OUT   Assigning Unique Permissions to a List

In this Try It Out, you modify the permissions on a Site Pages library so that only members of the Owners group can create new content. Even though all other site members can add content to other lists, it is important that you restrict the pages to allow only members of the Owners group to add new items. To accomplish this, you must stop inheriting permissions on the Site Pages list from the site. Similar to the scenario in the previous Try It Out, when you stop inheriting permissions for a list from a site, all rights are copied from the site into the list, so you must update the settings to reflect your requirements. For this exercise, you use the subsite from the preceding Try It Out, which has unique permissions from its parent.

1. From the main page of your subsite, select the Site Contents link from the side navigation menu.

2. Open the Site Pages list by clicking the icon next to the title.

3. Select the Library Settings option from the Library tab of the ribbon.

4. Select the "Permission for this document library" link. You are redirected to the Permissions management page for the list.

5. Select the Stop Inheriting Permissions option from the ribbon.

6. You receive a warning message. Click OK to confirm your action. The page refreshes, and a yellow message bar appears at the top of the screen indicating that the list has unique permissions, as shown in Figure 9-20.

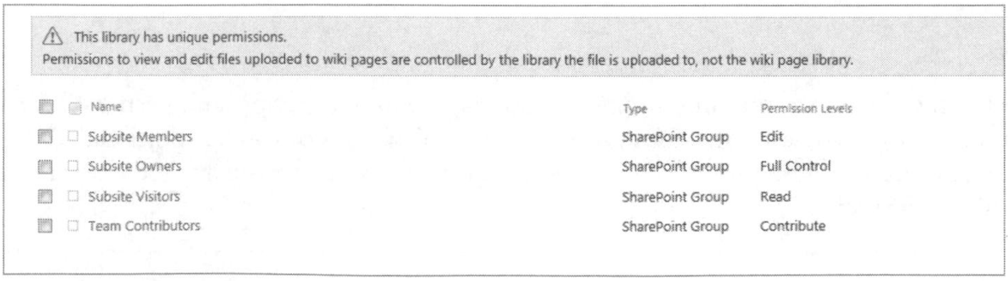

Name	Type	Permission Levels
⚠ This library has unique permissions. Permissions to view and edit files uploaded to wiki pages are controlled by the library the file is uploaded to, not the wiki page library.		
Subsite Members	SharePoint Group	Edit
Subsite Owners	SharePoint Group	Full Control
Subsite Visitors	SharePoint Group	Read
Team Contributors	SharePoint Group	Contribute

FIGURE 9-20

7. Select all groups except the Owners group, and click the Edit User Permissions option on the ribbon.

8. Select the Read permission level.

9. Click OK. You are returned to the library permissions page, and you should see that the permissions for the different groups have been updated. Figure 9-21 is an example of the updated permissions settings.

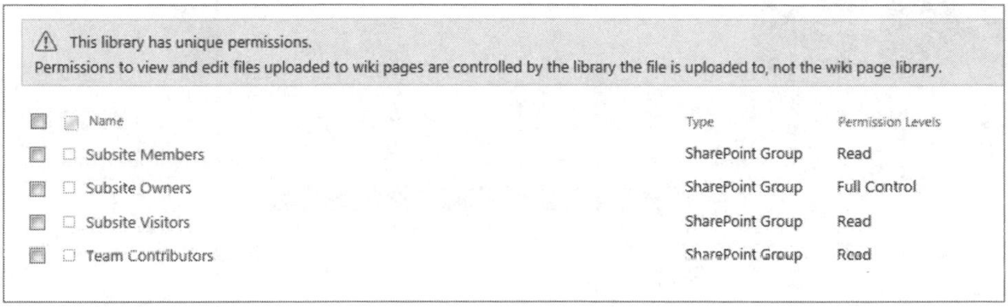

	Name	Type	Permission Levels
	Subsite Members	SharePoint Group	Read
	Subsite Owners	SharePoint Group	Full Control
	Subsite Visitors	SharePoint Group	Read
	Team Contributors	SharePoint Group	Read

⚠ This library has unique permissions.
Permissions to view and edit files uploaded to wiki pages are controlled by the library the file is uploaded to, not the wiki page library.

FIGURE 9-21

How It Works

When you disconnect from the permissions of the site, all rights and users are copied to the permissions scheme for the Site Pages library. Therefore, you must edit the rights of each group and user so that they can only read items. You selected every group except Owners and changed their rights to read-only.

Item Permissions

By default, access to an individual list item is inherited from the list or library in which it resides. However, you may need to better define this. For example, storing a policies and procedures document within a team's shared Documents library means anyone can contribute to it by adding items or modifying existing items; however, for legal reasons, only certain managers should have the right to edit it. You can restrict access to one document, even if it resides in a list or library to which everyone has access, as shown in the next Try It Out.

TRY IT OUT   Assigning Unique Permissions to a Document

In this Try It Out, you create a new document and restrict the rights so that only members of the Owners group have access to edit the document.

1. From the main page of the team site, select Documents from the Quick Launch bar.

2. Click the New Document option on the Document tab of the ribbon.

3. Save the document with a filename of **Team Policies and Procedures.docx**.

4. Select the ellipsis next to the document title and then in the information screen to open the menu. From the menu, select the Shared With link, as shown in Figure 9-22.

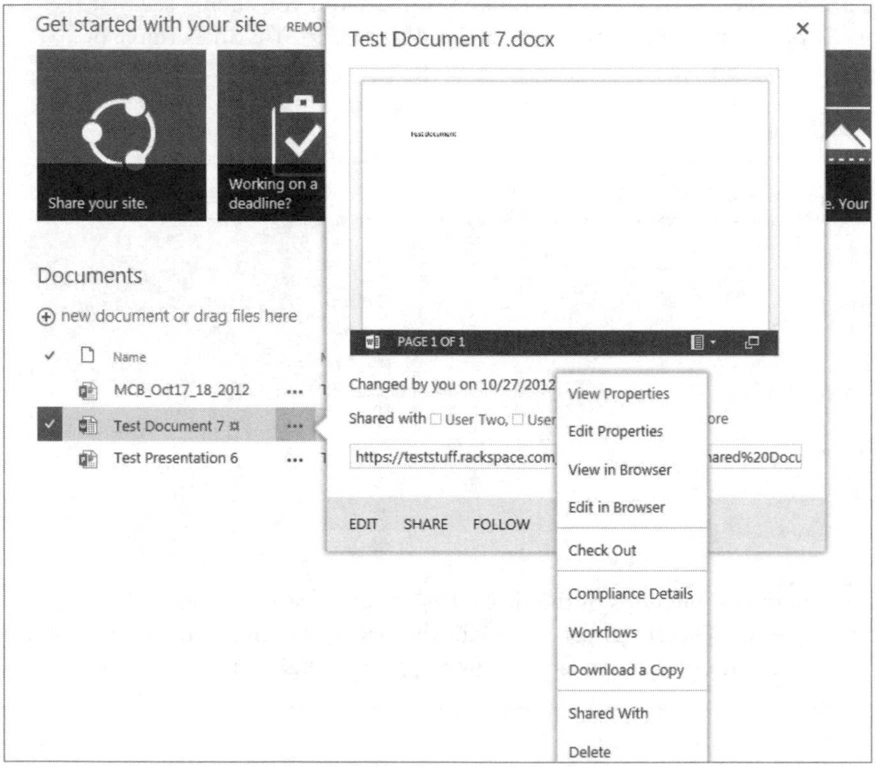

FIGURE 9-22

5. The Shared With page is displayed and shows you all the users that have access to the document.

6. Click the Advanced option to view the manage permissions page for the document.

7. Select the Stop Inheriting Permissions option from the ribbon. The page refreshes and a yellow message bar appears at the top of the screen indicating that the site document has unique permissions.

8. Select all the groups that you want to remove access for and click the Remove User Permissions link in the ribbon.

How It Works

In this example, you created a new document that had slightly different requirements over all other documents in the library. Rather than place it in a unique location, it's far more effective to manage the rights of this document independently of the library and make the required changes on an item-by-item basis.

> ### ITEM-LEVEL ACCESS IN A LIST
>
> SharePoint list applications have a feature, not available within document applications, that allows users to have access only to the content that they have authored. You configure this feature in the advanced settings for the list and it applies to all items in the list. This is a great alternative to managing item permissions.

TRY IT OUT   Customizing Item-Level Access Rights on a List

You can uniquely apply permissions to documents or list items in the same way as in the previous Try It Out. However, lists also have a unique function that allows a site manager to determine if users can view or edit their own items or the items of others. For example, it may be helpful to allow team members to view each other's appointments. However, a user should not be allowed to edit appointments that belong to a coworker. In the following example, you modify the default settings of the Calendar list so that users can view, but not edit, a coworker's items. You can do this on SharePoint lists but not with documents stored within document libraries.

1. From the main page of your team site, select Calendar from the side navigation menu. If your site does not have a calendar list, you will need to first create one before finishing this exercise.

2. Select List Settings from the Calendar tab of the ribbon.

3. Select Advanced Settings. The Advanced Settings page for the list appears, as shown in Figure 9-23.

4. In the Item-level Permissions section, under Read access, keep the default value of Read all items.

5. In the Item-level Permissions section, under Create and Edit access, select "Create items and edit items that were created by the user."

6. Click OK.

FIGURE 9-23

How It Works

In this example, you used some of the advanced list configuration options that allow for item permissions that can be managed at the list level. This keeps you from having to apply custom permissions to each item in the list.

Understanding the Share Option

Within SharePoint 2013 is a new feature that allows users to easily share content with others. This enables a more self-service type environment where users are directly able to proactively bring others to content so that they can collaborate together. In earlier versions of SharePoint, users had to contact the site administrators and ask them to give others permission to the site or to specific content within the site. In SharePoint 2013, users, regardless of their permission levels, can share the site with others, as long as the site is configured to allow for Site Access Request. The users who have enough access to manage permissions can assign permissions directly from the share link, but those who don't have elevated permissions are really just submitting a request to share the content to the site admin. The site admin can then approve or reject the request. When a site admin approves the request, the user who was invited to share the content will receive the request from the initial user who requested the share permission. Figure 9-24 shows the Share dialog box that appears when a user selects the share link from the homepage.

FIGURE 9-24

Once the share request has been submitted, the user assigned to manage the access requests will receive an e-mail notification that a new request has been made (see Figure 9-25).

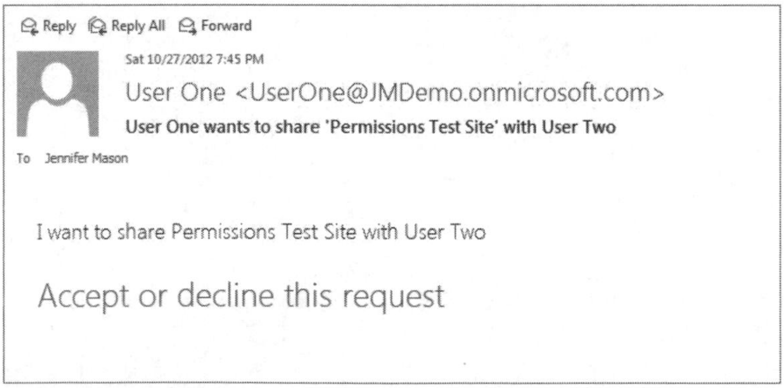

FIGURE 9-25

From this e-mail the request can either be approved or denied. Within the site, the request can also be managed from the Access Requests and Invitations link in the Users and Permissions group of the Site Settings page. From this page the site administrators can see all the requests that have been made and, with one click, approve or decline them. If the site administrator has any questions concerning the request, he or she can simply add a message to the request and the requestor will be notified of the message and given a chance to respond. These features are displayed in Figure 9-26.

FIGURE 9-26

Figure 9-26 shows the history for a single request and is displayed whenever the ellipsis is selected next to the request. Figure 9-27 shows an example of an Access Request history for a site collection. This history keeps a full record of the request comments as well as who approved the request. By default, the History portion of the page is hidden, but you can easily show it by selecting the Show History link at the bottom of the page.

FIGURE 9-27

Sharing is a concept in SharePoint 2013 that can occur at multiple levels, including sites, lists, and list items. By enabling these features, you are empowering users to take a more proactive role in working with others because they can quickly and easily share content. Because the requests are still processed through the site administrator, you can be assured that best practices in site management will still be followed. This is a great example of empowering users while maintaining control within the environment.

USER EXPERIENCE DEPENDS ON CONFIGURATION OF E-MAIL

For you to have the experience described in this section, your environment must be configured to allow for e-mails, and the site must be configured to allow user access requests. If these two items are not configured, you will notice different behaviors in the process of sharing content. The most notable difference is that you will receive an error when attempting to share content. This can be confusing and frustrating for users, so the recommended best practice is to enable Access Requests for each site collection.

You don't need to be concerned about users creating requests to share data with users who already have access to content, because they have very easy ways to review who has access to the content. In many cases this information is displayed in the same location as the Share command is, thus making it a natural thing for users to check who has access before requesting additional access. An example of this Share screen is displayed in Figure 9-28.

MANAGING PERMISSIONS

Managing permissions can be a very tricky and time-consuming process for site administrators. To help reduce the time spent on permissions management, it is important to engage in the proper level of planning and design to ensure that you have designed a solution that will be easy to manage in the

FIGURE 9-28

long run. Planning for permissions management at the onset of any new project greatly reduces the pain that can result from no planning. It's always best to manage permissions using the KISS (Keep It Simple, Stupid) method — the simpler the solution, the easier the management. And though simple isn't always something that can be associated with business process, a few tips and tricks can greatly reduce the level of effort required for management. Some of these tips are listed here:

➤ Avoid item permissions unless there is a strong business case that supports using them. If you must use them, you should evaluate having multiple lists or libraries and managing permissions at the list or library level.

➤ Include an approach for managing permissions in the design documentation that is created before the solution is built. Having this documented clearly will help avoid future issues as you transition to a new site collection administrator or as organization changes occur that could impact the structure.

➤ Give only a limited number of users the ability to manage permissions. Each of these users should be trained on managing permissions in SharePoint as well as have an understanding of the permissions structure that is required for your specific solution.

Even with the best of intentions, sometimes the process of managing permissions can get tricky. Thankfully, SharePoint offers the following features to make the task a little easier:

➤ Information bar

➤ Check Permissions option

Information Bar

Each permissions management page includes a yellow information bar that gives you important information about the security of the content. In most cases, a message is displayed, as well as a link to find additional information. Figure 9-29 shows an example of a message that appears on a site that has been configured with unique permissions.

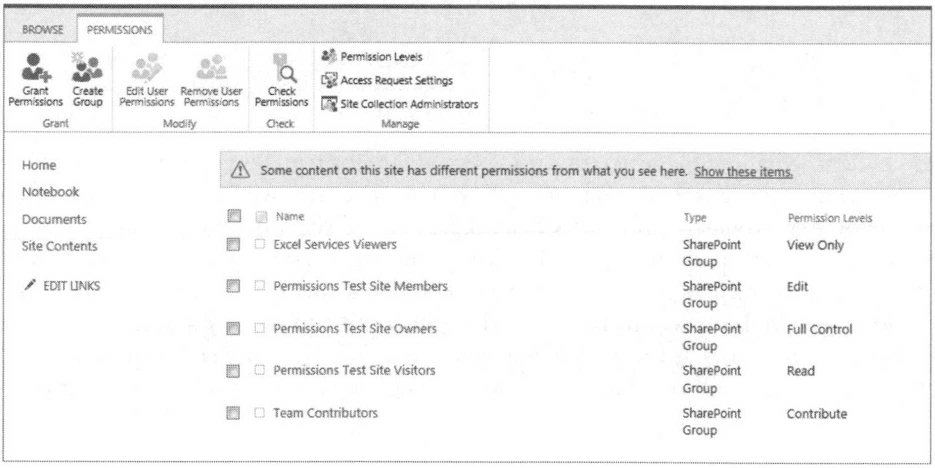

FIGURE 9-29

When you click a link within the message, another message appears with additional details about the content, as well as links to drill down into the data (see Figure 9-30). This additional information can be extremely helpful when you are trying to research information about the site, especially if you are trying to troubleshoot permissions issues.

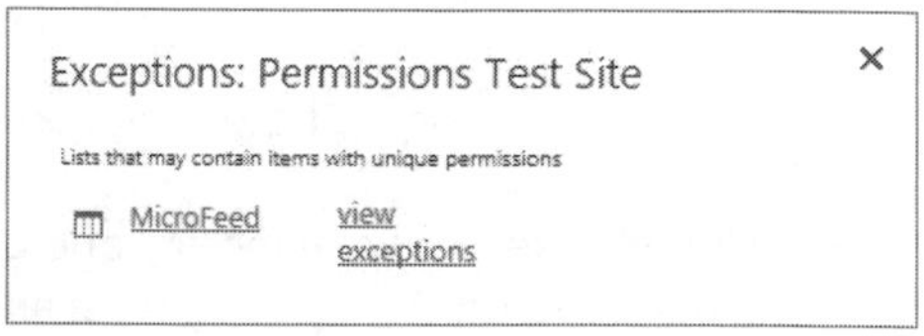

FIGURE 9-30

Check Permissions

The Check Permissions option is another tool for managing permissions for users or groups. You can find this option in the ribbon of any permissions management page. Figure 9-31 shows this option as it appears on the site collection Permissions management page.

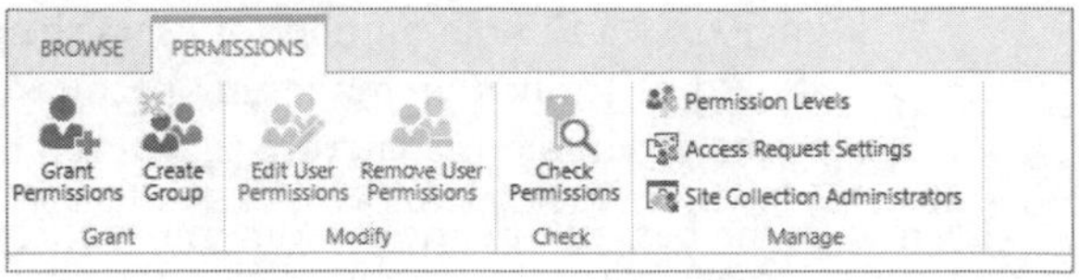

FIGURE 9-31

When you select the Check Permissions option, a dialog box appears that enables you to enter either a username or group and then view the permissions it has been assigned. Figure 9-32 shows the results of checking a user's permissions. Notice that in addition to seeing which rights a user has been given, you are also told how those rights were granted.

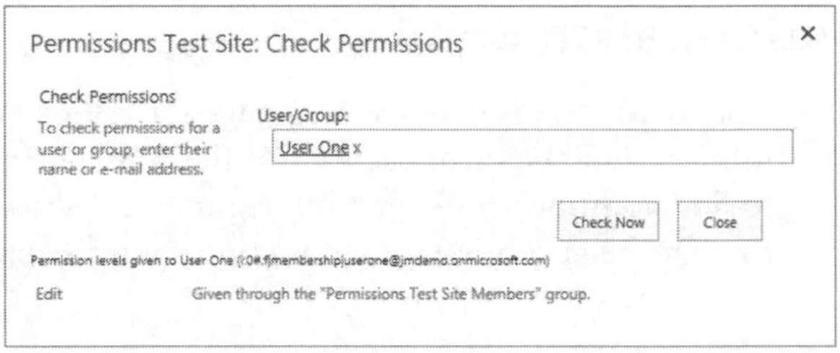

FIGURE 9-32

SUMMARY

In this chapter you learned about the different options available for managing permissions on your site through management of user access. User access is how you control who can view, edit, or create content in a SharePoint environment. You can define access on the site, document library, or list level through permission levels and site groups. For lists, you can also define rules for what content users can read or edit at the item level. In addition to developing a way for site administrators to manage permissions, you looked at controlled ways that allow users to quickly and naturally share content with other team members as the need arises. Because this is still managed through the site administrator, you don't have to fear having untrained users giving access to others without proper approval.

EXERCISES

1. What feature within SharePoint allows non-administrators to easily invite others to share content?

2. Name a tool within SharePoint that allows you to check the permissions that a user has.

3. True or false: You can modify one of the default permission levels by creating a new permission level based on the existing level and then modifying the new level's properties.

▶ **WHAT YOU LEARNED IN THIS CHAPTER**

TOPIC	KEY CONCEPTS
SharePoint Groups	A SharePoint Group is a defined role to which users can be added. These groups can then be assigned specific rights and permissions to different elements within SharePoint.
Permission levels	A permission level is a set of rights that can be assigned to a user or group in SharePoint.
Audiences	An audience is a group of people that share common characteristics. This helps create a relevant user experience for site members because they only see information that has been targeted to their role, but it is not a replacement for security.
Sharing content	Users who have the ability to manage permissions can quickly grant permissions to others throughout the site using the Share features. Users who don't have the ability to manage permissions can use the Share features to create requests to invite others to the site. The requests are then reviewed and completed by someone who is responsible for managing site access.

10

Working with Business Intelligence

WHAT YOU WILL LEARN IN THIS CHAPTER:

➤ The different types of business intelligence toolsets available in SharePoint

➤ Working with the out-of-the-box business intelligence features to configure charts, graphs, and spreadsheets

➤ Using Visio to publish content to a Visio Services Web Part

➤ How to create reports using SQL Server Reporting Services and Report Builder 3.0

You can use business intelligence (BI) to help provide tools that bring information directly to users through a single interface. This chapter digs into several different concepts, including how to get started and how to start bringing immediate value to the organization. If you are just getting started with BI, the chapter also looks at ways to progressively incorporate these features into your organization.

GETTING STARTED WITH BUSINESS INTELLIGENCE

The first step to getting started with BI is to understand what it is and how you plan to use it within your organization. "Business intelligence" is a very common buzz phrase, the type that your CEO will hear in a demonstration and march directly into your office explaining that you must have KPI and charts and dashboards, and you need them immediately. Though it is true that all those things will bring value to the organization, it is also true that there must be a plan in place and an end goal in sight. Having charts to have charts is never going to provide any business value. Instead, having charts that solve specific business problems or that provide information to a group of users will provide value and a return on investment. So, when faced with the CEO who has been bitten by the "demo bug," be sure to help him refocus what he has seen with your organization in mind. Once you have the end goal in mind, you can then select the tools to help you get there. The following list shows some common goals or phrases that describe different scenarios that you can resolve with the business insight tools within SharePoint. This list should give you some ideas and serve as a checkpoint that you can use to verify your goals.

➤ Show a visual representation of the task breakdown for our project.

➤ Show a visual indicator of issues that are present within a project, report, or collection of data.

➤ Provide information to the sales team from last year's sales numbers, so that they can make decisions for this year.

➤ Provide a single entry point into legacy business data so that users from one single location can drill into the specific information that they need for their current tasks.

There are many different reasons to deploy BI features within your environment. The key thing is that you understand your end goal and then work together with the business to provide the proper toolset to meet its specific needs. The tools available within SharePoint, specific to insights, are:

➤ **Visio Services:** This feature enables you to display a Visio web diagram within a SharePoint Web Part. You can connect the content within the Visio diagram to various data sources, and then use the information from those data sources to build connected solutions within SharePoint.

➤ **Excel Services:** This feature includes Web Parts that enable you to display data from an Excel workbook directly within a SharePoint Web Part. Within this Web Part you can also configure parameters that allow the data to be displayed based on the selections of the user. Excel Services Web Parts include various features from the Excel BI stack that enable you to take advantage of features from PowerView and PowerPivot.

➤ **PerformancePoint Services:** This feature enables you to easily create dashboards based on date that are distributed across various enterprise systems. These dashboards can then be migrated to other servers or site collections through the use of a collection of Windows PowerShell commands. These dashboards can also be viewed across multiple mobile devices, including iPads running the Safari web browser.

➤ **SQL Server Reporting Services:** This service enables you to create professional and printable reports for your enterprise. With Report Builder 3.0, self-service reporting is possible, which allows end users and power users to create their own reports. A server administrator must first install SQL Server Reporting Services on your SharePoint Server. Once it is in place, there are several different ways that you can architect your reporting structure and even create subscriptions to reports.

Like most things in SharePoint, there is a level of progression when working with these features. If you are just getting started, it is recommended that you first start by exploring and building an understanding of your internal data structures and the reports required by your organization. Once you are familiar with those elements, you should move on to Excel Services and Visio Services. Finally, once you have become familiar with those elements, you can begin working with PerformancePoint Services. Within any organization, the concept of BI is one that takes much planning, organization, and, often, development. In this chapter you see just a small glance of what is available out-of-the-box. It is recommended that you work with your organization to develop an overall BI strategy and a roadmap for achieving your goals. For most organizations, this roadmap will be one that is implemented over time using a phased approach.

PHASED APPROACH

In a *phased approach* for delivering BI solutions, you start with a small subset of features, such as Excel Services, and then, as your needs and experience grow, you begin to incorporate additional more advanced features, such as PerformancePoint Services.

One final note that you should be aware of is that working with different BI features requires the involvement of several key roles within the organization. The idea of BI is that you are pulling data from many locations and bringing it together via dashboards and Web Parts. This is a great concept that can provide tremendous value to the organization. However, it is important to note that the quality of the data returned is dependent on the quality of the data that is available. Don't be surprised if part of your process of moving to a comprehensive solution also includes an element of restructuring and verifying your current data structure.

Throughout the rest of the chapter, you review examples and learn the details of each of the components discussed in this section. You start with the Excel Services and Visio Services and end with a high-level overview of PerformancePoint Services. Each section builds on various examples, which will show you how you can combine all elements together to build a solution for your users.

WORKING WITH EXCEL SERVICES

Excel Services is the tool within SharePoint that allows users to interact with Excel workbooks directly from the browser. These features allow users to publish a workbook to a SharePoint library and then display it using a collection of Excel Services Web Parts. These Web Parts enable you to build dynamic dashboards through Web Part connections. Before we get into the details of working with Excel Services within a SharePoint site, it would be good to cover some of the basics of Excel

Services. Once you understand this basic foundation, you will easily see how you can combine Excel Services to build business solutions. At the core level, Excel Services consists of the following three components:

➤ Excel Calculation Services

➤ Excel Web Access

➤ Excel Web Services

These three components work together to provide the overall end-user experience. The Calculation Services engine is responsible for running all the calculations within the workbook. These calculations are run directly on the server without direct interaction from the users. This service is also responsible for maintaining sessions and refreshing data within each session. The Web Access components are the Web Parts that enable you to display the Excel information within SharePoint sites. These Web Parts also allow connections, enabling you to pass information to the Web Part that changes the data displayed, based on the input. Finally, the Web Services component provides an application programming interface (API) that developers can use to write custom applications to interact with the Excel workbook.

Once the workbook has been published to the SharePoint site, the site administrator can configure the Web Parts to display the Excel workbook. The Excel Web Parts can be configured to display the entire workbook or just a named region within the workbook. Once the workbook is displayed on the site, users can interact with it through preconfigured parameters. You create these parameters within Excel prior to its being published to the SharePoint site. Users will only be able to read the Excel document from the Excel Web Parts, but if they need to edit the content within the workbook, they can always use the Excel Office web application to make browser-based changes to the workbook.

Now that we have briefly covered the basics, in the following sections you explore the Excel Services features by working with the sample that is included in the Business Intelligence Center site template.

Creating a Business Intelligence Site Collection

Because this book focuses on SharePoint, you are not going to spend a lot of time on configuring the workbook. Instead, you use one of the Microsoft samples included in the Business Intelligence Center template. This sample contains several elements that will help you dive into the features available within Excel Services. In the first Try It Out in this chapter, you create a site collection based on the template that includes the sample file.

TRY IT OUT Creating a Site Using the Business Intelligence Template

The first thing that you do in this chapter is create a site based on the Business Intelligence site template. You do this from the Central Administration site; however, you can also complete the steps from any site that has the Enterprise Features enabled. You are creating this site collection so that you have a location to which to add content for the remaining chapter demos.

> **WARNING** *To create a new site collection in Central Administration, you must have farm-level permissions. If you don't have the required permissions, you should work with the server administrators to create a site collection for you.*

1. Open the Central Administration site.

2. Select the "Create site collections" link within the Application Management grouping, as shown in Figure 10-1.

3. Enter the following properties for the new site collection, as shown in Figure 10-2, and then click OK.

Application Management
Manage web applications
Create site collections
Manage service applications
Manage content databases

FIGURE 10-1

PROPERTY	VALUE
Web Application	Accept the default option, unless directed otherwise by your server administrator.
Title	BI Center
Description	Location to create and store dashboards and reports.
URL	/sites/BICenter
Select experience version	2013
Select a template	Business Intelligence Center
Primary Site Collection Administrator	Your Username
Quota Template	No Quota

4. Click the URL to open the new site collection. You will see that the site collection comes configured with a clean look and feel, as shown in Figure 10-3. In future exercises, you dig deeper into the content that comes preconfigured in the site collection.

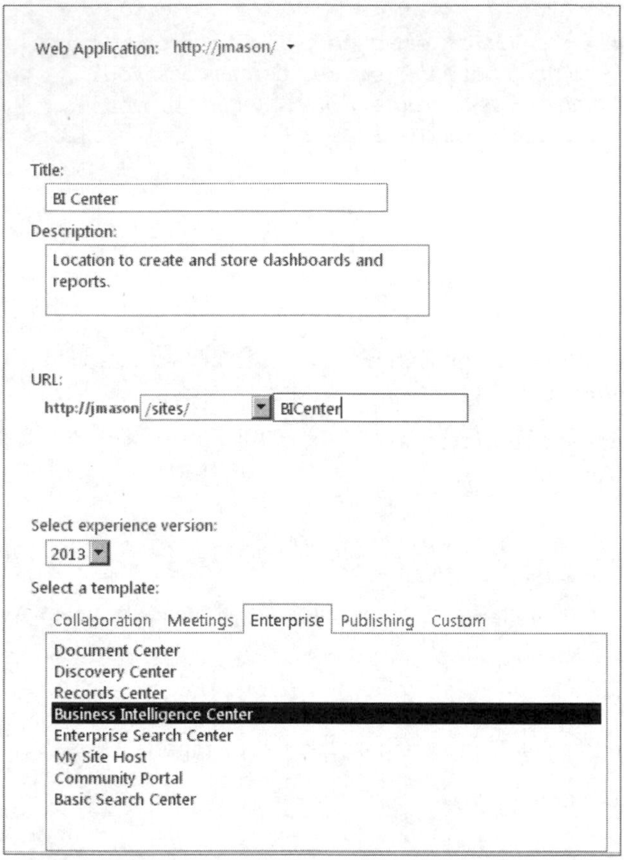

Web Application: http://jmason/
Title:
BI Center
Description:
Location to create and store dashboards and reports.
URL:
http://jmason /sites/ BICenter
Select experience version:
2013
Select a template:
Collaboration
Meetings
Enterprise
Publishing
Custom
Document Center
Discovery Center
Records Center
Business Intelligence Center
Enterprise Search Center
My Site Host
Community Portal
Basic Search Center

FIGURE 10-2

SharePoint
Newsfeed
SkyDrive
Sites
BI Center
BI Center
Home
Notebook
Documents
Site Contents
Site Contents
Empower the people in your organization to gain insights with ease using familiar tools. Learn More
Explore and Analyze Data
Create powerful data mash-ups of millions of rows of data from vario
Design Interactive Reports
Create presentation-ready reports that tell a compelling story using E
Share Dashboards
Publish dashboards that users can interact with using Excel Services.

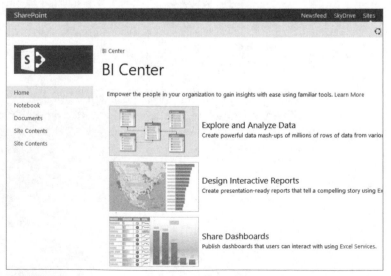

FIGURE 10-3

How It Works

When you create a site collection in Central Administration, you provide all the details for it, and then the site is provisioned for you and a link is returned. If you do not have access to Central Administration, you will need to follow your internal process for creating a new site collection.

PUBLISHING TO THE BI TEMPLATE

In the example, you are publishing the Excel document to a site that you created using the BI template. This template has already been preconfigured with many of the features you will be using, including:

➤ Dashboards library

➤ PerformancePoint library

➤ Data Connections library

We are doing this to expose you to the template; however, you could in theory publish to any team site where the publishing features have been installed and where the server administrators have marked the location as safe. If you are unsure whether your site is considered a safe location for publishing, you can check with your server administrator. You can complete the steps used in the preceding example and throughout the rest of the chapter within any site collection.

TRY IT OUT **Opening and Publishing an Excel Workbook to the SharePoint Library**

In this Try It Out, you open a sample Excel document that has been included in the template and then publish back to the site collection once you have reviewed it in the client.

1. Open the BI Center that you created in the previous exercise.

2. Click the Site Contents link in the quick launch area, as shown in Figure 10-4.

3. Open the Documents library.

4. Select the ellipsis and then click Edit in the document preview pane, as shown in Figure 10-5. Click OK or Yes on any security warnings that are displayed while the file is opening.

FIGURE 10-4

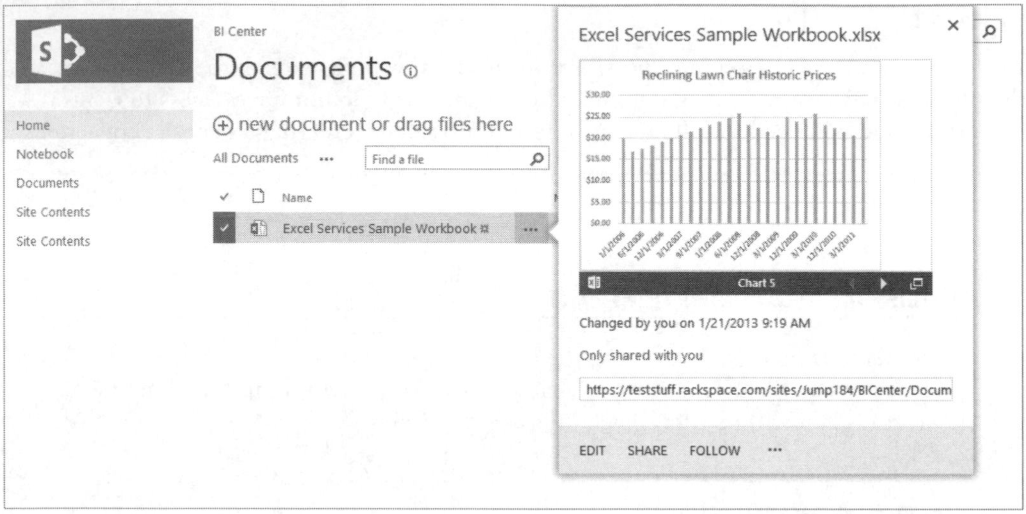

FIGURE 10-5

> **WARNING** *Document previews are available only when the farm is configured to use Office Web Apps. If your environment does not use Office Web Apps, you will see a slightly different image than what is shown in Figure 10-5.*

5. Click through the document and become familiar with the contents that have been included. Notice that multiple worksheets are included in this single sample file.

6. Select File and Save As to open the Backstage view.

> **WARNING** *Depending on your Office client settings, you might be required to enable saving before you can save the file. If you try to save without enabling, you will be prompted to enable and then you can complete step 6.*

7. Select the Current Folder Location to save the file back to the location from which it was opened.

8. When the Save As dialog box opens, click the button labeled Browser View Options to see the various configuration options for saving the file to SharePoint. These options are displayed in Figure 10-6. No matter what Excel file you save to SharePoint, these publishing options are

available to you. These options are what enable you to publish a chart without publishing the supporting data table. For this example, accept the default options.

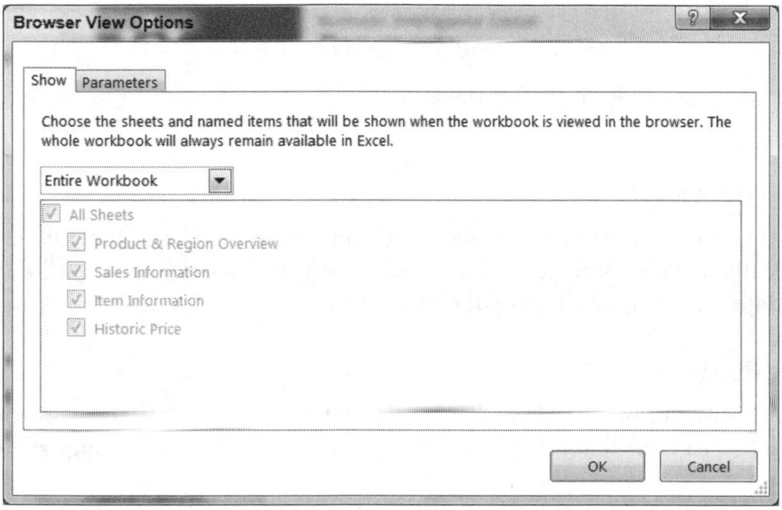

FIGURE 10-6

9. Click OK to close the options box.

10. Enter the filename of **Excel Services Sample Workbook**, and click Save.

How It Works

When you select the option to save to SharePoint, Excel publishes the document to the SharePoint library using the configurations you set under the publish options. You can publish any Excel file to SharePoint; however, for this example, you simply opened the sample file and republished back to the library.

Using the Excel Services Web Parts

Now that you have the workbook published to a SharePoint library, you can add a Web Part to display the workbook information. To get started, in the next Try It Out you create a new dashboard page. Later in the chapter we discuss this in greater detail, but for now you are going to create it just to get started. After creating the dashboard, you can add and configure the Excel workbook. Many different configuration options are available, so before you complete the examples, the following sections review the different options you have.

Toolbar and Title Bar

The toolbar and title bar options enable you to supply values for the various ways that you can configure the display of the Web Part. For the title bar, the Web Part is set to auto-generate the title and the link by default. If you would like to use your own title instead, you can deselect the option in this section and enter a custom title in the appearance settings. If you have this option selected, the title in the appearance settings is ignored and the Web Part title is auto-generated. The toolbar options enable you to select which commands you would like to make available to the users and include the following:

➤ Open in Excel, Download a Copy, Download a Snapshot

➤ Refresh Selected Connection, Refresh all Connections

➤ Calculate Workbook

➤ Named Item Drop-Down List

It is likely that each workbook you display using a Web Part could require a different combination of settings. By default, all the settings listed here are enabled, so if you don't want to use those features, you need to update the configuration of your Web Part.

Navigation and Interactivity

The navigation and interactivity options enable you to configure how the users can navigate and interact with the workbook. The table that follows describes each of the different settings available for configuration.

OPTION	DESCRIPTION
Hyperlink	If enabled, users will be able to use hyperlinks from within the workbook. These hyperlinks could link to other locations in the workbook or other sites.
Workbook Interactivity	If disabled, users will not be able to interact with the workbook through the features described in this table. Disable this if you want a quick way to remove all interactivity.
Parameter Modification	If enabled, users will be able to modify the content using parameters.
Display Parameter Task Pane	If enabled, users will be able to access a parameter tool pane that allows them to easily switch between the worksheet parameters.
Sorting	If enabled, users will be able to sort ranges within the worksheet.
Filtering	If enabled, users will be able to filter various items within the worksheet.
All PivotTable Interactivity	If enabled, users will be able to expand and drill down through the pivot tables within the worksheet.
Periodically Refresh if Enabled in a Workbook	If enabled, the worksheet will refresh periodically. A notification will be present during a refresh.
PivotTable & PivotChart Modification	If enabled, the worksheet will contain options that allow for the site users to conduct live modifications to the pivot tables and charts. This is a new enhancement available in SharePoint 2013.

Standard Web Part Tool Pane Settings

The remainder of the configuration options are the standard Web Part properties. When working with Excel Services Web Parts, one of the most common Web Part settings used is located within the appearance options. In many cases, you will want to manually configure the size of the Web Part so that your worksheet is displayed correctly on the page. Often the charts, tables, and graphs from the worksheet are larger than the default size of the Web Part, and when that occurs, scroll bars are displayed within the Web Part. To eliminate the need for the scroll bars, you can either shrink the content within Excel and republish the Web Part, or you can configure the Web Part to be large enough so that you don't need the scroll bars.

TRY IT OUT **Creating a New Dashboard**

You can easily create dashboards within the Business Intelligence site template. In this example, you create a dashboard so that you can have a location in which to add the Excel Services Web Part. Throughout the remainder of this chapter, you should refer to this exercise whenever you need to create an additional dashboard.

1. Open the site you created in this chapter's first Try It Out.

2. Select the Site Contents link in the Quick Launch toolbar and open the Dashboards application.

3. In the Files ribbon, select the New Document drop-down menu and then click to create a new Web Part Page (see Figure 10-7).

4. Enter the following properties for the dashboard, as shown in Figure 10-8.

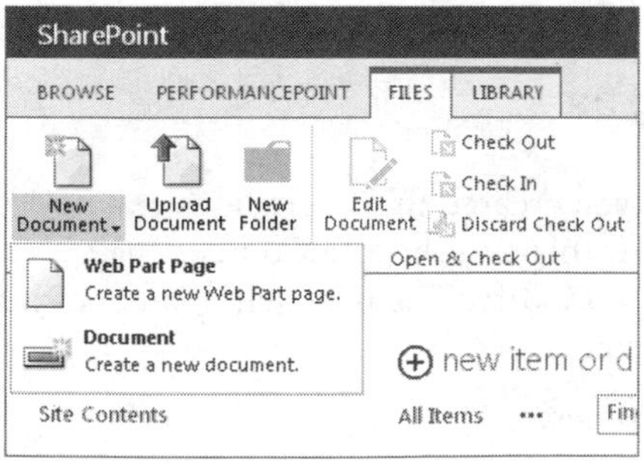

FIGURE 10-7

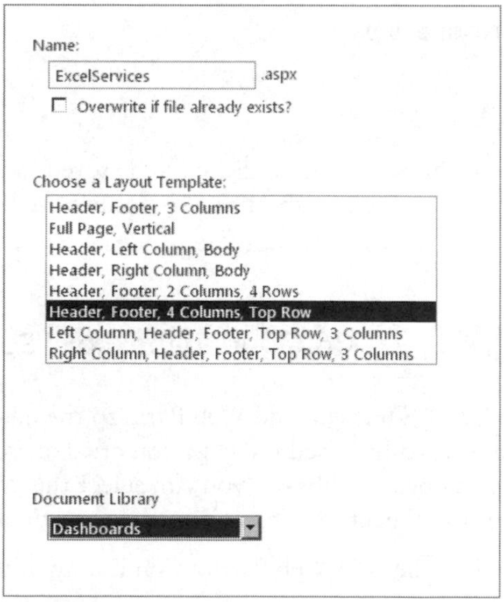

FIGURE 10-8

PROPERTY	VALUE
Name	ExcelServices
Choose a Layout Template	Header, Footer, 4 Columns, Top Row
Document Library	Dashboards

5. Click Create, and you are directed to the new dashboard page, as shown in Figure 10-9.

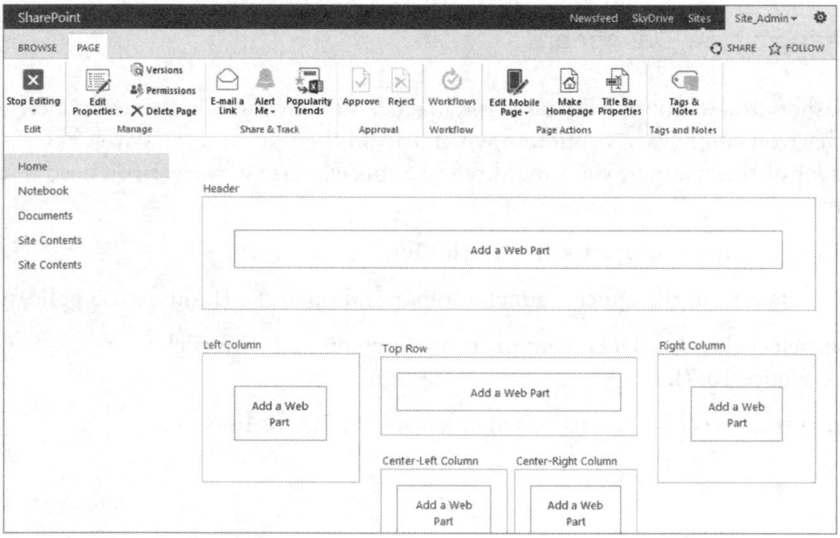

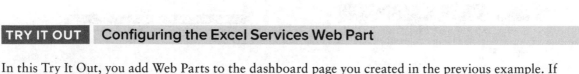

FIGURE 10-9

How It Works

A new dashboard page is created and stored in the Dashboards library application. You can access this page by accessing the library or by adding the link to the navigation.

TRY IT OUT   Configuring the Excel Services Web Part

In this Try It Out, you add Web Parts to the dashboard page you created in the previous example. If you have already closed the page you created, you can access it through the Site Contents page. Once you open the library, you can select the item you want to modify. The page will load and then you can use the Site Actions Gear to access the Edit Page option.

1. Click the Add Web Part option in any of the Web Part zones.

2. In the Business Data category list, select the Excel Web Access Web Part, as shown in Figure 10-10, and click Add.

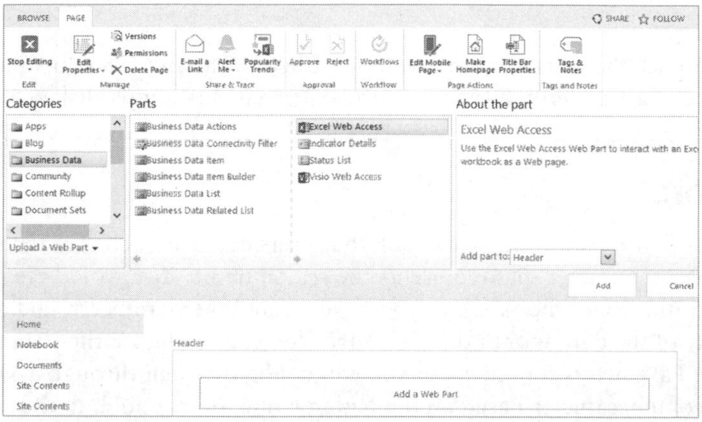

FIGURE 10-10

3. When the Web Part is added to the page, click the "Click here to open the tool pane" link within the Web Part.

4. Click the ellipsis next to the Workbook field to browse for the location of the document you published in the previous example, as shown in Figure 10-11. Click OK once you have selected the document.

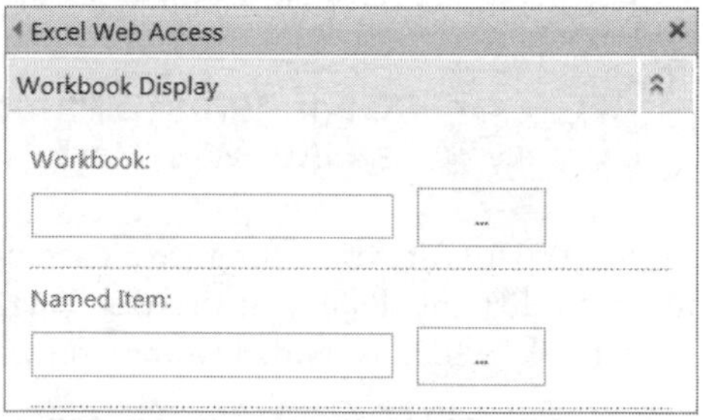

5. When you click OK, the document link is displayed in the Workbook field. Notice the remaining tool pane options. Each option was described previously in detail. For this example, accept the default configuration and click OK.

FIGURE 10-11

6. Select the Stop Editing option in the ribbon to view the page, as shown in Figure 10-12.

FIGURE 10-12

How It Works

You configured the Web Part to reference the document that you published to the site. The document's contents are displayed within the Web Part and are in sync with the data that is being published.

Working with Parameters

Parameters are the values you configure within the workbook that users can use to change the view of the data. An example of this is a parameter that represents the region name. You would create and configure the parameter within the workbook. Once you have created the parameter, end users could use it to modify the display of the data within the Web Part. You can configure the parameters within the Web Part through the Parameters tool pane, or you can configure them through a Web Part connection. In the example of a parameter based on the region name, users could, in theory, select only the regions that they are interested in comparing. Once those regions were selected, the Excel data would then be filtered based on the selection.

| TRY IT OUT | Configuring a Parameter Based on Product Name and Connecting with a Filter Web Part |

In this Try It Out, you configure a parameter within an Excel document so that you can use a filter to modify the display of the Web Part. You create a parameter within the Excel Services Sample Workbook, which is loaded to the site when the site is created.

1. Open the Documents library application in the site collection you created earlier in this chapter.

2. Open the Excel Services Sample Workbook that you used earlier in the chapter within the Excel client application.

3. Open the Product & Region Overview Worksheet and select any cells within the Sales by Region chart. In the Analyze ribbon, click the Field List to open the PivotTable Field List.

4. Add the Item Name field to the Report Filter section by selecting the Item Name field and dragging it to the Report Filter box. You should notice that there is now a filter drop-down above the table that is labeled Item Name, as shown in Figure 10-13. If you modify the selected value, the table is updated based on your selection.

FIGURE 10-13

5. Select the cell that contains the Item Name value. In the Formulas ribbon, select the Define Name option and name the cell **Item_Name_Filter**. Click OK to save the name changes. You will notice that whenever you have that cell highlighted, the name "Item_Name_Filter" is displayed in the toolbar, as shown in Figure 10-14.

FIGURE 10-14

6. Select the File menu to open the Backstage options.

7. Select the Save As option and the Save to SharePoint option.

8. Because you opened the document from SharePoint, you can save the document back to the current location. You first need to update the Browser View Options so that you can publish your parameter. Click the Browser View Options button. In the Parameters tab, select the Add option, and select the Item_Name_Filter parameter. Click OK twice to save the changes. In the Show tab, select the Items in the Workbook option and check all items.

9. Select the location for the Current Folder, and then click Save in the Save dialog box. Click Yes when prompted as to whether you want to save over the existing file.

10. Return to the BI Center Site Collection that you created earlier.

11. Using the steps in the earlier Try It Out called "Creating a New Dashboard," create a new dashboard called ExcelServices2.

12. When the dashboard page loads, click in any cell to add a Web Part.

13. Click the Add Web Part option in any of the Web Part zones.

14. In the Business Data category list, select the Excel Web Access Web Part and click Add.

15. When the Web Part is added to the page, select the "Click here to open the tool pane" link within the Web Part.

16. Click the ellipsis next to the Workbook field to browse for the location of the document you published in the previous example. Click OK once you have selected the document.

17. Configure the remaining tool pane options as follows:

PROPERTY	VALUE
Named Item	Chart 7
Remaining Options	Keep the Default

18. Select the Add a Web Part link in any of the Web Part zones and add the Choice Filter Web Part from the Filters category, as shown in Figure 10-15.

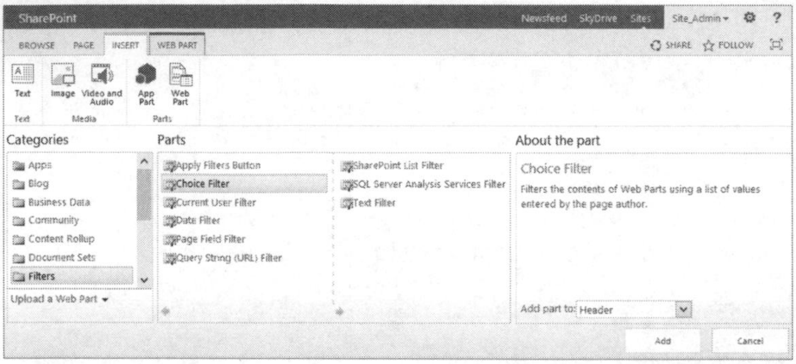

FIGURE 10-15

19. Open the Filter Web Part tool pane and add the Items data to the choice list box below the Filter Name in the properties tool pane. You can obtain this list by copying the data from the Excel spreadsheet. Keep the remaining default options, and click OK. It is likely that, when you implement this within your organization, you will instead work with an external content list that is referencing a back-end system that stores your client data. If that is the case, you could use the SharePoint list filter. To keep the example simple, you are going to enter the values manually.

20. The final step is configuring the Filter Web Part to pass values to the Excel document. Select the Filter Web Part drop-down menu and select the Connections option. Select the Send Filter Values To option and then select the Excel Web Access Web Part, as shown in Figure 10-16.

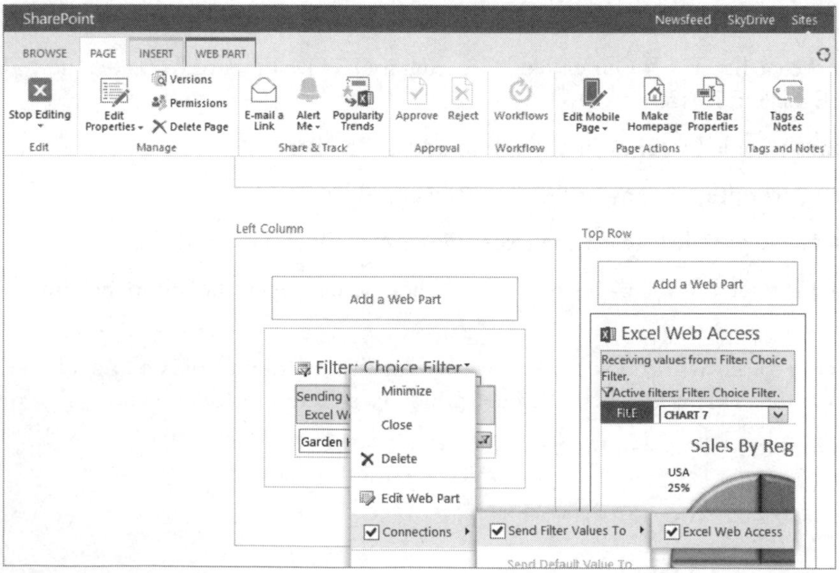

FIGURE 10-16

21. In the Configuration Wizard, set the connection type to Get Filter Values From: Filter Choice Filter. When the Configure Connection dialog page loads, select the Item_Name field for the Filtered Parameter option, and click then Finish.

22. Using the Page ribbon, select the option to Stop Editing the page.

23. Use the drop-down in the Filter Web Part to select a client. Once you press Enter, you should notice that the values in the chart are updated based on the value you selected (see Figure 10-17).

FIGURE 10-17

How It Works

The value passed from the Filter Web Part acts as the parameter filter in the Excel Web Access Web Part. Additional parameters can be created for any report that you have in Excel for which you would like to provide a way for users to filter the data within the Web Part.

Connecting to External Data Sources

Many times within Excel, worksheet connections are made to external data sources. These connections can be used for worksheets that are published to SharePoint, as long as the connections are stored within a trusted location. If you are planning on publishing Excel worksheets that contain connections to external data sources, you will need to work with your administrator to ensure that all of the data connections are configured correctly for use within your environment. In most cases, the connections will need to be created in a data connection file and then stored within the farm's data connection libraries.

Managing Permissions

There are two different ways to manage permissions for the content within the worksheet. The first option is to control what content is visible on the server. You configure this during the publishing process.

Any objects that you haven't selected will not be visible when the worksheet is viewed from the server. Figure 10-18 shows the configuration step from the publishing process that allows you to determine which items are published.

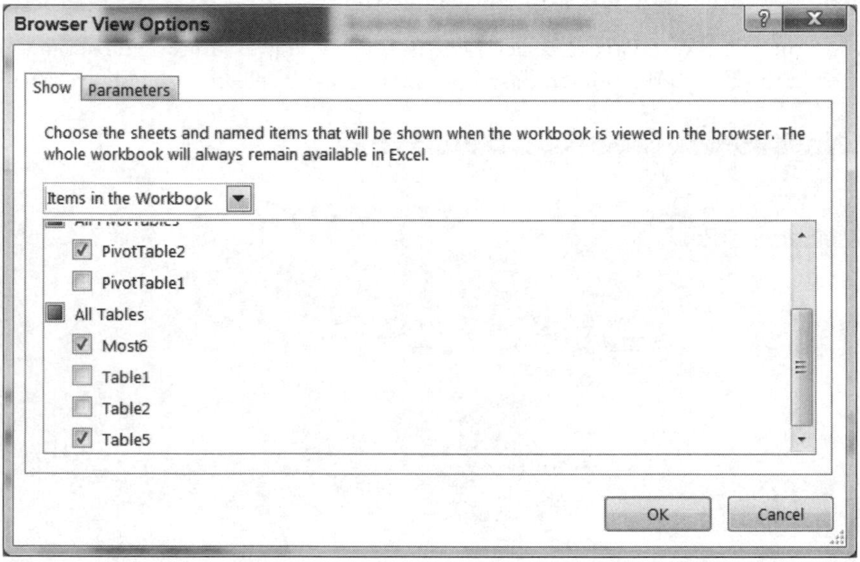

FIGURE 10-18

If you read the fine print in Figure 10-18, you will notice that the option applies to the server view only. If users open the workbook within the Excel client, they will have access to all the content. In most cases, this is probably not the desired result. Within SharePoint there is a way to configure permissions so that even if users open the worksheet, they have access only to the published information. You do this by using the View Item permissions. Users who have the View Item permissions will only be able to open a snapshot of the spreadsheet in the client. This snapshot will show only limited information and will prevent them from seeing the content that was not shared during the publishing process. The two lists that follow outline the different types of content that will be available within the snapshot and the types of content that will be removed from the snapshot:

➤ Available within a snapshot:

   ➤ Formatting

   ➤ Visible grid information

   ➤ Cell values

   ➤ Objects

➤ Removed from a snapshot:

   ➤ Private information

   ➤ Conditional formatting

➤ Hidden data

➤ Formulas

➤ Interactive data

➤ Connections

➤ Web-related content

WORKING WITH VISIO SERVICES

Visio Services is a new service application within SharePoint that enables you to interact with data from Visio diagrams. At the base level, a Visio Web Access Web Part is used to display the data from a published Visio diagram. The diagrams are first created in Visio and then published to SharePoint as web drawings. The Visio Web Part can then be added to any Web Part zone within the farm that is hosting the drawings. Keep in mind that, because the document is stored in SharePoint, the document will be rendered in the Web Part only for users who have at least View permissions for the document. Because you can point to any document within the farm, it is possible for you to render the information in many places, while still keeping a single entry point for the data.

The Visio Web Part supports Web Part connections, which allow users to interact with the published data. Some examples of possible configurations are:

➤ **Master/Detail:** You can use this when you have a step process; the master could display steps 1–4, for example. As you select a shape in the master diagram, the detail diagram is updated to display the detailed information for that step.

➤ **SharePoint List:** When your Visio diagram is connected to a SharePoint list, you can connect the diagram to the List Web Part and interact with the data. When you select items within the SharePoint list, the corresponding items in the diagram are highlighted.

You configure the connection settings within the Visio Web Access Web Part in the Connections menu option. As shown in Figure 10-19, the menu option provided for configuring the connection is very straightforward and easy to understand.

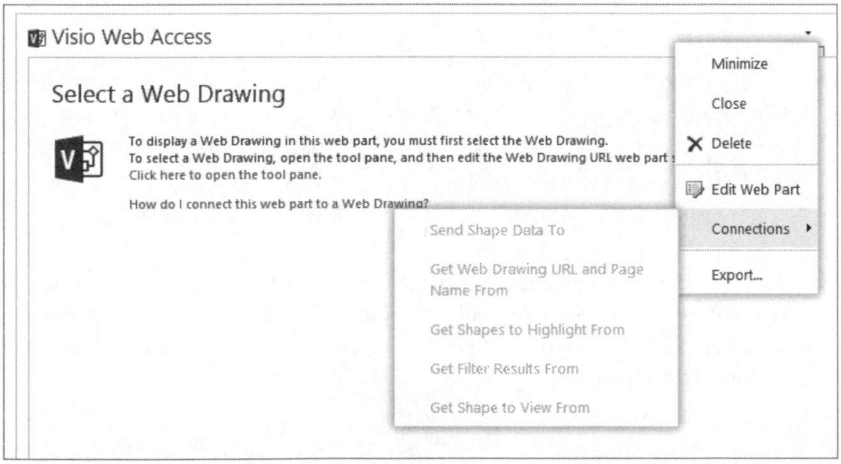

FIGURE 10-19

The following table describes the different connection options available, as well as an example of when you would use that particular connection:

CONNECTION TYPE	DESCRIPTION	EXAMPLE
Send Shape Data To	Send the data for the selected shape to another Web Part.	When you have to show diagrams in a master/detail relationship, you would send the shape data to the Details Web Part so that it would know what data to display.
Get Web Drawing URL and Page Name From	This connection enables you to dynamically accept the Drawing URL and Page name.	You can use this when you have a list of drawings and you want users to be able to easily select a drawing from a list and have the drawing displayed.
Get Shapes to Highlight From	This connection enables you to highlight shapes in the diagram. The connection will need to have the name of the shape and the color of the highlight.	You can use this if you want to be able to select from a list of items and have certain ones highlighted; for example, if you have a floor plan drawing and want to highlight all rooms that are 6 × 8.
Get Filter Results From	This connection filters the items in the Visio diagram based on the SharePoint list contents. This connection works only when the Visio diagram is connected to the SharePoint list and the only list that can pass the connection is the List Web Part of the connected list.	This highlights values that match the filtered SharePoint list. If you look again at the floor plan example, you could have a list that contains all of your information about each of the rooms. If you filter the list based on the fireplace option, all rooms with fireplaces would be highlighted in your Web Part.
Get Shape to View From	This connection enables you to change the zoom view for a specific shape.	This is useful, for example, if you want to have a list of values that, when selected, would cause a new view to display that zooms in to show all of the details.

As you can see from the table, you can configure and connect the Web Parts in many different ways. In the Try It Outs that follow, you work through several different examples. Once you complete these Try It Outs, you should have a good understanding of how these diagrams can be connected to provide valuable, dynamic information to users.

TRY IT OUT   Creating a Visio Services Document

The process for creating a Visio Services document is the same as for creating a standard Visio document. In this Try It Out, you upload two separate Visio files. The first one has several different pages, and the second one has only one page. Because the content is not relevant, you can use whatever Visio diagrams you have access to. If you do not have any, you can simply open Visio and create two separate diagrams with various shapes.

1. The first thing that you need to do is to create a document library in which to store your Visio documents. To do this, select the Site Contents link from the Home page, and then select the "Add an app" option. Select the Document Library template, enter the following value, and click Create:

PROPERTY	VALUE
Name	Diagrams

2. Open the first Visio document that you want to publish to the site. Select the File option to open the Backstage view. Select the Save As option and the Other Web Locations option, as shown in Figure 10-20. Select the option to Browse for a location, and set the file type to Web Drawing.

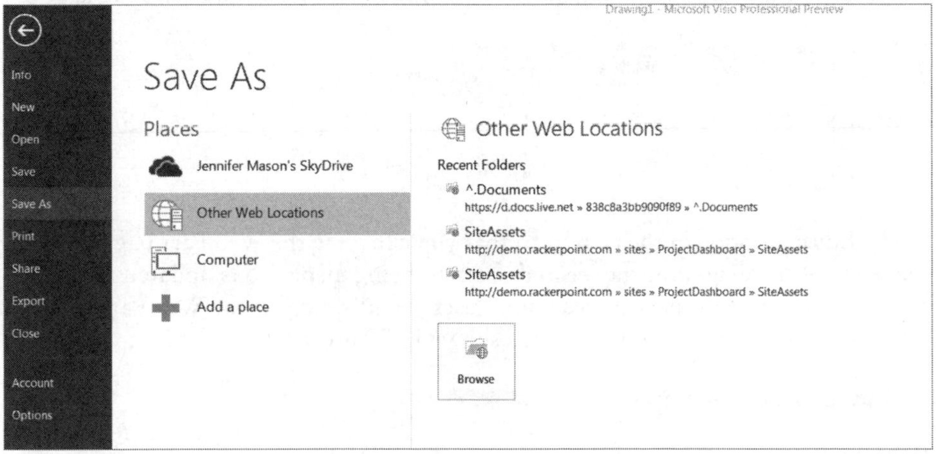

FIGURE 10-20

3. Enter the URL for the library that you created in step 1. When the library loads, enter the desired filename and click Save.

4. Repeat steps 2 and 3 for another Visio document. This will give you at least two different diagrams in your library.

How It Works

When you publish a document to a SharePoint site, the document is saved in a format that can be displayed within the Visio Access Web Part. In the next Try It Out, you configure the Web Part on a dashboard page.

TRY IT OUT Connecting a Visio Services Web Part to a List Web Part

In this example, you add the Visio Web Access Web Part to the page and connect it to the Diagrams library you created in the previous example. You create a connection between the two Web Parts so that the Visio Web Part will load the drawing you select in the Diagram Web Part.

1. Using the steps in the "Create a New Dashboard" Try It Out, create a new dashboard called VisioExample.

2. When the dashboard page loads, click in any column cell to add a Web Part.

3. Click the Add Web Part option in any of the Web Part zones.

4. In the Apps category list, select the Diagrams Web Part.

5. Select the zone next to the one you used for the Diagrams Web Part, and click the Add a Web Part option.

6. In the Business Data category list, select the Visio Web Access Web Part and click Add.

7. Select the Edit Web Part menu for the Visio Web Part, and click the Connections link.

8. Select the Get Web Drawing URL and Page Name option, and then click the Diagrams option.

9. In the Configure Connection dialog box, select the following options and click Finish:

PROPERTY	VALUE
Provider Field Name	Document URL
Consumer Field Name	Web Drawing URL

10. Select the Stop Editing option in the ribbon so that you can view the Web Part page. Notice that as you select each of the diagrams, the Visio document being displayed is updated to match the selected diagram. To make the page appear more user friendly, update the Web Part styles and views to provide a clean look for your users, as shown in Figure 10-21.

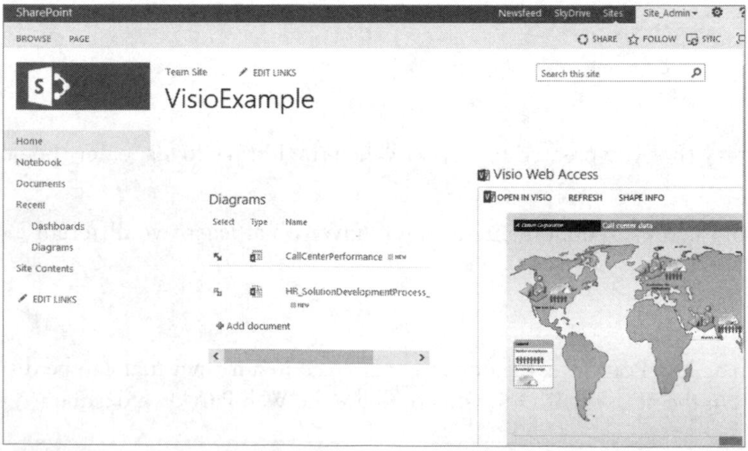

FIGURE 10-21

This is just one example of using the Visio Web Access Web Part. In this Try It Out, you used a Web Part connection to display the Visio documents. If you did not want to use a connection, you could configure the Web Part to display a single Visio document by entering the Web Drawing URL within the Web Part tool pane.

How It Works

The two Web Parts are added to the page and a connection is built between them. The values for the Web Document URL are passed from the Diagrams List Web Part. Doing this allows any user to select which diagram they want to be displayed.

TRY IT OUT **Connecting a Visio Services Web Part to a List and Using the List Values as a Web Part Connection**

In this Try It Out, you connect your Visio diagram to a list that stores information about various project stages. You then configure the Web Part to pass the process stage information to a document library. The documents in the document library have been tagged with their associated process stage and the connection between the diagram, and the process list enables you to filter the documents by process stage by selecting a shape in the Visio Web Access Web Part.

1. Following the steps from previous chapters, create the following site applications:

APPLICATION TYPE	NAME	ADDITIONAL COLUMNS	SAMPLE DATA
Custom List	Process Steps	None	Add a list item for each process stage. For our example, the following items will need to be created in the list: Step 1 Step 2 Step 3 Step 4
Document Library	Process Documents	Lookup column that adds the Title from the Process Steps list.	Add several documents to this library and configure the lookup column to have a sampling of values.

2. In addition to the items in this table, this example requires a Visio diagram that has been connected to the SharePoint list created in the table. To create this diagram, open Visio and create a new diagram with four connected shapes. An example is shown in Figure 10-22. Your diagram can vary slightly from the one in the example.

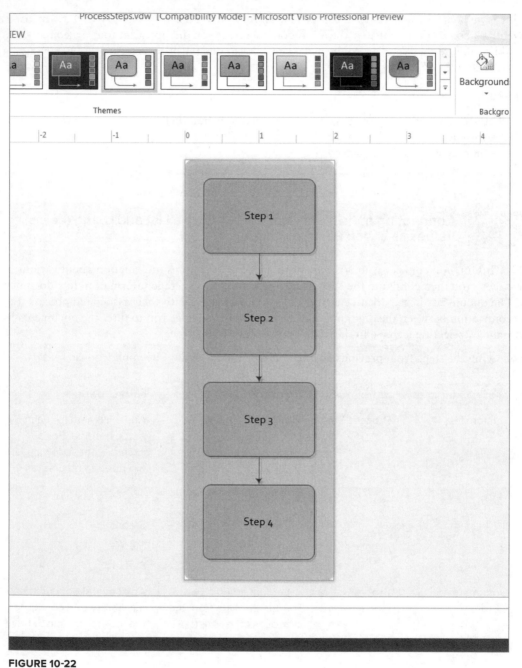

FIGURE 10-22

3. Once you have the diagram created, use the Data ribbon within Visio to Link Data to Shapes (see Figure 10-23).

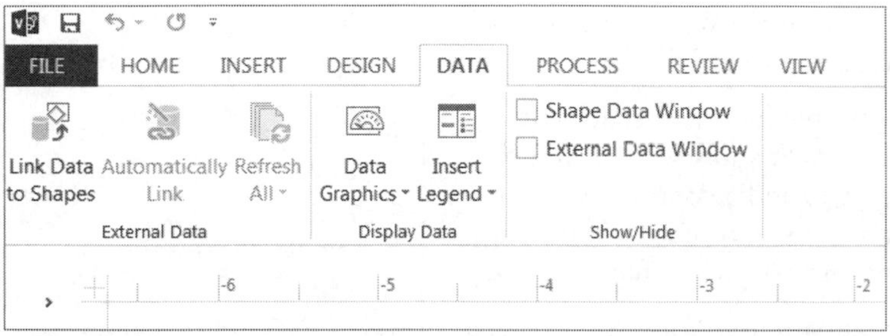

FIGURE 10-23

4. Follow the wizard to add a link to the Process Steps application that you created at the start of this exercise. Be sure to select Microsoft SharePoint Foundation List as the data type.

5. Once the external data is displayed, as shown in Figure 10-24, drag each of the line items in the dataset to the corresponding shape on the diagram. If the shape names and the items have the same names, you can use the Automatically Link Wizard located within the Data ribbon.

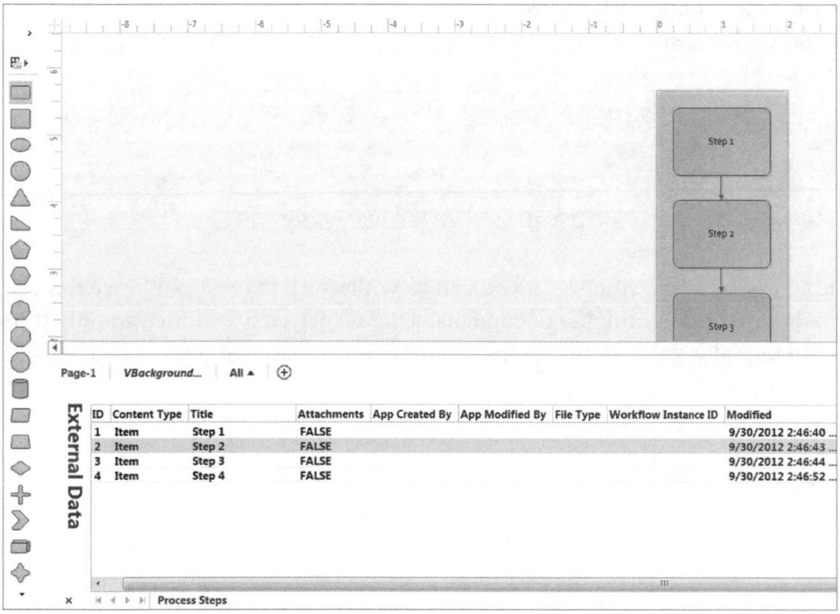

FIGURE 10-24

6. Use the Backstage View and Save As option to save the file.

7. Using the steps in the "Creating a New Dashboard" Try It Out, create a new dashboard called "Visio Process Example."

8. When the dashboard page loads, click in the left column cell to add a Web Part.

9. In the Business Data category list, select the Visio Web Access Web Part.

10. Open the Tool Pane and configure the Web Part to open the Process Diagram you created earlier.

11. Add the ID field to the "Expose the following shape data items to Web Part connections" field and select OK to save your changes. This enables you to add a connection to the Process Documents Web Part that will be added to the page. Figure 10-25 shows the configurations from steps 9 and 10.

12. Select the zone next to the one you used for the Visio Web Access Web Part, and click the Add a Web Part option.

13. In the Apps list, select the Process Documents Web Part and click Add.

14. In the Process Documents Web Part menu, select the Web Part Connections item.

15. Select Get Filter Values From, and then click the Visio Web Access option.

16. In the Configure Connection dialog box, select the following options and click Finish:

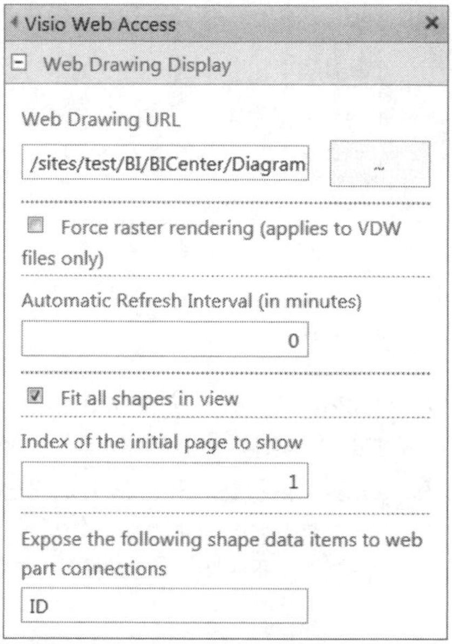

FIGURE 10-25

PROPERTY	VALUE
Provider Field Name	ID
Consumer Field Name	Process Step (lookup column created in step 1)

17. Select the Stop Editing option in the ribbon, so you can view the Web Part page. Notice that, as you select each of the shapes in the diagram, the documents being displayed are limited to only those that have been tagged with the same value in the lookup column of the list, as shown in Figure 10-26.

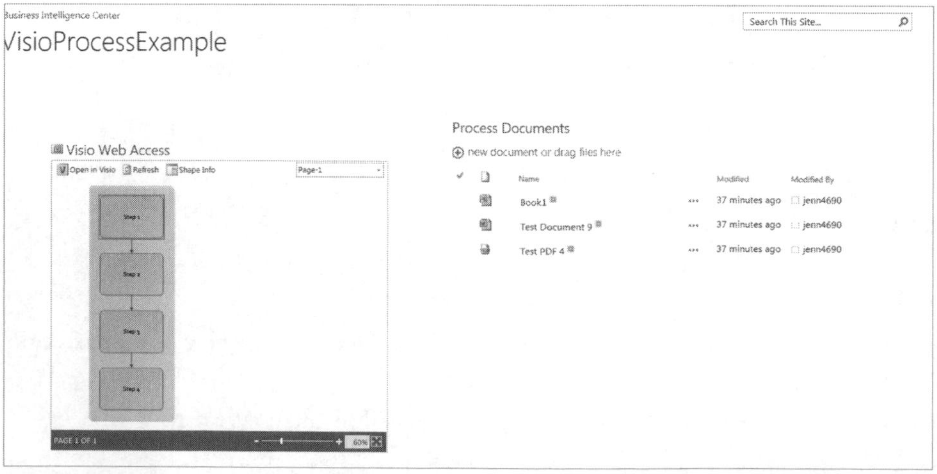

FIGURE 10-26

In this Try It Out, you used a Web Part connection to display the documents that were tagged with the same values that the corresponding Visio shape had been linked with. This approach enables you to add a level of visual process to your SharePoint solutions.

How It Works

The Visio file that you created was connected to a SharePoint custom list application. When you configured the Visio Web Access Web Part, you specified that the shapes in the diagram could use the custom list application data in Web Part connections. Because the documents application also had a lookup reference to the Process Steps custom application, you were able to use this as a connection between the two Web Parts. This enables you to select a shape in the diagram and use that to filter the documents that are associated with that phase only.

WORKING WITH PERFORMANCEPOINT SERVICES

PerformancePoint Services allows users to easily create rich reports, dashboards, scorecards, and KPIs using the Dashboard Designer. When the farm is configured, the SharePoint administrator will complete the process for configuring the PerformancePoint Services application. Once the configuration is complete, users with the appropriate permissions will be able to incorporate the PerformancePoint Services content into their sites.

One of the key benefits of PerformancePoint Services is that it allows you to design and build content using the Dashboard Designer. As you can see in Figure 10-27, this design environment is similar to that of other Office applications.

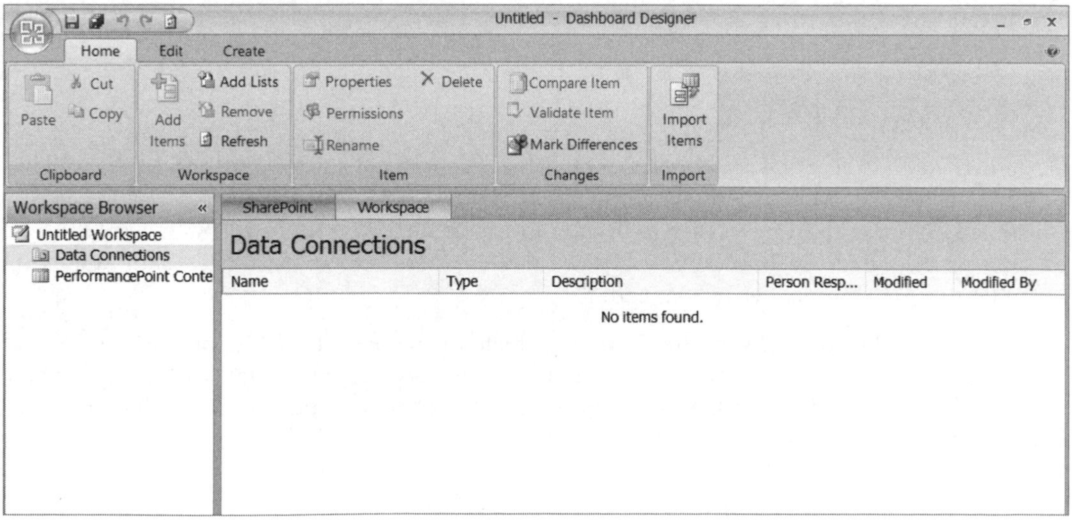

FIGURE 10-27

You can access the Dashboard Designer easily from any list created with the PerformancePoint Services content template. From within the list, the Dashboard Designer is launched whenever you create new content items. Figure 10-28 shows the menu you would use to launch the dashboard.

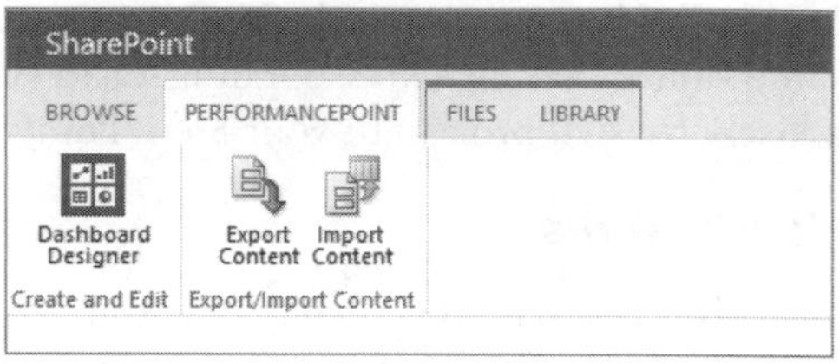

PerformancePoint Services is a very large component of reporting and business intelligence, and there is no way that a small section in a single chapter can do it justice. Because you do most of the work to create reports using PerformancePoint Services in the PerformancePoint Dashboard Designer, it is out of the scope of a beginning SharePoint solutions book.

FIGURE 10-28

WORKING WITH REPORTING SERVICES

Having reports available to see the state of a company can be invaluable. Reports enable information workers to make real-time decisions with access to all their pertinent data. With SharePoint, SQL Server Reporting Services (SSRS) is an additional service application that you can install. SSRS enables reports to be created and stored in document libraries. Following are some reasons to install SSRS:

➤ Professional reports can be created from a plethora of data sources.

➤ Reports are pixel-perfect when printed.

➤ Reports can be exported to various file types, such as PDF and Excel.

➤ Charts and graphs can easily be created and displayed in SharePoint.

➤ Self-service reporting enables power users to create reports directly in SharePoint.

➤ Reports can be created on a server by a report developer and deployed to SharePoint.

➤ Data alerts of changes in reports can be created.

Once a decision has been made to implement SSRS, there are some factors to consider, as well as steps that need to be taken by a server administrator. SQL (just Reporting Services) will need to be installed on one web front-end server in the SharePoint farm. Typically, the SQL database back end is on a separate server from the SharePoint Server(s); therefore, an extra license for SQL will be needed to also install it on a web front end.

Report Builder 3.0 is the software that is used to create the reports. This does not need to be downloaded or installed separately. As soon as anyone creates a report or dataset for the first time, Report Builder 3.0 will be installed automatically on his or her computer. This installation comes directly from the server, not from the Internet.

TROUBLESHOOTING REPORT BUILDER

When it comes to errors or issues with running or installing Report Builder, trouble-shooting typically is done on the client side. If there is a problem, try using different browsers and browser settings. Sometimes browsers have settings that disallow applications to be run.

> **NOTE** This book is not geared toward server administrators, so the server steps are covered at a high level. For detailed technical information, refer to the MSDN article "Install Reporting Services SharePoint Mode for SharePoint 2013" (http://msdn.microsoft.com/en-us/library/jj219068.aspx). Also, because this book is geared toward SharePoint beginners, the development and deployment of reports using Business Intelligence Development Studio (Visual Studio) is not covered.

The following are the general steps for getting SSRS up and running:

1. Run the SQL 2012 installation on a server on which SharePoint is already installed, and choose the following features:

   ➤ Reporting Services - SharePoint

   ➤ Reporting Services Add-in for SharePoint Products

2. Run the following commands in the SharePoint 2013 Management Shell:

```
Install-SPRSService
Install-SPRSServiceProxy
get-spserviceinstance -all |where {$_.TypeName -like
                                "SQL Server Reporting*"} |
    Start-SPServiceInstance
```

3. Create a SQL Services Server Application.

After the SharePoint Server administrator has performed the SSRS installation on the server, reports can be created and stored in SharePoint document libraries.

TRY IT OUT   **Creating a Library for Reports**

When a document library is configured to include the SSRS content types, SharePoint users can create reports directly in the library. In this Try It Out, you create a library that can be used for report creation.

1. In the browser, from the Corporate Intranet site you created in Chapter 1 of this book, click the Settings button at the top-right corner and choose "Add an app."

2. Click Document Library.

3. For the Name, type **Reports,** and then click Create.

4. Click the name of the new library, Reports, to go to the library page.

5. On the Library tab in the ribbon, click Library Settings.

6. Click Advanced Settings.

7. Change "Allow management of content types" to Yes, and click OK.

8. In the Content Types section, click "Add from existing site content types."

9. In the category called SQL Server Reporting Services Content Types, select the Report Builder Report and Report Data Source, and click Add. Click OK.

10. Click the name of the Document content type, and select "Delete this content type." Click OK to confirm the deletion. Figure 10-29 shows the Content Types section of the Settings page.

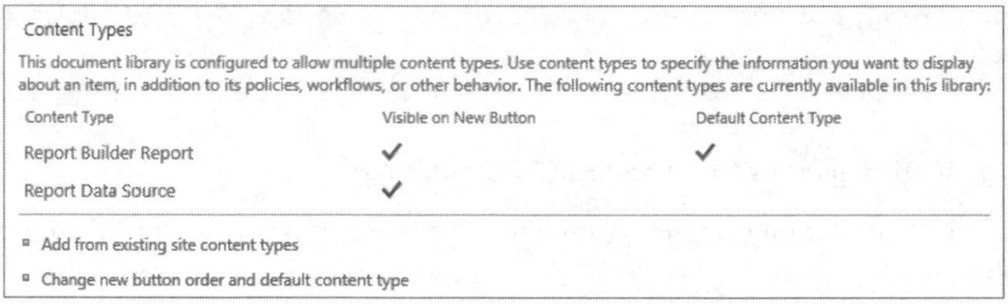

Content Types

This document library is configured to allow multiple content types. Use content types to specify the information you want to display about an item, in addition to its policies, workflows, or other behavior. The following content types are currently available in this library:

Content Type	Visible on New Button	Default Content Type
Report Builder Report	✓	✓
Report Data Source	✓	

▫ Add from existing site content types
▫ Change new button order and default content type

FIGURE 10-29

11. Click the Reports link at the top of the Settings page to go back to the main view of the library.

How It Works

In this Try It Out, you created a document library that enables end users to create data sources and reports. You can create this type of library on any type of site; it is not limited to a Business Intelligence site or site collection.

Technically, reports and data sources can exist in a library without the associated content types. The steps were taken to add data source and report content types to a library, to enable self-service reporting. This means that end users can create data sources and reports, so long as they have permission to access that library and add new items.

Working in a Report Library

When you create reports in SharePoint, they are stored in document libraries. We refer to it as a "report library," because it is a place to keep reports, but the libraries are simply created as document libraries. When a document library is created for the purpose of storing reports, there are some important concepts to understand, such as certain content types that are associated with reports. This section describes several common scenarios for using reports in SharePoint. You will learn about data sources, datasets, reports, and report parts, and how all of these are used with each other.

Data Sources

When creating reports, the first important question is, "Where is the data?" With SSRS, reports can be created based on data that is in SharePoint, and they can also be created based on data that lives in other databases that are external to SharePoint. The *data source* is where the data lives. A connection needs to be created to access that data. This chapter focuses on the SharePoint List data source, which means that it shows how to create reports off of information in lists and libraries.

TRY IT OUT   Creating a Data Source

In the preceding Try It Out, you created a document library in which to store reports and data connections. Before you can create a report, you need to create a data source, as demonstrated in this Try It Out.

1. In the browser, navigate to the Reports library that you created in the previous Try It Out.

2. On the Files menu in the ribbon, click the New Document drop-down. Select Report Data Source.

3. For the name, type **Intranet Site**; for the data source type, choose Microsoft SharePoint List; and for the connection string, type the URL of your SharePoint site, as shown in Figure 10-30. Click OK.

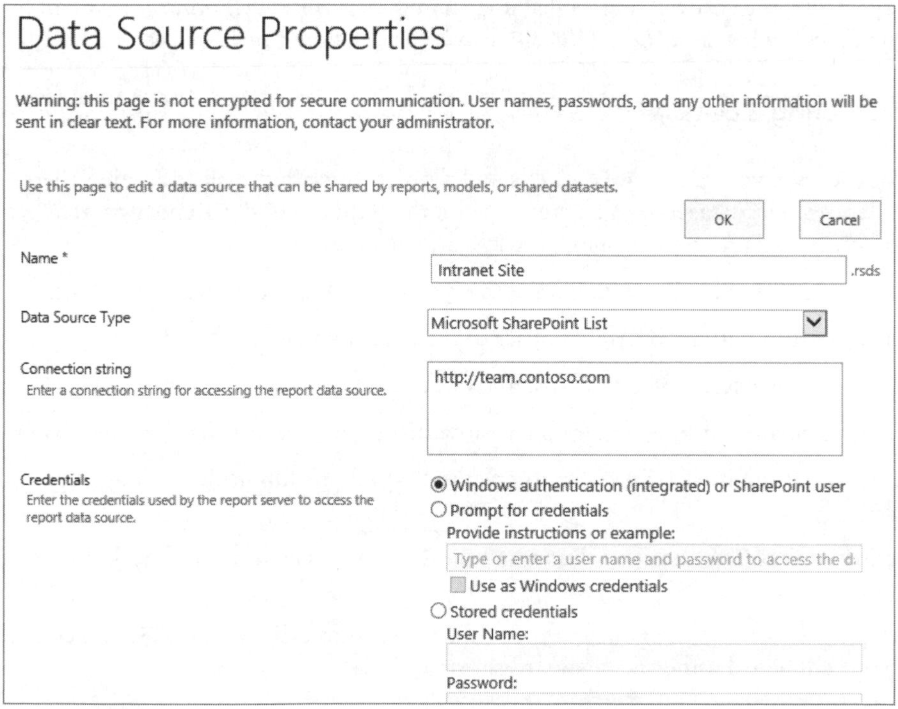

FIGURE 10-30

How It Works

The SharePoint List data source is actually the easiest type of data source to create. You can see that the site URL is all that is needed. For authentication, this example uses the default of Windows authentication. This means that if a user does not have access to a particular site or list, he or she will not be able to view that site's data in a report. This is the same security trimming concept that is seen throughout SharePoint. For example, if a user does not have permissions to a particular SharePoint list or library, he or she will not see it in the site's navigation.

> **NOTE** To connect to data sources other than SharePoint lists, you must use connection strings. For each type of data source, the syntax of the connection string is a bit different. For a connection string reference, go to www.connectionstrings.com.

Datasets

In SSRS, a *dataset* is a smaller subset of data within a data source. For example, if a data source is a SharePoint site, a dataset can be one list or library in that site. Likewise, if the data source is a SQL database, the dataset can be a specific table within that database.

Two different types of datasets exist: embedded and shared. An *embedded dataset* exists only within a specific report, whereas a *shared dataset* can be used by multiple reports.

TRY IT OUT   Creating a Dataset

After creating a data source, you can create datasets and reports. It is a bit misleading that there is no content type for a dataset, but datasets can be created with the Report Builder Report content type. In this Try It Out, you create a dataset; in the next Try It Out, you create a report.

1. In the browser, navigate to the Reports library that you created in the earlier Try It Out.

2. Click the Settings button at the top-right corner of the page, and choose "Add an app."

3. Click Tasks. Name this list **Important Tasks,** and click Create.

    The goal here is to create a task list and populate it with a lot of tasks so that it can be reported on.

4. Click the name of the Important Tasks list to open it. On the List tab in the ribbon, click Modify View.

5. Put a checkmark next to the Priority column and the Task Status column. Uncheck the Assigned To box, and click OK.

6. Open the sample file called `ImportantTasks.xlsx`. Select from cells A2 to D33, and copy the selection to your clipboard using the keyboard shortcut Ctrl+C.

7. Go back to the task list in the browser. On the List tab in the ribbon, click Quick Edit. Select the first Task Name cell, and use the Ctrl+P keyboard shortcut to paste the data from the spreadsheet. On the List tab in the ribbon, click the View button on the far left, which will show the full list of tasks, as shown in Figure 10-31.

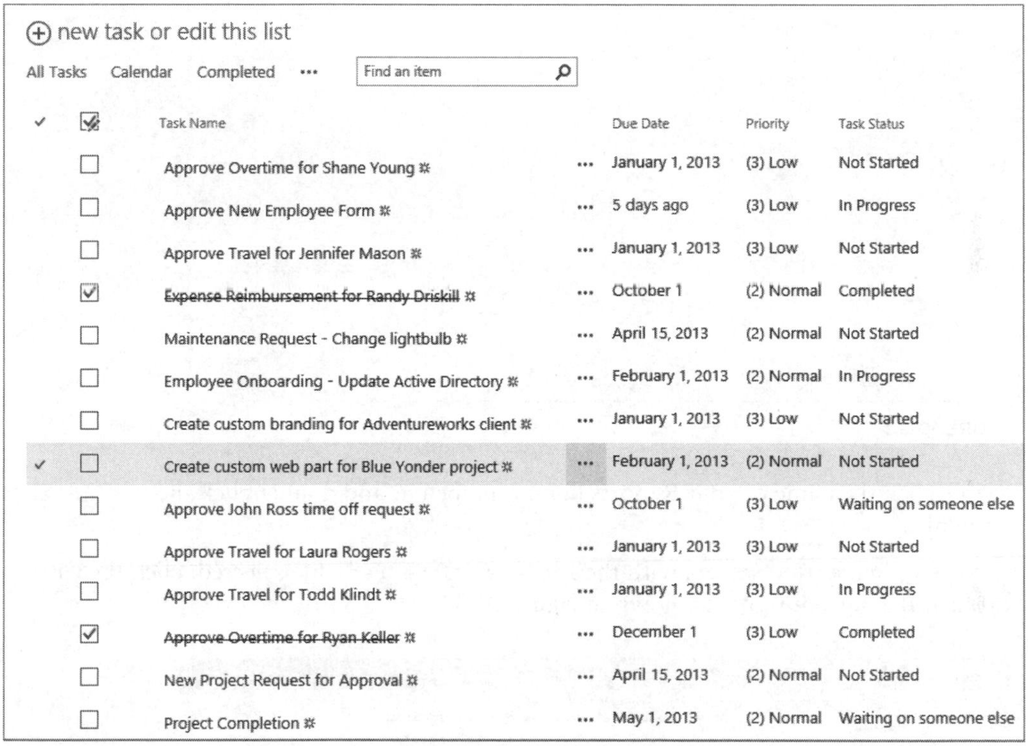

⊕ new task or edit this list

All Tasks   Calendar   Completed   ⋯   Find an item   🔍

		Task Name		Due Date	Priority	Task Status
✓	☑					
	☐	Approve Overtime for Shane Young ✳	⋯	January 1, 2013	(3) Low	Not Started
	☐	Approve New Employee Form ✳	⋯	5 days ago	(3) Low	In Progress
	☐	Approve Travel for Jennifer Mason ✳	⋯	January 1, 2013	(3) Low	Not Started
	☑	~~Expense Reimbursement for Randy Driskill~~ ✳	⋯	October 1	(2) Normal	Completed
	☐	Maintenance Request – Change lightbulb ✳	⋯	April 15, 2013	(2) Normal	Not Started
	☐	Employee Onboarding – Update Active Directory ✳	⋯	February 1, 2013	(2) Normal	In Progress
	☐	Create custom branding for Adventureworks client ✳	⋯	January 1, 2013	(3) Low	Not Started
✓	☐	Create custom web part for Blue Yonder project ✳	⋯	February 1, 2013	(2) Normal	Not Started
	☐	Approve John Ross time off request ✳	⋯	October 1	(3) Low	Waiting on someone else
	☐	Approve Travel for Laura Rogers ✳	⋯	January 1, 2013	(3) Low	Not Started
	☐	Approve Travel for Todd Klindt ✳	⋯	January 1, 2013	(3) Low	In Progress
	☑	~~Approve Overtime for Ryan Keller~~ ✳	⋯	December 1	(3) Low	Completed
	☐	New Project Request for Approval ✳	⋯	April 15, 2013	(2) Normal	Not Started
	☐	Project Completion ✳	⋯	May 1, 2013	(2) Normal	Waiting on someone else

FIGURE 10-31

8. Click the Reports library on the left. On the Files tab in the ribbon, click the New Document drop-down. Choose Report Builder Report.

9. If prompted to run the application, click Run.

10. After the application has installed or initiated, the first page of the Getting Started Wizard appears, as shown in Figure 10-32. Click the "Browse other data sources" link.

If any data sources have been selected in the past, they will be shown on this screen. In this case, you are not selecting an existing one; you are going to select the new one that you created in the previous Try It Out.

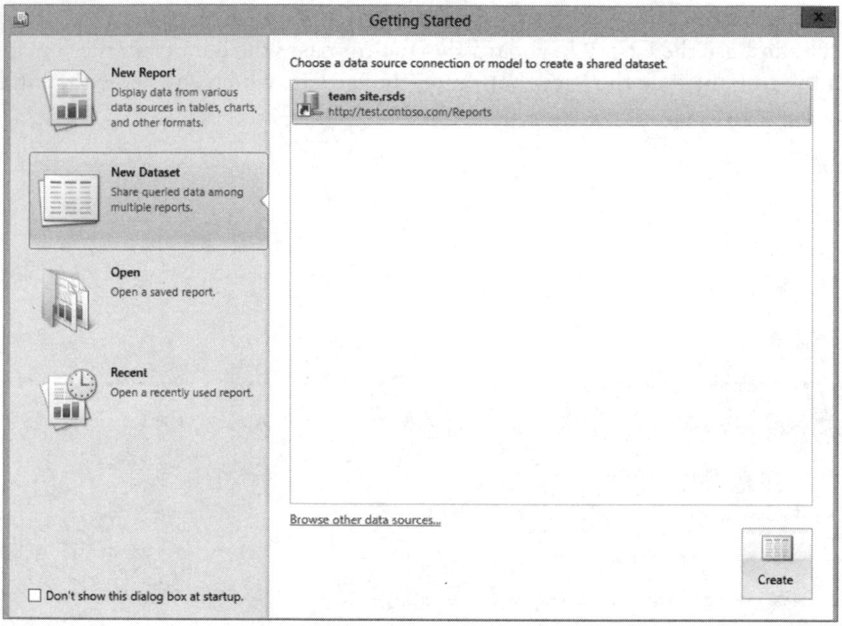

FIGURE 10-32

11. Double-click the name of your Reports library to open it, and double-click the `Intranet Site` `.rsds` file.

12. On the Getting Started screen, with the `Intranet Site.rsds` file selected, click the Create button at the bottom right, as shown in Figure 10-33.

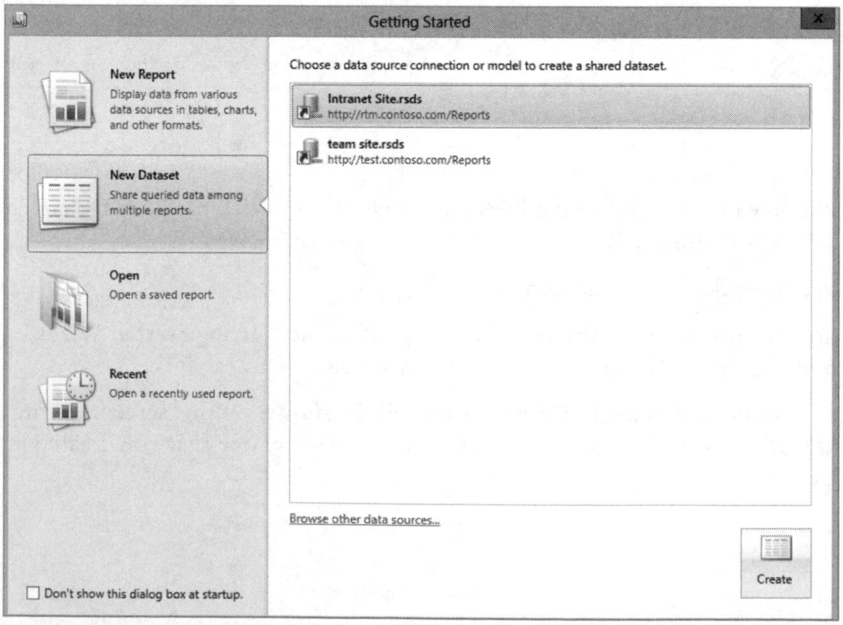

FIGURE 10-33

13. The next screen enables you to configure the dataset. Check the box next to the Important Tasks list on the left side, as shown in Figure 10-34. Click the Save button at the top left.

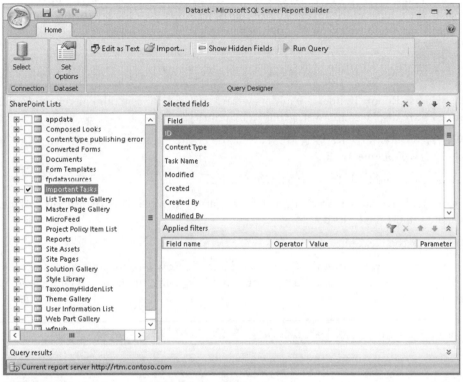

FIGURE 10-34

14. Double-click "Reports" to open the Reports library. Name the file **Important Tasks.rsd.** Close the Report Builder tool by clicking the X at the top-right corner.

How It Works

Notice when configuring the dataset, you can expand each list on the left. Instead of selecting all the columns in the list, you can optionally check boxes next to only specific columns that you need for the report. If you need to return only a filtered subset of data, you can filter the list. After checking the list that you need, you can use the Add Filter button next to Applied Filters. This is especially useful if a large list is involved. With a filter applied at this level, the report will load faster than if you filtered data within the report after it was loaded. If needed, you can use the Run Query button at the top to test the results of the selected data. Note that only one list or library (or table) can be selected at one time. If you later need to edit a dataset, click the ellipsis next to the name of the dataset in the library, click the next ellipsis, and then choose Edit in Report Builder.

Reports

Reports are a perfect way to display any type of business data in a professional-looking manner, with no programming required. As far as the look and feel of reports, the possibilities are virtually endless. Not only can you create several different types of reports, such as tables and charts, but you also can create dashboard-type interfaces within a report. Reports are stored in a library in SharePoint, which does not necessarily need to be the same location as the data sources and datasets.

TRY IT OUT   Creating a Report

In this Try It Out, you use Report Builder 3.0 and its wizard to create a basic tabular report. In this report, the list of tasks are displayed in a list, grouped by priority.

1. In the browser, navigate to the Reports library that you created in the previous Try It Out. On the Files tab, click New Document.

2. Choose New Report, and click Table or Matrix Wizard.

3. You've already created a dataset, so click the Browse button. Double-click the Reports folder, and double-click the Important Tasks dataset.

4. In the wizard, click the Next button.

5. On the Arrange Fields screen, drag the Priority field into the Row Groups box. Drag the following fields to the Values box: Task_Name, Task_Status, and Due_Date, as shown in Figure 10-35. Click Next.

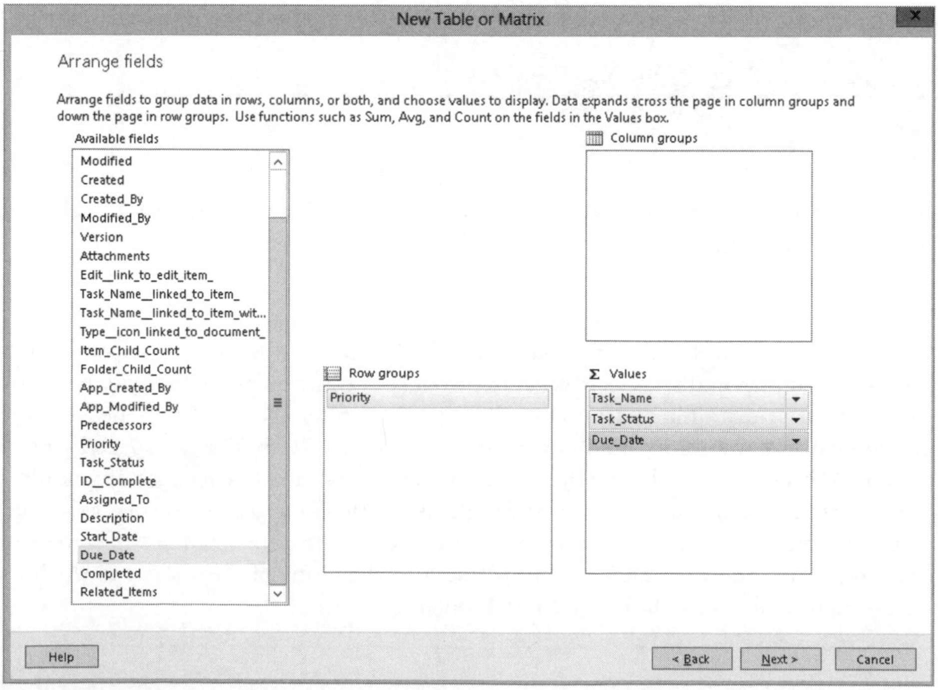

FIGURE 10-35

6. The Choose the Layout screen shows different options for subtotals and groups. Leave the defaults and click Next.

Once a report has been created, it is easy to remove subtotals and groups if they are not needed, but it takes a bit longer to create them from scratch. Leaving the defaults on this screen usually just saves time in the long run.

7. On the Choose a Style screen, pick a color scheme that you like, and click Finish.

8. Your report is now shown on the screen, in the Design view, as shown in Figure 10-36. Click the Run button at the top left to see a preview of the report. Notice that you can expand each priority group, and that the table is a bit too narrow for the fields.

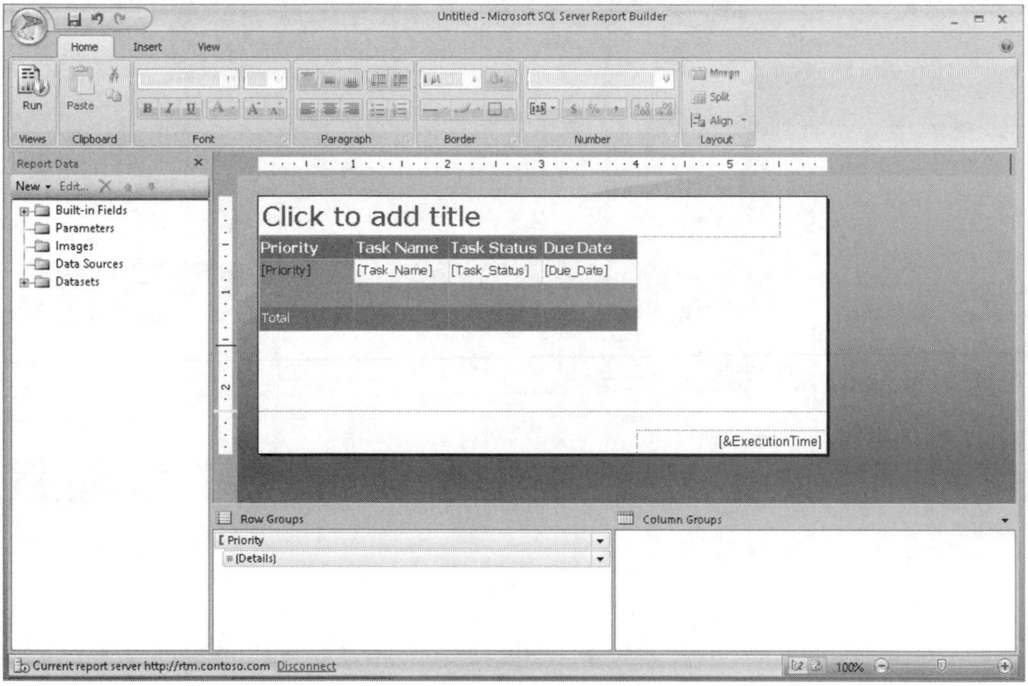

FIGURE 10-36

9. After previewing the report, click the Design button at the top left. This is a good time to save the report, so click the Save button at the top left. Double-click the Reports folder to open it. Name the report **Task Table.rdl**, and click Save.

10. Put your cursor in the table, inside of the priority cell. You're looking for the table to "light up" with gray boxes at the beginning of each column and row. Right-click the small gray box at the top left of the table, as shown in Figure 10-37, and choose Tablix Properties.

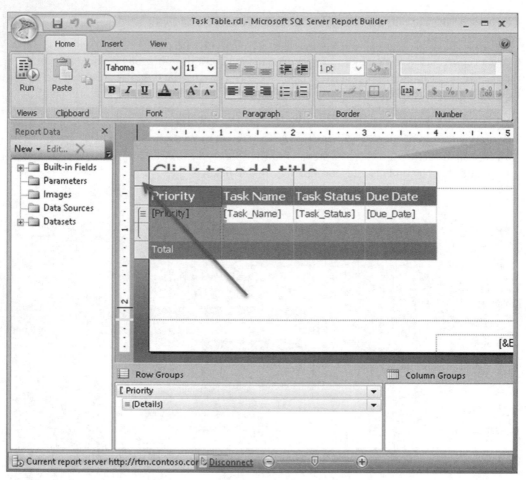

FIGURE 10-37

11. In the General section, the Name field currently says Tablix1. Change this name to say **Grouped_ Tasks**. Click OK.

This report has only one table; however, because any one report can have multiple tables and charts, it is a good idea to give them meaningful names. Note that no spaces are allowed in these names.

12. Put your cursor in the "Click to add title" box and type **Task Report**.

13. Save again, and close the Report Builder using the X at the top right.

14. Back in the browser, refresh the Reports library page. Click the name of the Task Table report to open it in the browser. Notice that the report opens within the browser, with interactivity so that the groups can be expanded and collapsed. The breadcrumb trail at the top of the report enables you to navigate back to the Reports library.

How It Works

At this point, you have created the first data source, dataset, and report in the Reports library. When creating the report (step 3), you may have noticed the option to create a dataset or browse for an existing one. It is not required for a dataset to be created before a report can be created. A dataset can be created in a report, and it just stays embedded in the report. This simply means that the dataset cannot be shared with other reports. It is a time saver to create shared datasets for data that is commonly reported on.

When viewing a report, a few important parts of the interface are going to be very useful for end users who care about this report data. Although the buttons at the top of the report, such as refresh and zoom, are self-explanatory, the Actions button has some options to take note of, as shown in Figure 10-38.

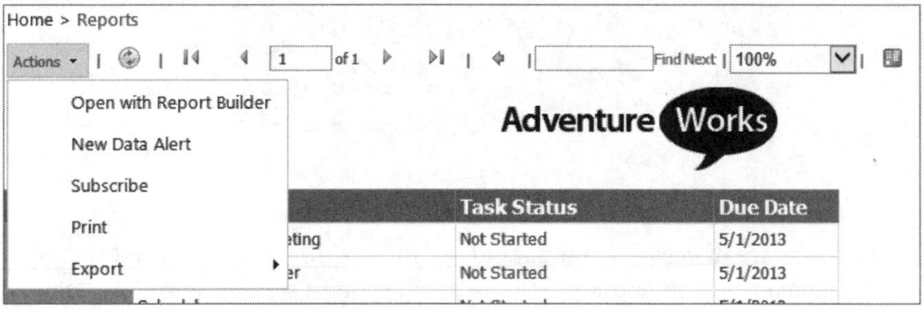

FIGURE 10-38

➤ **Open with Report Builder:** Use this to open the report using the client software instead of the browser or to edit existing reports.

➤ **New Data Alert:** Data alerts are new to SQL 2012, and the concept is similar to list alerts in SharePoint, but even better! Pick the report data name, such as the "Grouped_Tasks" tablix from step 11 in the preceding Try It Out. Data alerts enable you to set up rules so that you are alerted about the specific data that you are interested in. For example, you can set up an alert to notify you only when high-priority tasks show up in the report. You can set up a recurrence pattern and even determine a timeframe and specific recipients for the alert. Figure 10-39 shows an example of the data alert screen. For this example, if any high-priority tasks have not been started, I will receive an alert e-mail each day. I have checked the "Send message only if alert results change" box so that I will not receive an alert about the same task every day.

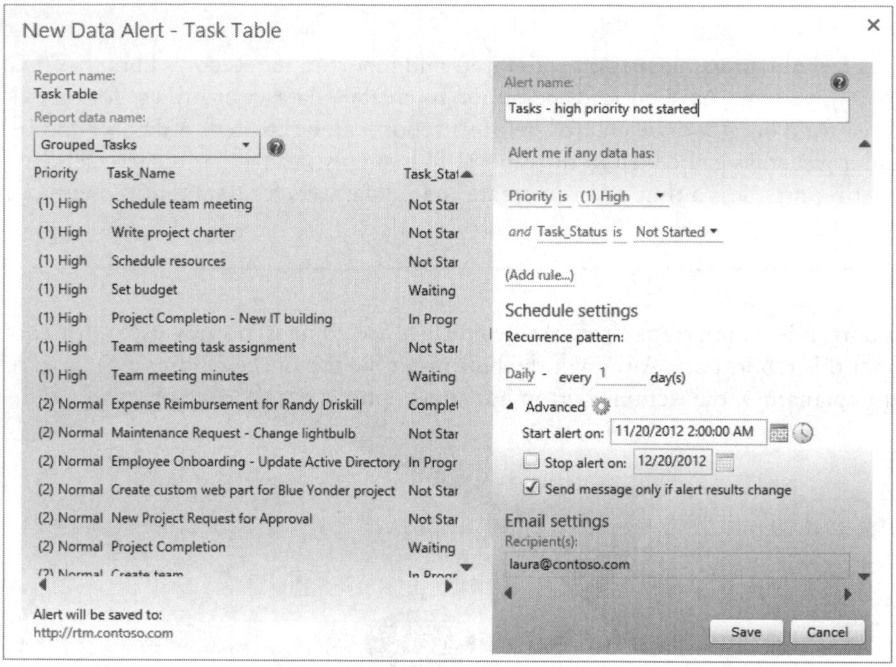

FIGURE 10-39

➤ **Subscribe:** Subscriptions are different from data alerts in that they are not based on any data that exists in the report. Subscriptions simply enable you to send a report to a certain location based on a schedule. That location can be a Windows file share, a SharePoint document library, or an e-mail. If your report has parameters, parameterized reports can be created on subscriptions. For example, if the report has a department name field that is set as a parameter, you can create a subscription to receive only the marketing department's report items in an e-mail or a document library every morning as a PDF.

➤ **Print:** Use this to send the report directly to your printer.

➤ **Export:** Pick one of the following file formats to export the report to: XML, CSV, PDF, Excel, TIFF, Word, or MHTML.

Report Parts

Any given report can contain a combination of several tables, charts, and graphs. This is a great way to create professional-looking dashboards! Report parts are a way to allow users to quickly piece together a report, using tables, charts, and graphs that have been pre-created. Report part files have an .RSC file extension. When report parts are used in reports, they maintain the relationship to the original so that if any individual report part is modified at a later date, each report that uses it will reflect the changes.

The following types of objects in a report can be re-used as report parts: charts, gauges, images, maps, parameters, rectangles, tables, matrices, and lists.

TRY IT OUT | Creating a Report Part

So far you have created a simple report. In this Try It Out, you add a company logo to the report. Then you create a report part from the table and a report part from the image. Once these exist, other users will be able to quickly drop them into other reports.

1. In the browser, navigate to the Reports library that you created in the previous Try It Out. Click the Task Table report to open it.

2. On the Insert tab in the ribbon, click Image. The cursor will look like a cross. Click in the top area of the report, to the right of the title.

3. For the name of the image, type **AW_Logo** on the Image Properties screen, as shown in Figure 10-40.

4. Click the Import button next to the "Use this image" box. Select the awlogo.png file, and click Open. On the Image Properties screen, click OK.

   On the Open screen, you might need to change the file type drop-down box to "PNG files" instead of the default of "JPEG files."

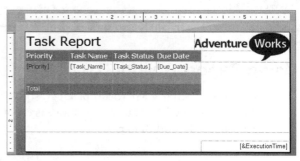

FIGURE 10-40

5. Drag the image and then drag the corners of the image so that it is displayed in the top-right corner of the report, as shown in Figure 10-41.

6. In Report Builder, click the File menu at the top-left corner (a round red logo). Click Publish Report Parts.

7. On the Choose SharePoint Document Library screen, select your Reports library from the drop-down box. Click OK.

8. Click the "Review and modify report parts before publishing" option.

FIGURE 10-41

   This enables you to add detailed descriptions of each part of the report, which makes the information more useful. Notice that both AW_Logo (picture) and the Grouped_Tasks (tablix) have checkboxes next to them. The dataset called ImportantTasks is grayed out because it has already been created as a shared dataset, so it cannot be used as a report part as well.

9. Click the small arrow next to AW_Logo to expand the section, as shown in Figure 10-42. Type the following description: **This is the Adventure Works logo**.

10. Click the arrow next to Grouped_Tasks, and type the following description: **This is the table of tasks, grouped by priority.** Click the Publish button.

11. At the bottom of the Publish Report Parts screen, you will see a message that states "0 report parts failed to publish, 2 published successfully." Click Close.

12. Click Save at the top left, and close Report Builder.

13. Go back to the browser and open the Reports library. If the library is already on the screen, refresh the page. Notice that there is a new folder called Report Parts.

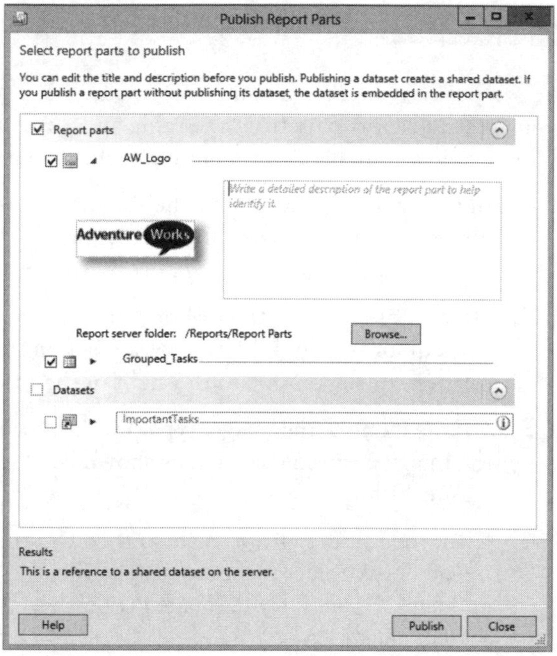

FIGURE 10-42

How It Works

In this Try It Out, you learned that report parts are a way to create a shortcut for future report creation. Some report parts have been published to the SharePoint document library and can now be used in other reports. In the following section, you work more with reports and use the report parts that you have created.

Using Report Builder 3.0

Report Builder 3.0 is a Microsoft product, so it has a look and feel that is similar to other products you have worked with. This makes it an easy tool to learn, especially for power users who do not have a lot of SQL and BI experience.

> **NOTE** When working with Report Builder and the different components of a chart or table, trying to figure out exactly where to click can be a bit tricky. A lot of functions are available when you right-click an object. If your cursor isn't in a specific spot with a specific object selected, you might see a different menu. Other than the right-clicking trickiness, most things you need to do in Report Builder are fairly easy and obvious.

Tables

A table is structured in rows and columns, and is similar to working in a spreadsheet. Tables can also be grouped by rows or columns. In the "Creating a Report" Try It Out, you used the Table or Matrix Wizard. You created your first table, which is also referred to as a *tablix*. By definition, tables and tablixes are not the same thing; however, for the purposes of this chapter, they are similar enough.

TRY IT OUT   Working with a Table

So far, you have created one simple report. Once a table has been added to your report, there are many customizations that can be made to it. In this Try It Out, you work in your existing report to improve its appearance. Some column widths and groupings are adjusted, and a logo is added to the top of the report.

1. In the browser, navigate to the Reports library that you used in the previous Try It Out.

2. Click the ellipsis next to the name of the Task Table, and then click the second ellipsis, as shown in Figure 10-43. Click Edit in Report Builder.

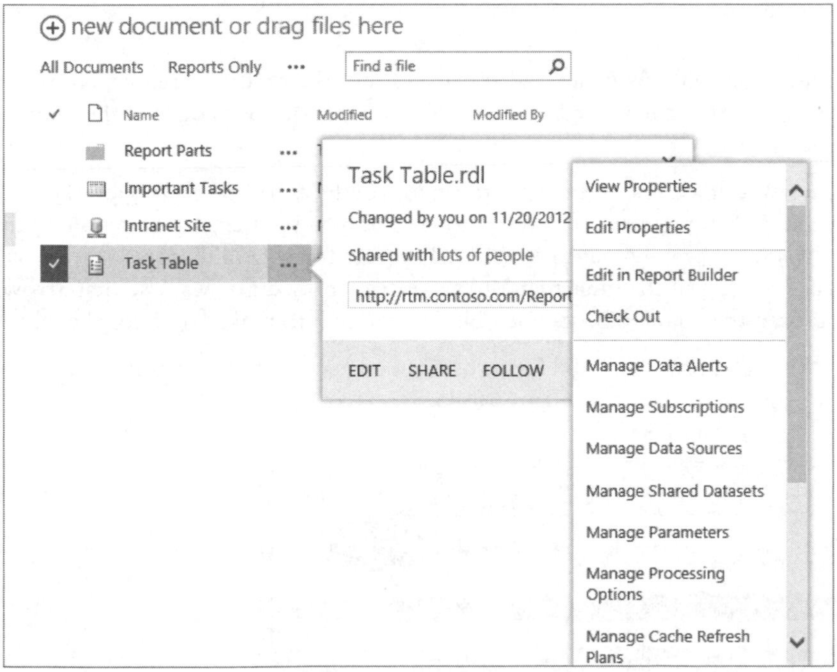

FIGURE 10-43

3. Click the Run button at the top left so that you can take a look at a few things that can be improved. Expand the priority sections to see what the report currently looks like. Click the Design button at the top left. Notice that the text is a bit too crowded.

4. Click the cursor inside of the table, such as in the Task Name column header. Gray boxes will appear around the table. Working with column widths is similar to working in Microsoft Excel. Drag the line between columns to widen the Task Name column.

5. Using the ruler at the top as a guide, drag the Task Name column to about 3.5 inches, and then drag the Task Status column to about the 5.5 mark, as shown in Figure 10-44.

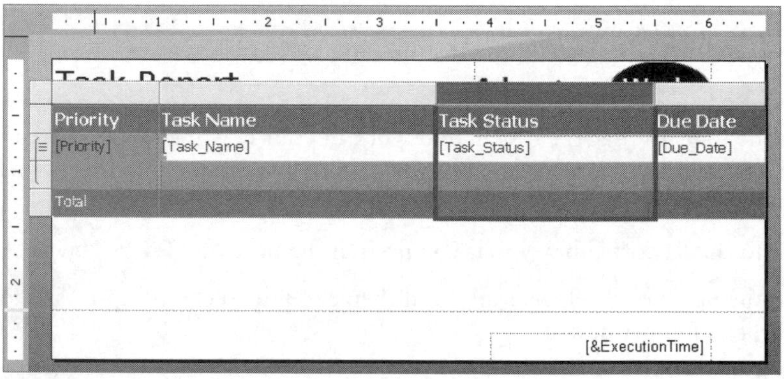

FIGURE 10-44

Notice that as you drag the columns wider, the whole width of the report increases, but the logo becomes hidden. Do not worry about the Due Date column yet; you focus on it in the "Functions" section later in this chapter.

6. To move the table down to make more room for the logo, you have to be able to grab the table and drag it down a bit. When you have the table selected and you see the gray boxes along the top and left, click the square gray box at the top left. The gray boxes will disappear, and you will see a small icon at the top left of the table that looks like crisscrossed arrows. Use that arrows icon to click on and drag the whole table down a bit, just enough to make room for the logo.

7. Click to select the "Task Report" title box. Drag the right edge of it so that it no longer overlaps with the logo. Your progress is shown in Figure 10-45.

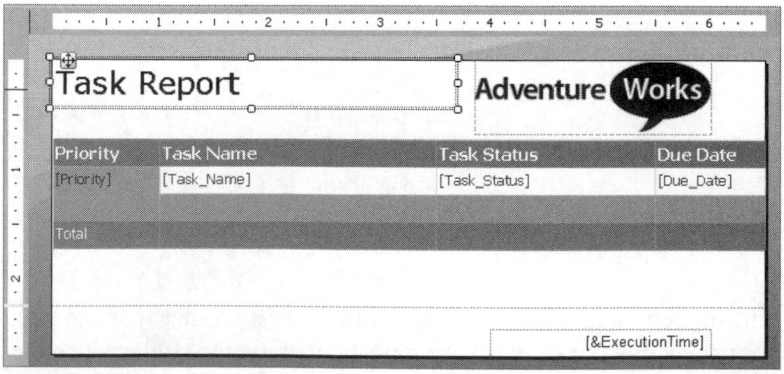

FIGURE 10-45

8. Now change the grouping so that the priority groups are expanded by default, instead of collapsed. At the bottom of the screen, in the Row Groups section, click the drop-down arrow next to the [Details] row, as shown in Figure 10-46, and select Group Properties.

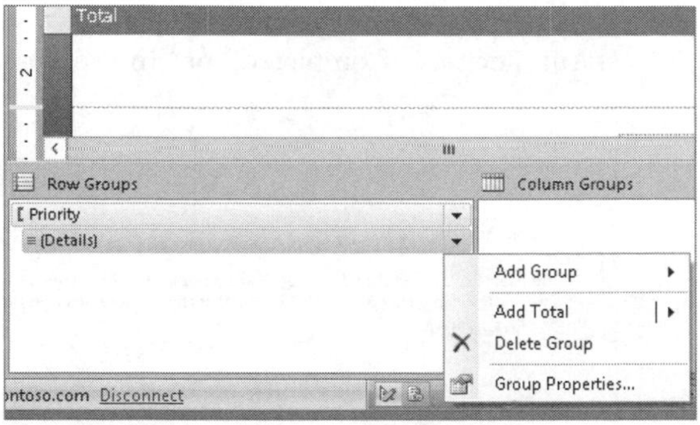

9. On the Group Properties screen, click Visibility on the left. Under "When the report is initially run," select Show. Click OK.

10. Click the Save button at the top left of the screen, and close Report Builder.

FIGURE 10-46

How It Works

When working in reports, you can drag each object around on the report and resize it as needed. When placing multiple tables and charts in a report, you can arrange and size them as necessary, so that they look neat on the page. Using the Insert tab, you can add new objects, such as images, gauges, and sparklines, to your report.

Charts

You can create many different types of charts in Report Builder: column, line, pie, bar, and area. The Chart Wizard walks you through all the steps of creating a chart. Charts can be on reports by themselves, or they can be added to existing reports to create the look and feel of a dashboard.

TRY IT OUT Creating a Chart

In this Try It Out, you create a chart. The goal is to display a pie chart that shows the statuses of all tasks that have not been completed yet.

1. In the browser, navigate to the Reports library that you used in the previous Try It Out.

2. On the Files tab in the ribbon, click the New Document drop-down and choose Report Builder Report.

3. With New Report selected on the left, click the Chart Wizard on the right.

4. In the "Choose an existing dataset in this report or a shared dataset" box, select the Important Tasks.rsd dataset that you used in earlier exercises. Click Next.

5. Click Pie. Click Next.

6. Drag the Task_Status field to the Series box. Drag the Task_Name field to the Values box.

7. Click the drop-down box next to the Task_Name field in the Values box. Select Count, as shown in Figure 10-47. Click Next.

Because you selected Count, the pie chart will represent the number of tasks that are at each status, such as "Completed" or "In Progress."

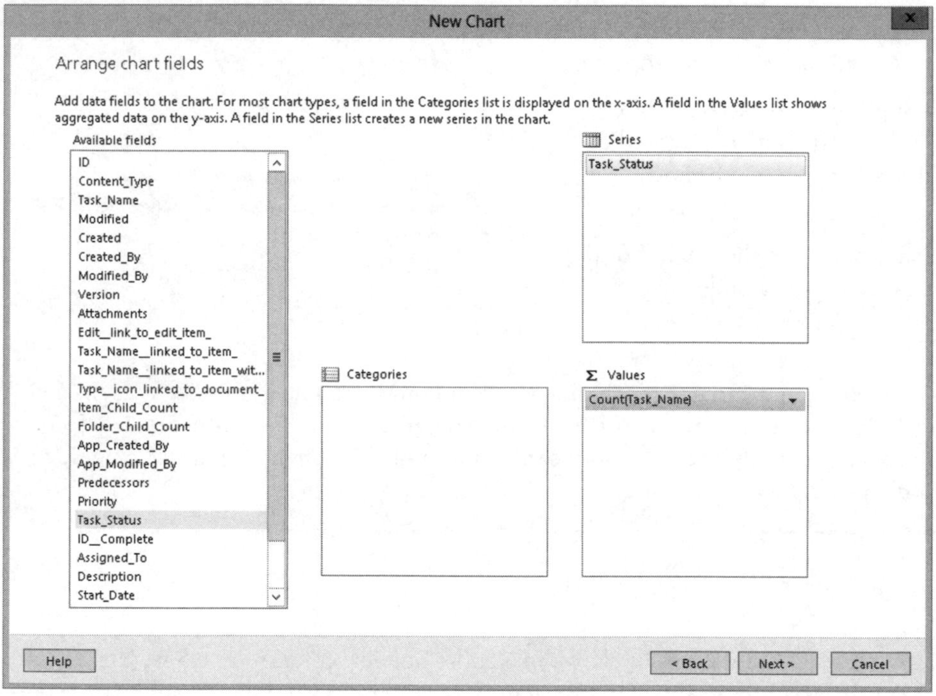

New Chart
Arrange chart fields
Add data fields to the chart. For most chart types, a field in the Categories list is displayed on the x-axis. A field in the Values list shows aggregated data on the y-axis. A field in the Series list creates a new series in the chart.
Available fields
ID
Content_Type
Task_Name
Modified
Created
Created_By
Modified_By
Version
Attachments
Edit__link_to_edit_item_
Task_Name__linked_to_item_
Task_Name__linked_to_item_wit...
Type__icon_linked_to_document_
Item_Child_Count
Folder_Child_Count
App_Created_By
App_Modified_By
Predecessors
Priority
Task_Status
ID__Complete
Assigned_To
Description
Start_Date
Series
Task_Status
Categories
Σ Values
Count(Task_Name)
Help
< Back
Next >
Cancel

FIGURE 10-47

8. On the "Choose a style" page, select the Mahogany style, and click Finish.
9. At the top-right corner, click the Run button to preview the report, as shown in Figure 10-48.
10. Click the Design button at the top left.
11. Right-click on the pie, and choose Show Data Labels. This displays the number of tasks inside of each piece of the pie.
12. Expand the Datasets folder on the left side of the screen in the Report Data pane. Right-click the ImportantTasks dataset and choose Dataset Properties.

Untitled
Run
Design
Zoom
First
Previous
of 1
Next
Last
Refresh
Stop
Back
Print
Page Setup
Print Layout
Views
Zoom
Navigation
Print
Chart Title
Completed
In Progress
Not Started
Waiting on som...
11/23/2012 9:37:48 AM

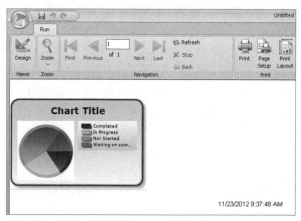

FIGURE 10-48

13. On the left side of the Dataset Properties screen, click the Filters button. Click the Add button.
14. For Expression, choose [Task_Status]. For Operator, choose <>. For the Value, type **Completed**, as shown in Figure 10-49. Click OK.

Now the data is filtered to show only the number of items that haven't been completed.

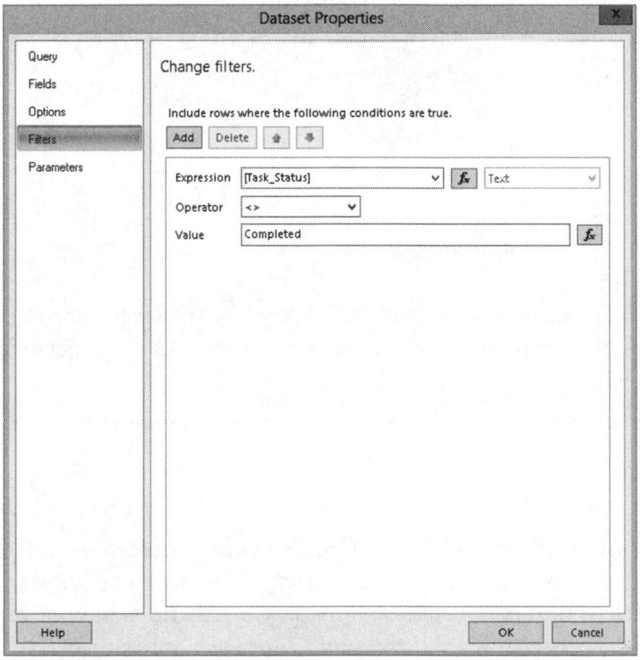

FIGURE 10-49

> **NOTE** *Data can be filtered on several different levels. When you create a shared dataset, the data can be filtered at that level. When working with large amounts of data, this is the most efficient place to apply the filter. Within the report that uses a shared dataset, the dataset can be filtered there also, as shown in the "Creating a Chart" Try It Out. Also, each element in a report can be filtered. For example, if your report contains a table and a chart, you can filter each differently. When you right-click a chart and choose Chart Properties, you see an area for creating filters: and when you right-click a table on the Tablix Properties screen, you see an area for creating filters as well.*

15. Double-click the black "Chart Title" to edit it. Rename it to say **Open Tasks**.

16. Select the outside edge of the red outline around the whole chart. Drag the edge to expand the chart to make it bigger. Drag it to about 4 inches wide by 3 inches high, using the ruler as a guide.

17. In the previous "Report Parts" section, you created two report parts. You insert one of them here. On the Insert tab, click Report Parts.

18. If you do not see any report parts in the Report Part Gallery on the right, type the word **adventure** in the search box and hit Enter. The AdventureWorks logo will show up. Drag the logo onto your report at the top right.

19. Click Run to preview the report. It should look like Figure 10-50.

20. Click the Save button at the top left, select the Reports folder, and name the file **Completed Task Status Chart.rdl**. Close Report Builder.

How It Works

In this Try It Out, you created a pie chart using the Chart Wizard. You can also edit existing charts in several places in Report Builder. In

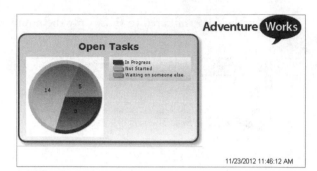

FIGURE 10-50

any chart, you can right-click the chart and select Series Properties. Right-click the legend for Legend Properties, and right-click the area around the chart to access Chart Area Properties. Settings exist in many places; simply right-click to find them.

Functions

Functions in Report Builder can be a powerful tool. If you are familiar with calculations in Excel, calculated columns in SharePoint, or functions in Microsoft Access, this is going to be an easy concept to understand. Functions enable you to create, use, and display calculations in your reports and data sources. You have hundreds to choose from, and the syntax for each one is displayed in an example box in the expression builder.

TRY IT OUT   **Creating a Function**

Functions can be created or displayed in countless places in reports. The example for this Try It Out is the due date field. Notice in the table that you created earlier, the due date is displayed as a long date and time field in the table. The goal is to show it as simply a date so that it will take up less space on the report. You have several places within the report to do this. The final place where you create the function is at the dataset level in the report.

1. In the browser, navigate to the Reports library that you used in the previous exercise and open the Task Table.rdl report in Report Builder, as described in previous exercises.

2. Right-click the [Due_Date] value field in the white part of the report (not the column header). Choose Expression.

This is the first place that you could add the expression to show the date only. However, in this case, this is not where you will add it.

3. Click Cancel.

4. Expand the Datasets folder on the left side of the screen in the Report Data pane. Right-click the ImportantTasks dataset, and choose Add Calculated Field. The Dataset Properties screen appears, as shown in Figure 10-51.

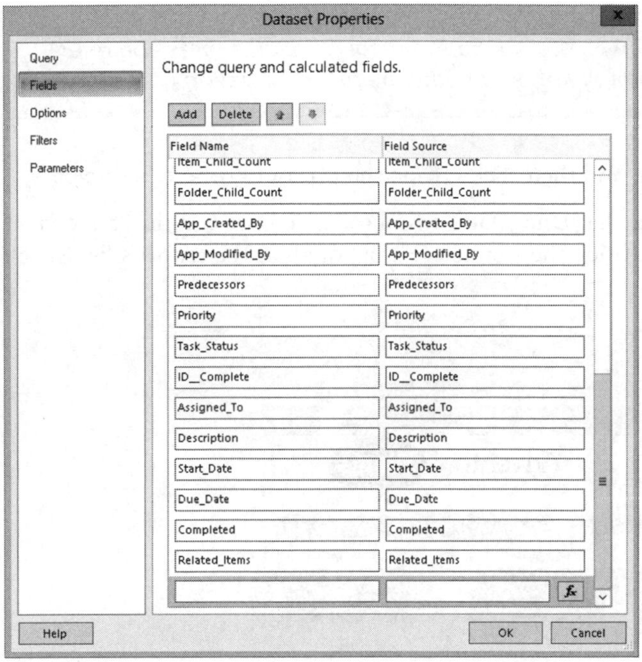

FIGURE 10-51

5. Notice that a new row has now been added to the bottom of the list of fields. In the Field Name column, type **DueDate_DateOnly** as the name of this new calculated field. Click the fx (function) button next to the Field Source box on the right.

6. In the expression builder, expand Common Functions on the left, and then select Date & Time. On the right, select FormatDateTime. Notice that the syntax is shown in the Example box. Double-click FormatDateTime to add it to your expression.

7. Type the following as your expression, as shown in Figure 10-52: **=FormatDateTime(Fields!Due_Date .Value,DateFormat.ShortDate)**.

The first part of the expression is where you select the field that you need to format. This is the due date field. The second part of the expression is the way you want the date formatted. In this case, we'll use the ShortDate.

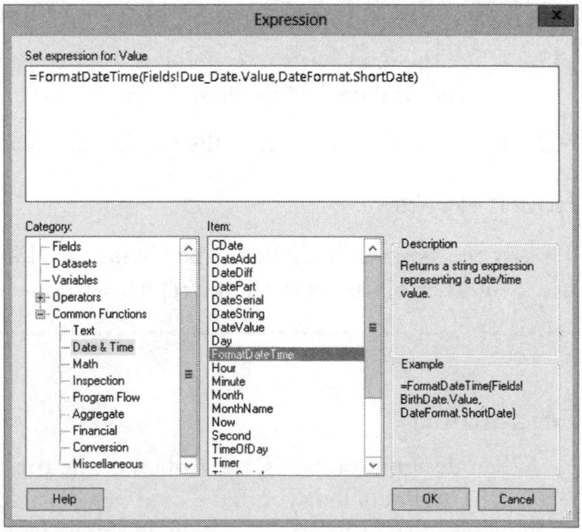

FIGURE 10-52

> **NOTE** *In Report Builder, when you use the F1 key for help, an expression reference is available, along with a plethora of other helpful information.*

8. Click OK on the Expression screen, and then click OK on the Dataset Properties screen.

9. On the report, when you hover over the [Due_Date] cell in the Due Date column, an icon appears, as shown in Figure 10-53. Click the icon to see a list of all of the report's fields. Select DueDate_DateOnly.

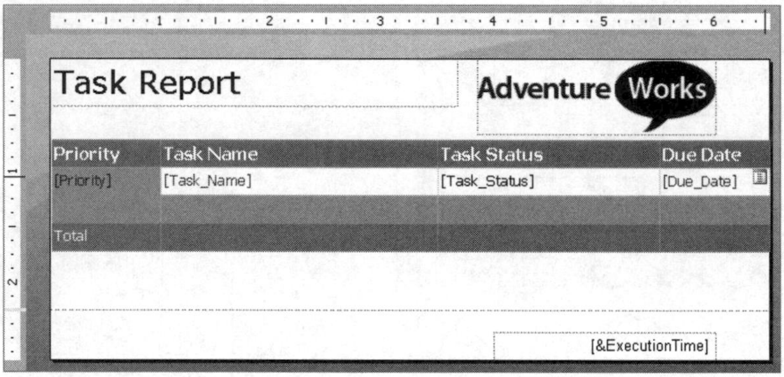

FIGURE 10-53

10. Notice that when you made this field change, a sum was automatically added to the two cells below the field. Delete these two sum formulas, because they are not necessary.

11. Click the Run button to preview. Notice that the Due Date column now shows only a date, instead of date and time.

12. Click the Save button at the top-left corner of Report Builder, and close Report Builder.

How It Works

This expression was created at the dataset level in the report so that if you need to use it again, you can use it in other places in the same report without having to re-create it.

Formatting

When designing reports, the ribbon at the top is the same familiar ribbon that exists in the Microsoft Office products that you have used before. Select any text or background in your report and use the buttons in the ribbon to quickly do things like change fonts, cell colors, borders, and much more.

When you used the report-creation wizard, there was a screen to select the style of the report, and different color schemes were available. Once a color scheme has been selected in the wizard and the report has been created, there is not a way to easily flip between color schemes again. If you need to change colors later, you can do so by selecting cells, rows, or columns and using the color and font options in the ribbon.

TRY IT OUT **Conditional Formatting**

In the Report Builder interface, changing fonts and colors is simple, just like editing in Word or Excel. However, there is a little trick to formatting items conditionally. In this Try It Out, you display a font in a certain color, based on the value of the field. For completed tasks, the word "Completed" is displayed in green.

1. In the browser, navigate to the Reports library that you used in the previous exercise and open the Task Table.rdl report in Report Builder.

2. Right-click the [Task_Status] box and choose Text Box Properties.

3. On the left, click Font. Next to the Color box, click the fx (function) button.

   It is time to create some conditional formatting so that if the status is equal to Completed, the text will show as green.

4. On the left, expand the Common Functions section and select Program Flow. Double-click IIf on the right, as shown in Figure 10-54.

   Notice that the proper syntax for each expression is shown on the right side of the screen as you select it, in the "Example" box.

FIGURE 10-54

5. On the Expression screen, type in the following expression, as shown in Figure 10-55:

   =IIf(Fields!Task_Status.Value="Completed", "DarkGreen","DimGray").

   You can simply type the expression in free form, or you can select fields, variables, and more from the Category box on the left. This expression states that if the status is completed, the text will show as dark green; otherwise, it will show as dim gray. Selecting the Constants category on the left enables you to select from the colors without having to know the names of them.

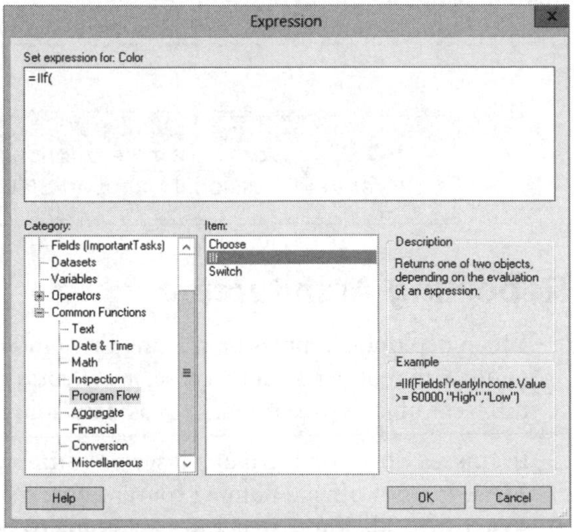

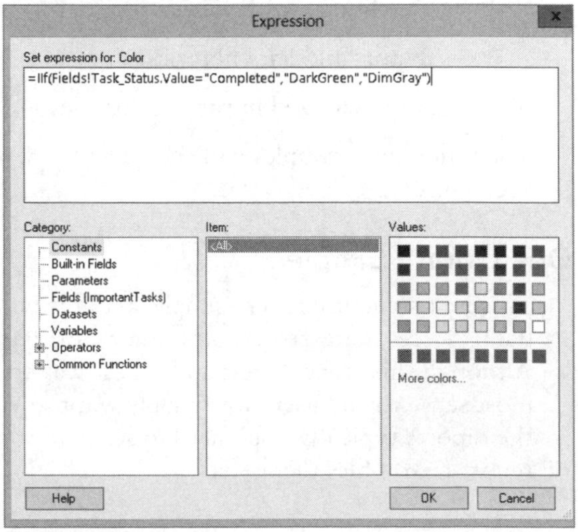

FIGURE 10-55

6. On the Expression screen, click OK. On the Text Box Properties screen, click OK.

7. Click Run to preview the report. Notice that the word "Completed" is shown in green in the task status column.

8. Save the report and close Report Builder.

How It Works

When you open the report again to view it, notice that all the completed tasks show the word "Completed" in green! Font colors are not the only thing that can be conditional. Backgrounds, font styles and sizes, borders, alignment, visibility, and many other components can be conditionally formatted using the IIf expression.

> **NOTE** *To learn a lot more about working with reports and reporting services, refer to* Professional Microsoft SQL Server 2012 Reporting Services *(Wrox, 2012).*

Reporting Architecture

When deploying reports or creating them in SharePoint, you can configure the architecture in many different ways. In this case, *architecture* refers to the way libraries are structured and where different objects are stored, such as data sources and reports.

In this section, you learn about several different methods of architecting your reporting structure. These are not official naming conventions; they are simply a descriptive way of referring to these structures. The three structures are going to be referred to as:

➤ One library simple

➤ One library with views

➤ Report and data libraries

➤ Parameterized in various libraries

The following examples will get you started, and once you try them out, you may think of even more!

One Library Simple

This first structure is very simple, and it is what you have worked with up to this point. All the data sources, datasets, reports, and report parts are created in one simple list within the library. Although this is the easiest and fastest way to architect it, this is not necessarily going to make the most sense to end users who simply want to view reports. End users who are simply consumers of the reports typically don't need to see data sources or datasets; they are just concerned with the report (.rdl) files themselves.

One Library with Views

Views in lists and libraries give you different ways of looking at the same set of information. Because reports have a specific file extension, it is easy to create a view that shows only reports and filters out all the other files, such as data sources. Views are also a great way to implement self-service reporting. For example, you could create a view called "My Reports" with the simple filter of "Created By" is equal to [Me]. This way, end users could create their own reports and see only their own in the list.

TRY IT OUT Creating a Library View

Your current library architecture uses the "one library simple" model. In this Try It Out, you create a new view in which only the reports are displayed. This displays a simple interface without the clutter of all the other file types that most users don't need to know about.

1. In the browser, navigate to the Reports library that you used in the previous exercise.

2. Go to the Library tab in the ribbon, and click the Create View button.

3. Click Standard View.

4. For the view name, type **Reports Only**. Scroll down to the Filter section, and in "Show the items when column" drop-down, choose the Type column. Underneath "Is equal to," type **rdl**, as shown in Figure 10-56. Click OK.

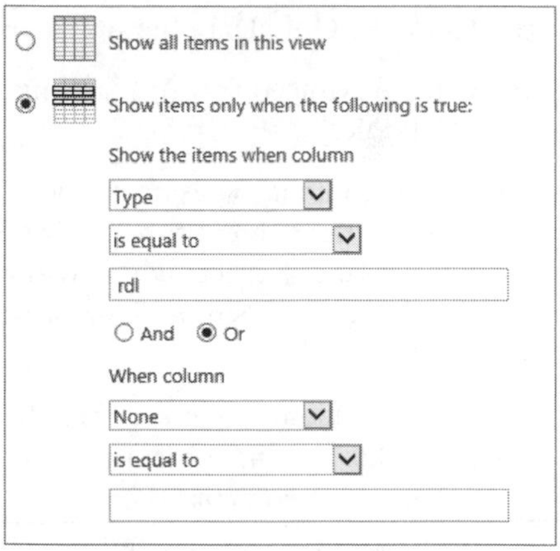

FIGURE 10-56

How It Works

Take a look at what is displayed in this new Reports Only view. Notice that only reports in your library are displayed, as shown in Figure 10-57. Also notice that you did not select the checkbox to make this the default view. In real-world scenarios, you may want to select this option so that end users are not initially presented with all the content in the library.

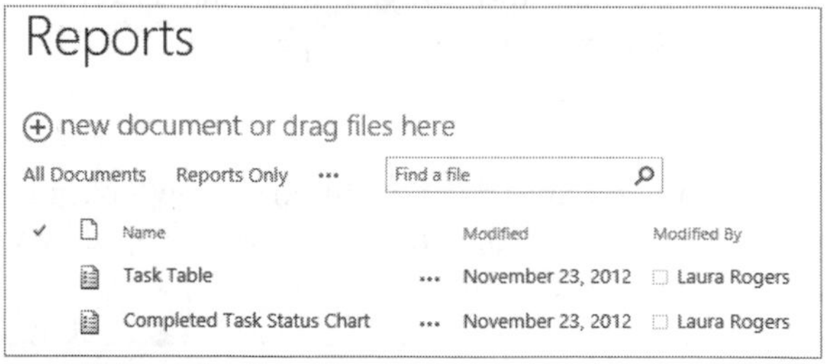

FIGURE 10-57

Report and Data Libraries

In this second model, different libraries are created for data and for reports. Instead of displaying reports in a separate view as in the previous model, reports are segregated into their own library. For security, different permissions and settings could be applied to the different libraries.

TRY IT OUT | **Creating Separate Libraries**

Your current library architecture uses the "one library simple" model. In this Try It Out, you create a new library just for data, and another new library just for reports. Content types play a role in separating these out, as you will see.

1. In the browser, click the Settings button in the top right, and choose "Add an app."

2. Choose Document Library, and for the name, type **Only Data**. Click Create.

3. In the browser, click the Settings button in the top right, and choose "Add an app."

4. Choose Document Library, and for the name, type **Only Reports**. Click Create.

5. Click the Only Data library to open it. On the Library tab in the ribbon, click Library Settings.

6. Click Advanced Settings, and under "Allow management of content types," choose Yes. Click OK.

7. In the Content Types area, click "Add from existing site content types." Double-click Report Data Source, which will move it to the right, as shown in Figure 10-58. Click OK.

8. In the Content Types section, click the name of the Document content type, and click "Delete this content type."

9. Click the Only Reports library to open it. On the Library tab in the ribbon, click Library Settings.

FIGURE 10-58

10. Repeat steps 6 through 8, this time selecting the Report Builder Report content type instead of the Report Data content type.

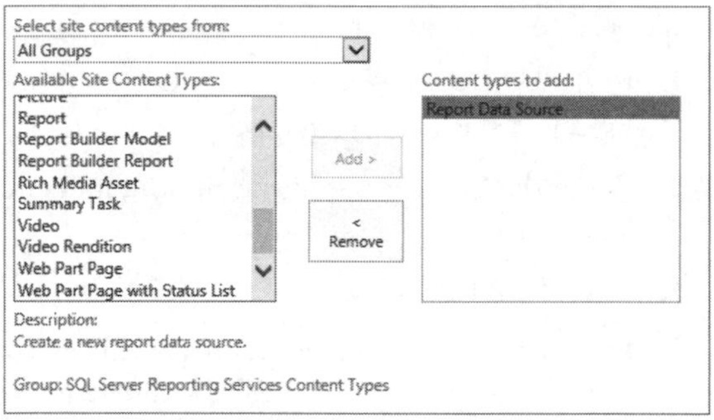

How It Works

When you look at each of the libraries you have just set up, go to the Files tab in the ribbon. Notice that when you click the New Document drop-down at the top left, it shows the name of the appropriate content type for that library.

Parameterized in Various Libraries

This third option is quite a bit more complex than the other ones. This is a great solution for reports in which only a small subset of data needs to be displayed. For example, if a report was needed that would display only the data pertinent to each of several departments, you have a couple of ways to go about it. One way would be to create a separate report for each department, in a library on each department's site. That is quite an efficient method, which leads me to introduce parameterized reports. What does this mean? In this example, the department field would be created as a parameter, which could then be used as a filter. A subscription can then be created, which can send a file to each department's respective site library on a schedule. This way, users see only the data pertinent to them, and the report creator only needs to create a single report.

REQUIRED EXECUTION ACCOUNT

In this section, you create report schedules and subscriptions in order to create parameterized reports. To use subscriptions in Reporting Services, an execution account needs to be set up on the server. This is a task that the server administrator will take care of. In Central Administration, under the Reporting Services service application, click the Execution Account setting, and type in an account and password of an administrator account that has access to all of the data that you will be reporting on.

TRY IT OUT Creating Parameterized Reports

In this Try It Out, you learn how to create a parameterized report. Although this is quite an advanced topic, it is a great skill to have under your belt when it comes to implementing reporting in your organization. You create a department field in your task list, and you create this field as a parameter. You also create two departmental sites. The report that displays tasks for each department will be deployed to each departmental sites' library. To keep it simple, you create this new report in the same Reports library that you have used since the beginning of this chapter.

1. In the browser, click the Settings button in the top right, and choose Site Contents.

2. Scroll down and click New Subsite. For the title, type **Human Resources**. For the URL name, type **hr**.

3. In the Navigation section, under "Display this site on the Quick Launch of the parent site," choose Yes. Under "Use the top link bar from the parent site," click Yes. Click Create.

4. Go back to the top-level site and repeat steps 2 and 3 to create a new subsite. For the title, enter **Information Technology**; for the URL, enter **it**.

   Each of your new subsites already has a document library called Documents, so that is where the parameterized reports will be deployed to. If you would like to go back and look at a previous day's versions of each report, you can turn on versioning for each library.

5. On the top-level site, navigate to your task list by clicking Important Tasks in the Quick Launch on the left. On the List tab in the ribbon, click Create Column.

6. For the column name, type **Department**. For the type, choose "Choice (menu to choose from)." In the box titled "Type each choice on a separate line," clear the box so that it is empty. Type **Human Resources**, hit the Enter key, and type **Information Technology**, as shown in Figure 10-59. Click OK.

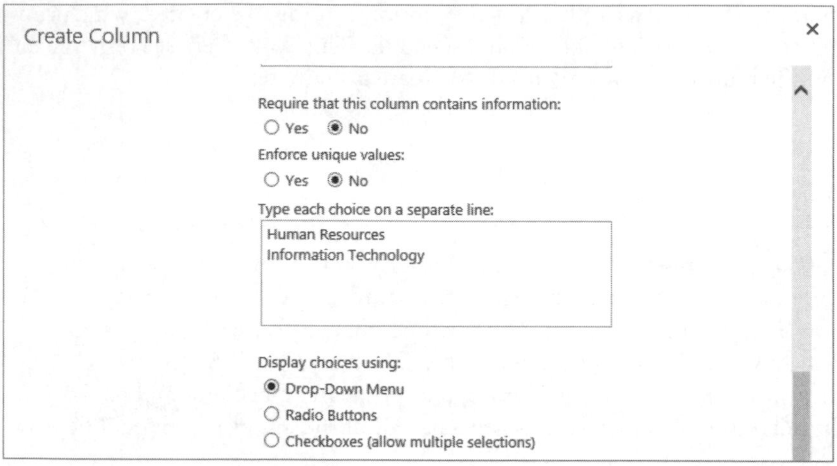

Create Column   ✕

Require that this column contains information:
○ Yes   ● No

Enforce unique values:
○ Yes   ● No

Type each choice on a separate line:

Human Resources
Information Technology

Display choices using:
● Drop-Down Menu
○ Radio Buttons
○ Checkboxes (allow multiple selections)

FIGURE 10-59

7. On the List tab in the ribbon, click the Quick Edit button.

8. In the Department column, fill in all of the cells so that each task has a department associated with it. Try to split it evenly between human resources and information technology. Remember that copy and paste works well in this quick edit view.

9. Go to the Reports library by clicking Reports in the Quick Launch on the left. On the Files tab in the ribbon, click the New Document drop-down and choose Report Builder Report.

10. On the left, select New Report. On the right, click Table or Matrix Wizard.

11. On the "Choose a dataset" screen, choose "Create a dataset" (instead of choosing an existing one). Click Next.

Remember that the previously created shared dataset was created before the "department" field was added, therefore it does not exist in that dataset. Instead of creating yet another shared dataset, you are saving time by quickly creating a dataset that will be embedded in this new report.

12. For the data source, select the `Intranet Site.rsds` file, and click Next.

13. Check the box next to the Important Tasks list on the left. Click Next.

14. Drag the following fields to the Values box: Task_Name, Priority, Task_Status, and Department. Click Next.

15. On the "Choose the layout" screen, click Next again. For the style, choose Forest and click Finish.

16. Right-click the Parameters folder on the left in the Report Data pane. Select Add Parameter.

17. For the Name, type **DepartmentParameter**, and for the Prompt, type **Department**, as shown in Figure 10-60. Click OK.

18. On the left, under the Datasets folder, right-click DataSet1. Choose Dataset Properties.

19. Click Filters on the left. For the expression, select the [Department] field. The operator is =, so leave that default. For the value, click the fx (function) button. Click Parameters on the left, and double-click the DepartmentParameter on the right to add it to the Expression box. Click OK. Click OK on the Dataset Properties screen, as shown in Figure 10-61.

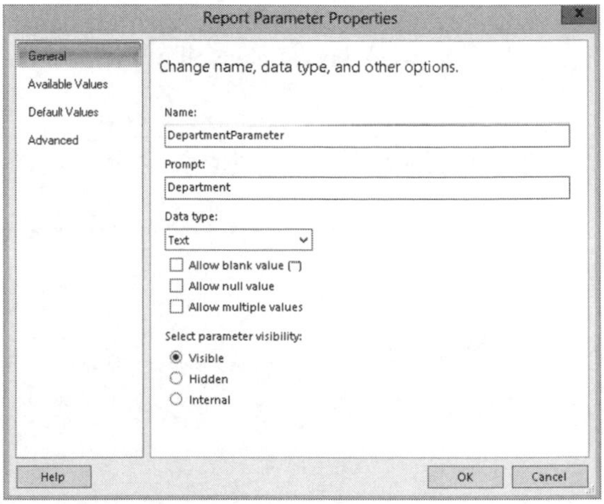

Report Parameter Properties

General

Available Values

Default Values

Advanced

Change name, data type, and other options.

Name:
DepartmentParameter

Prompt:
Department

Data type:
Text

☐ Allow blank value ("")
☐ Allow null value
☐ Allow multiple values

Select parameter visibility:
◉ Visible
○ Hidden
○ Internal

Help   OK   Cancel

FIGURE 10-60

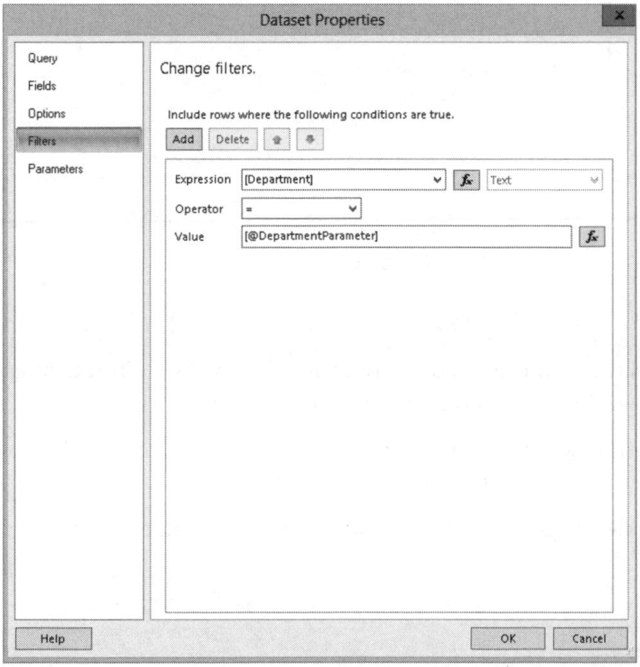

Dataset Properties

Query

Fields

Options

Filters

Parameters

Change filters.

Include rows where the following conditions are true.

Add   Delete   ⬆   ⬇

Expression [Department]   ▼   Text   ▼

Operator   =   ▼

Value   [@DepartmentParameter]   *fx*

Help   OK   Cancel

FIGURE 10-61

For the look and feel of the report, you are going to keep it super simple and not do anything with the formatting, because that was covered previously.

20. Click the Save button, select the Reports library, and name this report **Departmental Tasks.rdl**.

21. In the browser, click the Settings button at the top right of the SharePoint site. Choose Site Settings. In the Reporting Services section, click Manage Shared Schedules.

22. Click Add Schedule. For the schedule name, type **Daily**, and choose Day as the frequency. Select all of the weekdays. Leave all of the defaults, as shown in Figure 10-62, and click OK.

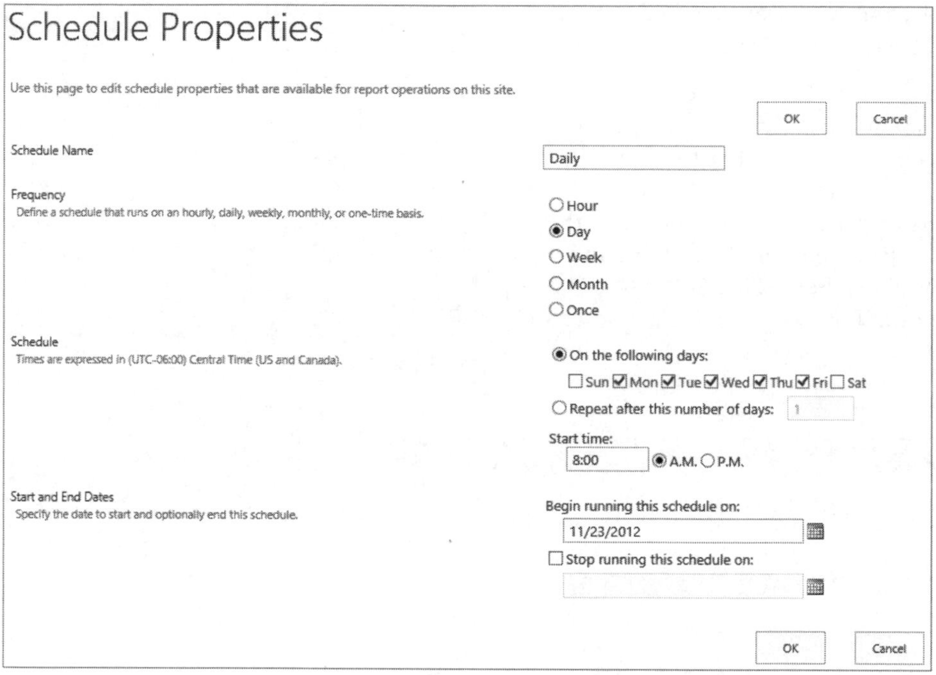

Schedule Properties

Use this page to edit schedule properties that are available for report operations on this site.

	OK	Cancel

Schedule Name

Daily

Frequency
Define a schedule that runs on an hourly, daily, weekly, monthly, or one-time basis.

- ○ Hour
- ● Day
- ○ Week
- ○ Month
- ○ Once

Schedule
Times are expressed in (UTC-06:00) Central Time (US and Canada).

● On the following days:
☐ Sun ☑ Mon ☑ Tue ☑ Wed ☑ Thu ☑ Fri ☐ Sat

○ Repeat after this number of days: 1

Start time:
8:00 ● A.M. ○ P.M.

Start and End Dates
Specify the date to start and optionally end this schedule.

Begin running this schedule on:
11/23/2012

☐ Stop running this schedule on:

	OK	Cancel

FIGURE 10-62

On this Manage Shared Schedules screen, you can add many different schedules. You can have varying schedules for hourly, daily, weekly, or monthly, with various settings.

23. Click your Reports library on the left. Click the ellipsis next to the new Departmental Tasks report, and then click the next ellipsis also. Choose Manage Subscriptions.

24. Click Add Subscription. Fill out the fields according to the following table, and click OK. This screen is shown in Figure 10-63.

FIELD	VALUE
Delivery Extension	SharePoint Document Library
Document Library	(browse to the URL of the Documents library in your new HR site), such as `http://team.contoso.com/hr/shared%20documents`
File Name	HR Tasks
Title	HR Tasks

Output Format	PDF
Overwrite Options	Overwrite existing file or create new version of file
Delivery Event	On a shared schedule: Daily
Parameters: Department	Human Resources

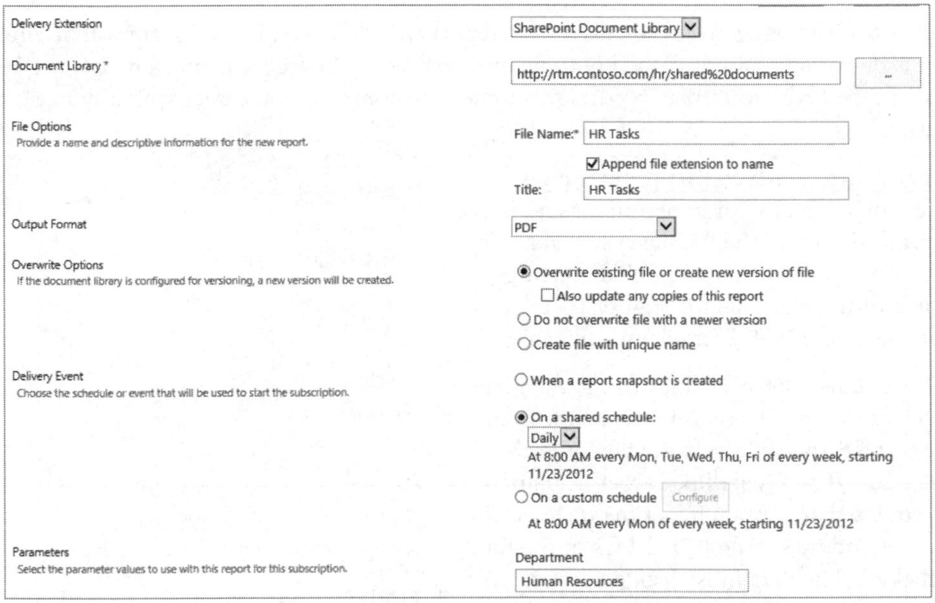

FIGURE 10-63

25. Click Add Subscription. You already added the HR report subscription, and now you will add the IT one. The document library URL will be to the IT site instead of HR, and the filename and title are both "IT Tasks." Most importantly, the department parameter is now "Information Technology."

How It Works

The next time the schedule report runs, which is 8AM by default, two different reports will be generated. You created a parameter and a filter by department on the report itself, and created a schedule for each of these department parameters. Each department site's library will have a new PDF file appear, which will be updated every morning at 8AM. Each department will only be able to see its own data. Think about the bigger picture here, of not just tasks, but enterprise data. One company-level report can be created and with parameters, it can become multiple reports every morning. With parameters you are saving a lot of time in report creation. One thing to remember, though, is that some of the report formats do not support the interactivity in the report, such as collapsing and expanding groups. For example, if a report with collapsed groups is created as a PDF file, the file will be flat with no ability to click and expand the groups. These reports are generated using the permissions of the execution account, so if that account does not have access to the data, such as the list, library, or database, the report will be blank.

Working with the Report Viewer Web Part

When it comes to displaying professional-looking reports to end users, it is important that vital information is delivered easily and quickly to people visiting the SharePoint site. The Report Viewer Web Part is a perfect way to display reports for immediate consumption directly on any page in your SharePoint site.

There are many different Web Part properties, and most of them correspond with something visual in the buttons that are shown in the Web Part's toolbar. In this section, you learn about the Web Part settings, and what each of them is used for. Figure 10-64 shows a portion of the Web Part settings screen.

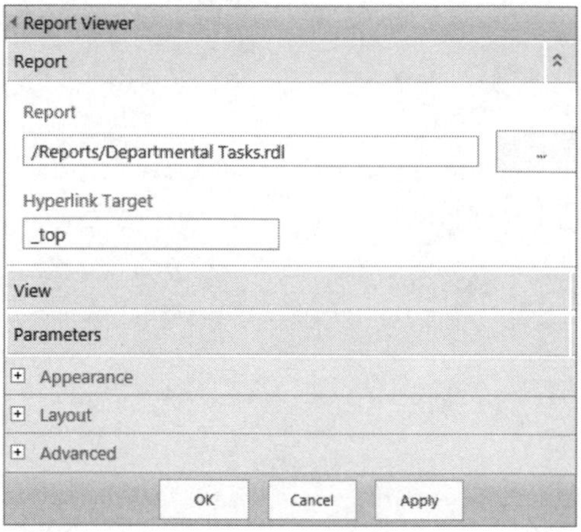

FIGURE 10-64

➤ **Report:** This section enables you to navigate to select the specific report that you would like to be displayed, from anywhere in the site collection. The Hyperlink Target field applies to reports that contain hyperlinks. Determine which window should be used when the link is clicked. The default is _top, which will open in the same window. Another commonly used target is _blank, which will open the link in a new window.

➤ **View:** The View section contains 19 different settings, mostly related to the way the report toolbar is displayed.

➤ **Parameters:** If a report contains parameters, you can click the Load Parameters button here. This enables you to either use the report's default value for the parameter, or to specify a new value. For example, this could be used with the parameterized department report you created. You could place this Web Part on the HR site and type "Human Resources" to override the report default (which is blank).

Figure 10-65 shows an example of a report displayed in the Report Viewer Web Part, with all of the options available in the View section of the Web Part settings.

Refresh button   Back button   Zoom control

Page navigation controls   Find controls   ATOM feed button

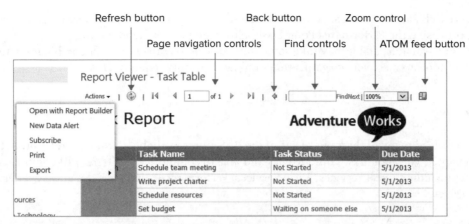

FIGURE 10-65

> **NOTE** *You can learn more about Web Parts in Chapter 7, "Working with Web Parts."*

IMPLEMENTING BUSINESS INTELLIGENCE IN YOUR ORGANIZATION

BI features are all powerful tools that, when combined, can be used to provide immediate, dynamic, and meaningful information to the users on demand. However, you have a few things to keep in mind as you move forward with the solutions you are building. This section covers some of the things that you should be thinking about as you begin to work with these tools.

Understanding the Organization

As you begin to look at the tools available and the information you want to present to the user, it is important to also look at the user. If you have been sending out an Excel document for five years and now you want to display it on the web page, what impact will that have on your users? It is very important that you consider this. You can build the best solution ever, but if users don't understand it, then it won't provide the value that you and they need. Be sure that you talk to your users to truly understand how they are currently working with the data and then formulate a plan that will empower them to do more with SharePoint.

Walking before You Run

Like with many things in SharePoint, BI is an area that has several levels of complexity. It is important that you understand each of these levels before you advance to the next one. This will keep you from over-customizing something when you could use the tools that are available out-of-the-box. To get started, you could work with the tools available out-of-the-box, such as the

Excel and Visio Web Parts, and, once you have explored those, you could build more custom and advanced reports using the PerformancePoint Dashboard Designer, or Report Builder 3.0. Many different tools are available, and it may take some time for you to realize the best combination and configuration of tools to meet your organization's unique reporting requirements.

SUMMARY

This chapter reviewed many of the key aspects of the BI features available within SharePoint. After reading this chapter, you should be familiar with and able to configure the different BI components within the site, including Excel Services, Visio Services, PerformancePoint Services, and SQL Server Reporting Services.

EXERCISES

1. Which site template comes preconfigured to support BI content?

2. True or false: In SharePoint, Excel Services content can be edited through the browser.

3. Which permission level would you need to apply so that users would be able to open only a snapshot of an Excel Services document?

4. Which file type do you have to save Visio files as so that they can be referenced in the Visio Services Web Part?

5. What is the easiest way to display only report (RDL) files in a document library that contains reports and data sources?

▶ WHAT YOU LEARNED IN THIS CHAPTER

TOPIC	KEY CONCEPTS
BI features	SharePoint has many features that provide the functionality to build dynamic, rich BI solutions, including Excel Services, Visio Services, PerformancePoint Services, and SQL Server Reporting Services.
Getting started with BI solutions	When getting started with building BI solutions, it is important to first understand all of the tools available. Once you have an understanding of the tools, you should evaluate your internal data to determine how the tools can be applied to your existing data. Whenever possible, take small steps to help ensure that you are getting the most benefit from the out-of-the-box tools.
SQL Reporting Services	Once an administrator has installed SSRS on your SharePoint Server, it is easy to get up and running creating your own professional reports, as long as you understand the basics of data sources, datasets and reports.
Visio Services	Visio Services provides much more than the simple ability to view Visio diagrams in the browser. You can do quite a lot with the Visio Web Access Web Part and Web Part connections.

11

Working with Social Features

WHAT YOU WILL LEARN IN THIS CHAPTER:

➤ Some concepts regarding personalization and social networking, as well as how they can be beneficial in an organization

➤ Examples of SharePoint My Sites functionality

➤ The concepts of tagging, note boards, and ratings, as well as the new out-of-the-box Web Parts related to personalization features

➤ The capabilities of blogs and wikis

➤ Targeting content to audiences, including the kinds of content that can be targeted, as well as how existing groups can be used as audiences

The term *Web 2.0* represents a fundamental change in the Internet in the past 10 years or so, in the way we interact with applications, content, and other people. The web is now a platform for promoting a collective intelligence, and so is SharePoint 2013. The new methods of content creation and participation, such as communities, tagging, and ratings, involve everyone in the enterprise in deeper and more meaningful ways.

In this chapter, you learn how to make the most of the social networking tools that exist in SharePoint and how they apply to you. This chapter also provides several walk-through scenarios for you to try out.

PERSONALIZATION OVERVIEW

Personalization and social networking tools are powerful things to put in the hands of business users. This chapter contains information related to how to work with the new social computing features, but before we get into the technical details, what is the big picture? In the grand scheme of things, what does Web 2.0 and social computing/networking mean to the company?

Engage People

Inherently, SharePoint is a collaboration platform. You are not simply feeding read-only information to people, you are giving them their own locations to upload and edit team and project documents and much more. Engaging employees in SharePoint has been taken to a new level in SharePoint 2013. Discussions, tags, and ratings can now be quickly added to content, which allows people to know that they have a hand in the creation and categorization of it. Individuals are now helping the online community in the organization by specifying which content they think has the greatest relevance and value.

Improve the Search Experience

Searching helps us find people and aggregate information. The rich and interactive search experience in SharePoint creates an environment in which people can find and engage each other. When participation is encouraged, this actually improves search results, because the tags and ratings have an effect on the search result ranking of the contents. Information workers typically spend a large part of their day searching for content. Getting the business community involved in tagging shortens the amount of time that is spent searching, thus increasing company efficiency and productivity.

Knowledge Mining

Knowledge mining is the concept of using the tags inside user profiles to mine for areas of expertise in the organization. People are encouraged to fill out their own profile information with their skills and interests, which makes experts easier to find. For example, if a manager would like to put together a team for a new project to create a company policy system, a people search for "policies" would provide a list of potential additions to the team.

The Informal Organization

In social computing, there's an organic element of self-organization, also known as a *user-generated taxonomy*, or *folksonomy*. This transcends the traditional organizational hierarchy. This informal organization lacks the rigidity of an ineffective, management-imposed organizational tree. When people in the organization come to an understanding as to the power of the social computing tools in SharePoint 2013, they will realize how much their contributions as individuals have shaped the collective information.

UNDERSTANDING MY SITES

When My Sites have been set up, each user in the organization gets his or her own landing page of SharePoint goings-on. This hub is where a list of the recent activities of colleagues is displayed. Users can update their own personal information and store personal or shared files. Your My Site consists of About Me, SkyDrive Pro, your newsfeed, and Sites.

About Me

The About Me page is where other people can read all about you. This page contains information about skills, projects you've worked on, ways to contact you, and a list of what you've been doing in SharePoint. Figure 11-1 shows the main page of About Me.

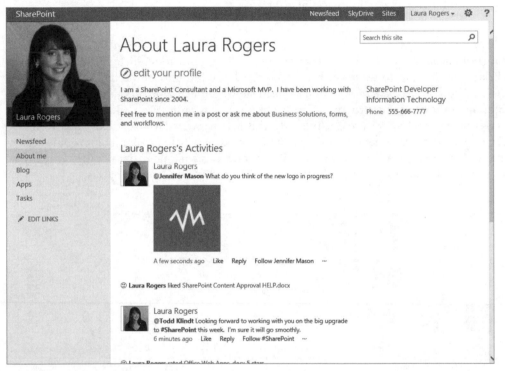

FIGURE 11-1

In the preceding figure, when Laura Rogers views her own profile, this is what she sees. The right side of the page contains basic information about how she can be contacted. SharePoint 2013 now contains an interactive newsfeed of activities, also known as *microblogging*. This same microblogging concept may be familiar to you as *Status updates* on Facebook, and as *tweets* on Twitter.

The following sections describe what you see when viewing someone's profile besides your own.

About a Person

Text describing the person is displayed, along with some links to quickly mention that person in a discussion, or ask her about her interests. Using these links is similar to writing on someone's wall on Facebook or mentioning them on Twitter.

Activities

This is a list of the most recent activities in SharePoint. Each activity contains a link to the item, such as a document that was tagged or rated.

➤ **Tags and Notes:** Click See All to take a look at items that the person has tagged recently and notes that he or she has made on note boards throughout SharePoint.

➤ **In Common:** This section displays who you have in common with that person. The first manager that you both share is displayed, as well as colleagues that you both know and the memberships that you both share. Click See All to see a full list of the people that the person follows and who follows him or her.

Org Chart

The organization chart is a very simple, text version of the organization, including names and job titles. Click anyone's name to see his or her profile. Click See More to view a dynamic Silverlight application called the *Organization Browser*, which shows a much more graphical and visual representation of the company structure. The structure itself is built automatically, based on the Manager field in each user's profile. Typically, this field is carried over to SharePoint from Active Directory (or other directory services), and is a read-only field in SharePoint profiles. The information in this organizational tree is only as accurate as the manager data in the company's directory. Figure 11-2 shows the Organization Browser, centered on Laura Rogers.

FIGURE 11-2

Tags and Notes

Click See All to take a look at items that the person has tagged recently and notes that he or she has made on note boards throughout SharePoint. Your social activities within SharePoint are logged and listed on the Tags and Notes page. Others who are interested in your work can take a look at what you have done to participate in the tagging of information, and they can see your opinions as note board notes. Each person uses this page to manage his or her own tags and notes. When viewing your own Tags and Notes tab, you will see that each item has a Delete button next to it, and you also have the ability to switch public items to private. Private items are visible only to you. Figure 11-3 shows this page as it appears to you when visiting someone else's My Site.

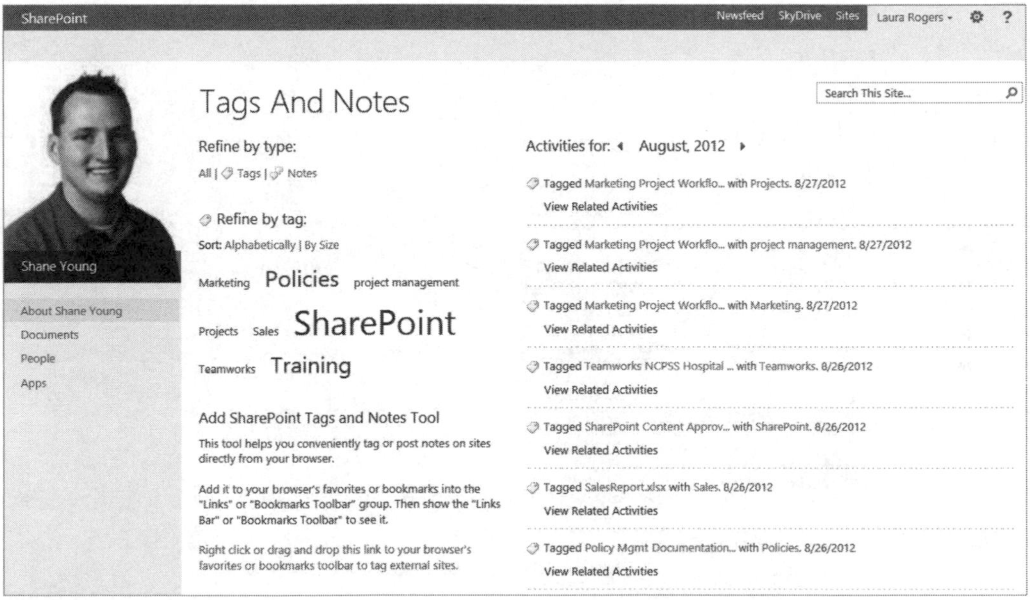

FIGURE 11-3

Narrow down the view of activities on the right by clicking the refinement links on the left. You can refine by type, such as tags or notes, and even refine by the tags themselves. A tag cloud displays all the tags that the person has used.

There is also a section called Add SharePoint Tags and Notes Tool. This tool provides a way to tag other Internet content that is not in SharePoint, and the instructions for using it are listed on the page.

> **NOTE** It is important to note that all tags and notes are ultimately managed by the SharePoint administrator, from Central Administration. In the User Profile service application, the administrator can perform searches by type, user, URL, date range, or keywords on the Manage Social Tags and Notes screen. The administrator can delete any content considered inappropriate.

Edit My Profile

Profiles tell a lot about people, and their skills and interests. Individuals can edit their profile, and are encouraged to be thorough when it comes to Ask Me About, Projects, and Skills. Filling out a profile accurately is helpful when it comes to knowledge mining, so that when someone is searching for an expert, the right people will be found.

Figure 11-4 shows the top portion of Basic Information about Todd Klindt.

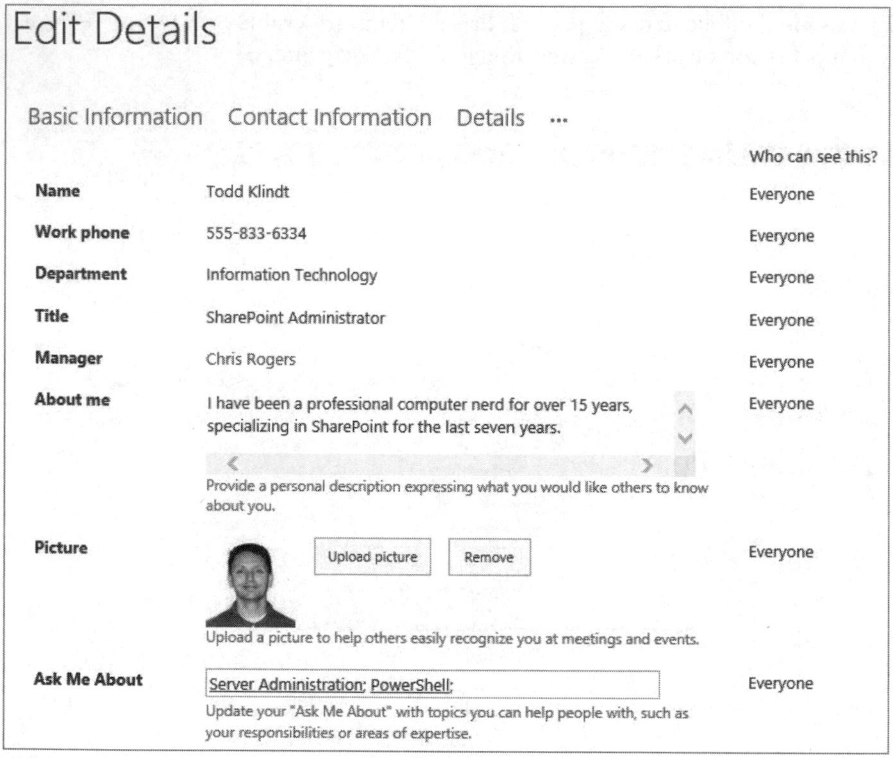

FIGURE 11-4

Some of the fields on the profile are editable, and some are not. These are called profile properties and are set up in Central Administration by the administrator. The "Who can see this?" column is displayed down the right side of the page, and indicates who can see which information. Some of the options in this column are editable, and some are not.

Click the cursor inside of the About Me box to see the Format Text tab of the contextual ribbon. The display of the information in this box can be customized to be more eye-catching, with font colors and sizes and the ability to edit the HTML code.

The Ask Me About information is an important part of making people findable in the organization. This is a list of proficiencies, and they are also tags that auto-fill as they are typed. The keywords typed here are displayed on the public profile, at the top of a Todd's About Me page.

The Contact Information tab of the profile lists the different methods by which Todd can be contacted. This screen can look different from organization to organization, because the SharePoint administrator configures the settings that determine which fields are read-only, required, or hidden. Notice that in the "Who can see this?" column, some items have drop-down boxes, whereas other items are static. This, too, is determined at the server level. Choose to either show a property to everyone or only yourself. Figure 11-5 shows an example of the Contact Information section. Todd has decided that only he can see his home phone number, and everyone in the company can take a look at all the other properties.

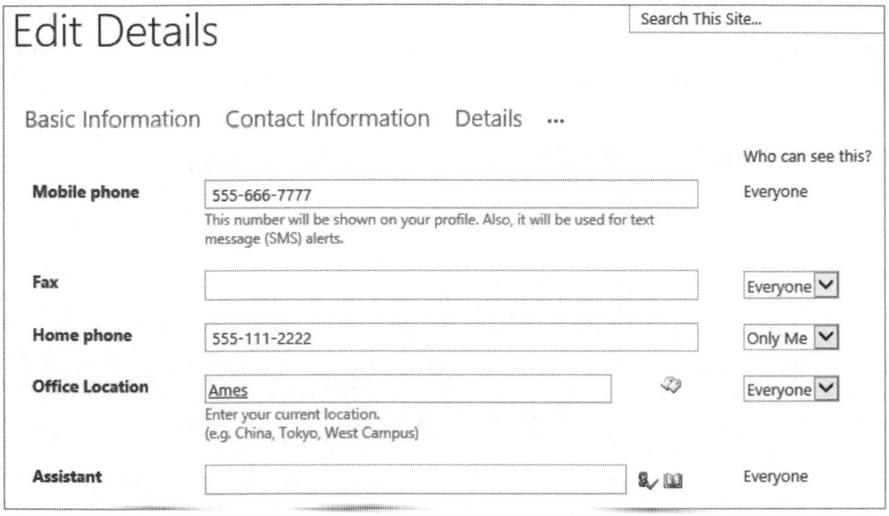

FIGURE 11-5

All the information that people share in profiles becomes part of SharePoint's searchable information. Social tags are covered in detail later in this chapter, but it is important to understand that each of the words that appear as underlined are tags. These keywords are stored in a database in SharePoint, so that any other type of item in SharePoint that has been tagged with one of these words is now in a sense *related* to this individual profile. This all ties back to the concept of SharePoint 2013 as an organic and dynamic platform in the organization.

To the right of the Contact Information tab is a Details tab, and then an ellipsis (three dots) button. Click the ellipsis to see a menu of more options. When you select Newsfeed Settings, there is a list of checkboxes within sections called Email Notifications and "Activities I want to share in my newsfeed." The e-mail notification options allow for granularly deciding what kinds of social activities you would like to receive e-mail notifications about. The "Activities I want to share in my newsfeed" checkboxes are options to narrow down the types of activities that you will share in your newsfeed. There is also a checkbox for "People I follow," a setting that allows others to see your follower information.

> **NOTE** *For the purpose of this chapter, most of the examples that have worked through will occur at the site level and on personal My Sites. If, after working through the chapter's activities, you are still looking for more in-depth administrative knowledge, refer to* Professional SharePoint 2013 Administration.

SkyDrive

Each user gets a personal site collection that contains a document library called Documents, which is referred to as *SkyDrive Pro*. You can quickly access this library via the toolbar at the top of any SharePoint site.

A new functionality exists in document libraries in SharePoint 2013. Libraries can be synchronized so that the files are available offline. At the top right of every SharePoint 2013 site is a Sync button that is used to initially start the offline sync of any library (see Figure 11-6).

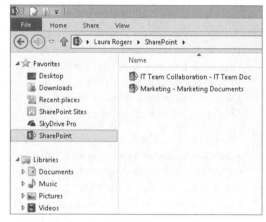

FIGURE 11-6

For SkyDrive Pro to work, it is optimal to have Microsoft Office 2013 installed. A new location will be created, which can be used in Office application, to quickly open or save SharePoint files. Your own SkyDrive is listed as SkyDrive Pro, and any other SharePoint libraries that you synchronize are listed under SharePoint. Figure 11-7 shows a view of Windows Explorer on a workstation, where the sync folders have been created by clicking the Sync button in SharePoint.

My Documents

The purpose of the document library known as SkyDrive Pro is to keep your own files and have the ability to access them from anywhere at any time. Notice that there is a folder called Shared with Everyone. By default, you can upload your personal files into this library, and if you would like to share other files with everyone, you can upload those into the Shared with Everyone folder.

FIGURE 11-7

> **NOTE** *For more information about sharing files, refer to Chapter 9, "Managing Permissions."*

Followed Documents

In SharePoint 2013, in every site, each file in a library has a button called Follow. The idea is to follow the files that are most important to you, and files that you work on the most. On the

SkyDrive page, click Followed Documents on the left to see a list of all the documents that you are following. To un-follow a document, click the star icon next to it.

Newsfeeds

Each person's newsfeed is their own stream of activities that they are following. These are things that are going on with people and topics that are of interest to the individual. Figure 11-8 shows an example of a newsfeed.

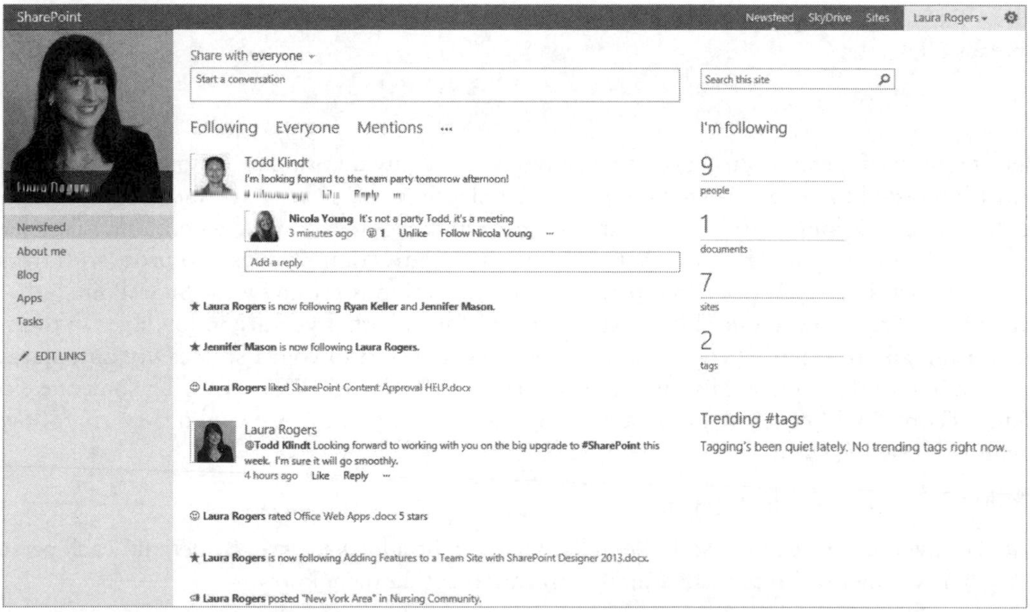

FIGURE 11-8

There is a lot going on in the newsfeed, and there is a lot more interactivity now than there was in the previous version of SharePoint. What used to be referred to as a one-way status update is now considered a "conversation." Here are some points to know about conversations:

➤ Conversations can be started by anyone.

➤ When starting a new conversation, select whether to share it with everyone, or with any site that you are following.

➤ When a conversation is shared with a site, it is posted in that site's newsfeed.

➤ Images and hyperlinks can be included in a conversation.

➤ To mention a specific person, type an @ symbol and then start typing his or her name.

➤ To mention a tag (also referred to as a *hashtag*), type a # symbol followed by that word.

➤ Reply to or "Like" any conversation in the newsfeed.

➤ Click the ellipsis (three dots) next to the Reply button, which brings up another menu with a Follow up option.

➤ Click Follow up to create a task for yourself to follow up with that conversation.

➤ Several site templates have newsfeeds. For example, each team site has its own newsfeed. This is where conversations about the site can be held.

At the top of the list of activities, click Everyone to see all activities, and click Mentions to see all the times that you have been personally mentioned in conversations. Also on the Newsfeed page, notice the nice summary information on the right side of the screen, called "I'm following." This area lists the number of people, documents, sites, and tags that you are following. Each of these numbers is clickable.

People

In SharePoint, each person can choose to "follow" other individuals. SharePoint assumes that you are most interested in people whom you work most closely with, so they are automatically added to the list of people you are following. Direct reports and people who have a common manager will already be on the list. This information comes into SharePoint profiles and properties from a directory service such as Active Directory, and the connection is set up by the SharePoint administrator. From the newsfeed, click the number of people that you are following. On this page, you can add or remove people manually. Adding a person to your list does *not* automatically add your name to that person's list of people he or she is following. When viewing someone else's My Site, "People" will be a link in the left navigation so that you can view who they are following and who is following them.

The following options are on this page:

➤ **Follow multiple people:** Multiple individuals can be added at once. By default, each person that is added will receive an e-mail notification letting them know.

➤ **Stop following people:** Click the ellipsis button next to a person, and click the Stop Following button.

➤ **Mention someone:** Click the ellipsis button next to a person, and click Mention to write a new discussion with that person's name in it.

➤ **See Followers:** To see a list of the people who are following you, click "My followers."

TRY IT OUT **Following Someone**

In this Try It Out, you pick someone in your organization whom you are not already following, and add him or her to the list. In the example's screenshots, the logged-in user is Randy Drisgill, and he would like to add John Ross as one of his colleagues. John is a SharePoint Consultant, and Randy would like to bring in more SharePoint expertise on a project he is working on.

1. On your homepage, click Newsfeed at the top of the page.

2. In the "I'm following" section on the right, click the number of people you are following.

3. Click the Follow button with the star next to it.

4. Type the name of the person that you would like to follow. (You can type more than one name here.) Figure 11-9 shows an example of this screen.

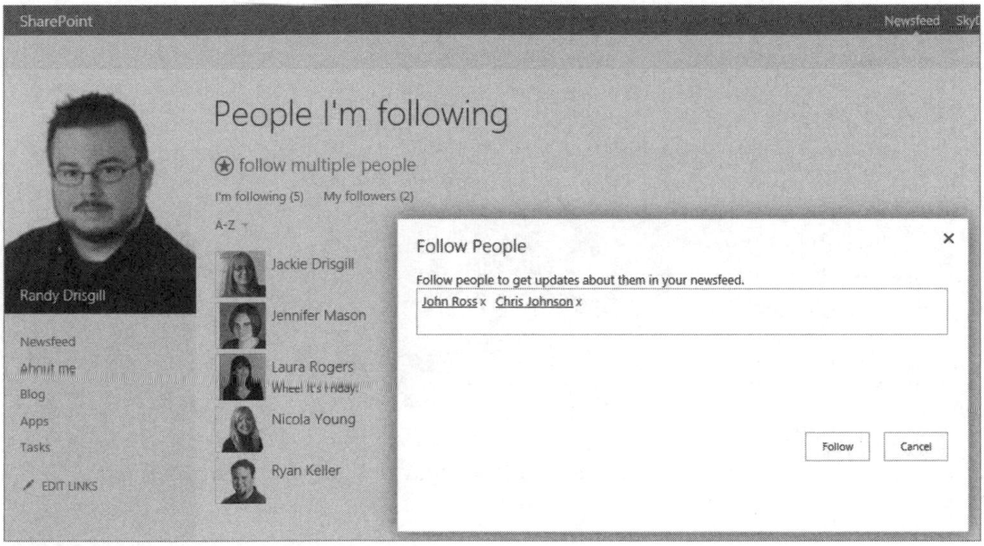

FIGURE 11-9

5. Click Follow.

How It Works

The new addition is now displayed in the list of colleagues. Click "My followers" to see who is following you, in case you would like to follow any of them back. How do you know if others can see your information about following/followers? When editing your profile, there is a section called "People I follow." The default setting is to allow others to see the people you are following and the people following you when they view your profile.

Tasks

Tasks is a new link on the left side, on the newsfeed page. Tasks are a familiar concept. They've been around in Outlook and in SharePoint for years. Tasks get assigned to people, and those people are supposed to complete their tasks. In the past, tasks have been spread out in different places, with it being up to the end users to remember what sites they are on, or synchronize them with their own Outlook clients.

Now in SharePoint 2013, all your assigned tasks are rolled up from *everywhere* in SharePoint, and displayed on this Tasks page. Figure 11-10 shows an example of a tasks page. The personal tasks are your own personal list of tasks. These tasks can only be assigned to you. Other than the personal tasks, the rest of the page contains tasks assigned to you, rolled up from various sites, grouped by the name of the site.

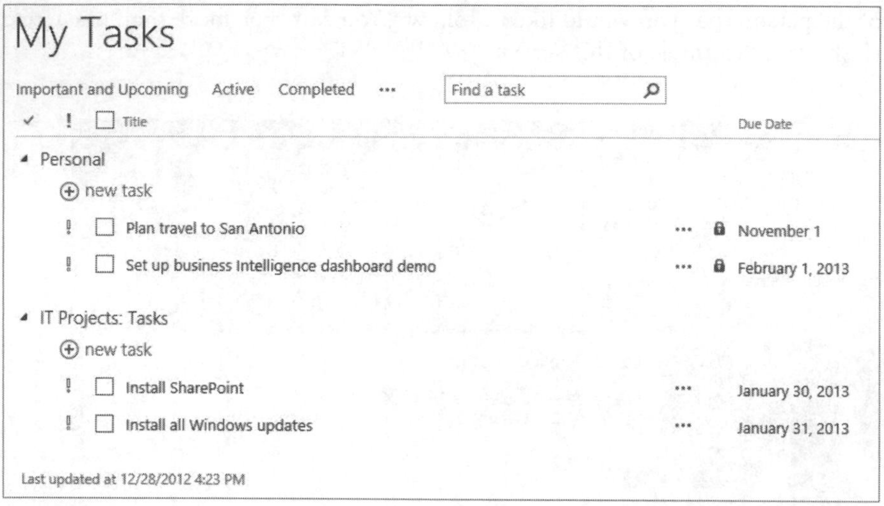

My Tasks

Important and Upcoming   Active   Completed   ⋯   Find a task   🔍

✓	!	☐ Title			Due Date
▲ Personal					
	⊕ new task				
	!	☐ Plan travel to San Antonio	⋯	🔒	November 1
	!	☐ Set up business Intelligence dashboard demo	⋯	🔒	February 1, 2013
▲ IT Projects: Tasks					
	⊕ new task				
	!	☐ Install SharePoint	⋯		January 30, 2013
	!	☐ Install all Windows updates	⋯		January 31, 2013

Last updated at 12/28/2012 4:23 PM

FIGURE 11-10

Click Important and Upcoming to see a graphical calendar timeline of your tasks.

Blog

The first time you click the Blog link on your own My Site, a new blog subsite is created automatically. This is your own personal blog. The Blog Tools section on the right contains the links you'll need to create and manage posts and comments. When viewing someone else's My Site, the Blog link will not show if they have not created their blog yet.

Apps

Each person's My Site can contain libraries and lists, just like any other SharePoint site. The Apps link is the same as clicking Site Contents on any other site. You can create and view the content in your own site, such as lists, libraries, and subsites.

Sites

This new page is perfect for following favorite SharePoint sites. Sites is a personal list that each user owns and manages. This section covers tasks like following sites, and information about places where this list can be found.

TRY IT OUT   Following Sites

In this Try It Out, you learn how to add favorite sites to your own personal Sites page. The goal is to make the sites that you do the most collaboration in readily available.

1. Create a site called **IT Team Collaboration**. This site is used by the information technology department.

2. Click the Follow button at the top-right corner of the site, as shown in Figure 11-11.

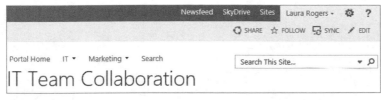

FIGURE 11-11

3. Click the Sites link at the top of the page.

4. Notice that the IT Team Collaboration site is now listed in the "Sites I'm following" section, shown in Figure 11-12.

5. Click the "Stop following" link under the IT Team Collaboration site to stop following it. The next time the Sites page is refreshed, this site will no longer be listed.

How It Works

You have now seen how to follow and stop following colleagues in SharePoint 2013. Your newsfeed will now automatically be populated with the activities of the people that you are following. The newsfeed is a good place to start in the morning, to see what's going on with your colleagues each day.

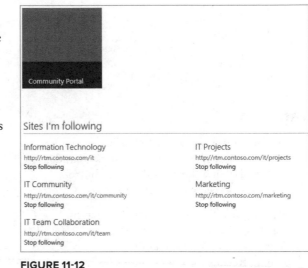

FIGURE 11-12

> **NOTE** *Notice in Figure 11-12 that the Community Portal is a larger button than all the others under "Sites I'm following." This Community Portal site was not followed by the individual but was pushed out from the server to all users who were in a certain audience. See the "Promoted Sites" section later in this chapter.*

TAGGING AND NOTE BOARDS

To tag objects in SharePoint is to assign keywords to them. The tags that are associated with any given item allow it to be found more readily when people in the organization perform searches that contain that tag. Note boards are areas where public comments can be posted about any given item. Participating in tagging and note boards is part of being an active member of the online community in your organization. In SharePoint 2013, everyone who visits the sites is encouraged to tag and make notes, which makes the experience organic and dynamic. Figure 11-13 shows the button that is used.

FIGURE 11-13

Where can you add tags and notes? Pretty much everywhere! The following is a list of some of the objects that you can tag.

➤ Pages

➤ Lists and Libraries

➤ Documents

➤ List Items

➤ Blogs

➤ Wikis

➤ Images

➤ Tag profiles

Tagging

This section describes the tagging interface, as well as how tags are used and managed. Click the Tags & Notes button to see the screen shown in Figure 11-14.

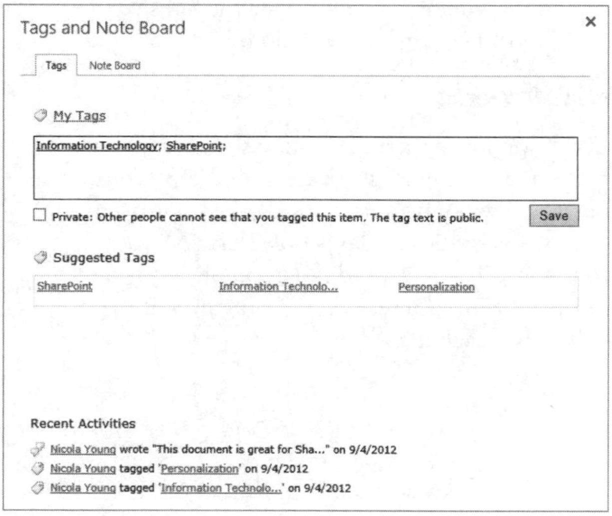

My Tags is a list of tags that the current user has added, and below it the Suggested Tags have already been added by other people. Recent Activities shows both tags and notes on the current item. Anyone can click the Private checkbox to set their own tags on that item to be visible only to themselves. When you add a new tag, click the Save button.

Any of the items in the Suggested Tags can be clicked to take further action. If that tag has not already been added to My Tags, there is an option to Add to My Tags. Each tag also has a tag profile, which is covered in the next section.

FIGURE 11-14

Tag Profiles

Every tag in the organization exists in a database on the server and can be managed by administrators in the Term Store Management Tool in Central Administration. There is also a tag profile to represent each tag. The tag profile is a page where the tag information is displayed, as well as a list of every time the tag was used, and a note board just for that tag. The tag description, categorization, and synonyms have been set up by the administrator. Figure 11-15 is an example of a tag profile for a tag called SharePoint.

FIGURE 11-15

The Get Connected section is a great tool for staying tuned in to all the activities related to the tag.

➤ **Follow this tag in My Newsfeed:** Click this button to add this tag to the list of interests in your profile. Tags that a user is interested in are displayed on his or her newsfeed.

➤ **Add to "Ask Me About" in My Profile:** Add this tag to your own profile's Ask Me About section.

➤ **View people who are following this tag:** Click this button to go to a search results page that displays all people who have this tag listed in their profile as responsibilities or interests.

Note Boards

Use note boards to make quick public notes about any object in SharePoint. In the example in Figure 11-16, Nicola Young is the currently logged-in user. Notice that Nicola has the ability to Edit or Delete only her own notes, not those of others. There are a couple of differences between newsfeeds and note boards. Note boards exist on many different levels, such as sites and items, whereas newsfeeds exist on sites and on My Sites. Also, newsfeeds can have threaded discussions and replies, whereas note boards are a much more simple running commentary.

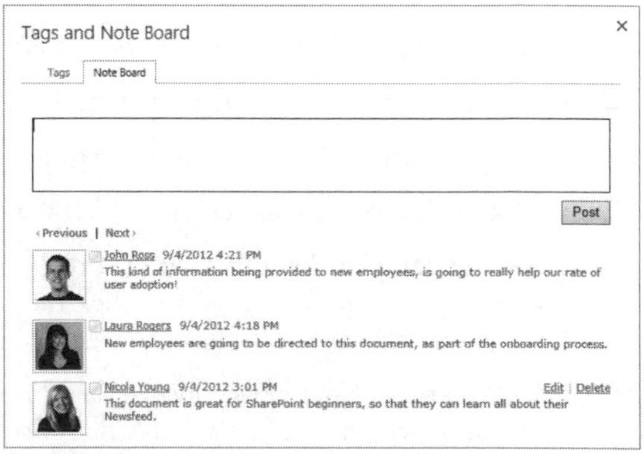

FIGURE 11-16

TRY IT OUT   Creating Tags and Notes

In this Try It Out, you participate in SharePoint social computing by creating new tags and notes on several different objects in a SharePoint site. The prerequisite is that you already have a document library with some files in it.

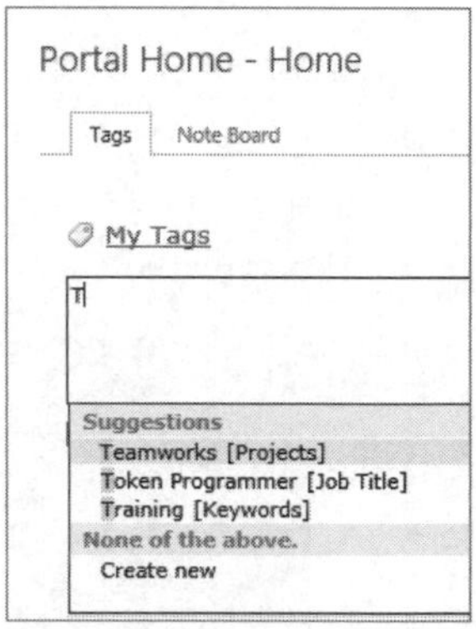

Follow these steps to create tags and notes in SharePoint:

1. Navigate to your SharePoint site's homepage, and click Page at the top-left corner.

2. At the top right, click the Tags & Notes button.

3. Type **Test Tag**. Type the letters slowly, and notice that a list of similar word suggestions is displayed underneath them, as shown in Figure 11-17. If the SharePoint Server is brand new, there may not be any suggestions yet, because the database of tags starts out empty.

4. After you type Test Tag, click Save. An underline is displayed under the phrase, and it is listed in the Suggested Tags section.

FIGURE 11-17

> **NOTE** In Figure 11-17, notice that there are different categories in square brackets next to each suggestion. These categories come from the Managed Metadata service application and are referred to as term sets. To administer the term sets, your SharePoint administrator can go to the list of service applications in Central Administration and click Managed Metadata Service.

5. Click the Note Board tab at the top.

6. Type the following: **This is a test note.**

7. Click Post. See that the new note is added to the top of the list of notes in the bottom part of the window.

8. Click the X at the top-right corner to exit.

9. Click the name of a document library, such as Documents, which takes you to that library's page.

10. Click the Library tab in the ribbon, and click the Library Settings button.

11. Click Enterprise Metadata and Keywords Settings.

12. Check both boxes to add enterprise keywords and to turn on Metadata Publishing. Click OK.

13. Click the name of the library at the breadcrumb trail at the top of the page to get back to the library's main view, and then click the Library tab. Click the Tags & Notes button. Tag this library with the Test Tag that you created in step 3. Click Save, and then click the X to close.

14. Select the row of one of the files in the library by clicking somewhere in the row (but not on the name of it, which would open the file). A selected file is displayed, as shown in Figure 11-18.

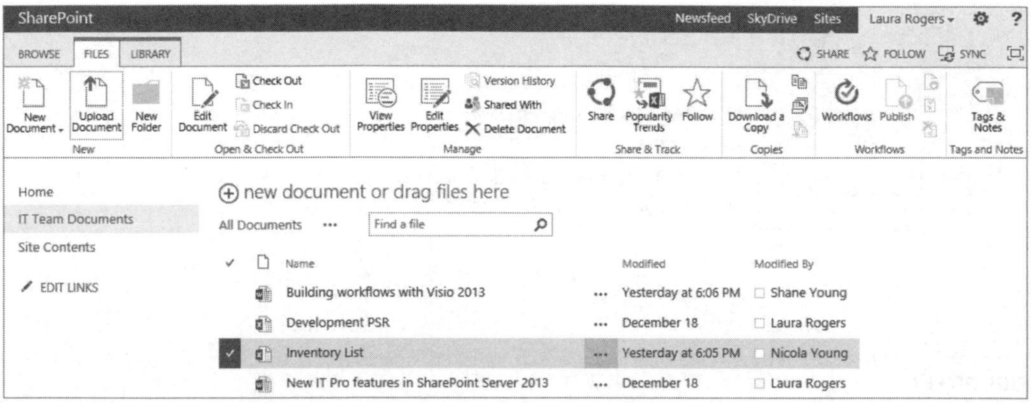

FIGURE 11-18

15. On the Files tab at the top, click Tags & Notes.

16. Type your own tag that is relevant to the content of the selected file, post a note board note, and close the Tags and Note Board screen.

17. Click your own name at the top right, and click About Me.

18. Click See All under Tags and Notes on the right.

19. Delete your last test tag or note by clicking the Delete button next to it on the right side of the page.

How It Works

Now that you've started participating in the continuously developing taxonomy of your own SharePoint environment, just keep going. Why stop now? Remember that tagging lists and list items works the same way as with libraries, but there is no pesky list level setting to enable in advance. Another thing to keep in mind is that when meaningful tags are associated with objects, this helps people find the item more quickly when searches are performed. Words that exist as tags on an item take precedence (relevance) before the words that exist inside of the document, for searching.

MANAGING CONTENT RATING

In SharePoint 2013 items can be rated on a scale of one to five, or with "likes." Content rating is yet another mechanism for engaging all the SharePoint users to participate on their sites, even if it simply involves clicking a star to quickly rate an item. Ratings can be used for any kind of list items, documents, and even wiki pages. When items are rated, this helps in determining their relevancy. SharePoint users will tend to lean more toward referencing documents that have more stars than toward the ones with fewer, and the higher-rated items will be returned first in search results.

The settings page for any list or library has a link called Rating Settings, as shown in Figure 11-19. This page describes what rating settings entail.

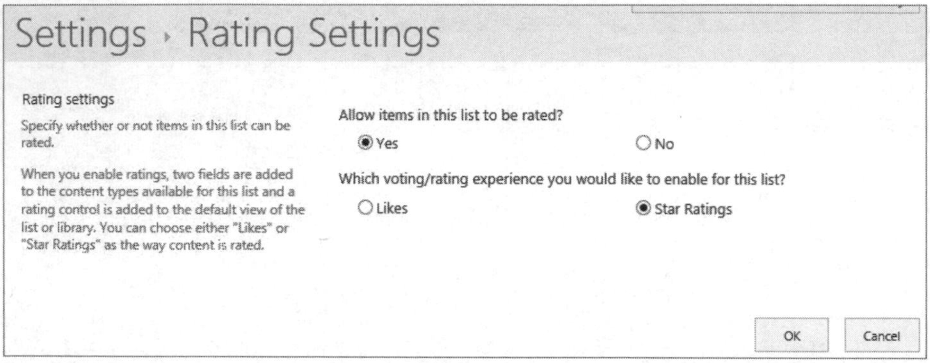

Settings › Rating Settings

Rating settings

Specify whether or not items in this list can be rated.

When you enable ratings, two fields are added to the content types available for this list and a rating control is added to the default view of the list or library. You can choose either "Likes" or "Star Ratings" as the way content is rated.

Allow items in this list to be rated?

- ⦿ Yes
- ○ No

Which voting/rating experience you would like to enable for this list?

- ○ Likes
- ⦿ Star Ratings

[OK] [Cancel]

FIGURE 11-19

TRY IT OUT   Content Rating

In this Try It Out, you use content rating in a document library, and you see the ratings in action. The prerequisite is that the document library has several items in it for rating.

1. In the Library tab of your document library, click Library Settings.

2. Click Rating settings, change the setting to Yes, and click OK.

3. A new column called Rating has been added to the default view of the library. Rate items in the library by clicking one of the stars next to each. When you hover your mouse over the set of stars for each item, a tooltip will let you know if you have already rated it and what that rating number is, or it will say "My Rating: not rated yet." Figure 11-20 shows a library of items that several people have already rated.

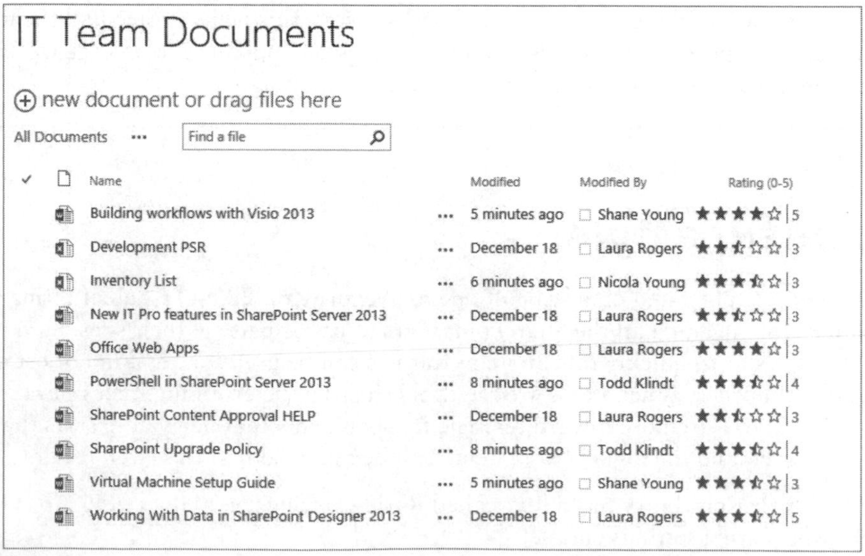

IT Team Documents

⊕ new document or drag files here

All Documents   ⋯   [Find a file   🔍]

✓	🗋	Name		Modified	Modified By	Rating (0-5)
		Building workflows with Visio 2013	⋯	5 minutes ago	☐ Shane Young	★★★★☆ | 5
		Development PSR	⋯	December 18	☐ Laura Rogers	★★⯨☆☆ | 3
		Inventory List	⋯	6 minutes ago	☐ Nicola Young	★★★⯨☆ | 3
		New IT Pro features in SharePoint Server 2013	⋯	December 18	☐ Laura Rogers	★★⯨☆☆ | 3
		Office Web Apps	⋯	December 18	☐ Laura Rogers	★★★★☆ | 3
		PowerShell in SharePoint Server 2013	⋯	8 minutes ago	☐ Todd Klindt	★★★⯨☆ | 4
		SharePoint Content Approval HELP	⋯	December 18	☐ Laura Rogers	★★⯨☆☆ | 3
		SharePoint Upgrade Policy	⋯	8 minutes ago	☐ Todd Klindt	★★★⯨☆ | 4
		Virtual Machine Setup Guide	⋯	5 minutes ago	☐ Shane Young	★★★⯨☆ | 3
		Working With Data in SharePoint Designer 2013	⋯	December 18	☐ Laura Rogers	★★★⯨☆ | 5

FIGURE 11-20

4. At the top of the document library, click the Library tab, and choose Modify View.

5. Scroll down and expand the Totals section. Next to Rating, choose Average, and click OK at the bottom of the page.

How It Works

The page now displays more information about the ratings. When multiple people have rated an item, the star that is displayed is an average rating, which is why some appear as half-stars. The number of ratings is displayed next to the average star for each item. The average at the top lets people know how valuable the information in the library is overall.

FOSTERING COMMUNITIES

In SharePoint 2013, there is a new concept of building community sites. Community sites consist of truly forum-style discussions, also referred to as *conversations*. Think of these sites as a great place to ask and answer questions, or to hold conversations around pertinent topics. In this section, all the great new functionalities are discussed and demonstrated. Communities can easily be created for each department in the organization. Another way to look at a community is to use it for job types, instead of just by department. For example, there may be Administrative Assistants spread out across many departments in the organization, but a community created just for this set of people will help them to communicate as a group, and not be isolated among different departments and groups.

TRY IT OUT Creating a Community Site

To see a community site and try all the activities in this section, the first step is to create your first community site. In the medical profession, a hospital system may have various sites for all the hospitals, but a nurse community site will be a great place for nurses. Instead of being confined to their own hospital's SharePoint site, they can have discussions with other nurses from across the other hospitals.

1. On any site in SharePoint, click the Settings button, and choose View Site Contents.

2. Scroll down and click "New subsite."

3. For the title of the new site, type **Nurse Community**. For the URL, type **community**. Pick the template called Community site.

4. Click Create.

How It Works

Now that the site has been created, the rest of the activities in this section will be based on it. The Community Site template can be used anywhere, as a site collection or as a subsite. If you would like a community site to have its own representative icon, go to Site Settings, click "Title, description, and logo", and insert a logo by uploading one or selecting it from within SharePoint.

The Community Portal

When several different community sites exist in SharePoint, there tends to be a need to see what communities exist. People in the organization like to feel like they have a way of contributing to conversations that are going on. A Community Portal is the best way to easily roll up and display every community site, from anywhere in the farm.

The Community Portal is fairly simple. There is a site collection template called Community Portal. Create a site collection using this template, and SharePoint search will take care of the rest. There is a Web Part on the homepage of the Community Portal that uses search results to show all community sites, along with their icons and some statistics. Figure 11-21 shows a Community Portal that displays four different community sites.

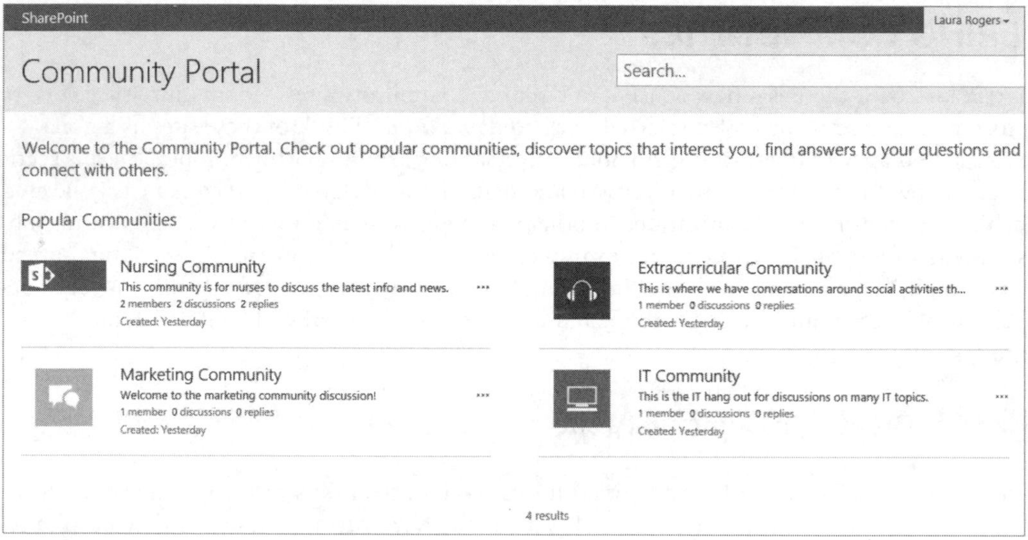

FIGURE 11-21

TRY IT OUT   **Creating a Community Portal**

To see the rolled-up view of all community sites, you can create a Community Portal. This activity requires access to SharePoint's Central Administration. If you are not a SharePoint administrator, this activity is only optional.

1. In Central Administration, click Create Site Collections.

2. Pick a web application, and type a title of **Community Portal**. For the URL, type **community**. For the template, click the Enterprise tab and choose the Community Portal template. Type your own name as the primary site collection administrator, and click OK.

3. The Community Portal rollup is based on search results, so you should run a search index so that the Nurse Community portal will show here. In Central Administration, click Manage Service Applications. Click Search Service Application, and click Content Sources on the left. Click the drop-down box on Local SharePoint sites, and choose Start Incremental Crawl.

How It Works

After the crawl completes, the Nurse Community site should appear on the homepage of the Community Portal. There is an out-of-box Web Part called *Content Search*. The Web Part on the homepage of the Community Portal is based on this Web Part. As with any search results, users will not see sites that they do not have access to.

Categorizing Conversations

Before adding new conversations, it is a good idea to add at least one or two new categories, so that the category interface can be explored. The simple purpose of categories is to categorize conversations, and there is a very nice looking user interface for viewing the list of categories. Figure 11-22 shows the Categories page on a community site. The mouse is hovering over the Social category, which shows more information, such as the description and number of discussions.

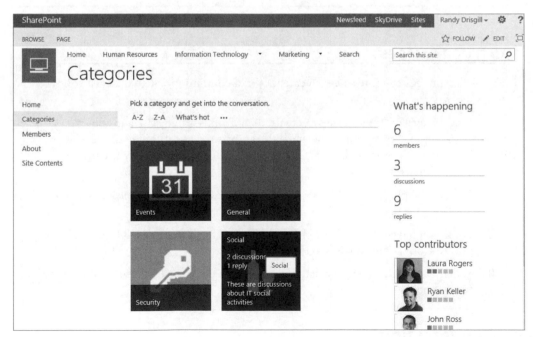

FIGURE 11-22

TRY IT OUT   Creating Categories

There is one default category called General. In this activity, you create two new categories on the Nurse Community site.

1. Go to the Nurse Community site that was created previously. In the Community tools box, click "Create categories."

2. Click "New item."

3. For the Category Name, type **Current Events**. For the description, type **Discussions about events going on in the field of nursing**. Click Save.

4. Click New item.

5. For the Category Name, type **Medical Equipment**. For the description, type **Discussions about common or new equipment that is used**. Click Save.

How It Works

Categories is just another list on the community SharePoint site. Creating categories is no different from adding items to any other type of list. Extra information will show when you click "Categories" in the left navigation and hover over each category. This functionality is built in, and no extra work is required for it to function.

CATEGORY IMAGES

To display images to represent each category in a community site, you must follow a few steps first:

1. Find images on the Internet or create them from scratch. Use a graphics program, or PowerPoint, which can be surprisingly useful in creating images. It is a good idea to make sure that the images for each category are of the same dimensions.

2. Upload the images to a library on your SharePoint, such as a picture library or an assets library.

3. Once you have uploaded the photos, you need to supply the URL for each photo. Copy a photo URL to the clipboard.

4. When creating or editing a category, paste the picture's URL into the Category Picture field.

Holding Conversations

Conversations in SharePoint 2013 are very interactive, with the ability to reply to and "like" questions or answers. There is a point system, and much more, so that community sites can be used as forums, if needed. In this section, you create some conversations, and then see an overview of the interface of the site.

TRY IT OUT   **Creating Conversations**

It's time to start up some conversations, so that the full capabilities of this site become obvious. It helps if you have more than one account to use, so that you have multiple members in your community. Logging in as different test accounts is a great way to go about this.

1. Open the Nursing Community site. Click "New discussion."

2. Create three new discussions, using the information in the following table:

SUBJECT	BODY	QUESTION	CATEGORY
October Convention	The big nursing convention is coming up this October, and I hear that there will be some great speakers.	No	Current Events
New York Area	Can anyone recommend a good medical equipment company in the New York area?	Yes	Medical Equipment
East Region	The company's east region meeting will be in November. Suggestions on meeting topics are welcome.	No	Current Events

3. Log in as a different user if possible. Click the name of a conversation, and reply to the New York Area conversation, and one other one. "Like" a conversation. Figure 11-23 shows one conversation with a reply. Also notice that there is a smiley face with a 1 next to it. This means that one person clicked the Like button.

4. Log back in as yourself. On the main page of the Nursing Community site, notice the names of several different views of the conversations, such as Recent, What's hot, and My discussions. Click the ellipsis next to My discussions. Notice the names of more views, such as Unanswered questions, and Answered questions.

5. Click "Unanswered questions."

6. Click the name of the New York Area discussion.

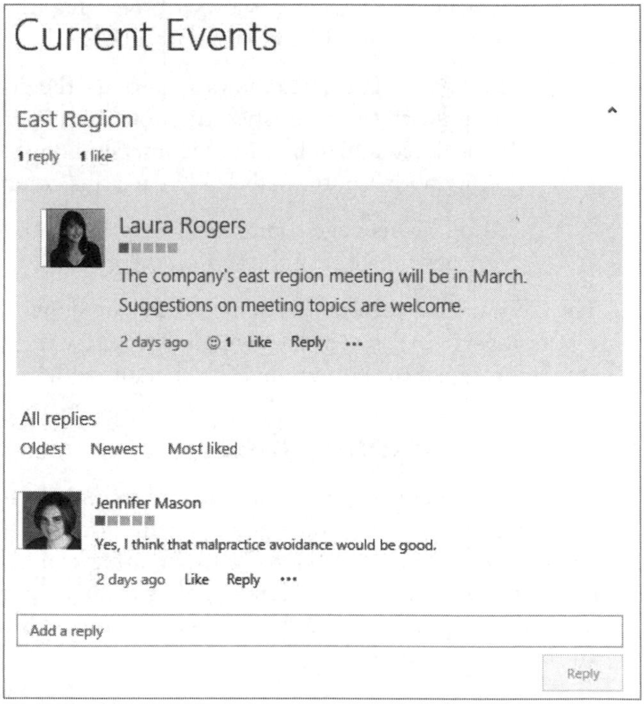

Current Events

East Region
1 reply   1 like

Laura Rogers
◼️◻️◻️◻️◻️
The company's east region meeting will be in March. Suggestions on meeting topics are welcome.
2 days ago   ☺ 1   Like   Reply   ...

All replies
Oldest   Newest   Most liked

Jennifer Mason
◼️◻️◻️◻️◻️
Yes, I think that malpractice avoidance would be good.
2 days ago   Like   Reply   ...

Add a reply

Reply

FIGURE 11-23

7. Find the reply, which is below the original question. Click the ellipsis next to the word Reply, which brings up another menu. Click "Best reply," as shown in Figure 11-24.

How It Works

Notice that the best reply is moved to the top. This is considered the answer to the question. The next time you go to the Unanswered questions view, there will be no items listed. When you look at the view called Answered questions, the "New York Area" conversation will be listed. On the left of the conversation, you will see a checkbox with "best reply," along with the numbers of replies and likes. This lets you know that this conversation does have a reply that was marked as the best reply.

New York Area

1 reply 0 likes

Laura Rogers

Can anyone recommend a good medical equipment company in the New York area?

2 days ago Like Reply ...

All replies

Oldest Newest Most liked

Jennifer Mason

There's a good one called AdventureWorks.

2 days ago Like Reply ...

Add a reply

Edit
Best reply
Delete

Reply

FIGURE 11-24

Now that there is some content in the site, it is time to go over the interface. First, the navigation:

➤ **Categories:** This page shows all the categories, with some additional views at the top, such as "What's hot" (refer to Figure 11-22).

➤ **Members:** This page shows a list of all the people who have contributed to the site, along with their statistics. As soon as any person has participated on the site, he or she is considered a member. My Membership on the right shows your own participation statistics, along with a button labeled "Leave this community."

➤ **About:** This page contains information about your community. Click the Edit button at the top right to change the text on the page.

The "What's happening" section on the right shows the number of members, and the number of discussions and replies in the community. Below the "What's happening" section is the list of "Top contributors" in the community. The person with the most points is listed first.

Managing Communities

A whole set of community tools are used to manage each community. Concepts such as "Top contributors" are based on a point system. For each different community site, the point system can be modified. There is also a badge system that can be different for each community. People obtain points for participating, and more points means higher levels. As the community moderator, you have control over which activities will earn people a certain number of points. This section covers all the community tools.

Community Tools

Community Tools is a Web Part on the homepage of your community site. All the links for administering the community are listed here. Not everyone can see this special Web Part, however. People who have Read or Contribute access to the site cannot see it at all. On the other hand, people who have Design permission on the site will only be able to manage discussions, create categories, create badges, and assign badges to members. If you have full control on the site, you will see all the following links.

➤ **Manage discussions:** This is a view of the Discussions list. All the discussions are in a list, with columns showing such information as who created each discussion, and how many replies there have been. Click the Moderation tab in the ribbon to select items and mark them as featured.

➤ **Create categories:** See a list view of the existing categories, and add or delete them.

➤ **Create badges:** Badges is a very simple SharePoint list with only one field, Badge Name. There are two badges by default: Expert and Professional. You can add or edit any badges in this list. When the list of community members is shown on the site, the name of a badge will show under each name if a badge has been assigned to that person.

➤ **Assign badges to members:** See a list view of all members. Use the Moderation tab in the ribbon to assign badges to people. *Badges* are words that will be displayed next to their photo in the list of members.

➤ **Reputation Settings:** Choose whether ratings can be used, such as likes or star ratings. The point system can also be enabled, and specific points can be set up for each type of activity, such as creating to a post or replying to one. Once members achieve points, they move up in achievement levels, which can also be modified here. By default, the achievement levels are displayed as blue bars, but they can be changed to text here instead. Scroll down and click "Manage the list of gifted badges" to add or change badges from the defaults of Expert and Professional.

➤ **Community Settings:** The established date will have a default value of the day that the site was created, but that value can be modified here. This date is displayed on the About page. There is another setting for enabling reporting of offensive content. When this box is checked, people can report items as offensive. The ellipsis button under each discussion and each reply will have a new option to Report to Moderator.

➤ **Review Reported Posts:** If the reporting of offensive content setting has been enabled, this link appears. This is a page where all the posts that have been reported as offensive can be reviewed. There is a tab in the ribbon called Moderation, which can be used when reading the comment of the person who marked it as offensive, to take the appropriate action.

Community Administration

If the Community tools box were to be removed from the homepage of the community site, there is still a way to perform management tasks. In Site Settings, there is a section called *Community Administration*, which contains all the same links that were listed in the Community tools box.

BLOGS AND WIKIS

When the Internet began, it was mostly composed of static HTML pages, and web page creation required knowledge of code languages. In the past 12 years or so, the web has evolved to become a much more interactive experience, and it has become easy for everyone to be participants. Now, people are collaborating, discussing, and forming online communities around topics. These collaborations can combine data, content, images, and multimedia from multiple sources to create personalized experiences.

Blogs

A *blog* is a personal journal written on the web, originally called a *web log*. Blogs can be written about any topic, ranging from daily life to information about a particular product, to opinions on politics. Within SharePoint in the enterprise, blogs are usually of a business-related nature. Here are a few blog concepts you should be familiar with:

➤ **Blog posts:** Using the concept of a blog being a journal, blog posts are the individual journal entries.

➤ **Comments:** Blog readers can enter their own input about each blog post, for a running commentary.

➤ **Blog site:** The blog site is the SharePoint site in which the blog posts and comments reside.

➤ **Blog account:** The account comprises the URL to the blog site and the associated user login information.

Wikis

"Wiki-wiki" is the Hawaiian word for quick. Wiki pages are web pages that can be quickly edited by typing directly into the browser. Use wikis to maintain a knowledge base, obtain community input on a topic, or simply to take personal notes.

Here are the major differences between blogs and wikis:

➤ A blog is a whole site, whereas a wiki can be a wiki site or simply a wiki library on an already existing site.

➤ Comments can be made on blogs, but not on wikis.

➤ This table lists the items that can be inserted into a blog versus a wiki:

TYPE OF ITEM TO INSERT	BLOG	WIKI
Table	Yes	Yes
Picture	Yes	Yes
Video and Audio	Yes	Yes

Link	Yes	Yes
Upload File	Yes	Yes
Reusable Content	No	Yes
Web Part	No	Yes
Embed Code	Yes	Yes

> **NOTE** *Sites in SharePoint 2013 have a feature called a* Wiki Page Home Page. *This means that the whole homepage itself is a wiki page onto which images and text can be added directly. Inserting a Web Part (or anything else) is done from the Insert tab in the ribbon. To turn off the wiki page, click the Settings button and choose Site Settings. In the Site Actions section, click "Manage site features," and then click the Deactivate button next to the Wiki Page Home Page feature.*

TARGETING CONTENT TO AUDIENCES

In SharePoint, you can target specific content to groups of people who have certain attributes in common, known as an *audience*. For example, you can create a "Marketing" audience that includes everyone involved in the organization's marketing campaign. Content on a SharePoint page can be set up to be displayed to only members of a specific audience. Audience targeting is not the same as security, though. That an item is not targeted to a particular user does not mean the user will not be able to navigate to that item or find it in a search. Utilize targeting to personalize the page according to information about the logged-in user, so that any given person will automatically see the information that is relevant to them.

In this section, you learn how to target content to audiences and how to create new audiences.

Web Parts

Each individual Web Part on a page can be targeted to an audience. This helps to clean up the clutter of many Web Parts being presented, and helps to eliminate scrolling. Target each Web Part to only those users for whom the content is relevant. In the Web Part tool pane, expand the Advanced section. Target Audiences is the last option in this section, and the names of the audiences can be filled in here. Read more about Web Parts in Chapter 7, "Working with Web Parts."

Pages

Pages can only be targeted if audience targeting is enabled for the page library. In the library's settings, on the Audience targeting settings screen, check the box to Enable audience targeting. Each page's settings will have a box to fill in the names of the target audiences. In the site's navigation settings, when the Show Pages checkbox is selected, the pages that are displayed in navigation will be visible only to their target audiences.

Navigation Links

When new links are manually created in the site's navigation settings, each link can be targeted to an audience. This applies only to sites that have the publishing feature enabled. On the Navigation Settings page, click Add Heading or Add Link to see the page where the link's audience can be selected, as shown in Figure 11-25.

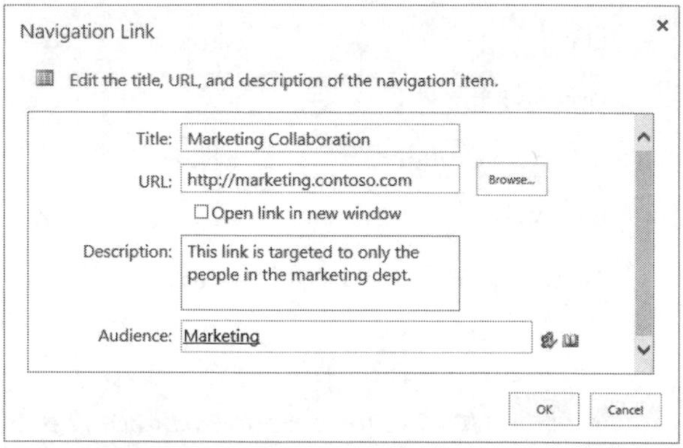

FIGURE 11-25

> **NOTE** *Remember that, aside from any audience targeting, navigation items will automatically be security trimmed. This means that if you don't have access to a site, list, or library, you won't see it in the navigation.*

Promoted Sites

The list of Promoted Sites is managed by a SharePoint administrator. Promoted Sites are links that are only displayed on the Sites page that was mentioned earlier in this chapter. Use these types of links to target sites to specific groups of people. Although an owner's name is required for each link, it is not tied to any type of security. The owner's name is used purely for informational purposes. In Central Administration, open the User Profile service application and click Manage Promoted Sites to create these links.

Publish Links to Office Client Applications

Also in the User Profile service application, links can be created for use in Microsoft Office applications, such as Word and Excel. In Central Administration, a SharePoint administrator can open the User Profile service and click Publish Links to Office Client Applications. When links are created here, users in the target audiences will see their links in Office when viewing the Open or Save As screens.

An administrator can create and define audiences at a global level, but this is not required to make use of audiences. Active Directory or SharePoint groups can be used as audiences. The following table compares the different methods of targeting content to show what kinds of audiences can be utilized with each one. This is useful when determining when it may or may not be necessary to elicit the help of the SharePoint Administrator.

METHOD	GLOBAL AUDIENCE	DISTRIBUTION/ SECURITY GROUP	SHAREPOINT GROUP
Web Parts	Yes	Yes	Yes
Pages	Yes	Yes	Yes
Navigation Links	Yes	Yes	Yes
Promoted Sites	Yes	No	No
Publish Links to Office Client Applications	Yes	No	No

CREATING AUDIENCES

With access to Central Administration, you can create global audiences. Navigate to the User Profile service application. In the People section, click Manage Audiences. This is where the audiences and their rules can be created or modified. Also in the People section, you can use the Compile Audiences section to compile them after they have been created.

THE OUTLOOK SOCIAL CONNECTOR

The Outlook Social Connector, included as part of Outlook 2013, allows you to configure Outlook to display information from your social networks. The included networks are Facebook, LinkedIn, and SharePoint.

When your social network login information is added, a new contacts list is added to Outlook, and the contacts from each network are imported. When you correspond with these contacts, a People pane appears at the bottom of the page. This pane contains information such as the person's picture, along with a list of the most recent activity associated with that person, such as e-mails and calendar appointments.

In Outlook 2013, click Contacts in the bottom navigation pane, and then click "Connect to a social network" in the left navigation pane. Check the box next to each social network, as shown in Figure 11-26, and type your login name and password to connect it.

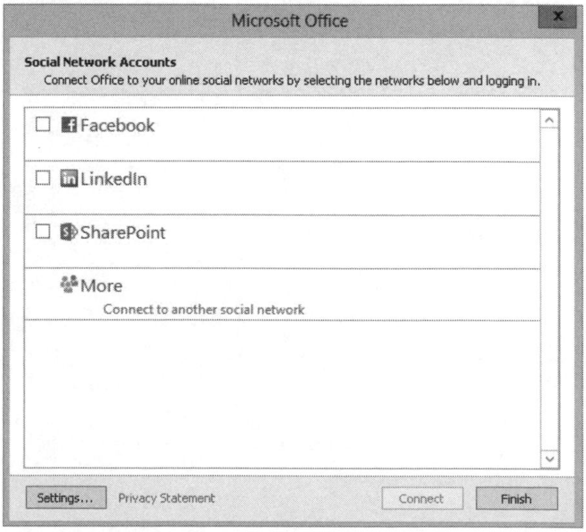

FIGURE 11-26

SUMMARY

Personalization and social networking in SharePoint 2013 are fundamental aspects of how people will share, categorize, and find information. In this chapter, you learned why these social concepts are important and how they are applied in the organization. You also learned how to go about making use of these tools as part of day-to-day work in SharePoint. The more people that get involved in social computing in your company, the easier it will be to find content and people. When people participate and feel like they are making a contribution to the community of the organization, they will not only be more efficient at their jobs, but will feel valued as individuals.

EXERCISES

1. You need to see where in the organizational chart a person named Misty Parker fits in. How can you find that information about her?

2. Charlotte complains that the activity feed on her My Site is sending her too many e-mails, especially about conversations. What changes do you recommend for her settings?

3. Katie Schmidt uses the Projects library on the Marketing site quite frequently. She would like it to be more readily available to her within the Office applications. How can she add this shortcut?

4. Todd has added the Tag Cloud Web Part to his team site. He wants to know if he can configure it to display the number of times each tag was used. What is the answer?

5. Management has decided that the Marketing homepage should be displayed on everyone's "Sites" page. How can this be accomplished?

▶ **WHAT YOU LEARNED IN THIS CHAPTER**

TOPIC	KEY CONCEPTS
My Sites	These are used by individuals to keep up with the daily activities of people and tags that they are interested in.
SkyDrive	These document libraries are stored in personal site collections where files can be stored as personal or shared with everyone.
About Me	This is an important page to fill out so that others will know where your expertise lies.
Contributing socially	Newsfeeds, tagging, and note boards are all over the place, which makes it extremely simple for people to contribute to the categorization of content.
Content rating	Ratings can be turned on for any list or library, and it is a quick way to let people rate the worth of an item. These ratings can be quantified and summarized.
People search	Searching for people is a rich and dynamic experience, with detailed information being displayed about each person. The refinement panel allows quick filtering of the results page, to find the person you are looking for.
Blogs and wikis	Blogs and wikis both offer quick ways of posting content directly to web pages in the browser, and they each have pros and cons.
Audience targeting	Audiences in SharePoint are not used for security but do allow for content targeting of several different types of objects. SharePoint groups or distribution lists can be used for targeting in some cases, or global audiences can be created.
Community sites	Community sites are places where people can come together and help each other or hold discussions on relevant topics. Point systems and moderation can also be done here.

12

Managing Forms

WHAT YOU WILL LEARN IN THIS CHAPTER:

➤ Information collection techniques with InfoPath 2013

➤ How to create an InfoPath form template

➤ How to create different types of business logic rules

➤ How to connect to external data using InfoPath

WROX.COM DOWNLOADS FOR THIS CHAPTER

The wrox.com downloads for this chapter are found at www.wrox.com/remtitle
.cgi?isbn=1118495896 on the Download Code tab. The files are in the Chapter 12 download
and individually named according to the names throughout the chapter.

An important aspect of working in a business environment and collaborating with others is
the collection of information. A common challenge is to identify ways to make this process
more efficient and effective. One solution is to collect information in a form that contains
preconfigured fields for the data you want to receive. This ensures that all the required
information is collected, and it also helps consolidate information that you can use for
comparison or calculations. For example, by collecting feedback from your customers on their
satisfaction level with your services, you can identify trends or averages in their responses. If
the average of all customer satisfaction ratings is 4.5 out of 5, and a customer submits a rating
of 3 out of 5, it is easy to see that the response is below average. If all customer feedback were
submitted verbally or via a less structured format such as e-mail or paper, it would be less
efficient to compare results in a calculated manner.

Forms simplify the task of gathering important information. In Microsoft Office, you can use
InfoPath Designer to create electronic forms that you can then publish to team members and

others through SharePoint. InfoPath is straightforward enough that nonprogrammers can use it for a simple forms creation system, yet flexible enough for programmers to create sophisticated forms-based applications.

After reading this chapter, you should feel comfortable identifying scenarios in which the use of InfoPath forms would be beneficial for your organization for the collection of information from various key stakeholders. This chapter requires that you use Microsoft InfoPath Designer 2013 for the creation of form templates. In addition, for users to complete forms created in InfoPath Designer, you must design the forms to be browser compatible; otherwise, the users will need to have Microsoft InfoPath Filler installed on their systems. For the majority of the exercises in this chapter, you will be creating browser-based forms. The Enterprise version of SharePoint Server 2013 is required to create browser-based forms, because this is the only version of SharePoint that contains InfoPath Forms Services. Without InfoPath Forms Services, forms can be created as "Filler forms," but not as browser-based forms.

WHAT IS INFOPATH?

InfoPath is an application that integrates with SharePoint to collect and present data. InfoPath forms are XML-based documents that you can design to help collect data in ways that the standard SharePoint interface cannot. Although you can use InfoPath on its own, it truly excels as a data collection tool when combined with SharePoint. Some ways of using InfoPath within an organization include:

➤ **Team reports:** Team members can create weekly status reports from which the team's manager can create a single report that tracks the team's progress. This involves creating a form template that features fields related to weekly activities and publishing it to a shared location, such as the team's SharePoint site. Every week, the manager can access a special view that displays all the forms, and then she can merge them into a single document. This consolidation reduces the amount of work that a manager must perform each week. She can even customize that single document to present to her own management team.

➤ **Data connections:** Salespeople can use forms to report on customer information from a centralized database containing details on the customer and previous purchases. They can also attach a document with a record of meetings and communication with the customer so that colleagues can access this later. Again, you must create a form template and store it on a centralized team site, but this template features special data connections that display customer data directly from the database. This reduces duplicate data by eliminating the need to re-create this content in SharePoint because it already exists in the database, improves data access, and allows the sales team to make accurate decisions. With Info Path, you can also submit information to other data systems via a web service, which means that you don't have to enter data into two separate systems.

➤ **Travel requests:** Employees can visit a SharePoint page and complete an electronic form to request to go on a trip. The form is submitted securely to a location, and the employee is supplied with the status as it changes. A special feature of InfoPath, when utilized with the Enterprise version of SharePoint Server, is the ability to create forms that customers can view and edit via the browser. This eliminates the need for users to have special software on their computers.

CREATING AND CUSTOMIZING AN INFOPATH FORM

You use InfoPath in situations when you need to improve how information is shared or collected in your organization. One of the primary advantages of using InfoPath is that you can make the interface very simple and intuitive for users to add and complete information. Figure 12-1 shows an example of a typical InfoPath form.

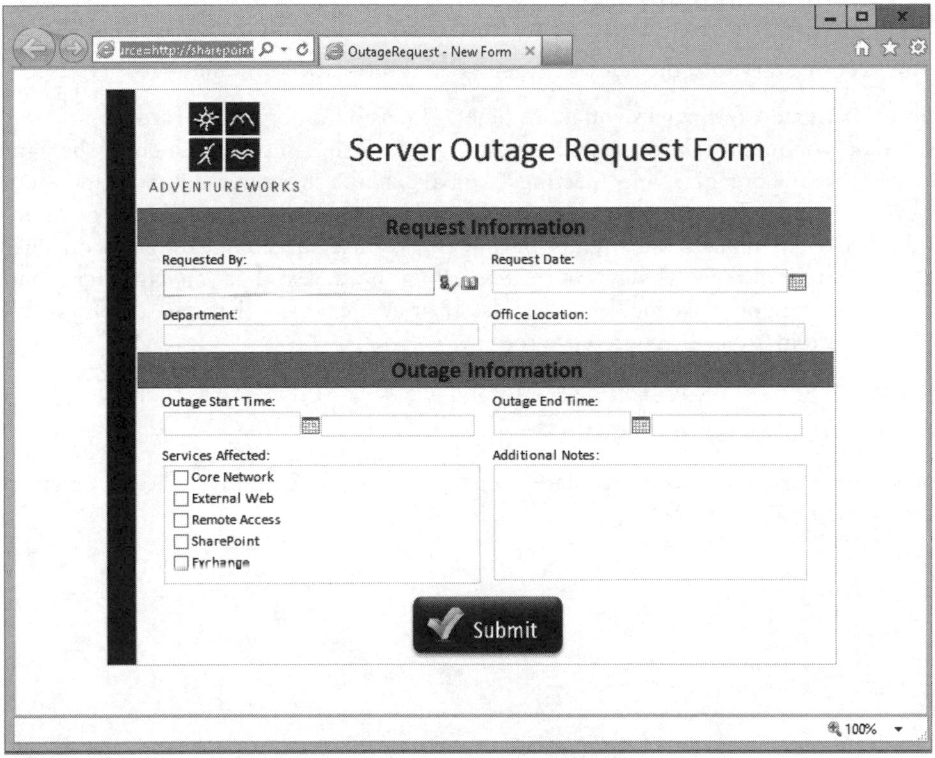

FIGURE 12-1

Before a user can complete an InfoPath form, you must start with a form template, which someone using the InfoPath Designer application creates. An InfoPath form template is a file with an .xsn extension. You then have to publish the template to a location where users can complete the form by adding information. Each time a user completes and saves the form, a new file is created. The data file that is created when a user completes a form has an .xml extension. For example, if you take the example of the weekly status reports described in the introduction of this chapter, a single form template exists that contains all the required and optional fields that the form should contain. This form template would be published to the SharePoint site. Each team member would then click the New Document button in the library to open a new instance of the form. Once the form is completed, the team member would submit it to the library, which would create a new XML data file. If a team consists of five members, five new form data files are created in the library each week as the team members create their status reports. However, there would be only one form template file for the status reports.

To get started using InfoPath, you must first create or design a form template. In the first Try It Out in this section, you open an existing sample template in InfoPath Designer 2013 and modify a field to make it more appropriate for your organization. You can also make modifications to the form to give it a look and feel that is more appropriate for your organization. This may include adding a company logo to the various form views or adopting a color scheme that matches that of other company documents and interfaces. The second Try It Out in this section illustrates how to do this.

Creating an InfoPath Form

The examples in this section start with the `MeetingAgenda.xsn` InfoPath form template file.

Using a starting point to create a form gives you more time to focus on tailoring the form to fit your needs. In this Try It Out, you modify the existing Meeting Agenda form template to include the names of staff members who typically organize your meetings. You also make this a mandatory field because, in your company, every meeting should have an identified meeting room. Giving users a list of values rather than a standard text box reduces the amount of time it takes users to complete the form. The list of values also enables you to build special views in the SharePoint library so that you can filter them via the meeting room. For example, this enables you to select or create a view that only displays meetings that are being held in a specific conference room.

1. Open the Microsoft Office InfoPath Designer 2013 application.

2. From the New tab of the ribbon, select Open.

3. Locate the `MeetingAgenda.xsn` form template from this chapter's materials and click Open. The form opens, as shown in Figure 12-2.

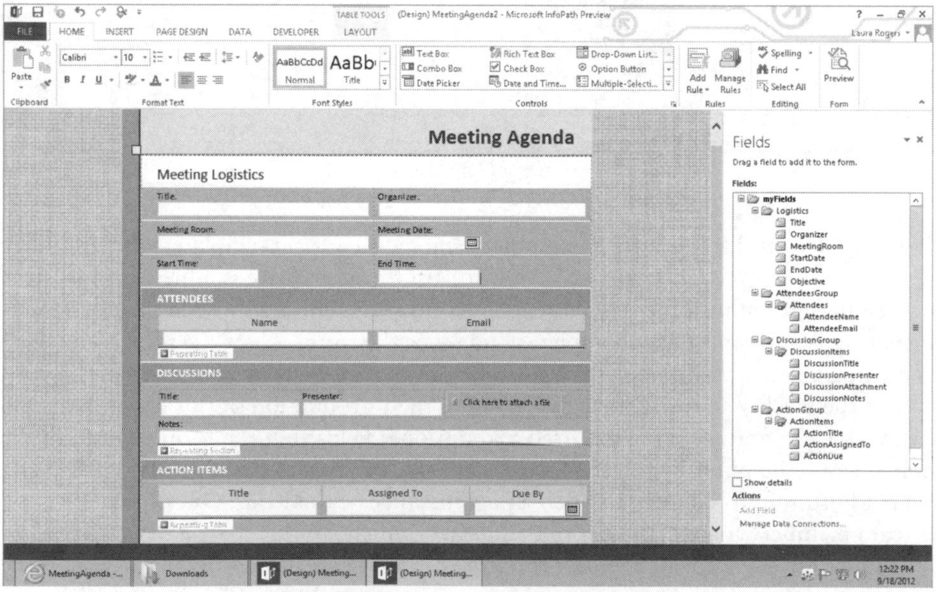

FIGURE 12-2

4. Click to select the Meeting Room field.

5. Right-click and select Change Control, then Drop-Down List Box from the menu. Notice that the Organizer field changes from a standard text box (as shown in Figure 12-3) to a drop-down list box.

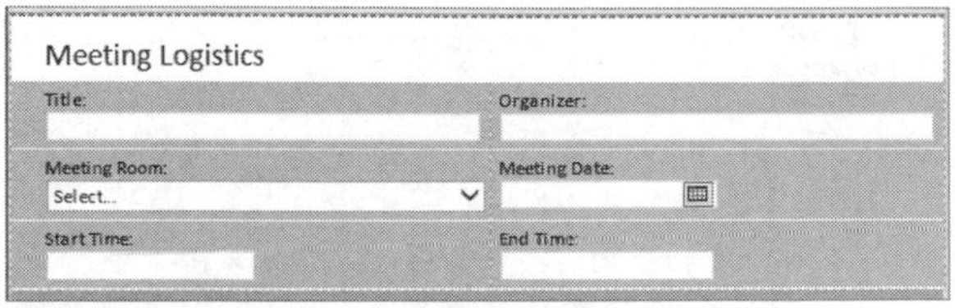

FIGURE 12-3

6. Right-click again, and this time select Drop-Down List Box Properties. The Drop-Down List Box Properties dialog box appears.

7. Check the Cannot be blank checkbox under the Validation section.

8. From the List box choices section, click Add. The Add Choice dialog box appears.

9. Enter a name for a meeting room. For this example, enter **Conference Room A** in the Value and Display Name fields. When you enter the text for the Value field first, it is added automatically to the Display Name field.

10. Click OK. You will now see Amanda Perran as a value listed in the properties of the field.

11. Repeat this process by clicking Add again and entering another meeting room. In this case, enter **Conference Room B** as a value for the drop-down, and then enter a third room name as a value, such as Conference Room C. Figure 12-4 shows an example of the Drop-Down List Box Properties.

12. Click OK.

13. Select Save As from the File tab of the ribbon menu.

14. Save the file on your computer in the location containing the resource files for this chapter. Name the form template **CH12meetingagenda.xsn**.

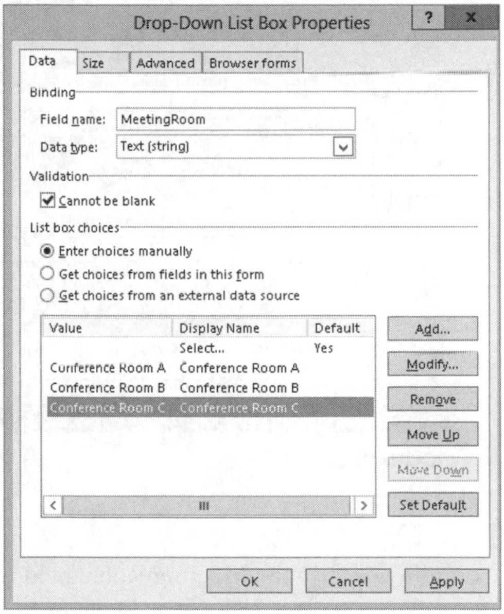

FIGURE 12-4

15. Select the Preview option from the right-hand side of the Home ribbon menu. Your form opens in preview mode, as shown in Figure 12-5.

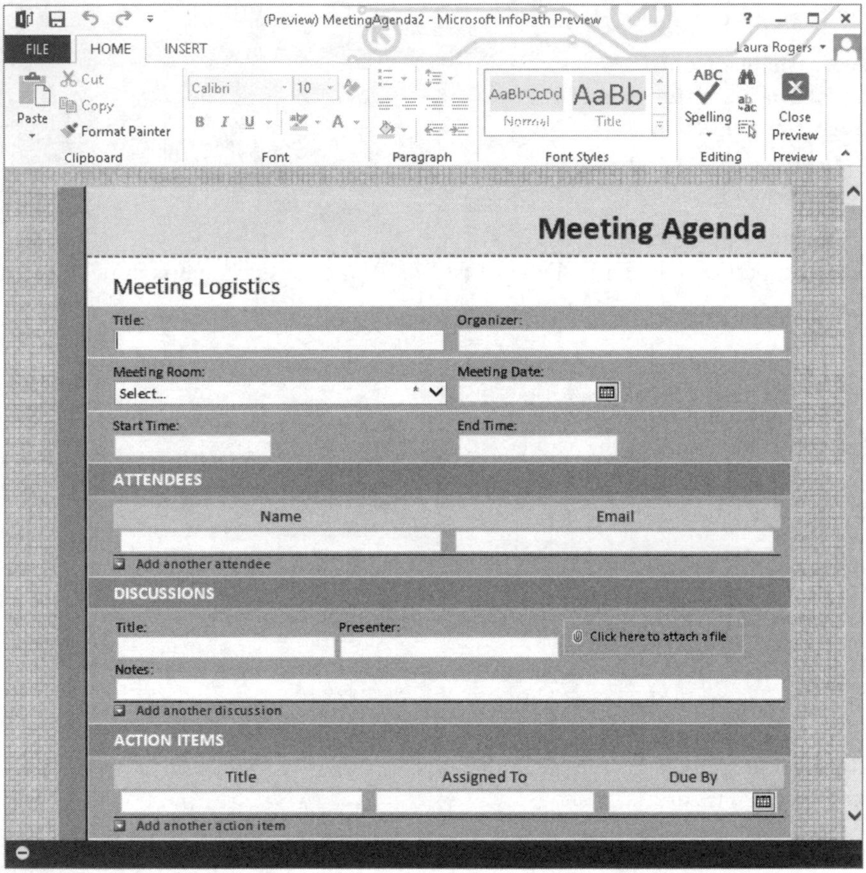

FIGURE 12-5

You now see that the Meeting Room field is a drop-down list box featuring the names you entered in the previous steps. Click Close Preview.

TRY IT OUT Customizing the Look and Feel of a Form Template

All the examples in this section use the Ch12MeetingAgenda.xsn InfoPath form template file that was created in the previous Try It Out.

In this Try It Out, you add your company's logo to the form template so that it appears whenever users view or print the form. Branding forms and document templates helps create a more professional image for your forms and can help customers identify you as a company. Also, it's good to have a standardized template with a logo for conducting business activities so that people can clearly identify the official company template.

For this example, you make slight look-and-feel changes to the form template. Note that any alterations you make should be reviewed with the appropriate departments in your organization such as communications or marketing. If these departments do not exist in your organization, consider reviewing changes with stakeholders. By allowing others to participate in the design and planning stages, you can increase the probability of solid end-user adoption because you are more likely to directly address their needs and requirements.

1. Open the form template you designed in the previous example called `CH12meetingagenda.xsn` using the same method described in the previous Try It Out.

2. Right-click the header of the form just to the left of the words Meeting Agenda, as shown in Figure 12-6.

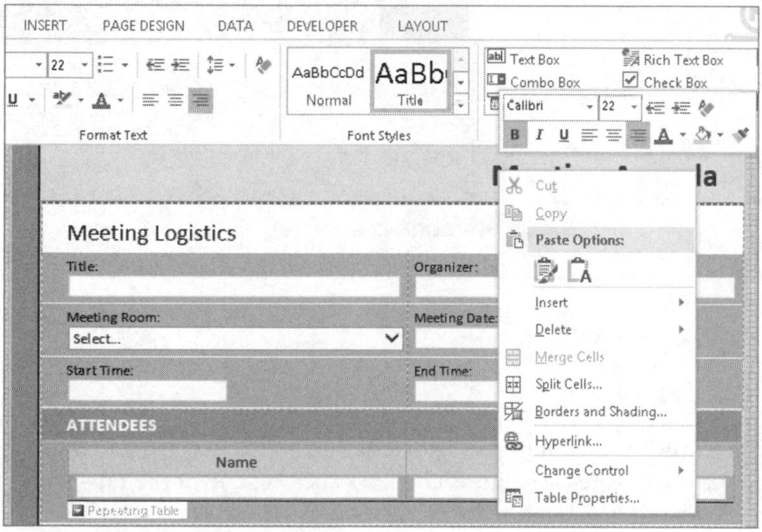

FIGURE 12-6

3. Select Borders and Shading. The Borders and Shading dialog box appears.

4. Select the Shading tab.

5. Select the light-blue color. Notice that the background color of the heading changes to match your selection.

6. Right-click the header of the form just to the right of the words Meeting Agenda and select Split Cells. A dialog box appears, requesting information on the format you want to create for your table.

7. Enter 2 for the number of columns, keep the value of 1 for number of rows, and click OK. The table is reformatted as specified.

8. Click in the right-hand column of the header. Click the Insert tab of the ribbon and select the Pictures option. A file selection window appears, as shown in Figure 12-7.

9. Browse to the resource files from this chapter and select `awlogo.png`.

10. Click the Insert button. The form refreshes, displaying the AdventureWorks logo, as shown in Figure 12-8.

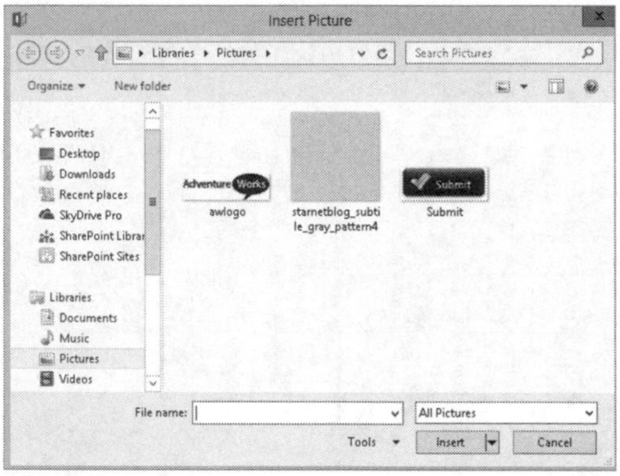

FIGURE 12-7

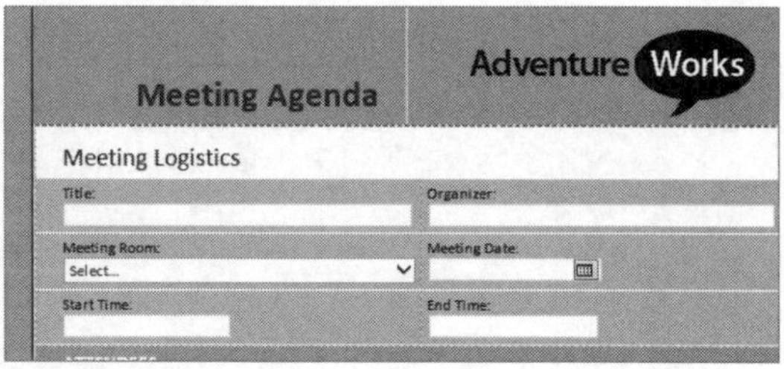

FIGURE 12-8

CORE CONCEPTS

In InfoPath, the ribbon contains the most common design activities and concepts related to customizing or developing a form template (see Figure 12-9). By clicking any of the tabs, you get a listing of actions relevant to that subject.

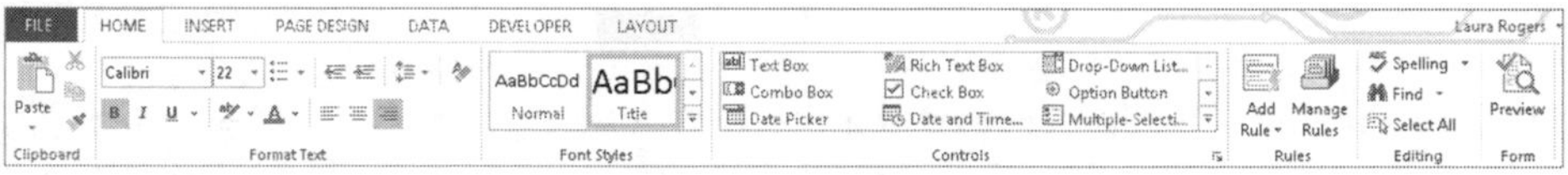

FIGURE 12-9

You start with a blank form template, and it launches with fields or controls. You may choose to apply a layout to the form. As you add controls to the form in InfoPath Designer 2013, fields automatically appear in the form's data source to support the use of these controls. The data source represents all the available fields that have been added to the form template. You can view the data source by clicking the Show Fields option on the Data tab of the ribbon. Next, you can create various views for the form, which are similar to the concept of those discussed in Chapter 4 related to lists and libraries, but in this case they are specifically located in the form. You can basically create a set of criteria that displays your data in different ways, depending on what you want to collect or represent. You then check your design to make sure that it's compatible in the browser where it will operate. Some field types are not suitable for use in a web browser, so when creating a form for the browser, it is important to include only elements that are supported. InfoPath has a Design Checker mode that helps support you with this. Finally, you publish your form template so that others can use it and so that you can begin collecting data.

> **NOTE** To learn how to create and publish a form template, see the next section, "Working with Form Templates."

If you are not creating your form from an existing file, you should take time to plan it out. By considering your information requirements in advance and sketching out a form on paper, you can determine what your form and data source elements should be before you even start creating the form template.

Page Design

The Page Design tab enables you to create tabular layouts in your form to control how information is presented. Quite often, to create a form that contains multiple columns of information you need a table to effectively organize everything. From the Page Design tab, you can:

➤ Insert a predefined layout into your form template that corresponds to your need.

➤ Create or change views.

➤ Apply style changes or themes to your form.

➤ Apply page settings such as margins or print settings (not applicable for browser-based forms).

➤ Configure header and footer settings (not applicable for browser-based forms).

Controls

Once you lay out a form and define its overall structure, the next step is to add the fields that the form will contain. InfoPath offers a variety of controls that you can use to effectively collect and display information in a form, including text boxes, rich text boxes, selection list boxes, date pickers, checkboxes, option buttons, buttons, and sections.

Adding controls is closely linked to creating the form's data source, which is covered in the next section. You can start with a blank form template and create the fields by adding controls to the form. As you add a control to the form, a field is created automatically in the data source to represent that control. You can add a control by selecting the area in the form where the field is to appear and clicking the control from the Home tab of the ribbon menu. You should name your fields as you add the controls. You can rename a field by selecting it and editing the Name property in the ribbon menu, as shown in Figure 12-10, or by right-clicking the field and selecting Properties. The name cannot contain spaces and should be intuitive. When you open the Properties dialog box, you will see other aspects of the field that you can customize, such as default values, display options, or selection values. Each type of control has its own set of unique attributes and properties. Some controls are not supported in browser-based forms and are available only when using the InfoPath Form Filler tool for the completion of forms. Therefore, when planning your forms, it is important to consider the medium by which they will be completed and the availability of specific controls to support your requirements.

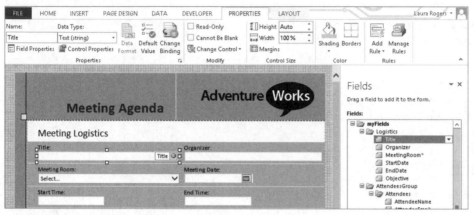

FIGURE 12-10

Text Box

A text box can hold all sorts of information types such as Name, Phone Number, or Currency. When you edit the properties of a text box, you can determine in what format the information should be stored by selecting the Data Type. When designing a form using this field type, you can have default values populated based on a user's selection for other fields. InfoPath also supports the use of customizable rules that enable you to perform actions such as switch views or set a field's value based on the user's selection of an item or activity within the form. You can also include tooltip text that demonstrates to users the type of information that the field should contain or how they can complete the item. Some of the options related to the Text Box control are listed in Figure 12-11, including some of the formatting and display alternatives.

➤ **Enable AutoComplete:** This option suggests words or phrases to a user as she is completing a form based on previously entered options. Sometimes AutoComplete can make the process for filling out a form easier for the users. However, it is not typically appropriate for forms where information entered may be of a sensitive or confidential nature.

➤ **Enable spelling checker:** This enables spell checking on content stored in the field.

➤ **Multi-line:** By using this option, you can specify whether a text box can include paragraph breaks or if text can wrap. This is helpful for situations where the text may exceed a single line. If you do select Multi-line, you can determine whether the control should allow scrolling or expand to display the text when it exceeds a single line.

➤ **Limit text box to:** This option enables you to specify the number of characters a field can contain. You can use this option when accepting information, such as a phone number or Social Security number, where the number of characters is limited to a fixed number. If you enable the Multi-line option listed previously, this option is disabled.

➤ **Placeholder:** You can use placeholder text to include suggestions in a text box or field to represent the text a user might enter or provide instruction on how he or she should complete a field. For example, for a name field, you might have placeholder text that states "Enter Name Here." As soon as a user clicks the field, the text is erased.

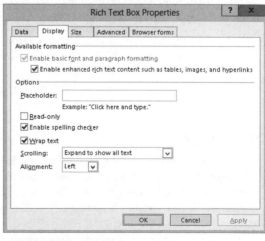

FIGURE 12-11

> **WARNING** *The auto-correct, spell checker, and placeholder settings are not applicable with browser-based forms. Any autocomplete that happens in the form is a result of the browser's settings, not InfoPath's. Because placeholder text will not show in a browser form, go to the Advanced tab and type text in the Screentip box. This text will show when you hover your mouse over the text box in the browser.*

Rich Text Box

You use the rich text box to collect more detailed information from a user, such as a description or background information. This field type or control has many of the same customization features as the text box, including spell check, placeholder, conditional formatting, and wrapped text. When customizing this field type, you can choose to support basic rich text formatting or enhanced rich text. An example of the additional formatting options available within an enhanced rich text field is shown in Figure 12-12.

Selection List Box

Selection list box field controls include drop-down list boxes, combo boxes, list boxes, and multiple selection list boxes. Depending on the type of

FIGURE 12-12

information you are collecting from your users and whether you intend to make the form available in the browser, your implementation choices may vary:

➤ **Drop-down list box:** This type of box allows users to select from fixed sets of values. If you have many items, you can select a drop-down list box to save room because it shows only one item until the user clicks a down arrow. Having too many items can negatively affect the user experience, so consider applying a filter so that only a relevant set of items are displayed based on a user's selection in another field. For example, if the user enters the United States as his country, you could filter a field for State or Province selection to display only states because there is no requirement to display provinces.

➤ **List box:** This option allows users to select from a fixed set of values. The items are displayed in a listing, inside of what looks like a vertical text box, and are viewable all at once. This is different from the drop-down box for that reason and is typically suitable only when you have less than 10 or so values. Otherwise, the control will take up a large amount of space, and selecting from too large a set of values may be difficult for some readers.

➤ **Combo box:** The combo box is very similar in presentation to the drop-down list box; however, it also allows users to enter their own values in a list. Therefore, if the item they want to select is not listed in the drop-down, they can type in their own value.

➤ **Multiple-selection list box:** The multiple-selection list box is similar to the list box but contains checkboxes for each item and can also optionally allow users to enter their own values into the list. An example of a multiple selection list box is shown in Figure 12-13.

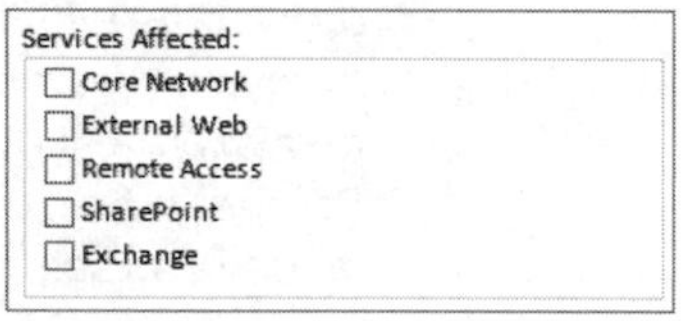

FIGURE 12-13

➤ **Person or group picker:** This selection field integrates with the membership listing of your SharePoint environment to allow for the selection of users or groups through this field. By using this field type, you can link a user's profile directly within a form, rather than merely entering his or her name in a text box. This field is very similar to the person or group column type that was explored in Chapter 4.

➤ **External item picker:** This selection field integrates with the Business Connectivity Services feature of SharePoint Server to allow for the selection of external business data within an InfoPath form. If an external application has been defined in SharePoint Server through the Business Connectivity Services feature, you can associate it with this field type.

Date Picker

This feature helps a user select a date, which is especially helpful when you have regional variations in date formats. For example, 05/06/07 can represent a completely different day in Canada than it would in the United States. An example of the date picker control as seen by an end user on the completed form is shown in Figure 12-14.

FIGURE 12-14

You can configure the date picker to contain certain default values including special functions, such as today(), which sets the default date to the current date of when the user is completing the form.

Checkbox

In many of the exercises in this book, you selected a checkbox to enable an option for an application. The same logic applies in a form template. You can have a single checkbox to provide a Yes or No type answer to a question. For example, if a checkbox were associated with a to-do list, a blank box would indicate that the task had not been completed, whereas a selected checkbox would be an indication that task was complete. Alternatively, you have checkboxes that allow a user to select one or more items from a group of choices, as shown with the "toppings" in the Pizza Order Form in Figure 12-15. Although each choice is an individual field, you can group the checkboxes in a section or table for data organization purposes.

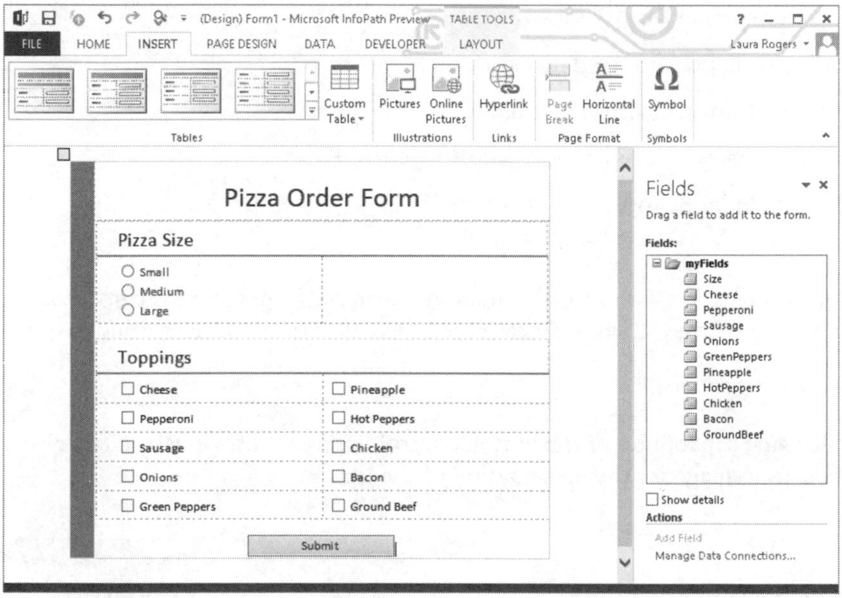

FIGURE 12-15

Option Button

The option button, sometimes referred to as a *radio button*, gives users a choice between items. Instead of allowing users to select more than one item, you give them a list of choices and allow them to select only one of them. In Figure 12-16, users can select only a single size when ordering their pizza.

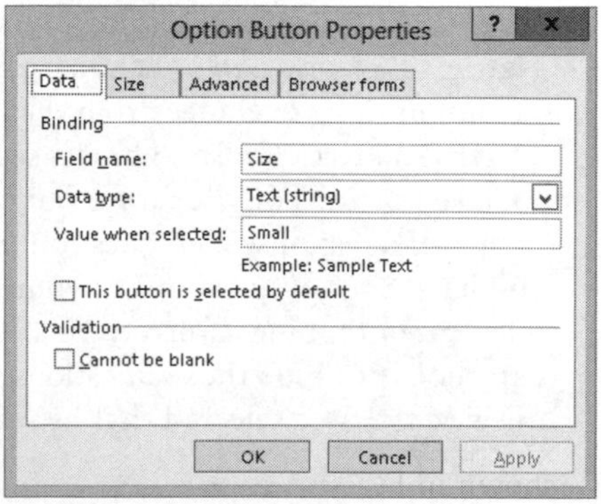

You select how many choices you want to give the user, and you assign each option button a unique value that makes it easy for you to identify the user's selection. Figure 12-16 shows the properties of the radio button for

FIGURE 12-16

the small size selection. The "Value when selected" is Small. Also, if you wanted Small to be the default size, you could check the box next to "This button is selected by default".

> **NOTE** *Take a look at the list of fields on the right side in Figure 12-15. Notice that because only one size can be selected, there is only one field for size. Because multiple toppings can be selected, each topping has its own field.*

Button

You can add a button to launch a new activity or series of rules on a form. When the user clicks the button, the activity or rule triggers. You can use buttons to launch a number of actions, including:

➤ Change views in a form.

➤ Submit to a data connection.

➤ Retrieve (query) information from a data connection.

➤ Launch a new form (InfoPath Form Filler only).

➤ Launch a message window or display box (InfoPath Form Filler only).

➤ Set the value for a field in the form.

➤ Close a form.

By implementing rules in combination with special conditions, a simple form template can become a dynamic application and drive specific business processes in a way that is very intuitive and easy to use.

Picture Button

A picture button has the same capabilities of the button control described previously, but it also enables you to select a custom image for the presentation of the button.

Section

Sections give elements structure and are, therefore, important when you design a form's data source and display needs. You can add, remove, or hide sections within a form template. As shown in Figure 12-17, you can select an option to have a section initially excluded from the form or added by a user. You can choose to hide a section if you want to have portions of your form only appear based on a user's response to a question. For example, if you have a set of questions in your form related to what pizza toppings a user wants on his pizza, you can choose to hide those questions if, in a previous answer, the user selected that he wanted to order hamburgers.

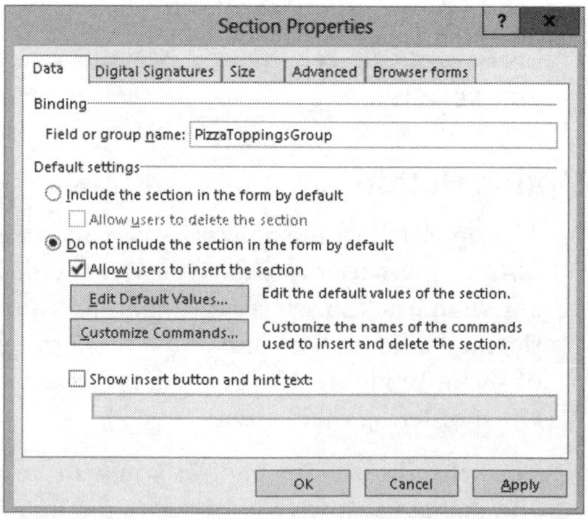

FIGURE 12-17

It is generally a good idea to add sections to your form templates to group information that is similar or related. You should name sections appropriately so that you can better identify a set of related fields within the form's data source.

Other Controls

The previously listed field types are just a few of the standard controls available for use in an InfoPath form. Additional control types include:

➤ **Table:** You can include tables in your form for users to complete. Each table can contain a number of fields and may include repeating rows so that users can add more information or items to the table as required.

➤ **Master/detail:** In some cases, you may have two controls or sections whereby the selection in one dictates the detail displayed in another. An example of this might be a product category list and a product details listing. If a user selects a category, the details listing should be reformatted to display only the items related to the selected category. This field is supported only for forms that will be completed using InfoPath Filler.

➤ **Lists:** A list can be a more informal control that allows a user to add a bulleted or numbered list in his response. You may include a list in a form that asks a user to submit ideas for a new product or accomplishments for a particular time period.

➤ **File attachment:** It may be appropriate or beneficial to have a user attach a file to his form instance. This file becomes embedded in the form document and others can access it later when reviewing the form.

➤ **Picture:** This control enables you to create a field that will either upload and embed a picture in the form or link to a picture stored elsewhere.

➤ **Ink picture:** For users with a drawing tablet or Tablet PC, InfoPath has built-in support for Ink, which allows a user to write directly into a form with a digital pen. This field supports the drawing of an image directly within the form. This field is supported only for forms that will be completed using InfoPath Filler.

➤ **Hyperlink:** This control enables end users to insert a hyperlink into the form whereby they can specify the hyperlink address and display text.

➤ **Calculated value:** More advanced users can use this control to enter an XPath expression that can perform advanced calculations on data stored in the form. The results of the calculation are displayed in the form.

➤ **Vertical label:** For design purposes, you may want to have a vertical label added to your form. This control presents the form designer with a text box within which text can be added. This text is displayed vertically on the form. This field is supported only for forms that will be completed using InfoPath Filler.

➤ **Regions or groups:** Similar to sections, regions and groups are organizational elements that you can add to pages to support fields or text.

Data Source

The primary data source of your InfoPath form is basically the skeletal information structure of your form. In order to have a field in the form, it must be tied to an element in the data source. When you create your form by adding controls, data source elements are automatically added in the primary data source for you. You can also have secondary data sources, such as external data connections that you can use to display information in the form. For example, you may have a secondary data source that is a database. You can drag information from your database onto the form and select which fields or controls should be used to display the information.

As described in the previous section, the data source is very closely tied to the controls. You should name your fields as you add the controls. This will automatically update the data source. The name cannot contain spaces and should be intuitive. You can also add groups, tables, or sections in your form's data source so that you can easily track elements or items that are related to one another. You can also create fields in the fields section before dragging them to the design surface. It is not required that every field be represented by a control on the design surface. Sometimes there may be a need to have fields, which can be used behind the scenes, that end users never see.

You can import the primary data source of a form based on an XML file, or you can generate it from a data connection. The available options for creating a new form from a data connection are displayed in Figure 12-18. This approach is more advanced; a formalized data structure is imported into the form and then controls are added to the form to represent the data.

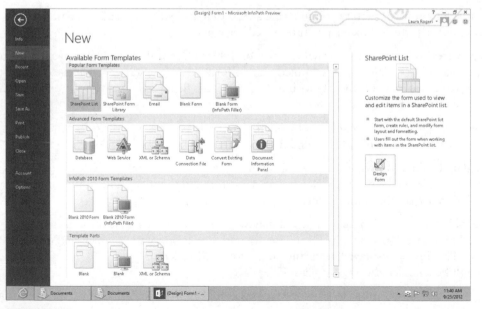

FIGURE 12-18

If you are not creating your data source from a data connection or XML schema file, you should take time to plan it out. Consider your information requirements, and sketch a form out on paper. By considering what some of the information requirements are in advance, you can generate a good idea on what your data elements should be before you even start creating the form template.

> **NOTE** *When you remove a control from a form's view, the field is not automatically removed from your data source. If you need to delete a field permanently, right-click the field in the list of fields on the right, and choose Delete. Views are discussed in the next section.*

In addition to the primary data source of a form template, other data sources become available as you add new data connections to the form. An example of this is shown in Figure 12-19.

Similar to the behavior of the primary data source, you can drag elements within a secondary data source onto the page. This can help provide some data reporting from external data sources within the form itself. You can add items either as sections or tables and then format them as required. For example, in a form template that tracks information about a customer, the primary data source of the form may contain items such as the customer's phone number, company name, and e-mail address, and you might create a secondary data source that connects to the orders database. You can drag information from this secondary data source onto the form to show a salesperson all the products the customer has purchased.

FIGURE 12-19

Views

In Chapter 4, you saw how to create custom views for lists and libraries to display different records and columns from a single data source. With InfoPath, you can also create multiple views from a single form. The views can either act as reports or pages in a form where they can represent completely unique steps related to the completion of a process. For example, you can have a form template with four different views: one for customer requests; a second that logs troubleshooting issues that an employee must resolve; a third that tracks correspondence with customer; and a final one that tracks customers' comments on the level of service they've received.

You can create views from the Page Design tab of the ribbon menu by selecting New View. When you create a view, it is blank. You must drag layout elements such as tables onto the form and add controls as needed. You can add a single field to multiple views. For example, you may have a field for customer name. You can add this field to every view in your form. You can also change unique characteristics related to the presentation of the field on each view. Though the data remains the same, the presentation of a field on each view can be slightly different. For example, on one page the customer's name may appear in large bold letters in read-only format, and on another it may appear in a drop-down box. However, the data of the field remains the same. Therefore, if "Graphical Wonder" is listed as the customer in one view, it will also be listed on all other views in that field.

You can add buttons to each view of the form, to toggle between each of the available views. In some cases, you can implement multiple views and buttons on a form to collect information from a user in steps. You essentially add a button to a view that, when selected, launches another view using the Rules capabilities of buttons. This replicates the experience of a wizard and can help simplify the experience of the user as she completes the operation. If you don't use custom buttons, you can have users switch between various form views within the form itself, using the Current View menu, as shown in Figure 12-20. This is a great method to use for very long forms, so that scrolling is not needed.

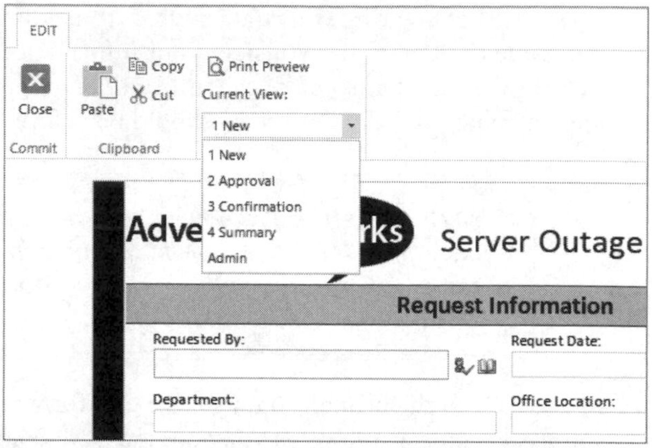

FIGURE 12-20

This view drop-down box is an optional setting that you can configure in the Advanced Form options available from the File menu. Each view's property screen also has a checkbox to determine whether that view should be visible in the View drop-down box on the form.

Design Checker

As previously stated, not all form controls are supported for use within browser-based forms. Therefore, you need to consider who the audience for your form will be and how they will access it. If the form has to be available for use on the browser, careful consideration is required to ensure that the experience is positive. This may seem like a lot to understand if you are just getting used to creating these forms. Therefore, a Design Checker exists with the InfoPath application to guide you by highlighting anything you may have in your form that would not be compatible with the browser or previous versions of InfoPath.

If you decide that a form should be browser-compatible after you have already begun the form design process, you can change the setting by selecting the Web Browser Form within the Compatibility settings under Form Options, as shown in Figure 12-21.

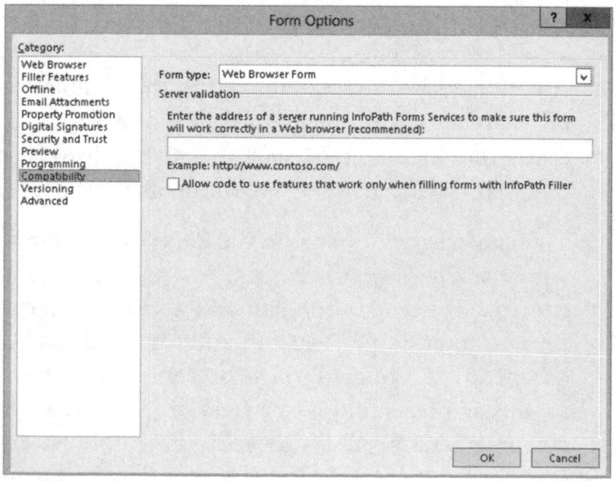

Another option in this same interface is a URL to test whether the form will be compatible with the destination SharePoint Server. If you specify a URL, the Design Checker displays alerts and messages indicating items in your form that may affect compatibility with either the browser or older versions of the application.

FIGURE 12-21

Publish Form Template

You can always save a template in a location for your personal use and to edit further, but to make your form available to others, you need to publish the template to a central location. You can publish an InfoPath form template to any of the following locations:

➤ A SharePoint Server with Enterprise Features (supports browser-based forms or the use of InfoPath Filler)

➤ A SharePoint Server with Standard Features (requires InfoPath Filler on each client machine)

➤ A SharePoint Foundation Server (requires InfoPath Filler on each client machine)

➤ A shared network location, such as a file share (requires InfoPath Filler on each client machine)

➤ An e-mail message to recipients (requires InfoPath Filler on each client machine)

Depending on the environment in which you are working and what tools you have available, you can select any one of these options when completing the Publishing Wizard.

> **NOTE** *The next section, "Working with Form Templates," walks you through examples of publishing an InfoPath form to a SharePoint server, including publishing a form directly to a document library, creating an InfoPath Form content type, and uploading an administrator-approved form template.*

If you publish your form template to any of these locations, you must first save a local copy of the template on your computer. If you want to make updates to the form template later, you can make them to your local copy and complete the Publishing Wizard to update your form template in its shared location. However, you should be confident that no edits were performed directly on the template in its shared location. If edits are made by other form administrators, you could end up overwriting them by publishing an older version of the form. It is a good idea to identify and define development policies and procedures related to your organization's custom InfoPath forms to ensure that such situations do not occur. Once the initial publishing process has completed, future updates can be delivered to the server using the Quick Publish feature. This republishes the form using the same settings as previously defined in the last publishing process.

> **NOTE** *To ensure that you are editing the most recently published version of a form (as opposed to your local copy), go to the document library settings, click Advanced Settings, and click the Edit Template link.*

WORKING WITH FORM TEMPLATES

Now that you know the design-related functions of an InfoPath form template, you can start creating some actual form templates that can help you collect and view information. This section discusses creating a new form template and then addresses some options for publishing and customizing the form to further meet the business requirements. Customizing SharePoint list forms with InfoPath is also covered to demonstrate some differences.

Designing a New Form

Before you can begin creating a new form, you need to figure out the form's requirements. This might involve gathering information from the group or sponsors who are requesting the form. However you gather the information, you should know the following:

➤ What types of information should the form collect?

➤ How should you present the information, and what special rules are there for submitting the information? For example, you should create Name and Email fields because they are required to contact employees after they submit feedback.

➤ How should you format the Data fields? For example, you can apply special formatting or filtering that disables a field based on a user's input in another field. This is helpful to ensure that users have to deal only with the fields they are required to complete.

➤ Is there additional data that is stored in an external system that should be available within your form?

➤ What is the defined life cycle of any given form? If the form needs to be "read-only" after completion, you can create a read-only view in the form.

Once you have the information you need, it's time to do the actual work of creating the form template.

Although the next Try It Out contains many steps, they represent a small portion of the steps required to create the most basic of electronic forms.

TRY IT OUT   **Customizing a List Form**

In this Try It Out, you create a SharePoint contact list and customize it using InfoPath. You will see that with a few simple changes, you can format a form very professionally, and you can add validation to fields so that they must consist of a specific type of information, such as an e-mail address. This form will be published by you, and filled out by anyone who has at least contribute permissions on the library.

1. Open your SharePoint site in the browser. Click the Settings button at the top right, and choose Add an app.

2. Click Contacts, and for the name, type **Vendors**. Click Create.

3. In the Quick Launch area on the left side of the site, click the name of the new list, Vendors.

4. Click the List tab at the top, and click the List Settings button. Click the Advanced Settings button. For Attachments, choose Disabled. Scroll down to the Dialogs setting, and choose Yes for "Launch forms in a dialog." Click OK. Click OK to the warning about disabling attachments.

5. Click Vendors at the top, click New Item, and fill out some information for a new vendor. Notice how simple and plain the interface is, and how all of the fields go down the page vertically, as shown in Figure 12-22. Click Save.

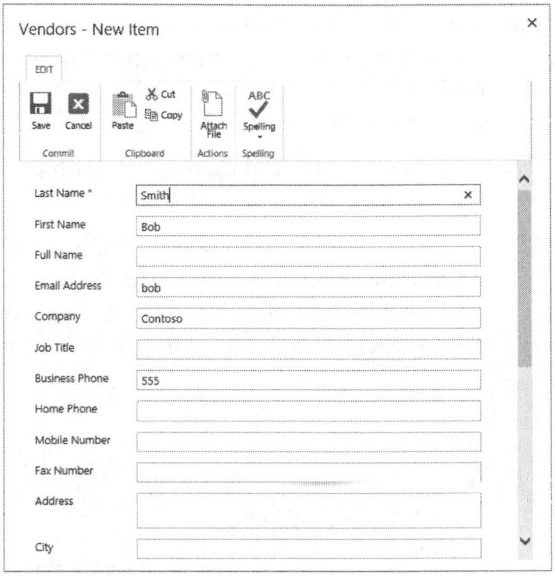

6. Click the List tab, and click the purple Customize Form button. If prompted with a security prompt, click Allow.

7. With the form now opened in InfoPath, you can now customize it to be a bit more streamlined and professional looking. Put the cursor in the top cell of the table, above Last Name. Type **New Vendor Form**. In the font style section of the homepage, choose the Title style, and center the text.

8. On the Page Design tab, choose the theme "Playground - Azure," or any theme that you would like. Click Yes to the prompt about using Microsoft Office 2013 styles.

FIGURE 12-22

9. Select the Full Name field, and use the Alt+Enter keyboard shortcut to open the field's properties. Click the function (fx) button next to the default value box.

10. The first and last name are concatenated together to form the full name. Use the Insert Function button to insert the concat function.

11. Double-click to insert the first field, and select First Name. Delete the second instance of "double click to insert field," and replace it with " ". Double-click the last "double click to insert field", and select the Last Name field. Figure 12-23 shows the resulting formula. Click OK, and click OK again.

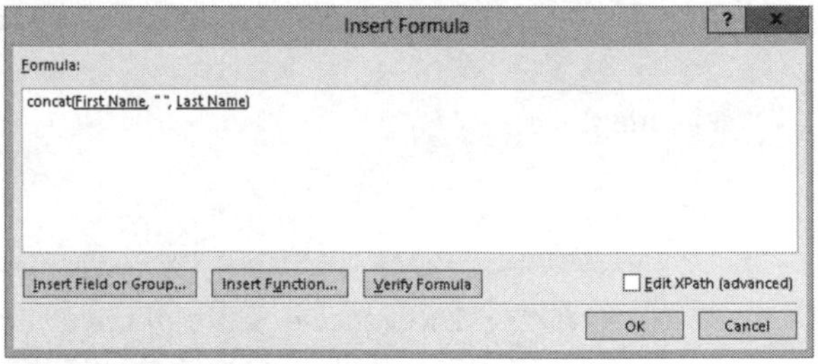

FIGURE 12-23

12. Select the First Name box, and in the Properties tab, check the box for Cannot be blank.

13. Select the Full Name box, and in the Properties tab, check the box for Read-Only.

14 Click to select the Email Address box. On the Home tab, click the Add Rule drop-down box, choose Is not an E-mail Address, and choose Show Validation Error.

15. Click to select the Business Phone box, and repeat step 14. In the Rules pane on the right, click to select the condition. Instead of "does not match pattern" Email, change the pattern to Phone number, and click OK. Click OK again. For the screen tip in the rules pane, type **Enter a valid phone number**.

16. Put the cursor at the very bottom of the table, under Notes. From the list of controls on the Home tab, select Button. This puts a gray button at the bottom of the form. Center the button. Double-click the button, and go to the Properties tab in the ribbon. From the Action drop-down box, choose Submit.

17. Click the X at the top right of InfoPath to close the form. You are prompted to save and publish. Click the Save and Publish button.

18. In the vendors list, click New Item. Notice that when the first and last names are filled in, the full name is automatically populated. Also, notice that a proper e-mail address and phone number must be filled in before the form can be submitted, as shown in Figure 12-24. Click Save at the top, or click the Submit button at the bottom.

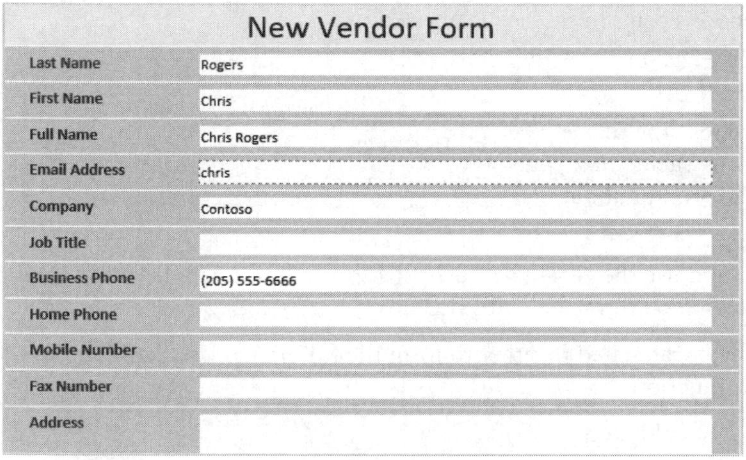

New Vendor Form	
Last Name	Rogers
First Name	Chris
Full Name	Chris Rogers
Email Address	chris
Company	Contoso
Job Title	
Business Phone	(205) 555-6666
Home Phone	
Mobile Number	
Fax Number	
Address	

FIGURE 12-24

> **NOTE** *When changes are made to the list, such as columns being edited or added, a message pops up the next time you click the Customize Form button that says "One or more fields in the SharePoint list have been changed. Do you want InfoPath to update the set of available fields? . . ." Click Yes. In general, changes that are made on the List Settings page will not automatically be propagated to the form. For example, if a new field were added to the list and not showing on the design surface as a control in InfoPath Designer, find it in the list of fields on the right and drag it onto the form's surface. You can add and rearrange table rows to accommodate for new or changed fields.*

Now that you have created and customized a fairly simple form from a SharePoint list, the next step is to try creating a Form Library form.

Designing a New Form Template

For this Try It Out, you start from scratch and first set up the layout of the form. This helps mold the canvas for how the form will look. It is also recommended that prior to opening the InfoPath application you should always sketch out how you want the form to look on a piece of paper, or use any type of mockup software. This is something that can be helpful for collecting feedback from your sponsors prior to starting any development work. As you see in the Try It Out, sometimes there can be many steps to creating even the most basic of forms. Therefore, it is always a good idea to have a solid roadmap before you start.

Once you define the layout, you begin adding controls and creating the data source. In this situation, every time you add a new control to the page, it creates a new data source field. You name the fields as you go along to keep things organized and easy to follow. This is very important as forms become more complex, and you create large numbers of fields.

1. Open the Microsoft InfoPath Designer 2013 application. The new form template selection window appears.

2. Select the option to create a blank form. Your selection is displayed on the right side of the window, as shown in Figure 12-25.

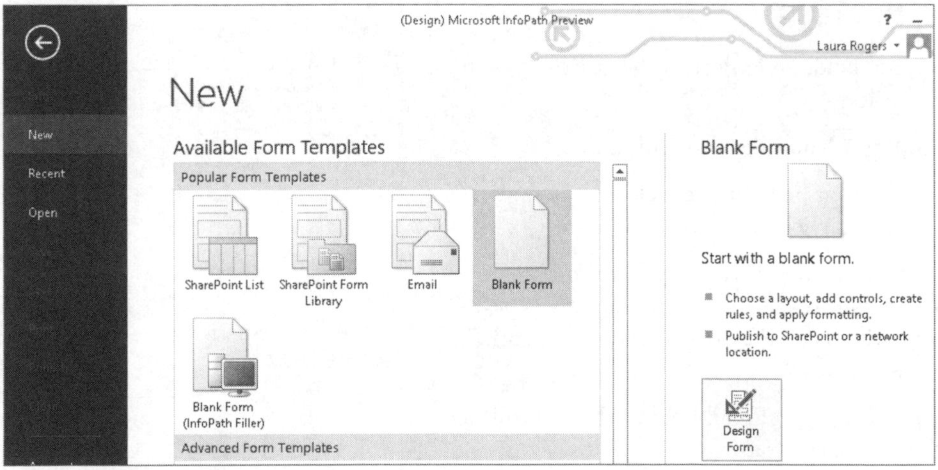

FIGURE 12-25

3. Click the Design Form button. A blank form template opens.

4. Delete the table, so that the view is completely empty. On the Page Design tab, click Page Layout Templates and choose Color Bar.

5. Click in the title area and enter **Employee Feedback** for the form title.

6. Click within the second row of the form template, and select the Insert tab of the ribbon. Insert the table layout called Two Column with Emphasis 4. Your new form layout is displayed, as shown in Figure 12-26.

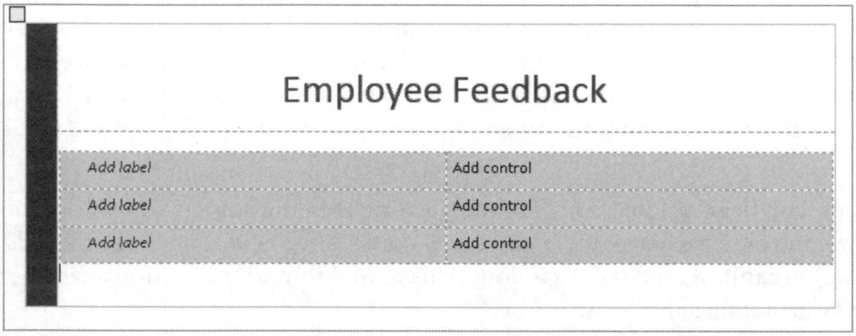

Employee Feedback

Add label	Add control
Add label	Add control
Add label	Add control

FIGURE 12-26

7. Click within the left column of the first row of the new table, and enter **Employee Name**.

8. From the Home tab of the ribbon, select the Text Box control. A new text box field appears below the Employee Name label.

9. Right-click the field, and select the Text Box Properties option.

10. Specify **EmployeeName** for the field name.

11. Check the "Cannot be blank" checkbox, as shown in Figure 12-27, and click OK.

12. In the list of fields on the right, right-click MyFields and choose Add…. For the Name, type **EmployeeEmail**, check the box "Cannot be blank," and click OK.

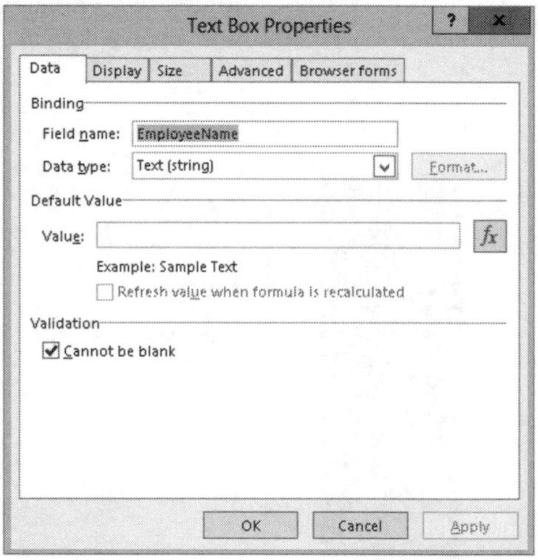

FIGURE 12-27

13. Drag the new EmployeeEmail field to the cell to the right of the Employee Name.

14. Notice that the font in the left column looks a bit different from the right column. Select the left column of the table, and on the Home tab, click Normal in the Font Styles.

15. Put the cursor underneath the two-column table, but still within the main Employee Feedback table.

16. On the Insert tab, click to insert the table called Single-Column Stacked 2.

17. In the spot that says Click to Add Heading, enter the text **Tell Us What You Think**.

18. With the cursor in the next cell down, from the Home tab of the ribbon menu, select the Rich Text box. A new field is added to the form.

19. Select your newly created field, and click the Properties tab of the ribbon menu.

20. Enter **EmployeeFeedback** in the Name field, as shown in Figure 12-28.

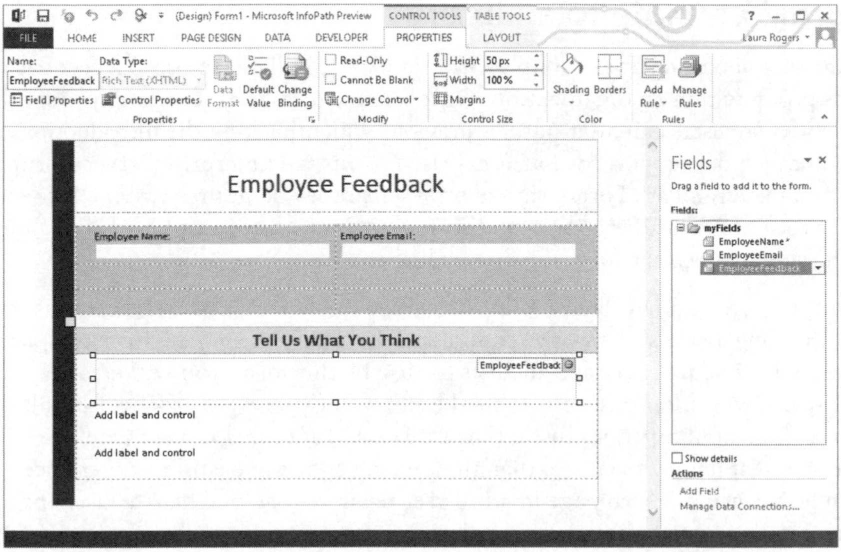

FIGURE 12-28

21. Select the Cannot Be Blank checkbox from the ribbon.

22. You have two empty rows in each of the tables in the form. To clean up and save some real estate, select each of the empty rows and use the Delete key to remove them.

23. From the File tab, select the Save as button.

24. Save the form in the folder containing this chapter's resource files using the name **EmployeeFeedback.xsn**.

25. From the Home tab of the ribbon menu, click the Preview button.

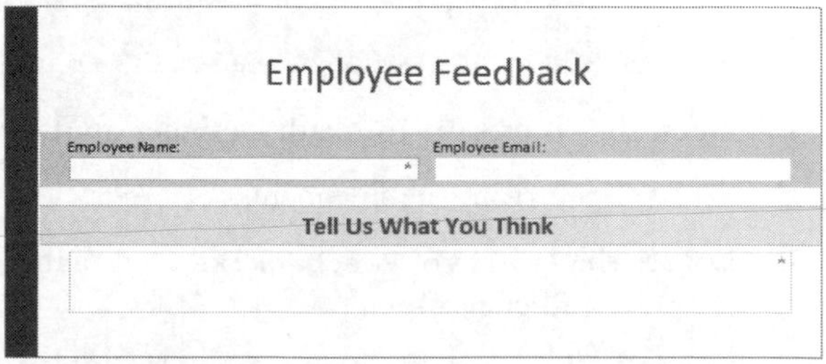

How It Works

After you finish adding fields and save the form, you preview it. Figure 12-29 demonstrates that each field has a special character within it that communicates to the user that the fields are

FIGURE 12-29

required. Keep in mind that although you ask for the employee's name in the form, the form library in SharePoint will always have the Created By column, which shows the name of the person who submitted each form. Also, the Modified By column shows the last person who edited the form. So, unless people need to fill out forms on behalf of other people, it is not always necessary to ask for the submitter's name in a form. In the list of submitted forms in the library, click the name of anyone in the Created By column to see more information about them, such as their e-mail address and department.

Publishing a Form Template to a Library

In the previous example, you created a very simple form for users to fill out to provide feedback to a communications group within an organization. Once you create a form template, you must publish it to a location where users can fill it out. As previously mentioned in the introduction of this chapter, SharePoint includes support for *browser-based forms*, an Enterprise Server feature that allows users to complete InfoPath Forms via the browser so they do not require the InfoPath application. For a site to support this functionality, this Enterprise feature must be activated on the site collection and the site to which the form is being published.

In the next Try It Out, you create a new SharePoint site named "Communications" that uses the Blank site template. Creating a new site is not a requirement for publishing a new form template; however, because you will be adding very specific lists for use by this form, you will create a brand-new site from which to work. Once you create the site, you explore the process for publishing a form template to a document library. Finally, in the last Try It Out of this section, you learn how to configure a document library to ensure that all users have the same editing experience, and specify that the form be opened as a web page in a browser regardless of whether the users have the InfoPath application installed on their computer.

TRY IT OUT   Publishing a Form Template to a Document Library

All the examples in this section use the `EmployeeFeedback.xsn` InfoPath form template file that was created in the first Try It Out in this chapter.

1. From the Corporate Intranet Site you created in Chapter 1 of this book, create a new site called "Communications" based on the Blank site template.

> **NOTE** *You can find detailed steps for creating a new site in the first Try it Out of Chapter 2.*

2. Open the Microsoft InfoPath Designer application.

3. Select Open from the File menu.

4. Locate the `EmployeeFeedback.xsn` template that you created in the first Try it Out of this chapter, and click Open.

5. Select Publish from the File menu. The Publish window appears, as shown in Figure 12-30.

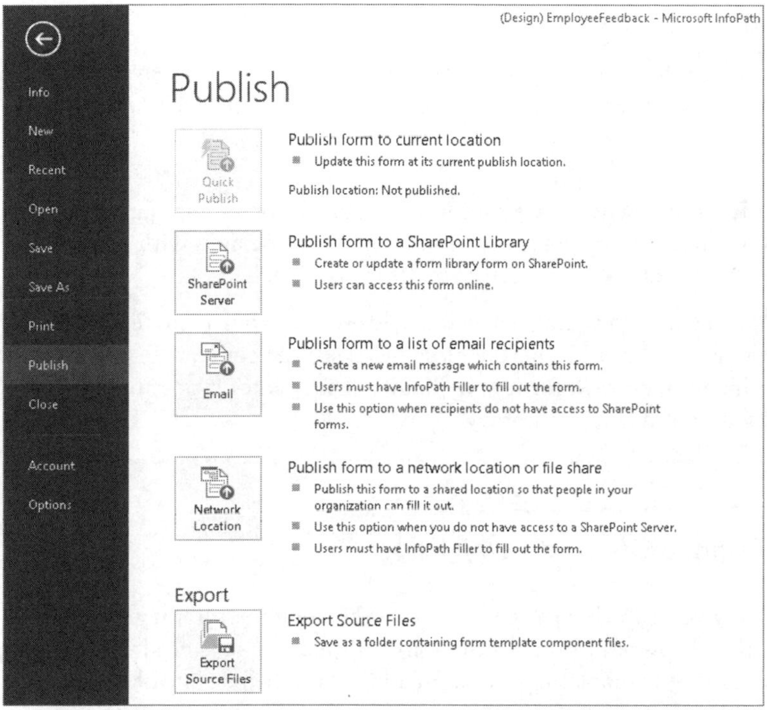

FIGURE 12-30

6. Select the option to Publish form to a SharePoint Library.

7. Enter the URL of the site you created in the first step of this Try It Out. Click Next.

8. Ensure that the checkbox is selected to Enable this form to be filled out using a browser. Select the option to publish to a Form Library, and click Next.

9. Select the option to Create a New Form Library, and click Next.

10. Enter **Feedback** as the name of the library. For Description, enter the following:

Electronic form for collecting feedback from employees on new communications website.

11. Click Next. The wizard continues to the field selection stage of the publishing process.

12. In the section for column names at the top, click Add.

13. Select the EmployeeName field from the list of fields, as shown in Figure 12-31. Click OK.

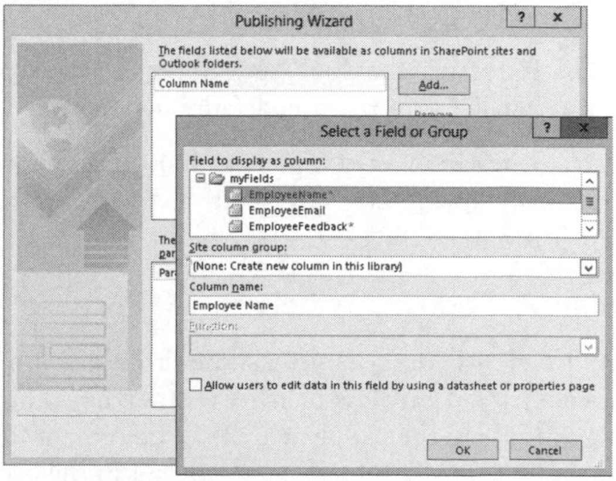

FIGURE 12-31

14. Repeat steps 12 and 13 for the remaining fields in the form. Click Next.

15. Click the Publish button. Upon the successful publishing of your form, you receive a confirmation window containing a link to view the form within the browser and to open the form library.

How It Works

In this example, you created a new document library on the Communications site as part of the form-publishing process. This document library has the form template associated with it so that whenever a user enters the site and clicks the New button, the form is launched.

During the publishing process, you chose to promote specific fields within your form template to become columns within your document library. This enables you to see the contents of the forms in a view in the library without having to open each form individually. This makes it possible to create custom reports on data stored within a document library.

TRY IT OUT   **Forcing a Form to Open as a Web Page**

In this Try It Out, you review how you can change the setting on the document library to force everyone to open the form within a browser. In some situations, this technique is used to ensure that all users have a consistent experience when completing forms. In addition, it helps control the interface so that only items exposed within a specific view are displayed to the user. You can use this same process to force the form to open in either the browser or the InfoPath Filler application.

1. From the main page of your Communications site, click the Feedback link on the left.

2. Select the Library Settings option from the Library tab of the ribbon.

3. Click the Advanced Settings link.

4. For the Opening Documents in the Browser value, select "Open in the browser," as shown in Figure 12-32. Click OK.

5. Return to the document library by clicking Feedback in the breadcrumb navigation.

6. Click the New Document link to fill out a new form. Take a look at the form and the toolbar. Click Close.

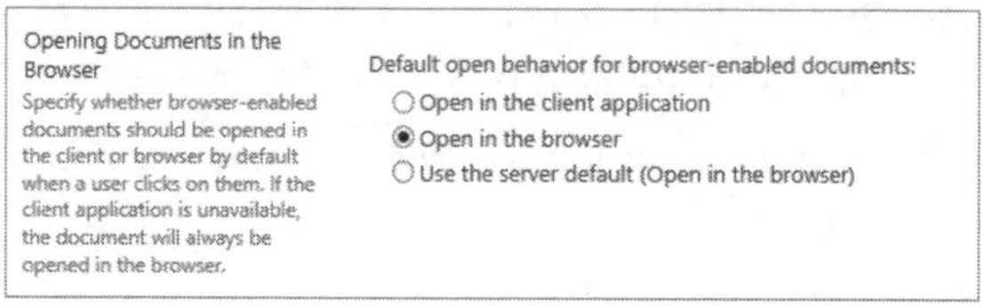

Opening Documents in the Browser
Specify whether browser-enabled documents should be opened in the client or browser by default when a user clicks on them. If the client application is unavailable, the document will always be opened in the browser.

Default open behavior for browser-enabled documents:
○ Open in the client application
● Open in the browser
○ Use the server default (Open in the browser)

FIGURE 12-32

How It Works

As previously described, in some situations it may be necessary to ensure that all users open a form as a web page regardless of whether they have the InfoPath Filler application installed. In this exercise, you modified the properties of the document library to ensure that all browser-enabled documents, including InfoPath forms, are opened in the browser.

Now that you have published your form template to the site, users can enter the site and complete the form template. When they are done, they can save the form back to the library by using the toolbar buttons. However, after giving the matter some consideration, you have decided that it would be nice to add a Submit button to the form, which will save the document back to the library and name it automatically. This is the subject of the next section.

CUSTOMIZING A FORM TEMPLATE

Once you have created a template and published it to a library, you can still edit and enhance it to further address business needs. As a form designer, you should consult with business users to identify ways in which the form can evolve to better suit their needs. This may include improving how data is submitted or saved to a library as well as how the form is presented to users.

In this section, you review some of the enhancements and changes you can make to a form template that might make it a more effective tool for a team. In the first Try It Out, you look at how you can add a button to a form as well as a submit data connection that will save the form to a destination library without requiring a user to select Save or Save As from the File menu. These approaches help ensure that a proper naming scheme is followed for saved forms because the name can be derived from form data upon submission. It also makes the user experience better for those completing the form because they do not have to bother with understanding the details of where and how they should save the form. Once you add a Submit button, there may no longer be a need to expose the Save buttons on the form's toolbar to users. Therefore, in the second Try It Out of this section, you learn how you can customize the form's toolbar to suit your needs. You then look at how you can add a data connection to a form template to retrieve information from another content source.

TRY IT OUT   Adding a Submit Button to a Form Template

In some cases, rather than having users select Save As and manually name their form file, it's more appropriate to offer a Submit button at the bottom of the form that users can select when they complete the form. This makes the submission process easier because the users do not have to be concerned with where the file is being saved and what the filename will be.

In this exercise, you edit the Employee Feedback form to include a Submit button that saves the file to your library and automatically generates a name based on information stored within the form.

1. Open the Microsoft InfoPath Designer application.

2. Select Open from the File menu.

3. Locate the `EmployeeFeedback.xsn` template that you created in the first Try it Out of this chapter, and click Open.

4. In the list of fields on the right, right-click MyFields and choose Add.

5. For the field name, type **Date**, and for the data type, choose Date and Time. Click OK.

6. In the list of fields on the right, double-click the new Date field to open its properties. Click the fx function button next to the Default Value box. Insert the function called Now(). Click OK.

7. On the Field or Group Properties screen, it is very important to uncheck the box "Refresh value when formula is recalculated." Click OK.

8. Place the cursor in the bottom-most empty cell in the Employee Feedback table, below the bottom-most Text Box control.

9. Add the Button control from the Controls section of the Home ribbon. Click the Center button, also on the Home tab of the ribbon.

10. Select the button that you just inserted, and select the Control Tools ribbon. The Properties tab of the Control Tools ribbon appears, as shown in Figure 12-33.

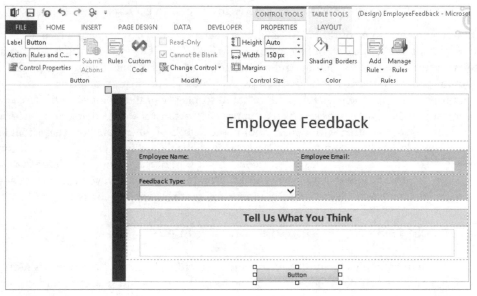

FIGURE 12-33

11. From the Action drop-down, select Submit. The Submit Options window appears.

12. Select the option to "Allow users to submit the form." The submit options are enabled. Select the option to Send form data to a single destination and select SharePoint document library from the associated drop-down menu. Click Add.

13. The Data Connection Wizard appears. Enter the URL for the document library you created for feedback forms.

> **NOTE** If you are unsure of the exact URL, visit the document library and copy the URL. Be sure to include only the URL of the library. If the URL of the library is `http://team.contoso.com/communications/_layouts/15/start.aspx#/Feedback/Forms/AllItems.aspx`, the example of the trimmed-down URL is shown in Figure 12-34.

14. For the File Name field, click the fx button to the right of the field.

15. Enter the following into the Formula field, as shown in Figure 12-34. Click OK.

concat(EmployeeName, " ", Date)

On the Insert Formula screen, input the EmployeeName and the Date fields by selecting them with the Insert Field or Group button.

16. Still in the Data Connection Wizard, check the "Allow overwrite if file exists" checkbox, and then click Next.

FIGURE 12-34

17. Click Finish. Click OK on the Submit Options screen.

18. Click the Quick Publish button, which is a small icon next to the Save button at the top left.

19. In the browser, complete the form with sample data, and click the Submit button.

20. You should see a form successfully submitted to the library, as shown in Figure 12-35.

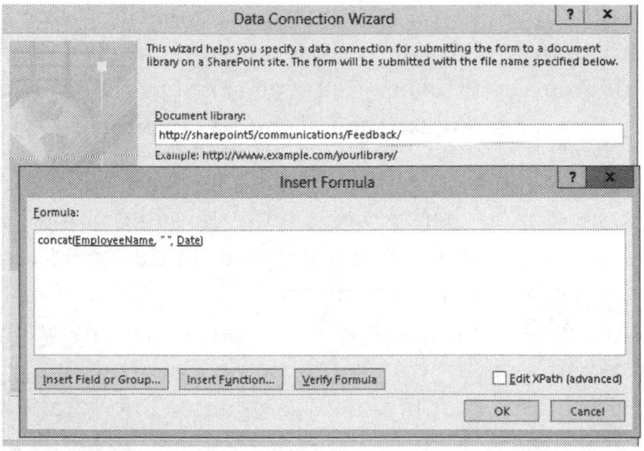

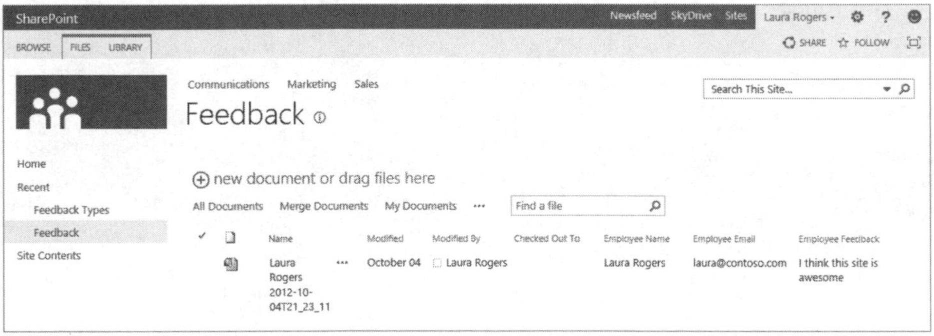

FIGURE 12-35

How It Works

In this example, you made a modification to the form template to allow users to more easily submit their changes to the document library. Previously, you had to rely on users to click the Save As button from the toolbar or menu. From that point, users were required to name the file on their own. This could lead to major inconsistencies in naming practices and the ability to easily identify specific differences between forms.

You implemented a Submit button on the form. You had a number of different methods you could use to submit the form, including the use of web services or e-mail. However, in this situation, because all completed forms are being saved to the same document library you are using to launch the form, it makes sense to use the Submit to Document Library option.

In addition to specifying where you can submit a form, you can also select how the form should be named and whether items with the same name should be overwritten, along with what actions take place once the form is submitted. In this situation, you chose to name the forms based on the name of the employee submitting the form in addition to the exact date and time at which the form was filled out. Although this does not create a visually appealing filename, you can be sure that it will be very easy to identify who submitted each form, and you can ensure that filenames will be unique. You also determined that if a file was updated and resubmitted, the existing form record should be overwritten rather than creating a completely new record. The reason you put the Now() function in a separate field instead of directly in the data connection is because in this case, you don't want a new XML file to be created each time the same form is opened and submitted. When a single form needs to be opened and submitted multiple times, such as in an approval process, the desired result is typically to keep the same filename for a single form throughout that process.

TRY IT OUT Customizing the Browser-Based Form Toolbar

There is still another set of changes that you need to make to the form to make it more usable and intuitive. In Figure 12-36, you see a screenshot of what the form looks like in its current state.

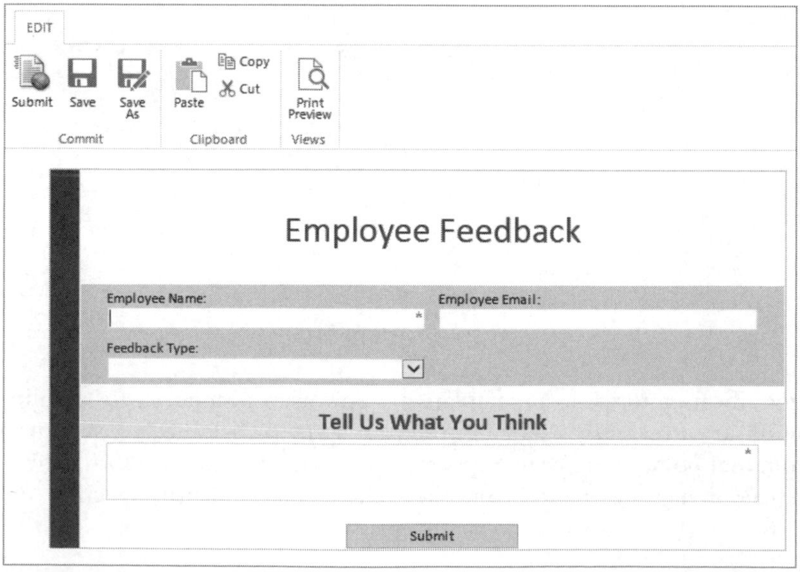

FIGURE 12-36

The users now have to choose between the custom Submit button, a Save button, and a Save As button. This can lead to some users choosing to save their forms using their own naming structure, and thereby eliminates any benefits associated with a standardized naming scheme that has been introduced with the custom button. Most importantly, for a very simple form you are offering users far too many choices. This leads to confusion and possibly even frustration. So in this example, you customize the toolbar that is automatically added to the browser-based forms to display only the Print View option, because this is something that users might find useful.

1. Return to your local copy of the Employee Feedback template featuring the changes you implemented in the previous example.

2. Select Form Options from the File tab of the ribbon. The Form Options appear, as shown in Figure 12-37.

3. Uncheck all commands except Print Preview. Click OK.

4. From the File tab of the ribbon menu, select the Quick Publish option. Once the form has been published, you will receive a message confirming that the operation has completed successfully.

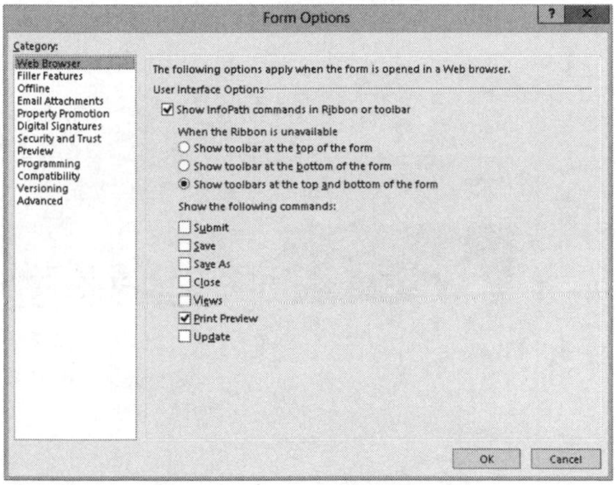

FIGURE 12-37

How It Works

In this example, you used the Form Options menu to customize what commands are displayed in a toolbar when users view the form via the browser. You did this to simplify the interface so that users can easily identify what they should select when it comes time for them to submit their information to the site. As in most cases, it is far more important for users to focus on the information they are submitting rather than the steps they are taking to submit it. Once your changes were complete, you used the Quick Publish option in InfoPath to republish your changes to the previously published location.

TRY IT OUT Adding a Data Connection to a Form Template

So far, you have reviewed how to create a custom template that supports browser-based viewing and editing. You created a data connection in the form template to allow for the form to be submitted to the document library using a standardized naming scheme. However, you can also use data connections to display information in a form from an external data source, such as a SharePoint list or web service.

In this example, you discover how data entry can be made easier by allowing information to be pulled directly from a central source. For this example, you use a SharePoint list of types of feedback, from your site.

1. On the Communications SharePoint site in the browser, click the Settings button at the top right, and choose Add an App. If no apps are displayed on the screen, type **Custom** in the Find an app box, and click the search button.

2. Click Custom List, and for the name, enter **Feedback Types.** Click Create.

3. Click Feedback Types on the left side of the screen, and use the New Item link to create each of three new feedback types: Suggestion, Complaint, and Compliment. Figure 12-38 shows the completed list.

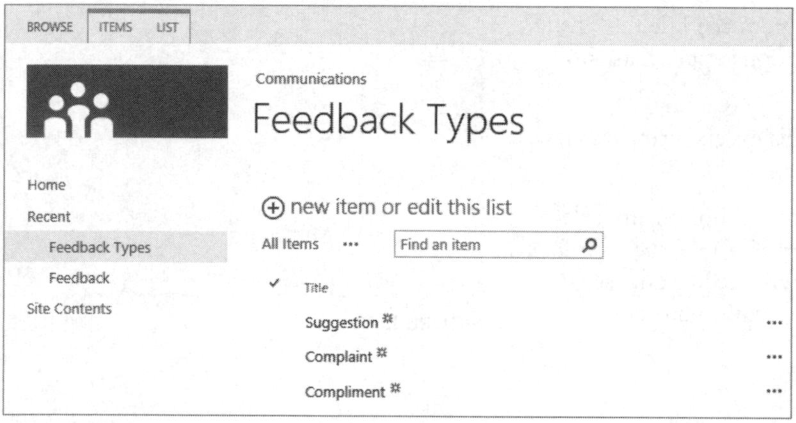

FIGURE 12-38

4. Return to your local copy of the Employee Feedback template featuring the changes you implemented in the previous example.

5. In the Fields pane on the right, right-click MyFields and choose Add. Name the field **FeedbackType** and click OK.

6. Put the cursor in the table cell with Employee Email. When you click the Tab key on the keyboard, a new row is created in the table.

7. Drag the FeedbackType field from the list of fields to the newly created row on the design surface. Notice that the name of the field is automatically added.

8. Select the FeedbackType text box on the form's design surface, and click the right mouse button. Select Change Control, then Drop-Down List Box. The field is transformed into a drop-down list box.

9. With the FeedbackType box selected, use the Alt+Enter keys as a shortcut to open the Drop-Down List Box Properties screen.

10. From the "List box choices" section, select the "Get choices from an external data source" option, as shown in Figure 12-39.

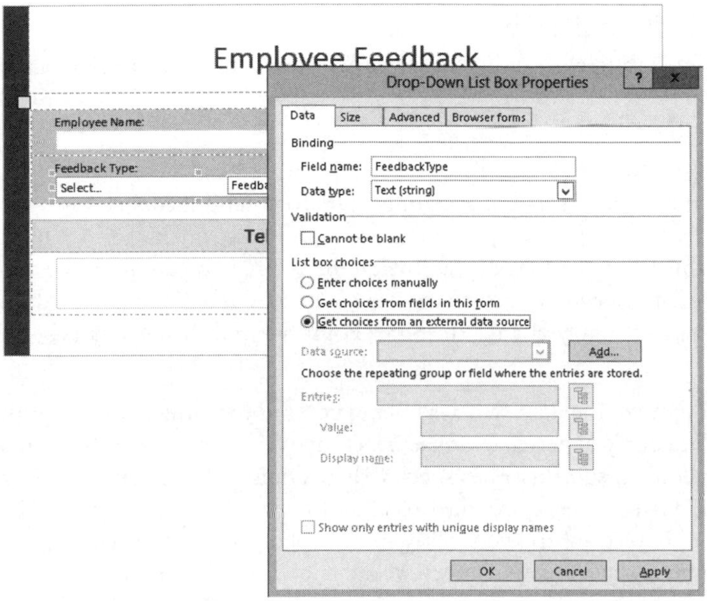

FIGURE 12-39

11. Click Add to launch the Data Connection Creation Wizard.

12. Select the Create a New Connection To option button, and select Receive Data. Click Next.

13. Select SharePoint library or list, and click Next.

14. Enter the URL of your communications site, such as http://team.contoso.com/communications. Click Next. A listing of all lists in that site is returned.

15. Select the Feedback Types list. Click Next.

16. Select the Title field, select Title in the Sort by drop-down box, and click Next. Click Next again.

17. Retain the default settings for the data connection name and synchronization settings. Click Finish.

18. Click the button to the right of the Value field. Select the Title field and click OK.

19. Click the button to the right of the Display Name, select the Title field, as shown in Figure 12-40, and click OK. This means that for whichever feedback type is selected, the actual name of that feedback type will be stored in this field, as opposed to just the ID of it.

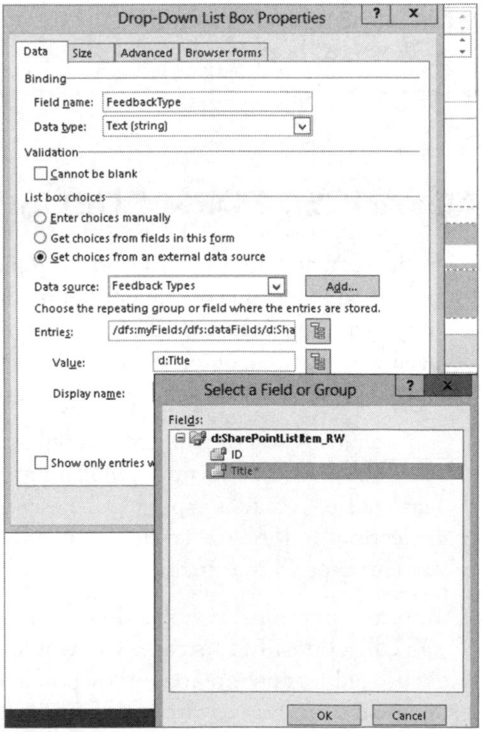

FIGURE 12-40

20. On the Drop-Down List Box Properties screen, click OK.

21. Click the Save button on the File tab to ensure that your changes are committed to the template. Quick Publish the form.

How It Works

You added a feedback type field to the form. Instead of allowing users to enter a feedback type in a free-form text box, you decided to let them select a type from a drop-down list of choices. In addition, rather than manually maintaining this list of feedback types inside the form, you can draw the value list from an external data source. Any time you need to change the list of feedback types, you do not need to modify the form itself — you can simply change the SharePoint list and the new values will be reflected in the form.

In addition to a requirement to standardize the data that was being entered for name, you recognized a need to reduce and simplify the data entry experience of users as they were completing the form. For example, it seemed somewhat ridiculous to some users to specify their e-mail address because they were logged in to the network as registered users. Therefore, the organization should already have an e-mail address associated with them. You did not want to just strictly remove the field because your goal might be to later e-mail all users who complete the form. Therefore, you decided that it would be useful to retain the Email Address field but have its value auto-populated based on the selection of a user's name.

Once the data connection was configured, you connected the drop-down list box to the data connection. By default, all items in the SharePoint list are returned and displayed in the drop-down list box. When you click the Preview button after making the changes, you should see the feedback types in the drop-down list box.

ADVANCED FORM-PUBLISHING OPTIONS

In the section "Publishing a Form Template to a Library," you learned how a form template is published to a single document library. This approach is suitable for scenarios where a form is required only in a single location and where multiple groups or sites do not reuse the form. However, you may need to make a form template available to multiple sites in a site collection or multiple site collections. In each of these cases, you can choose one of the advanced form publishing options.

For scenarios where you want to publish a form template to multiple sites or libraries in the same site collection, the optimal publishing choice is to publish as a content type. In Chapter 6, you learned how content types can be associated with multiple libraries and locations in a single site collection. In the first Try It Out of this section, you publish your meeting agenda form template as a content type so that it can be added to multiple libraries.

In some situations, you may have a single form template that you want to make available in multiple site collections. In this case, you would choose to publish your template as an Administrator-Approved form template and then upload it via the Central Administration site. From there, form templates can be activated to site collections from one central location. This method is also the only supported choice for advanced form templates containing custom code or highly complex data connections.

| TRY IT OUT | Publishing a Form Template as a Content Type |

All the examples in this section use the `MeetingAgendaFinal.xsn` InfoPath form template file.

You now know how to publish a form template directly to a SharePoint document library. The next step to look at is the process for creating a content type by publishing a form template. For this example, you use the Meeting Agenda Final form. However, you open it in InfoPath Designer 2013 and choose a different publishing location and type. You publish the form template as a content type so that you can deploy it to multiple sites and libraries in the same site collection.

1. From the practice files, locate the file called `MeetingAgendaFinal.xsn`, and open this template within InfoPath Designer.

2. From the File tab, select the Publish option. Select SharePoint Server from the list of Publish choices.

3. If you have previously published this form, a URL may already exist. Remove it and enter the URL of your corporate intranet portal, which should be the root of the site collection (example: `http://team.contoso.com`), and click Next.

4. Check the Enable the Form to Be Filled Out by Using a Browser checkbox, select Site Content Type (Advanced), and click Next.

5. Select the "Create a new content type" option, as shown in Figure 12-41, and click Next.

6. For the name of the content type, specify **Meeting Agenda Form**, enter the following for the description, and click Next:

   This content type is an electronic form for meeting agendas to be filled out and used by various departments.

7. Click the Browse button to specify a location where the form template can be stored within the site collection.

FIGURE 12-41

8. Select the Form Templates document library, and click Open.

9. Enter the name in the Filename field as **meetingagenda.xsn**. Click Save and then Next.

10. Use the Add button to promote the MeetingTitle, Organizer, MeetingRoom, Start Date, and End Date fields as columns to document libraries within the site collection. Click Next and then Publish.

11. Click Close to complete the wizard.

How It Works

One of the primary advantages of a content type is being able to add a single content type to multiple locations throughout a site collection. Using the previously explored method of publishing directly to a document library, the form template could only be pushed out and associated with a single library. There would be no way to add it to other libraries without republishing it manually in a series of redundant and unrelated processes. Data connections in the form are unrelated to the location that the form is published to. In our example, the form was published to a content type, but there is no data connection specifying where the file will be submitted to when users fill it out.

When it's time to edit this content type template again, of course, you can edit the local copy as in previous exercises. If this XSN file does not exist, there is another way to edit the template. At the top level of the site collection, go to the Site Settings screen and click Content Types. Click the name of your content type, click Advanced Settings, and then click the Edit Template link.

If the form had a single submit data connection, all submitted forms would end up in the same form library, no matter which library users used to fill out the form. All users submitting forms would also need to have Contribute permissions to the library to which the forms were being submitted. This model is great for collecting all forms in a single location; however, in this example, you are going to assume that the goal is for each department to manage its own list of meeting agendas. This requires a different submit connection for each different library.

TRY IT OUT **Creating Multiple Submit Connections**

The form has been published as a content type, and now it is time to associate this content type with two different libraries on different sites in the same site collection. Sales will manage their own list of agendas, and Marketing will manage theirs.

1. On the Communications site in the browser, create a new subsite called Sales (using the Team Site template), and another one called Marketing.

2. On the Sales site, click Settings at the top right, and choose Add an app. Click Form Library, name it **Sales Meetings**, and click Create.

3. On the Marketing site, create another form library called **Marketing Meetings**.

4. Click the name of the Marketing Meetings library, and in the Library tab in the ribbon, click Library Settings.

5. Click Advanced Settings, and under Allow management of content types, choose Yes. Click OK.

6. On the library settings page, under Content Types, click "Add from existing site content types."

7. On the left side, click Meeting Agenda Form, click Add, and click OK. The content types are shown in Figure 12-42.

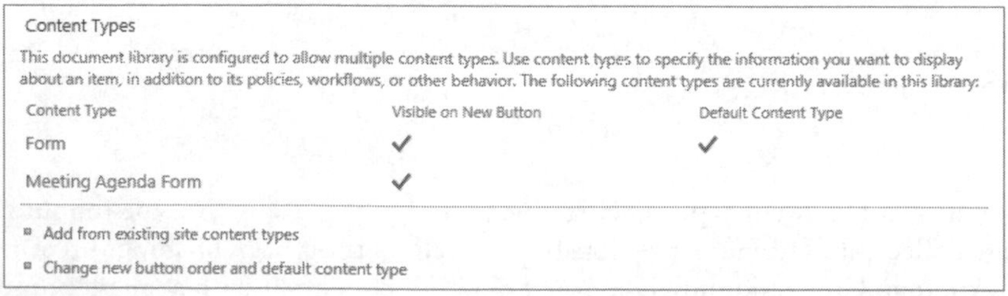

Content Types		
This document library is configured to allow multiple content types. Use content types to specify the information you want to display about an item, in addition to its policies, workflows, or other behavior. The following content types are currently available in this library:		
Content Type	Visible on New Button	Default Content Type
Form	✓	✓
Meeting Agenda Form	✓	

▫ Add from existing site content types

▫ Change new button order and default content type

FIGURE 12-42

8. Under Content Types, click the name of the Form content type, click Delete this content type, and click OK.

9. Scroll down to the bottom of the library settings page, and click Create view. Choose Calendar View.

10. Name the view **Calendar**. In the Begin drop-down box, choose Start Date. In the End box, choose End Date. For the Month View Title, Week View Title, and Day View Title, choose the Meeting Title field. Click OK.

11. Repeat steps 4 through 10 on the Sales Meetings library.

12. In the form in InfoPath Designer, right click MyFields on the right, and choose Add. Name the field **CurrentSite**, and click OK.

13. Double-click to open the CurrentSite field properties. Click the fx function button next to the Default Value box. Click the Insert Function button.

14. In the category called URL, double-click to select the function called SharePointSiteURL(), as shown in Figure 12-43. Click OK, and click OK again.

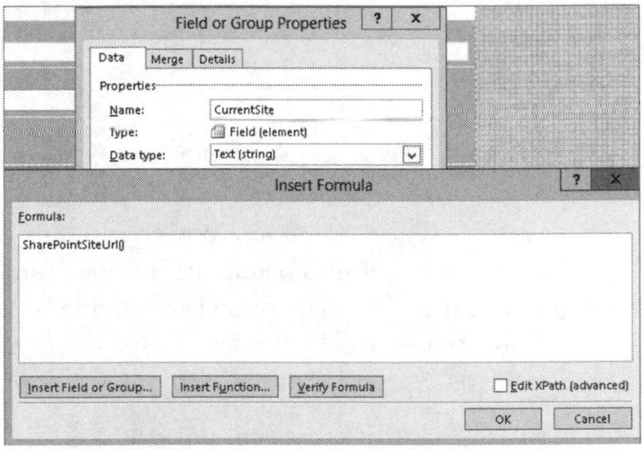

15. On the Data tab, click To SharePoint Library.

16. Enter the URL of the Sales Meeting library, and for the form name, concatenate the MeetingTitle with the StartDate field. (You can see more details of this screen in the previous activity called "Adding a Submit Button to a Form Template".) Check "Allow overwrite if file exists" and click Next.

FIGURE 12-43

17. Change the name of the data connection to Sales Submit, and uncheck the box to set it as the default submit connection. Click Finish.

18. Repeat steps 12 through 14 for the Marketing Meetings library, using the URL to the marketing library, and naming the connection Marketing Submit.

How It Works

In this exercise, you created two different data connections. The idea is that if a user fills out this form from the marketing site, the form will be submitted to the marketing library, and on the sales site, it will go to the sales library. It is time to automate the form, so that end users do not need to concern themselves with the location to which the form is being submitted.

> **WARNING** When fields are used as part of the filename, such as MeetingTitle and StartDate were in this example, it is important that they are set as required fields. If the filename depends on a meeting title existing, the filename will not follow the proper syntax when the form is submitted without one. Also, if the meeting title or start date is changed later, a new XML file will be created the next time that same form is submitted. These are just some considerations to make regarding filename syntax. In the exercise called "Add a Submit Button to a Form Template," you learned a method of creating a unique date/time field to be used as part of the filename. If you want to ensure a unique filename, one method is to use only that unique date/time. This creates files that are not necessarily the best looking, but are always unique.

WORKING WITH RULES

Rules in InfoPath represent a powerful set of functionalities in order to create logical statements in a visual manner, with no code necessary. You can create one or more rules on each control in the form, and they are triggered when a field's value changes, or when a button is clicked. Form load rules, located on the Data tab, are automatically triggered when the form is opened. Each rule may have one or more conditions, and one or more actions that happen.

There are three different types of rules:

➤ Validation rules

➤ Formatting rules

➤ Action rules

Validation Rules

These types of rules enable you to create conditions in which a field will be required, or you can create them in order to require that a certain value or format exists in a field. In the "Customizing a List Form" Try It Out earlier in this chapter, you set up an e-mail address field to allow only actual e-mail addresses to be typed in. Another example is that you can set a field to be required, only if another field contains a certain value.

Formatting Rules

Formatting rules enable you to hide or disable a control according to a condition. You can also apply certain colors. For example, if a field called priority is set to High, that field can show with red text and/or a red background. Also, you can hide a section or button if a certain value does not exist in a field.

Action Rules

The most commonly used rules, action rules allow a certain action or multiple actions to take place when a value is changed in a control, or when a button is pressed. With browser-based forms, you can use six different types of actions:

➤ Switch views

➤ Set a field's value

➤ Query for data

➤ Submit data

➤ Close the form

➤ Send data to web part

For a quick example of a way to use the "Set a field's value" action, picture a form with two buttons at the bottom: Save Draft and Submit for Approval. These can even be pretty picture buttons. Each button has different rules. When Save Draft is clicked, a field called Status is set to a value of Draft, and the form is submitted and closed. When Submit for Approval is clicked, the Status field is set to a value of Submitted, and the form is submitted and closed. Then, you can add a formatting rule to the Save Draft button so that if the form's Status field has a value of Submitted, it is hidden.

TRY IT OUT   Creating Conditional Rules for Submission

In this exercise, you create a submit button on the existing Meeting Agenda form, with conditions, so that the form is automatically submitted to the correct library. Because you have two different data connections, it is not a good idea to use any of the default submit functionality. Therefore, you apply custom rules to the submit button.

1. Return to your local copy of the Meeting Agenda template featuring the changes you implemented in the previous example.

2. Put the cursor at the bottom of the form, and from the Home tab, insert a new Button control. Notice on the Properties tab that the default action is Rules and Custom Code. Change the label of the button to say **Submit Agenda** instead of Button.

3. On the Home tab, click the Manage Rules button. The Rules pane shows on the right side of the screen.

4. Click the New button, and choose Action. In the Details for box, type **Sales Submit**.

5. Under Condition, click the link that says None - . For the first drop-down box, choose CurrentSite if it is not already selected.

6. Change the second box to contains, and in the third drop-down box, choose Type text. Type the word **sales**, as shown in Figure 12-44. Note that this condition is case-sensitive. Click OK.

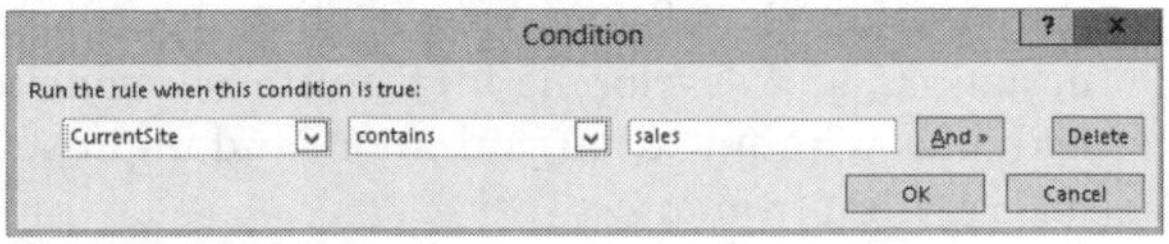

FIGURE 12-44

7. In the Rules page, under Run these actions, click the Add button, and choose Submit data.

8. Choose the Sales Submit data connection, and click OK.

9. At the top of the Rules pane, with the Sales Submit rule selected, click the Copy Rule button. Click the Paste Rule Button.

10. Now there is a copy of the rule that you can modify. Instead of Rule 1, name this new rule **Marketing Submit**. Click the condition to open it, and change it to say CurrentSite contains "marketing" instead of "sales." Click OK.

11. Under Run these actions, click the Submit action that's already in there to open it, and change the Data Connection drop-down box to Marketing Submit. Click OK.

12. There is one more rule to create. Because closing the form is not conditional, and you want it to happen each time a form is submitted, you can create a third rule. Click the New button, and choose Action.

13. Name this rule **Close Form**. Click the Add button, and choose Close the form. Click OK.

14. From the File menu, click Form Options. Uncheck the boxes next to Save and Save As. Click OK.

15. Click the Quick Publish button.

How It Works

In this exercise, you created rules on a submit button, so the form gets submitted to the appropriate library, depending on what site the form is filled out from. Because the form was published as a content type, changes to the form only need to be made in one place, and they are applicable in every library that is using that content type. To try out this form, navigate to the Sales Meetings library in the browser, and click New Document to fill out a form and submit it. Do the same in the Marketing Meetings library. When submitted, each form file will end up in the correct library.

SUMMARY

This chapter discussed how you can use and integrate a Microsoft Office application for creating electronic forms with SharePoint, using InfoPath Forms Services.

You learned about the various design-level tasks and elements associated with an InfoPath form, including its layout, controls, data source, design check, and publishing functions. You saw some of the standard controls you can add to a form, some of the publishing possibilities for a form template, as well as an overview of how rules work.

This chapter offered several step-by-step examples showing how to create form templates and use them within SharePoint. After reading this chapter, you should feel comfortable planning, designing, and developing InfoPath form templates that can map directly to specific business activities within your organization, and improve the efficiency and effectiveness of collecting information from users.

EXERCISES

1. Explain the reasons why you would decide to create a form that supports editing in the browser.

2. Explain the different scenarios by which you can publish a form template.

3. Describe a template part.

4. Explain the difference between a control and a data source element.

5. True or false: InfoPath cannot submit to a data connection. It can only retrieve information.

▶ **WHAT YOU LEARNED IN THIS CHAPTER**

TOPIC	KEY CONCEPTS
InfoPath	InfoPath is an application that integrates with SharePoint to collect and present data. InfoPath is comprised of two tools: InfoPath Designer, which is the tool used to create form templates; and InfoPath Filler, which is a tool that is used to fill out InfoPath Forms.
The difference between a form template and a form data file	An InfoPath form template is designed and published to a shared location by a forms designer. It has an `.xsn` file extension. An InfoPath data file is created when a user completes a form, and it has an `.xml` file extension.
Rules	Rules are created in order to create business logic in forms. With validation rules, formatting rules, and action rules, automation can be built around field values and button actions.

13

Working with Access Services

WHAT YOU WILL LEARN IN THIS CHAPTER:

➤ How to build an Access app using Microsoft Access 2013

➤ The main components of an Access database

➤ How to work with an Access database within SharePoint

Microsoft Access is a relational database product that has been around for many years. It has come a long way since good old Access 1.0 back in 1992. Over the years, and with the proliferation of networks and the Internet, the way that we get to our data has changed significantly. Access has always been a great tool for power users to create business solutions on the fly, but with more business processes taking place in a browser interface for the past few years, Access just didn't fit the bill. SharePoint 2010 introduced Access Services. These web-based forms can be used in any modern web browser. These forms also don't require any add-ins or extensions like ActiveX or Silverlight. This was a great improvement to requiring users to have the Microsoft Access client software installed on their computers.

In this chapter, you learn how to work with the new Access Services in SharePoint 2013, using Access 2013. This new version of Access has been tremendously improved over Access 2010. Many behind-the-scenes changes have been made, such as the structure and storage of the database, and also very obvious changes to the user interface.

All the step-by-step instructions in this chapter build on each other. The first Try It Out walks you through creating your first database, which you will use in all the other Try It Outs. You will need either a SharePoint 2013 site or an Office 365 SharePoint Online site. Also, you will need Microsoft Access 2013 installed on your computer.

Creating a New Database

To create your first database with Access Services, follow these steps. It is assumed that you already have created a SharePoint site from previous chapters, and that you have installed Microsoft Access 2013.

1. From the homepage of your SharePoint site, click the Settings button at the top right and choose "Add an app."

2. Scroll down until you find Access App, and click it.

Each page of apps shows only 16 at a time, so you may have to click the arrow button to go to the next page of apps.

3. For the App Name, type **My Test App** and click Create.

It will take a couple of minutes before your app is ready (the icon will be light blue until it is). Refresh the Site Contents page to see when it is updated.

4. The new app icon will be red when your app is ready. Click it to open the new app.

5. The welcome screen appears, as shown in Figure 13-1. Click "Open this app in Access to start adding tables."

If the browser prompts you to open or save the `My Test App.accdw` file, click Open.

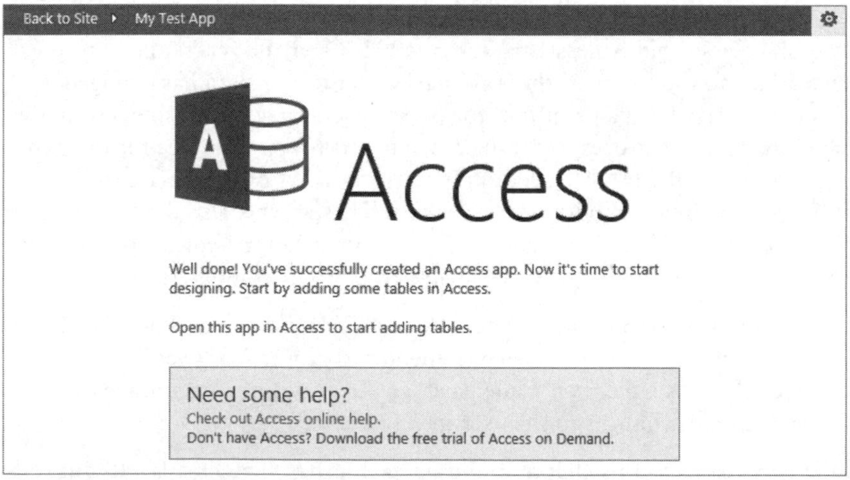

FIGURE 13-1

> **NOTE** *A prompt or two may come up for your authentication to the SharePoint Server. This occurs with the Access software but will not happen when users visit the Access site via the browser.*
>
> *The next screen will be very helpful in getting started, because it gives suggestions as to types of database tables that can be created or imported.*

How It Works

Your new database exists as an "app" in SharePoint. When users interact with the database, such as adding, editing, and deleting records, they are using the browser. As the database administrator, you change the design of the database, such as modifying tables, queries, and forms, via the Access 2013 client on your computer.

UNDERSTANDING TABLES

Tables are the basis for every Access database. A table in Access is the same concept as a table in any database, a list in SharePoint, or even a spreadsheet. It is comprised of columns and rows of data.

> **Columns:** Columns are also referred to as *fields*, and they can be likened to columns in a spreadsheet or a SharePoint list.

> **Rows:** Rows are also referred to as *records*. If you had a simple phone list of contacts, a single contact in the list would be referred to as a record.

Primary Key

The *primary key* is a field in each table that is unique for each record. This is a data type of AutoNumber, which is a number field that automatically increments up for each row in the table. This can be likened to the ID field, which exists in every list and library in SharePoint.

Creating Tables

There are two ways to create tables in Access 2013. You can create each table from scratch, and manually create all the fields in each table. Or, you can use one of the many templates available. You can add one or many of these table templates to your database to save time. For example, if your database is going to be used to track SharePoint projects and clients, you can choose several table templates to use in conjunction with each other to put together a single solution. You can also create tables from other types of existing data sources, such as other Access databases, Excel spreadsheets, SQL Server/ODBC data, Text/CSV, and even SharePoint lists. When creating a table from a SharePoint list, you can choose whether to simply do a one-time import or link to the existing data.

In the example database in this chapter, you create a client and project database. You create the first table using templates, and create the last one manually.

TRY IT OUT Creating a New Table Using a Template

To create your first table with Access Services, follow these steps.

1. From the Start menu on your computer, open Microsoft Access 2013, and from the list of your recently opened files, open the My Test App database from the previous exercise.

2. In the "Create a new table using our templates" box, type **customer** and hit Enter. Notice that there is an option in the list called Clients, as shown in Figure 13-2, which appears to suit your needs. Click Clients. Notice that the Clients table now appears on the left-side navigation.

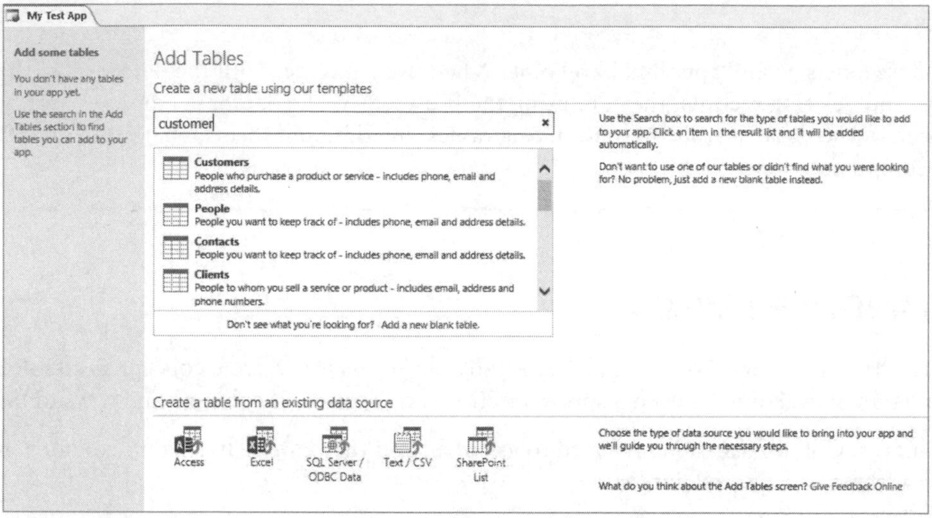

FIGURE 13-2

3. Next, you are going to have projects associated with the clients, so type **project** in the search box and hit Enter. In the list of results, click Projects. You now have Projects, Employees, and Tasks as new tables on the left. These tables are already related to each other.

4. Type **hours** as the next search, and then click Billable Hours. This set of tables includes Hours, Rates, and Clients. Because the Clients table already exists, a duplicate was not created.

5. Figure 13-3 shows your app with tables listed in the left navigation pane. You can click each table to see what the default form looks like. If you needed more tables, you could use the Table button in the ribbon.

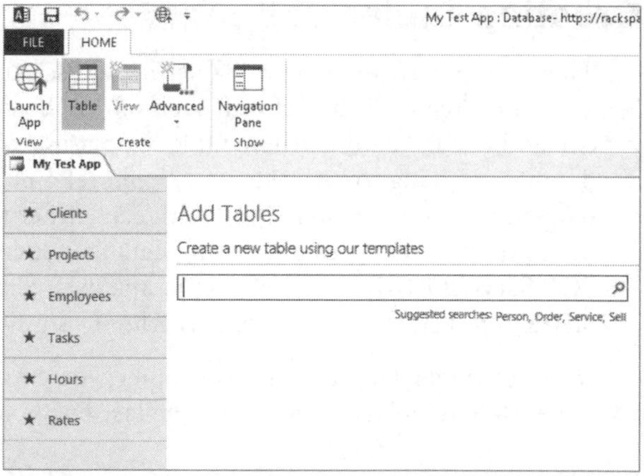

How It Works

These table templates are great for getting started, especially when you are first learning Access. This allows you to dig in and look at how everything works, especially when you start creating your own tables and forms from scratch.

FIGURE 13-3

Now that you have created some tables using a template, the next step is to create one manually, so that the whole process is better understood.

Working in Design View

Now that a simple database and some tables have been created, the next step is to explore getting around in the design surface in Access. If you've used Access in the past, you'll notice that it is quite a bit trimmed down and simplified when working with web databases in Access Services. Figure 13-4 shows an example of what it looks like to design a table. To get to this view, right-click any table name on the left and click Edit Table.

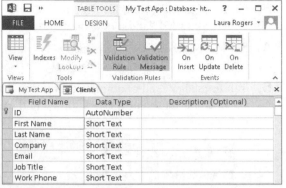

FIGURE 13-4

Each table consists of a set of fields, and the table design surface consists of three columns. The concept of creating fields is very similar to creating columns in a SharePoint list or library. The columns are Field Name, Data Type, and Description:

> **Field Name:** Give each field a short but descriptive name.

> **Data Type:** The data types are short text, long text, number, date/time, currency, yes/no, hyperlink, image, calculated, and lookup.

> **Description:** This is optional, and is simply used to further describe the purpose of each field.

Notice that the bottom half of the table design surface is labeled Field Properties. Once fields are created, each field will have more properties displayed at the bottom as it is selected. Each data type will have different property options available. Here are some examples of field properties:

> **Label Text:** If you would like a different name displayed as the field name, instead of the actual field name, this is called the label. For example, you may want a field called StartDate displayed as "Start Date."

> **Default Value:** A default value can be set for all data types except for images and calculations.

> **Required:** Decide whether data is required to be filled out in each field.

> **Indexed:** You have three options here: No, Yes (Duplicates Okay), Yes (No Duplicates).

TRY IT OUT　Creating a Table Manually

In this Try It Out, you create a table to keep track of states and the sales associate who is in charge of each state. To create a table manually in Access, follow these steps:

1. From the Start menu on your computer, open Microsoft Access 2013 and open the My Test App database from the previous exercise.

2. On the Home tab in the ribbon, click the Table button.

3. On the right side, look for the small text "Don't want to use one of our tables..." and click the hyperlink called "add a new blank table."

4. Notice that there is already one field created. This is the ID, and it is an AutoNumber. Put your cursor in the second row of the Field Name column, and type **State**.

5. Tab to the next cell and notice that the default data type is short text. In the properties area at the bottom, set the properties shown in the following table. The other properties can keep their default values.

PROPERTY	VALUE
Character Limit	2
Label Text	State Abbreviation
Required	Yes
Indexed	Yes (No Duplicates)

6. Put your cursor in the next blank Field Name cell under State, and type **StateName**. In the Label Text property below, type **State Name**. This field is also short text. Figure 13-5 shows your progress so far.

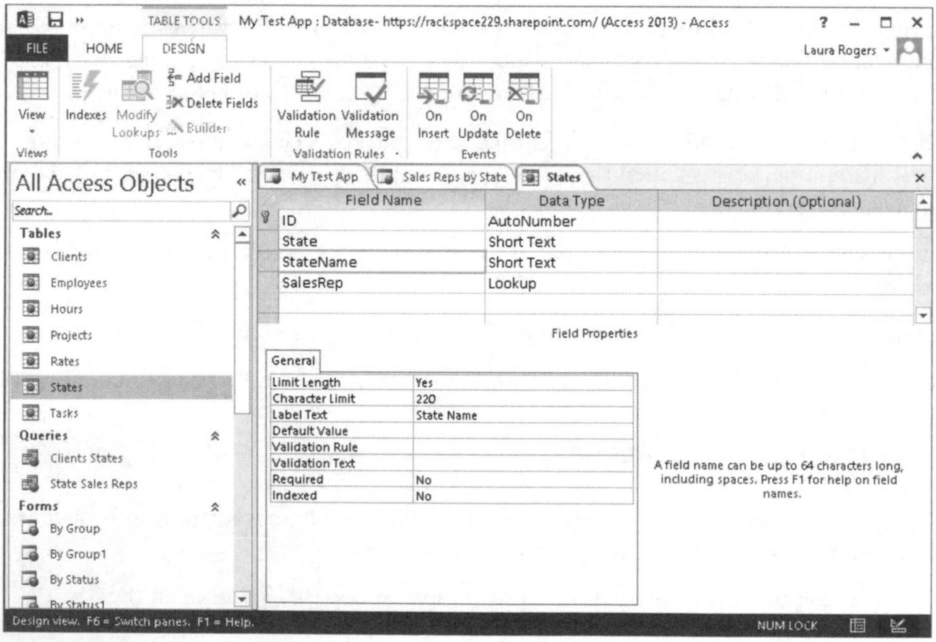

FIGURE 13-5

7. For the next Field Name, type **SalesRep**. For Data Type, select Lookup. This elicits the Lookup Wizard.

8. Choose "I want the lookup field to get the values from another table or query."

9. For the table, choose Table:Employees, and for the value, choose Display Name First Last.

10. Keep the rest of the default settings as shown in Figure 13-6, and click OK.

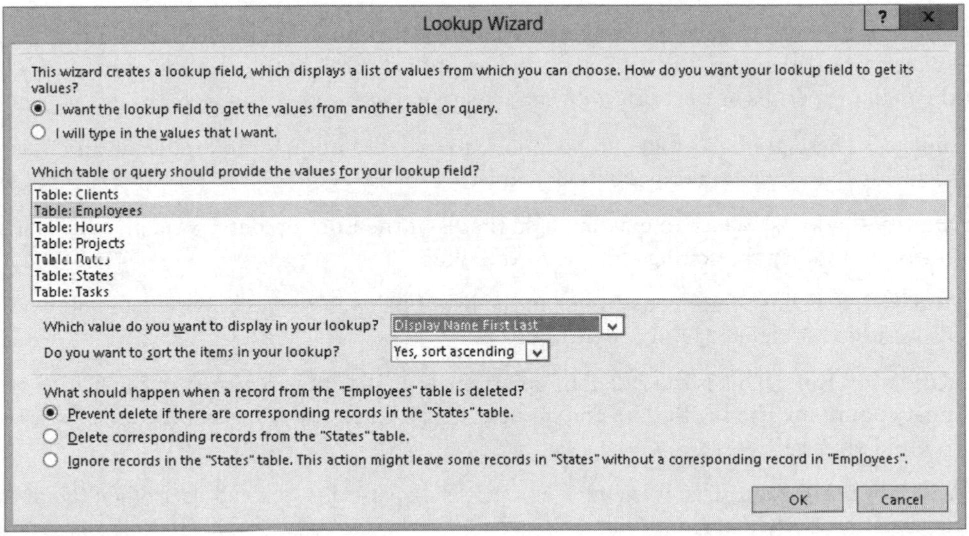

Lookup Wizard dialog box:

This wizard creates a lookup field, which displays a list of values from which you can choose. How do you want your lookup field to get its values?

- ● I want the lookup field to get the values from another table or query.
- ○ I will type in the values that I want.

Which table or query should provide the values for your lookup field?

Table: Clients
Table: Employees
Table: Hours
Table: Projects
Table: Rates
Table: States
Table: Tasks

Which value do you want to display in your lookup? [Display Name First Last]

Do you want to sort the items in your lookup? [Yes, sort ascending]

What should happen when a record from the "Employees" table is deleted?

- ● Prevent delete if there are corresponding records in the "States" table.
- ○ Delete corresponding records from the "States" table.
- ○ Ignore records in the "States" table. This action might leave some records in "States" without a corresponding record in "Employees".

[OK] [Cancel]

FIGURE 13-6

11. For this SalesRep field, in the Field Properties at the bottom of the screen, set the Label text as Sales Associate.

Notice that above the Label Text property, it shows that the Number Subtype is a whole number. When a field is set up as a lookup, values are stored in the lookup as numbers. The number is going to be a relationship to the ID field in the table in the lookup.

12. Now that all the fields have been created, click the Save button at the top-left corner of Access. Name this table **States** and click OK.

13. Click the View button at the top left to switch to Datasheet view, and add a few states, filling out the state and the state name.

Note that you will not be able to select any employees yet for the SalesRep field, because no data exists in that list yet.

14. Click the View button again to switch back to the Design view.

How It Works

When creating fields in a table, you can use several types of data. Depending on what you select in the Data Type column, different properties will be available in the Field Properties pane at the bottom of the screen. Just as with SharePoint data, be careful about changing the data types after users have already started populating the database with information. For example, if you change a text field to a number field, you would lose all the text that users have already typed in that column.

Now that your table and a few fields have been created, it is time to explore the table design interface a bit more. Take a look at the ribbon. Some of the buttons in the ribbon are redundant to some of the field properties at the bottom of the screen:

➤ **Indexes:** These are fields that can be unique to each record in a table, such as an ID, or they are fields that are commonly queried against.

➤ **Modify Lookups:** Select an existing field that is of the Lookup data type, and click this button to modify the settings for the field lookup.

➤ **Add/Delete Fields:** Place your cursor in the list of fields in the location where you would like a row added or deleted, and use this button.

➤ **Validation Rule:** This is the rule that determines what data is required in the field. This is most commonly used with date and number fields. Click the ellipsis button in this property to build your rule.

➤ **Validation Message:** This is the message that is displayed to the end user when the data has not been properly entered in the field.

➤ **On Insert/Update/Delete:** Clicking one of these buttons elicits the macro builder. A macro is similar to a workflow. For example, click the On Insert button to create a set of actions that will take place when a new row is added to the table.

TRY IT OUT   Creating a Relationship

Now that the States table has been completed, it is time to close it and hide it. Other tables that need to reference the list of states can be modified to include this new lookup.

1. If the States table from the previous exercise is still opened, click the X at the top right of the States table, which is not the same as the X at the top right of Access.

2. Back on the main screen of your app, right-click the States table on the left, and choose Hide.

3. There is a State field in the Clients table. Right-click the Clients table on the left, and choose Edit Table.

4. Find the State field, and change it from a data type of Short Text, to a Lookup.

5. Choose "I want the lookup field to get the values from another table or query." Choose States, choose State as the value, as shown in Figure 13-7, and click OK.

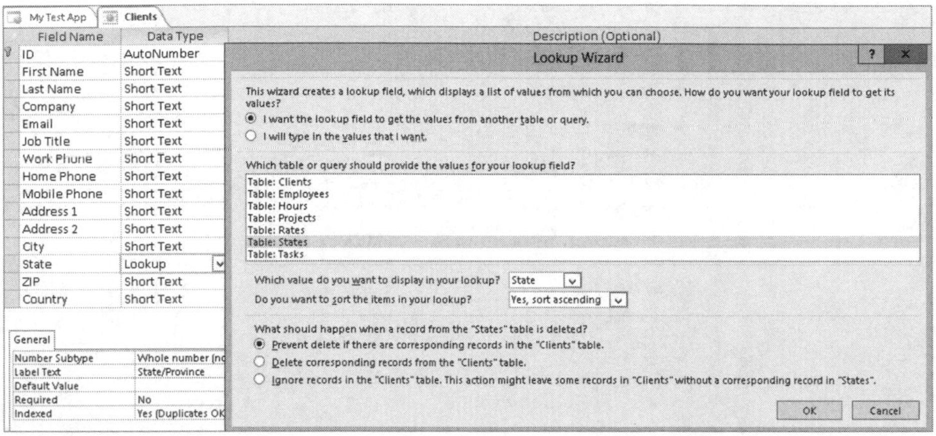

FIGURE 13-7

6. Click the Save button at the top left, click Yes, and close the Clients table.

7. Now that the States table has been completed, it's time to fill in some data in all the tables. Right-click the Clients table on the left, and choose View Data.

8. Create two new clients in the list by filling out data in every column.

How It Works

When you create lookup fields in Access 2013, relationships are created automatically between tables. Every table has an AutoNumber field called ID, which is always unique. This ID is the value that is stored in the table that looks up to another table. For example, if "Alaska" is the first item that you type in the list of states, it will have an ID of 1. If you edit a client in the list of clients, and select Alaska as his or her state, the number 1 is the actual value that is stored in the "State" field in that client's record. Unique IDs help to maintain consistency. If you later edit the state to be called "AK" instead, all the clients that reference the Alaska state will still maintain their lookup values of 1, because the ID didn't change, only the state name.

TRY IT OUT Exploring the App

Now that the test app has been created, it's time to explore all its capabilities. A lot of functionality exists out-of-the-box with Access apps. In this Try It Out, you create data in all the tables and take a look at how the user interface works. In the previous exercise, you created rows (records) in a table directly. Here you fill out the existing forms via the browser.

1. If the Access database from the previous exercise is not still opened, in the ribbon at the top, click the Launch App button.

2. Your app looks almost the same in the browser, and the Clients table is selected by default, as shown in Figure 13-8. Close Microsoft Access.

FIGURE 13-8

3. Add another client by filling in the fields on the page. Click the Save button on the form when the new client is complete.

Notice that when you fill in the State/Province field, as you type the state abbreviation, the field automatically finds the list of matching selections. Also, if the value you type does not exist in the states list, there is a link to "Add a new item." You alter this functionality in a later exercise.

4. When each client on the left is selected, your screen will look similar to Figure 13-9. Click the Add icon (+) to create one more client.

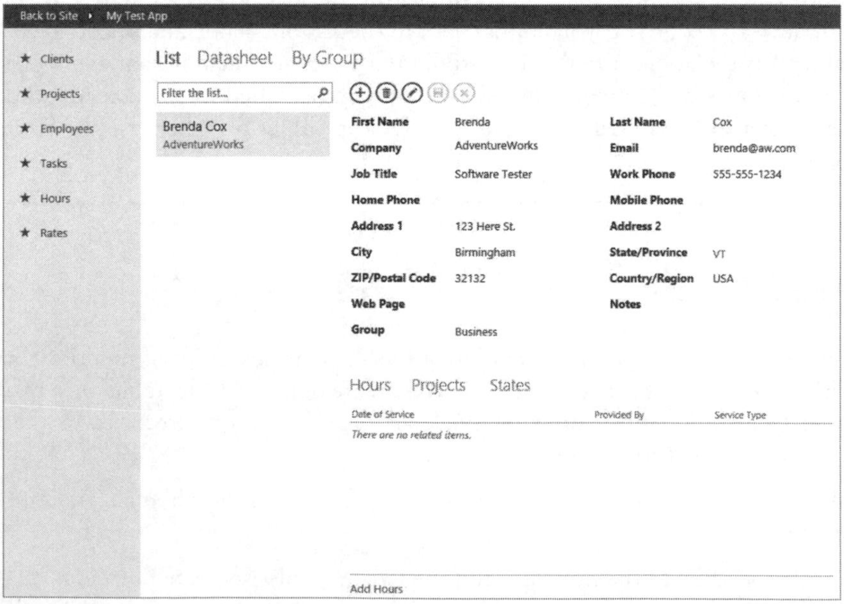

FIGURE 13-9

5. Click the Save icon to save the client.

Notice that on this client list, as clients are added, they are listed in a column on the left. Click any client name to go to their record. Also, at the bottom of each client record are related tables such as Hours, Projects, and States.

6. With one of your clients selected, click Projects on the bottom half of the screen (refer to Figure 13-8). Scroll down to the very bottom of the screen, and click Add Projects.

7. Create a project called **Company Policy Upgrade**, and fill in the rest of the fields with your own data.

As you are filling out the new project form, notice that the name of the customer was automatically populated, because you started this form from that specific customer's record. Also, notice that for the owner field, the options available will come from the list of clients that you have created. Do not check the Active checkbox because it is disabled.

8. Click the Save icon at the top of the form to save this new project. Close the project window. Figure 13-10 shows your client with the project that is now associated with them.

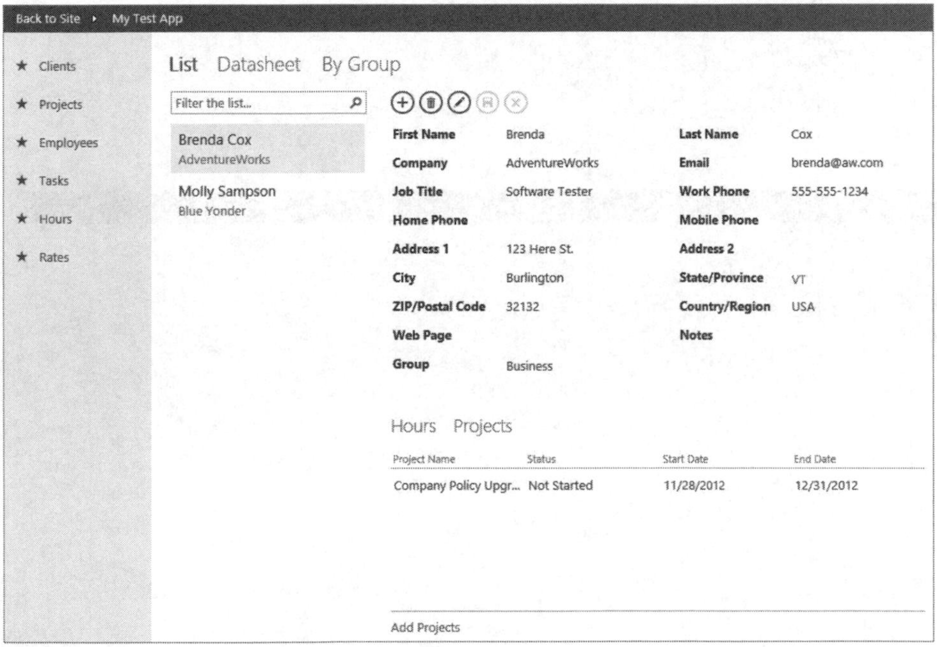

FIGURE 13-10

9. Click the Projects table in the left navigation.

10. Click the Add icon to create one more project, and name it **Onboarding Workflow**. Fill in all the fields on the screen, and click the Save icon.

11. Click the Add Tasks link at the very bottom of the project form.

12. Name this task **Requirements document**. Fill in all the fields with any data, and click the Save icon. Close the new task window.

13. Click the Tasks table in the left navigation. One task is already listed. Click the Add button, and make up another task. For the Project field, type the name of the Company Policy Upgrade project. After all the fields are filled in, click the Save button.

14. Click the Hours table in the left navigation.

Notice that this Hours form is a bit difficult to fill out because the Customer, Service Type, and Provided By fields are all lookup fields. Without drop-down boxes, it is sometimes difficult to know what your options are. Click the name of the Datasheet view at the top of the page, and notice that this is another method of filling out table data, but there are still no drop-down boxes.

15. Click the Rates table in the left navigation. Add the following three rates, as shown in Figure 13-11.

TITLE	RATE
Ad-Hoc	200
Pre-Paid	175
Project	150

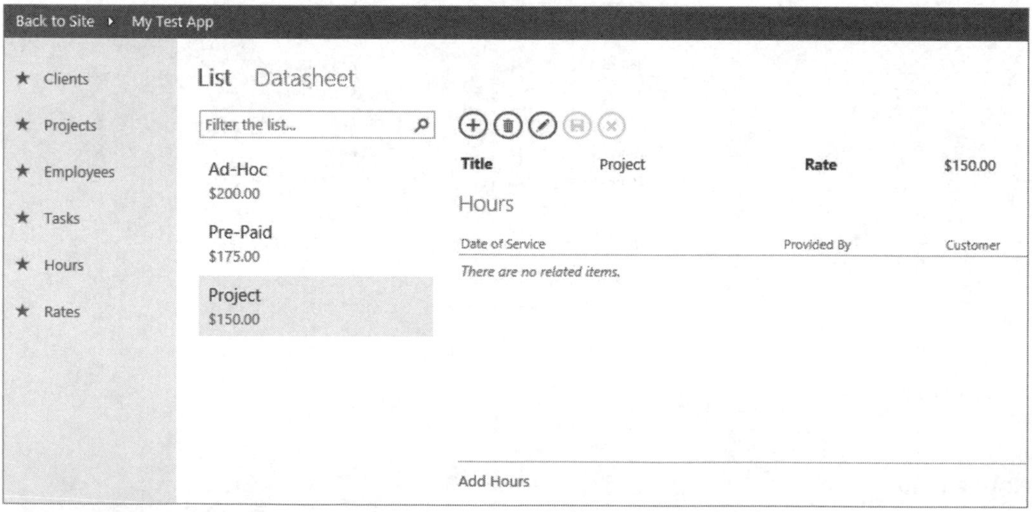

FIGURE 13-11

16. Now that some data has been filled in within each table, there is one more thing that is missing. When you created the States table, you created a column for _, which can be filled in now. Because the States table is hidden, this data cannot be edited in the browser, but in Access instead. At the top-right corner in the browser, click the Settings button, and choose Customize in Access. If prompted by the browser, click the Open button. Close the browser.

17. Right-click the States table on the left, and choose View Data.

18. In the Sales Associate column, enter the names of people who are in the employees list. Fill in a sales associate for each state in your list. Close the States table.

How It Works

Having a sales associate correlated with each state will help you to understand who is in charge of each territory. This leads to the next section, where you create a query across multiple tables. With relationships and queries across tables, you harness the real power of an Access database, in comparison to lookups across regular SharePoint lists. You can also see that the pane at the bottom of each form has tabs that represent each table that the current table is related to. For example, the Clients form has Hours and Projects at the bottom so that you can quickly see all records in those two other lists, which are related to the current client.

UNDERSTANDING QUERIES

The definition of a query is that it is a request for information. In Access, a query is a way to ask a question about the data that is in your database. Queries can be created to find out about a subset of information, which could come from one or more tables. For example, a query could simply be a list of all employees who live in Alabama. Queries that go across tables use a common value in both tables to marry the information together. For example, a database could have a table of sales transactions and a table of products. Each transaction has the name of a product, but the list of products has much more detailed information about each product. In this case, the product would be the common field, which would be the basis of the relationship between the transactions and the products.

In this section, you learn about queries by creating a new one, and explore relationships and how they work.

Creating Queries

When you are creating a query, the design surface has the following ribbon buttons (see Figure 13-12):

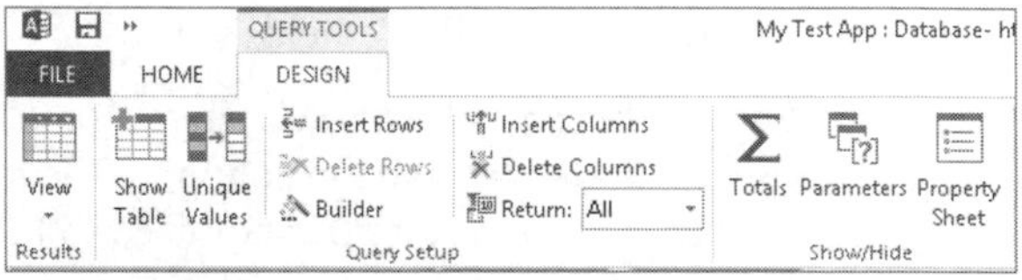

FIGURE 13-12

➤ **View:** Use this button to switch back and forth between the Design view and the resultant list of data, referred to as the *Datasheet view*.

➤ **Show Table:** When a query is first created, you are prompted to add tables to the query. If more tables need to be added later, click this button.

➤ **Unique Values:** With this toggle button pressed, the results of your query will never show two records that have all duplicate information in their fields.

➤ **Insert/Delete Rows:** These buttons apply to the bottom half of the screen, with regards to the criteria.

➤ **Insert/Delete Columns:** Select a column at the bottom half of the screen to delete it or insert a new one next to it.

➤ **Builder:** Click this button to create a new calculated query field. For your calculation, you can only choose from the fields that have been added as columns to the bottom half of the screen. You can use more than 50 different functions here. These calculations are similar to calculated columns in SharePoint, and you can even create expressions that include fields from multiple tables.

➤ **Return:** When working with a large amount of data, you may only want to see a small amount of data returned in the query. This drop-down box enables you to choose to return only the first few records. Records are returned in the order that you specify with your sorting.

➤ **Totals:** When this toggle button is pressed, a new row appears in the bottom half of the screen, called Total. By default, each field's total says Group By, but you can choose other options like Sum and Average. This is done on a per-field basis.

➤ **Parameters:** The parameters button brings up a list of parameters for the query. These are going to be data that is passed to the query from somewhere else, such as a prompt, or from a selection on a form.

➤ **Property Sheet:** This toggle button is used to display a property pane on the right side of the screen, which pertains to whichever object is currently selected.

➤ **Sort:** This row on the bottom half of the screen is used to indicate how each field is sorted. If more than one field is sorted, the sort will be applied from left to right in the order that the columns are displayed.

➤ **Criteria:** Criteria exist for each field on the bottom half of the screen. This is equivalent to a filter. For example, if there is a field called Department, and you want to only show items in the HR department in you results, you can go to the department column, and type **HR** in the Criteria box. Every row below the row labeled Criteria is also for criteria. Therefore, your query can be quite complex with multiple filters for each column. Also, right-click in any criteria box and choose Build to build more complex criteria that involves functions and multiple fields.

➤ **Show:** This checkbox is seen in each column in the bottom half of the screen. Uncheck this box if you would like the column to be hidden in the query results. Why would you add a field as a column if it does not need to be displayed? Sometimes a field is needed in the query because it is a part of a calculation in another field, or for a filter, but it just does not need to be seen in the list of results.

TRY IT OUT Creating a Query

Your database includes a list of states with a sales associate associated with each state. There is also a list of employees, which contains a lot of detailed contact information for each person. In this example, suppose you want to see a list of states with not only the name of the sales associate, but all his or her contact information as well. It would be a bad idea to duplicate all this information — that is, you would not want to go into the States table and add phone number and e-mail address columns to it. With this bad practice, each time a sales associate's info had to be changed, it would need to be changed on two different tables. This is why queries are extremely useful. You can keep a single version of the truth, and query across multiple tables as long as you have at least one common field. In this example, the common field is the employee's name. The goal here is to display a simple list of states with the sales associate and contact info for each.

1. If the Access database called My Test App is not already opened, start Access and open it from the list of recent databases.

2. In the ribbon, click the Advanced button and choose Query. The query design surface is shown in Figure 13-13.

3. In the Show Table dialog box, select the Employees table and click the Add button.

4. Select the States table and click the Add button. Click Close.

5. Notice that the two tables now appear on the query design surface. From the States table, drag the StateName field to the first column, and drag the SalesRep field to the second column at the bottom half of the screen.

   Notice that any fields can now be added to the query by dragging them to a column at the bottom of the screen. If you wanted to add all fields in a table, you could drag the asterisk from that table (which is above the ID field in each table). Columns at the bottom can also be rearranged by selecting them and dragging them back and forth. You can also use your cursor to drag the employees and states boxes around to arrange them, or expand them to make them taller.

6. From the Employees table, drag the Email field and the WorkPhone field to the empty columns at the bottom of the screen. Figure 13-14 shows the appearance of the query design surface so far.

7. Click the Save button at the top left, and name this query **State Sales Reps**. Click OK.

FIGURE 13-13

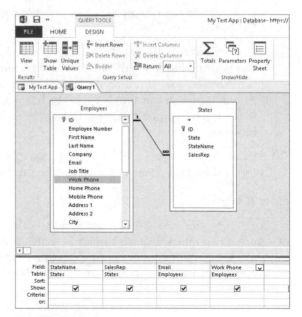

FIGURE 13-14

8. At the top-left corner in the ribbon, click the View button to switch to Datasheet view. This shows the results of the query, as shown in Figure 13-15.

The View button is a great way to flip back and forth between the design and the results of the query as you go. My states list only has eight states in it, which is why only a few are listed. There are three sales associates, and their contact information is displayed next to each state.

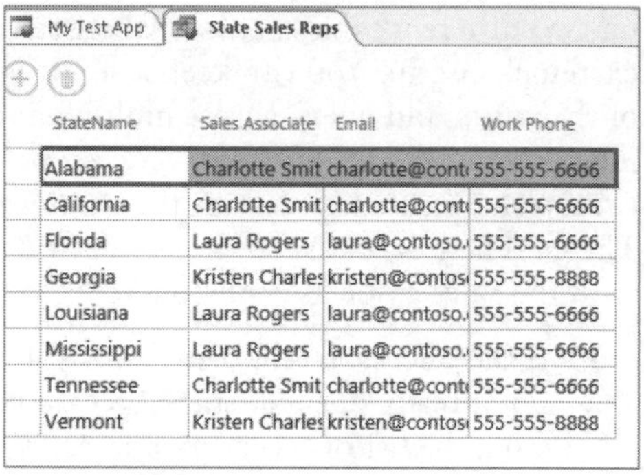

9. Close the query window. In the ribbon, click the Navigation Pane button.

	StateName	Sales Associate	Email	Work Phone
	Alabama	Charlotte Smit	charlotte@cont	555-555-6666
	California	Charlotte Smit	charlotte@cont	555-555-6666
	Florida	Laura Rogers	laura@contoso.	555-555-6666
	Georgia	Kristen Charles	kristen@contos	555-555-8888
	Louisiana	Laura Rogers	laura@contoso.	555-555-6666
	Mississippi	Laura Rogers	laura@contoso.	555-555-6666
	Tennessee	Charlotte Smit	charlotte@cont	555-555-6666
	Vermont	Kristen Charles	kristen@contos	555-555-8888

FIGURE 13-15

Although you can't see the new query anywhere in the app, you can see that it exists. In this navigation pane, the objects are grouped by tables, queries, forms, and so on.

10. Click the Navigation Pane button again to hide it. Click to select the Employees table on the left in the gray pane. In the ribbon, click the View button.

Because there is not a quick way to include the query in the web interface of this app, this query must be added to a view to be able to display it in the browser.

11. Name this view **Sales Reps by State**. For the View Type, select Datasheet, and for the Record Source, choose State Sales Reps, as shown in Figure 13-16. Click Add New View.

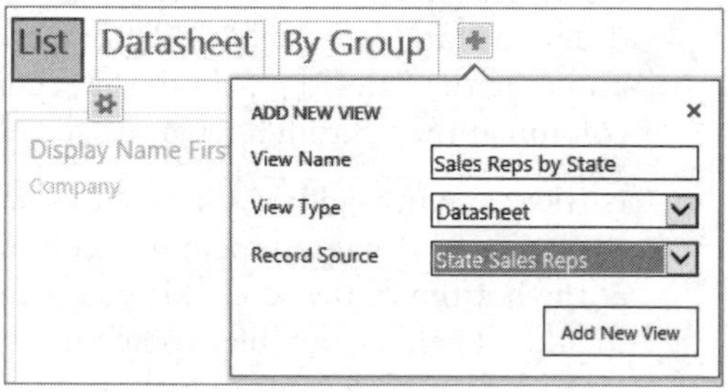

12. Click the Save button at the top left, and click the Launch App button. If the app is already open in the browser, you do not need to click the Launch App button; you can simply click My Test App in the top navigation to refresh the app in the browser.

FIGURE 13-16

13. Click the Employees table on the left, and click the name of the "Sales Reps by State" view at the top. Take a look at the list of states and their sales associates.

How It Works

Notice that on this view, you cannot add and delete records. Because this query is just a read-only view of a join of two tables, records cannot be edited here. Also notice that the columns are a bit too close together. The "Understanding Forms" section in this chapter covers how to edit forms. Queries are perfect for creating lists of related items, which can then be displayed on various forms in your Access app.

Creating Relationships

Tables can be related to each other. This means that one field in a table matches up with a field in another table. For example, there can be more than one employee who works at each store. There could be a table called Stores, and a table called Employees. To define who works where, you can create a lookup column in the Employees table, to pick the associated store. At that point, there would be a *one to many relationship* of stores to employees. One store can have many employees. Each relationship between one field and another is referred to as a *join*.

In Access 2013, working with relationships is a bit different than in previous versions of Access. Previously, there was a screen called Relationships that you could look at and modify, and it was a matrix of all tables with lines between them representing all the relationships. Now instead of that, relationships are configured as part of each lookup column in tables. They can also be separately edited in each query that you create.

TRY IT OUT   Working with Relationships and Queries

There are a few relationships in your test database already. In this Try It Out, you explore relationships and how they are created, as well as how they can be modified.

1. In your app called "My Test App" in Access 2013, right-click the Clients table on the left and choose Edit Table.

2. Put your cursor in the field called State, and click the Modify Lookups button in the ribbon.

You created this lookup in the previous "Creating a Relationship" Try It Out (refer to Figure 13-7). This is where you defined the relationship between the clients and the states.

3. Click Cancel.

4. On the Home tab of the ribbon, click the Advanced button and choose Query.

5. Double-click the Clients table and the States table to add them both to the design surface. Close the Show Table box.

6. The black line between the two tables represents the relationship between the clients and the states (see Figure 13-17).

You can scroll down within the Clients table, so that the State field is visible, and you can also use your cursor to expand the sizes of the two boxes.

7. There are many clients, and each client can have an address in any state. The symbols on the black line represent 1 state to many clients. The little infinite loop symbol next to the state field

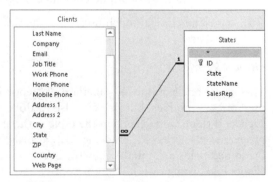

FIGURE 13-17

means "many." Double-click the black line to see the Join Properties dialog box, as shown in Figure 13-18.

8. Notice that this relationship has option 1 selected, which is "Only include rows where the joined fields from both tables are equal." Click Cancel, and click Save. Name this query **Clients States**.

FIGURE 13-18

You have added eight states to your list of states, but there are only two clients in the list of clients. With this type of join, you are always going to have the smaller number of returned records in your query. Because two is smaller than eight, you have two records in your query. To see some examples, you'll add data from both tables to this query.

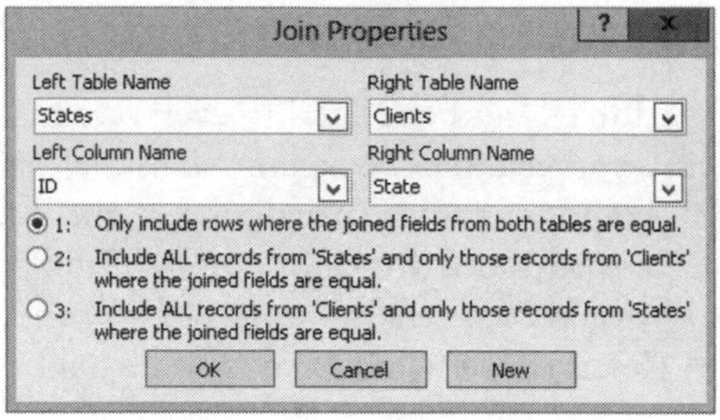

9. From the Clients table, drag the Company and City fields to the first two columns at the bottom. From the States table, drag the State and StateName fields to the next two columns.

10. Click the View button at the top left to see the Datasheet view. Notice that the records displayed have values that come from both tables. Click the View button again to go back to the design surface.

11. Double-click the join between the two tables again. Change the relationship to option 2: "Include ALL records from 'States' and only those records from 'Clients' where the joined fields are equal." Click OK.

This second option means that the query will return everything in the states list, whether it has an associated client or not.

12. Click the View button again. Because there are eight states in your states list, and only two of them have clients associated with them, Figure 13-19 shows some states listed with no companies next to them.

13. Save and close all open tables and queries in the database.

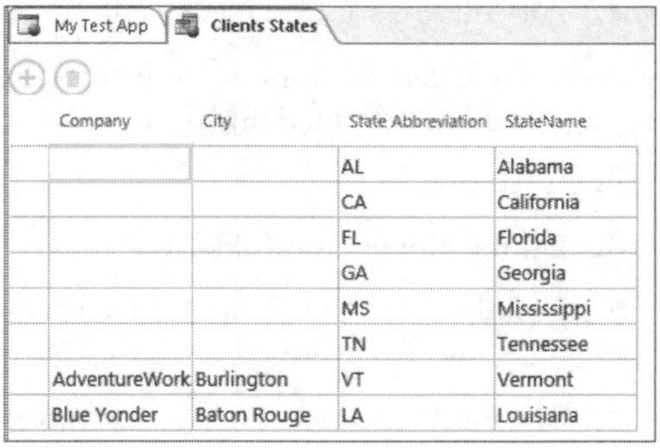

FIGURE 13-19

How It Works

This is just one example of a method of "reporting" off of data across multiple tables. This example used only two tables, but this can also be done with multiple tables. There could be a third scenario, such as if there were clients in the table without the state field filled in. If the third option in the join properties was selected, "Include ALL records from 'Clients' and only those records from 'States' where the joined fields are equal," then the query results would show the full list of clients, whether those clients had a state or not. Another option to note is that when creating queries, you can not only edit existing relationships, but you can add and delete them. This modification has no effect on the lookups that exist in the underlying tables, and only goes as far as the scope of the query.

> **NOTE** *In the query design surface, drag a field from one table over to a field in another table to quickly create a relationship between them.*

UNDERSTANDING FORMS

Forms are the way that we present data to end users in the browser in an Access 2013 app. Because tables and queries cannot be directly accessed in the browser, any front-facing data needs to be placed in a form. Forms can be used for the purposes of allowing users to fill in or edit data, or they can simply be used to display data. Within Access 2013, many forms are created by default for you when tables are created, and you do have the ability to add your own forms or edit the existing ones. When new views are created, these are also forms. In this context, a view is actually the same thing as a form.

The Form Design Surface

What is a form comprised of? Forms are mainly comprised of controls, data, formatting, and actions. In this section, you will become oriented as to how to work in the new design surface for these web app forms in Access 2013. If you are familiar with Microsoft Office InfoPath, a lot of these concepts will be familiar. Figure 13-20 shows an example of a form, which happens to be called "Clients List" and is used for adding new clients.

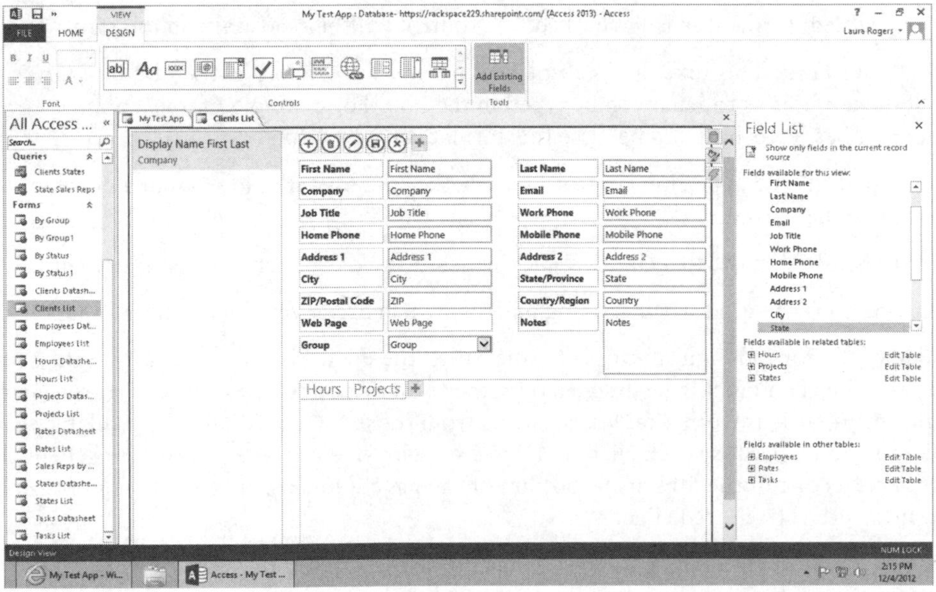

FIGURE 13-20

When you are designing a form, the ribbon displays the Design tab, which provides controls for changing font sizes and colors, as well as a list of controls that can be added to the form. Notice that there is no ability to change the background color or text box color to anything but white.

The design surface itself starts out as a blank white slate. Controls can be added to the form, and can be dragged around to rearrange them. Right-click a control to see more options. Figure 13-21 shows the three buttons that let you configure each control when you select it. The buttons, in order, are as follows:

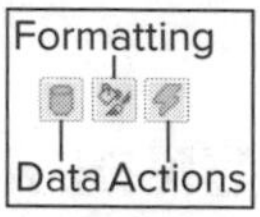

FIGURE 13-21

➤ **Data:** Data is comprised of settings that vary according to which type of control you are using. The most common are listed here:

   ➤ **Control Name:** A unique name for the control on the form, which describes the field it is linked to as well as what type of control it is, such as FirstName_TextBox. This is unique on the form.

   ➤ **Control Source:** This is typically the name of the field to which the control is bound.

   ➤ **Default Value:** Optionally assign a default value to exist in this control. This can be separate from the default value that may have been assigned when the table was designed.

➤ **Formatting:** This option is comprised of the following most common settings, which pertain to how the control acts in the browser:

   ➤ **Tooltip:** When filling out the form, if a user hovers her mouse over the control, this small box is displayed with your tooltip.

   ➤ **Visible:** Set the control visible to users, or hidden.

   ➤ **Enabled:** If this box is unchecked, the control will be read-only on the form.

   ➤ **Input Hint:** This text can be displayed in a text box before users fill it out. Give them a hint as to what can be typed in the box. For example, if it is a phone number, your hint can be "Use this format: ###-###-####."

   ➤ **Open In:** For hyperlink controls, set whether the link should open in a new window or in the current one.

   ➤ **Label For:** With label controls, pick which text box the label is associated with.

➤ **Actions:** Actions are used when creating macros, which are covered later in this chapter.

On the right side of the form design surface is a pane called the Field List. The fields from the table are listed here, and they can quickly be dragged onto the form to be added as controls. If the current table has relationships with any other tables, the fields from those tables will also be available to add to the form. For example, because each client is associated with one or more projects, the clients list form shows Projects as one of the tabs at the bottom of the page. Quickly view the list of projects that are associated with the selected client.

Each view will have a set of standard square buttons at the top, referred to as the *action bar* (see Figure 13-22). These buttons are not editable, and perform the basic commands Add, Delete, Edit, Save, and Cancel.

FIGURE 13-22

In addition to using the basic commands, the green plus button at the far right enables you to add more actions. This is another place where macros come into play. The action bar can be completely hidden if you would like to add your own set of buttons by adding the button control to the form. Figure 13-23 demonstrates how to click the Formatting button for the view to see the ActionBar Visible option.

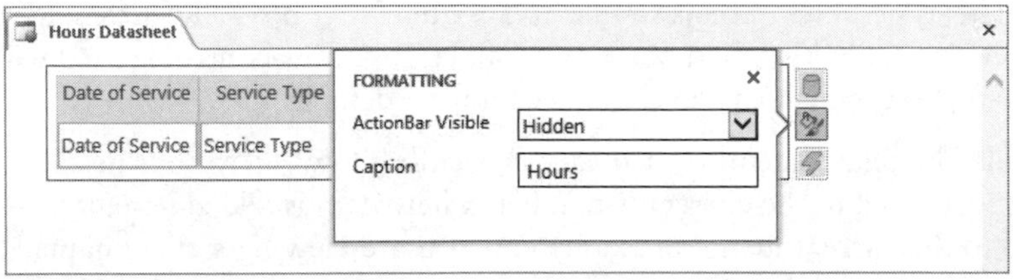

FIGURE 13-23

Working with Controls

Controls enable end users to interact with the data in the browser form. When on the design surface of a form, controls are available on the Design tab in the ribbon. In this section, you learn about all the available controls and how they can be used. Figure 13-24 shows the set of controls.

FIGURE 13-24

➤ **Text Box:** A text box allows users to type free-form data. Use your cursor to drag the box to make it bigger if a lot of text needs to be typed in a particular field.

➤ **Label:** The label is simply the name next to each control.

➤ **Button:** In addition to the default square buttons on each form, use the button control to add buttons anywhere on the form, which can perform custom actions using macros.

➤ **Web Browser Control:** Embed secure browser content in this control by entering a specific Default URL in the control's data settings.

➤ **Combo Box:** This is a drop-down box. For the control source, choose from an existing data source such as a table or query, or type in a list of values.

➤ **Check Box:** This is a simple checkbox. The data settings allow you to set a default of yes or no.

➤ **Image:** Enter the URL of a specific picture, and it will be displayed on the form. This is not a control that users input information into.

➤ **Autocomplete Control:** An autocomplete control points to a specific source like a drop-down box does, but the user interaction is different. Instead of clicking a drop-down box to look at choices, the user is expected to start typing the value that belongs in the field, and similar choices will start appearing as options.

➤ **Hyperlink Control:** This control allows end users to enter a hyperlink. They are prompted to fill in the URL address as well as the display text.

➤ **Subview:** This is a form inside of a form. The subview is typically related to the main form in some way. In the data options, pick another form as the source object. This means that the subview needs to already exist as another form. If there is a relationship, type the name of the master field in the current form, and the related child field in the subview.

➤ **Multiline Text box:** This type of text box is similar to a regular text box. The difference is that whereas a text box is used with a field of the type Short Text, this control is used with a field with the type Long Text, which has no character limit by default.

➤ **Related Items Control:** The related items control automatically shows up to four fields from another list that is related to the current list. When a new item is added here, it is automatically related to the current item. For example, if you are viewing a client named Brenda Cox, and there is a related items control that shows projects, you can click the Add Projects button to add projects that are associated with this client.

TRY IT OUT   Modifying a Form

Earlier in this chapter, you created a database, and sample data was filled in for most tables. No hours have been filled in yet, though, because the hours form is a bit confusing. The form contains three auto-complete boxes, but without knowing what the options are, it is difficult to know what to start typing. This is a great example of a reason to use a combo box instead. In this Try It Out, you edit the hours list form, and change some fields to combo boxes.

1. In Microsoft Access 2013, open the app called My Test App, which you created in previous exercises.

2. On the left, click the name of the Hours table in gray. The form called Hours List is displayed on the page. Click the Edit button in the middle of the page, as shown in Figure 13-25.

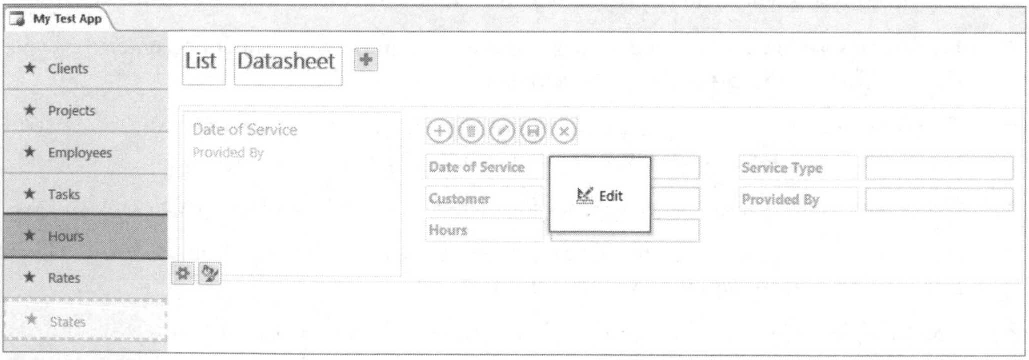

FIGURE 13-25

3. Click to select the Service Type field and delete it. There should now be a blank space above the Provided By field.

4. On the Design tab in the ribbon, click the combo box control. Drag this new control into the spot where the Service Type field was.

5. Click to select the combo box, and click the Data button underneath it. Figure 13-26 shows this dialog box.

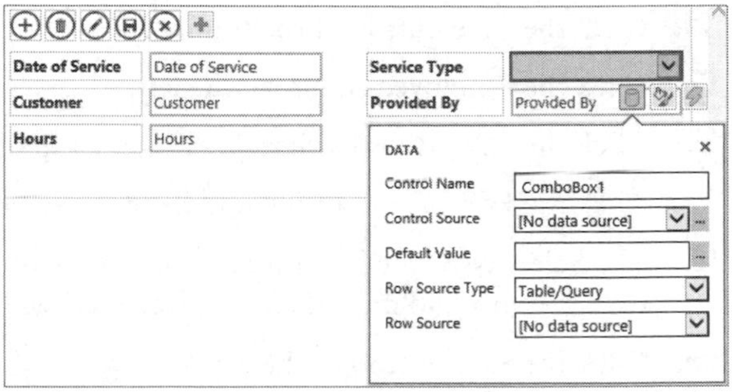

6. To fill in the data fields, use the information in the following table.

The fields below the Row Source field will not appear until the Rates table is selected as the row source. Leave the Default Value blank.

FIGURE 13-26

FIELD	VALUE
Control Name	ServiceTypeCombo
Control Source	Service Type
Row Source Type	Table/Query
Row Source	Rates
Bound Field	ID
Display Field	Title
Popup view	(leave this blank)

7. In the Field List pane on the right, expand the Rates section. Drag the Rate field to the form so that it is below the Service Type, and above the Provided By field.

Because the rates list is very simple and consists of only the rate title and dollar amount, there is no need to open up a popup view to see more information. This is why the Popup view field has been left blank. Instead, because the rate is the only other field, you are going to display it on the form. When you select a service type from the drop-down, the rate of that service type appears below it. This field will not be editable because it is a fixed value that comes from another table.

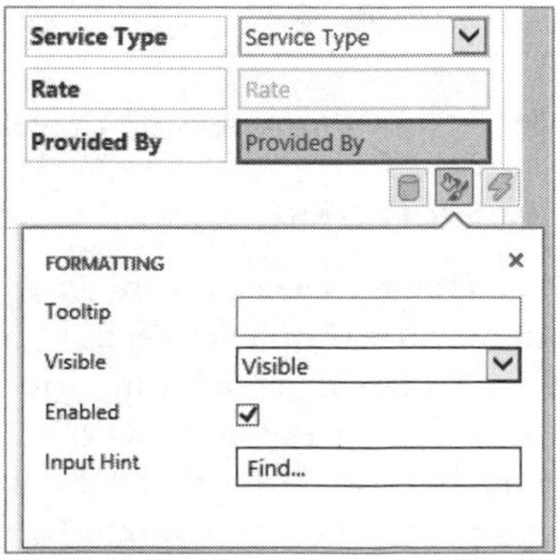

8. Click to select the new Rate text box. Click the Formatting button underneath it. Uncheck the box called Enabled.

9. Select the Provided By text box. Click the Formatting button underneath it, as shown in Figure 13-27.

10. In the Tooltip box, type **Who logged these hours?**. In the Input Hint box, type **Type your name....**

FIGURE 13-27

11. Click the Save button at the top left.

12. Click the Employees table on the left.

13. Click the Sales Reps by State view at the top of the form.

14. Click the Edit button in the middle of the screen.

15. The Sales Associate and Email columns are too narrow. Use your cursor to select each of these two columns and drag them to twice their widths.

16. Click the Save button at the top left.

17. If your app is already open in the browser, go to the browser and click My Test App in the breadcrumb trail at the top to refresh the changes. If your browser is not currently open, click the Launch App button in the Home tab.

18. In the browser, click Hours on the left. Enter at least 10 different hours entries, filling out all the fields for each record. Figure 13-28 shows a filled-in list of hours.

FIGURE 13-28

19. Click Employees on the left. Click the Sales Reps by State view at the top.

How It Works

The Hours table is now much more useful for people filling out the form. Instead of users needing to know what the choices should be, they are provided with a drop-down box to simply make a selection. Notice that each time you save a new record, the Rate field on the list view is populated with the rate associated with the selected service type. You can use the Datasheet view at the top to enter them quickly. Also notice that the column widths look much better since they have been widened. The only way that end users will interface with the data will be through forms, so it is important to know how to modify forms to look and behave as needed.

WORKING WITH MACROS

In Microsoft Access, macros can be likened to workflows. They are a set of conditions and actions that take place when a field is clicked or updated. Macros can be created at the top level of your app, and reused in multiple locations in your app. They can also be created directly on a control or button in a form, or on form load.

Understanding Program Flow

In a macro, program flow is regarding the way that the macro is organized. When comparing this to SharePoint Designer workflows, program flow can be likened to steps and comments.

➤ **Comment:** Add comments to a macro to simply make notes for yourself as to what the macro is doing. These comments are purely for documentation and troubleshooting purposes.

➤ **Group:** This is a way to organize your macro, which is similar to steps in a workflow. Put several conditions and/or actions in a group. A great thing about groups is that they can be collapsed and expanded.

➤ **If:** Use this to create conditions in your macro. If a certain condition exists, then take certain actions. Otherwise, take different actions.

Working with Actions

Actions are the things that happen when each macro runs. Actions come in five different categories, which are data entry operations, database objects, filter/query/search, macro commands, and user interface commands. You have a plethora of actions from which to choose:

➤ **Data Entry Operations:** These actions are related to working with records in a table.

➤ **Delete Record:** On a form, this deletes the current record.

➤ **Edit Record:** On a form that you are viewing, this behavior is the same as clicking the Edit button at the top of the form.

➤ **New Record:** This action is equivalent to clicking the New button on a form to begin filling out a new record.

➤ **Save Record:** Save the edits that you have made to a new or existing record on a form.

➤ **Undo Record:** Undo the last changes that were made to the current record on a form.

➤ **Database Objects**

➤ **Go To Control:** Move the focus to a specific control on the form. The control name is required. You can start

FIGURE 13-29

typing a control name, and the field will auto populate, as shown in Figure 13-29.

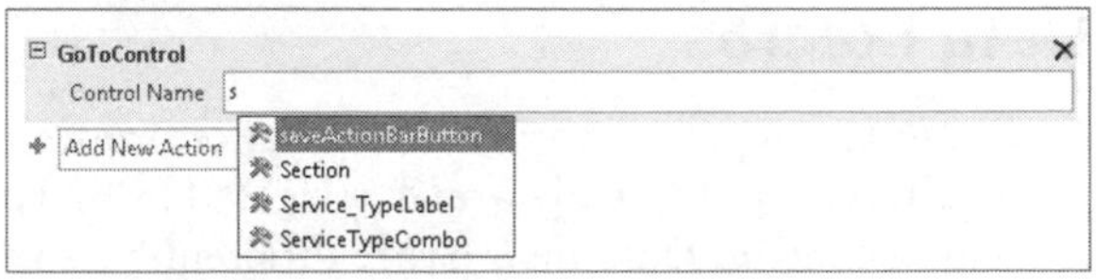

➤ **Go To Record:** Pick from previous, next, first, or last to jump directly to that record in the form.

➤ **Set Property:** Type the name of a control on the form and then select which property to set. The choices for Property are enabled, visible, forecolor, backcolor, caption, and value. For the forecolor and backcolor, the hex value for the color is needed. For example, if you wanted the color to be yellow, use #F0F000.

> **NOTE** *You can find a great reference for hex color hues at* `www.lynda.com/resources/hexpalette/hue.html`.

➤ **Filter/Query/Search**

➤ **Requery Records:** This lets you re-query the list of records. Use a SQL WHERE statement, and type the name of a field to order the records by.

➤ **Macro Commands**

➤ **Run Data Macro:** If there is an existing data macro in your database, this is where you can trigger it to run.

➤ **Run Macro:** Pick the name of an existing macro to trigger it here.

➤ **Set Variable:** Type the name of a variable, and use the expression builder to set what the value of that variable needs to be.

➤ **Stop Macro:** Simply stops the currently running macro.

➤ **User Interface Commands**

➤ **Change View:** Manually type the name of the table and the name of the view that you would like to switch to. Also, optionally type a SQL WHERE clause to set a filter, and fill in the order by information.

➤ **Close Popup:** If the current form is open in a popup window, this action closes that window.

➤ **Message Box:** A small message box pops up, displaying the text that you type in the properties of this action.

➤ **Open Popup:** Select any view in the database to show in a popup window on top of the current window. Optionally type a SQL WHERE clause to set a filter, and fill in the order by information.

Data Macros

Data macros enable you to add logic to forms, in a different manner from regular macros. The macros covered already are all triggered by an action, such as a form being opened or interactivity with a control. Data macros are different because they are triggered by events such as records being added, edited, or deleted. These triggers are similar to the way in which SharePoint Designer workflows can be triggered. The concept of program flow is no different than in regular macros, but the actions are in groups called data blocks and data actions. When you click the Advanced drop-down button on the Home tab, you can click Data Macro to create one. The actions are as follows:

➤ **Data Blocks**

➤ **Create Record:** Pick a table in which to create a record, and add an action to take place. Several actions are available within this data block, such as SetField. If you want the macro to create a record and put a value in a field, you would choose SetField, and then type the name of the field and the value that needs to be in it. You can use the expression builder to create the value, or just type a set value in quotes.

➤ **Edit Record:** Pick an action to run within this data block, type the name of the field, and build or type the name of the value to set in it.

➤ **For Each Record:** For each record in a certain table, where a certain condition exists, what actions do you want to take? For example, you could use this to say that for each record in the Tasks table, where the project is equal to X, set all the task statuses to completed. Pick a table, and then create your "where" condition. Add an action to happen on all those records that meet that condition.

➤ **Lookup Record:** Look up a record in a certain table that meets a defined condition, and take action on that record. You have many actions to choose from, such as editing a record or running another macro.

➤ **Data Actions:** The data actions cannot be added to the data macro alone. They need to exist within one of the data blocks. Not all data actions are available within every type of data block.

➤ **Cancel Record Change:** This action behaves as if the item were being edited and then you clicked the Cancel button on that form.

➤ **Delete Record:** Delete the record and optionally type in a record alias.

➤ **Exit For Each Record:** When using the For Each Record data block, use this action to stop the "for each record" from happening any more. The macro will stop iterating through all of the records.

➤ **Raise Error:** This makes an error pop up while the macro is running. Just type the text that the error needs to say.

➤ **Run Data Macro:** Pick the name of an existing data macro to run.

➤ **Set Field:** Type the name of the field and the value that needs to be in it. You can use the expression builder to create the value, or just type a value in quotes.

➤ **Set Local Var:** Create a new variable and set a value in it, or type the name of an existing variable and set a value.

➤ **Set Return Var:** Set the name and value of a variable to be returned to the caller.

➤ **Stop Macro:** Terminate the current macro immediately.

Macros in Action

In this section, you create your own macros and see a couple of common examples of how to use them.

Creating Macros

When looking at tasks in the Tasks table, you might want the high-priority ones to stand out. In this Try It Out, you create a macro that runs when the form opens that colors the text in red.

1. If your app called My Test App is not already opened, open Access 2013 and open this database from the list of recent files.

2. On the left, click the Tasks table.

3. Click the Edit button in the middle of the List view.

4. Notice the three icons for Data, Formatting, and Actions down the right side of the view. Click Actions, as shown in Figure 13-30.

FIGURE 13-30

5. Click the On Current button.

6. In the blank drop-down box for Add New Action, select If. Figure 13-31 shows the added If condition in the macro.

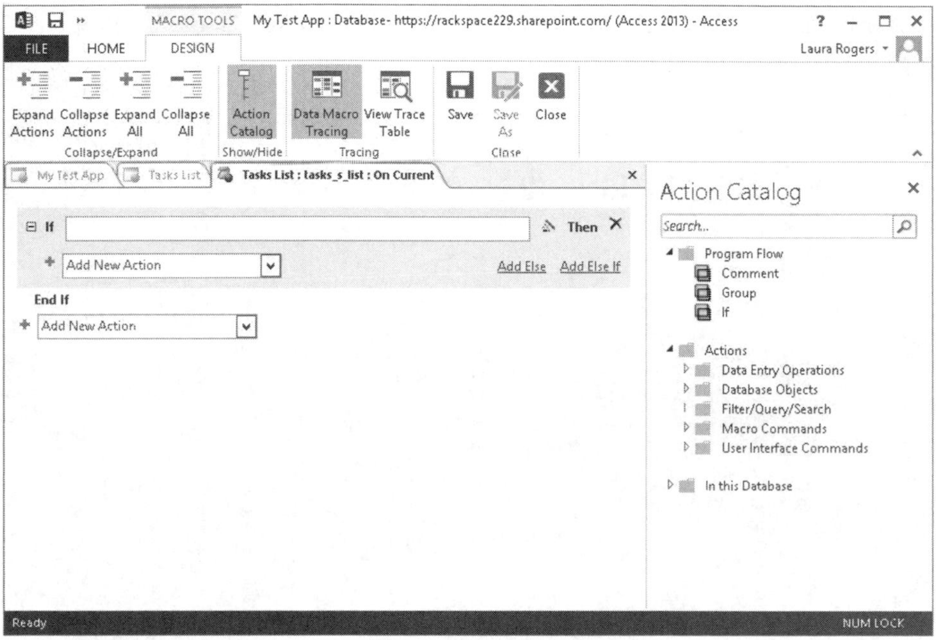

FIGURE 13-31

7. Click the Expression Builder button to the right of the If box. It looks like a magic wand.

8. In the Expression Categories section on the Expression Builder screen, double-click the PriorityComboBox.

9. In the expression box, type **= "1 - High"** as shown in Figure 13-32. Click OK.

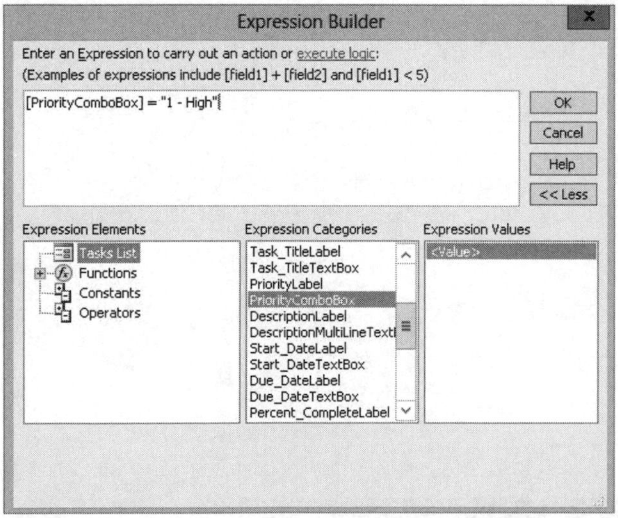

FIGURE 13-32

10. Directly under the If box, click the Add New Action drop-down box. Choose Set Property. The macro looks like Figure 13-33 so far.

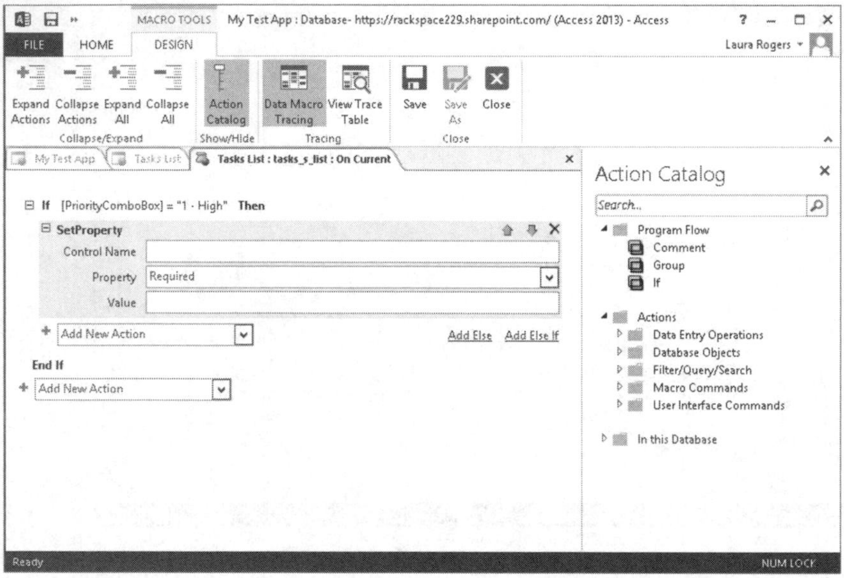

FIGURE 13-33

11. In the Control Name box, type **PriorityComboBox**. In the Property drop-down box, choose ForeColor. For the Value, type **#990033** and then click your cursor anywhere outside of the If statement, as shown in Figure 13-34.

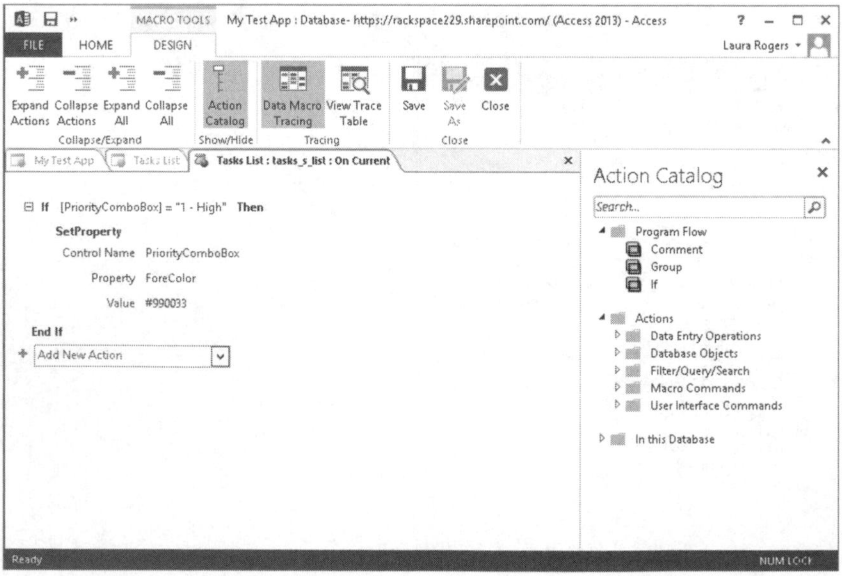

FIGURE 13-34

12. Click the Save button at the top left, and close the macro.

13. Click the Save button again, and close the Tasks form.

14. Click the Launch App button on the Home tab.

15. In the browser, click the Tasks table on the left. In the list of tasks, click the names of the tasks. Notice that when a task is high priority, the Priority field shows as a different color!

How It Works

In this Try It Out you learned how to create a macro that runs on a form. Each control on a form can have macros that run when the item is clicked or after it is edited. Another place you'll find macros is on the Advanced drop-down box on the Home tab.

SUMMARY

In this introductory chapter, you learned the basics of getting around in Microsoft Access 2013 apps with SharePoint 2013. Once you understand the fundamentals of tables, queries, and forms, you can create your own apps. Using table templates is very helpful in your learning process, because you have the ability to dissect the tables and forms to see how they work. As you create more databases, you can always reference these templates to see how things are done. With your new fundamental knowledge, you can keep learning and create your own powerful relational databases.

> **NOTE** *For further reading and research, try the following links:*
>
> ➤ **Microsoft Access on Wikipedia:** `http://en.wikipedia.org/wiki/Microsoft_Access`
>
> ➤ **Database Design Basics:** `http://office.microsoft.com/en-us/access-help/database-design-basics-HA001224247.aspx`

EXERCISES

1. Is there a way to view SharePoint list data in an Access 2013 app? What are some other types of data that can be linked or imported into Access?

2. Where are relationships between tables created?

3. What are the names of the default buttons in the action bar of every form? Can additional buttons be added to the action bar in a form?

4. What type of macro gets created when you create an action from a control in a form?

▶ **WHAT YOU LEARNED IN THIS CHAPTER**

TOPIC	KEY CONCEPTS
Access databases	Access databases consist of tables, queries, forms, and macros.
Forms	Forms are the same thing as views in Access 2013. Some forms are created by default, but you can also create custom forms.
Queries	The relationships in queries can be based on lookup fields that have already been created. Alternately, you can create and modify the relationships between tables within your query. Once a query exists, you have the ability to create lists of records that contain columns from multiple tables.
Macros	Macros have concepts that are similar to what you may be familiar with in workflows. They consist of conditions and actions, and can be created for forms and controls in forms.

14

Branding and the User Experience

WHAT YOU WILL LEARN IN THIS CHAPTER:

➤ Why organizations brand

➤ Best practices for enhancing the user experience

➤ Working with themes

➤ An introduction to the Design Manager

➤ Working with master pages

WROX.COM CODE DOWNLOADS FOR THIS CHAPTER

The wrox.com code downloads for this chapter are found at `www.wrox.com/remtitle .cgi?isbn=1118495896` on the Download Code tab. The code is in the Chapter 14 download and individually named according to the names throughout the chapter.

The previous chapters discussed the basics of creating sites and working with Web Parts/apps to extend those sites, bringing users rich features that will help them to more easily store, share, and find people, processes, and information within their organization.

This chapter delves into the world of user experience and the role branding plays in its success. More specifically, it attempts to uncover the layers of a successful brand strategy and unleash the secrets to user adoption, the ultimate compliment and purpose of any brand.

Finally, the chapter dives into the more technical features of SharePoint branding, working with the Design Manager and familiar tools such as Dreamweaver to create master pages. The ability to leverage common HTML/CSS tools such as Dreamweaver is new to SharePoint 2013, and one of the biggest improvements to the way we deliver user interfaces and experiences through SharePoint.

WHY ORGANIZATIONS BRAND

The reasons to brand are many and may differ slightly from organization to organization, but there are a few consistent underlying motivations across the board, and that is where we will focus our attention.

Most organizations strive to build a trusted image that encompasses the core values and general purpose the organization represents. That image or brand is often broken down into a set of tools, patterns, and practices that, when combined and used consistently, build a common experience that people begin to remember, identify with, and ultimately trust.

This subliminal trust is the key to a positive user experience, which ultimately leads to user adoption. Successful user adoption often means the sale of products or services in most scenarios. In this situation, however, we are not selling a product or service; we are selling the methods by which users create, share, and find people, processes, and information. It is important to keep those requirements front and center.

Microsoft has helped develop a trust in the SharePoint platform that having a unified infrastructure upon which to build business applications will ultimately make organizations more efficient. To make this possible, however, an organization needs to ensure that its employees adopt the tool and use it frequently to best leverage the investment. Simply deploying SharePoint (or any tool) and demanding usage by employees is not enough. This is where branding and user experience comes in. This is why organizations brand their SharePoint portals, to ensure that the portal falls in line with other tools, patterns, and practices used across the organization. Essentially, by branding you are building a more familiar and better user experience, which will lead to greater user adoption and, ultimately, a more successful deployment. Users will become less focused on the technology aspect of the tool and see the application as an integrated portion of their business.

The payoff is more effective sharing of people, processes, and information, leading to a more efficient organization overall.

BEST PRACTICES FOR ENHANCING THE USER EXPERIENCE

As with most things there are best practices for enhancing the user experience. These best practices are the lessons learned as a result of several iterations of the SharePoint platform (2001, 2003, 2007, 2010, and now 2013). Several years of implementing different tactics and listening to the feedback from users has yielded many different points of view, but a few keep coming up time and time again, and those are the practices we will focus on.

Likely the most significant best practice for enhancing user experience is one that is not specific to SharePoint, but rather relates to the mentality with which you should approach most any project, and that is "KISS," or "Keep it simple, stupid." To quote Albert Einstein, "Everything should be made as simple as possible, but not simpler." This should apply to every level of your branding initiative, from your plan, to your tactics, to your execution. The simpler your roadmap, the less risk that is involved, and similarly, the easier things are to use, the better experience your users will have, and the faster users will adopt your tools.

Another common best practice and general rule of thumb when it comes to branding is consistency. People are creatures of habit, and few feel positive toward a lot of change in their day-to-day activities. For this reason, it is imperative that you align your branding initiatives with tools, patterns, and practices already in place. For example, if users currently store the majority of their documents in a shared folder called G-Drive, then to keep things consistent for the users, you might want to consider naming your new store, such as a SharePoint document library, G-Drive. Although more descriptive names are better as a general rule, by limiting the amount of change you are introducing to how employees do their work, you will create a sense of familiarity across current practices and applications, and ultimately users will have a better experience.

Follow existing brand guidelines. Some organizations feel that because the intranet is not publicly available, all rules go out the door. Unfortunately, this could do more harm than good when it comes to user experience and, ultimately, user adoption. If your corporate color scheme is made up of blues, then stick with blues on your intranet. If your main heading fonts are Helvetica and standard copy is Verdana, then keep those also. If your users click your logo in the top left to return to the homepage, then don't change that either; the more familiar the practices and processes are, the better the experience will be for the users of the system.

Stick with best practices for web design; after all, SharePoint is a web-based platform. Keep your user interface easy to navigate, and ensure you use easy-to-read typography and colors (no yellow on red!).

Less is more. Having all of your organization's information at your fingertips and presented within a single page might seem like a good idea, but it is much better to stick with the information that is important to your users and getting their job done. That way your page will not be cluttered, and you can focus on what is important.

CHANGING THE SITE LOGO

A common requirement most organizations have is to have their company logo displayed predominantly within the site's prime header area. Each site within SharePoint has a setting to allow site administrators to specify a custom image to be displayed in the header of their site. If you apply this setting to the top-level site within your site collection, it will be applied to all subsites as well if an alternate image is not specified.

TRY IT OUT   Associating a Custom Logo with Site

This Try It Out reviews the process for setting the site image (`AWlogo.png` in this chapter's resource files).

1. From the top-level site of your site collection, select Site Settings from the Settings menu. Formerly Site Actions, Settings is now available by clicking the gear icon in the upper right of the screen.

2. From Look and Feel, select Title, Description and Logo.

3. Give your logo a Title and Description of **Home**.

4. In the Insert Logo section, select FROM COMPUTER, as shown in Figure 14-1.

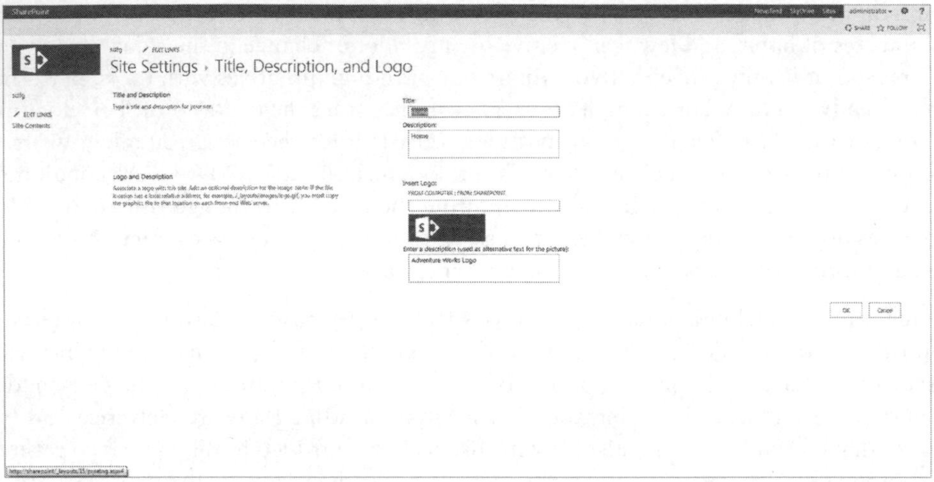

FIGURE 14-1

5. Upload the `AWlogo.png` file.

6. Enter the description **AW Logo** and click OK.

7. Click the logo in the top left to return to your site.

8. You should notice a bar toward the top of the screen, as shown in Figure 14-2. Click "Publish this draft" to publish your changes.

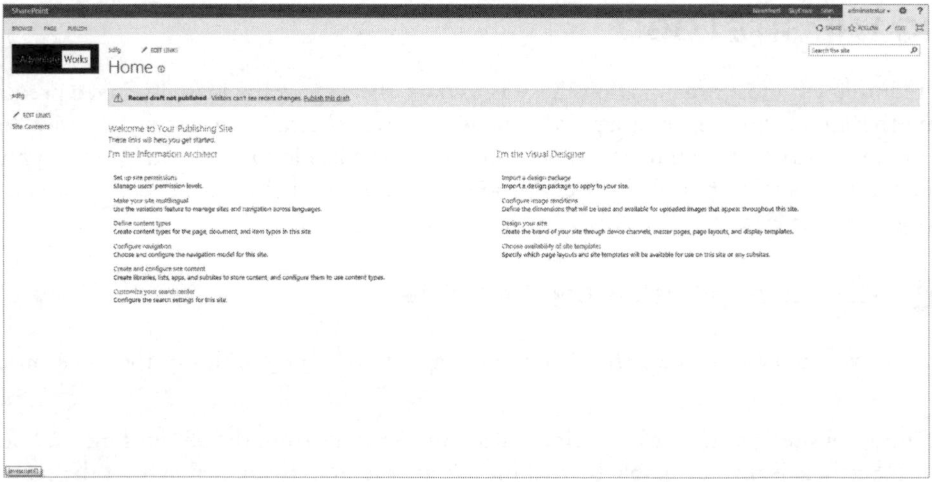

FIGURE 14-2

9. The page refreshes and your image is displayed in the top left of your site, as shown in Figure 14-3.

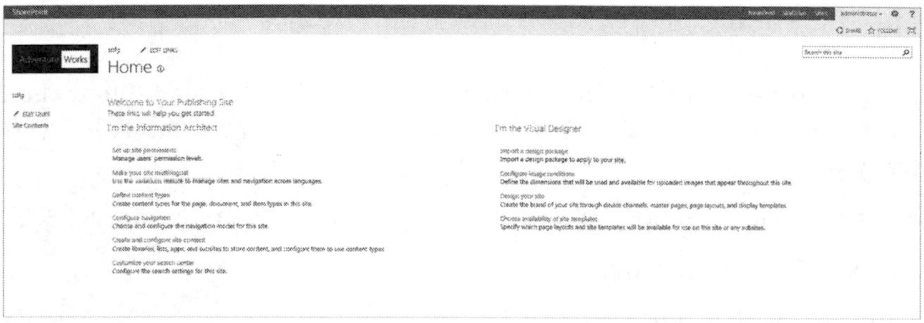

FIGURE 14-3

How It Works

When you configure your top-level site with a logo as detailed in this Try It Out, you will notice that all pages of your site and associated subsites display the image in the top-left corner of the page. Clicking this image returns you to the homepage of whatever site you are currently on. You can further customize your site logo to appear in different locations or contain a hyperlink to return you to the homepage of the top-level site of the site collection by editing the master page. We review this type of customization later in this chapter.

WORKING WITH THEMES

Themes have changed considerably in SharePoint 2013, but they still enable you to make basic color scheme and font changes to visual elements within your site. In earlier versions of SharePoint, only users who were skilled in the use of CSS were able to modify themes within a SharePoint environment. SharePoint 2013 offers built-in tools that provide users with the appropriate privileges the ability to apply and modify existing themes. Figure 14-4 displays the tools available on each SharePoint site for site owners or designers.

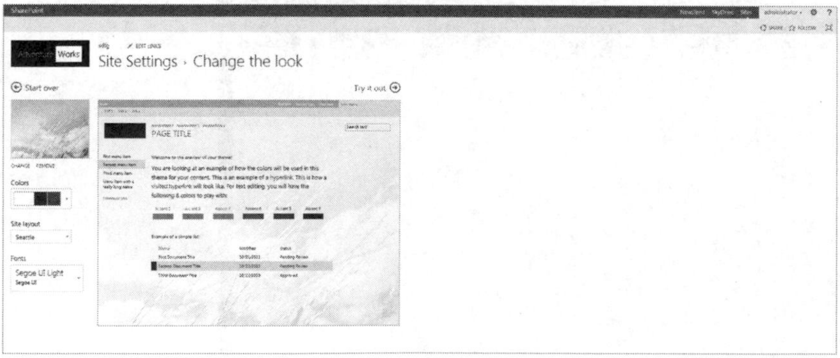

FIGURE 14-4

SharePoint 2013 enables you to change a theme by selecting "Change the look." The process by which you apply and modify an existing look is demonstrated in the steps in the next Try It Out.

TRY IT OUT   Changing the Theme of an Existing SharePoint Site

In this Try It Out, you apply an out-of-the-box SharePoint theme to a team site. You can follow these steps to apply a theme to any site in SharePoint 2013. You have several ways to get to the "Change the look" area, but for consistency you will use the Settings icon.

1. From the top-level site of your site collection, select Site Settings from the Settings menu.

2. From Look and Feel, select "Change the look."

3. Select the Sea Monster theme, as shown in Figure 14-5.

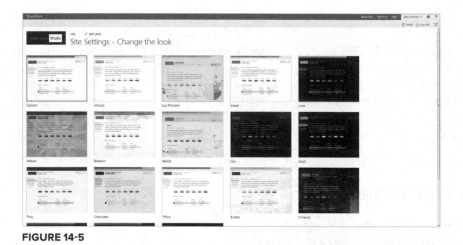

FIGURE 14-5

4. Click the "Try it out" link. The theme is applied and a preview appears, as shown in Figure 14-6, displaying a preview of your site with the Sea Monster theme applied.

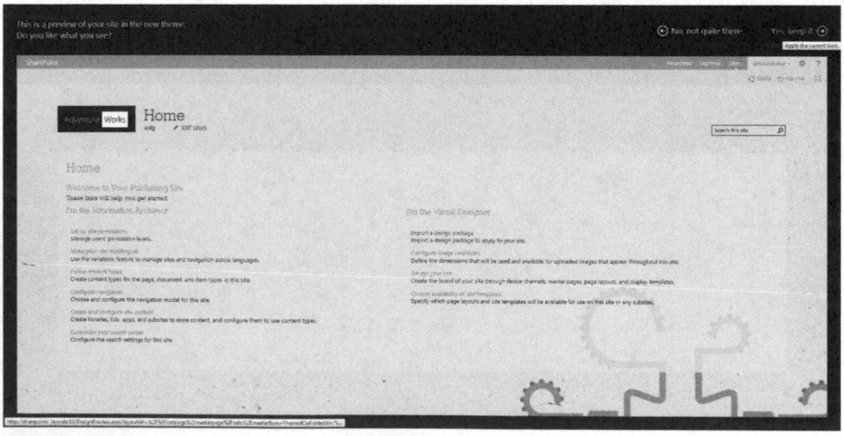

FIGURE 14-6

5. To apply the theme, select "Yes, keep it" in the top right of the screen. You are returned to the Site Settings page of your site, and the new theme is applied.

How It Works

From the "Change the look" area, you can select any of the existing themes. When you select a theme, an image appears, as shown in Figure 14-6, to give you a high-level preview of the theme's color scheme.

By selecting the "Yes, keep it" option, you apply the selected theme to the current site.

TRY IT OUT   **Customizing an Existing Theme**

In this Try It Out, you customize an existing theme further to suit your specific preferences.

1. From the top-level site of your site collection, select Site Settings from the Settings menu.

2. From Look and Feel, select "Change the look" to be redirected to the list of available themes.

3. Select the Sea Monster theme.

4. From the Colors drop-down on the left, select a different color scheme as shown in Figure 14-7.

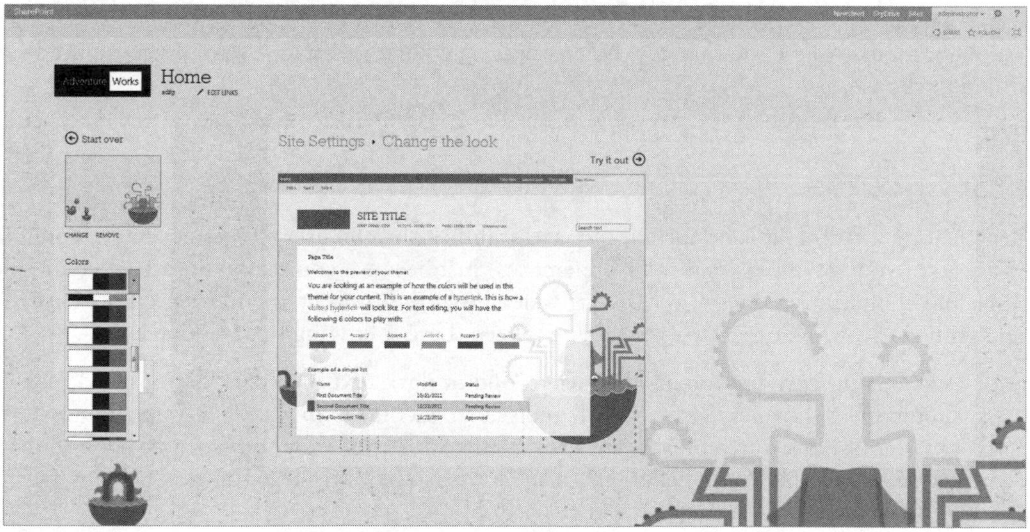

FIGURE 14-7

5. In the Fonts drop-down, select Georgia and Segoe UI. The preview image in the center of your screen changes, as shown in Figure 14-8.

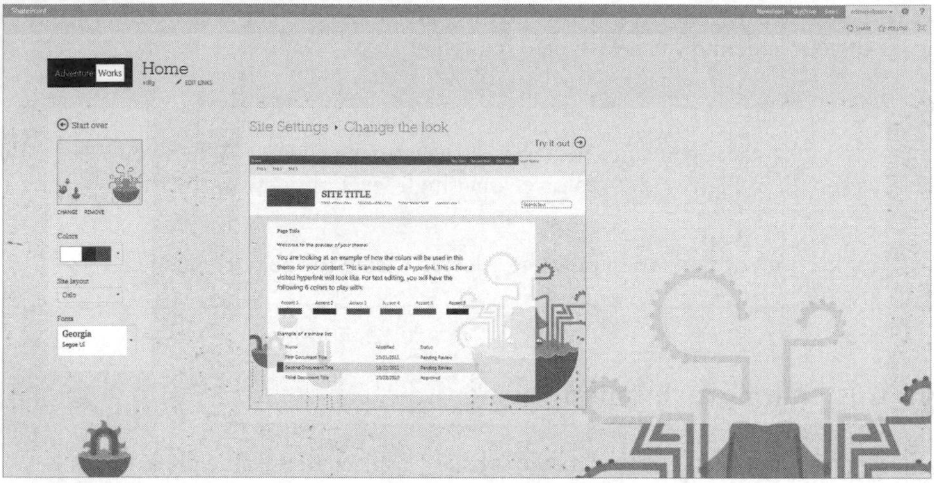

FIGURE 14-8

6. Select "Try it out" to preview the changes as they will apply to the site.

7. To accept the changes, select "Yes, keep it" in the top right of the screen.

How It Works

In this Try It Out, you started with an existing theme applied and then customized the theme to suit your needs. To change the colors of the theme, you used the built-in color selection feature. Using this feature did not require any code changes. When selecting colors, you had several preconfigured sets from which to choose.

Tips for Success

When creating a theme, it is important to place usability and the user experience of your site's members ahead of your own personal color preferences. Just because you really like a particular color scheme and combination does not necessarily mean that the content and navigation are easily readable by others. So when designing your themes, keep these following tips in mind:

➤ Avoid using light text on a light background or dark text on a dark background. Text should always be very easy to read, and selecting contrasting colors is important. Most users will find it hard to read text if the chosen color does not stand out strongly from the background color that is applied to an area. This is particularly true for users who may be color blind or have a visual impairment or disability.

➤ If you select a custom font for either the Heading Font or Body Font, be sure to select a font that is commonly used, easy to read, and likely to be installed on the systems of users of your site. Common choices include Verdana, Arial, Tahoma, Helvetica, and Times New Roman.

➤ If you choose to apply a background image to your theme, make sure to examine it for easy readability once it's applied. If it is difficult to read or feels overbearing, these may be signs that your background image is not suitable.

When to Use Themes

Themes allow for the basic modification of site visual elements without requiring any modifications to code or knowledge of style sheets. These are intended for use in scenarios where slight changes to the visual look and feel are required without the need for advanced styling techniques such as layout changes. Themes are most appropriate for shared environments and collaborative scenarios where strict brand guidelines may not exist and long-term management requirements are low. They require very little effort to create and deploy; however, there are limitations on the number of changes you can apply.

For more complicated scenarios where strict brand guidelines exist or where long-term changes must be accommodated in a well-defined and governed process, applying customizations to master pages and style sheets is recommended because it allows for more flexible and consistent changes to be applied in a unified fashion across all sites. We describe these types of customizations in detail in the following sections.

WORKING WITH MASTER PAGES

Master pages are one of the most powerful tools in your arsenal when it comes to branding your portal and building a consistent user interface. Before we begin, it is important to note that this requires some basic web development knowledge, because this is a slightly more technical aspect of branding involving code. Unlike previous versions of SharePoint, SharePoint 2013 enables you to use any HTML editor such as Dreamweaver to create your designs. For simplicity however, you will leverage SharePoint Designer 2013, a free download from Microsoft.

> **NOTE** To edit the master pages, you will make use of SharePoint Designer 2013, a free download from Microsoft, available at the following URLs:
>
> Download 32-Bit SharePoint Designer 2013:
>
> `http://download.microsoft.com/download/7/E/D/`
> `7EDC5BE7-811C-4854-8502-EAFDEBB981B0/sharepointdesigner_en-us_x86.exe`
>
> Download 64-Bit SharePoint Designer 2013:
>
> `http://download.microsoft.com/download/7/E/D/`
> `7EDC5BE7-811C-4854-8502-EAFDEBB981B0/sharepointdesigner_en-us_x64.exe`

What Is the Design Manager?

Before delving too deep into master pages, we need to take a closer look at one of the big improvements in SharePoint 2013, the Design Manager. The Design Manager is a site consisting of links to tools and instructions that can help take your designs to new heights, faster and easier than ever before. Figure 14-9 shows a preview of the Design Manager.

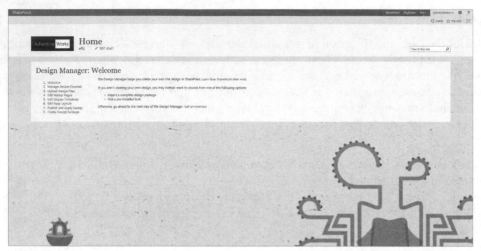

FIGURE 14-9

The Design Manager can help to guide you through the process of creating and publishing your HTML designs to SharePoint 2013 sites that work in a variety of mediums, including mobile phones, tablets, and desktops. In the following section you learn more about what a master page is and how to use the Design Manager to convert a static HTML design to a working SharePoint 2013 master page, a feature new to SharePoint 2013.

What Is a Master Page?

A *master page* essentially is a template that defines the chrome of your site. The chrome refers mainly to the parts of a site that are shared across all pages, items such as a top or side navigation bar or the header and footer. In a nutshell, by using master pages you can make SharePoint look less like SharePoint and more like any website you might visit online. In fact, there is really nothing that can be done on a typical website that cannot be done in SharePoint — a common misconception.

Using master pages drastically reduces efforts associated with branding in the future, because it enables you to make sweeping changes to the look and feel of all pages in your site by modifying a single file, the master page.

Master pages work in conjunction with another type of template called a "page layout" to produce the page that you see in the browser after clicking a link. A page layout is to content what the master page is to the user interface chrome. A page layout enables you to customize the look and feel of content on your page.

For example, when you click a link called "products" in the navigation menu, a process takes place in the background. The master page and page layout associated with the products page merge and form a single page, `products.aspx`, which is presented to the user. This framework gives you immense flexibility in both the chrome and the content of your website, offering true separation of your presentation from the content of your site.

The master page contains a variety of controls and placeholders. The controls remain consistent across pages and are usually used for items such as the global navigation, current navigation, and search, while the placeholders allow page layouts to inject content or controls. This is done by matching IDs with content placeholders in the master page with content controls in the page layout. For example, if you request a page that has a content placeholder with an ID="productmap", and the page layout associated with the page you requested has a content control with an ID="productmap", the content from the page layout with the ID="productmap" will be inserted into the master page's content placeholder, and subsequently displayed to the user. The most common example of this is the content placeholder in the master page with the ID="PlaceHolderMain". This is where the page layout is inserted and basically means this is where all your content is inserted, as shown in Figure 14-10.

FIGURE 14-10

Understanding the Relationship between Master Pages and Style Sheets

The presentation of items on a master page is controlled by a combination of XHTML and cascading style sheets (CSS). Presentation refers to things such as the colors, fonts, and placement of items on a page.

By default, a filesystem-based style sheet (CoreV15.CSS) is applied to new sites, but you can override this by using an out-of-the-box feature called *Alternate CSS*. The Alternate CSS is applied after the default style sheet and hence overrides any identical selectors (Classes and IDs). The Alternate CSS, while still a style sheet, should not be confused with themes, which we discussed earlier in this chapter. Later in this chapter, you are guided through the process of applying and editing both the master page and an alternate style sheet.

Best Practices for Branding SharePoint

As is the case with any project involving the modification of files and code, there are best practices to follow to mitigate risks associated with upgrades or patches and to ensure your site is running smoothly.

There are several rules of thumb to follow when branding SharePoint. The following are some of the more important ones:

➤ Never modify the filesystem files because this can lead to complications during patches or upgrades. Instead, make a copy of the file and modify the copy.

➤ When modifying master pages, never remove placeholders. If you prefer not to have a certain control displayed, simply hide it using CSS or use the more common practice of hiding it at the bottom of your page in an ASP panel that is set to HIDDEN.

➤ Always store files in the correct locations. Some of the rich features of SharePoint, such as browsing to files, work better and faster when the files are in a location (or path) that is selected by default.

Some of the more common file locations you will be using are:

➤ **Master Pages:** Master pages (and page layouts) are stored in the Master Pages and Page Layouts Gallery, which is accessible by selecting the Settings icon from the top menu and then selecting "Master pages and page layouts" from the Web Designer Galleries group of links. The master page is also accessible via the left-hand menu when editing your site in SharePoint Designer 2013 under the Master Pages folder.

➤ **Alternate CSS:** Always store your style sheets in the Style Library. In cases where you are managing multiple brands within a single collection, it is strongly recommended that you create a folder per site within the Style Library to house the CSS to make it easier to identify for future editing. It will also make it easier to store images specific to that site and style sheet. The Style Library is accessible by clicking the Settings icon and selecting Site contents.

➤ **Images:** In most scenarios, images are used in two specific ways:

➤ Images that are shared and used within content, photos, or headers, for example. These images should be stored in the Site Collection Images library.

➤ Images that are used specifically with the style sheet such as background images. These images are most effective when stored with your style sheet. It is recommended that you create an images folder inside the folder you created to store your CSS; this will make referencing your images via the CSS much easier.

➤ There is also a Site Assets library that can be used to store these file types.

TRY IT OUT   Creating a New Master Page from a Standard HTML Page

The marketing department has informed you that a new corporate look and feel is required for the company intranet. After researching the various options, you decided to have your intranet shadow your public-facing website to create a more familiar atmosphere for users and, hopefully, aid in the user adoption process. To accomplish this, you decide to leverage the Design Manager to convert a standard HTML page into a master page, a new feature in SharePoint 2013. This Try It Out uses the CSS, Images, and HTML assets inside the Marketing folder in this chapter's resource files.

1. Before you begin, you must upload your static website using the Design Manager. From the top-level site of your site collection, select Design Manager from the Settings menu.

2. From the links on the left, select Upload Design Files, and then select the link that reads `http://yourdomain/_catalogs/masterpage`. A file explorer window appears, as shown in Figure 14-11. For easy access, it is best to create a shortcut to this network folder.

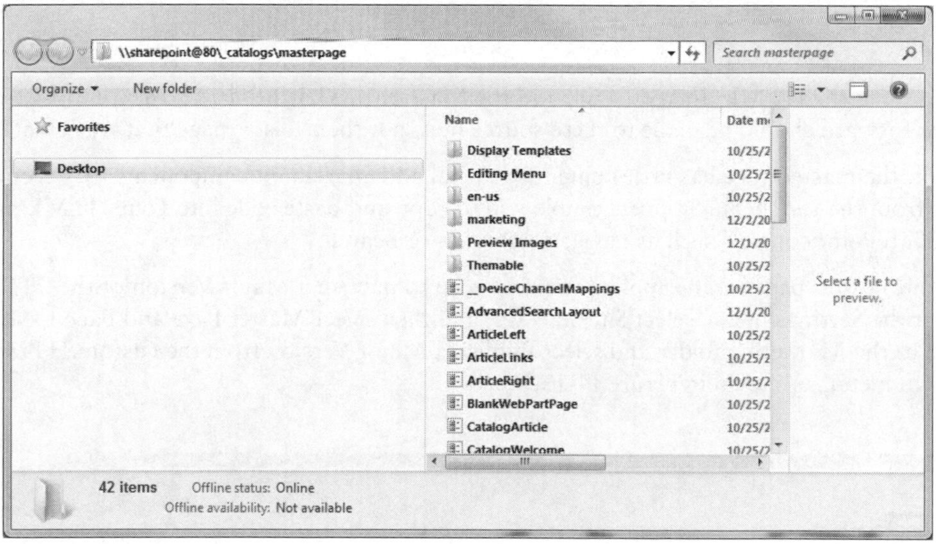

FIGURE 14-11

3. Upload the contents of the Marketing folder.

4. Select the "Convert an HTML file to a SharePoint master page" link, and a window appears.

5. Select the Marketing folder, select the `custom.html` file, and finally, select Insert. You should see Custom added to the list, along with a status of Conversion Successful. A page refresh might be required to see the newly added file

6. Select Custom. You are directed to your new master page, as shown in Figure 14-12.

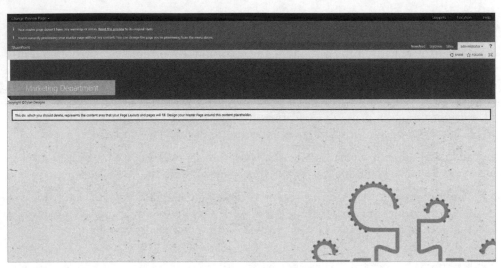

FIGURE 14-12

7. A link between the HTML, Images, CSS, and the Master Page has been created. Changes from this point forward should be made to these source files, not the .Master page that was created.

8. By default, the master page has little content. You can add SharePoint components by selecting Snippets from the top menu. Snippets enable you to copy and paste code into your HTML page to display SharePoint controls such as navigation menus or Search.

9. Before your master page can be applied you will need to publish a Major Version of the .HTML file. Select the Settings menu, select Site Settings, and then select Master Page and Page Layouts. Navigate to the Marketing folder and select Publish a Major Version from the custom.HTML drop-down menu, as shown in Figure 14-13.

FIGURE 14-13

How It Works

In this example, you set the stage for branding your intranet by converting a standard HTML file into a master page using the Design Manager. SharePoint 2013 creates a link between the HTML file and master page, enabling you to modify the HTML file moving forward using your editor of choice.

This process is new to SharePoint 2013 and allows you greater flexibility to create stunning user interfaces without worrying about how your design will work in SharePoint.

TRY IT OUT   Adding an Alternate Style Sheet

To best separate the presentation (such as layout and colors) from your master page markup, you will be using a cascading style sheet in this Try It Out. In an earlier Try It Out, you referenced a style sheet using a traditional `STYLE` tag. SharePoint also allows you to reference an alternate style sheet, which lets you override any default styles. You use that method in the following example.

1. From the top level of your site collection, select Site Settings from the Settings menu. The Site Settings page appears.

2. Select Master Page from the Look and Feel list of links. The Site Master Page Settings page appears, as shown in Figure 14-14.

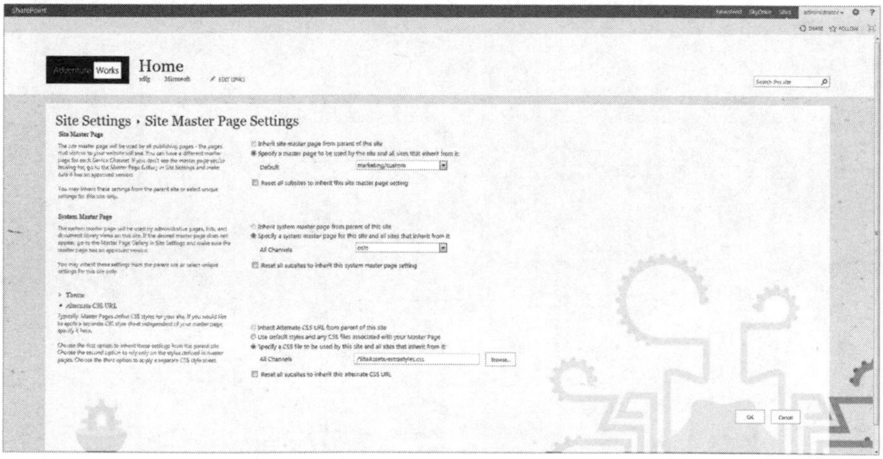

FIGURE 14-14

3. Select the Alternate CSS URL link to expand the options.

4. Select the option "Specify a CSS file to be used by this site and all sites that inherit from it," and then select Browse.

5. Select Style Library, and then select "Click to add new item." The Add a document dialog box appears.

6. Select Browse, and then navigate to the CSS Extras folder supplied with the chapter materials. Open it, select the `ExtraStyles.css` file, and then click the Save button.

How It Works

In this example, you set the stage to use the Alternate CSS feature to control the look and feel of your master page by uploading a new style sheet to the Style Library, where it can be applied to your site and subsequently be accessible in SharePoint Designer 2013 or an editor of your choice, where it will be modified.

This helps to ensure that the default style sheet remains untouched. This is of particular importance during upgrades or patches, where the risk is highest for default file replacement.

TRY IT OUT Applying a MasterPage

The master page and Alternate CSS are so closely linked that they are applied in the same place, as demonstrated in this Try It Out.

1. From the top level of your site collection, select Site Settings from the Settings menu. The Site Settings page appears.

2. From the Look and Feel section, select Master Page.

3. From the Site Master Page section, ensure that Custom is selected in the drop-down menu, as shown in Figure 14-15.

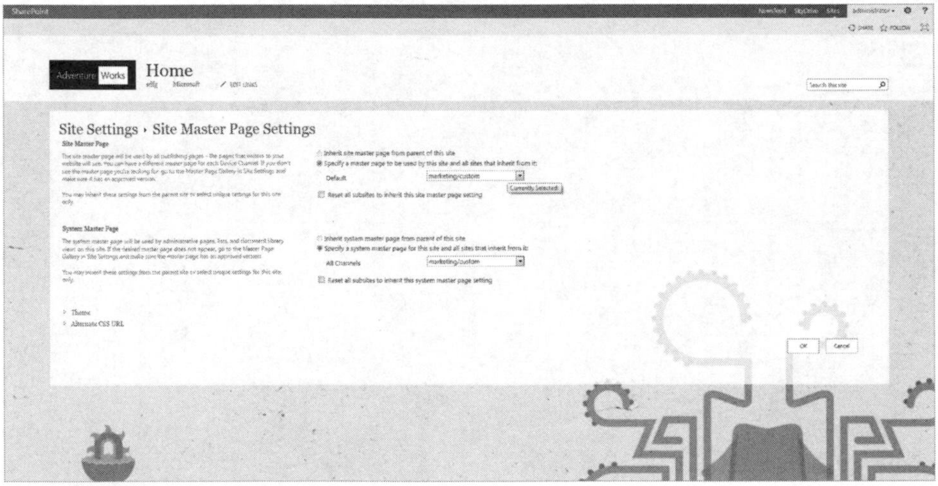

FIGURE 14-15

4. Select the checkbox labeled "Reset all subsites to inherit this site master page setting."

5. From the System Master Page section, also select Custom from the drop-down and select the checkbox labeled "Reset all subsites to inherit this system master page setting."

6. From the Alternate CSS URL section, ensure that extrastyles.css is selected, as shown in Figure 14-16.

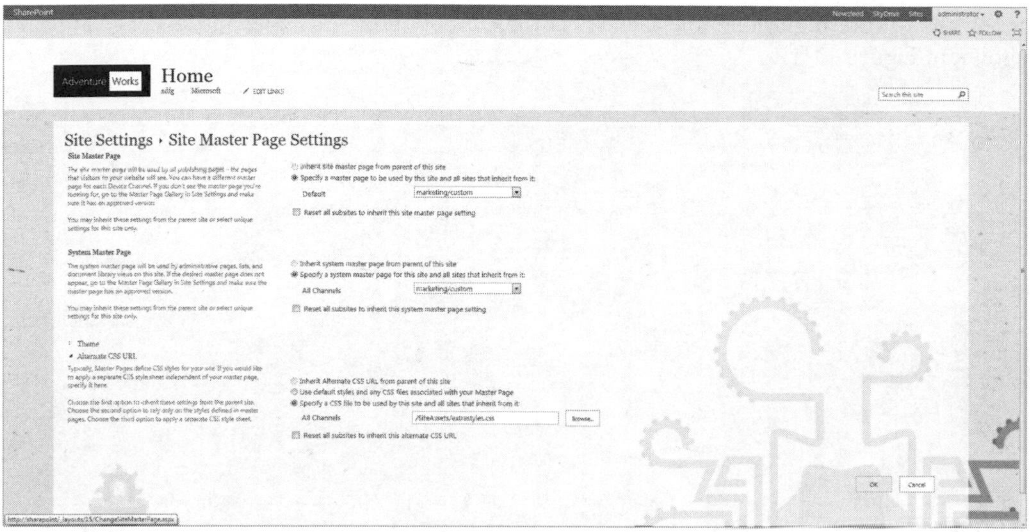

FIGURE 14-16

7. Click OK.

8. Select the checkbox labeled "Reset all subsites to inherit this alternate CSS URL."

9. Click OK. You have applied your master page and alternate style sheet to the site.

How It Works

In this exercise, you applied a custom master page and an alternate style sheet to a site. These files will override the default look and feel of the site, allowing you to transform the out-of-the-box SharePoint site into a vibrant intranet that is more in line with corporate brand standards used on your public-facing website. Because SharePoint 2013 allows you to use any editor to modify your files, you can map the file locations on your local drive and modify the HTML and CSS or you can still connect the traditional way with SharePoint Designer 2013.

TRY IT OUT   Modifying Your Custom HTML Page Using SharePoint Designer 2013

You are now ready to dig into the more technical parts, dealing with the markup of the master page and style sheet. To do this, you will be connecting to your site using SharePoint Designer 2013.

1. Open SharePoint Designer 2013.

2. Select Open Site. The Open Site dialog box appears.

3. Type the URL of your site in the Name area of the dialog box window and click OK. SharePoint Designer 2013 connects to your site.

4. From the left-hand menu under Site Objects, select Master Pages. The master pages library is displayed to the right.

5. Select the Marketing folder, and then select the `custom.html` file. The options page appears, as shown in Figure 14-17.

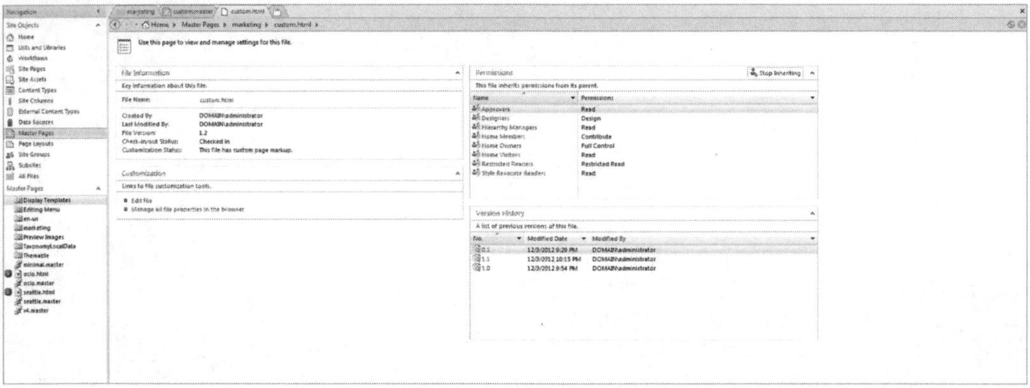

FIGURE 14-17

6. Under Customization, select "Edit file." If prompted to check out, choose Yes. The HTML file associated with the master page opens, as shown in Figure 14-18.

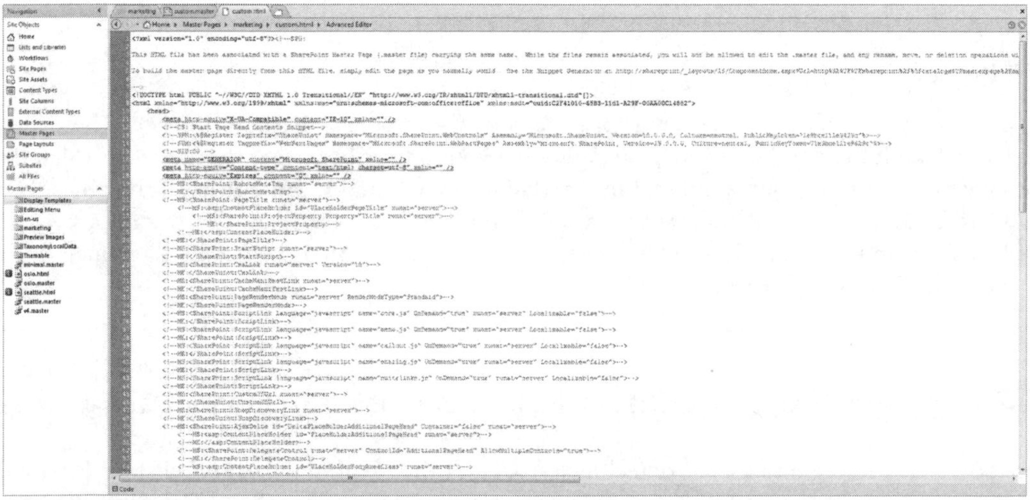

FIGURE 14-18

7. Locate the following code in the page. This is where Page Layout (Content) for your page is inserted.

```
<div id="s4-bodyContainer">
```

8. As a simple example, you will add a bar under the ribbon. To do this, place the following code immediately under the preceding tag:

```
<div class="custom_bar">Master Page Editing Example</div>
```

9. Select File ➪ Save as to save the master page.

10. Select Master Pages, Marketing Library from the Site Objects menu on the left.

11. If required, Check in and Publish a Major Version.

12. Your site now shows a bar just under the ribbon, as shown in Figure 14-19.

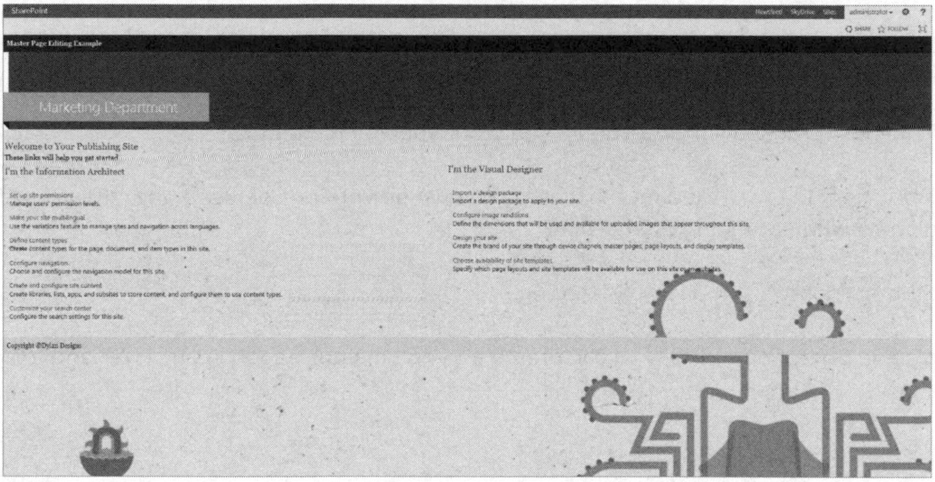

FIGURE 14-19

How It Works

In this example, you connected to your site using SharePoint Designer 2013 to access the master page and style sheet. Using a combination of HTML, CSS, and images, you can completely transform your intranet site from a vanilla SharePoint site into a more aesthetically pleasing work of art — a site more in tune with corporate brand standards.

SUMMARY

In this chapter, you delved into the world of corporate branding and how that applies to the SharePoint world. This chapter touched on many facets of a successful brand strategy, starting with the purpose of branding, which we concluded was ultimately to drive user adoption by creating a better user experience.

After reading this chapter, you should now have a working knowledge of the following branding components:

➤ Best practices for branding and creating positive user experiences in SharePoint

➤ SharePoint themes

➤ Master pages and style sheets

➤ Using SharePoint Designer or any HTML editor for the modification of branding related files

➤ A basic understanding of the Design Manager

EXERCISES

1. True or false: Themes and master pages require an understanding of CSS in order to apply branding changes to a SharePoint site.

2. According to best practices, where should you store your style sheets?

3. Why is it important to create and modify copies of existing versions of files rather than modifying the default files when branding SharePoint?

4. Describe the purpose of the Design Manager.

5. True or false: In SharePoint 2013, you can create and edit master pages in any HTML editor.

▶ WHAT YOU LEARNED IN THIS CHAPTER

TOPIC	KEY CONCEPTS
Themes	Themes allow for the basic modification of site visual elements without requiring any modifications to code or knowledge of style sheets. These are intended for use in scenarios where slight changes to the visual look and feel are required without the need for advanced styling techniques such layout changes.
Master pages	A master page is essentially a template that defines the chrome of your site. The chrome refers mainly to the parts of a site that are shared across all pages, items such as a top or side navigation bar or the header and footer. By using master pages, you can make SharePoint look less like SharePoint and more like any typical website you might visit online.
Design Manager	The Design Manager is a website that consists of a list of links to tasks and instructions that will guide you through designing your sites for access on a variety of devices, including mobile phones, tablets, and desktops.
Converting an HTML page to a master page	In SharePoint 2013, you can build a website using any HTML editor and then convert that design to a working SharePoint site.
Why organizations brand SharePoint	By branding, you are building a more familiar and better user experience, which can lead to greater user adoption and a more successful deployment. Users will become less focused on the technology aspect of the tool and see the application as an integrated portion of their business.

15

Getting Started with Web Content Management

WHAT YOU WILL LEARN IN THIS CHAPTER:

- ➤ What is web content management?
- ➤ How to use SharePoint to publish web content in a single or multiple languages
- ➤ How to create custom page layouts and templates
- ➤ What is cross-site publishing?
- ➤ How to configure metadata navigation

With more and more business activities taking place online, web content management systems (WCMS) have become increasingly important for businesses. *Web content management* is the process of creating and managing web content either on the Internet or an intranet. Where possible, a good WCMS should support a variety of information and provide tools to users for updating this content with minimal effort.

In the past, a major roadblock to managing web content has been the lack of effective tools, which meant relying on expensive, labor-intensive, and time-consuming processes. You don't have these roadblocks using a WCMS such as SharePoint, however. In this chapter, you take a look at web content management and how SharePoint 2013 can make teams and processes more efficient.

WEB CONTENT MANAGEMENT OVERVIEW

A traditional challenge in many organizations has been the reliance of business users on technical teams to publish new content and to improve communication with stakeholders on the web. SharePoint 2013 makes business users more independent in their content publishing activities, which empowers them to more effectively publish up-to-date information and communicate with their target audience through their website.

So, how can SharePoint's WCMS work in your situation? If your company headquarters is in one part of the world, with support teams in other locations, your employees can still collaborate by accessing a company website, regardless of location. Website content owners create lists and libraries and supply employees with the materials they need to perform their day-to-day duties. Managers can create and update a tasks list that outlines what the team needs to do and who is responsible. Teams everywhere can log in to the portal and instantly access important information or even create it for someone in another country. Employees can create e-mail alerts on the important lists and libraries so that colleagues are instantly notified of new or changed content. Specifically, SharePoint has the following features for managing and publishing content:

➤ **Page layouts and master pages:** Enforce consistency across your website and ensure that all new pages that are created follow your corporate brand.

➤ **Creating web pages from the browser:** Allows users without knowledge of HTML code to create web pages that inherit the site's look and feel.

➤ **Workflows:** Automate the process of publishing or approving content. For example, you might create content for a website and then send it through a workflow system where it is approved and finally published to your website.

➤ **Content versioning:** Ensures that you are always using the most up-to-date versions of your documents and allows you to restore to a previous version by keeping an electronic paper trail as the document evolves.

➤ **Reporting dashboards:** This is a great way to get a high-level overview of your content.

➤ **Check in/check out:** Ensures that multiple people are working on the same up-to-date content so that you can check your documents out and in during editing.

WORKING WITH PUBLISHING FEATURES

Publishing refers to the act of creating content such as a new page in your site or modifying content such as a block of text or a picture. By using built-in publishing tools explained throughout this chapter, you can quickly and easily modify your web content without the need for code. With SharePoint's publishing features, you can publish web content for pages and run content approval workflows directly from the browser or edit text right on the page. SharePoint has various templates, such as the Publishing Portal template, that have the publishing features already enabled. However, you can enable the publishing features on a regular team site, such as a blank site, at any time to give it the publishing capabilities.

Creating a Publishing Portal

If you are planning to create a site that is going to be highly customized and feature many pages of content, you may select the Publishing Portal template as the site template for your site collection. You can select this template only as a top-level site within a site collection. In the next Try It Out, you create a publishing portal site that acts as a sample site for the remainder of this chapter.

TRY IT OUT Creating a Publishing Portal Site

In this Try It Out, you create a new site collection that acts as a host for your company's public Internet site. This site contains news articles and company information pages, as well as information on various ski products and services in multiple languages. In the past, creating a public-facing Internet site required in-depth knowledge of HTML and other related technologies.

To create a new site collection, you must visit the Central Administration site of your SharePoint environment and be authorized to perform this action. This action typically is performed by the SharePoint farm administrator. If you are unsure what the address for this site is, you should contact your system administrator or the person who installed SharePoint. You may also access the Central Administration site by logging directly in to the server and selecting SharePoint 2013 Central Administration from the Microsoft SharePoint 2013 Products option on the Programs menu.

1. Log in to the SharePoint Central Administration site for your server farm.

2. Select Create Site Collections from the Application Management group of links.

3. The first item in your list of things to identify is the web application on which you will create the site. Make sure that the web application you select is the correct application. If it is not, you can click the down arrow to the right of the selected web application and click Change Web Application.

4. You must provide a title, description, and URL for the site. Name the site **AW Ski Company**, and enter the following description:

Corporate Website for AW Ski Company

5. For the Web Site Address name, select /sites/ from the drop-down menu and enter **internet** in the blank field to the right of the drop-down, as shown in Figure 15-1.

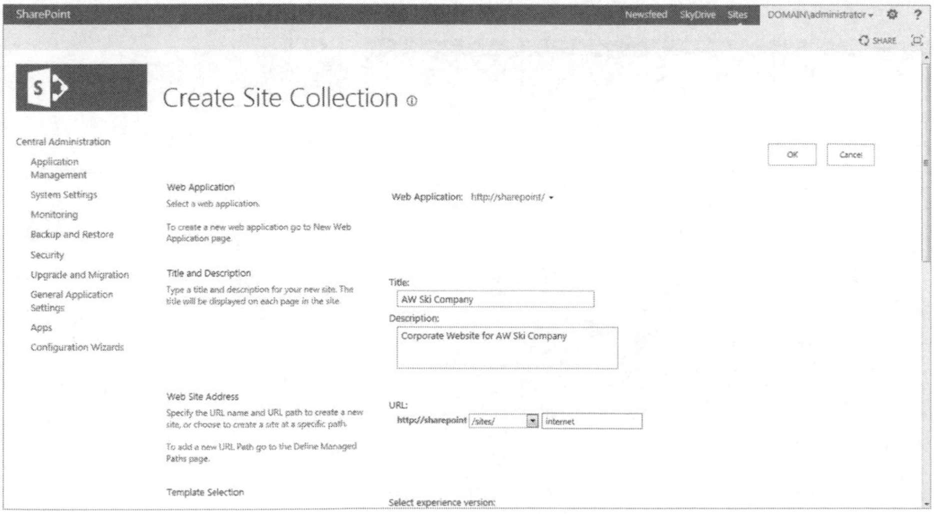

FIGURE 15-1

6. Select 2013 for the experience version.

7. Select the Publishing Portal template from the Publishing tab.

8. Enter your own name as the primary site collection administrator.

9. Click OK. The process for creating your site takes a few minutes. After it is completed, you are redirected to a page advising you that the process has completed successfully, and a URL will be displayed for you to select to visit your site, as shown in Figure 15-2.

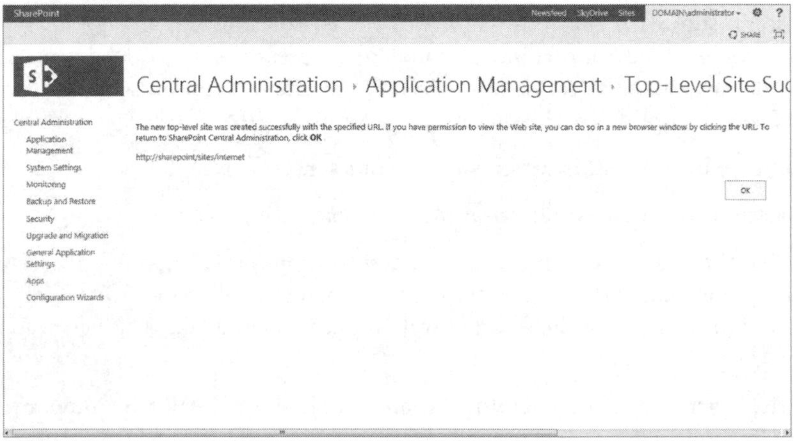

FIGURE 15-2

How It Works

A publishing portal is created with many of the initial lists and libraries that you will need to get started on your website. Figure 15-3 shows an example of how the Internet site will look upon creation.

FIGURE 15-3

The Publishing Portal's Lists and Libraries

As mentioned in the previous Try It Out, a publishing portal comes with lists and libraries to get you started, including the ones shown in the following list. In addition to these lists, the site collection contains two subsites, for Press Releases and Search. You can create new subsites to represent the various sections of your company website. So, although you may think of a company website as a single site, in fact, it contains multiple subsites. As you create each subsite, the navigation updates to reflect your changes. The navigation controls allow visitors to your site to browse the various sections in a seamless and intuitive manner that does not make them feel as though are actually visiting multiple sites.

➤ **Documents:** This library stores documents and files to which your website's various content pages link. You can add columns, content types, or views to suit your specific requirements. By default, this library has versioning enabled; however, unlike SharePoint 2010, content approval is not enabled. A version of this library is created in each publishing subsite for files and documents unique to that site.

➤ **Form Templates:** This is a useful location for storing central templates used by InfoPath forms utilized throughout your site collection.

➤ **Images:** This system-generated library stores images for display in the current site that has versioning enabled, although content approval is not enabled. A version of this library is created in each publishing subsite for images unique to the site.

➤ **Pages:** This holds the various pages you create for the content of your website, including the default page. It has a series of special content types that allow you to create site content and pages. Only one pages library can exist within a single site; however, each subsite will have its own version of this pages library.

➤ **Site Collection Documents:** This document library acts as a centralized store for documents and files that are required and accessed throughout the site collection. Various publishing controls can access documents in this library. You can select Site Collection Documents from the left menu when editing either of these controls, as shown in Figure 15-4.

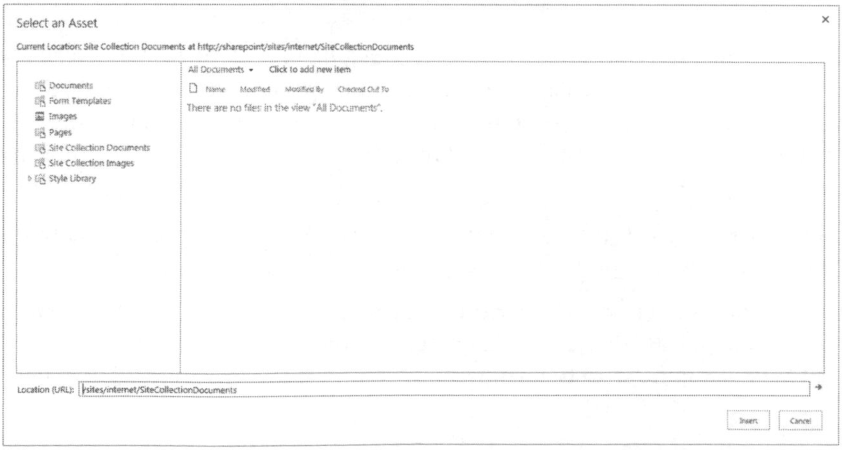

FIGURE 15-4

➤ **Site Collection Images:** This document library stores the images that a site collection requires. Like the Site Collection Documents library, this is available directly via the interface when you use the various image publishing controls.

➤ **Style Library:** This system-generated library contains many of the style elements that your site requires, including custom XSL styles and CSS files; however, you can also add your own style sheets, which you can reference from within the site collection.

➤ **Content and Structure Reports:** This system list contains special queries within each list item that help to generate the reports available on a publishing site from the Manage Content and Structure section of the site. Reports are helpful for identifying tasks and content that exists throughout the publishing site collection. An example of such a report is shown in Figure 15-5.

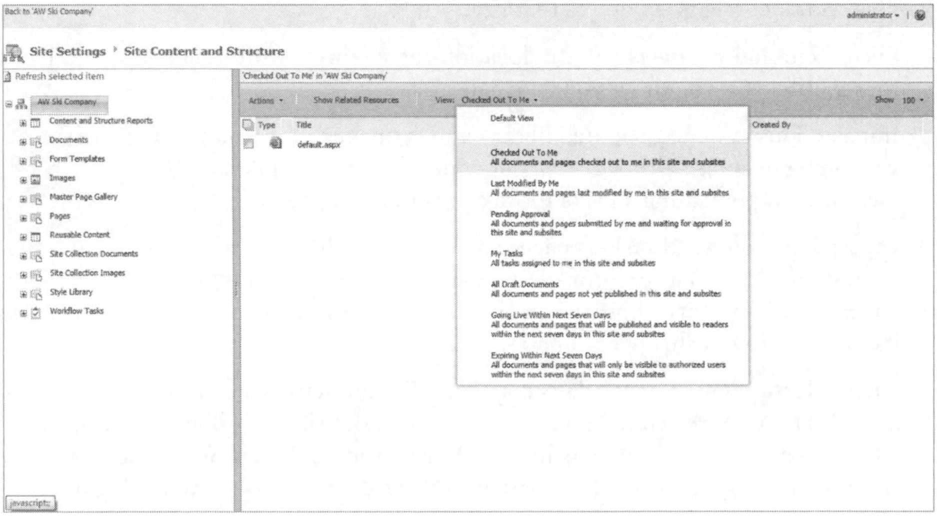

FIGURE 15-5

➤ **Reusable Content:** You may need to display content in multiple Web Parts or locations that are pulled from a single centralized source. This system-generated list contains content that you can display within specific Web Parts. You can opt to link it back to the source so that as content updates in the list, the areas within the site that are using this content will also automatically be updated.

➤ **Workflow Tasks:** This system-generated task list tracks the workflow tasks that are created as a result of the various publishing workflows.

In addition to the seamless navigation experience that SharePoint offers users between sites, it also has support for creating portals in multiple languages. In the next section, you see how to take a company website and configure it so that content users can view it in multiple languages.

WORKING WITH VARIATIONS

When you design an Internet-facing website or corporate intranet, you may need to present it in multiple languages. This may simply mean providing users with access to documents in multiple languages, or you may need all your content, including web pages and interface elements, in multiple languages. In the latter case, if your content is in one language, such as English, you must translate documents into other languages, but the system should support and manage this process.

SharePoint has the Variations feature, which you can use to create a website hierarchy for content in multiple languages. For example, the site may be where customers from multiple languages can view information about the company's products and services, or a corporate intranet site where employees live in different regions of the world and need access to information in their primary languages. In previous versions of SharePoint, there was no ability to have content translated for you. SharePoint 2013 has addressed this, and content can be automatically translated to other languages. Basically, you create content in a source language and then provision the content out to other sites, which represent the other required languages. This happens via workflow, which also notifies appropriate users that they are required to perform the translations. Figure 15-6 represents a site hierarchy with support for English and French versions of the website. Besides English and French, Variations can support any other languages, such as Spanish, Japanese, and German.

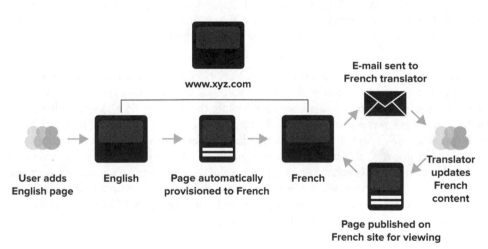

FIGURE 15-6

In this section, you learn how Variations work, including how to enable this feature. You then learn how to create labels for each language on your site, and, finally, how to manage the workflow so that you have all the pieces you need for a working site with multiple language pages.

How Variations Work

After users log in, the version of the site that users see is determined by their preferred language setting in their browser, as shown in Figure 15-7. If, for some reason, a user has a requirement to change the site language to something other than his or her default language, he or she may do so using the global navigation or a language selection control. If that page does not exist or is not published yet, the user is directed to the next page in the site hierarchy, which is typically the parent page.

For a site to become available in multiple languages, you must first enable the publishing features. By default, the Publishing Portal template has these features enabled. Enabling Variations on a publishing site or site collection is fairly simple in comparison to the benefit and functionality it provides to an organization. In the next example, you configure a site collection to support this feature. You use the Ski Company site for this example. There have been slight adjustments to the process for creating Variations in SharePoint 2013 over SharePoint 2010, but the core concepts remain similar.

FIGURE 15-7

TRY IT OUT   Enabling Variations on a Site Collection

Your ski company has customers throughout the United States and Canada, which means you need content in both English and French. To do this, you enable the Variations feature. Because this functionality applies to the entire site collection, you enable this feature from the Site Collection Administration page.

Variation options are configured across a couple of pages, Variation Labels and Variations Settings. In this Try It Out, you start your Variations at the root of your site collection, subsequently making English your main language variation. You also opt to automate the creation of pages for other languages. This means that if you create a new page on the English site, a new page is created automatically in the French site. You then select to re-create any deleted target pages when you republish the source page. You also opt to have Web Part modifications made in one site carry over into the second site. Whether you decide to update Web Parts has to do with the level of Web Part customization you plan to do between languages. For example, if you want unique views available on a product's Web Part for each language, you may opt not to update Web Parts so that the English Web Part doesn't overwrite changes you want on the French Web Part. Finally, you choose to send an e-mail when variation pages have been updated, and choose to share resources with the source variation rather than creating new copies.

1. From the main page of your AW Ski Company site collection created in the first Try It Out of this chapter, select Site Settings from the Settings menu.

2. Select Variations Settings from the Site Collection Administration group of links. Note that this group of links is available only to members of the Site Collection Administrators role. The Variations Settings page appears.

3. Under the Site, List, and Page Behavior options, select the option most applicable to your organization. For this example, keep the default setting of Create Everywhere.

4. Under the Recreate Deleted Target Page options, select the "Recreate a new target page when the source page is republished" option. This setting is likely already selected by default.

5. Under the Update Target Page Web Parts section, select the "Do not update Web Part changes to target pages when variation source page update is propagated" option.

6. Select the checkbox to "Send an e-mail notification to site and page contacts when a new site or page is created or a page is updated by the variation system." This setting is likely already selected by default, as shown in Figure 15-8.

7. Click OK. The Variations feature will be enabled, and you will be redirected to the Site Settings page of your site.

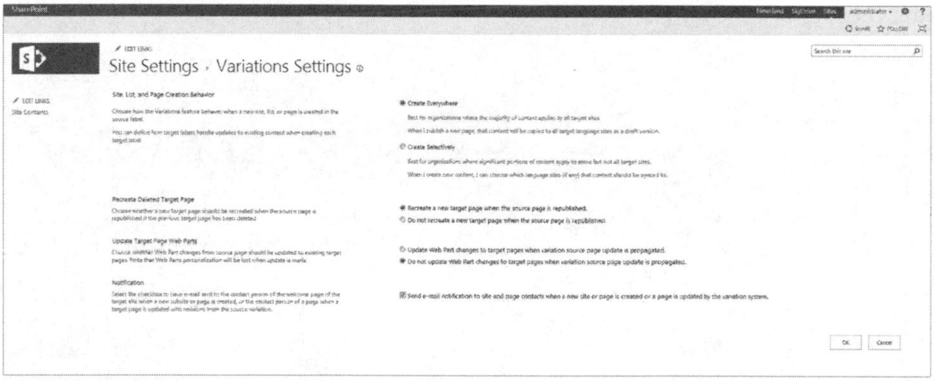

FIGURE 15-8

How It Works

The Variations feature is enabled for your site collection with the options you selected in this Try It Out. Once you enable Variations, the next step is to create labels to represent the sites for the various languages you want to support, as discussed in the following section.

Understanding Labels

In Variations, you create a label for each language you want to represent within the site collection. The label defines the language of the site, the display name, the locale, as well as the hierarchy and source hierarchy. For each language, a sub-hierarchy is created below the root site.

➤ **Language:** This value dictates the language for which you are creating a site.

➤ **Locale:** This further tailors your site to reflect the nuances in variations on the same language. For example, you can define whether your French-speaking audience is French Canadian or from France. Likewise, you can distinguish between an English speaker from the United States and a speaker from Great Britain.

➤ **Variations Home:** This option specifies where your site will be created. In this example, you will be creating your variation sites as the root of your site collection.

➤ **Label name and description:** These values are for organizational purposes only. It is important to be descriptive when entering a description for your label so that it is clearly understood by all site administrators.

➤ **Display Name:** You next define the display name for each site hierarchy. This is the name as it displays in the navigation menu. You generally make the display name the name of the language as it would appear to native speakers, so that they can recognize it and select it. For example, for the French display name, you enter **Français**. This is particularly helpful for viewing the structure of the site in reports such as the Content and Structure Report, as shown in Figure 15-9. If you have difficulty entering the ç character, press the Alt key while typing the number 135.

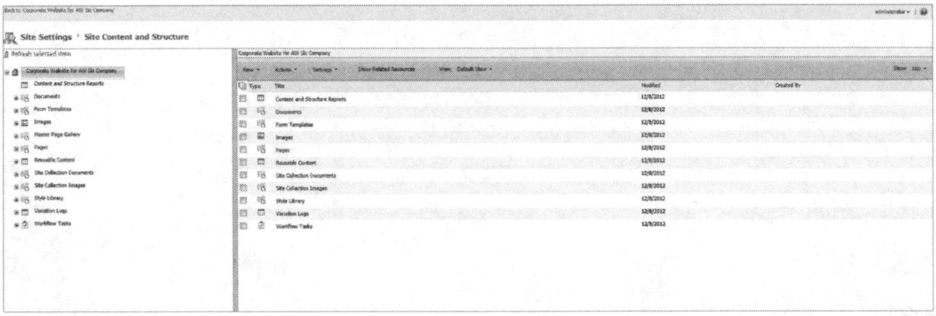

FIGURE 15-9

➤ **Publishing Site Template:** The template that is used to create a top-level source and target variation sites.

➤ **Label Contact:** If e-mail notifications are enabled, label contacts will receive e-mails when the source variation sites are created.

TRY IT OUT   Creating Labels for Each Language

In this Try It Out, you create labels for each of the languages in which you want your Ski Company site to be available. Each label represents a major language, which in turn represents a unique site hierarchy containing all the elements related to that language. In this Try It Out, you make the Ski Company site available in both English and French, but you can expand into other languages later by adding additional labels.

1. Return to the Site Settings page of your site collection. You may already be there after completing the previous exercise.

2. Select Variation labels from the Site Collection Administration links. Note that this group of links is available only to members of the Site Collection Administrators role.

3. Click the New Label link, as shown in Figure 15-10. The Create Variation Labels window appears.

FIGURE 15-10

4. In the Language section, select English from the Site Template Language.

5. Specify the locale of the site to be English (United States) by selecting it from the drop-down.

6. In the Variations Home section, put / in the location field. This specifies that your variation sites be created at the top level of your site collection.

7. Verify that the Label Name is en-us. This should have been prepopulated based on an earlier selection, if not enter **en-us** in the Label Name field now.

8. For Description, enter **English Site**.

9. For Display Name, enter **English**. This is the value that end users see on the site.

10. For Publishing Site Template, select Publishing Site with Workflow, as shown in Figure 15-11.

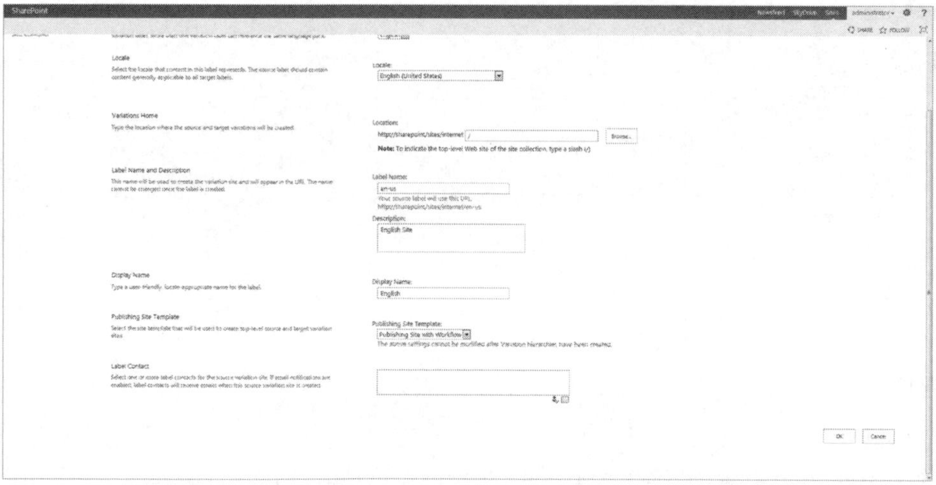

FIGURE 15-11

11. In Label Contact, add your name; if e-mail notifications are enabled, an e-mail is sent to the contact when the variation source site is created.

12. Click OK. You are redirected to a page with a message informing you that your Variations are on their way. Click OK again to finish.

13. Select the New label link once more. The Configure Your Target Label page appears.

14. In the Language section, select French from the Site Template Language. This option will appear only if you have installed the language packs for SharePoint Server.

15. Select the locale of the site to be French (Canada) and click Continue. The Name Your Target Label page appears.

16. Verify that the Label Name is fr-ca; this value should be pre populated; if not, that enter it now.

17. For Description, enter **French Site**.

18. For Display Name, enter **Français**.

19. For Hierarchy Creation, select the Publishing Sites, Lists with Variations, and All Pages option. Click Continue. The Translation Options page appears.

20. In the Create Translation Package section, select "Disable human translation on this target label."

21. In the Machine Translation section, select "Allow Machine Translation on this target label."

22. From the Machine Translation Language drop down, select French and click Continue. The Target Label Behavior page appears.

23. In the Page Update Behavior section, select "Automatically update target variation pages."

24. For Label Contact, type your name and click Continue. The Review Label Settings page appears, as shown in Figure 15-12.

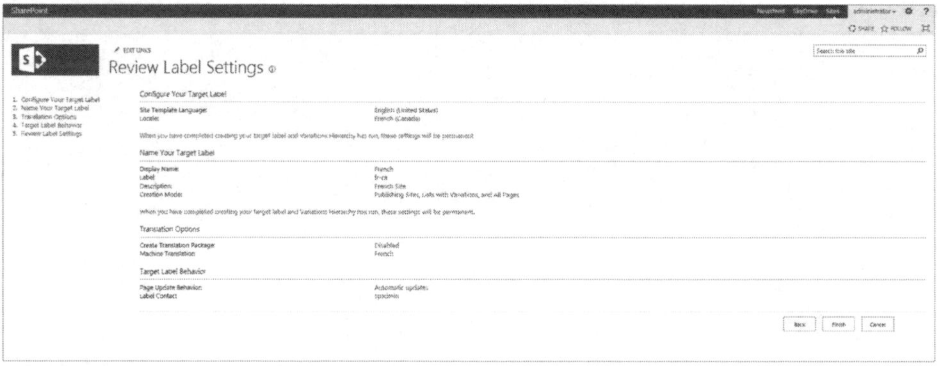

FIGURE 15-12

25. Click Finish. You are redirected back to the Site Settings, Variation Labels page.

26. Click the Create Hierarchies link. You are redirected to a page with a message informing you that your Variations are on their way. Click OK again to finish. Upon completion, the hierarchies are created, as shown in Figure 15-13.

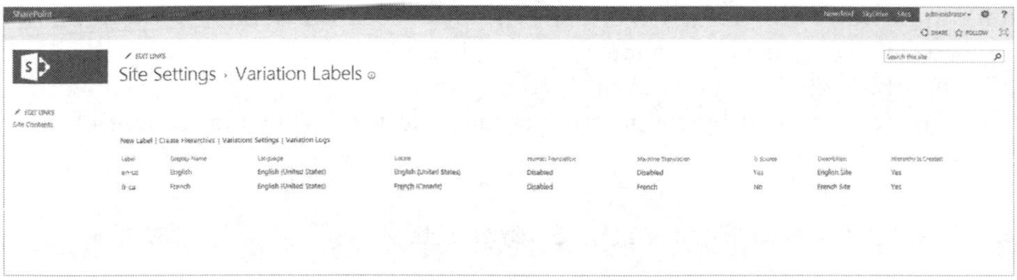

FIGURE 15-13

How It Works

Depending on the language preference that a user has set in the browser, a user is taken to the site with the appropriate language, which, in this example, is English. If a user defines a language preference that does not exist on the site, he or she is redirected to the source language.

In this example, although you created labels for two languages, you can still add new languages later. So, if you were to develop a requirement to offer the Ski Company website in Spanish, you could do so by creating a label for Spanish and then clicking the Create Site Hierarchies link again.

The hierarchy will be created based on the configuration of the Variations Create Hierarchies Job Definition Timer job on your server. The frequency at which this job runs can be updated from the Central Administration site.

Although you can specify that content be human updated, you may also have noticed the option for machine translation while creating labels. Unlike previous versions of SharePoint, SharePoint 2013 can perform machine translation of content.

Managing Translation Workflows

To ensure that pages are translated into the required language of the destination sites as they are created, you can tie your site to a special workflow. As the preceding section showed, pages are automatically created in the language of the source site. The process works something like this: You create content for the source language page. When you check the page in, this launches an approval process. The group that is set to approve the page is notified, and a task is assigned to them in a task list. When the source language page is approved, Variations automatically creates the pages for other languages, and e-mail notifications are sent to translators notifying them that new content has been added to their sites. They translate the page to the appropriate language and, upon checking in the page, start a second approval process. In cases where machine translation is selected, content is automatically translated. Best practices often dictate that the machine-translated content be validated by a human.

This section features two Try It Outs that show you the inner workings of the workflow. In the first Try It Out, you create a new page in the source site, which is English. The page is created in the French site, and both sites go through the content editing and approval stages. In the second Try It Out, you create the site's hierarchy by adding subsites that reflect the two main sections of the website: About Us and Products.

TRY IT OUT | **Creating a New Page in the Source Site**

In this Try It Out, you create a contact information page in your English site and check it into the system to launch an approval workflow. Because you are a member of the Approvers group, you would normally receive an e-mail notification and task assignment; however, for the sake of this example, you can clearly see that the page is pending based on the UI.

1. From the homepage of your Ski Company website, select Add a Page from the Settings menu. A dialog window appears.

2. Enter **Contact Us** for the name of the page.

3. Click Create. You are redirected to an empty page, as shown in Figure 15-14.

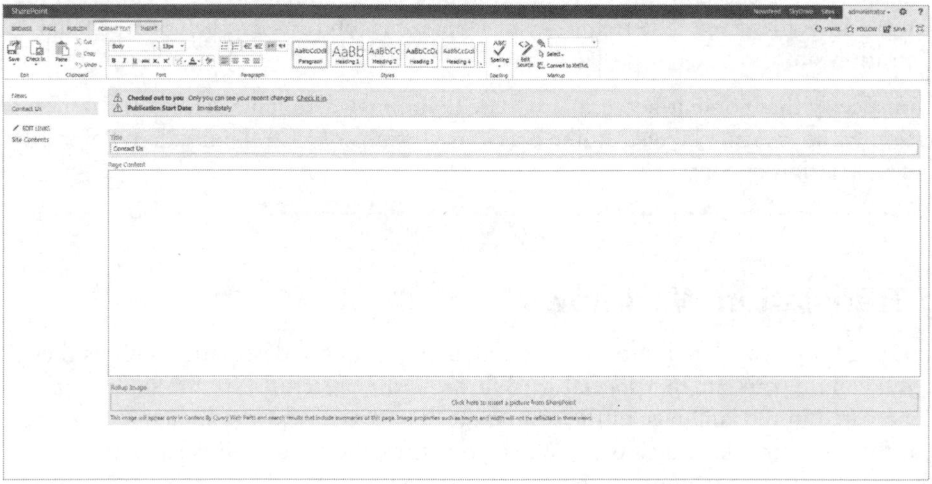

FIGURE 15-14

4. From the Page Layout option on the Page tab of the ribbon, select Image on Right. The page will reformat to display a layout containing a Page Image control on the right, as shown in Figure 15-15.

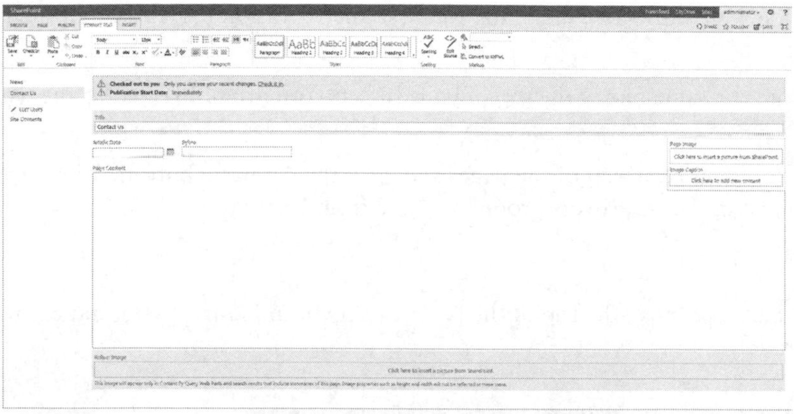

FIGURE 15-15

5. Enter today's date for the Article Date and some basic text the Page Content field.

6. For the Page Image control, select the "Click here to insert a picture from SharePoint" link. The Edit Image Properties window appears.

7. Click the Browse button to the right of the Selected Image field. The Select an Asset window appears.

8. From the left panel, navigate to an area on the site where you have images stored. If you do not have an image, select the Site Collection Images library from the left and select the home.jpg image.

9. From the Image Rendition drop-down, select Display Template Picture 3 Lines (100 x 100).

10. Click the OK button on the Edit Image Properties window to save your image details.

11. Select the Check In button from the Page tab of the ribbon.

12. Add some comments. These will be useful to you and others later when reviewing the page's version history.

13. Click the Continue button.

14. Click "Publish it," which should now be displayed in the bar at the top of your screen. A workflow form appears, as shown in Figure 15-16.

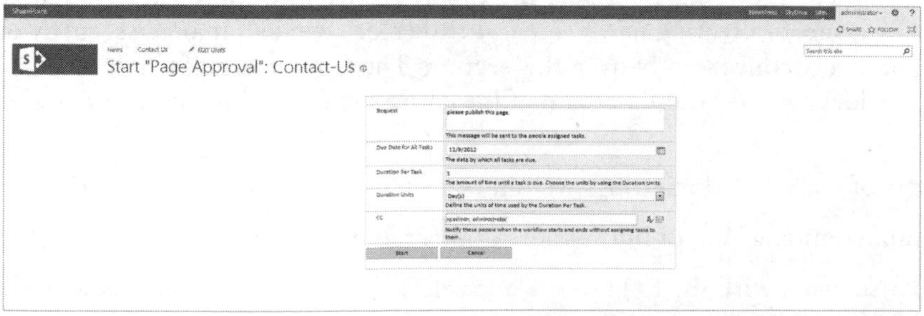

FIGURE 15-16

15. Enter details to describe your workflow, including Request and Duration Per Task, and then click the Start button.

16. Click "Approve it" from the same bar at the top of your screen. You are redirected to the workflow approval form.

17. Add comments related to your approval of the page, and click the Approve button. To approve content, you need to exist in the Approvers group available from Settings.

How It Works

After the workflow runs, a bar appears at the top of the page, as shown in Figure 15-17, indicating that the page is waiting for approval.

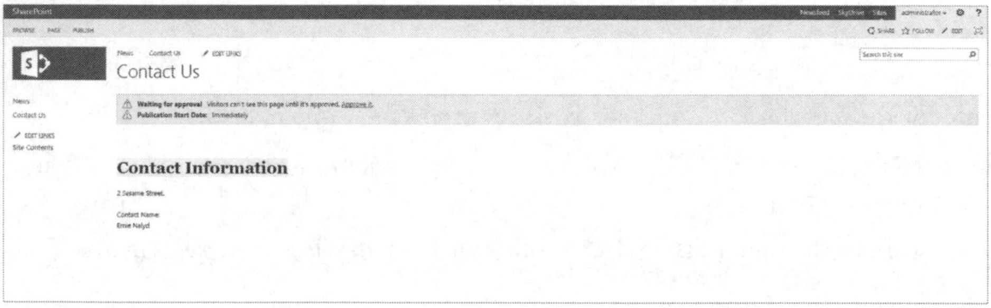

FIGURE 15-17

The workflow was automatically assigned to the built-in Approvers group. Upon approval of the English page, the French page for Contact Us will be created, and content owners from the French site will receive e-mail notifications. This process might take a few minutes, depending on the configuration of your server. Content owners can then edit a draft page that the system creates, and then publish the page. Content approval workflows are also launched for this page, and the approvers of this page are notified.

TRY IT OUT   **Creating a Site Hierarchy of Publishing Sites**

In this Try It Out, you walk through the steps of creating two subsites for your publishing site collection. Because you need to create multiple subsites, you should use the Manage Content and Structure interface, shown in this example. From this interface, you can activate many administrative functions, such as copying or moving a site, or creating new content. In addition, you can manage security or content across multiple sites very conveniently from this section. The Content and Structure window, shown in Figure 15-9, provides a good visual diagram of the entire site collection and its various content elements.

1. From the main page of your AW Ski Settings website, select Site Settings from the Settings menu.

2. From the Site Administration group of links, select Content and Structure.

3. Expand the menu associated with the English site and select the option to create a new site, as shown in Figure 15-18.

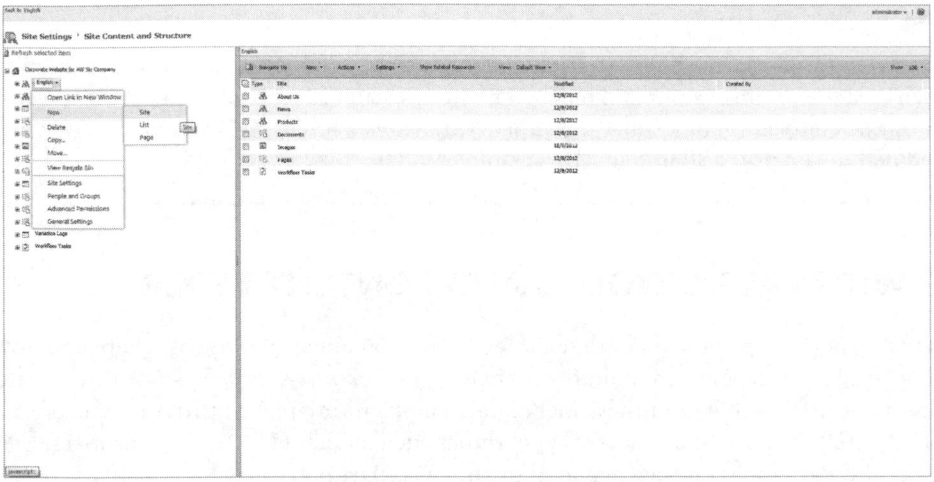

FIGURE 15-18

4. Enter a title and URL for the site. For this example, enter **About Us** for the title; **About Us Section** for the description; and **aboutus** for the URL.

5. Select the Publishing Site template.

6. Select the option to use the same permissions as the parent site.

7. Select the Yes option for Use the Top Link Bar from the Parent Site.

8. Click Create.

9. Repeat steps 2-6, but this time enter **Products** for the Title; **Products Section** for the Description; and **products** for the URL Name in step 4.

10. Browse to the newly created About Us site and select Site Settings from the Settings menu.

11. From the Site Administration group of links, select Site Variation Settings.

12. Select the checkbox for the fr-ca site, as shown in Figure 15-19, and click the Continue button. You are redirected to a confirmation message page. Click OK to return to the Site Settings page. A French variation of your site is added.

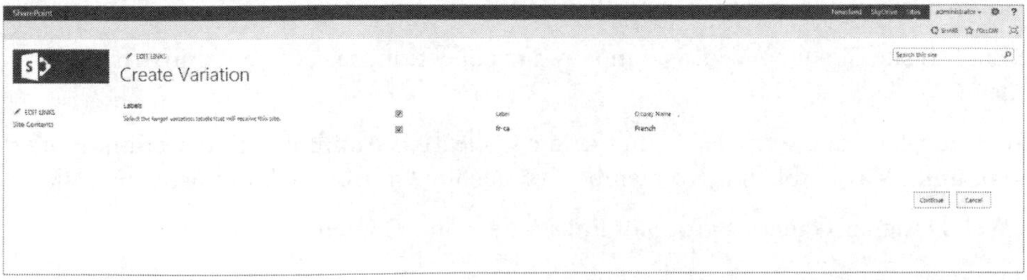

FIGURE 15-19

How It Works

As you create a new site and run the Site Variation Settings utility, a variation of the site is created in the languages selected — in this example, French. The site creation is scheduled based on server settings and relies on the completion of a timer job called *Variations Propagate Sites and Lists Timer Job*. This job is scheduled to run every 30 minutes by default.

WORKING WITH PAGE LAYOUTS AND CONTENT TYPES

Page layouts control the type of content that can be created on a page as well as where and how that content is displayed. Page layouts are built on content types. A *content type* has one or more metadata columns associated with it, and these metadata columns ultimately control the type of information associated with that particular content type, things such as rich HTML fields or images. You can also place Web Part zones on the page to allow for Web Part placement.

In previous versions of SharePoint, you would define page layouts either through Microsoft Office SharePoint Designer 2013 or via the browser. Although those options are still possible, a welcomed new addition to SharePoint 2013 is the ability to create page layouts using your HTML editor of choice. By default, when you use the browser method, which is described in the first Try It Out in this section, the controls are all added to the page from the top down, stacked one after another, with little control over how the various controls on the page are presented or positioned.

When you require full control over the layout of the page, you can use your HTML editor of choice, such as SharePoint Designer 2013, to create the page layout. If you are comfortable editing a page in SharePoint Designer, you can get started by following the steps in the second Try It Out in this section.

Because SharePoint Designer 2013 is required, it is recommended that only experienced web developers or professionals attempt this type of customization.

In the final Try It Out, you learn how to create a new page based on your custom page layout.

TRY IT OUT   **Creating a Page Layout Based on a Content Type**

In this Try It Out, you create a new content type using the methods described in Chapter 6, "Working with Content Types," which includes columns that describe the products your company sells. You then create a Product Details page layout based on this content type. You leverage the Design Manager to create the page layout, a new feature in SharePoint 2013.

1. From the English site of your AW Ski Company site collection, select Site Settings from the Settings menu.

2. Select "Go to top-level site settings" from the Site Collection Administration section. Note that this group of links is available only to members of the Site Collection Administrators role.

3. From the Web Designer Galleries group of links, select Site Content Types.

4. Click Create.

5. Create your content type with the following settings:

PROPERTY	VALUE
Name	Product Details
Description	Information page on AW Ski Company Products
Select Parent Content Type From	Page Layout Content Types
Parent Content Type	Article Page
New Group	Marketing

6. Click OK.

7. Select the "Add from new site columns" link at the bottom of the page and create site columns for each of the following:

COLUMN NAME	COLUMN TYPE
Product Name	Single line of text
Product Category	Choice
Product Description	Full HTML content with formatting and constraints for publishing
Product Image	Image with formatting and constraints for publishing
Promo Video	Rich media data for publishing

8. Click each of the following columns and change the Column Setting to Hidden. These columns will not be required in your page layout.

➤ Page Content

➤ Page Image

➤ Contact

➤ Contact E-Mail Address

➤ Contact Name

➤ Contact Picture

➤ Byline

➤ Article Date

9. Return to the top level of your site collection.

10. From the Settings menu, select Design Manager. The Design Manager appears.

11. Select Edit Page Layouts from the links on the left, as shown in Figure 15-20. The Edit Page Layouts page appears.

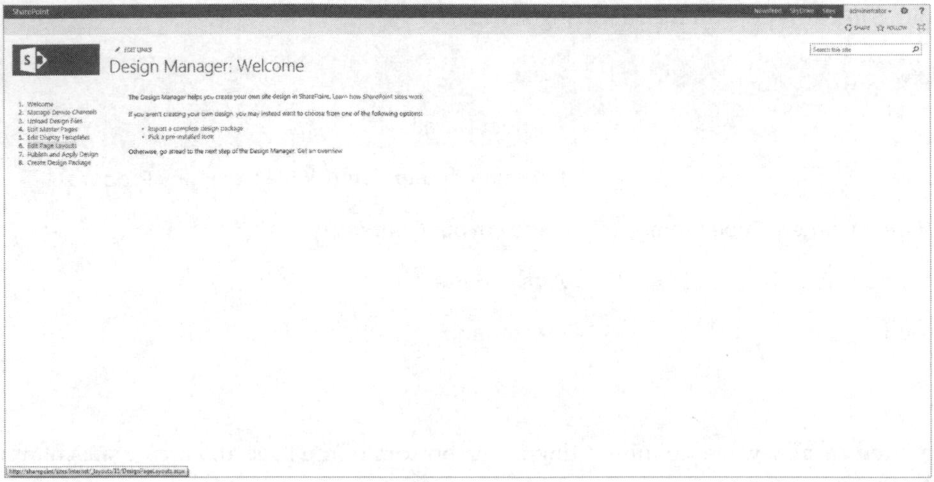

FIGURE 15-20

12. Select Create a Page Layout.

13. In the Name field, enter **Product Details Page.**

14. Leave the master page as-is.

15. For the content type, select Product Details.

16. Click OK. You are redirected to the Edit Page Layouts page.

17. Select your Product Details page layout. A preview of your page layout appears, as shown in Figure 15-21. From here you can make additional modifications.

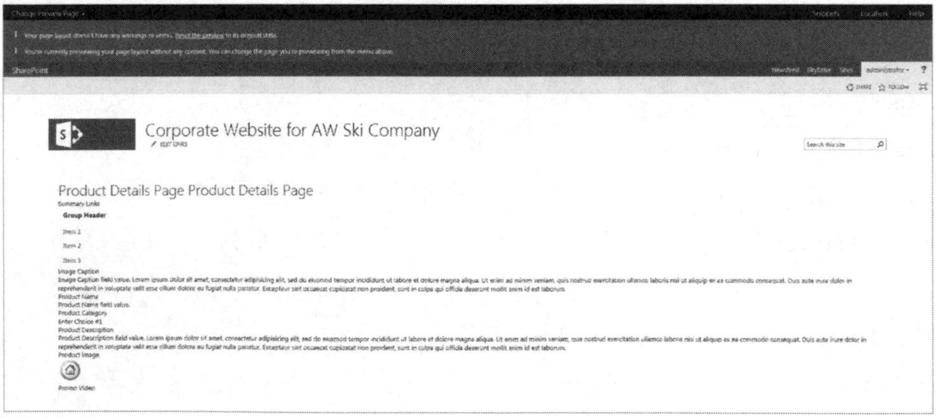

FIGURE 15-21

How It Works

New to SharePoint 2013, once you have created a page layout, it is available in the Design Manager. If you prefer the SharePoint 2010 method of creating page layouts, the layouts are available via the Add a Page option in the Settings menu, or when you are using the ribbon to add a page layout from the Master Pages and Page Layouts library, as shown in Figure 15-22.

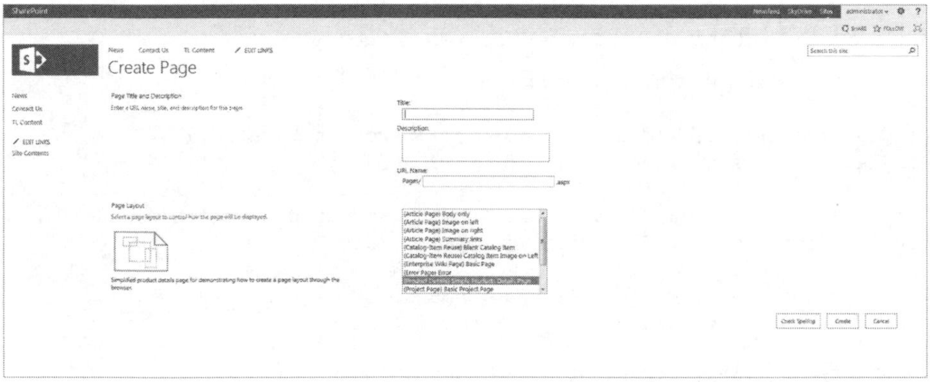

FIGURE 15-22

TRY IT OUT   Creating a Page Layout Using SharePoint Designer 2013

Page layouts set the stage for the type of content you want to allow on a particular page. For example, you might allow someone to place an image and description on a page. These pieces of content are actually columns in the content type you built your page layout on. These columns are accessible in your HTML editor of choice, such as SharePoint Designer, as content controls in the SharePoint Controls section of the ribbon. It is important to note that the content controls should be placed inside the placeholder labeled *PlaceHolderMain*.

1. In SharePoint Designer 2013, open your AW Ski Company website.

2. Select Page Layouts from the left-hand navigation.

3. Click the New Page Layout option from the ribbon menu. A dialog box will appear, as shown in Figure 15-23.

4. From the Content Type Group drop-down, select Marketing.

5. From the Content Type Name drop-down, select Product Details.

6. In the URL Name field, enter **moreproductpage**.

7. In the Title field, enter **More Product Details**.

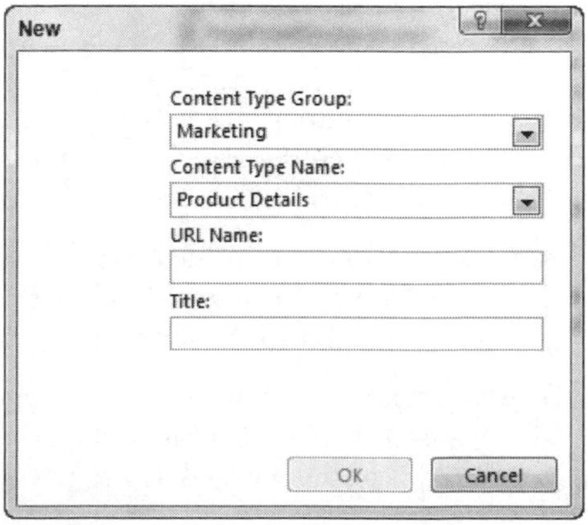

FIGURE 15-23

8. Click OK.

9. Your page layout should open for editing. What you have just done is create a blank page layout ready for customization.

10. SharePoint Designer 2013 no longer has a Design view, so you will already be in Code view. Locate the `PlaceHolderMain` tag. This is the main content area of the page where you want to make any changes to layout or content.

11. Add the following sample code between the `PlaceHolderMain` tags:

```
<div style="float:left; width:80%; margin:auto;">

    <div style="float:left; width:40%;" id="num1">Product Name</div>
    <div style="float:left; width:40%;" id="num2"></div>

    <div style="float:left; width:40%;" id="num3">Product Decription</div>
    <div style="float:left; width:40%;" id="num4"></div>

    <div style="float:left; width:40%;" id="num5">Product Photo</div>
    <div style="float:left; width:40%;" id="num6"></div>

    <div style="float:left; width:40%;" id="num7">Product Video</div>
    <div style="float:left; width:40%;" id="num8"></div>

</div>
```

12. When you create a content type, you attach metadata columns to the content type. These columns are the content you place in your page layout that ultimately becomes the content that the users will add to the page. These columns are visible from the Insert tab of the ribbon, as shown in Figure 15-24. It is recommended that you show the Toolbox by selecting View from the ribbon, then View Task Panes, and then Toolbox. The Toolbox will appear on the right.

FIGURE 15-24

13. Place your cursor inside the `div` tag with `id="num2"`. From the Toolbox, locate Content Fields, right-click the Product Name field, and select Insert to add it to the selected `div` tag, as shown in Figure 15-25.

14. Place your cursor inside the `div` tag with `id="num4"`. From the Toolbox, locate Content Fields, right-click the Product Description field, and select Insert to add it to the selected `div` tag.

15. Place your cursor inside the `div` tag with `id="num6"`. From the Toolbox, locate Content Fields, right-click the Product Image field, and select Insert to add it to the selected `div` tag.

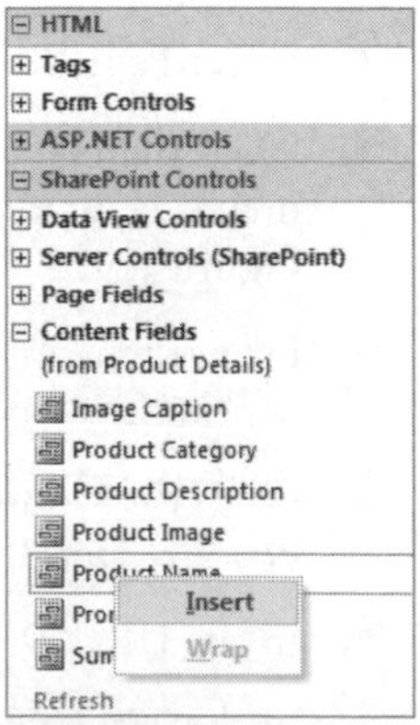

FIGURE 15-25

16. Place your cursor inside the `div` tag with `id="num8"`. From the Toolbox, locate Content Fields, right-click the Promo Video field, and select Insert to add it to the selected `div` tag.

17. Save and close the page layout.

18. Page layouts are protected by source control, and you need to check them out for editing, and check them in and publish them when they are final. From the Page Layouts tab of SharePoint Designer, right-click `moreproductdetails.aspx` and choose Check In.

19. Select Publish a Major Version.

How It Works

You can now put your page layouts to work by creating new pages based on these layouts. To create a new page, you must specify a page layout. By selecting the product details page that you just created, you generate a page to which you can add a product title, description, image, and video, just as you specified in the page layout (see Figure 15-26).

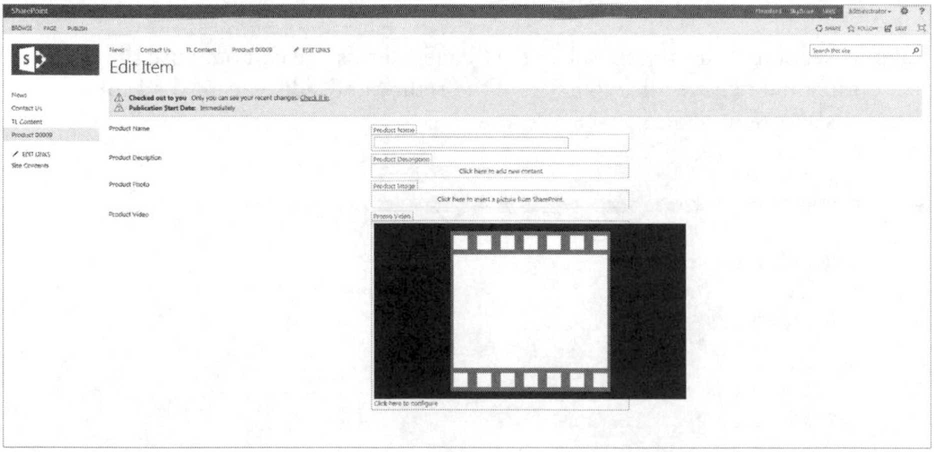

FIGURE 15-26

TRY IT OUT   Creating a Page Using a Custom Page Layout

As you learned earlier in this chapter, you can select from a number of page layouts when creating a page. The page layouts that are available for selection can be limited by the site administrator. In this Try It Out, you configure your Products site to allow the use of only your More Product Details page layout to create new pages. You then create a new page using the More Product Details page layout.

1. From the Products subsite of the English site of your AW Ski Company site collection, select Site Settings from the Settings menu.

2. Select Page Layouts and Site Templates from the Look and Feel section. The Page Layout and Site Template Settings page will appear, as shown in Figure 15-27.

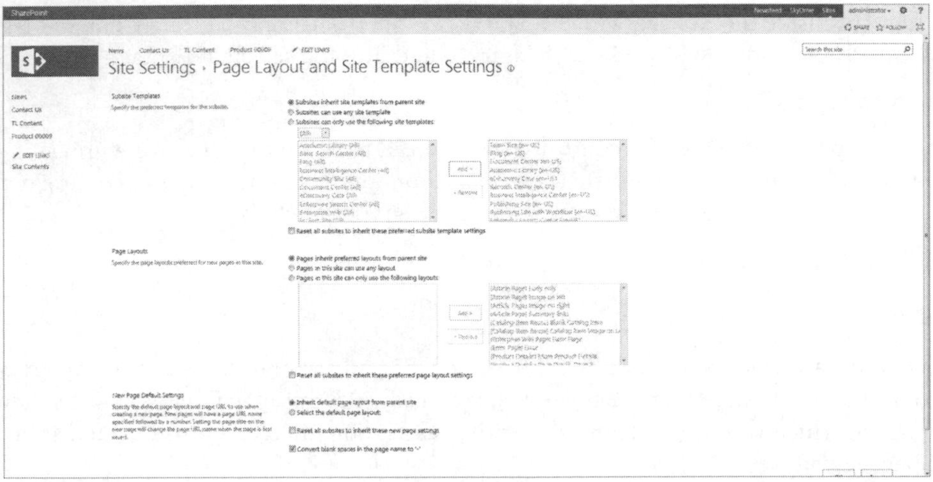

FIGURE 15-27

3. From the Page Layouts section of the screen, select the "Pages in this site can only use the following layouts" option and remove all layouts from the right-hand side, except the More Product Details Page, as shown in Figure 15-28.

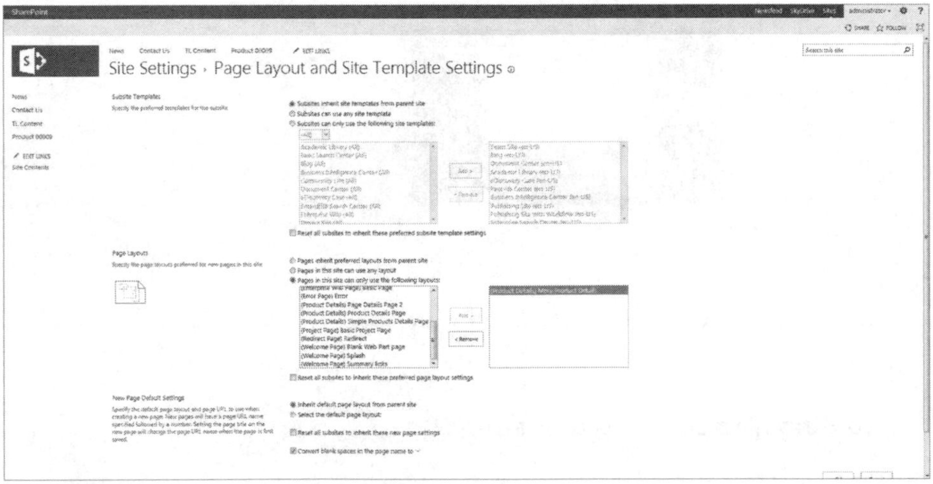

FIGURE 15-28

4. In the New Page Default Settings section, select the More Product Details Page as the default page layout.

5. Click OK.

6. Return to the main page of your Products site by clicking the logo in the top left.

7. Select Add a Page from the Settings menu. The Add a Page dialog box will appear.

8. Enter **Bamboo Skis** as the New Page Name, and click Create.

How It Works

Your new page will be created, and you will be able to specify content in the associated content areas as defined in your page layout (refer to Figure 15-26).

ENABLING PUBLISHING ON A TEAM SITE

The examples to this point have worked with the Publishing Portal site template. This is primarily because this template contains many of the components and elements you need to create a web-facing site. However, you may need to make use of publishing features within a standard team site or workspace, and to do so means you have to enable the publishing features. Switching on the publishing features means you can transform any team site into a publishing site, complete with content approval workflow and new lists and libraries.

TRY IT OUT   Enabling the Publishing Features on a Team Site

In this Try It Out, you have a team site that your ski company is using to create content and track progress across various initiatives. However, to track team announcements and news, you decide to enable the publishing features on the site. To do this, you visit the Settings page for the site and select Activate for the publishing features.

When you enable the publishing features on a collaborative site, such as a team site or a blank site, you can no longer save that site as a template. This is something you should be aware of before making the choice to enable specific features or functionality on existing sites.

1. From the SharePoint Central Administration site, create a new site collection from the Application Management section using the Team Site template called "Ski Team Site."

2. From the main page of your new team site, select Site Settings from the Settings menu.

3. Select Site Collection Features from the Site Collection Administration links. Note that this group of links is available only to members of the Site Collection Administrators role.

4. Click the Activate button next to the SharePoint Server Publishing Infrastructure feature.

5. Return to the Site Settings page of your site.

6. Select Manage Site Features from Site Actions links.

7. Click the Activate button next to the SharePoint Server publishing feature.

How It Works

Enabling publishing features creates new lists and libraries, automatically adds content approval workflow, and expands the Site Actions menu so that you can create pages.

ADVANCED PUBLISHING CONCEPTS

We have reviewed the core concepts when it comes to creating content and configuring sites for web content management. SharePoint 2013 also introduces more advanced features, discussed at a high level in the following sections.

Cross-Site Publishing

So far in, we have reviewed multiple benefits of using SharePoint as a WCMS, such as its easy content authoring, multilingual support, and template capabilities. Because of these strengths, many organizations opt to use SharePoint as their public-facing website platform. This allows them to take advantage of the rich publishing capabilities and easy authoring features for their public content.

Although it is possible to create a public-facing website using SharePoint that is authored directly by content owners, it can sometimes be risky from a security perspective to allow direct authentication and publishing from the Internet site. Instead, many organizations opt to have an authoring environment that is separate from the published environment that public users access for information. This allows for tighter control over logins and access but also provides greater flexibility in how the content is created, reviewed, and approved prior to appearing on the public website. It allows organizations to take advantage of all the features that SharePoint provides from a collaboration, document management, and publishing perspective without having to implement all those features within a public-facing Internet site.

SharePoint Server 2013 offers a new content-authoring capability: It allows for authoring site collections to be created based on a special template specifically designed for use in a scenario where an organization has product information that is to be maintained and authored within a site collection that is accessible to authorized employees on the network. This site collection can be configured to support *cross-site publishing*, whereby the content on that site can appear in another site collection that is publically accessible (or accessible via an alternate audience) via search-driven content Web Parts. These Web Parts were discussed briefly in Chapter 7.

Another benefit of cross-site publishing is that content can be stored in standard lists or libraries rather than requiring end users to populate all web-based content into pages. This enables users to focus on the content they want to maintain without requiring additional knowledge or skill sets related to managing publishing pages. It can also provide greater control for system administrators over the content that is displayed on each page. Content publishers will update a list that impacts a single Web Part on a page, rather than being empowered to edit all content on the page. This may be preferred in scenarios where a page contains additional controls or Web Parts that the content publisher is not familiar with.

This topic is not explored in depth in this beginner's book; however, the process by which such an environment is created would resemble the following:

1. Create a new site collection, called "Product Data," based on a template, such as the Product Catalog site template. This site will be the authoring site collection where information about each product, including title, price, category, and image, is stored. For information on creating site collections, see Chapter 8, "Working with Sites."

2. Activate the cross-site publishing feature on the Product Data site collection. This is not required if you are using the Product Catalog site collection, as the feature is activated by default. For information on activating features, see Chapter 8.

3. Create site columns, content types, and page layouts on the authoring site, as required. For information on creating site columns and content types, see Chapter 6.

4. Update and create terms sets, as required, in Managed Metadata Service Application. By default, a term exists called Product Hierarchy for the Product Catalog site. However, you can add others, as desired.

5. Add items to the Products list and specify appropriate metadata, as needed.

6. Configure the catalog settings for the Products list that is associated with the Product Data site collection. This is done by accessing List Settings from the Products list and modifying the Catalog Settings. Figure 15-29 shows a sample of this page. You must enable the Catalog Sharing option in order for the items in this list to appear in the Internet site. In addition, if these items are to appear in the Internet site collection to users who are not logged into the site, click the "Enable anonymous access" button.

7. Ensure that the search index associated with your farm is updated by performing a crawl. Depending on your configuration, this may happen automatically or require action from you to start the process. The search configuration settings are displayed for your convenience on the Catalog Settings page (refer to Figure 15-29). For more on search indexing and creating crawls, see Chapter 17, "Working with Search."

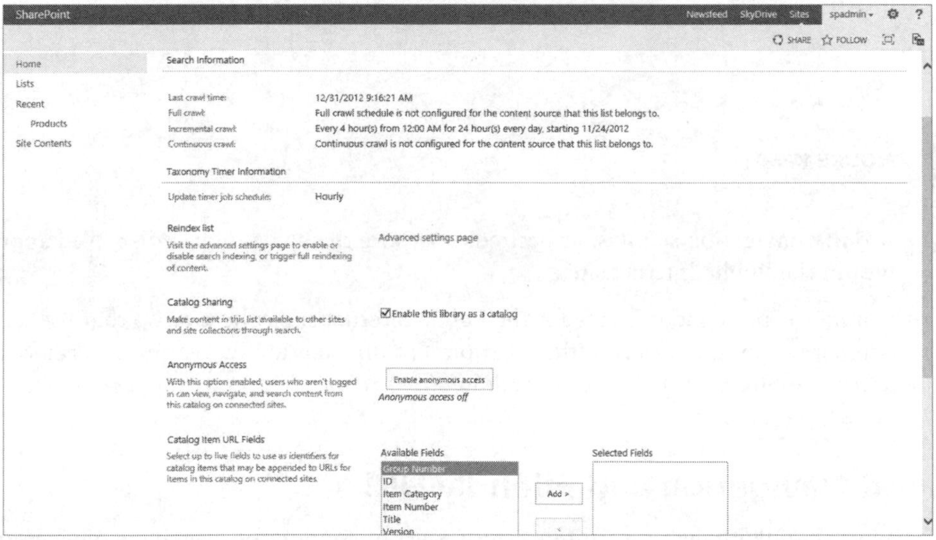

FIGURE 15-29

8. Create a new site collection, called "Public Internet," based on the Publishing Portal site template. This site will be where all content is published and displayed to public Internet users.

9. Connect to the catalog associated with the Products list. This is done by visiting the Site Settings page of the Public Internet site and clicking the "Manage catalog connections" link. You will be redirected to a page that lists any existing catalogs (see Figure 15-30). If you do not see any items listed but you have shared them as described in step 5, you may need to run the search index associated with the farm again to ensure that the settings have been picked up by the search service.

Clicking the Connect link will redirect you to a page where you can choose to integrate the catalog into your site directly. This will update links in the navigation to include items from your products list. Alternatively, you can choose to connect but not integrate to the catalog, which will allow you to manually configure search Web Parts and content.

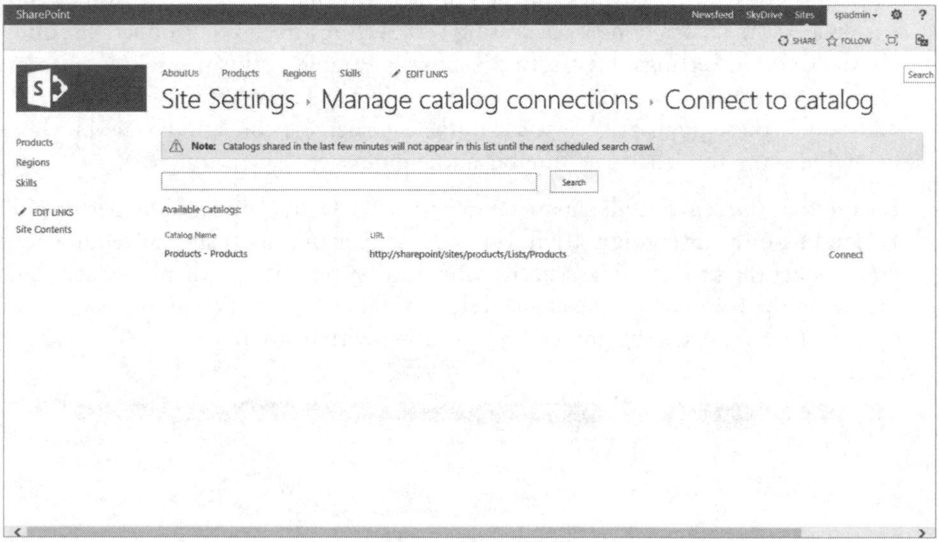

FIGURE 15-30

10. Modify navigation settings, as desired, to ensure the navigation is displayed appropriately within the Public Internet site.

11. Configure anonymous access for the Public Internet site collection so that users can view content without requiring authentication. For information on planning permissions and access for SharePoint 2013 sites, visit `http://technet.microsoft.com/en-us/library/cc262939.aspx`.

Managed Navigation and Friendly URLs

Previously in SharePoint, as a site administrator, the only option for displaying navigational links was to generate the global and current navigation links on the structure of the site. In other words, you could display links to sites and pages based on where they existed in the site hierarchy. You explored this concept in Chapter 8 when it demonstrated that by creating a site collection for projects, you could have the navigation display a listing of all project sites that were located directly below the top-level site in the global navigation.

SharePoint 2013 has introduced a new concept that allows you to create navigational structures based on metadata — specifically, managed metadata (explored in Chapter 16, "Managing

Records"). Using this option, you can create a term set, a managed set of metadata values that can be associated with a site column. Term sets are more complex than standard metadata values that would be available in column types, such as Choice lists, because they can be hierarchical in nature, have synonyms, and be moved or changed over a period of time to reflect changes in the organization. Figure 15-31 shows an example of a term set that is accessible via Managed Metadata Service Application in Central Administration or via the Term Set Management link within the Site Settings of a site. You can create a term set to define the core structure of your site.

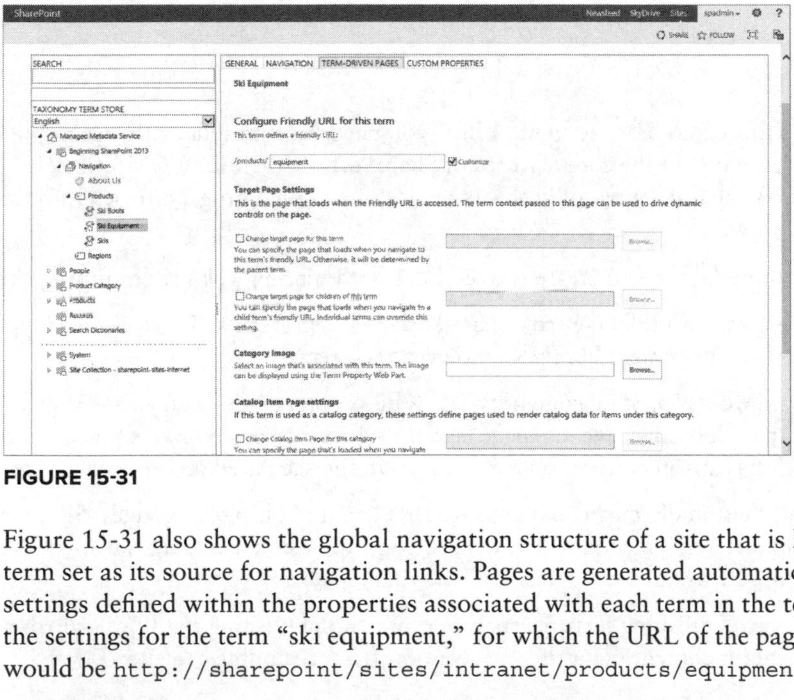

FIGURE 15-31

Figure 15-31 also shows the global navigation structure of a site that is leveraging the Navigation term set as its source for navigation links. Pages are generated automatically in the site based on the settings defined within the properties associated with each term in the term set. Figure 15-32 shows the settings for the term "ski equipment," for which the URL of the page associated with that term would be `http://sharepoint/sites/intranet/products/equipment`.

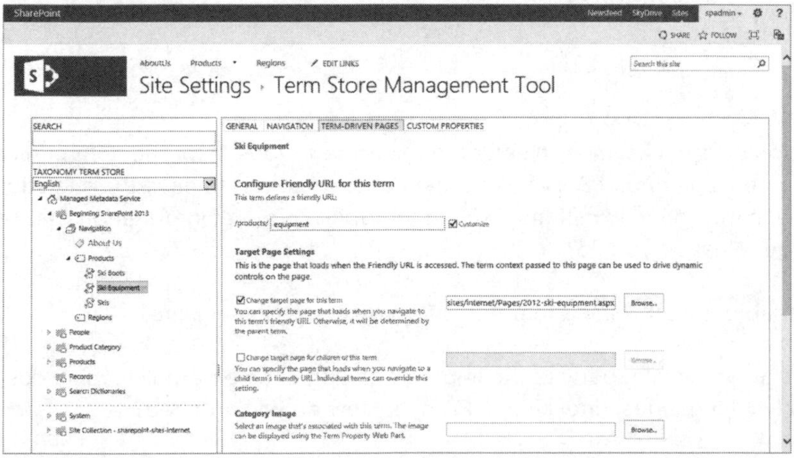

FIGURE 15-32

Using the managed navigation feature, you can set custom URLs for the pages so that they display in a clean and easy to read manner for end users. This is often referred to as a *friendly URL*. You can also set which page is displayed when the link is clicked. This is helpful if you don't want to use a system-generated page for the term, but instead want to have greater authoring control of your page. When the page is viewed by end users, the URL will display as you have specified and will also exclude details such as references to the pages library of the site, which is not intended to be accessed directly by end users. You can also use this feature to combine friendly URLs, managed navigation and the cross-site publishing feature described in the previous sections.

SUMMARY

As your business publishes more and more content online, you need tools to efficiently accomplish this task. This chapter covered one of the core features of SharePoint Server, its WCMS, which enables users to perform tasks that once required the expertise of a skilled programmer. From this chapter, you learned the following:

➤ You can use publishing features to create web content without any web programming skills.

➤ Using content types, you can fully control what content a user creates. These content types can be attached to lists, document libraries, and even web pages.

➤ You can create page layouts based on content types. While content type controls the type of content that you can have on the page, the page layout itself can be customized to position and style the content. Users can later create content or pages in the site based on these page layouts.

➤ Doing business internationally means having sites that are in multiple languages. SharePoint can help you set up different calendars and local settings in various languages using Variations, regional settings, resource files, and language packs.

➤ You can use advanced publishing features such as cross-site publishing to allow contributors to modify and maintain content in a different location from the published site.

➤ You can leverage managed metadata term sets to define how the navigation of your site should be displayed and how the URLs associated with your content can be displayed to end users.

EXERCISES

1. Your manager informs you that you have been selected to create a website for the communications department on the new SharePoint Server. The main requirement is to have the site allow nontechnical employees in the communications division to publish product information that can be viewed as a web page. What do you do?

2. True or false: You can enable the publishing features after you create a team site.

3. The sales manager says a recent sale requires the implementation of an externally facing customer support portal in two languages, English and French. How do you proceed?

4. True or false: You can use your HTML editor of choice to create page layouts in SharePoint 2013.

▶ WHAT YOU LEARNED IN THIS CHAPTER

TOPIC	KEY CONCEPTS
Web content management	Web content management features allow business users or content publishers to create web content for a site without the requirement for custom code or HTML knowledge. This may include the creation of web pages or the publishing of images or video.
Variations	Variations is a feature available within SharePoint to support scenarios where multiple sites may exist around a common topic but have slight differences, such as language. A change in content in one site can then be automatically copied to the other sites.
Page layouts	Page layouts are web page templates that contain specific content fields pre-configured and laid out on a page so that they can be completed by a content publisher.

16

Managing Records

WHAT YOU WILL LEARN IN THIS CHAPTER:

➤ The essential components of a records-management solution

➤ How to create a file plan

➤ How to create a classification plan

➤ About Records Declaration

➤ How to use the archival approach

➤ How to use In-Place Records Management

➤ How to use records retention and disposition

➤ How to use eDiscovery and holds

WROX.COM CODE DOWNLOADS FOR THIS CHAPTER

You can find the wrox.com code downloads for this chapter on the Download Code tab at www.wrox.com/remtitle.cgi?isbn=1118495896. The code is in the Chapter 16 download and individually named according to the names throughout the chapter.

As the amount of paper and digital information continues to increase within our organizations, the effective retention, organization, and disposal of this information becomes more and more critical. Records management is becoming a larger area of focus for many organizations today. SharePoint Server 2013 provides multiple features to assist organizations with their records-management requirements whether they are just getting started or have a highly defined and well-governed records-management practice.

GETTING STARTED WITH RECORDS MANAGEMENT

Records management is the practice of organizing and maintaining documents within an organization based on a series of predetermined rules. These rules control things such as where files are stored, how long they are retained, how they should be disposed of, and who is responsible for these files. An organization may practice records management for either operational or regulatory purposes. This chapter provides you with a greater insight into the activities that are related to implementing a records-management solution within your organization.

If you are new to records management, you may be wondering about how you should approach the establishment of a records-management practice or solution for your organization. It is important to be specific to your organization's needs when devising a plan. Although some fundamental elements are consistent across most organizations, records management is not a one-size-fits-all concept. Following is a high-level listing of the key elements of a records-management solution.

Key Roles and Responsibilities

It is important to clearly identify the key roles and responsibilities related to your records management implementation. Typically, this includes records administrators who are the key managers and enforcers of your records-management strategy. Members of this group are closely familiar with the rules and regulations within your organization related to records declaration, retention, and disposal. They are responsible for managing and maintaining the file and classification plan as well as ensuring that these items evolve as the organization changes and develops. These members must have the buy-in and support of the organization's decision makers in order to define, implement, and govern the policies appropriately to ensure the successful adoption of the practice.

In addition to the records administrators, it is important to clearly understand and communicate the involvement of standard end users of the system. How should they be involved in the identification and declaration of records? Should they be empowered to classify content and identify the appropriate stage at which a document becomes an official record, or should such stages be identified automatically by the system independent of the involvement of the end users of the system? Should end users be allowed to view or edit a document once it has been declared an official record?

Finally, you must consider the involvement of the technical system administrators of your solution in the management and configuration of various technical aspects of the system. What level of access should they be given to the records within the system?

These are questions that you must consider and clearly answer as part of the planning stage of your records-management implementation. Although some similarities exist across organizations, you should base the answers to the preceding questions on the specific needs of your organization — its size, the maturity of its information-management processes, regulatory or legal requirements, and the complexity of the organization's structure and information.

The File Plan

A core element of every records-management solution is the identification, planning, and subsequent creation of a file plan. The file plan typically includes the following information:

➤ The categories of documents that exist within the organization. Examples may include Sales, Marketing, Human Resources, and so forth. Depending on the complexity of the organization, there may be multiple layers of categories and subcategories.

➤ The individuals or groups responsible for the governance of each category of documents.

➤ The types of documents that exist within each category. Examples within the Human Resources category may include Personnel Records, Forms, Policies, and so forth.

➤ The location of the records associated with a specific category. This location may be a library or folder within the solution or it may refer to a physical storage location for paper records.

➤ Details of the regulatory or organizational rules related to how long the records should be stored within the system (retention) or when they should be removed from the system and whether they should be deleted or moved to another location (disposal).

➤ Details related to when an item should be considered a record and any associated restrictions that should be placed on the item at that point. For example, in some organizations, once an item is declared a record, it should no longer be available for editing or deletion by users of the system. In other organizations, a document is a record as soon as it is created.

It may seem overwhelming to address these aspects of a records-management plan, if you have not yet begun the process. In fact, it does require a significant amount of planning and effort. However, a key strategy to effectively executing the development of your file plan is taking an iterative approach to planning and including key stakeholders within your organization in the process. The file plan is not something that should be created by a single member of a technology team, but rather should be a joint effort between the appropriate experts within the business.

When identifying the categories, subcategories, and associated document types within an organization, it is helpful to create a mind map or hierarchy diagram to assist with the visualization of such information. A sample of how this may look is provided in Figure 16-1.

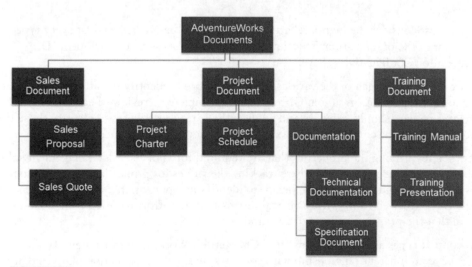

FIGURE 16-1

It may take multiple iterations and revisions to get a final listing. Once you have effectively identified all categories and subcategories, you typically then assign a unique identifier to each and begin planning for the storage location for each. It is important to be flexible enough to accommodate changes over time, while still providing the appropriate level of detail to suit your requirements today. Figure 16-2 is an example of a document library that has been configured to represent a single category of documents with subfolders to represent the associated subcategories.

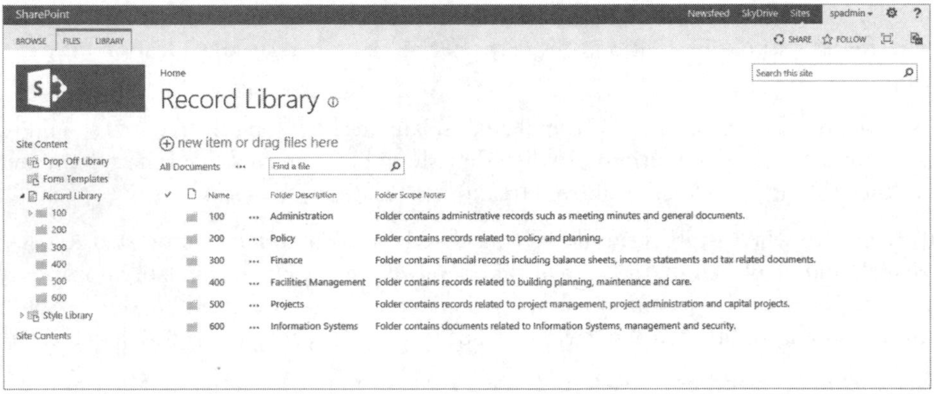

FIGURE 16-2

The Classification Plan

Once you have identified the various document types within your organization, the next step is to identify the attributes or metadata that you must track with each of the various documents within that type. This process is once again quite iterative and requires the involvement of key business stakeholders and decision makers to ensure that the appropriate level of detail is captured.

When identifying attributes for your various document types, it is important to approach the process from two angles:

> ➤ First, you must consider the high-level attributes that must be tracked against every type of document in the organization. This may include properties such as Document ID, Department, or Confidentiality Level.

> ➤ You must then review each of the various document types to identify the attributes that are specific to that type of information. Once you have completed a review of each individual document type, you should compare and analyze the various attributes to identify those that are common or can be combined for maximum efficiency in maintenance.

It is important when identifying the properties that are required for your records-management solution to not over-classify items to the point where tracking the values for properties related to documents becomes tedious for end users. It is important to identify an appropriate balance between the benefit that will be received from tracking certain items with the effort required from content authors to ensure that the properties are up to date and accurate.

You may recall content types and site columns from Chapter 6, "Working with Content Types." Document types have an inherent relationship with content types, and classification plans and attributes have an inherent relationship with site columns. The goal is to define your document types and classification attributes down to a level that translates into the creation of content types and site columns to support these requirements. Figure 16-3 demonstrates an example of the attributes required for individual document types. This can then become an outline for how you must configure your content type within the solution.

Title	Category	Attributes
Sales Proposal	Sales Documents	Title Client Sales Lead Document Status Document Owner Submission Date
Sales Quote	Sales Documents	Title Client Sales Lead Document Status Document Owner Submission Date
Sales Contract	Sales Documents	Title Client Sales Lead Approval Status Document Owner Signature Date

FIGURE 16-3

Figure 16-4 demonstrates how you can define each individual attribute. This can then become an outline for how you can configure your site column within the solution.

Site Column	Type	Group	Required	Configuration Notes
Approval Status	Choice	Sales Documents	Yes	Value List: Pending Submission In Review Approved Display as: Radio Buttons Allow Fill In: No Default Value: None

FIGURE 16-4

IMPLEMENTING A CLASSIFICATION PLAN

SharePoint offers a feature known as the *Managed Metadata Service* and an associated concept known as the *Term Store*. These features are important to the creation of structured classification plans in SharePoint.

Using the Managed Metadata Service and Term Store, you can define attributes once centrally within the entire solution, and then reuse them throughout the organization in multiple site collections. Attributes are defined as *term sets*. You can create a term set either directly within the system through the browser or import it from a file. Several benefits of the term set feature include:

➤ Term sets support the definition of metadata as a hierarchy. This is a major improvement over standard choice columns in SharePoint, which support only one level of information.

➤ You can define unique users or groups as Owners of a specific term set and subsequently empower them to manage the values associated with a single term set.

➤ You can provide synonyms for individual terms. This makes it easier for end users to specify an attribute using their own wording; however, you provide a suggestion for the appropriate wording. Figure 16-5 shows an example of the interface for defining synonyms.

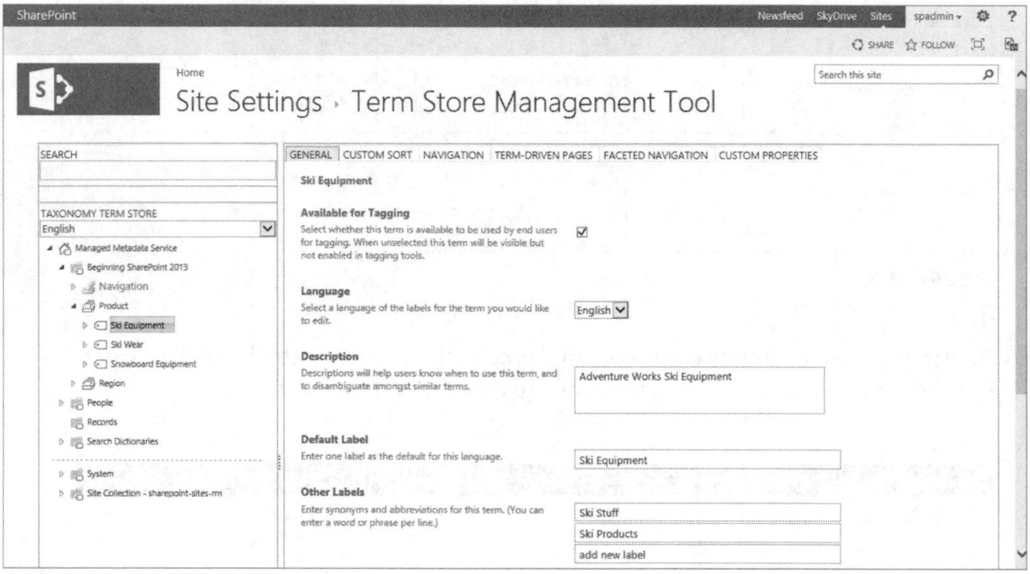

FIGURE 16-5

➤ You can add, reorganize, merge, or deprecate terms over time to address the changing needs of the organization.

➤ You can promote unstructured terms or keywords to structured values over time based on their usage within the system.

➤ You can share term sets across the system and use them within multiple site collections.

➤ You can define terms for multiple languages so that users can view terms in their preferred language.

Working with Managed Metadata

In the next few exercises, you gain some experience working with the Managed Metadata Service and creating custom term sets within the Term Store. You start by creating a simple term set directly through the browser. Then you create a more advanced hierarchy of terms by importing a term set via a custom .csv file. Finally, you create a site column based on the Managed Metadata Service and point it to your custom term set.

> **NOTE** To complete these exercises, it is assumed that you have been given
> the appropriate permissions to access the Term Store and Managed Metadata
> Service. If you cannot access these interfaces, please see your system adminis-
> trator about being given access to manage the Term Store.
>
> To make yourself a Term Store Administrator, visit the Central Administration
> site, select Manage service applications, select your Managed Metadata Service
> Application, click Manage from the ribbon menu, and add yourself as a Term
> Store Administrator.

TRY IT OUT   Creating a Term Set Manually

Your organization has decided that a key attribute related to the classification of content is the region
in which it was created. In this Try It Out, you create a custom term set called "Region" in the Term
Store.

1. From the top-level site of your site collection, select Site Settings from the Settings menu.

2. Select Term Store Management from the Site Administration group of links. You are redirected to
   the Term Store Management Tool, as shown in Figure 16-6.

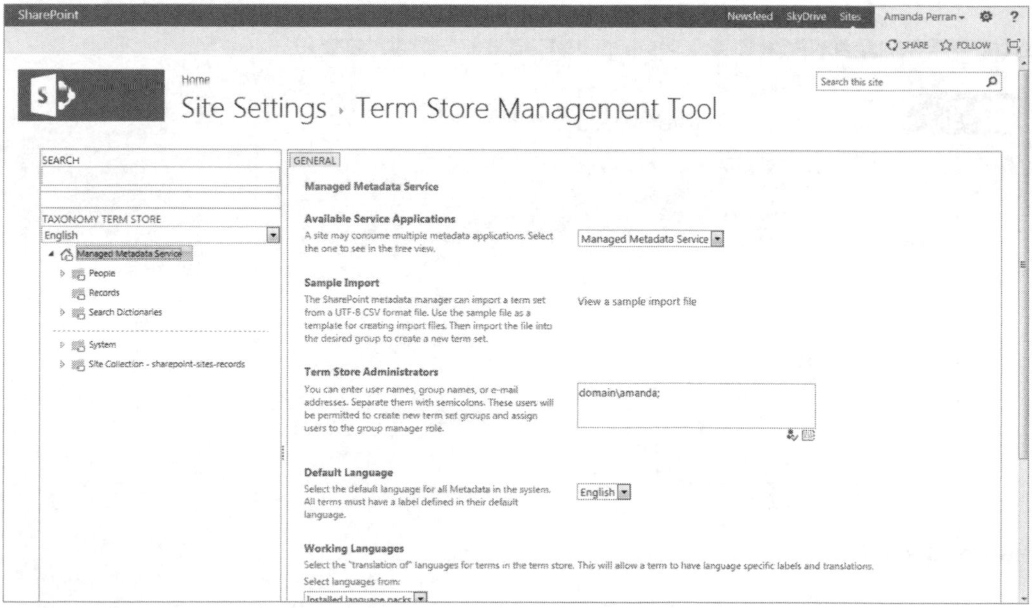

FIGURE 16-6

3. Hover over the Managed Metadata Service item in the left-hand panel and select the arrow that
   appears on the right-hand side to expand the menu, as shown in Figure 16-7.

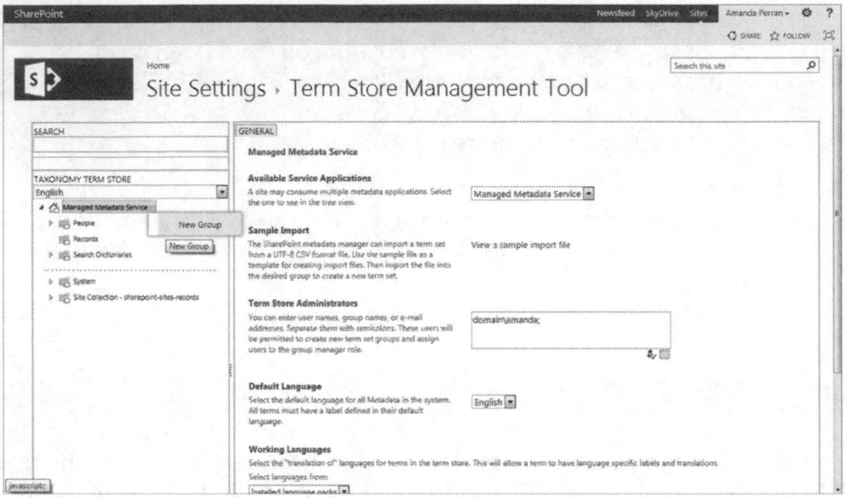

FIGURE 16-7

4. Create a New Group called **Beginning SharePoint 2013**.

5. Expand the menu associated with your new group, and select the New Term Set option.

6. A new branch is added to your hierarchy. Enter **Region** as the name of your term set. The page refreshes to display the available settings for your term set, as shown in Figure 16-8.

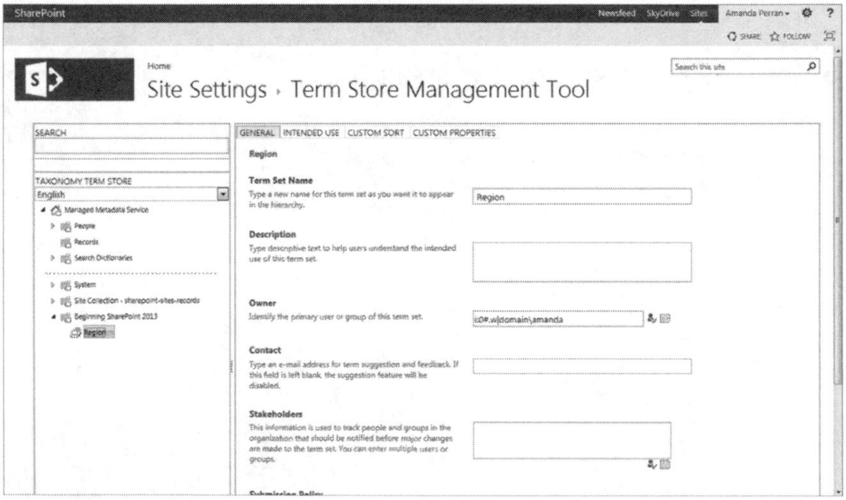

FIGURE 16-8

7. Expand the menu associated with the Region term set, and select the Create Term option.

8. Enter **Eastern** as your term and hit Enter. A placeholder for a new term automatically appears in the listing. If you click away from an empty term, that placeholder will be deleted. Optionally, you can return to the Region term set and select the Create Term option. Create new terms for the following:

> ➤ Central
> ➤ Western
> ➤ Northern
> ➤ Southern

9. Select your Eastern term.

10. Enter **East Region** and **East Coast** as values in the Other labels field. Enter each value on its own line.

11. Click Save. Your term set is now created, and all associated settings have been saved.

How It Works

To start, you created a custom group. Groups can be helpful in organizing your various terms as well as for delegating responsibility over the management of certain terms. Once you created the group, you could have specified details related to the description of the group or identified group managers and contributors. By adding these users, you empower them to make changes related to the terms stored within this group.

You then created your custom term set for Region. When defining a term set, you have the ability to identify stakeholders that should be notified before changes are made to a term set. You can also specify whether a specific term set is open or closed. If a term set is open, users can add new values to the term set through the Managed Metadata interface, as shown in Figure 16-9. If a term set is closed, only the values that are entered by the term manager or contributor can be selected.

FIGURE 16-9

Finally, before completing the configuration of your term set, you updated the Eastern value with two additional synonyms that end users of the system can enter instead of the predefined value.

Creating a Term Set Using an Import File

In addition to region, another key attribute related to the classification of content in your organization is product name. Because products are categorized in groups, you create a term set that utilizes a hierarchy of values. Although you could create this hierarchy manually using the steps outlined in the previous Try It Out, in this exercise you generate the values by importing a file. This is a more effective method for creating large or complex term sets.

1. From the top-level site of your site collection, select Site Settings from the Settings menu.

2. Select Term Store Management from the Site Administration group of links.

3. Hover to the right of your Beginning SharePoint 2013 group so that a small arrow appears. Click the arrow to expand the menu associated with your Beginning SharePoint 2013 group, and select the Import Term Set option, as shown in Figure 16-10.

4. The Term Set Import dialog box appears. Browse to the location of this chapter's resource files and select `Products.csv`.

5. Click OK.

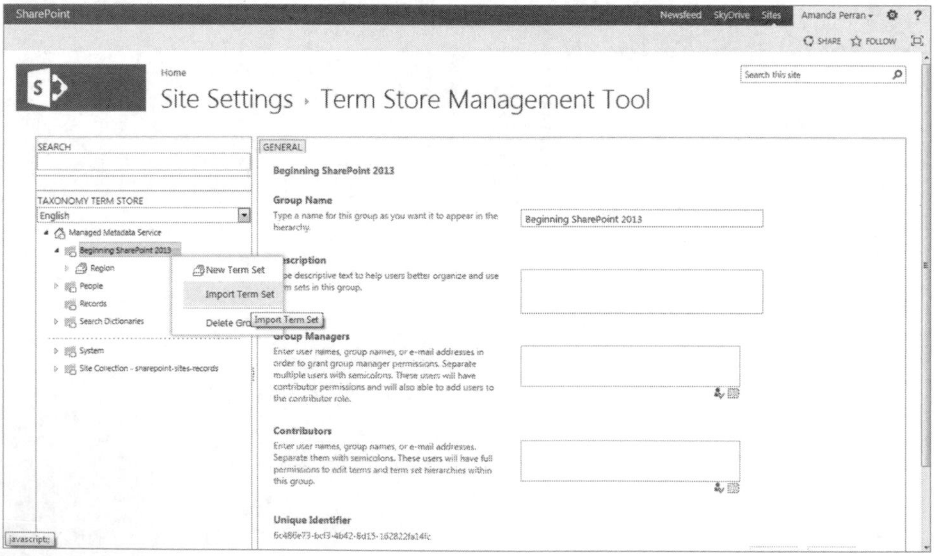

FIGURE 16-10

How It Works

Once the file import is complete, your new term set is created with all associated properties. Depending on the size of your import file, this process may take anywhere from a few seconds to a few minutes.

Term sets can support a large number of values and complex hierarchies; however, it is recommended that you try not to exceed more than 5000 values within a single term set. Values higher than this may have an adverse impact on the performance of the system. In fact, from a user-experience perspective, it is recommended that you avoid such high numbers, because it will be tedious for the end users to navigate such a large list within the Managed Metadata selection interface or Metadata Navigation interface.

TRY IT OUT   **Creating a Site Column Based on Managed Metadata**

In this Try It Out, you create two new site columns based on the custom term sets you defined in the previous two Try It Outs. You then create a custom content type that utilizes these site columns using the same methods described in Chapter 6.

1. From the top-level site of your site collection, select Site Settings from the Settings menu.
2. Select "Site columns" from the Web Designer Galleries section of links.
3. Click Create.
4. Create a new site column using the following properties:

PROPERTY	VALUE
Column Name	Region
The type of information in this column is:	Managed Metadata
Group (New Group)	Chapter 16
Display format	Display term label in the field.
Term Set Values	Use a managed term set (Select the Region Term Set).

5. Click OK. You are returned to the Site Column Gallery.
6. Click Create.
7. Create a new site column using the following properties:

PROPERTY	VALUE
Column Name	Product
The type of information in this column is:	Managed Metadata
Group (New Group)	Chapter 16
Display Value	Display the entire path to the term in the field.
Term Set Values	Use a managed term set (Select the Product Term Set).

8. Click OK. You are returned to the Site Column Gallery.

9. Select Site Settings from the Settings menu.

10. Select Site Content Types from the Web Designer Galleries group of links.

11. Click Create.

12. Create the content type using the following settings:

PROPERTY	VALUE
Content Type Name	Sales Contract
Select parent content type from:	Document Content Types
Parent content type	Document
Group (New Group)	Chapter 16

13. Click OK. You are redirected to the administration page for your new content type.

14. Select the option to add from existing site columns.

15. Select the Chapter 16 group and add both the Region and Product columns. You may get a message that this type of column may not be supported by all client versions. This is because earlier versions of Microsoft Office may not be able to display this type of column in the document information panel.

16. Click OK.

How It Works

Once you create your new content type, you can add it to document libraries throughout your site collection. Users will be able to specify the metadata when uploading new sales contracts using the Managed Metadata selection interface. Figure 16-11 is an example of the Products column as it would appear to end users of the solution when specifying a product to be associated with a sales contract.

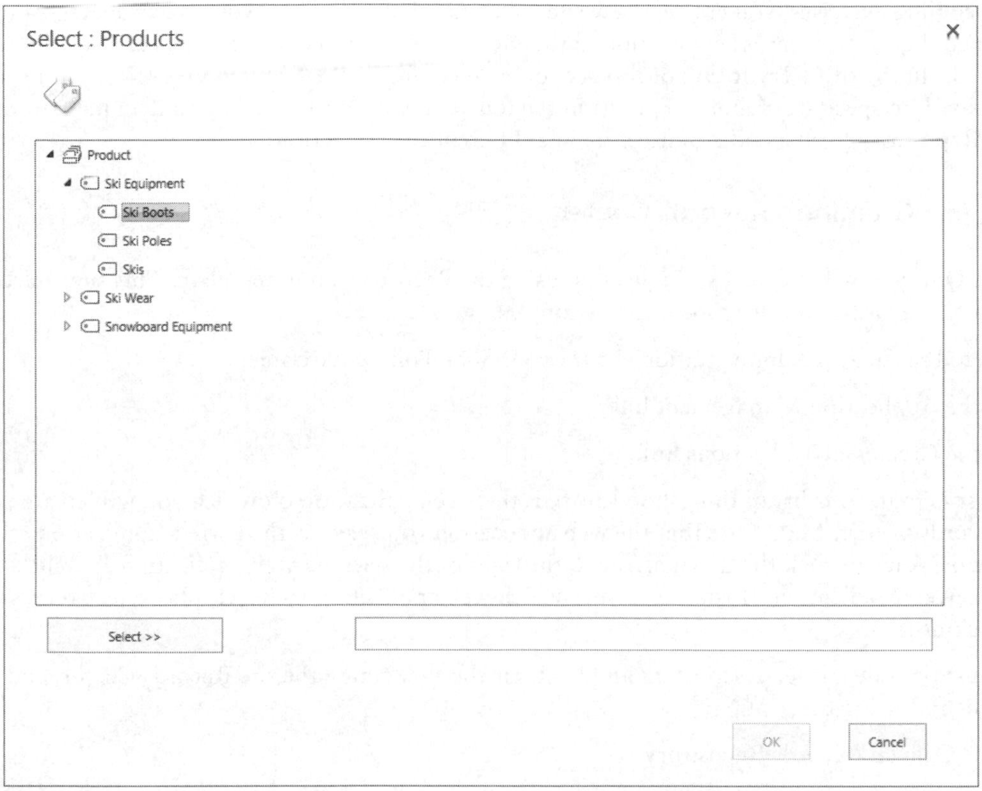

FIGURE 16-11

CONFIGURING THE RECORDS REPOSITORY

An important aspect of any records-management solution is, of course, the repository in which all records will be stored. Due to the flexibility of SharePoint as a records-management platform, a number of options exist related to how the repository is configured and structured.

The Archive Approach

A common approach to records management is to submit a record to a Records Repository once it has been recognized as an official record. This record submission, also referred to as *Records Declaration*, can be either a manual or automated process. When a file is declared as a record, it is either copied or moved to a Records Repository, often referred to as a *Records Center*. Within the Records Center the file can be either queued for manual filing by a records manager or it can be automatically moved to the correct location within the file place based on its metadata or properties. The feature that controls the automatic filing of records based on properties is known as the *Content Organizer*.

In the upcoming exercises, you create a new site collection that will act as your Records Repository. You then configure an external connection to this Records Repository so that users can submit documents to it. In the third Try It Out of this section, you configure the Content Organizer to move content based on specific attributes. Finally, in the fourth Try It Out you submit a document to the Records Repository from a collaborative site in a different site collection.

TRY IT OUT   Creating a Records Center

In this Try It Out, you will create a site collection using the Records Center template. This site collection will be your records repository for future examples.

1. Log in to the Central Administration site for your SharePoint environment.

2. Select the Application Management link.

3. Select the Create Site Collections link.

4. The first item in your list of things to identify is the web application on which you will create the Records Center. Make sure that the web application you select is the correct application. If it is not, you can click the down arrow to the right of the selected web application and click Change Web Application. If you are unsure which web application to select, please see your server administrator.

5. You must provide a title, description, and URL for the site. Name the site **Records Center**, and enter the following description:

> **Official Records Repository**

6. For Web Site Address name, select /sites/ from the drop-down menu and enter **rc** in the blank field to the right of the drop-down.

7. Select the Records Center template from the Enterprise tab.

8. Enter your own name as the primary site collection administrator.

9. Click OK. The process for creating your site takes a few minutes. After it is completed, you are redirected to a page advising you that the process has completed successfully, and a URL is displayed for you to select to visit your site.

How It Works

Depending on your requirements, you may elect to have the Records Center be a site within an existing site collection, a separate site collection, or a completely separate web application. You should base your decision on security, scalability, and integration requirements. In this example, you selected a separate site collection. Once you create your Records Center, it will look similar to Figure 16-12.

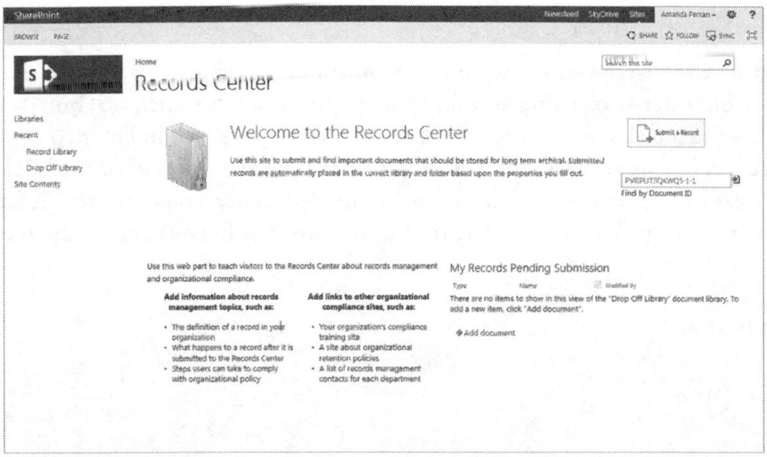

FIGURE 16-12

TRY IT OUT | **Defining a Records Connection**

In this Try It Out, you will create a connection in SharePoint so that users can send documents from any site collection to the Records Center created in the previous Try It Out.

1. Log in to the Central Administration site for your SharePoint environment.

2. Select the General Application Settings link.

3. Select the Configure Send to Connections link. You are redirected to a page where you can define connections that will be available to users from within a document library.

4. Select the correct web application.

5. Select New Connection, as shown in Figure 16-13.

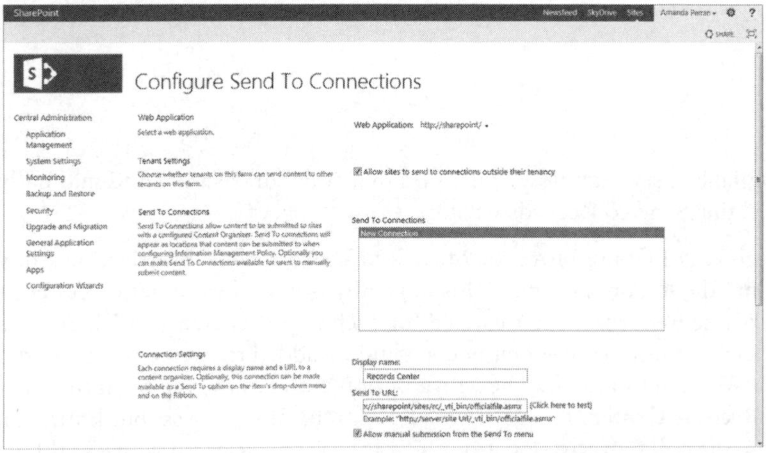

FIGURE 16-13

6. Enter **Records Center** as the Display Name.

7. Enter the URL of the Records Center web service. Based on the naming convention used in the previous Try It Out, you should enter something similar to **http://sitecollectionurl/_vti_bin/officialfile.asmx,** where `sitecollectionurl` represents the URL that users would enter to access your Records Center created in the previous Try It Out. Be sure to keep the portion of the URL that contains `/_vti_bin/officialfile.asmx`, because it is required. After you enter the Send to URL, select the "Click here to test" link to verify that the connection has been specified correctly.

8. For Send to Action, select Move and Leave a Link.

9. Click the Add Connection button.

10. Click OK.

How It Works

In this example you created a Send to Connection. A Send to Connection is a location that appears in document libraries whenever a user selects a file, as shown in Figure 16-14.

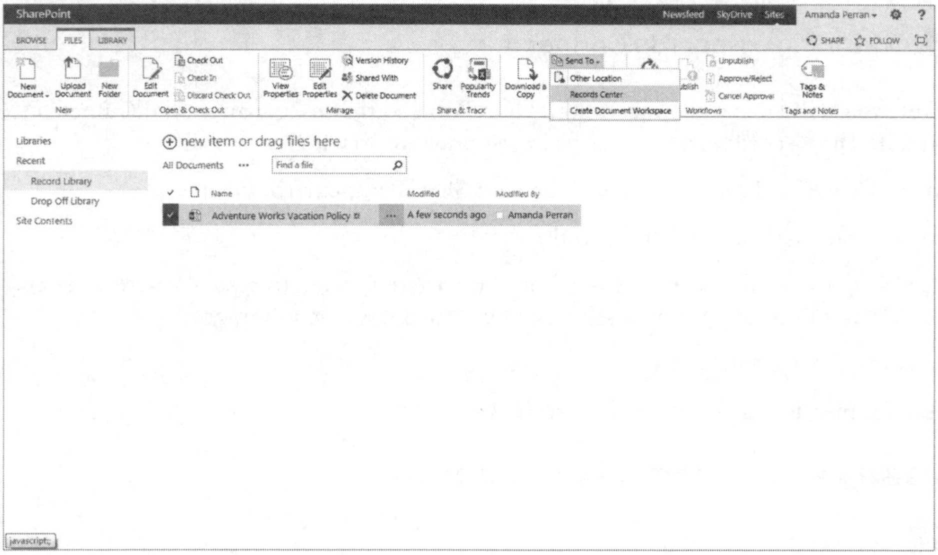

FIGURE 16-14

By making this connection available, users can now select files in a collaborative site and manually declare them as records by selecting Send to Records Center.

For Send to Action you had a choice of Copy, Move, or Move and Leave a Link. By selecting Copy, a duplicate of the file is copied into the Records Center. This normally is not a best practice but could be beneficial for cases where a separate Records Center existed for each legal case with which an organization was involved. Then copies of important documents could be added to each case site without impacting the existing collaborative environment. The Move option removes the file from the collaborative site and places it into the Records Center. This is effective for archival purposes, but limits standard user access to the file from the collaborative location. In this case you selected Move and Leave a

Link, which moves the file into the Records Center and supplies a link to the Records Center location. When users click the link, they are redirected to a page that describes that the file has been moved with a link to its new location.

Configuring a Records Center Site

In this Try It Out, you will perform some basic steps related to configuring libraries within the Records Center site collection.

1. From the Records Center site you created in the first Try It Out of this section, select Manage Records Center from the Settings menu. You are redirected to a specialized page designed to assist in the configuration of a Records Center site, as shown in Figure 16-15.

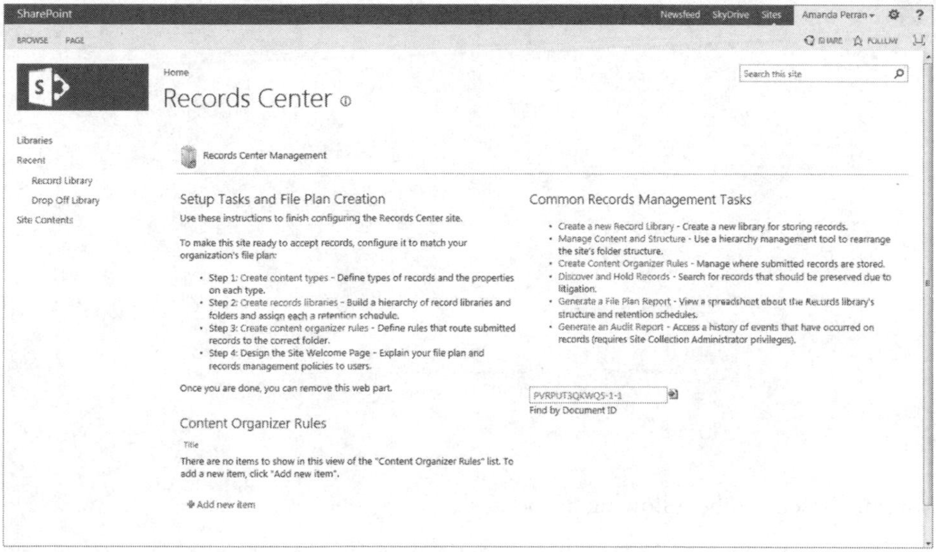

FIGURE 16-15

2. Select the Create Record Libraries link. You are redirected to a page listing the various templates for lists and libraries.

3. Select the Records library template.

4. Enter 01 as the Name.

5. Click Create.

6. Click Library Settings from the Library tab of the ribbon.

7. Select the List name, description and navigation link.

8. Change the name of the library to **01 Human Resources** and click Save. You can then return to the library by clicking 01 Human Resources in the breadcrumb.

9. Create new folders with the following names in the library by clicking New Folder from the Files tab:

➤ 01 Policies

➤ 02 Forms

➤ 03 Templates

➤ 04 Personnel

10. Select the Manage Records Center link from the Settings menu.

11. Select the "Add new item" link associated with the Content Organizer Rules section of the page. You are redirected to the Content Organizer Rules list. A form appears, as shown in Figure 16-16.

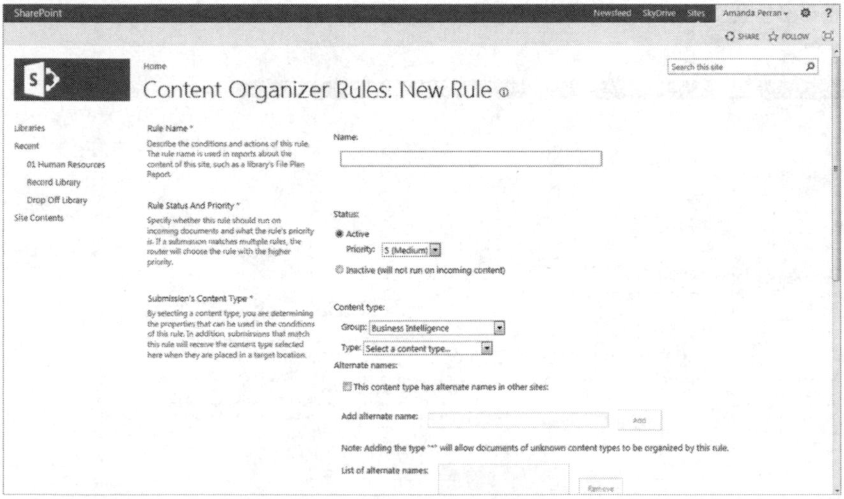

FIGURE 16-16

12. Define your rule based on the following properties:

PROPERTY	VALUE
Name	0101 Policy
Status	Active
Content Type (Group)	Document Content Types
Content Type (Type)	Document
Property Based Conditions	Title Contains all of Policy
Target Location	/sites/rc/01/01 Policies (Browse to the location of the 01 Policies folder within the 01 Human Resource library.)

13. Click OK.

How It Works

In this example, you started to create the file plan for your Records Center by creating a library for human resources files. When a list or library is first created, the URL is the value that is entered for Name. However, if the list or library is renamed later, it will still retain the original value that was entered as the name for its URL. Because 01 was chosen as the unique identifier for the Human Resources category of documents, you named the library 01 upon initial creation and then later renamed it 01 Human Resources. This ensures that the path to the Human Resources library is a simple URL.

Once you created the Human Resources library, you added subfolders to the library to reflect the structure of the file plan. You then created a Content Organizer rule that will intersect any files that are added to the Records Center and review the properties to determine where the destination location in the Records Center should be. In this example, you selected that any document with "policy" in the title should be routed to the HR library's Policy folder. This rule, though easy to create for demonstration purposes, may not be a practical solution for real life and, therefore, it is recommended that you base your rules on more discrete properties, such as content type and other uniquely identifying metadata.

TRY IT OUT   Submitting a Document to a Records Center

In this Try It Out, you submit a document from a collaborative location to the Records Center you defined in the previous example.

1. From any collaborative site in your SharePoint environment, upload the `AdventureWorks Vacation Policy.docx` file that is included in this chapter's resources.

2. Select the file in the library. Ensure that the file is checked in.

3. Select the Send to Records Center item from the Files tab of the ribbon, as shown in Figure 16-17. Depending on the size of your screen and available space, you might see only the icon displayed.

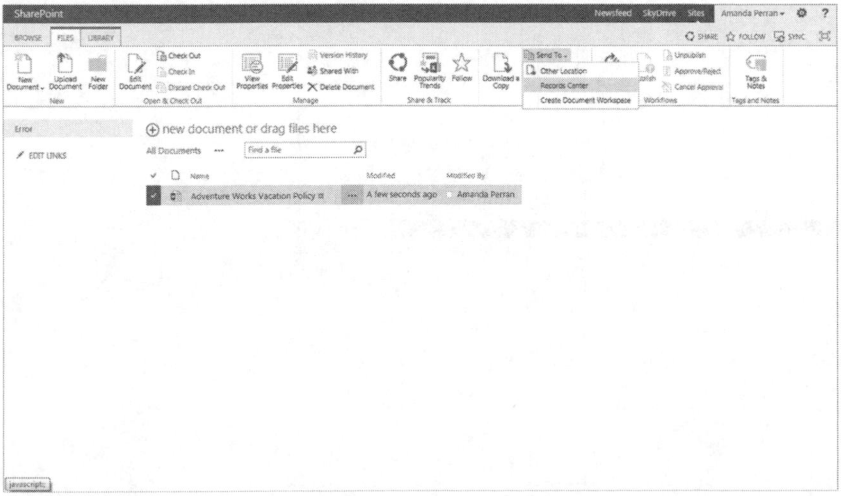

FIGURE 16-17

4. You receive a warning dialog box advising you that you are about to move the file and create a link. Click OK.

How It Works

The file will now be moved to the Records Center. This operation may take a few moments, but when it is complete a confirmation message appears, as shown in Figure 16-18.

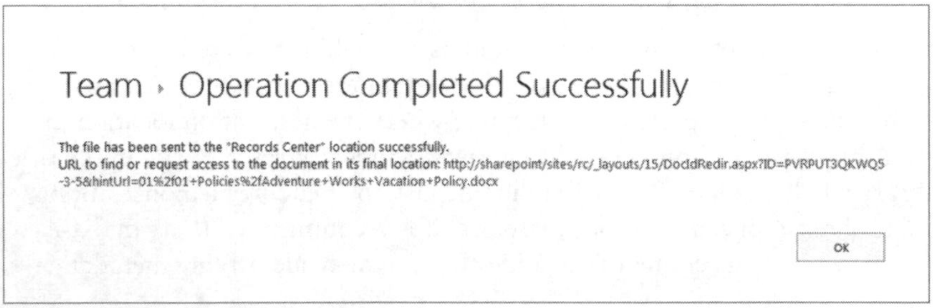

Team › Operation Completed Successfully
The file has been sent to the "Records Center" location successfully.
URL to find or request access to the document in its final location: http://sharepoint/sites/rc/_layouts/15/DocIdRedir.aspx?ID=PVRPUT3QKWQ5-3-5&hintUrl=01%2f01+Policies%2fAdventure+Works+Vacation+Policy.docx
OK

FIGURE 16-18

If you visit the Records Center, you will notice that the file has been automatically placed into the Policies folder of the Human Resources library as defined in the Content Organizer rule you created in the previous example. Similarly, if you return to the library from which you sent the file originally, you will notice that clicking the link to the file redirects you to a page describing that the file has been moved (see Figure 16-19). An icon appears on the link in the library similar to that shown in Figure 16-20.

SharePoint
Newsfeed
SkyDrive
Sites
Amanda Perran
SHARE
FOLLOW
Team
Error
EDIT LINKS
Search this site
Documents : Adventure Works Vacation Policy
This document was moved to a new location
New Location
http://sharepoint/sites/rc/_layouts/15/DocIdRedir.aspx?ID=PVRPUT3QKWQ5-3-5&hintUrl=01%2f01+Policies%2fAdventure+Works+Vacation+Policy.docx
Reason for move
Move Date
11/13/2012 11:53:59 PM
Moved By
Manual submission by i:0#.w|domain\amanda

FIGURE 16-19

SharePoint
Newsfeed
SkyDrive
Sites
Amanda Perran
BROWSE
FILES
LIBRARY
SHARE
FOLLOW
SYNC
Team
Error
EDIT LINKS
Search this site
Documents
Error
EDIT LINKS
new document or drag files here
All Documents
Find a file
Name
Modified
Modified By
Adventure Works Vacation Policy
4 minutes ago
Amanda Perran

FIGURE 16-20

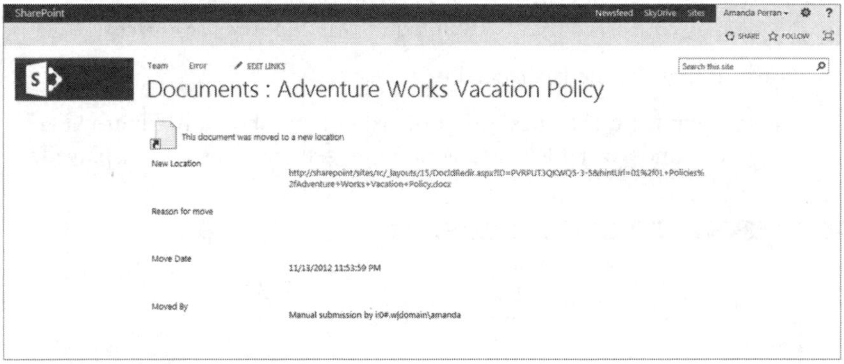

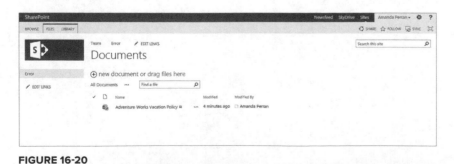

The In-Place Approach

Previously in SharePoint and in many other applications, records-management activities were managed separately from collaborative activities. As a result, there was often a great risk of certain documents "falling between the cracks" and not being properly submitted to the Records Repository. SharePoint 2013 includes a feature called *In-Place Records Management* that allows teams to declare records while collaborating in their standard environment. The records are not moved from the system, but instead are stored within the same library with a visual indicator, as shown in Figure 16-21.

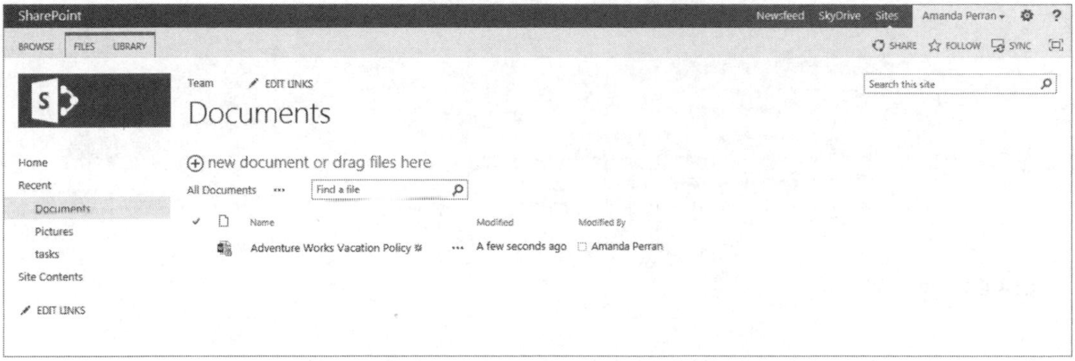

FIGURE 16-21

When an item is declared as an in-place record, restrictions can still be put in place to disable the editing capabilities of users, as well as the ability to delete items. However, the file stays in the library in which it was originally created, which can be helpful for teams that may have a requirement to access the file after it has been declared a record. An example of this is a collaborative project site. The project scope document is created at the start of the project and approved by a client. Once the scope document has been approved, it is automatically (or manually) declared a record. The file is then locked for editing and deletion; however, it will continue to exist in the document library, along with all other project documents, throughout the duration of the project. This allows team members to continuously reference the original scope document for informational purposes.

By default, the In-Place Records Management feature is not enabled on a collaborative site. Therefore, you must enable it. You explore how to do this in the next Try It Out.

TRY IT OUT   **Activating the In-Place Records Management Feature**

In this Try It Out, you will activate the In-Place Records Management feature, which enables users to declare items as in-place records from within a document library on the site.

1. From the top-level site of your site collection, select Site Settings from the Settings menu.

2. Select Site Collection Features from the Site Collection Administration group of links. You are redirected to the Site Collection Features page, shown in Figure 16-22.

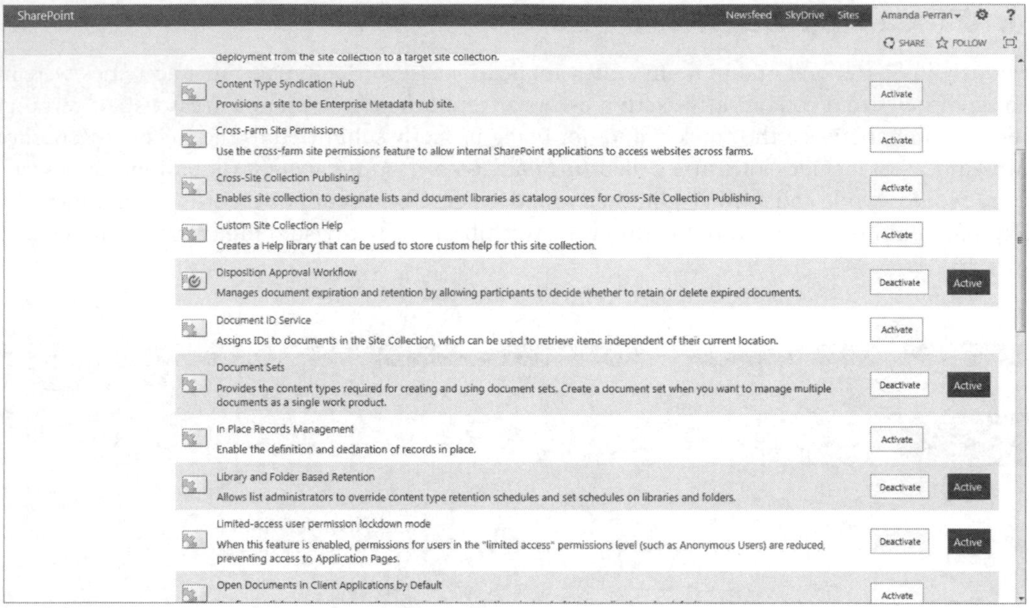

FIGURE 16-22

3. Click the Activate button next to the In-Place Records Management item.

How It Works

In this Try It Out, you activated In-Place Records Management. By activating this feature, the functionality to declare records within libraries will be enabled. However, you will still have to set the Records Declaration settings for the site to determine whether users are allowed to manually declare items as records in all locations. You do this in the following Try It Out.

TRY IT OUT   Modifying Records Declaration Settings on Site Collection

In this Try It Out, you will configure the Records Declaration setting for a site collection to determine which actions can be performed on files once they have been declared a record and whether the ability to declare records will be available in all locations.

1. From the top-level site of your site collection, select Site Settings from the Settings menu. For this example, you are using the intranet site collection you created in Chapter 1, "Understanding SharePoint."

2. Select the Records Declaration Settings link. You are redirected to the Records Declaration Settings page, shown in Figure 16-23.

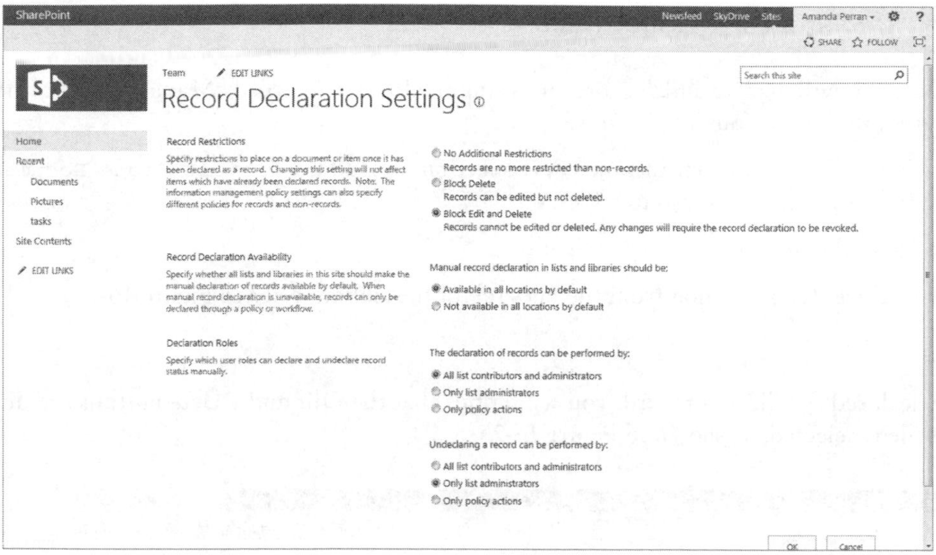

FIGURE 16-23

3. For Records Restrictions, select the Block Edit and Delete option. This may be the default setting in your environment.

4. For Records Declaration Availability, select the "Available in all locations by default" option.

5. Click OK.

How It Works

Now that you have enabled the In-Place Records Management feature on your site collection and configured the Records Declaration settings, each library in the site collection will support the declaration of records from the ribbon, as shown in Figure 16-24.

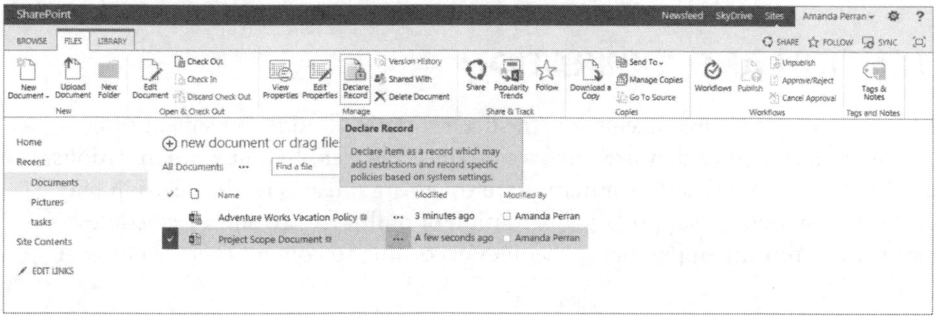

FIGURE 16-24

In step 3, you selected the option to Block Edit and Delete once a file has been declared a record. As a result, these options are grayed out from the ribbon whenever a file is declared as a record. You could also identify the roles in your organization that have the ability to declare a record as undeclared within your site collection. In this exercise you went with the default setting.

TRY IT OUT   Declaring an In-Place Record

In this Try It Out, you will declare a file as a record using the In-Place Records Management features that you configured in the previous Try It Outs.

1. From a collaborative site in your intranet site collection, upload the `Project Scope Document .docx` file from this chapter's resource files.

2. Select the file in the library.

3. Select the Declare Record option from the Files tab of the ribbon (refer to Figure 16-24).

How It Works

Once you have declared the file as a record, you will notice that the Edit and Delete buttons are disabled when the file is selected, as shown in Figure 16-25.

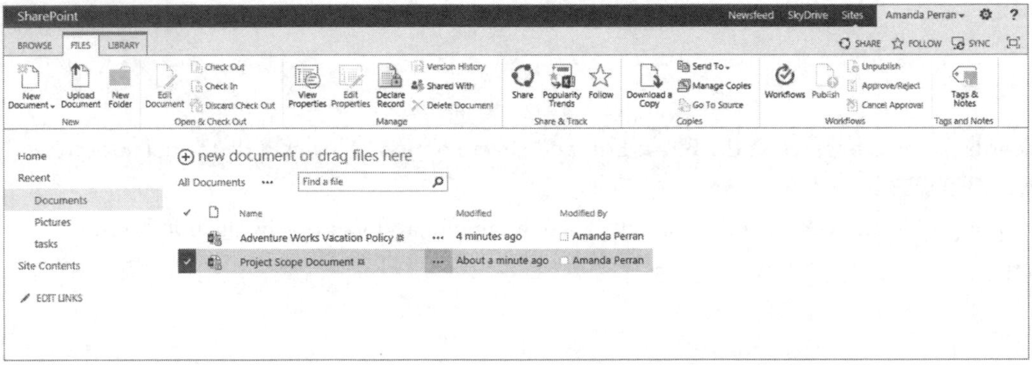

FIGURE 16-25

RECORDS RETENTION AND EXPIRATION

Another important aspect of records management is the determination and management of how long records should be retained before they are removed from the system. In many organizations, there may be regulatory reasons for this determination. In other organizations, the decision may be more operations based. SharePoint supports the definition of multistage retention schedules for records and nonrecords. You can apply these schedules according to content type or physical location.

When defining a retention schedule, you must identify an event that must occur to initiate the actions that will follow. You can define an event using date-based properties of the document, such as two years after it has been last modified or seven years after it has been created. You can also define the event according to a programmatic formula that is installed on the server.

Once you have set a schedule for an event, you can identify an action that takes place after that event has occurred. These actions may include one of the following options:

➤ **Move to recycle bin:** This delete activity provides a "soft delete," which can be undone by a user with appropriate privileges.

➤ **Permanently delete:** This delete activity represents an action that cannot be undone. The intent is to remove the document from the system without any opportunity for review or reconsideration. In many cases, this action is selected for regulatory reasons.

➤ **Transfer to another location:** In some cases, once an event has occurred, the file should be added to a new location. This may result in the file being copied, moved, or moved with a link. A logical scenario for this action would be to remove the file from the collaborative location where it was created and add it to a Records Repository.

➤ **Start a workflow:** In some cases, further review or consideration is required before the appropriate action for a file can be determined. Therefore, you may elect to have a review workflow launched to determine if the file should be deleted from the system or moved to an alternate location.

➤ **Skip to next stage:** For a particular stage, there may be no specific activity other than to move to the next stage of the life cycle for the document.

➤ **Delete previous drafts:** This activity removes all minor versions of a document. This may be relevant for cases where it is not necessary to keep all draft versions after a certain period, and because it is unlikely for the document to be updated further, it is logical to conserve on disk space and purge all pervious draft versions. All major versions of the document are still retained.

➤ **Delete all previous versions:** This activity removes all versions, including major and minor versions.

In the next two Try It Outs, you create retention schedules for a content type as well as a physical location. In the final Try It Out for this section, you review the compliance details of a document for which a retention schedule has been defined.

TRY IT OUT Creating a Retention Schedule for a Content Type

In this Try It Out, you create a retention schedule for the Sales Contract content type you created earlier in this chapter.

1. From the top-level site of your site collection, select Site Settings from the Settings menu.

2. Select Site Content Types from the Web Designer Galleries section.

3. Select the Sales Contract content type.

4. From the Content Type Administration page, select Information Management Policy Settings. You are redirected to the Edit Policy page, as shown in Figure 16-26.

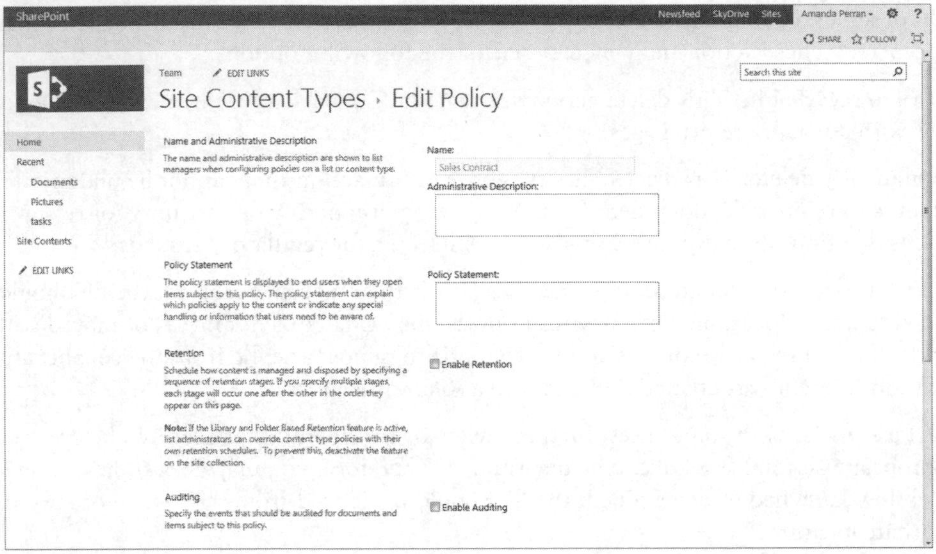

FIGURE 16-26

5. Select the Enable Retention checkbox. The retention options for this content type are displayed.

6. Under the Non Records section, select the Add a Retention Stage link. A Stage properties window appears, as shown in Figure 16-27.

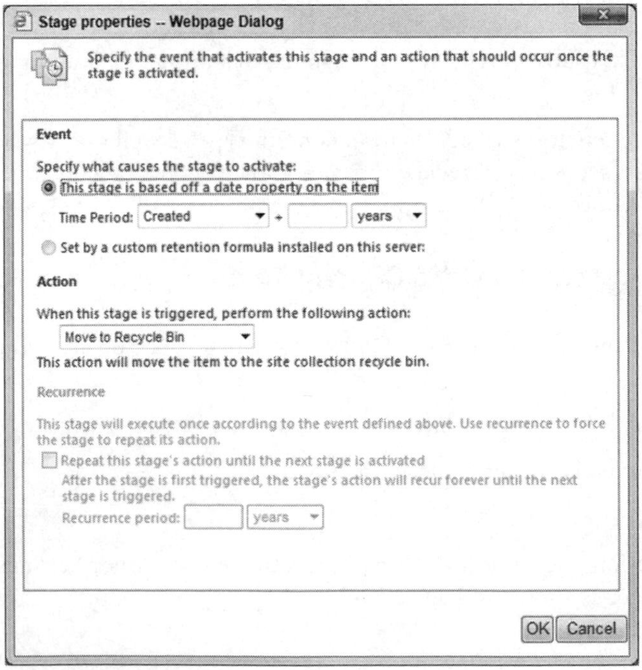

FIGURE 16-27

7. Select the option to create the event based on a date property.

8. Select Modified as the date from the drop-down and enter **5 years** in the textbox.

9. Select the Move to the Recycle Bin action and click OK.

10. From the Records section of the Retention Policy page, select the "Define different retention stages for records" option and click the "Add a retention stage for records" link.

11. Select Declared Record as the date from the drop-down and enter **3 years** in the textbox.

12. Select the Transfer to Another Location action.

13. For Type of Transfer, select "Move and leave a link," as shown in Figure 16-28.

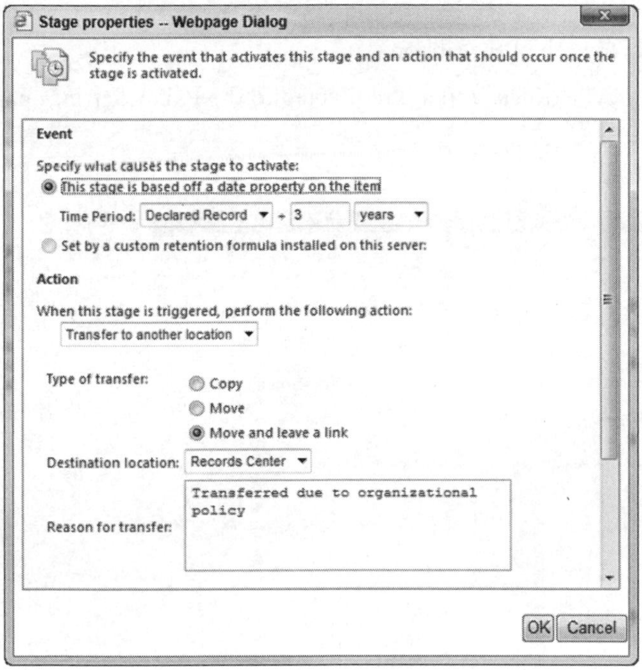

FIGURE 16-28

14. For Destination Location, select Records Center.

15. Click OK.

16. Click OK on the Edit Policy page.

How It Works

When you enabled retention for the content type, you had the option to define unique rules for nonrecords and records. If you had enabled this feature, your document would have had a unique retention schedule up until the point at which it was declared a record. This is a way of ensuring that proper expiration and handling rules are applied to nonrecords as well as records within your system.

In this example, you selected the option that nonrecords should be deleted five years after they have been modified. If a document is declared a record, it should be moved from the collaborative location where it is stored to the Records Center after three years. Once it is in the Records Center, it is managed by the retention schedule defined for that location.

TRY IT OUT   Creating a Retention Schedule for a Library

In this Try It Out, you will define a retention schedule for a library that is not related to a content type.

1. From the main page of the Records Center site collection that you created in a previous exercise, select the 01 Human Resources library.

2. Select Library Settings from the Library tab of the ribbon.

3. Select Information Management Policy Settings. You are redirected to the Policy Settings page for the library, as shown in Figure 16-29.

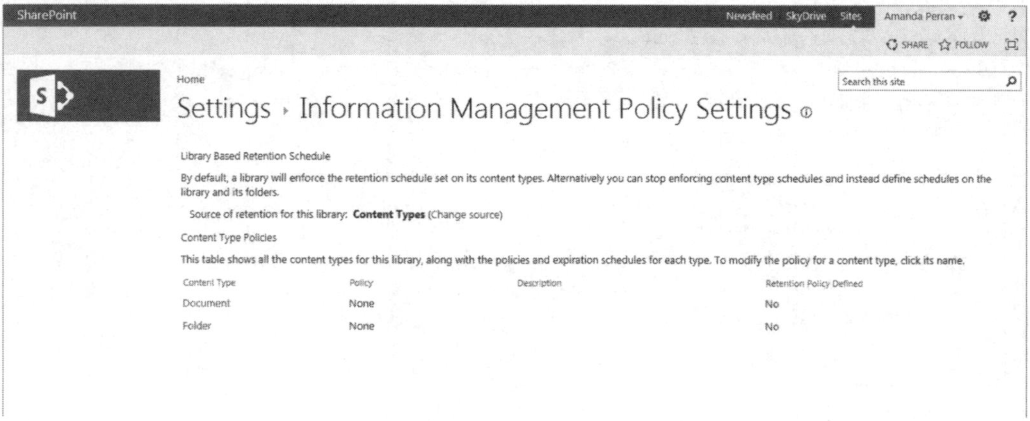

FIGURE 16-29

4. You should notice that at the top of the page, the retention source for the library is listed as Content Types. Select the "Change source" link.

5. Select Libraries and Folders as the source of retention.

6. You receive a warning message. Click OK to accept it.

7. Click the "Add a retention stage for records" link.

8. Define the rule that states seven years after the file has been declared a record, it should be permanently deleted. The settings for this rule are displayed in Figure 16-30.

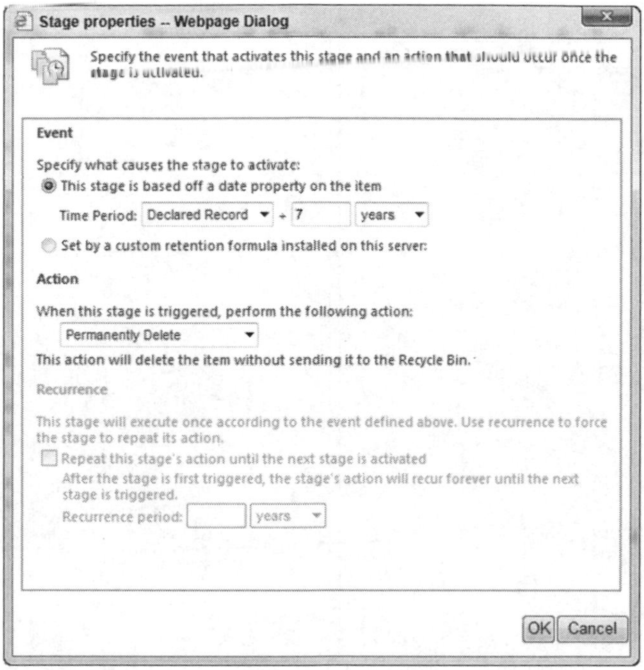

FIGURE 16-30

9. Click OK to save the rule.

10. Click Apply, then OK to save the settings for the library.

How It Works

In this example, you created a retention schedule for a library that was independent of content type. This is a relevant scenario in cases where a formalized file plan exists and content is organized and grouped according to properties such as retention and expiration requirements. In this case, you defined the rule that seven years after a file has been declared a record, it should be permanently deleted. This rule applies to all folders and documents in the library by default. However, in the next example you review how you can define a unique retention schedule for an individual folder that will override that of the library.

TRY IT OUT   Creating a Retention Schedule for a Folder

In the previous Try It Out, you configured a retention schedule for a library. In this Try It Out, you will configure a retention schedule for a folder within the library.

1. From the 01 Human Resources library of your site, hover over the Policies folder to expose the context menu, and then select Compliance Details. The Compliance Details report appears for the folder, as shown in Figure 16-31.

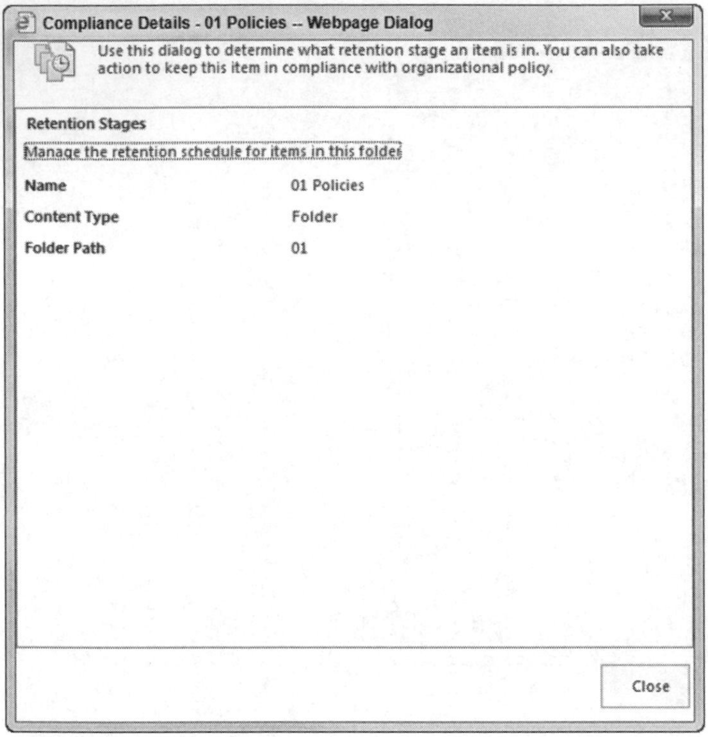

Compliance Details - 01 Policies -- Webpage Dialog

Use this dialog to determine what retention stage an item is in. You can also take action to keep this item in compliance with organizational policy.

Retention Stages

Manage the retention schedule for items in this folder

Name	01 Policies
Content Type	Folder
Folder Path	01

Close

FIGURE 16-31

2. Select the "Manage the retention schedule for items in this folder" link. You are redirected to the Folder Based Retention Schedule page.

3. Select the "Define retention stages" link.

4. Select the "Add a retention stage for records" link.

5. Define the rule that states five years after the file has been declared a record, it should be permanently deleted.

6. Click OK to save the rule.

7. Click Apply, then OK to save the settings on the folder.

How It Works

In this example you created a retention schedule for the Policies folder that was unique from that of the Human Resources library. In this case, files in the Policies folder will be deleted five years after they are declared a record, versus the seven-year rule that exists for the library.

TRY IT OUT Viewing Compliance Details for a Document

In this Try It Out, you will look at a file known as *Compliance Details*, which includes retention schedules, content type information, and details related to any exemptions or holds to which the file may be subject.

1. From the 01 Human Resources library of your site, select the Policies folder.

2. Expand the menu associated with the AdventureWorks Vacation Policy document and select Compliance Details. The Compliance Details report for the document appears, as shown in Figure 16-32.

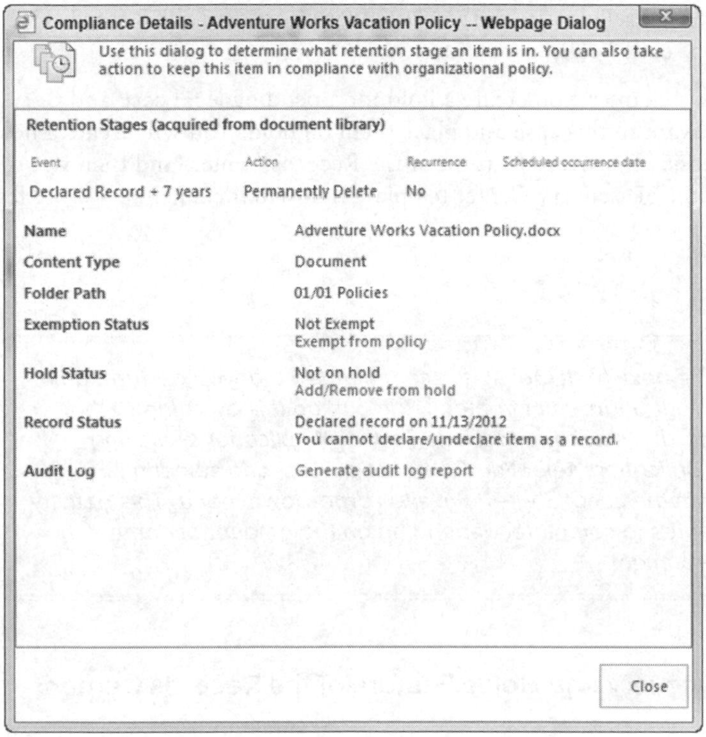

FIGURE 16-32

How It Works

In this example, you can see that the AdventureWorks document is scheduled to expire seven years after it is declared a record. You can also view the date on which the file was declared a record. In Figure 16-32, the file was declared a record on November 13, 2012. You can also perform activities such as generating an audit log report to view details of how the file has been accessed.

EDISCOVERY AND HOLDS

In certain cases, an organization may be involved in legal proceedings or regulatory reviews that require the collection of evidence or documentation related to a specific topic or subject. In these situations, it is critical that important documents be accessible to stakeholders involved in the proceedings or investigation. As a result, it may be appropriate to place holds on the records, which temporarily exempt the files from any retention or expiration policies that have been defined for them. If a record's expiration date passes while it is on hold, it will not expire. However, once the file is removed from the hold, all normal policies will resume, and the file will be queued for expiration according the defined policy.

A key aspect of adding a document to a hold is searching for and locating the file. You do this through two different methods in SharePoint 2013: the *eDiscovery* feature of the Records Center and a dedicated site template type called *eDiscovery Center*.

In the final few Try It Outs of this chapter, you create a hold for a pending legal case and then search for files that might be relevant to this case and place them on hold. You will create a hold and search for items using the basic eDiscovery features of the Records Center, and then you will create a site collection based on the eDiscovery Center template that will include many more features related to querying and holding files.

> **NOTE** *To complete the next Try It Out, it is recommended that you perform an incremental crawl of your SharePoint content. You can do this by going to the Central Administration site, selecting Manage Service Applications, clicking the Search Service Application, selecting Content Sources, and selecting Start Incremental Crawl from the Local SharePoint sites drop-down menu. This activity may take several minutes to complete, depending on the amount of content in your SharePoint environment.*

TRY IT OUT   Using the eDiscovery and Holds Feature of the Records Center

In this Try It Out, you will configure the eDiscovery and Holds feature of the Records Center.

1. From the main page of the Records Center, select Manage Records Center from the Settings menu.

2. From the Common Records Management Tasks Web Part, select the Discover and Hold Records link. You are redirected to the Search and Add to Hold page, as shown in Figure 16-33.

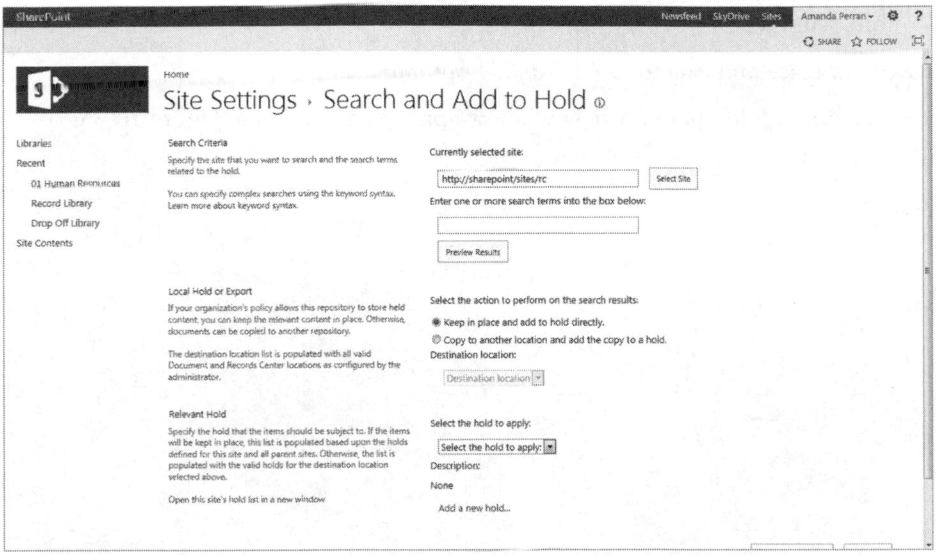

FIGURE 16-33

3. Select any site collection on which you want to perform your search. For this exercise, retain the default setting to search the Records Center for items.

4. Enter the word **Policy** into the search box.

5. Click the Preview Results button. A new window appears, as shown in Figure 16-34, showing items in your site collection that contain the word "policy."

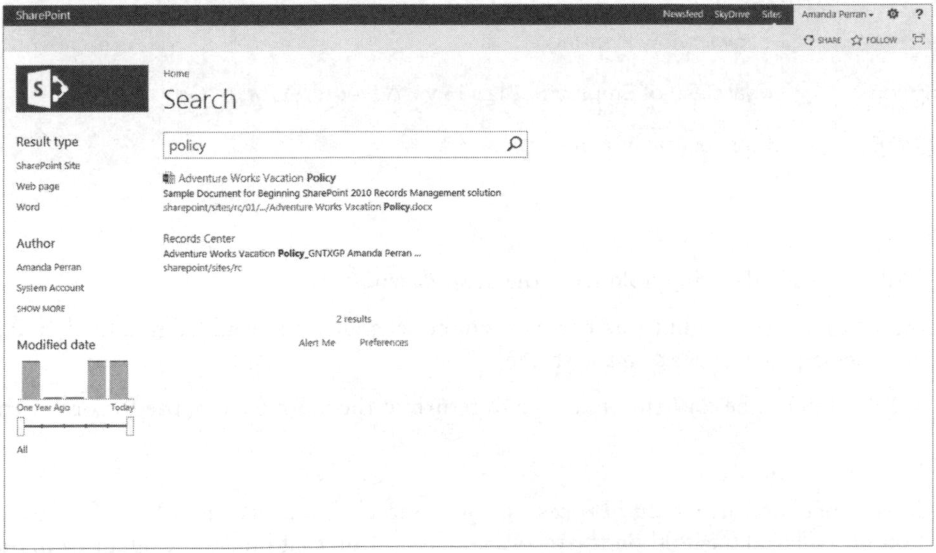

FIGURE 16-34

6. Close the results window.

7. Select the Keep in Place and Add to Hold Directly option.

8. Select the Add a New Hold option. A new window appears, as shown in Figure 16-35.

Holds - New Item   ✕

```
EDIT

  💾      ✖       📋      ✂ Cut     📄        ABC
 Save   Cancel   Paste   📋 Copy   Attach    ✓
                                    File     Spelling
                                             ▾
 Commit          Clipboard        Actions   Spelling
```

Title *   [   ]

Description   [   ]
                   [   ]
                   [   ]

Managed By   [Enter a name or email address...]

                              [Save]   [Cancel]

FIGURE 16-35

9. Enter the details of the hold, as follows:

PROPERTY	VALUE
Title	Policy Review Hearing
Description	Legal Case of Employee #12345 vs. AdventureWorks
Managed By	Enter your own name

10. Click Save.

11. Select the Policy Review Hearing hold from the drop-down.

12. Click the Add Results to Hold button. The files will be scheduled to be added to a hold, and a confirmation message will appear on the screen.

13. Click the OK button on the confirmation page to return to the main page of the Records Center.

How It Works

There is a scheduled job, called *Search and Process*, on your server that processes all pending hold requests. Once you have placed the hold on the records, items within that hold are exempt from their standard retention schedules. Figure 16-36 is an example of the Compliance Details report for the AdventureWorks Vacation Policy document, which has now been placed on hold.

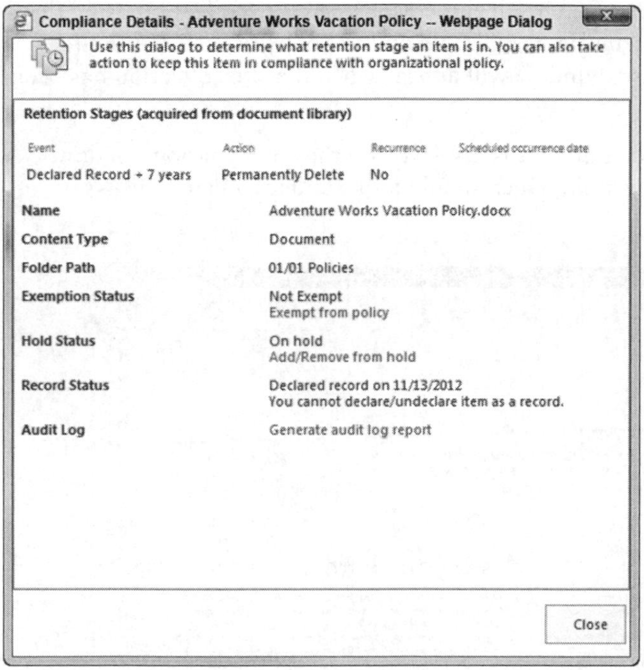

Compliance Details - Adventure Works Vacation Policy -- Webpage Dialog

Use this dialog to determine what retention stage an item is in. You can also take action to keep this item in compliance with organizational policy.

Retention Stages (acquired from document library)

Event	Action	Recurrence	Scheduled occurrence date
Declared Record + 7 years	Permanently Delete	No	

Name	Adventure Works Vacation Policy.docx
Content Type	Document
Folder Path	01/01 Policies
Exemption Status	Not Exempt Exempt from policy
Hold Status	On hold Add/Remove from hold
Record Status	Declared record on 11/13/2012 You cannot declare/undeclare item as a record.
Audit Log	Generate audit log report

Close

FIGURE 16-36

In addition, you can go to the Site Settings of your Records Center at any point and click the link to view Hold Reports. This report is generated based on a scheduled task on the server called *Hold Processing and Reporting.* This job is scheduled to run daily, by default, and will generate a report for each hold that lists the files that have been placed on hold.

TRY IT OUT **Creating an eDiscovery Center**

In this Try It Out, you will create a more advanced eDiscovery environment than was used in the previous exercise. Using this environment, you can perform searches against either SharePoint or Exchange content.

To search against Exchange content, you must have an appropriately configured environment that includes Exchange Server 2013 and a trusted connection between SharePoint and Exchange. For more information on configuring Exchange and SharePoint for eDiscovery, see the article at `http://technet.microsoft.com/en-us/library/fp161514(v=office.15)`.

After creating an eDiscovery Center, you can create cases within the site collection. This is how you might store information you discover related to each individual legal case that you are involved in.

Within each case, you can create eDiscovery sets, predefined sets of properties that can include details about the source you want to search, the query or filter you want to assign, and the content that you want to place a hold on.

1. From the Central Administration site of your environment, create a new site collection using the eDiscovery Center as the template. This template is available on the Enterprise tab of the site template selection interface. A confirmation window will appear when the site collection has been created.

2. Once the site collection is created, click the link that is displayed on the confirmation window. You will be redirected to the new site collection, which should look similar to Figure 16-37.

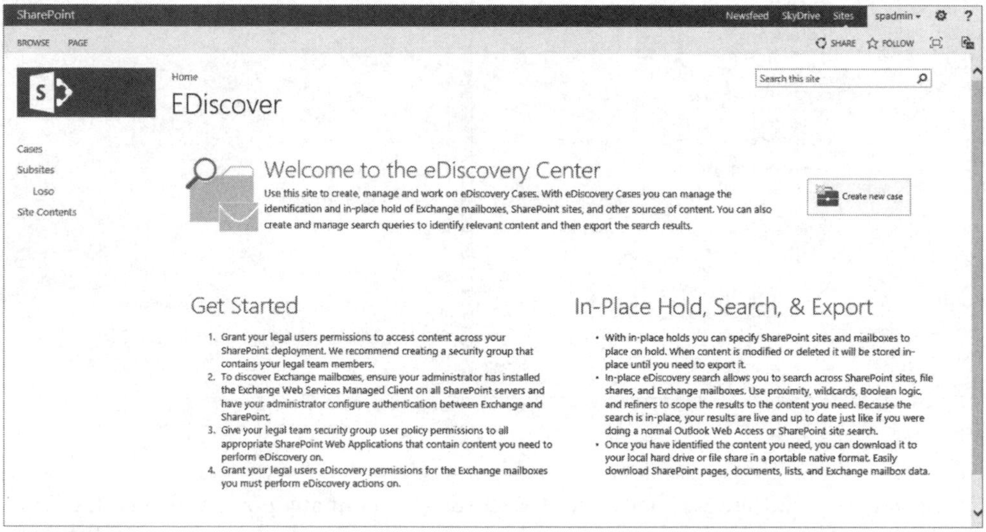

FIGURE 16-37

3. Click the "Create new case" link. This will launch the site creation page.

4. Enter the following details for your case:

PROPERTY	VALUE
Title	Low Sodium Foods
Description	Legal case related to the proposed lack of low sodium foods in the corporate cafeteria
Web Site Address	loso
Display this site on the Quick Launch of the parent site?	Yes
Use the top link bar from the parent site?	Yes

5. Click the Create button to create your site. Once the site for your case is created, you will be redirected to a page similar to Figure 16-38.

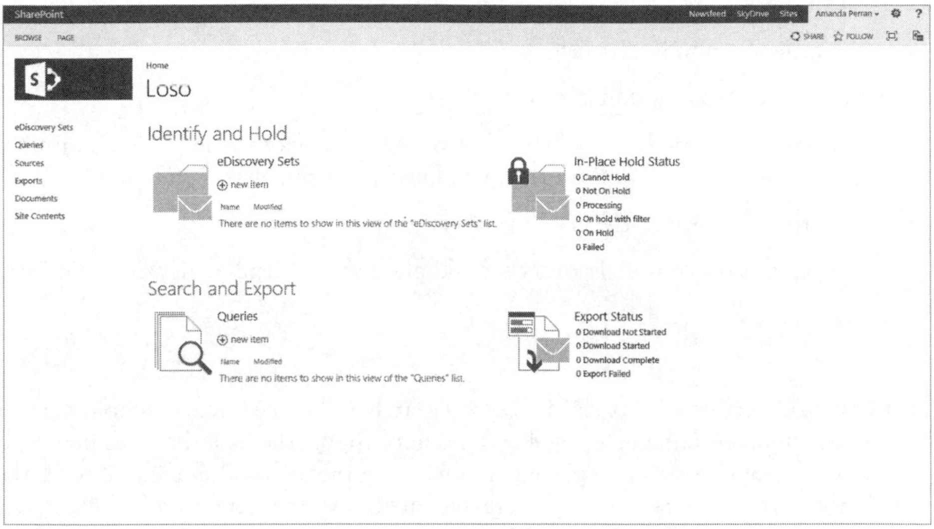

FIGURE 16-38

6. From your case site, you can now create an eDiscovery set. Click the "new item" link below the eDiscovery Sets heading.

7. Enter **Authored By Your Name** (use your own name) for eDiscovery Set Name.

8. Click the Add & Manage Sources link. A window will appear, as shown in Figure 16-39.

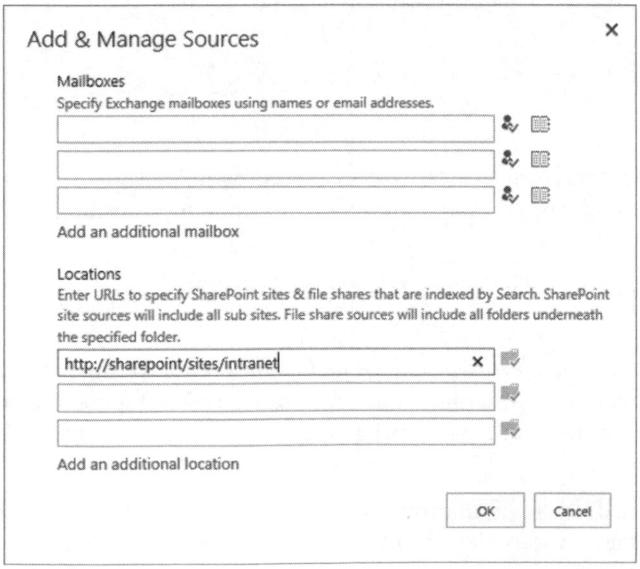

FIGURE 16-39

9. Specify the URL of a site collection within which you have authored contented. You are required to enter only the top-level site address, as all subsites will also be searched.

10. Click the OK button.

11. Enter your name in the Author/Sender field.

12. Click the Enable In-Place Hold option button.

13. Click the Preview Results button to view items that would be subject to the hold. A pop-up window will appear. To see the SharePoint content, you must select the SharePoint tab.

14. Click the Close button to return to the eDiscovery Set page.

15. Click the Save button to save your eDiscovery set and place the applicable files on an In-Place Hold.

How It Works

In an earlier Try it Out, you performed a basic eDiscovery search and placed items on hold. The hold was limited to preventing items from being deleted and did not support the idea that files may be edited over time and further changed. Once a file is placed on hold using this method, it cannot be further edited or changed. In the preceding Try it Out, you created an eDiscovery Center and case site. This is a location where you can create multiple eDiscovery sets to query for content related to a common topic. Once you identify the content, you can place it on an In-Place Hold, which captures the content as it exists at the point in time the hold was placed but still allows the file to be edited by others or deleted. This allows business users to continue working without any knowledge that the file is on hold. This can be a good thing in cases where sensitive cases or investigations are ongoing and you do not want to make it obvious to end users that files are being reviewed. It is also more practical than the traditional holds, in that it may take a long time to review all relevant information related to a hold or case and, therefore, the file does not have to be disrupted during this time.

SUMMARY

In this chapter, you learned the fundamental elements of creating a records-management solution in SharePoint 2013. After reading this chapter, you should have a complete understanding of the following:

➤ Identifying roles and responsibilities related to your records-management implementation is important.

➤ A file plan is a critical element of your records-management solution that outlines the categories and types of documents that exist within your organization. Developing a detailed file plan is an important step that must take place prior to configuring any technical elements of SharePoint.

➤ A classification plan is a detailed listing of all properties and attributes that should exist related to your records. It is important to identify a classification plan that is detailed enough to support your informational and organizational needs, but still manageable for end users to populate and maintain.

➤ In SharePoint 2013, you can manage records separately in a dedicated archive (known as the *Records Center*), or you can keep them "in place" within the collaborative sites in which they were created.

➤ You can create rules to determine how long records can exist within the solution based on dates such as when they were created, last modified, or declared a record.

➤ Unique retention rules can exist for non-records and records.

➤ You can place files on hold for investigative or regulatory reasons. If a file is added to a hold, it cannot be removed from the system until the hold is removed.

➤ You can also place files on an In-Place Hold, which allows the files to be changed or deleted and a copy of the file is preserved to reflect its condition and content at the point in time the hold was placed.

EXERCISES

1. What is the difference between a file plan and a classification plan?

2. How is In-Place Records Management different from archive-based records management?

3. True or false: A file cannot be deleted if it has been declared a record.

4. Can retention schedules be applied to folders or content types?

▶ **WHAT YOU LEARNED IN THIS CHAPTER**

TOPIC	KEY CONCEPTS
Records management	Records management is the practice of organizing and maintaining documents within an organization based on a series of predetermined rules. These rules control things such as where files are stored, how long they are retained, how they should be disposed of, and who is responsible for these files.
Holds	In regulatory or legal cases, it is critical that important documents be accessible to stakeholders involved in the proceedings or investigation. As a result, it may be appropriate to place holds on the records, which temporarily exempt the files from any retention or expiration policies that have been defined for them.
Archive-based records management versus In-Place Records Management?	Archive-based records management focuses on the movement or copying of a file to a centralized location where all records are stored. In-place records management focuses on retaining the record within the same repository it has been created and stored in along with all other documents that relate to the same topic or subject.

17

Working with Search

WHAT YOU WILL LEARN IN THIS CHAPTER:

➤ Basic search

➤ Building search queries

➤ Customizing the search experience

➤ Search Center

➤ Managing search features

➤ Search-driven content

➤ Search usage reports

Thus far, this book has covered the various ways you can store and interact with documents and content via SharePoint 2013. After configuring your system to fit your business requirements, you need to configure it so that users can easily find the information. When users visit a website, they expect to be able to find the relevant content that they are looking for quickly and easily by searching the site. SharePoint is no exception to this expectation. The tools covered in this chapter can be combined to help you build powerful search solutions for your users.

UNDERSTANDING SHAREPOINT SEARCH

The search facilities in SharePoint enable users to easily locate content stored in the various SharePoint sites as well as other external content sources, such as file shares, Exchange public folders, and line-of-business (LOB) applications. Before you start working through this chapter's Try It Out exercises, you need to familiarize yourself with some of the core concepts of SharePoint Search.

Key Terms

Quite a few components make up the SharePoint Search application; in fact, entire books have been dedicated to explaining how to best configure, manage, and use the search features of SharePoint. Although this book won't go into as much detail, it will cover all the search basics and give you enough information to start using Search within your solutions. To get started, let's review some common search terms that you are likely to hear.

Content Sources

The search must have a content source, which is the location where SharePoint looks for information when you enter search terms into the SharePoint interface. By default, one content source represents all the sites in the SharePoint environment. However, you can add more content sources so users can search content stored in other locations, including:

➤ Other SharePoint sites

➤ Standard websites

➤ File shares

➤ Exchange public folders

➤ External business systems

Once content sources have been defined within the system, the search engine schedules them to be crawled so that data from these content sources can be located via the SharePoint Search features.

Indexes

An *index* is the location that contains details on all the information in the content sources. When users perform searches, the index is queried for content that matches the user-entered terms. For a search to be accurate and effective, the system must update the index regularly based on a schedule that you define. The index is comprised of both the metadata and content of the files contained within the system. In some cases, a particular file type might not be recognizable by the system out-of-the-box, so additional configuration, such as the installation of an iFilter, may be required to allow for the handling of such files. However, by default, SharePoint Server is able to view the contents of files such as Microsoft Office files, PDF, XML, and web pages.

Crawl Schedules

Crawling is the process that the SharePoint Server uses to access the data within the content source and build the search index. Once a content source has been defined within the system, an administrator can define specific schedules by which the content will be crawled. You should define schedules appropriate to the type of information that a content source contains and the probability of it being updated. For example, if you had a file share location that you used to store old project information that is no longer updated, you would probably not need to update the index often. On the other hand, your SharePoint sites are likely very active and dynamic, and should be crawled on a frequent basis.

There are two types of crawls:

➤ **Incremental crawls** check for updates to content and new items since the last crawl.

➤ **Full crawls** are required less frequently — after significant configuration changes to the search application, such as the addition of a new managed property, changes to the search service account, or the installation of a service pack or update.

When defining incremental and full crawl schedules, try not to create schedules that are too frequent. This can cause excess load on the server and result in performance challenges for the environment. If you want to have frequent updates of your SharePoint content, you might want to enable continuous crawls. This feature will crawl SharePoint content in 15 minute intervals by default but can be set to a more frequent setting if desired. Once enabled, the ability to schedule incremental crawls of the SharePoint content source is disabled. This type of crawl can only be created for SharePoint content sources.

Queries

When you conduct a search by entering a keyword or phrase into one of the available search boxes, you are creating a *query*. This query will be performed against the content index to identify content that contains a match for a keyword or phrase that you have entered. The search system will return a listing of items that match your query. These are referred to as *search results*.

Result Sources

To get the most out of your search, you might need to define a result source to segment certain types of content so that they can be searched in a narrower fashion than searching against all content within the index. For example, if you lose your keys while in the front lobby of a building and go back to search for them, you limit your search to that lobby, not the entire building. In previous versions of SharePoint, this concept was addressed through search scopes. In essence, result sources tell SharePoint which sections of an index to search by restricting queries to a subset of content. Using result sources, a server administrator, site collection administrator, or site owner can define rules that must be met by the content in order for it to appear in a result source. You may have result sources that represent smaller subsets of data such as user profiles or the human resources site.

Result Types

SharePoint 2013 enables administrators to customize how search results are displayed to users of their sites based on the type of results they are viewing. For example, when a user performs a search query, he or she will be returned a set of results that matches that query. Hovering over a Word document search result will allow a user to view a preview of the document as well as view some basic metadata related to the document. However, using result types, administrators can create additional conditions and actions that will allow for unique display templates to be displayed based on the type of content that is returned. For example, content that is identified as a procedure might display with a unique set of metadata, as opposed to what typically would be displayed in the hover pane for a Word document.

Search Center

The Search Center is a site that contains many of the typical configurations you would make related to a site that is dedicated to the purpose of Search. You can create multiple Search Centers within your environment by including one or more within each site collection. Alternatively, you can have a single site collection or site that acts as the central search location for your entire organization. Within a Search Center, you can create custom pages and tabs to help guide users to a specific type of search, as shown in Figure 17-1.

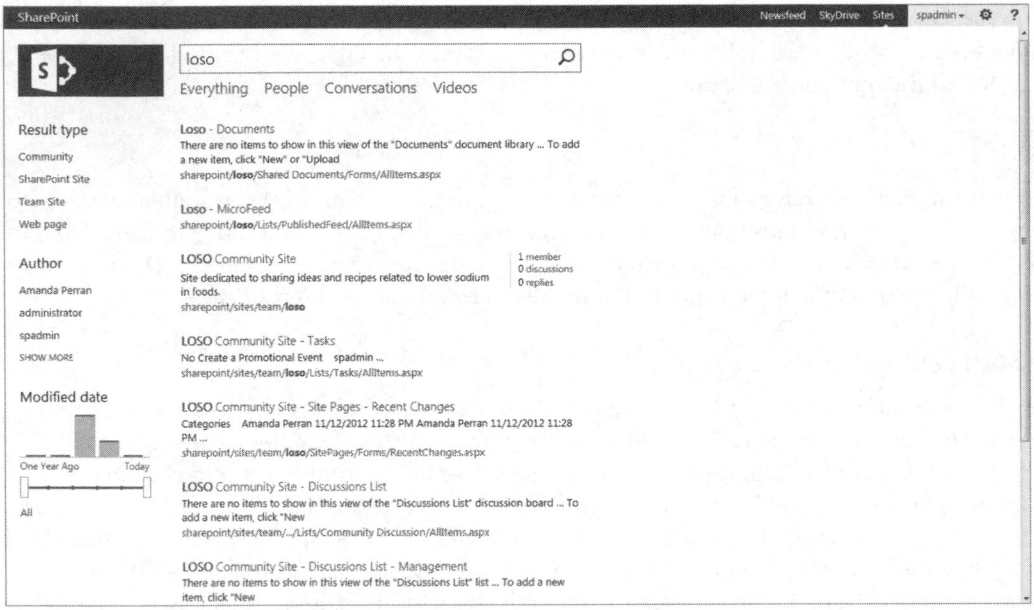

FIGURE 17-1

Now that you have learned about the core concepts of Search in SharePoint, you will now begin to look at the process of interacting with the Search application by creating basic queries and advanced searches, and configuring the search interfaces.

You can interact with and manage searches in SharePoint in multiple ways. The following sections discuss the two most common search interfaces:

➤ **Basic search:** The most common search query in which users type simple keywords and phrases that the Search application uses to find file content, filenames, and properties.

➤ **Advanced search:** A more detailed search interface that filters based on properties, file types, and languages. It includes more detailed options for how keywords are searched, such as if all keywords appear in a specific order or if none of the words exist.

Basic Search

Every out-of-the-box site in SharePoint has a basic search box in the top-right corner, as shown in Figure 17-2, where users can enter terms or words that allow them to find content. SharePoint searches the titles and column data associated with documents as well as the content within the document.

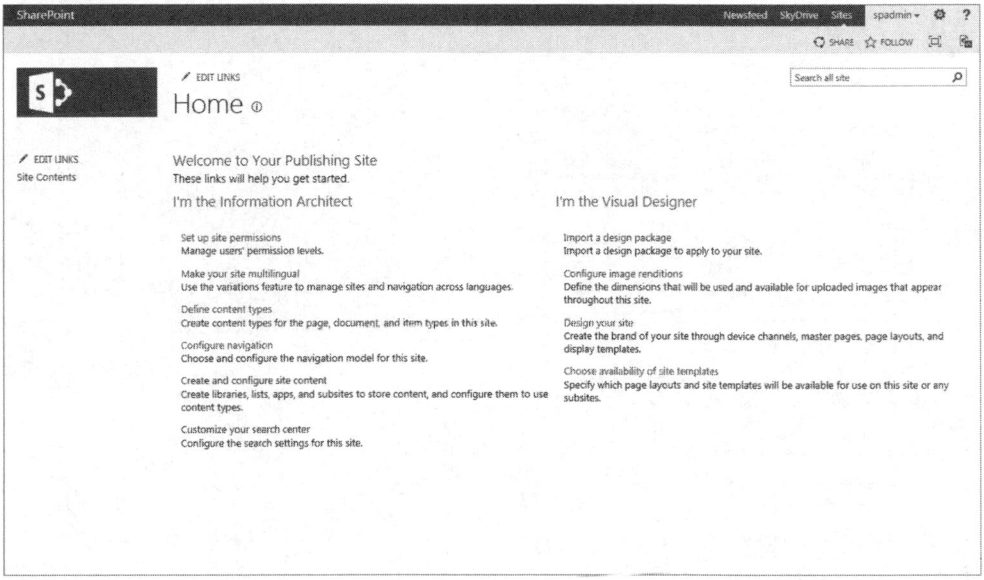

FIGURE 17-2

When a user adds a value to the search box and presses Enter, the value is translated into a query string that is passed to the search results page. For example, when a user enters the term "camping" into the search box and presses Enter, he or she is redirected to a search results page, and any items that contain the phrase "camping" appear in the search results. If you look at the URL when you arrive at the search results page, you will notice that your search term is part of the page URL. The URL for this example is `http://sharepoint/sites/intranet/_layouts/15/osssearchresults.aspx?u=http%3A%2F%2Fsharepoint%2Fsites%2FIntranet&k=camping`. The following table describes each element.

VALUE	TRANSLATION
`http://sharepoint/sites/intranet/_layouts/15/OSSSearchResults.aspx`	The search results page.
`u=http%3A%2F%2Fsharepoint%2FIntranet`	The site on which the search was performed. This URL is the same as `http://sharepoint/sites/intranet;` however, some of the characters have been formatted differently.
`k=camping`	The keyword search value.

Figure 17-3 shows an example of the search results page, including the URL. Search results pages can be shared with other users or bookmarked for reference at a later time. You review the process for subscribing to a search in an upcoming Try it Out.

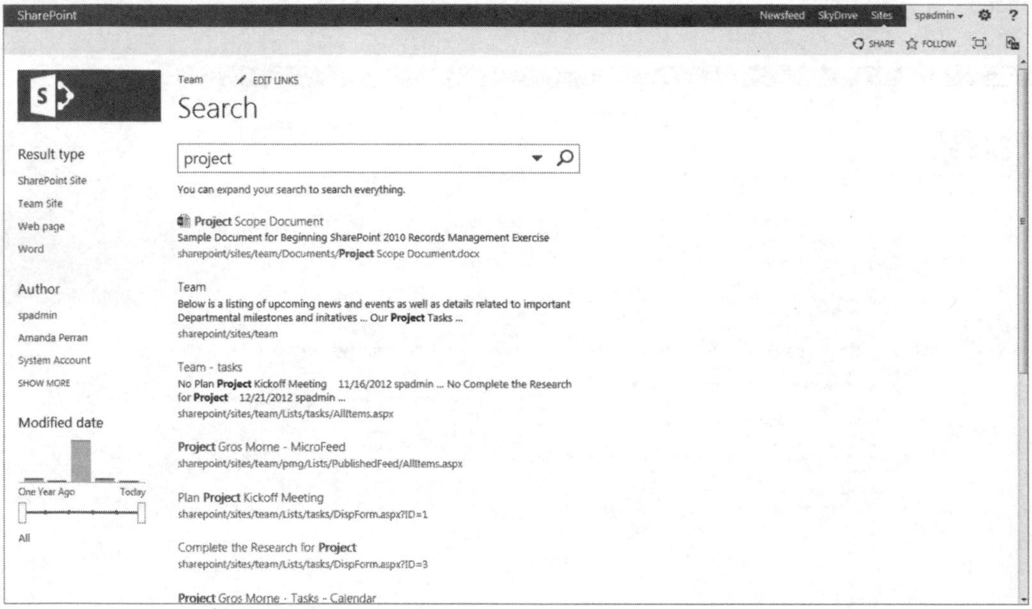

FIGURE 17-3

TRY IT OUT Performing a Basic Search

To quickly get a feel for how search works, in this Try It Out, you complete a basic search. To get started, log in to the home page of your SharePoint site.

1. From the home page of your SharePoint site, enter a phrase, such as sales, in your search box, as shown in Figure 17-2.

2. Click the Search icon to the right of the search box. This will redirect you to a search results page as shown in Figure 17-3.

3. From the search results page, review and select an option in the left panel to further refine your search. For example, by selecting Word in the refinement panel on the left, the search results on the right portion of the screen will be filtered to show only Word documents.

How It Works

For the search you conducted, you entered a search query in the search box. The search query was conducted against the search index, and all SharePoint content that contained the term "sales" was returned as part of the search results.

Now that you have completed a basic search query, take a few minutes and review the search results page. At the top of the page there is a search box that contains the search that you have performed. If you wanted to conduct a new more detailed search, you could update the query and click the search icon. This would conduct a new search and update the search results.

On the left of the page a refinement panel allows you to refine your search results based on attributes, such as Result Type, Author, and Modified Date. For example, if you know that you are looking for a document that was edited by "Dylan Perran" within the past month, you can refine the Result Type to "Word" and the Author to "Dylan Perran," and select the date range to be between one month and one week ago. This will refine your search results and subsequently make it easier to locate your document.

TRY IT OUT | **Subscribing to a Search**

In this Try It Out, you subscribe to a search results page so that if any new items are added to the index that match your search, you can receive an e-mail notification. This can be helpful if you are responsible for a particular topic in your organization or you are interested in learning more about something. It allows you to receive notifications whenever new content is created related to that topic without having to visit each library or list where content could be stored to create an individual alert.

1. From the main page of your site, perform a search for a term, such as "sales." Be sure to select a term for which there would be results within your own environment.

2. Once you have been redirected to the search results page, scroll to the bottom of the page.

3. Select the Alert Me link. You will be redirected to a page containing options for how you wish to be alerted, as shown in Figure 17-4.

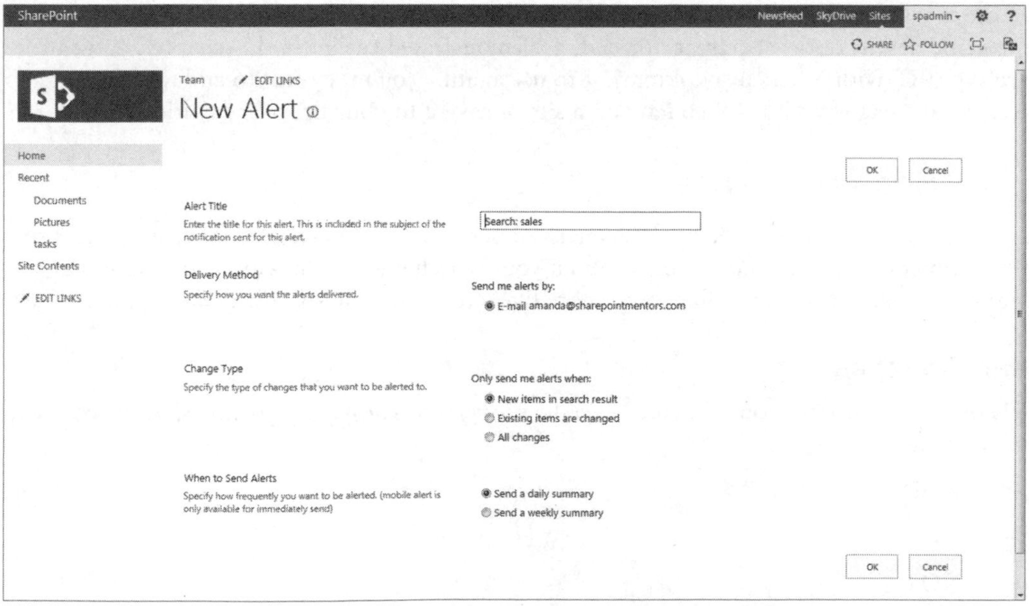

FIGURE 17-4

4. Modify the Alert Title to something informative. By default, the title will display your search query, which will look something similar to "Search: sales." However, it is a good idea when creating alerts to type in something informative since this title will be the subject line of the e-mails you receive related to this alert in the future. A good example might be "New Items Added to Sales Topic."

5. Select the option to Send me alerts by e-mail. This will likely already be selected for you.

6. Select the option to receive alerts when New items appear in search results. This setting will send you an e-mail when new documents or content items get added to SharePoint related to sales. The other settings will notify you when any of the existing items are updated in addition to new items being added.

7. Select the option to receive a weekly report. This will allow you to receive a weekly update on any items that might have been added related to the topic of sales in the past week.

How It Works

In this Try It Out, you subscribed to a search result so that whenever new results are added, you receive an e-mail alert. This might be relevant if you are following a specific topic in your organization and want to know when new content is added.

Saving Searches

A common request or requirement is for users to be able to share or save specific searches with others. For example, if you work in a shoe factory, you may conduct a search for a specific shoe brand. This would allow you to identify everything in the system related to that brand. You might then want to send it to other members of your team or post a link to that search on your team site. Because every search in SharePoint is done via a URL, and the search results page contains the specific details of the search performed, as demonstrated earlier in this chapter, you can share the URL with others or bookmark it to use again. You may want to add the URL of a search results page to a links Web Part on a site or save it to your browser favorites.

Building Search Queries

Now that we have reviewed the basic elements of performing a search, let's take a moment to review ways in which you can be more specific about your search query. This can help ensure that your initial set of search results is refined and more likely to return the specific content you are seeking.

Boolean Searches

Boolean searches allows you to include specific properties, known as *operators*, with your search term, including:

➤ AND

➤ OR

➤ NOT

You can enter these properties in the search box along with your search query to perform more advanced searches. Consider a scenario where you want to search for sales presentations but you want to ensure that items related to a product line called "loso" are not included. You would enter the following into the search box:

> "sales" and "presentations" NOT "loso"

You can also use Boolean searches against specific managed properties related to a file. For example, if you know that the search file you are looking for has a title that includes either the words "salt" or "sodium," you can enter the following into the search box:

> title: "Salt" OR title: "Sodium"

Entering this search query would return all items that contain "Salt" or "Sodium" in the title. It is important to note that when you use Boolean operators, they must be entered in all caps so that the system recognizes them as Boolean operators; otherwise, they are treated as standard search terms.

Prefix Matching

At times you may be searching for something and only know the first part of the terms you are looking for. For example, you might be looking for something that relates to Admin, Administration or Administrative topics. You can then enter Admin* and items that started with Admin would be returned within the Search results. An example of this is shown in Figure 17-5, where the user searched for "lo*" but results were returned for words that started with "lo." Or you may be looking for things that were created by Amanda but you are unsure if it was Amanda Murphy or Amanda Perran, as her name had changed due to a recent marriage. You could search for "Author: Amanda*," and results would be returned for anything where the "Author" started with "Amanda."

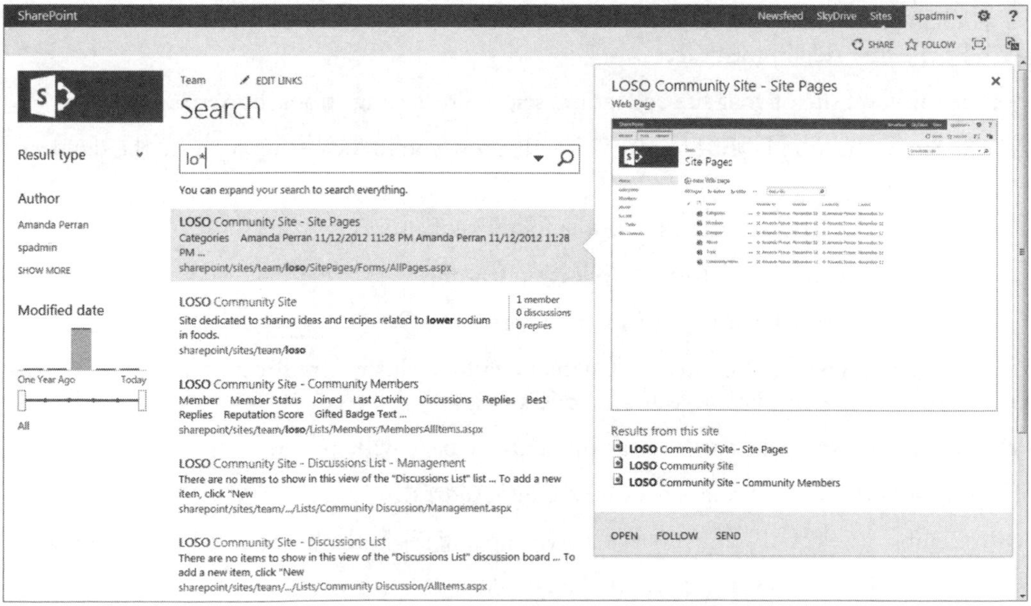

FIGURE 17-5

LOCATION OF THE *

Keep in mind that this type of wildcard search is a prefix matching search only, so the * must come at the end of the phrase. Using the * at the beginning of the phrase is considered "suffix matching" and is not supported.

Phonetic Search

It is possible that at times you want to perform a search for someone or something that can be spelled a number of ways. For example, you are looking for "Neal" but he spells his name "Neale." Through the Phonetic Search in SharePoint, the search results will return correct results for either.

Search Center

So far, we have discussed how to work with the basic search features of SharePoint. However, you might want to have a wider variety of features and customization options for your search centers. There is an Enterprise Search Center template that includes more options for searching. Next, we look at creating an Enterprise Search Center and some of the options for creating a more advanced search experience.

TRY IT OUT   **Creating an Enterprise Search Center Site**

To allow you to perform more advanced customizations and search queries, you start by creating a site that is dedicated to performing searches. Since you want to take full advantage of the features installed, you are going to create a Search Center using the Enterprise Search Center template. Because this is an enterprise template, it requires that you have some of the Enterprise features enabled, so enabling these features will be the first step in the process.

1. From the top-level site of your site collection, select Site Settings from the Settings menu.

2. Click the Site Collection Features link. This will allow you to locate and activate the required search settings.

3. If they are not activated, activate each of the following features:

➤   SharePoint Server Standard Site Collection features

➤   SharePoint Server Publishing Infrastructure

4. From the Settings menu, select the Site Contents option. This will redirect you to a location where you can create a new subsite for your site collection.

5. Click the New Subsite link. The New SharePoint Site page will appear.

6. Enter **Search** as the Title of your site and Web Site Address.

7. For the Template Selection, click the Enterprise tab and select the Enterprise Search Center.

8. Select the option to Use same permission as parent site. Typically, you do *not* want to have unique permissions for a Search Center, as the results are security trimmed, and you want to ensure that all users can access the pages.

9. Select the Yes option to use the top link bar from the parent site.

10. Click the Create button. The page will reload and your new Search Center will be displayed.

How It Works

The Search template is a site definition that is preconfigured with all the different Web Parts and lists that are needed for configuring a Search Center. Creating this site is the first step in configuring the search experience for users.

TRY IT OUT **Associating a Search Center with a Site Collection**

Now that you have created the Search Center, you need to configure the site collection to use that site as the location where all search results will be displayed.

1. Click the Settings menu and then Site Settings

2. Click the Search Settings link in the Site Collection Administration group of links.

3. Specify the URL of the site you created in the preceding Try It Out as the Search Center URL (see Figure 17-6).

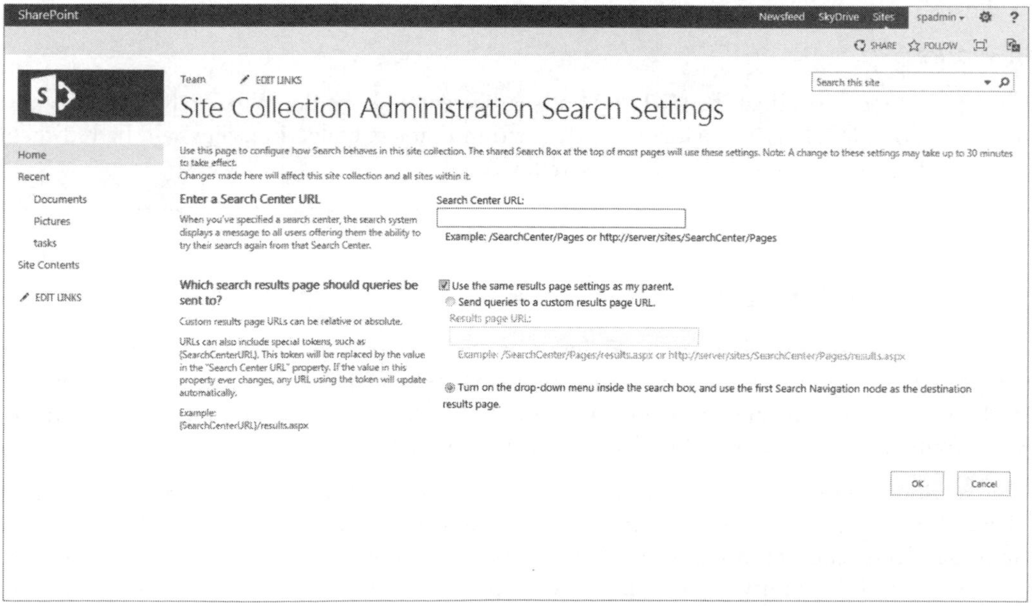

FIGURE 17-6

You can also set a Search Center to be the global Search Center for the entire farm. This will be the location where all searches go, regardless of from where they were initiated. To specify your site as the Global Search Center, visit the Central Administration site and click the Set a Search Center URL link, as shown in Figure 17-7.

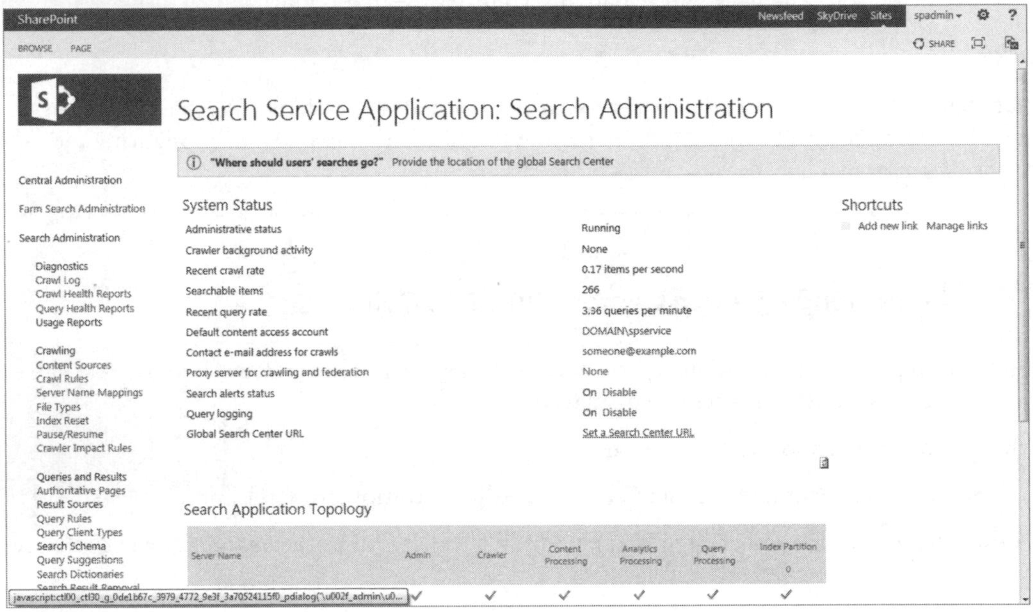

FIGURE 17-7

How It Works

In this Try It Out, you specified the URL of your search center as the default search results location for your site collection. When users perform a search within that site collection, they will be redirected to the search results pages from the Enterprise Search Center.

Administering Search

As previously mentioned, SharePoint can index multiple content sources so that data from multiple business systems can be accessed via the search interface. The default content source is the SharePoint content associated with a farm. However, authorized system administrators can add custom content sources, such as file shares, websites, or business applications.

In this section, we review the process for adding a new content source to the search engine and how to define crawl schedules for each content source to ensure that the data contained within the index is up to date and accurate. Most of the Try It Outs are intended for a user with administration rights on the server and the ability to manage service applications. Therefore, if you do not have those privileges in your environment, you might have difficulty completing the exercises in this section.

Managing Content Sources

This section reviews the options for managing and creating new content sources within the SharePoint Search application. In the first two Try It Outs, you will add two new content sources to your SharePoint environment, so that you can index a site to gather further information about a topic of interest to us as well as a file share location. You will then modify the crawl schedule associated with your SharePoint content sources so that crawls occur on a regular basis.

TRY IT OUT   Creating a New Content Source (Non-SharePoint Site)

In this example, you create a new content source that will allow users of your SharePoint site to search for content contained in your company's Internet-facing website that is not a SharePoint site.

1. Log into the Central Administration site for your SharePoint environment.

2. Click the Manage service applications link within the Application Management group. You will be redirected to a page listing all service applications for your farm. These service applications represent specialized functionality and features that are available to the entire farm and not just a single site collection or site.

3. Click the link for the Search Service Application. The default name of this link is Search Service Application, as shown in Figure 17-8; however, your environment might be named differently.

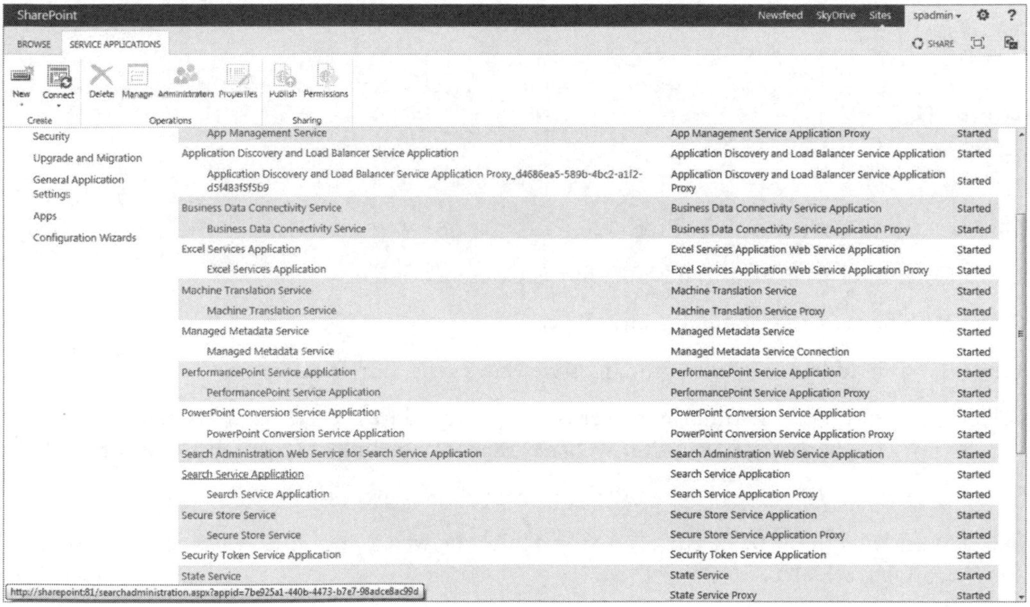

FIGURE 17-8

4. From the Search Administration screen, select the Content Sources link from the Crawling section on the left navigation. You will be redirected to the Manage Content Sources page, which lists all existing content sources associated with the farm as well as details related to their most recent crawls and upcoming scheduled crawls, as shown in Figure 17-9.

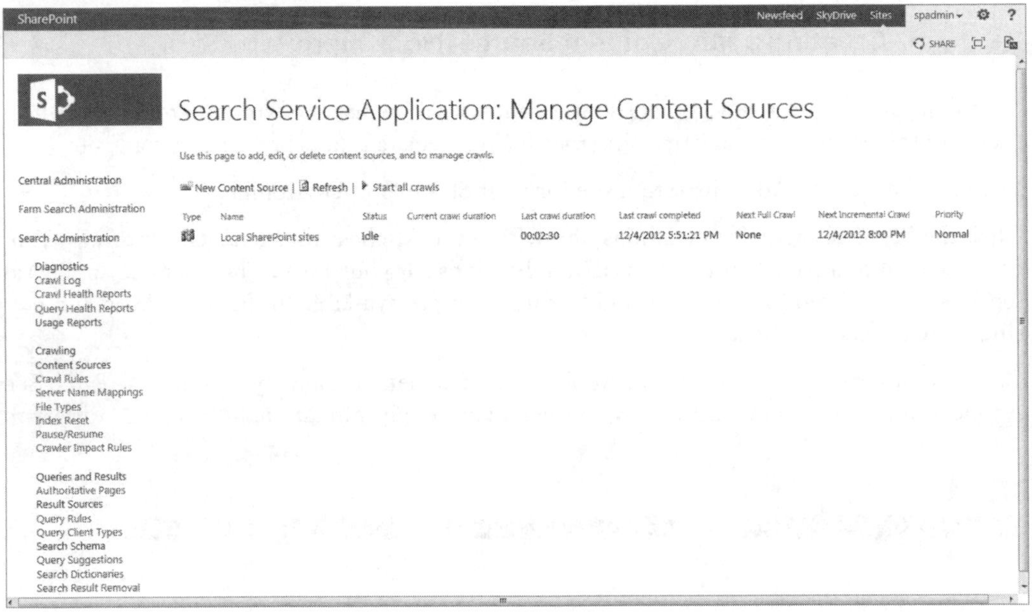

FIGURE 17-9

5. Click the New Content Source link.

6. Enter **Corporate Website** as the Name of the Content Source.

7. Select Web Sites as the Content Source Type.

8. Enter the web address of your company's website as the Start Address.

9. Select the "Only crawl within the server of each start address" setting. This helps to ensure that you do not crawl content from other websites that may be linked from your Corporate Website.

10. Select the Create Schedule link below the Incremental Crawl title.

11. Select Weekly as the Type, Saturday as the day of the week, and 3:00 AM as the Starting time, as shown in Figure 17-10.

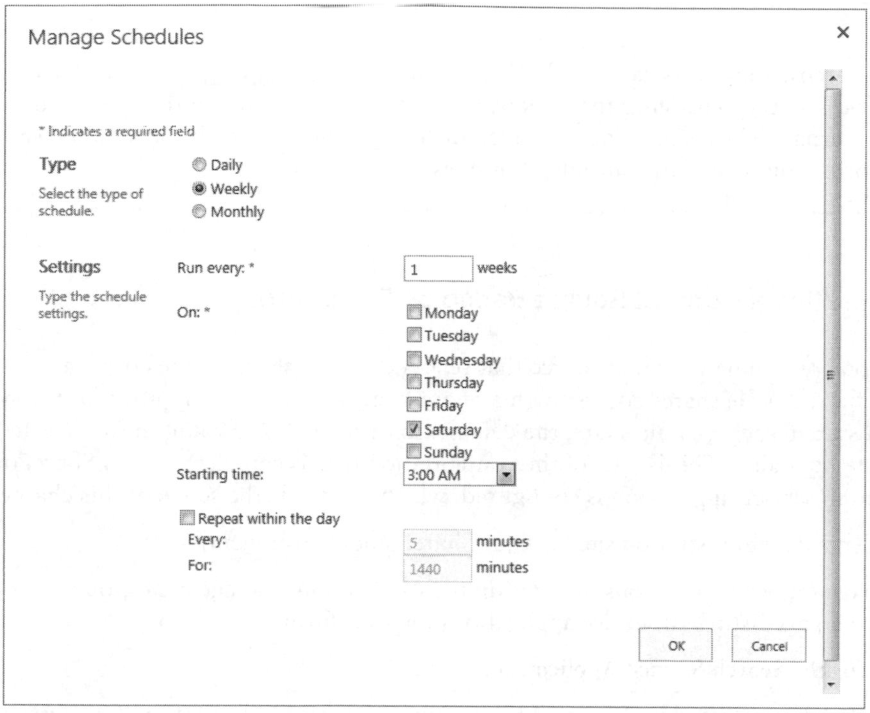

FIGURE 17-10

12. Click the OK button.

13. Hover over the Corporate Website content source you just created to expose the menu associated with it, as shown in Figure 17-11, and select the Start Full Crawl option. This will index the website for the first time so that content will be available via search.

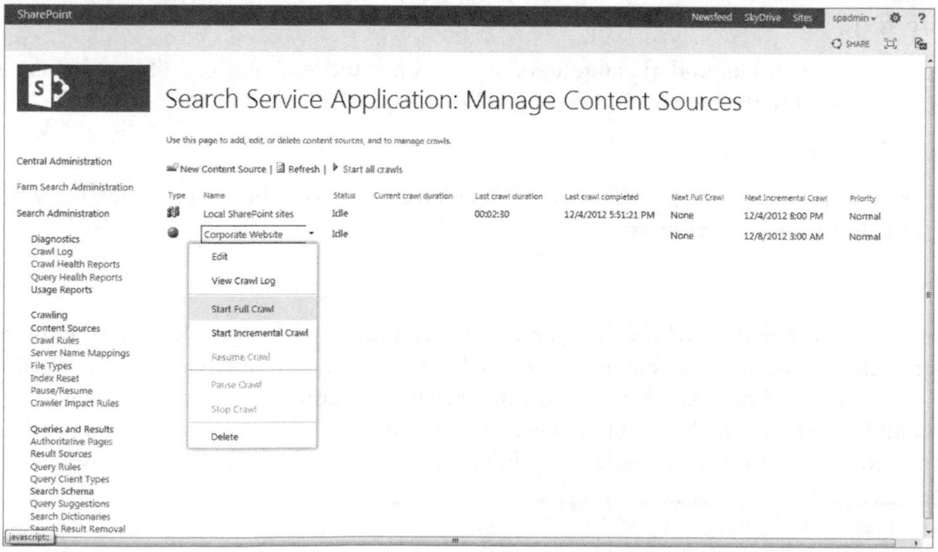

FIGURE 17-11

How It Works

Once you finish these steps, your users can search the company's Internet-facing website. This creates a more unified content-discovery experience for all your company's information, both public and private. Other examples of external websites that you can index include partner sites or informational sites that contain valuable information related to your line of business.

TRY IT OUT   Creating a Content Source Based on File Shares

In this Try It Out, you create a new content source that references a file share on the corporate network. This is useful when file shares coexist with a SharePoint environment. In order for the system to crawl an external system such as a file share, the default Content Access Account must have access to that location to create the index. This is part of the configuration that is completed when SharePoint is installed and the Search service application is configured, which is outside the scope of this chapter.

1. Log into the Central Administration site for your SharePoint environment.

2. Click the Manage service applications link within the Application Management group. You will be redirected to a page listing all service applications for your farm.

3. Click the link for the Search Service Application.

4. From the Search Administration screen, select the Content Sources link from the Crawling section on the left navigation.

5. Click the New Content Source link.

6. Enter **File Share** as the Name of the Content Source.

7. Select Web Sites as the Content Source Type.

8. Enter the address of a shared drive on your network, in the format of **\\server\directory** or **file://** server/directory.

9. Select the "Crawl the folder and all subfolders of each start address" option. This will ensure that all folders associated with that path, including subfolders, are included in the crawl.

10. Click the OK button.

11. Hover over the File Share content source you just created to expose the menu associated with it, and select the Start Full Crawl option.

How It Works

By creating content sources that crawl the file shares, users can take advantage of the SharePoint Search interface to locate all the important documents. In this Try It Out, you are indexing an old file share that no longer is updated and has been set to read-only, because all content that is being updated will not be modified and saved within SharePoint. Therefore, you did not set a crawl schedule on this content source. If the content is not being regularly updated, there is little value in regular crawls.

Crawl Schedules

So far, we have looked at setting the crawl schedule for a custom content source, such as your Corporate Website. For your non-SharePoint content sources, you might run a crawl only once a day or once a week, depending on the expected level of updates to the content. However, when it comes to your SharePoint content, it is very likely that you will want to have the crawl running on a regular basis to ensure that newly created or uploaded content is available as soon as possible to users via search. One often misunderstood point is that content will not appear within search results until a crawl has been performed. Therefore, if you upload a new document, no user will be able to locate it in the search until the next crawl takes place.

As described in the opening of this chapter, you have options on the type of crawls that can be performed. A full crawl will search through all content regardless of the time of its last update. It is a deeper level crawl and is required for major system updates or configuration changes. An incremental crawl searches only for items that have changed since the last update. There is also an option for a continuous crawl setting, which disables the ability of scheduling an incremental crawl and instead allows the system to determine when it is required to update. The continuous crawl can adjust to run more frequently so that new content is identified almost immediately.

TRY IT OUT   **Creating a Crawl Schedule**

In this Try It Out, you define a crawl schedule for your farm. You enable the continuous crawls feature so that content is regularly crawled, as needed, and a full crawl occurs on a monthly basis.

1. From the Central Administration site, click the Manage Service Applications link within the Application Management group. You will be redirected to a page listing all service applications for your farm.

2. Click the link for the Search Service Application.

3. From the Search Administration screen, select the Content Sources link from the Crawling section on the left navigation.

4. Hover over the Local SharePoint sites content source to expose the menu associated with it, and select the Edit option.

5. Select the Enable Continuous Crawls option. With this option selected, there is no requirement to create an incremental crawl schedule.

6. Create a full crawl schedule that occurs on the first day of every month at 12 AM.

7. Click the OK button.

How It Works

In this Try It Out, you configured the crawl schedule for your farm so that a complete crawl of all content will take place on a monthly basis. You also enabled the continuous crawl feature, which ensures that as new content is added to the system, it is crawled and made available within the Search application within minutes.

Advanced Search

Once you have created a Search Center site, you can further customize the search experience for users and provide a more flexible environment for creating search queries. One example of this is the Advanced Search page, as shown in Figure 17-12. From this page, users can create more specific searches by using drop-down and selection boxes to refine their search terms.

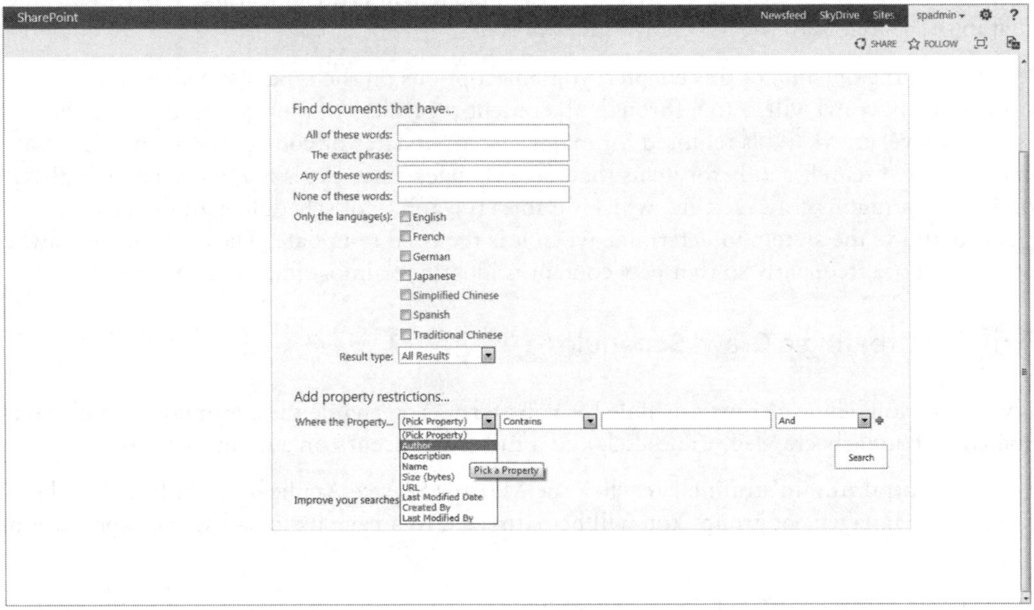

FIGURE 17-12

In addition to being able to type exact phrases for your search criteria, you can specify the type of file you're searching for in the "Result type" drop-down, or you can search based on specific column data in document libraries. By default, SharePoint offers the following properties:

➤ Author

➤ Description

➤ Name

➤ Size

➤ URL

➤ Last Modified Date

➤ Created By

➤ Last Modified By

In addition to these properties, you can create your own properties. This is helpful for locating items in specific columns that are used as properties for multiple lists, libraries, or content types throughout the environment. We review how to add additional properties as an activity in the "Managed Properties" section.

TRY IT OUT Performing an Advanced Search

In this Try It Out, you use the Advanced Search interface so that you can perform more refined search queries.

1. From any page within your site collection, perform a search for a term that is likely to provide results. This example uses the term "sales" again. You should notice that after you perform the search, you are redirected to a search results page within your Search Center. If not, ensure that you have specified the Search Center URL correctly in the earlier "Associating a Search Center with a Site Collection" Try It Out.

2. Make note of the number of items that have been returned in your search as well as the different Result Types options that are displayed on the left of the screen. In this example search, as shown in Figure 17-13, you will see that we have received results for Word files and web pages.

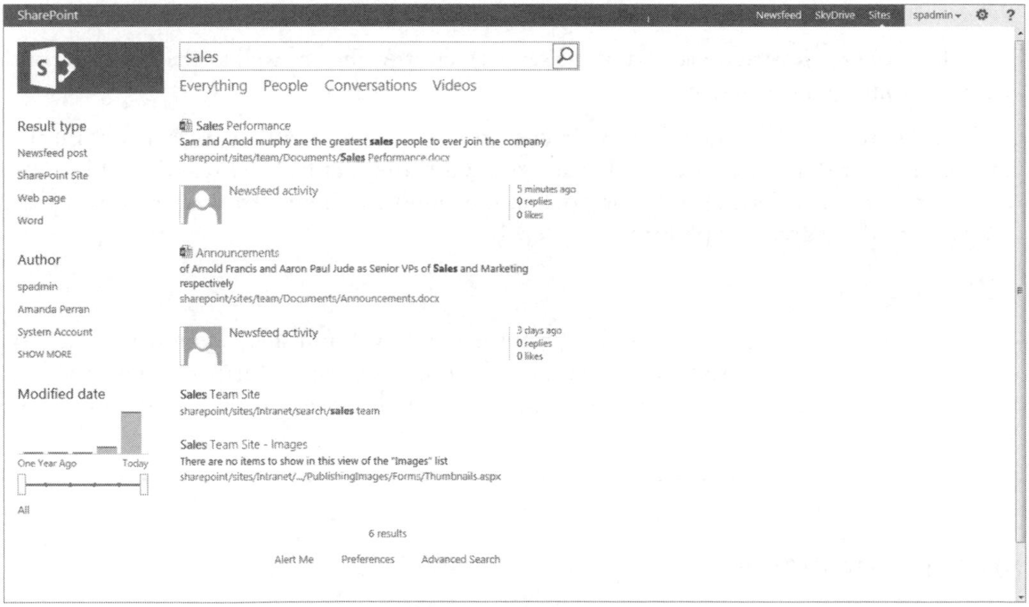

FIGURE 17-13

3. From the search results page, scroll to the bottom of the page and click the Advanced Search link.

4. From the Advanced Search page, enter the same term that you entered in step 1 into the "All of these words" field.

5. From the Result type drop-down, select Word Documents, as shown in Figure 17-14.

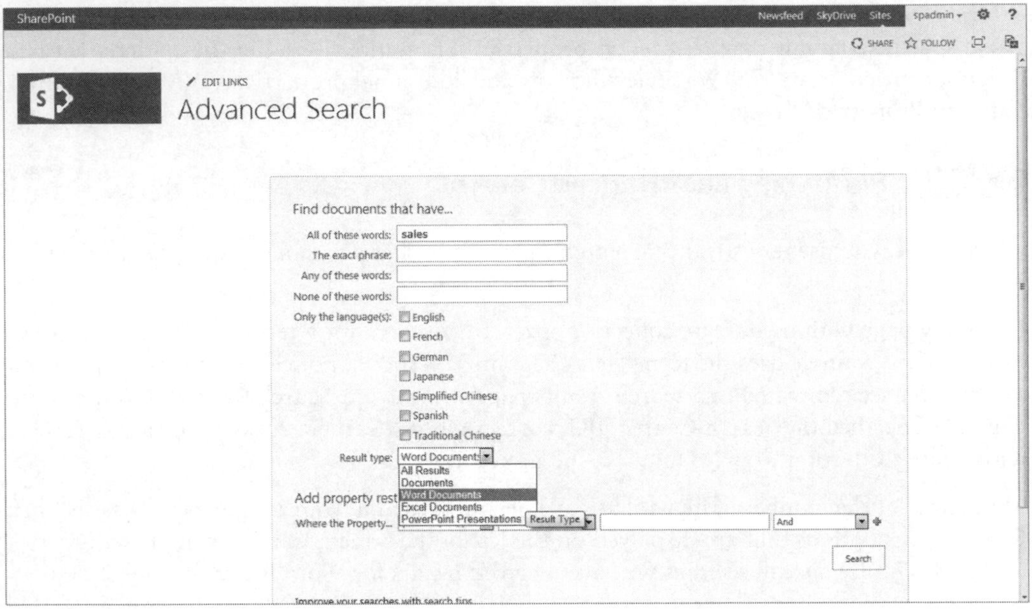

FIGURE 17-14

6. From the Property Restrictions area of the screen, select Author as well as the Contains option, and enter your own first name.

7. Click the Search button. You will be redirected to a results page with items that contain the term you searched for that are only of the Result type Word and that have been authored by users with your first name. As a comparison, look at the number of items returned for this search, as compared to the search you performed in step 1.

How It Works

By typing the phrase in the box in the searches performed in step 1 and step 6, you would have typically received the same search results. However, in your second search, to further refine your search, you limited the results to include only Word documents and added a refinement based on the Author property.

Managed Properties

In the previous example, you performed a search where the Author property was restricted to values that contained a specific name. These types of searches can be very useful in cases where an organization requires the ability to perform searches for very specific data. For example, a legal company might want to have the ability to search by case number or lawyer. *Managed properties* are defined metadata elements that can be created at either a site collection or service application level, and that map to crawled properties; they can be used for more advanced queries in tools such as the Advanced Search or Result Source rules.

In the next Try It Out, you create a new managed property within a site collection. While the majority of these steps are performed from within your site collection, you are required to conduct a full crawl of the SharePoint Server in order to complete the exercise. For this, you will either require access to the Central Administration site for SharePoint and the associated Search service application, or you will require assistance from your Server administrator.

TRY IT OUT Creating a Managed Property

In this Try It Out, you create a new site column called "Case ID" and associate it with a library in SharePoint. You then add some sample content to that library and specify the column. Finally, you complete a full crawl of the Search service so that the new property can be identified by the search engine.

1. From the top-level site of your site collection, create a new site column, called *Case ID*, using the methods described in Chapter 4, "Managing and Customizing Lists and Libraries." This column should be a "Single line of text" column.

2. Associate the Case ID column with a document library by visiting Library Settings and selecting the "Add from existing site columns" option.

3. Upload several documents to the library or update existing documents so that the Case ID column has information within it.

4. Log into the Central Administration site and initiate a full crawl. Wait for the crawl to complete before proceeding with the next step.

5. From the Site Settings page of the top-level site of your site collection, click the Search Schema link. You will be redirected to a page that lists all managed properties that exist within the system.

6. Click the New Managed Property link.

7. Enter **CaseID** as the name of your Managed Property.

8. Select Text as the type of information.

9. Click the Searchable checkbox. This will ensure that the values associated with the managed property are returned as part of the search. Note that you can also adjust the weighting of your managed property with respect to other instances of the term as part of the full text search capabilities of the system by clicking Advanced Searchable Settings.

10. Select the Queryable checkbox. This will allow users to perform searches such as CaseID:123456 to query directly against the property.

11. Select the option for the term to be Retrievable so that the contents of the property will be returned in the search results.

12. Scroll down to the "Mappings to crawled properties" section and click the Add a Mapping button. The "Crawled property selection" window will appear.

13. Search for the term "case" and click the Find button. Two results should appear. Select the ows_Case_x0020_ID value and click OK to close the window.

14. Click OK to save your changes to your managed property. Note that you should launch another crawl of the content source prior to performing searches for the property to ensure that the latest changes are recognized by the system. However, once a crawl has completed, you can search for documents based on this property, as shown in Figure 17-15.

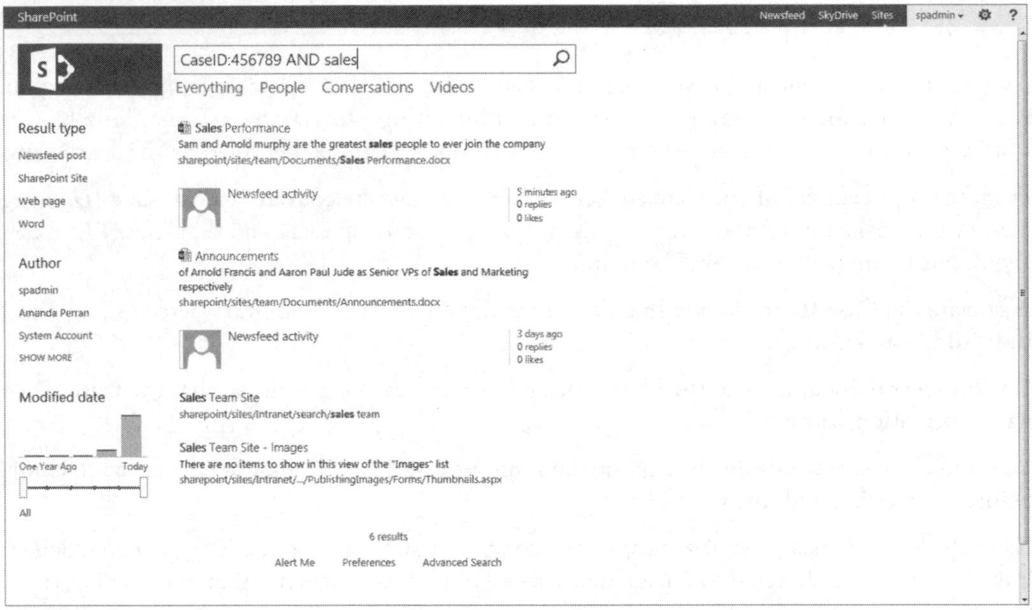

FIGURE 17-15

How It Works

In this Try It Out, you created a managed property in the Search Schema for CaseID so that users could use it in Search to further refine their queries. When a term such as CaseID:123456 is entered in the search box, the system returns only items for which the value 123456 was included in the CaseID property.

SEARCH-DRIVEN CONTENT

Search sometimes can be an underused feature in many organizations. One potential cause of this may be related to the fact that many users are focused on browsing to find content and have become accustomed to finding information based on navigation. One of the new features introduced in SharePoint 2013 is the concept of search-driven content Web Parts that allow site administrators to highlight content that may be of interest to users based on common or expected search terms. By doing this, site administrators are able to perform searches for content that users might be seeking and make the content easy to find. Using the search-driven content Web Parts, a site administrator can also display content from other site collections within his or her own site. This provides enterprise content rollup capabilities that were previously not possible in earlier versions.

In the next Try It Out, you add a Web Part to a page that will display a listing of items that have recently been updated in a site collection using a search-driven content Web Part.

TRY IT OUT   Using Search-Driven Content

In this Try It Out, you add a Web Part to the main page of your site collection that will display items that have been recently updated.

1. From the homepage of the top-level site of your site collection, select Edit Page from the Settings menu.

2. Scroll to the Header Web Part zone and click the Add a Web Part link.

3. Select the Search-Driven Content category. Take a moment to review the various options for adding search-driven content to your page by clicking each Web Part and reading the description that is provided in the About the part section of the page.

4. Select the Recently Changed Items Web Part and click the Add button.

5. By default, the Web Part is added to the page and displays three thumbnails in a vertical list, with the name of the item to the right. Edit the Web Part to display the Web Part tool pane.

6. Change the "Number of items to show" to be 5, and change the Display template from List to Slideshow.

7. Click Apply and the OK buttons to save your changes. You will now see the slideshow preview of the five items within the header Web Part zone of your page, as shown in Figure 17-16.

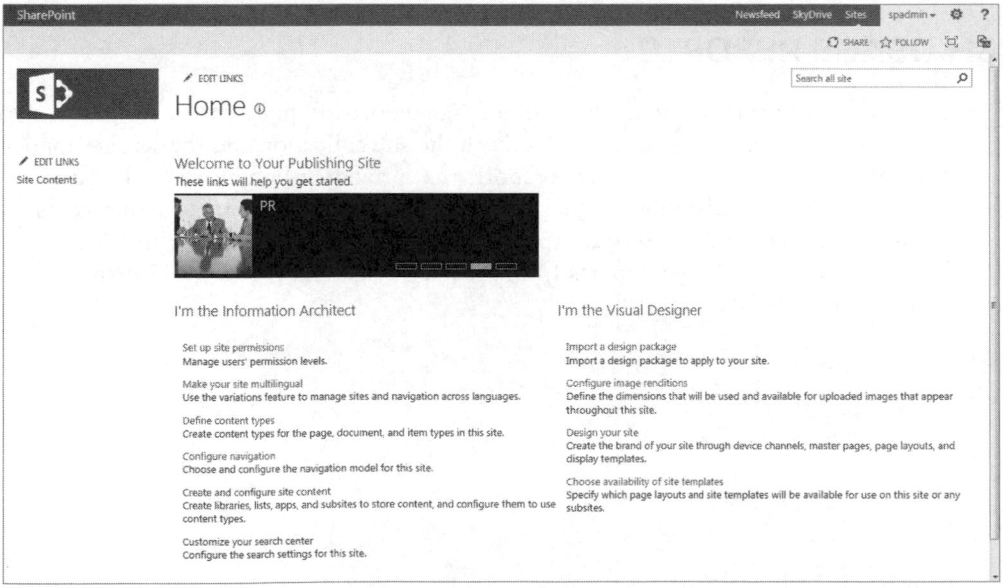

FIGURE 17-16

How It Works

In this Try It Out, you added the Recently Changed Items Web Part to the page. This Web Part displays items that have recently been updated in a listing. You adjusted the number of items and the display options to suit your needs.

EDISCOVERY

SharePoint 2013 offers capabilities around the electronic discovery (eDiscovery) of content for managing records and identifying information that might be useful for legal proceedings or regulatory reviews. Basic eDiscovery of content has been available in previous versions, in that the search service was leveraged to identify relevant data within SharePoint that might be useful for a case, and then a records manager or authorized user could choose to place the items returned within the search results "on hold." When content is placed on hold, the content is not expired or disposed of in the typical manner defined for such content.

> **NOTE** *eDiscovery and holds are explored further in Chapter 16, "Managing Records." In addition, see the article at* `http://technet.microsoft.com/en-us/library/fp161513(office.15)`.

In addition to leveraging the search features of SharePoint to identify content that is stored in SharePoint related to a specific topic, administrators can now configure the SharePoint eDiscovery engine to search through Exchange 2013 information.

SEARCH USAGE REPORTS

The final area to cover in this chapter is the search usage reports. Reports that detail the usage of search within your environment are generated at both the site collection and the service application levels. At the application level, you can access reports that provide information on the Number of Queries, the Top Queries, Abandoned Queries, and the No Result Queries. These reports are available by going to the Search Service Application Administration area within Central Administration and selecting Usage Reports from the left navigation. Figure 17-17 displays a listing of some of the reports available.

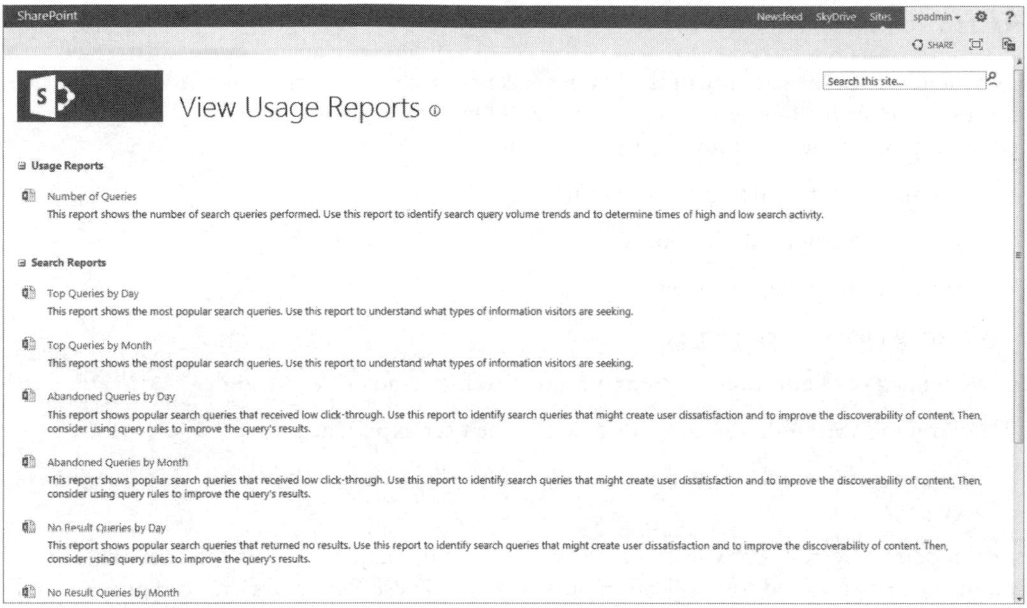

FIGURE 17-17

Search usage reports can be very helpful for monitoring your usage of search over time. By reviewing these reports on a regular basis, you will have a good understanding of how users are interacting with search and how you can use the tools discussed in this chapter to improve their experience. Figure 17-18 shows an example of the Top Queries by Day report. By identifying the things that users are searching for most often, you can do things to highlight content within the site further so that it is more easily found.

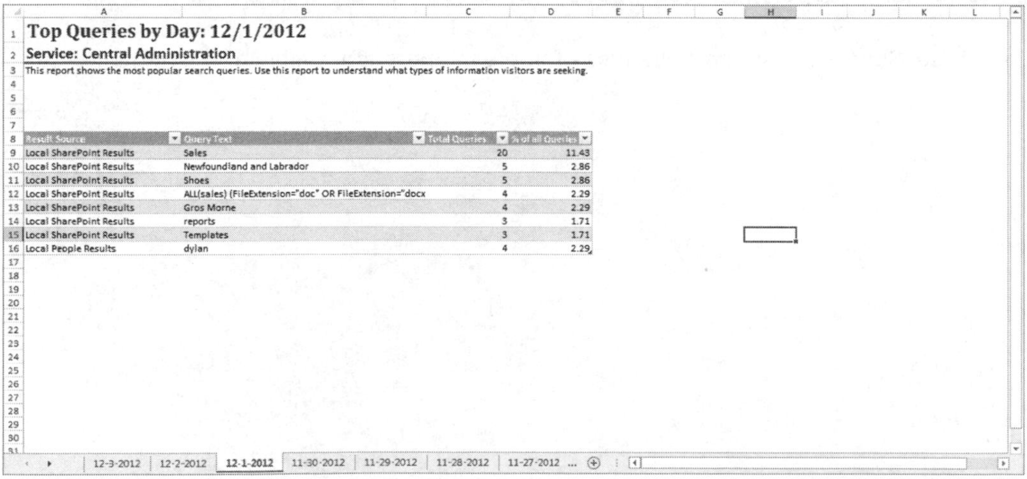

FIGURE 17-18

SUMMARY

In this chapter, we reviewed many of the key aspects of search and worked through some of the key configurations. After reading this chapter, you should be familiar with and able to configure the different search components within the site, including:

➤ Using the default search features within a site

➤ Creating a custom Search Center

➤ Performing advanced searches

➤ Creating managed properties

➤ Managing configurations related to content sources and crawl schedules

➤ Leveraging search-driven content to add to the user experience

➤ Reviewing the search usage reports to determine how effective your users' searches have been over time

The most important lesson that you can take away from this chapter is to understand that search is simply a query that is passed to a collection of Web Parts. These Web Parts are configurable and can be customized to meet your specific needs. Once you have this understanding, you will really be able to customize your users' search experience and build organization-specific search solutions that will provide great benefit for everyone who uses it.

EXERCISES

1. Where do you need to make configurations if they need to be accessed by every site within the farm?

2. You have a group of users who want to be able to quickly search for documents based on a specific metadata property, such as Product Name. How would you help them configure this?

3. True or false: SharePoint supports the use of Boolean operations within a search query.

▶ WHAT YOU LEARNED IN THIS CHAPTER

TOPIC	KEY CONCEPTS
Building search queries	Out-of-the-box, SharePoint provides the ability to search directly from any site collection. Users can enter search queries into the search box, and their results are displayed using the standard out-of-the-box search results page (`/_layouts/OSSSearchResults.aspx`).
Customizing the search experience	SharePoint provides several templates and various Web Parts that can be configured to customize your search experience.
Search service application configurations	SharePoint Search is managed at the farm level as a service application. Changes made at the service application level are global and apply to all site collections that are consuming that service.

18

Building Solutions in SharePoint

WHAT YOU WILL LEARN IN THIS CHAPTER:

➤ Combining techniques to build a single solution

➤ Planning for successful projects

➤ Planning for user adoption

The goal of this book is to provide you with experience using the tools and features of SharePoint to develop powerful, no-code business solutions. This chapter reviews some of the issues to consider as you build different composite solutions within your environment. You see how to combine the various concepts and techniques discussed in previous chapters to build powerful solutions that can bring great impact to your organization.

BUILDING COMPOSITE SOLUTIONS

Composite solutions combine multiple items to create a single solution. Within SharePoint, composite solutions are the primary way that you can bring value to the organization. For example, consider a standard SharePoint list. Alone, a list is a powerful feature that enables you to track data points, but when combined with Web Parts, pages, and connected Web Parts, it enables you not only to provide data to users, but to give them a level of context to the data that may not have been as easily available if you were just considering the task list by itself. Composite solutions range from very simple to very complex and can be created in no-code scenarios as well as used with custom development. This range of availability is a great feature because it enables you to build unique solutions that best match your organization's specific needs.

The types of solutions that you can develop within SharePoint are practically limitless. Because SharePoint can be customized, you can build solutions based on the factors that impact your needs. This flexibility allows your organization to have several different solutions. SharePoint then becomes a single platform that you can use to truly transform how your organization works. Before you dig into the details of developing internal solutions, consider the following example of a composite solution within SharePoint.

BUDGET PROCESS EXAMPLE

The fictional organization Rossco Tech Consulting offers professional services and technology mentoring to startup companies. Internally, Rossco follows multiple business processes for various business requests. One process that currently takes a great deal of time to manage is its budget request process. Rossco determined that using SharePoint to implement this process would provide the control, organization, and management the process requires. The overall solution includes the following elements:

➤ Visio diagram for the process

➤ Document library for the process templates

➤ Task list for assigning the process tasks

➤ Workflows for task notifications

From the preceding list, you can see a small example of using various elements combined into one single solution. Figure 18-1 provides an example of Rossco's budget request solution.

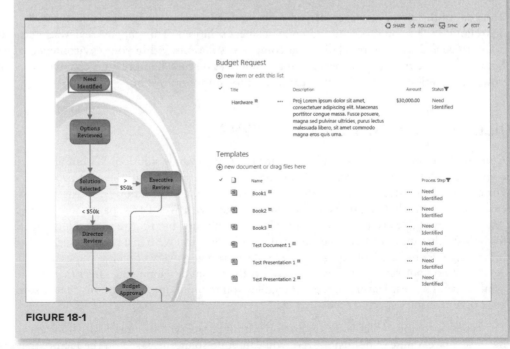

FIGURE 18-1

WORKING WITH THE BUSINESS

The central key to building any solution is to focus first on the needs of the business. If the business is not at the center of the solution, the odds of the solution being adopted and embraced are very slim. A solution comprised of the latest techniques and bells and whistles is just noise if the organization doesn't adopt it. A simple solution can be the most relevant and impactful if users adopt it and use it to enhance how they work. The trick isn't in building the most advanced and technical components, but rather in matching what you build to the exact needs of the users. If you are able to truly listen to what they need and build an application that addresses the core of their issues, they will adopt the solution and the organization will be enhanced. As the organization continues to adopt and use new solutions, the organization and the culture within the organization will grow. Technology can truly help an organization grow and develop, so long as the technology meets the users where they are and helps them take the needed steps to get to the next level. Because SharePoint enables you to build customized solutions without code, you can build a solution that can easily be enhanced over time.

Identifying Reality

The first step in building a business-focused solution is to dig into the issue at hand and identify what is really happening. What are users currently doing to address the need for which you have identified a potential solution within SharePoint? You can complete this process by understanding the following:

➤ **The data:** By looking at the type of data and information users are currently working with, you will be able to better identify all the components that need to be included in the solution. Some of the data points could include e-mails, documents, charts, graphs, and even conversations.

➤ **The users:** Understanding the users will help you to determine which elements must be included in the solution to make it successful. Remember, only solutions that really speak to users are likely to be adopted, so be sure that your solution caters to its primary user base. By taking the time to map out each of the types of users that have to interact with your solution, you will likely be able to uncover some things that you might have missed if you didn't take the time to complete this step of the process.

➤ **The desired outcome:** You don't want to get too far into planning for your solution before considering the end results. Is the solution meant to help users complete a set of current tasks, or is the solution meant to make things easier to find at a later date? Or, does the solution require a little of both? These types of questions, which frame the type of solution that you will develop, are best answered long before the solution is developed. By providing a clear solution that leads to a desired outcome, you allow users to appreciate the value that the potential solution brings to the organization — and they will be more inclined to adopt it.

Planning for the Culture

In addition to spending time looking into the users and the things they need to do with your solution, you need to consider the organization's culture. In many cases, an organization's culture will impact how the organization responds to change. Because SharePoint solutions often are put in place to drive change, it would be foolish to build a solution without reviewing how culture could impact it overall. After identifying how the organization responds to change, you can help it more easily adopt the solution. In many cases, the culture determines how complex or simple your solutions should be. The following are some of the factors that could greatly influence an organization's culture:

➤ **Remote workforce:** If a large percentage of your workers are mobile, they will have different needs than a local workforce. Your solution will need to address this head on in order for it to be successful.

➤ **Technical skill:** The solution you build should play directly into the technical level of your organization. If you are dealing with a workforce that isn't very technical, you will want to approach things with great simplicity and have a plan to add enhancements over time. On the other hand, if you have a technically advanced workforce, you will want to include some of the newest technology to help drive excitement for the solution. If the workforce is somewhere in the middle, your solution should employ a balanced approach.

➤ **Security:** How an organization deals with security often has a great impact on how it adapts to new solutions. An example of this is when you try to get a group of people who are used to working in a controlled structure to instead use an open and collaborative approach. They will likely need to be assured of the level of security within the new solution before they will embrace it and use it to communicate freely. Although SharePoint can easily provide a secured collaborative environment, the users will likely question it and be leery of jumping right in without additional assurance.

These are just a few examples of cultural elements that can impact your solutions. By planning for the organization's culture, you can include elements in your solution to drive its adoption.

Setting Realistic Goals

Setting realistic goals for your solution will help you address something that users can relate to. If the goals you have for the organization are too large, the solution could cause them to feel out of touch or unable to accomplish the desired outcome. By setting realistic goals, you help to promote a level of ownership that can be achieved through the use of the new solution. This approach helps move the focus from the technology to the need. In most cases, users are oblivious to the types of technology within the organization and simply want to have access to a set of tools that enables them to complete their expected roles successfully. Users will embrace a solution that helps them do this.

WORKING WITH THE BUSINESS

A new budget request at Rossco Tech involves several groups working together to complete the required forms. This example reviews the various items that Rossco identified for the data, users, and desired outcome as it planned to build this solution. Although there are no specific actions for you to complete here, it serves as an example of the data you would need to gather for the solutions you are building within SharePoint.

Data

The budget request process includes the following types of data:

➤ Process flow chart that is used by the organization to see the required process for all new requests. This flow chart provides a visual representation of the process required for each new request.

➤ Templates managed by the legal and accounting departments and completed by the person requesting the funds. These templates are currently Word and Excel documents stored on a file server.

➤ Completed budget requests. The requestor opens the required templates for each new request, completes them, and sends them via e-mail to the required parties.

Users

The budget request process included the following user profiles:

USERS	WHAT THEY WILL DO	HOW THEY WORK	OTHER NOTES
Legal	Access completed documents so they can review and send for signature.	In their offices, connected to the network.	They prefer substance over style.
Requestors	They make the requests and need to have additional information to ensure they are completing the tasks appropriately.	They split their time between the office and traveling to various client sites.	They want a clear set of instructions to follow.
Managers and Approvers	They need to check requests and update the status of approvals.	They need only what they need to see, when they need it.	Simple is best for them so they can work quickly with little additional training required.

continued

continued

Goals

This budget request process will achieve the following goals:

Create a single location for people to submit any budget request.

Create an archive that can be referenced in the future that identifies the various stages completed along with the required documentation.

This example looked at the various components that Rossco considered when developing a budget request solution that they would like to build within SharePoint. Each element in this example describes specific components that will need to be included in the solution. In order for the solution to be successful, it must address each of the components.

UNDERSTANDING YOUR AUDIENCE

After examining the data and how your users will work with it, the next important step is to spend some time understanding your users. By exploring your proposed solution through their eyes, you should be able to gather valuable insights that will help you build the best solution for them. Users relate best to a solution that speaks directly to their needs and preferences, so the more impact those have on the solution, the greater likelihood you have for a high adoption rate. Understanding your audience takes time and should be an ongoing process, because the organization is likely to morph over time and circumstances. As soon as you lose touch with the audience, you run the risk that your solution will not speak directly to them. At its core, SharePoint is about empowering your user base to be more efficient, accurate, and informed. If users can relate to your solution, they will be able to adapt to it without much transition.

Communicating Effectively

Your ability to communicate effectively with your audience as you build and implement your solution can have a large impact on its overall success. Each organization is comprised of many different groups, personalities, and skill sets. Within each group is a standard style of communication and working together, based on the type of work and the work environment. For example, consider the work environments and styles of the following departments:

> **Marketing:** A typical marketing department is interested in the way things are presented. It is a pretty mobile group that acts quickly and usually takes in a lot of data. It is always looking for the best way to tell a story, and often uses the latest technology and adopts the newest fads.

> **Legal:** A typical legal department is concerned with content and will go to great lengths to keep content organized. It is slow to adopt new things and typically likes to prove things out before moving too fast. It is more interested in content than design.

These are just simple summaries of two departments. The important thing is not to fall into stereotypes and categories, but to understand how different people may work differently. In this example, the solution for the marketing department should focus on how the data is presented. The solution for the legal department should present a clear structure that allows members of the department to drill down into the data to dissect it for their tasks. By not catering the solution to the audience, you run the risk of presenting the right data in the wrong way, thereby limiting the solution's overall acceptance.

Timing Your Solution Deployment

Not only is it important to speak the user's language within your solution, it is also important to plan the deployment of your solution at a time that makes the most sense for the users. If you work in a sales-based organization, there is likely a time of the month that is focused on closing out the numbers and meeting the assigned quotas. If you assume that this occurs at the end of every month and you need to deploy a new solution to help the sales team, it should be obvious that any type of deployment that occurs at the end of the month wouldn't be in a good position for success. In this scenario, your chances of success will increase significantly by scheduling a deployment early in the month. In many cases, though, if you don't take the time to understand and work with your specific audience, you run the risk of building an excellent solution but deploying it at the wrong time.

Planning for Multiple Scenarios

There is really no true scenario that can be a cookie-cutter deployment where all things considered line up and allow for an easy deployment of a new solution. The previous examples in the chapter identified two very different types of users. What if, instead of having a solution for each of them, you had to build a solution that was used by both unique groups of users? In the real world, this is the more typical scenario. The important thing is that you focus on the data, the context of the information you need to provide the users, and the action that you want to drive them to. By looking at these areas, you can make the best decisions given the scenario and then plan for any identified gaps. At least this way you are going into the deployment with your eyes open and with a plan in place. Although you might not be able to design each solution to be exactly what the users want or expect, using this approach you can start to think the way users think and develop a plan for deployment that answers the questions and concerns that they might have before they can even ask them!

UNDERSTANDING YOUR USERS

Rossco Tech Consulting's budget approval process will be accessed by several different types of users, each with a different need to work with the data. A user requesting a new item wants to be able to easily add new requests, whereas managers who need to approve items need to look at the bigger picture. The solution needs to be built in a way that makes it easy for both types of users to complete their tasks. The plan for this solution is to show the high-level information on the homepage and display a secondary information page when users make a new budget request. This will keep managers from being bogged down with information, and make it easy for users with requests to get all the assistance they need.

continued

continued

Because there are several types of users with varying needs, it would be difficult to build a single, intuitive solution for everyone. To address this concern, Rossco opted to place information strategically in a single solution, enabling the display of the same data in multiple formats, based on the needs of the primary user of that page. An example of the homepage is shown in Figure 18-1, and the secondary page for making new requests is shown in Figure 18-2.

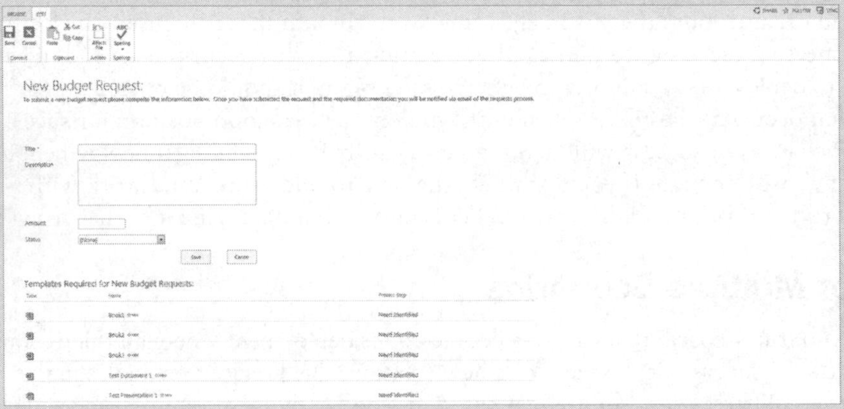

FIGURE 18-2

GATHERING REQUIREMENTS

Now that you have reviewed the business requirements and the types of users that will be accessing your solution, it is time to focus on the specific and detailed requirements of the solution. It is important to first map out the business aspect of the solution so that you can bring everyone to the same starting point, but now is the time to start looking at the very specific items that will be required within the solution.

You can take many approaches to finalizing these requirements. Because this topic is so varied, this section just highlights some of the tools that are valuable to SharePoint solutions. It is likely that your organization uses standard templates for requirements gathering, so these techniques are just things that can be added to your existing process. Remember, though, that your situation is likely unique, so it is good for you to review approaches and templates and then just select what will work best for you. The main thing you need to keep in mind is the end goal. The tools used to get there aren't nearly as important as arriving at the end goal.

Visual Mockups

One of the greatest points of confusion can be in how you visually represent the information you are given. If you described your solution to all the users in your organization and then asked them to go to the whiteboard and draw it, each person likely would draw something slightly different. Many times what users are visually expecting will have a large impact on how they accept the solution. Incorporating visual mockups into your requirements enables you to help reduce any confusion because users will be able to see what you have in mind before you develop the solution. As the saying goes, a picture is worth a thousand words.

EXAMPLE MOCKUPS

For the budget request solution that Rossco Tech Consulting is developing, the team responsible for the requirements wanted to be sure to clearly map out how the solution would look for the users prior to completing any development. To complete this task, they used Visio 2013 to design a mockup of the homepage and the new request page. Figures 18-3 and 18-4 show the mockup from the homepage and from the accounting dashboard, respectively.

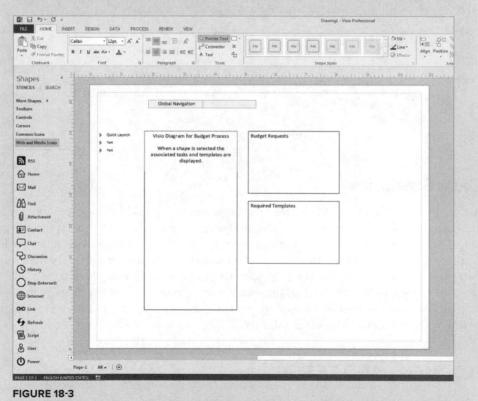

FIGURE 18-3

continued

continued

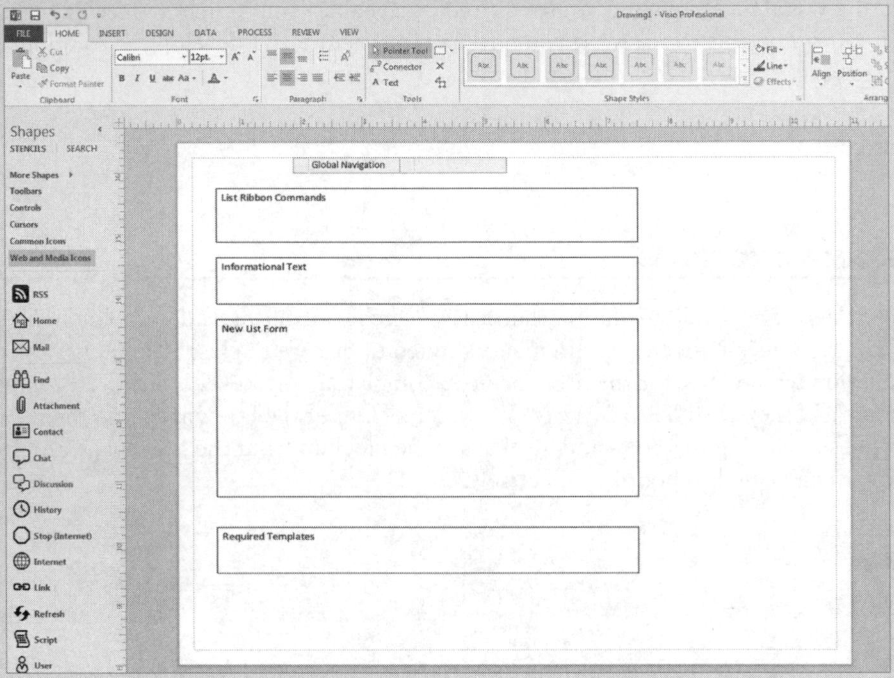

FIGURE 18-4

Use-Case Scenarios

To validate that your solution satisfies the business scenario it is addressing, you should map out specific business cases for testing and validation. For each of your primary users, there should be an associated use-case scenario that walks them through the process of using your solution. They can review this prior to development to ensure that the solution addresses the primary functions that will be completed in the solution. Once the solution has been developed, these same scenarios can then be used for testing to validate that the solution satisfies each of the use cases. If the use cases are written in a language that is common to the users, they will be able to take a very proactive stance in helping you craft the specific solution.

DEVELOPMENT AND TESTING

Once you have completed the design and requirements phases, it is time to start on the actual development of the solution. In this phase, you build the solution and then work with users to validate that it matches the specifications.

How SharePoint Differs from Other Solutions

An important thing to know about developing composite solutions for SharePoint is that all development is meant to be done in the production environment. Because you are using out-of-the-box tools to build your solution, it is intended that you can build the solution directly in the production environment. This drastically cuts down on the time it takes to get a solution ready for release. In many environments, this concept is very hard to implement, and much time is spent trying to find a workaround that enables you to bypass it. By attempting to find a work around, you are really trying to make SharePoint behave in a way that it wasn't designed to work and will in many cases run into issues as you try to work around the designed process for development.

The theory behind wanting to have the solution first built in test is so that you can validate the approach you are working on. One way to accommodate this type of validation is to create a secondary site collection within the production environment that you can use to validate your approach before you make the changes to the production site. You can use this site as a testing area where you can try new things without having to fully develop them. Once you validate that your approach will achieve what you have in mind, you can simply move to production and use the approach you validated in the test area.

Guidelines for Testing

When it comes to testing your solution, you should focus on the overall goals and requirements. There should be adequate testing to ensure that the solution technically satisfies the requirements. The testing that applies to the fulfillment of the goals should be completed by the users. This will validate that the users are satisfied with the solution and will support its full deployment to the organization. In most cases, this testing involves the creation of various use cases that allow the users of the solution to test specific business scenarios within the solution. For the Roscco example that has been used in this chapter, the use cases for testing would include the following scenarios:

➤ Creating a new budget request

➤ Approving/rejecting a budget request

➤ Searching for a past budget request

PLANNING USER ADOPTION

Now that you have built and tested the solution, you might think you are ready to deploy. Although you are close, there is one large area to focus on before implementing your solution: planning user adoption. As mentioned previously, the best technical solution can be the worst solution if users don't adopt it. In fact, you can be successful in planning, developing, and testing and still have the entire thing fall apart because the solution's users don't embrace it.

Gauging User Adoption

The culture of an organization is a unique thing and, in many cases, can be used to predict how an organization will adapt to new solutions. But this prediction is just an assumption about what could happen and needs to be tracked along the way so that you can adjust your plan based on how the solution is being accepted. By default, your adoption plan should include checkpoints, which gives you the freedom to adjust your plan based on the success of the current activities. It is important to have a long-term vision of what your deployment will look like, but it is also important to build some flexibility into the plan so that you can adjust along the way as you deploy the solution.

For example, suppose that you develop a training scenario that requires two days of onsite training to equip users to use the solution. Then, as you start the training, the organization has to respond to a major change in the industry and no one is able to dedicate two days away from his or her normal activities to attend training. What could be done in this case to ensure that adoption still happens, given the changes to the environment? You could adjust the solution by offering training in smaller batches over several weeks. This would allow users to receive the same level of training, but spread out over time so that they can keep up with their current tasks and responsibilities. This is an example of using a flexible approach to deployment. An initial plan was created to deliver the training, but as the environment changed, so did the approach.

The way to manage this type of approach is to develop a plan that includes checkpoints and validation marks. Your plan should allow the project team to switch directions and take a different path that will ultimately provide greater value. Because you are working with the business, they will need to buy into this approach. They should be brought into the planning stages early so that they see you are willing to try multiple approaches until you get the one that works best.

Adapting along the Way

Using a flexible deployment approach works only if you have determined in the beginning that you can adapt and change directions midstream. The decision to follow this approach can be risky, because you don't want to invest a great deal of effort into an approach if it isn't going to work. In scenarios that require a great deal of resources, you should consider starting a small pilot group to validate your approach. Based on the feedback from that group, you can determine if the investment is worth it and if it will provide you with the desired outcome. An example of this could be the development of training materials. It is not recommended that you spend a great amount of resources to develop a set of training materials only to discover that the training isn't getting you the desired results and requires you to take a different approach. By working with a pilot group, you could make a minimal investment into the training to first validate the approach.

THINK BIG, START SMALL, AND KEEP GROWING

Much of this chapter can be summed up as an approach that enables you to Think Big, Start Small, and Keep Growing. You look at the organization as a whole and determine how your solution can impact the environment and bring additional value. Once you have the big picture in mind, start with a small subset of users and take the time to build a solution that addresses their business needs and relates to them in a way that is clear and easy to understand. You can then repeat this approach on the next solution you are tasked to deliver. Over time, as you continue to deliver value to the organization, your environment will grow to become the go-to tool for the organization. Because your solution focused on the business, they will begin to see SharePoint as a tool that can be customized to directly address their business needs.

SUMMARY

This chapter provided guidance around combining all the techniques covered in this book to build composite solutions. By listening to the needs of the organization, you can accurately record the requirements and then translate those requirements into the different features within SharePoint. Doing this as the first step to any new SharePoint solution greatly increases your odds of implementing a successful business solution.

EXAMPLE COMPONENTS

The example in this chapter was based on various concepts covered throughout the book. The following table highlights some of the chapters where you can find additional information:

TOPIC	CHAPTER REFERENCE
Custom lists	Chapter 2, "Working with List Apps"
Document libraries	Chapter 3, "Working with Library Apps"
Lookup columns	Chapter 2, "Working with List Apps"
Visio Services Web Parts and data connections	Chapter 10, "Working with Business Intelligence"
Connected Web Parts	Chapter 7, "Working with Web Parts"

EXERCISES

1. What is the first thing that you should do when a user requests a new solution within SharePoint?

2. What are some tools or techniques that can be used as part of your solution planning process?

3. What makes a SharePoint solution a success?

▶ **WHAT YOU LEARNED IN THIS CHAPTER**

TOPIC	KEY CONCEPTS
Communicating with users	Speak in the language of the business so that users can relate to what the solution is going to do. The technology shouldn't matter.
Requirement-gathering tools	Use cases and visual mockups can be great tools to help ensure that your solution is satisfying the requirements of the users.
Flexibility	Be flexible in your implementation plan so that you can adjust to the way the users are adopting the solution.

A

Installing SharePoint Server 2013

In this appendix, you learn how to install SharePoint Server 2010 so that you can establish a test environment to complete the book's Try It Out exercises. Prior to completing this task, you should review the following resources:

➤ **Hardware and Software Requirements for SharePoint Server 2013:** http://technet .microsoft.com/en-us/library/cc262485.aspx

➤ **Administrative and Service Accounts Required for Initial Deployment of SharePoint Server 2013:** http://technet.microsoft.com/en-us/library/ee662513.aspx

➤ **Installation Instructions for SharePoint Server 2013:** http://technet.microsoft .com/en-us/library/cc303424.aspx

➤ **SharePoint Server 2013 Resource Center:** http://technet.microsoft.com/en-us/ sharepoint/fp142366

When installing SharePoint Server 2013, you have a choice between installing a SharePoint farm within a single server or across multiple servers. One option leverages a full version of SQL Server and is often referred to as a *complete installation*. You also have the option to install a single server with a built-in database. This is sometimes referred to as a *standalone installation*. The standalone option does not leverage the full version of SQL Server but instead installs Microsoft SQL Server 2008 R2 SP1 Express Edition.

You will have very little choice in how specific services are configured, and the entire farm will be deployed to a single server. This type of installation does not scale beyond 10GB of data and is recommended only for product evaluation or demonstration scenarios; it is *not* advisable for use in production environments.

> **NOTE** *For details on how to create a single server with a built-in database type of installation, see* `http://technet.microsoft.com/en-us/library/cc263202.aspx`.

The complete installation type, which is most commonly chosen by system administrators, provides greater flexibility and control over the configuration of specific SharePoint components. It is the recommended installation for long-term use of a system and will be the installation type we review in this appendix.

To complete the following Try It Out, you should have already installed Windows Server 2008 R2 with Service Pack 1 or Windows Server 2012 on the server you want to install SharePoint on. In addition, you should have already installed and configured SQL Server 2008 R2 with Service Pack 1 or SQL Server 2012 so that it is available for use by your SharePoint farm. For more information on this, refer to the Hardware and Software requirements resource listed previously.

TRY IT OUT   Installing SharePoint Server 2013

In this Try It Out, you install SharePoint Server 2013 so that it can be used for other exercises in this book.

1. Open the install media location for SharePoint Server 2013. This may be available to you on a DVD or through an ISO image that you have mounted within your environment.

2. Run the `prerequisiteinstaller.exe` file. The SharePoint 2013 Products Preparation Tool appears, as shown in Figure A-1.

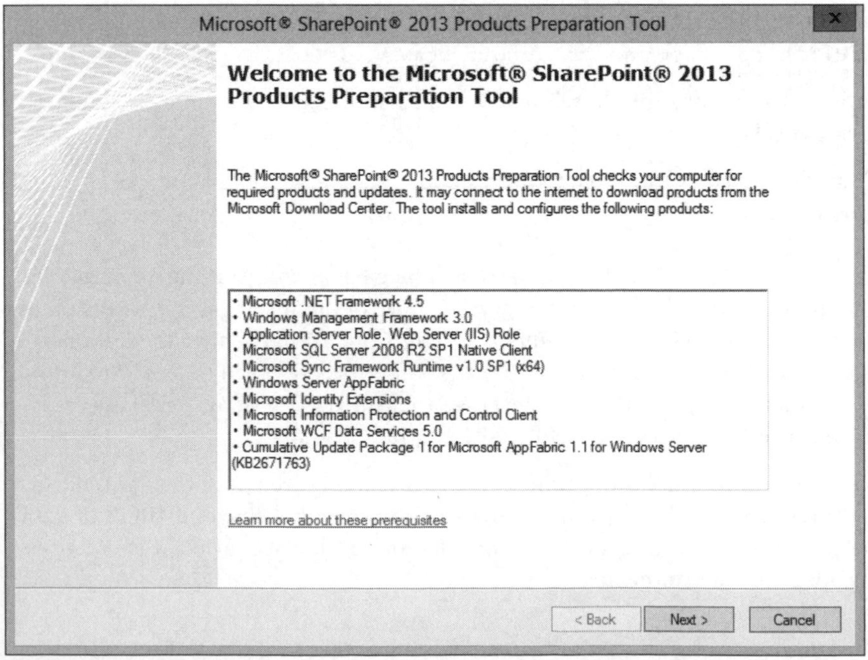

FIGURE A-1

3. Note that you must have an active Internet connection in order to download the prerequisite software on your server.

4. Click Next.

5. Review and accept the terms of the License Agreement.

6. Click Next to download and install the prerequisite software on your server. This process may take several minutes depending on a number of factors, such as the speed of your network connection and server. Once all components have been successfully installed, the Restart Confirmation window will appear, as shown in Figure A-2.

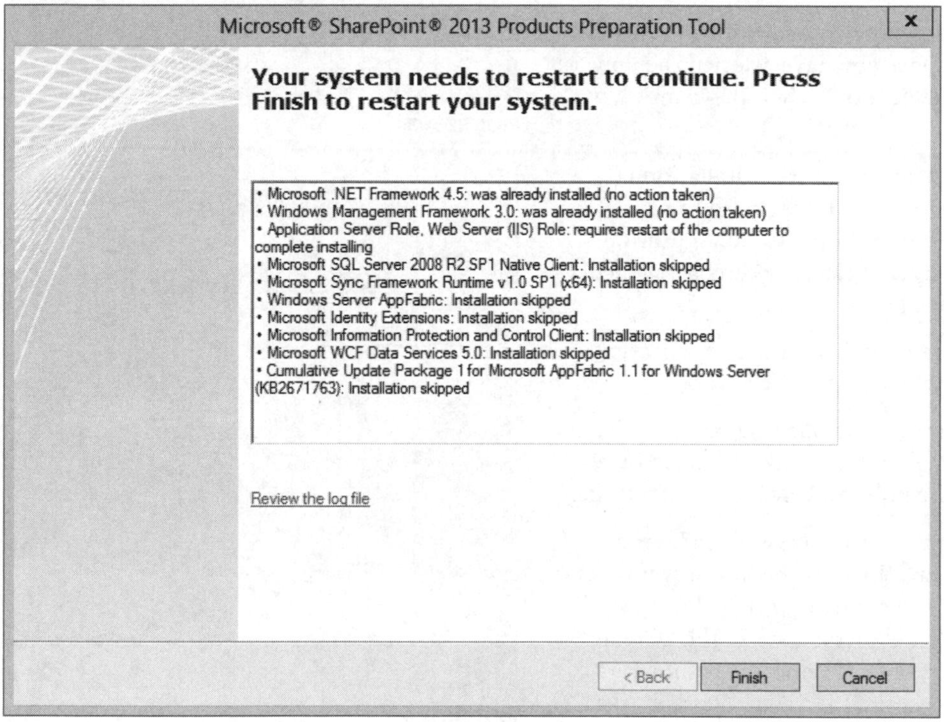

Microsoft® SharePoint® 2013 Products Preparation Tool [X]

Your system needs to restart to continue. Press Finish to restart your system.

- Microsoft .NET Framework 4.5: was already installed (no action taken)
- Windows Management Framework 3.0: was already installed (no action taken)
- Application Server Role, Web Server (IIS) Role: requires restart of the computer to complete installing
- Microsoft SQL Server 2008 R2 SP1 Native Client: Installation skipped
- Microsoft Sync Framework Runtime v1.0 SP1 (x64): Installation skipped
- Windows Server AppFabric: Installation skipped
- Microsoft Identity Extensions: Installation skipped
- Microsoft Information Protection and Control Client: Installation skipped
- Microsoft WCF Data Services 5.0: Installation skipped
- Cumulative Update Package 1 for Microsoft AppFabric 1.1 for Windows Server (KB2671763): Installation skipped

Review the log file

[< Back] [Finish] [Cancel]

FIGURE A-2

7. Your system will require a restart to complete the process. Click Finish. Due to the required installation and configuration of certain features, it may take several minutes for the system to restart. Once the system has restarted, you will need to log in to complete the installation of components. Depending on your system's configuration, additional restarts may be required. Once finished, you will receive an Installation Complete window, as shown in Figure A-3. Click the Finish button.

8. Return to the SharePoint Server 2013 install media location and run the `setup.exe` file.

9. The product key window will appear. Enter the SharePoint Server key Microsoft provided to you based on your licensing agreement, and click Continue.

10. Review and accept the Microsoft Software License Terms.

11. Click Continue.

12. The Choose a File Location window will appear. Once you have selected the appropriate file locations, click the Install Now button.

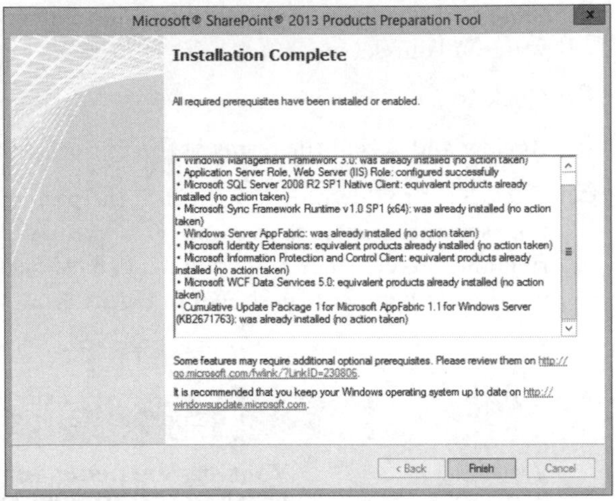

13. Once the core software installation is finished, you will be required to run the SharePoint Products Configuration Wizard. Ensure the checkbox is selected and click Close.

14. The SharePoint Products Configuration Wizard will launch. Click Next.

15. You will receive a warning message that certain key services will be started or reset during the process. Click Yes to continue.

16. The "Connect to a server farm" window will appear. If this is the first server of a multiple server farm, or if you are installing on a single server, select the "Create a new server farm" option, as shown in Figure A-4, and then click Next. If you are adding new servers to an existing SharePoint farm, select the "Connect to an existing server farm" option.

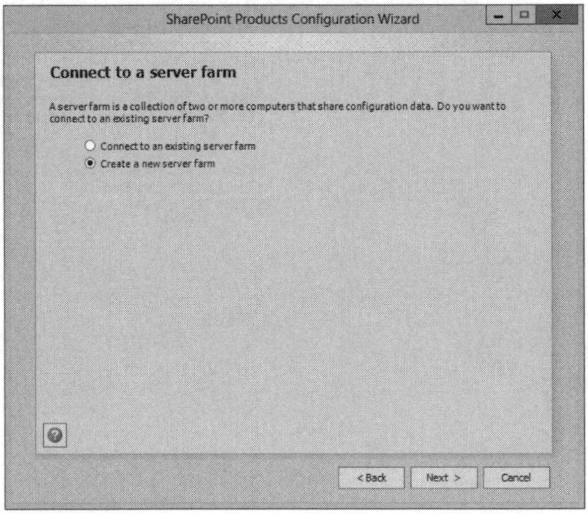

FIGURE A-3

FIGURE A-4

17. The Specify Configuration Database Settings window will appear. Enter the name of your database server and the credentials for your database access account, and click Next.

> **NOTE** *For more information on which permissions this or other service accounts should have, see* `http://technet.microsoft.com/en-us/library/cc678863 .aspx`.

18. You will be asked to provide a passphrase for the farm, which is required when joining additional servers to the farm. Enter your passphrase in the required fields and click Next. Note this passphrase in case it is required at a later time.

19. You will then be redirected to the Configure SharePoint Central Administration Web Application step. For this step, you must specify a port number for your web application. Ideally, it would be best to enter something that will be memorable. Next, select an authentication provider. For this example, select NTLM, as shown in Figure A-5.

FIGURE A-5

20. The Completing the SharePoint Products Configuration Wizard screen will appear, with all the selected settings displayed for your review. Click Next.

21. The SharePoint Configuration Wizard will run. This process may take several minutes to complete. Once this process has finished, a successful configuration message will appear. Click Finish.

22. The Central Administration Site will appear. The next step will be to configure the various service applications for your SharePoint farm, as shown in Figure A-6. You can select to configure the services via the Farm Configuration Wizard or manually. For this example, run the Farm Configuration Wizard by selecting the Start the Wizard button. However, for production scenarios, you should consider configuring these services manually to allow for greater control and to ensure the service applications are configured to suit your specific needs.

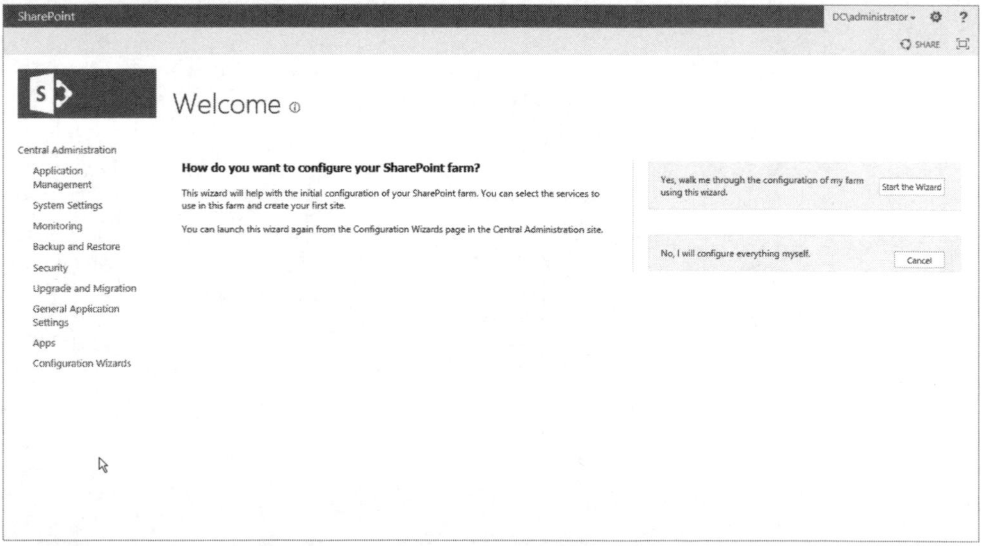

FIGURE A-6

23. Specify the Service Account that you want to run each service with.

24. Ensure each service is selected.

25. Click Next. The Farm Configuration Wizard will create and configure each service. This may take several minutes.

26. Once the services are configured, you will be redirected to a page where you can create the first site collection for your SharePoint farm.

27. Enter **Beginning SharePoint 2013** for the Title field.

28. For the Template Selection, select the Publishing tab and select the Publishing Portal.

29. Click OK. Your new site collection will be created and the Farm Configuration Wizard will complete.

30. Click Finish.

B

Exercise Solutions

CHAPTER 1

Exercise 1 Solution

A site is a single location that stores lists and libraries related to a common subject. A site collection represents a group of sites.

Exercise 2 Solution

There are many reasons that organizations invest in portal technologies. Two major reasons are:

➤ People need to connect with information that will help them make informed business decisions regardless of their physical location. Because portals are web-based and are available via the browser, large numbers of users can access information from a centralized location.

➤ Portal technologies scale with an organization as it grows and can accommodate business processes and information management.

Exercise 3 Solution

False. The collaboration features of SharePoint are the baseline features that are included within all versions of SharePoint. The feature sets that require SharePoint Server are the Enterprise features.

CHAPTER 2

Exercise 1 Solution

To receive an e-mail notification every time a new item is added to a list, you would create an alert. You create an alert by selecting Alert Me from the List tab of the Ribbon.

Exercise 2 Solution

A choice column features a value list, from which you can select options that a site manager has manually entered into the column. A lookup column displays a value list based on the contents of an existing column from another list on the site.

Exercise 3 Solution

You can export SharePoint list views to an Excel spreadsheet from the Ribbon menu. This means you can take information from the SharePoint site, customize it, and send it to team members or partners who do not have direct access to the SharePoint list.

Exercise 4 Solution

True. SharePoint includes a concept known as *branching logic* in surveys that define what the next question is that a user should answer based on his response to a specific question.

CHAPTER 3

Exercise 1 Solution

In this situation, you would browse the available versions of your document to find the version submitted earlier in the week. Once you have found the correct version, you would restore the previous version and finally resubmit the newly restored version.

Exercise 2 Solution

Browse to the library that you want to use to archive your documents, select the files you want to copy, and drag them into the document library.

Exercise 3 Solution

In this situation, you could open your library in Quick Edit mode (available from the Library tab of the ribbon). While in Quick Edit mode, you can update a particular column for multiple documents, and change them all at the same time.

CHAPTER 4

Exercise 1 Solution

By creating a site column for Region, lists, such as the contact list, can feature custom views that filter items to only show items for a specific region. The sales manager can use a list view that shows items across all regions, and each regional office can have its own view that filters out information from regions other than its own. A list-centric column for Region would work specifically for this scenario as well. However, because you can assume this type of behavior is desired for other content lists on the site, a site column may be a better implementation choice.

Exercise 2 Solution

You can accomplish this by creating a custom view that has a filter to only show items where Created By is equal to [me]. It may also be beneficial to make the custom personalized view the default view so that users can see that view first when they enter a list.

Exercise 3 Solution

By creating a Calendar view on the list, you can display visual indicators of items based on the date of initial contact and expected date of sale. The sales manager can easily identify the ones that are taking the longest to close.

CHAPTER 5

Exercise 1 Solution

Open the workflow in SharePoint Designer 2013, click Edit Workflow, and choose Visual Designer from the Views drop-down button in the ribbon.

Exercise 2 Solution

Use the "Start a task process" action. Put the Taxation group of people in the Participants box, with the order as Parallel. In the Task Options section, make sure there is a check in the box next to "Assign a task to each member within groups."

Exercise 3 Solution

In the Task Options section, select "Wait for percentage of a response" from the Completion Criteria drop-down box. In the Required percentage box, type 50, and for the Required Outcome, choose Approved.

Exercise 4 Solution

In the workflow in SharePoint Designer, hover the mouse over the "Send an email" workflow action that you have already added. Click the drop-down box on that action and choose Properties. Select the Body row and click the ellipsis button toward the right. This will open the String Builder, which lets you directly edit the e-mail's code.

Exercise 5 Solution

Bob should click on the item name in the list, and click Workflows. The workflow he needs is not displayed in the Start a New Workflow section because it is already in the Running Workflows section. The status is Error Occurred. Click on this running workflow's name, and click Terminate This Workflow.

CHAPTER 6

Exercise 1 Solution

This is somewhat of a trick question, so the answer is both true and false. Prior to enabling content type management via the Advanced settings of a document library, you can associate only a single document template with a document library. However, if you enable content type management on your library, you can then manage multiple content types from that single location and have more than one document template associated with the library.

Exercise 2 Solution

You have two primary methods for accomplishing this.

➤ Your first method is to add the words Private and Confidential to all the standard document templates within the organization. This method is tedious and requires you to constantly add these words to all new document templates. Also it's difficult to prevent users from removing the text directly from their documents themselves.

➤ The second method involves creating an information management policy on the base document content type so that all child document content types inherit the policy. This method also supports the creation of new content types that maintain the same information management policy setting. There is a setting on the label configuration that allows you to enter custom text such as Private and Confidential, and you can select a checkbox option to prevent users from removing the label or changing it after it's been added.

Exercise 3 Solution

To manage approval processes around specific types of information such as job postings, you associate an Approval workflow template with the Job Postings content type. You can define the workflow activity to launch whenever an item is either created or modified. You can also select who needs to provide the approval for new content. Because the workflow is configured on the content type level, no matter how many location job postings exist throughout the portal, you can apply the same business process.

CHAPTER 7

Exercise 1 Solution

You should edit the main page of the Corporate Intranet and add a Web Part that displays a list of contacts. You can either use a Contacts list app and its associated Web Part, or you can use the Summary Links Web Part, which supports the creation of links to users.

Exercise 2 Solution

Web Parts can be dragged from one Web Part zone to another. Alternatively, you can edit the properties of a Web Part and select which zone the Web Part appears in.

Exercise 3 Solution

Each list app Web Part allows for the selection of a list view that is to be displayed in that Web Part. Therefore, you can create a new view that displays the information you want to have displayed in the Web Part and specify that view in the Web Part properties. Alternatively, you can edit the Web Part properties and select the Edit This View link to make minor modifications to the existing Web Part view.

Exercise 4 Solution

Each list and library app in SharePoint has its own Web Part. You can display upcoming events by adding the Web Part associated with a Calendar list app. You can also have a Calendar list app aggregate information from other Calendar list apps by using the Calendar Overlay option on the Library tab of the Calendar list. So, if you have event information stored in multiple Calendar lists, you can add the Web Part to the page and then use the Calendar Overlay feature to aggregate events from other Calendar lists. Finally, your third option is to use the Content Query Web Part to aggregate events from within the site collection.

Exercise 5 Solution

For this scenario, you can use the new search-driven content Web Parts, or you can use the Picture Library Slideshow Web Part.

CHAPTER 8

Exercise 1 Solution

A site collection is a container that holds many different types of content, including sites. Site collections have galleries associated with them that store content that can be used for all sites within the site collection. A site is created within a site collection. Sites are used to store different lists and libraries.

Exercise 2 Solution

The Community Site template is a site that contains a discussion forum and supports the rating of answers to questions and the awarding of contributor badges.

Exercise 3 Solution

Most sites can be saved as a template by visiting the Site Settings page for that site. The only exception would be if the site has publishing features enabled or is based on a Records Center template. Those sites cannot be saved as templates.

CHAPTER 9

Exercise 1 Solution

The Share feature allows non-administrators to easily share content. From the site or from list items, users can click the Share option in the menu to invite others to work with them on the site.

Exercise 2 Solution

The Check Users Permission feature on the Permissions page allows you to enter a User Name or Group and then search for the permissions they have been assigned within the location you are searching.

Exercise 3 Solution

True. This approach allows you to copy existing permission levels to create more appropriate levels for use within your solution.

CHAPTER 10

Exercise 1 Solution

The Business Intelligence Center template comes preconfigured to support BI content.

Exercise 2 Solution

True. Content can be edited through the browser when the server is configured with the Office Web Applications.

Exercise 3 Solution

If you grant users the View Item permission to an Excel Services document, they will only be able to access the snapshot.

Exercise 4 Solution

Visio files should be saved as web drawings so that they can be referenced in the Visio Web Part.

Exercise 5 Solution

Create a filtered view in the library, which only shows files of the file type RDL.

CHAPTER 11

Exercise 1 Solution

In SharePoint's top navigation bar, click Newsfeed. Click the "follow" hyperlink, and then click the "follow" hyperlink on the "People I'm following" page. Type the person's name and click Follow. When the person is in the list of people you are following, click on his or her name. On the right side of the screen, under the Org Chart, click the SEE MORE link.

Exercise 2 Solution

Here are the instructions to give Charlotte: At the top right, click your name and choose About Me. Click "edit your profile." Click the ellipsis to the right of Details and choose Newsfeed Settings. In the Email Notifications section, you can uncheck the boxes next to "Someone replied to a conversation that I started," "Someone replied to a conversation that I replied to," and "Someone replied to my community discussion post." Click "Save all and close."

Exercise 3 Solution

When Katie is on the Projects library page, she can click the Library tab in the contextual ribbon, and then click Connect to Office and Add to SharePoint Sites. If a prompt labeled "Connect Office to your portal" comes up, she can click Yes.

Exercise 4 Solution

In the Tag Cloud Web Part properties, Todd can check the box next to Show Count. This will display a number in parentheses next to each tag in the cloud.

Exercise 5 Solution

In the User Profile Service Application in Central Administration, the SharePoint administrator can add the Marketing site link as a new promoted site. Click Manage Promoted Sites, and click New Link to add it.

CHAPTER 12

Exercise 1 Solution

Because not all users have access to the InfoPath application, creating a form template that is supported by the browser can expose the form to a wider audience. In addition, because the browser removes some of the interface elements that the InfoPath form itself offers, such as a view switcher or formatting controls, it may be a more controlled environment to have users complete and review form data. Finally, by using Forms Services to present the form to users, they see the form as a standard web-based form and can spend less time focusing on the technology and more time thinking about the information they are supplying and the decisions they are required to make as part of a business process.

Exercise 2 Solution

A form template can be published to SharePoint directly from a document library. This is suitable for scenarios where the form is only required to be hosted in a single location. Another alternative is to publish the form as a content type to a SharePoint Server. This method is most appropriate when there is a requirement to publish the form to multiple locations within a single site collection. Finally, there is an option to upload the form template via the Central Administration site as a server administrator. This method is most appropriate for complex forms featuring advanced customizations or custom code. It is also suitable for situations where a form template needs to be accessible across multiple site collections within a single server farm.

Exercise 3 Solution

A template is a reusable component that is comprised of form fields, controls, and customizations that can be saved as a single control and added to other form templates. An example of a template part might be a group of fields for entering contact information within a form. Because these fields are often exactly the same across all forms, it would be advantageous to save them once as a template part for reuse in other form templates.

Exercise 4 Solution

A data source element represents information and data that can be collected within a form. However, a control is the mechanism by which the data will be entered or viewed within the form. One single data source element may use multiple controls across different views depending on the requirements for data entry or viewing. However, each instance of a control that is added to a form can only be mapped to a single data source.

Exercise 5 Solution

False. InfoPath can submit data to an external data source as well as receive data.

CHAPTER 13

Exercise 1 Solution

On the screen where tables can be added to your database, one of the options is SharePoint List. You can create a link directly to a list or copy the list data into your database. The other types of data on that screen are Access, Excel, SQL/ODBC, and Text/CSV.

Exercise 2 Solution

When lookup columns are created in a table, to look up to other tables, this automatically creates a relationship between the tables.

Exercise 3 Solution

The buttons are Add, Delete, Edit, Save, and Cancel. Yes, additional buttons can be added.

Exercise 4 Solution

An action macro is created. If a data macro needs to be run, you can use the action called "Run data macro" in your action macro.

CHAPTER 14

Exercise 1 Solution

False. Although an understanding of CSS is helpful for customizing master pages, it is not required for the use of themes, as these types of visual changes are made through the browser interface.

Exercise 2 Solution

Style sheets should be stored in the Style Library of a site collection.

Exercise 3 Solution

It is important to not change system files or default files. Doing so may cause compatibility issues with future updates and can make it difficult to revert back to the state prior to customizations being performed. Whenever performing any type of customization, it is important to ensure that changes can always be undone.

Exercise 4 Solution

The Design Manager can help to guide you through the process of creating and publishing your HTML designs to SharePoint 2013 sites that work in a variety of mediums, including mobile phones, tablets, and desktops.

Exercise 5 Solution

True. You can use the Design Manager to create and edit master pages from any HTML editor.

CHAPTER 15

Exercise 1 Solution

In this situation, you begin by creating a publishing portal. You would first create a Newsletter content type to have columns that represent such things as a title, body text, and a picture. Next, you create a page layout based on this content type. You would call the page layout "Newsletter," and the types of content you can create on this page would be the columns title, body text, and picture.

Exercise 2 Solution

True. Although initially you can create a website using a collaboration template, such as the team site, you can make it publishing-capable at a later date using the power of Features. You enable Features from the Site Collection Features and Site Features pages, which you access from the Site Settings page. After enabling the publishing features on a team site, all publishing lists, libraries, and functionality are made available on your team site.

Exercise 3 Solution

In this situation, you first create a publishing portal, the standard template for Internet-facing sites. To make your site accessible in two languages, you first enable and set up Variations on your site. You then create labels for your languages, one named English and one named French. You must specify one of the sites as the source site. The source site is where users initially create content. As content is created, it can be automatically replicated on the other sites and translated either via a workflow or machine translation.

Exercise 4 Solution

True. You can create page layouts in any HTML editor and then import the files via the Design Manager.

CHAPTER 16

Exercise 1 Solution

A file plan outlines the types of documents and information that exist within your organization, as well as the rules that exist related to where the files must be stored and for how long. The classification plan focuses more specifically on the data that must be tracked related to each document type and is typically completed as a secondary step to the creation of the file plan.

Exercise 2 Solution

In-Place Records Management focuses on the declaration and storage of records within the contextual location from which they are created and collaborated on, whereas archive-based records management focuses on the copy or movement of a file to a Records Repository where it will be stored outside of its original context.

Exercise 3 Solution

Either. This is determined based on the Records Declaration Settings for the site collection, as outlined in Chapter 16.

Exercise 4 Solution

Both. When defining retention schedules, you must determine whether they are applied to the content type or the folder that the file is stored within.

CHAPTER 17

Exercise 1 Solution

Changes that are global in nature and need to be referenced by the entire farm should be made in Central Administration.

Exercise 2 Solution

The metadata property would be created as a managed property and added to Advanced Search interfaces.

Exercise 3 Solution

True. SharePoint supports Boolean operations, such as AND or NOT, in search queries.

CHAPTER 18

Exercise 1 Solution

You should work with the users to determine the business requirements of the solution. The requirements should be focused on the users, not the technology.

Exercise 2 Solution

One very effective tool used as part of the solution planning process is a solution mockup. This mockup helps to ensure that the users of your solution agree with the initial approach you are taking to build the solution.

Exercise 3 Solution

A solution is a success when users within the organization adopt the solution and use it freely. A successful solution directly addresses the business needs of the users.

INDEX

X

Y

Z